THE BEST 159 LAW SCHOOLS

THE BEST 159 LAW SCHOOLS

2006 EDITION

Eric Owens, Esq., John Owens, Esq., Julie Doherty and The Staff of The Princeton Review

Random House, Inc.
New York
www.PrincetonReview.com

The Princeton Review, Inc.
2315 Broadway
New York, NY 10024
E-mail: bookeditor@review.com

ISBN: 0-375-76498-4

Editorial Director: Robert Franek
Production Editor: Christine LaRubio
Production Manager: Scott Harris
Account Manager: David Soto
Editor: Erik Olson

Manufactured in the United States of America.

9 8 7 6 5 4 3 2 1

2006 Edition

ACKNOWLEDGMENTS

Eric Owens would like to say, "Thank you, John Katzman, for pretty much everything."

Thanks also to Erik Olson for support and guidance on this book and many others and to Bob Spruill for his LSAT expertise.

In addition, much thanks should go to David Soto and Ben Zelevansky for spearheading the law school data collection efforts. Their survey, along with the support and assistance of Andrew Baker and Itala Souza allowed for the completion of a totally cohesive stat-packed guide. And Chaitra Ramanathan deserves a standing ovation for her tireless work coordinating student surveys and profile reviews at 159 law schools.

A special thanks must go to our production team: Scott Harris and Christine LaRubio. Your commitment, flexibility, and attention to detail are always appreciated in both perfect and crunch times.

—Eric Owens

I'd like to send my thanks:

To Eric Owens, my quasi-cousin, who kept me in mind for this project.

To Erik Olson, who trusted me (and the other EO) enough to give me the chance.

To The Princeton Review for deciding to bring *The Best Law Schools* back into circulation.

To my family & friends, who support me in the things I do.

To the law students who took the time to complete the law student survey.

—John Owens

I would like to thank my parents, Brucine and Francis Doherty, Erik Olson of The Princeton Review, and Arturo Meade.

—Julie Doherty

CONTENTS

PREFACE

Welcome to *The Best 159 Law Schools*, The Princeton Review's truly indispensable guide for anyone thinking about entering the law school fray. This is not simply a reprint of the garden-variety fluff from each law school's admissions booklet. What we have attempted to do is provide a significant amount of essential information from a vast array of sources to give you a complete, accurate, and easily digestible snapshot of each and every law school in the country. Here you'll find a wealth of practical advice on admissions, taking and acing the Law School Admissions Test (LSAT), choosing the right school, and doing well once you're there. You'll also find all the information you need on schools' bar exam pass rates, ethnic and gender percentages, tuition, average starting salaries of graduates, and much more. For 159 ABA-approved law schools, you'll find descriptive profiles of the student experience based on the opinions of the only true law school experts: current law school students. Indeed, with this handy reference, you should be able to narrow your choices from the few hundred law schools in North America to a handful in no time at all.

Never trust any single source too much, though—not even us. Take advantage of all the resources available to you, including friends, family members, the Internet, and your local library. Obviously, the more you explore all the options available to you, the better the decision you'll make. We hope you are happy wherever you end up and that we were helpful in your search for the best law school for you.

Best of luck!

ALL ABOUT LAW SCHOOL

CHAPTER 1
So You Want to Go to Law School . . .

Congrats! Law school is a tremendous intellectual challenge and an amazing experience. It can be confusing and occasionally traumatic—especially during the crucial first year—but the cryptic ritual of legal education will make you a significantly better thinker, a consummate reader, and a far more mature person over the course of three years.

The application process is rigorous, but it's not brutal. Here's our advice.

WHAT MAKES A COMPETITIVE APPLICANT?

It depends. One of the great things about law schools in the United States is that there are a lot of them and standards for admission run the gamut from appallingly difficult to not very hard at all.

Let's just say, for example, you have your heart set on Yale Law School, arguably the finest law school in all the land. Let's also say you have stellar academic credentials: a 3.45 GPA and an LSAT score in the 99th percentile of everyone who takes it. With these heady numbers, you've got a whopping 2 percent chance of getting into Yale, at best. On the other hand, with this same 3.45 GPA and LSAT score in the 99th percentile, you are pretty much a lock at legal powerhouses like Duke University School of Law and Boston College Law School. With significantly lower numbers—say, a 3.02 GPA and an LSAT score in the 81st percentile—you stand a mediocre chance of getting into top-flight law schools like Case Western or Indiana. But with a little bit of luck, these numbers might land you at George Washington or UCLA.

> ***Fascinating Acronyms***
>
> ***LSAC:*** *Law School Admission Council, headquartered in beautiful Newtown, Pennsylvania*
>
> ***LSAT:*** *Law School Admissions Test*
>
> ***LSDAS:*** *Law School Data Assembly Service*
>
> ***ABA:*** *American Bar Association*

This is good news. The even better news is that there are several totally respectable law schools out there that will let you in with a 2.5 GPA and an LSAT of 148 (which is about the 36th percentile). If you end up in the top 10 percent of your class at one of these schools and have even a shred of interviewing skills, you'll get a job that is just as prestigious and pays just as much money as the jobs garnered by Yale grads. Notice the important catch here, though: You *must* graduate in the top 10 percent of your class at so-called "lesser" schools. Almost every Yale Law grad who wants a high-paying job can land one.

Ultimately, there's a law school out there, somewhere, for you. If you want to get into a "top-flight" or "pretty good" school, though, you're in for some pretty stiff competition. Unfortunately, it doesn't help that the law school admissions process is somewhat formulaic; your LSAT score and your GPA are vastly more important to the process than anything else about you. But if your application ends up in the "maybe" pile, your recommendations, your major, the reputation of your college alma mater, a well-written and nongeneric essay, and various other factors will play a larger role in determining your fate.

THE ADMISSIONS INDEX

The first thing most law schools will look at when evaluating your application is your "index." It's a number (which varies from school to school) that is made up of a weighted combination of your undergraduate GPA and LSAT score. In virtually every case, the LSAT is weighted more heavily than the GPA.

While the process differs from school to school, it is generally the case that your index will put you into one of three piles:

(Probably) Accepted. A select few applicants with high LSAT scores and stellar GPAs are admitted pretty much automatically. If your index is very, very strong compared to the school's median or target number, you're as good as in, unless you are a convicted felon or you wrote your personal statement in crayon.

(Probably) Rejected. If your index is very weak compared to the school's median or target number, you are probably going to be rejected without much ado. When admissions officers read weaker applications (yes, at almost every school every application is read) they will be looking for something so outstanding or unique that it makes them willing to take a chance. Factors that can help here include ethnic

Admission Decision Criteria

According to the Law School Admission Council (LSAC), there are no less than 20 factors that law schools might consider in deciding to admit or reject applicants. They are:

- *LSAT score*
- *Undergraduate grade point average (UGPA)*
- *Undergraduate course of study*
- *College attended*
- *Graduate work*
- *Improvement in grades and grade distribution*
- *Extracurricular activities in college*
- *Ethnic background*
- *Character and personality*
- *Letters of recommendation*
- *Writing skills*
- *Personal statement/essay*
- *Work experience and other relevant experience*
- *Community activities*
- *Motivation and reasons for studying law*
- *State of residency*
- *Difficulties overcome*
- *Pre-college preparation*
- *Past accomplishments and leadership*
- *That old catchall: anything else about you*

background, where you are from, or very impressive work or life experience. That said, don't hold your breath because not many people in this category are going to make the cut.

Well . . . Maybe. The majority of applicants fall in the middle; their index number is right around the median or target index number. Folks in this category have decent enough LSAT scores and GPAs for the school, just not high enough for automatic admission. Why do most people fall into this category? Because for the most part, people apply to schools they think they have at least a shot of getting into based on their grades and LSAT scores; Yale doesn't see very many applicants who got a 140 on the LSAT. What will determine the fate of those whose applications hang in the balance? One thing law schools often look at is the competitiveness of your undergraduate program. On the one hand, someone with a 3.3 GPA in an easy major from a school where everybody graduates with a 3.3 or higher will face an uphill battle. On the other hand, someone with the same GPA in a difficult major from a school that has a reputation for being stingy with A's is in better shape. Admissions officers will also pore over the rest of your application—personal statement, letters of recommendation, resume, etc.—for reasons to admit you, reject you, or put you on their waiting list.

ARE YOU MORE THAN YOUR LSAT SCORE?

Aside from LSAT scores and GPAs, what do law schools consider when deciding who's in and who's out? It's the eternal question. On the one hand, we should disabuse you hidebound cynics of the notion that they care about nothing else. On the other hand, if you harbor fantasies that a stunning application can overcome truly substandard scores and grades, you should realize that such hopes are unrealistic.

Nonquantitative factors are particularly important at law schools that receive applications from thousands of numerically qualified applicants. A "Top Ten" law school that receives 10 or 15 applications for every spot in its first-year class has no choice but to "look beyond the numbers," as admissions folks are fond of saying. Such a school will almost surely have to turn away hundreds of applicants with near-perfect LSAT scores and college grades, and those applicants who get past the initial cut will be subjected to real scrutiny.

Less competitive schools are just as concerned, in their own way, with "human criteria" as are the Harvards and Stanfords of the world. They are on the lookout for capable people who have relatively unimpressive GPAs and LSAT scores. The importance of the application is greatly magnified for these students, who must demonstrate their probable success in law school in other ways.

CAN PHYSICS MAJORS GO TO LAW SCHOOL?

"What about my major?" is one of the more popular questions we hear when it comes to law school admissions. The conventional answer to this question goes something like "There is no prescribed, pre-law curriculum, but you should seek a broad and challenging liberal arts education, and yadda, yadda, yadda."

Here's the truth: It really doesn't matter what you major in. Obviously, a major in aviation or hotel and restaurant management is not exactly ideal, but please—we beg you!—don't feel restricted to a few majors simply because you want to attend law school. This is especially true if those particular majors do not interest you. Comparative literature? Fine. American studies? Go to town. Physics? No problem whatsoever. You get the idea.

Think about it. Because most would-be law students end up majoring in the *same* few fields (e.g., political science and philosophy), their applications all look the *same* to the folks in law school admissions offices. You want to stand out, which is why it is a good idea to major in something *different*. Ultimately, you should major in whatever appeals to you. By the way, of course, if you want to major in political science or philosophy (or you already have), well, that's fine too.

DOES GRAD SCHOOL COUNT?

Your grades in graduate school will not be included in the calculation of your GPA (only the UGPA, the undergraduate grade point average, is reported to the schools) but will be taken into account separately by an admissions committee if you make them available. Reporting grad school grades would be to your advantage, particularly if they are better than your college grades. Admissions committees are likely to take this as a sign of improvement with maturation.

> ***Waiting Lists***
>
> *If a law school puts you on its waiting list, it means you may be admitted depending on how many of the applicants they've already admitted decide to go to another school. Most schools rank students on their waiting list; they'll probably tell you where you stand if you give them a call. Also, note that schools routinely admit students from their waiting lists in late August. If you are on a school's waiting list and you really, really want to go there, keep your options at least partially open. You just might be admitted in the middle of first-year orientation.*

ADVICE FOR THE "NONTRADITIONAL" APPLICANT

The term "nontraditional" is, of course, used to describe applicants who are a few years or many years older than run-of-the-mill law school applicants.

In a nutshell, there's no time like the present to start law school. It's true that most law students are in their early to mid-twenties, but if you aren't, don't think for a minute that your age will keep you from getting in and having a great experience. It won't. Applicants for full-time and part-time slots at all manner of law schools all over the fruited plain range in age from twenty-one to seventy-one and include every age in between. Some of these older applicants always intended to go to law school and simply postponed it to work, travel, or start a family. Other older applicants never seriously considered law school until after they were immersed in another occupation.

Part-time attendance is especially worth checking into if you've been out of college for a few years. Also, dozens of law schools offer evening programs—particularly in urban centers.

MINORITY LAW SCHOOL APPLICANTS

Things are definitely looking up. Back in 1978, according to figures published by the American Bar Association's Committee on Legal Education, over 90 percent of the law students in the ABA's 167 schools were white. In recent years, though, the number of nonwhites enrolled in law school has nearly doubled, from about 10 percent to more than 20 percent. Taking an even longer view, figures have tripled since 1972, when minority enrollment was only 6.6 percent. These days, the American Bar Association and the legal profession in general seem pretty committed to seeking and admitting applicants who are members of historically under-represented minority groups.

WOMEN IN LAW SCHOOL

During the past decade, the number of women lawyers has escalated rapidly, and women undeniably have become more visible in the uppermost echelons of the field. Two women sit on the United States Supreme Court, for instance. Also, according to statistics compiled by the American Bar Association (ABA), more than 16 percent of all law firm partners are women and women comprise more than 29 percent of all lawyers.

> ***Engineering and Math Majors Make Great Law Students***
>
> *A disproportionate number of law students with backgrounds in the so-called "hard sciences" (math, physics, engineering, etc.) make very high grades in law school, probably because they are trained to think methodically and efficiently about isolated problems (which is what law students are supposed to do on exams).*

More and more women are going to law school as well. At a solid majority of the ABA-approved law schools in the United States, the percentage of women in the student population is 49 percent, and women make up well over half of the students at a handful of schools.

Gender discrimination certainly lingers here and there, though. You might want to check certain statistics on the law schools you are interested in, such as the percentage of women on law review and the percentage of female professors who are tenured or on track to be tenured. (Nationally, nearly 33 percent of all full law school professors are women, and 25 percent of tenured faculty are women.) Also, go to each law school and talk with female students and female professors about how women are treated at that particular school. Finally, see if the school has published any gender studies about itself. If it has, you obviously ought to check them out, too.

CHAPTER 2
CHOOSING A LAW SCHOOL

There are some key things you should consider before randomly selecting schools from around the country or just submitting your application to somebody else's list of the Top 10 law schools.

GEOGRAPHY

It's a big deal. If you were born and raised in the state of New Mexico, care deeply about the "Land of Enchantment," wish to practice law there, and want to be the governor someday, then your best bet is to go to the University of New Mexico. A school's reputation is usually greater on its home turf than anywhere else (except for some of the larger-than-life schools, like Harvard and Yale). Also, most law schools tend to teach law that is specific to the states in which they are located. Knowledge of the eccentricities of state law will help you immensely three years down the road when it comes time to pass the bar exam. Even further, the career services office at your school will be strongly connected to the local legal industry. And, as a purely practical matter, it will be much easier to find a job and get to interviews in Boston, for example, if you live there. Still another reason to consider geography is the simple fact that you'll put down professional and social roots and get to know a lot of really great people throughout your law school career. Leaving them won't be any fun. Finally, starting with geographic limitations is the easiest way to reduce your number of potential schools dramatically.

SPECIALIZATION

Word has it that specialization is the trend of the future. General practitioners in law are becoming less common, so it makes sense to let future lawyers begin to specialize in school. At certain schools, you may receive your JD with an official emphasis in, say, taxation. Specialization is a particularly big deal at smaller or newer schools whose graduates cannot simply get by on their school's established reputation of excellence. Just between us, though, it's kind of hard to specialize in anything in most law schools because every graduate has to take this huge exam—the bar—that tests about a dozen topics. Most of your course selections will (and should) be geared toward passing the bar, which leaves precious few hours for specialization. You'll almost certainly specialize, but it's not something to worry about until you actually look for a job. All of that said, if you already know what kind of law you want to specialize in, you're in good shape. Many schools offer certain specialties because of their location. If you are very interested in environmental law, you'd be better off going to Vermont Law School or Lewis and Clark's Northwestern School of Law than to Brooklyn Law School. Similarly, if you want to work with children as an attorney, check out Loyola University Chicago's Child Law Center. So look at what you want to do in addition to where you want to do it.

Dean's List

According to a letter signed by just about every dean of every ABA-approved law school in the country, here are the factors you should consider when choosing a law school:

- *Breadth and support of alumni network*
- *Breadth of curriculum*
- *Clinical programs*
- *Collaborative research opportunities with faculty*
- *Commitment to innovative technology*
- *Cost*
- *Externship options*
- *Faculty accessibility*
- *Intensity of writing instruction*
- *Interdisciplinary programs*
- *International programming*
- *Law library strengths and services*
- *Loan repayment assistance for low-income lawyers*
- *Location*
- *Part-time enrollment options*
- *Public interest programs*
- *Quality of teaching*
- *Racial and gender diversity within the faculty and student body*
- *Religious affiliation*
- *Size of first-year classes*
- *Skills instruction*
- *Specialized areas of faculty expertise*

JOINT DEGREE PROGRAMS

In addition to offering specialized areas of study, many law schools have instituted formal dual-degree programs. These schools, nearly all of which are directly affiliated with a parent institution, offer students the opportunity to pursue a JD while also working toward some other degree. Although the JD/MBA combination is the most popular joint degree sought, many universities offer a JD program combined with degrees in everything from public policy to public administration to social work. Amidst a perpetually competitive legal market, dual degrees may make some students more marketable for certain positions come job time. However, don't sign up for a dual-degree program on a whim—they require a serious amount of work and often a serious amount of tuition.

YOUR CHANCE OF ACCEPTANCE

Who knows how law schools end up with their reputations, but everything else being equal, you really do want to go a to a well-respected school. It will enhance your employment opportunities tremendously. Remember, whoever you are and whatever your background, your best bet is to select a couple "reach" schools, a couple schools at which you've got a good shot at being accepted, and a couple "safety" schools where you are virtually assured acceptance. Remember also that being realistic about your chances will save you from unnecessary emotional letdowns. Getting in mostly boils down to numbers. Look at the acceptance rates and the average LSATs and GPAs of incoming classes at various schools to assess how you stack up.

The Dreaded Bar Exam

Once you graduate, most states require you to take a bar exam before you can practice law. Some state bar exams are really, really hard; New York and California are examples. If you don't want to take a bar exam, consider a law school in beautiful Wisconsin. Anyone who graduates from a state-certified Wisconsin law school does not need to take the state bar exam to practice law in the Badger State, as long as they are approved by the Board of Bar Examiners.

PERSONAL APPEAL

A student at a prominent law school in the Pacific Northwest once described his law school to us as "a combination wood-grain bomb shelter and Ewok village." Another student at a northeastern law school told us her law school was fine except for its "ski-slope classrooms" and "East German Functionalist" architecture. While the curricula at various law schools are pretty much the same, the weather, the surrounding neighborhoods, the nightlife, and the character of the student populations are startlingly different. An important part of any graduate program is enjoying those moments in life when you're not studying. If you aren't comfortable in the environment you choose, it's likely to be reflected in the quality of work you do and your attitude. Before you make a $10,000 to $80,000 investment in any law school, you really ought to check it out in person. While you are there, talk to students and faculty. Walk around. Kick the tires. *Then* make a decision.

EMPLOYMENT PROSPECTS

Where do alumni work? How much money do they make? What percentage of graduates is employed within nine months of graduation? How many major law firms interview on campus? These are massively important questions, and you owe it to yourself to look into the answers before choosing a school.

YOUR VALUES

It is important that you define honestly the criteria for judging law schools. What do you want out of a law school? Clout? A high salary? A hopping social life? To live in a certain city? To avoid being in debt up to your eyeballs? A noncompetitive atmosphere? Think about it.

MAKE A LIST

Using these criteria (and others you find relevant), develop a list of prospective schools. Ideally, you'll find this book useful in creating the list. Assign a level to each new school you add (something like "reach," "good shot," and "safety").

Did You Know?

According to the people who take the LSAT, the average applicant applies to four or more law schools.

At your "reach" schools, the average LSAT scores and GPAs of incoming students should be higher than yours are. These are law schools that will probably not accept you based on your numbers alone. In order to get in, you'll need to wow them with everything else (personal statement, stellar recommendations, work experience, etc.).

Your "good shot" schools should be the schools you like that accept students with about the same LSAT scores and GPA as yours. Combined with a strong and *cohesive* application, you've got a decent shot at getting into these schools.

At your "safety" schools, the average LSAT scores and GPAs of their current students should be below yours. These schools should accept you pretty painlessly if there are no major blemishes on your application (e.g., a serious run-in with the law), and you don't just phone in the application. They hate that.

CHAPTER 3
APPLYING TO LAW SCHOOL

Our advice: Start early. The LSAT alone can easily consume 80 or more hours of prep time, and a single application form might take as much as 30 hours if you take great care with the essay questions. Don't sabotage your efforts through last-minute sloppiness or let this already-annoying process become a gigantic burden.

WHEN TO APPLY

Yale Law School's absolute final due date is February 1, but Loyola University Chicago's School of Law will receive your application up to April 1. There is no pattern. However, the longer you wait to apply to a school, regardless of its deadline, the worse your chances of getting into that school may be. No efficient admissions staff is going to wait for all the applications before starting to make their selections.

If you're reading this in December and hope to get into a law school for the fall but haven't done anything about it, you're in big trouble. If you've got an LSAT score you are happy with, you're in less trouble. However, your applications will get to the law schools after the optimum time and, let's face it, they may appear a bit rushed. The best way to think about applying is to start early in the year, methodically take care of one thing at a time, and *finish by December*.

Early Admissions Options. A few schools have "early admissions" options, so you may know by December if you've been accepted (for instance, New York University's early admission deadline is on or about October 15). Early admission is a good idea for a few reasons. It can give you an indication of what your chances are at other schools. It can relieve the stress of waiting until April to see where you'll be spending the next three years of your life. Also, it's better to get waitlisted in December than April (or whenever you would be notified for regular admission); if there is a "tie" among applicants on the waiting list, they'll probably admit whoever applied first. Of course, not every school's early admission option is the same (and many schools don't even have one).

Rolling Admissions. Many law schools evaluate applications and notify applicants of admission decisions continuously over the course of several months (ordinarily from late fall to midsummer). Obviously, if you apply to one of these schools, it is vital that you apply as early as possible because there will be more places available at the beginning of the process.

Applying Online. Almost all law schools are allowing applicants to submit applications online. The LSAC online service (www.lsac.org) has a searchable database and applications to ABA-approved schools. For students applying for 2006 admission, all LSDAS (see below) registrants will have free access to online applications for all ABA-approved law schools.

LAW SCHOOL ADMISSIONS COUNCIL: THE LAW SCHOOL APPLICATION MAFIA

In addition to single-handedly creating and administering the LSAT, an organization called the Law School Admissions Council (LSAC) maintains a stranglehold on communication between you and virtually every law school in the United States. It runs the Law School Data Assembly Service (LSDAS), which provides information (in a standard format) on applicants to the law schools. They—not you—send your grades, your LSAT score, and plenty of other information about you to the schools. You'll send only your actual applications directly to the law schools themselves. Oh, by the way, the fee for this service is $106 of your hard-earned money plus $12 (or more) every time you want LSDAS to send a report about you to an additional law school.

THE BIG HURDLES IN THE APPLICATION PROCESS: A BRIEF OVERVIEW

Take the LSAT. The Law School Admission Test is a roughly three-and-a-half-hour multiple-choice test used by law schools to help them select candidates. The LSAT is given in February, June, October (or, occasionally, late September), and December of each year. It's divided into five multiple-choice sections and one (completely useless) writing sample. All ABA-approved and most non-ABA-approved law schools in the United States and Canada require an LSAT score from each and every applicant.

Register for LSDAS. You can register for the Law School Data Assembly Service at the same time you register to take the LSAT; all necessary forms are contained in the *LSAT and LSDAS Registration Information Book* (hence the name). It can also be done, of course, online.

Get applications from six or seven schools. Why so many? Better safe than sorry. Fairly early—like in July—select a couple "reach"

LSDAS Fees

LSDAS Subscription Fee: $106 (This buys you an LSDAS "subscription" for 12 months and a single, solitary report to one law school.)

LSDAS Law School Reports: $12

A Legal Education: Priceless

schools, a couple schools to which you've got a good shot at being accepted, and a couple "safety" schools where you are virtually assured of acceptance. Your safety school—if you were being realistic—will probably accept you pretty quickly. It may take a while to get a final decision from the other schools, but you won't be totally panicked because you'll know your safety school is there for you. If, for whatever reason, your grades or LSAT score are extremely low, you should apply to several safety schools. Most schools won't post online applications until mid-September at the earliest. Still, it is a good idea to familiarize yourself with the previous year's applications as soon as possible, as law schools tend not to radically alter components of their applications from one year to the next.

Write your personal statement. With any luck, you'll only have to write one personal statement. Many, many schools will simply ask you the same question: basically, "Why do you want to obtain a law degree?" However, you may need to write several personal statements and essays—which is one more reason you need to select your schools fairly early.

Obtain two or three recommendations. Some schools will ask for two recommendations, both of which must be academic. Others want more than two recommendations and want at least one to be from someone who knows you outside traditional academic circles. As part of your LSDAS file, the LSAC will accept up to three letters of recommendation on your behalf, and they will send them to all the schools to which you apply. This is one of the few redeeming qualities of the LSAC. The last thing the writers of your recommendations are going to want to do is sign, package, and send copies of their letters all over the continent.

Fee Waivers

Taking the LSAT, subscribing to LSDAS, and applying to law schools at $50–75 a pop will cost you an arm and a leg (though these costs are but a drop in the bucket compared to the amount of money you are about to spend on your law school education). The LSAC and most law schools offer fee waiver programs. If you are financially strapped and are accepted into the LSAC program, you get to take the LSAT and subscribe to LSDAS for free. You also get three LSDAS law school reports and a complimentary book of three previously administered LSATs.

You can download a Fee Waiver form at www.lsac.org, request that one be sent to you at 215-968-1001, or request one in writing at:

Law Services
Attn: Fee Waiver Packet
Box 2000
661 Penn Street
Newtown, PA 18940-0998

Update/create your resume. Most law school applicants ask that you submit a resume. Make sure yours is up-to-date and suitable for submission to an academic institution. Put your academic credentials and experience first—no matter what they are. This is just a supplement to the rest of the material; it's probably the simplest part of the application process.

Get your academic transcripts sent to LSDAS. When you subscribe to LSDAS, you must request that the registrar at every undergraduate, graduate, and professional school you ever attended send an official transcript to Law Services. Don't even think about sending your own transcripts anywhere; these people don't trust you any farther than they can throw you. *Make these requests in August*. If you're applying for early decision, start sending for transcripts as early as May. Law schools require complete files before making their decisions, and LSDAS won't send your information to the law schools without your transcripts. Undergraduate institutions can and will screw up and delay the transcript process—even when you go there personally and pay them to provide your records. Give yourself some time to fix problems should they arise.

Write any necessary addenda. An addendum is a brief explanatory letter written to explain or support a "deficient" portion of your application. If your personal and academic life has been fairly smooth, you won't need to include any addenda with your application. If, however, you were ever on academic probation, arrested, or if you have a low GPA, you may need to write one. Other legitimate addenda topics are a low/discrepant LSAT score, DUI/DWI suspensions, or any "time gap" in your academic or professional career.

An addendum is absolutely not the place to go off on polemics about the fundamental unfairness of the LSAT or how that evil campus security officer was only out to get you when you got arrested. If, for example, you have taken the LSAT two or three times and simply did not do very well, even after spending time and money preparing with a test prep company or a private tutor, merely tell the admissions committee that you worked diligently to achieve a high score. Say you explored all possibilities to help you achieve that goal. Whatever the case, lay out the facts, but let them draw their own conclusions. Be brief and balanced. Be fair. Do not go into detailed descriptions of things. Explain the problem and state what you did about it. This is no time to whine.

Send in your seat deposit. Once you are accepted at a particular school, that school will ask you to put at least some of your money where your mouth is. A typical fee runs $200 or more. This amount will be credited to your first-term tuition once you actually register for classes.

Do any other stuff. You may find that there are other steps you must take during the law school application process. You may request a fee waiver, for example. Make extra-special sure to get a copy of the LSAC's *LSAT/LSDAS Registration and Information Book,* which is unquestionably the most useful tool in applying to law school. It has the forms you'll need, a sample LSAT, admissions information, the current Law Forum schedule, and sample application schedules.

The Princeton Review	**LAW SCHOOL APPLICATION CHECKLIST** (suitable for framing)
January	• **Take a practice LSAT.** Do it at a library or some place where you won't be interrupted. Also, take it all at once.
February	• **Investigate LSAT prep courses.** If you don't take one with The Princeton Review, do *something.* Just as with any test, you'll get a higher score on this one if you prepare for it first.
March	• **Obtain an *LSAT/LSDAS Registration and Information Book.*** The books are generally published in March of each year. You can get one at any law school, by calling the LSAC at 215-968-1001, or by stopping by The Princeton Review office nearest you. You can also download one in .pdf format at www.lsac.org.
April	• **Register for the June LSAT.** • **Begin an LSAT prep course.** At the very, very least, use some books or software.
May	• **Continue your LSAT prep.**
June	• **Take the LSAT.** If you take the test twice, many schools will avenge them. Your best bet is to take it once, do exceedingly well, and get it out of your hair forever.
July	• **Register for LSDAS.** • **Research law schools.**
August	• **Obtain law school applications.** You can call or write, but the easiest and cheapest way to get applications is via the Internet. This is, of course, only necessary if you plan to send in paper applications. Go to www.lsac.org to access and submit online applications. • **Get your undergraduate transcripts sent to LSDAS.** Make sure to contact the registrar at each undergraduate institution you attended.
September	• **Write your personal statements.** Proofread them. Edit them. Edit them again. Have someone else look them over for all the mistakes you missed. • **Update your resume.** Or create a resume if you don't have one. • **Get your recommendations in order.** You want your recommenders to submit recommendations exactly when you send your applications (in October and November).
October	• **Complete and send early decision applications.**
November	• **Complete and send all regular applications.**
December	• **Chill.** • **Buy holiday gifts.** • **Make plans for New Year's.**

CHAPTER 4
THE LSAT

As you may know, we at The Princeton Review are pretty much disgusted with most of the standardized tests out there. They make us a lot of money, of course, and we like that, but they are hideously poor indicators of anything besides how well you do on that particular standardized test. They are certainly not intelligence tests. The LSAT is no exception. It is designed to keep you out of law school, not facilitate your entrance into it. For no good reason we can think of, this 101-question test is *the single most important factor in all of law school admissions*, and, at least for the foreseeable future, we're all stuck with it.

Unfortunately, with the possible exception of the MCAT (for medical school), the LSAT is the toughest of all the standardized tests. Only 23–24 of the 101 questions have a "correct" answer (Logic Games), as opposed to Arguments and Reading Comprehension, where you must choose the elusive "best" answer. As ridiculous as they are, the GMAT, GRE, SAT, MCAT, and ACT at least have large chunks of math or science on them. There are verifiably correct answers on these tests, and occasionally you even have to know something to get to them. *Only the LSAT requires almost no specific knowledge of anything whatsoever, which is precisely what makes it so difficult.* The only infallible way to study for the LSAT is to study the LSAT itself. The good news is that *anybody* can get significantly better at the LSAT by working diligently at it. In fact, your score will increase exponentially in relation to the amount of time and work you put into preparing for it.

HOW IMPORTANT IS THE LSAT?

The LSAT figures very prominently in your law school application, especially if you've been out of school for a few years. Some law schools won't even look at your application unless you achieve a certain score on your LSAT. Most top law schools average multiple LSAT scores, so you should aim to take it only once. By the way, each score you receive is valid for five years after you take the test.

LSAT STRUCTURE

Section Type	Sections	Questions Per Section	Time Per Section
Logical Reasoning (Arguments)	2	24-26	35 minutes
Analytical Reasoning (Games)	1	23-24	35 minutes
Reading Comprehension	1	27-28	35 minutes
Experimental	1	????	35 minutes
Writing Sample	1	1	30 minutes

Each test has 101 questions. Neither the experimental section nor the writing sample counts toward your score. The multiple-choice sections may be given in any order, but the writing sample is always administered last. The experimental section can be any of the three types of multiple-choice sections and is used by the test writers to test out new questions on your time and at your expense.

Not only is the writing sample not scored, but it is also unlikely that anyone other than you will ever read it. However, the law schools to which you apply will receive a copy of your writing sample, so you should definitely do it. A blank page would stand out like a sore thumb, and you wouldn't want the folks in the admissions office to think you were some kind of revolutionary.

WHAT'S ON THE LSAT, EXACTLY?

We asked the experts in the LSAT Course Division of The Princeton Review for the lowdown on the various sections of the LSAT. Here's what they had to say:

> ***Registering for the LSAT***
>
> *You can register for the LSAT by mail, over the phone, or online. To register by mail, you will need a copy of the Registration and Information Bulletin, which you may either request from Law Services or pick up from your pre-law advisor. You may also register for the LSAT online at www.lsac.org. The LSAT fee is currently a whopping $115; if you're late, it's an extra $58. To avoid late fees, mail your registration form at least six weeks—six weeks—before the test. Also, by registering early, you are more likely to be assigned your first choice of test center.*
>
> *You can reach the Law School Admissions Council at:*
>
> *Phone: 215-968-1001*
>
> *www.lsac.org*
>
> *lsacinfo@lsac.org*

Analytical Reasoning: If you've ever worked logic problems in puzzle books, then you're already somewhat familiar with the Analytical Reasoning section of the LSAT. The situations behind these problems—often called "games" or "logic games"—are common ones: deciding in what order to interview candidates, or assigning employees to teams, or arranging dinner guests around a table. The arrangement of "players" in these games is governed by a set of rules you must follow in answering the questions. Each Analytical Reasoning section is made up of four games, with five to seven questions each. Questions may ask you to find out what must be true under the rules, or what could be true under the rules; they may add a new condition that applies to just that question; or they may ask you to count the number of possible arrangements under the stated conditions. These questions are difficult mostly because of the time constraints under which they must be worked; very few test-takers find themselves able to complete twenty-four questions on this section in the time allotted.

Logical Reasoning: Because there are two scored sections of them, Logical Reasoning questions on the LSAT are the most important to your score. Each Logical Reasoning—sometimes called "arguments"—question is made up of a short paragraph, often written to make a persuasive point. These small arguments are usually written to contain a flaw—some error of reasoning or unwarranted assumption that you must identify in order to answer the question successfully. Questions may ask you to draw conclusions from the stated information, to weaken or strengthen the argument, to identify its underlying assumptions, or to identify its logical structure or method. There are most often a total of 50 or 51 argument questions between the two sections—roughly half of the scored questions on the LSAT.

Reading Comprehension: Reading Comprehension is familiar to anyone who's taken the SAT or virtually any other standardized test. The Reading Comprehension section is made up of four passages, each roughly 500 words in length, with six to eight associated questions. The material of these reading passages is often obscure or esoteric, but answering the questions correctly doesn't depend on any specialized knowledge. Questions may ask you to identify the passage's main idea, to identify descriptions of its structure or purpose, to evaluate the purpose of specific examples or contentions, or to understand its argumentation. Although the form of this section is familiar, the language and length of passages, questions, and answer choices make it challenging; like the Analytical Reasoning section, the Reading Comprehension section is for many test-takers simply too long to finish in the time allotted.

We strongly recommend that you prep for this test. Although we provide the best prep for the LSAT, you certainly don't have to take The Princeton Review's course (or buy our book, *Cracking the LSAT*, or sign up for our awesome distance learning course), as much as we'd obviously like it. There are plenty of books, software products, courses, and tutors out there. The people who make the LSAT will gleefully sell you plenty of practice tests as well. The key is to find the best program for you. Your first step should be taking a free full-length practice LSAT given under realistic testing conditions (we offer them across the country), so you can gauge where you stand and how much you need to improve your LSAT score. Whatever your course of action, though, make sure you remain committed to it, so you can be as prepared as possible when you take the actual test.

WHEN SHOULD YOU TAKE THE LSAT?

Here is a quick summary of test dates along with some factors to consider for each.

JUNE

The June administration is the only time the test is given on a Monday afternoon. If you have trouble functioning at the ordinary 8 A.M. start-time, June may be a good option. Furthermore, taking the LSAT in June frees up your summer and fall to research schools and complete applications. On the other hand, if you are still in college, you'll have to balance LSAT preparation with academic course work and, in some cases, final exams. Check your exam schedules before deciding on a June LSAT test date.

OCTOBER/SEPTEMBER

The October test date (which is sometimes in late September) will allow you to prepare for the LSAT during the summer. This is an attractive option if you are a college student with some free time on your hands. Once you've taken the LSAT, you can spend the remainder of your fall completing applications.

DECEMBER

December is the last LSAT administration that most competitive law schools will accept. If disaster strikes and you get a flat tire on test day, you may end up waiting another year to begin law school. December testers also must balance their time between preparing for the LSAT and completing law school applications. Doing so can make for a hectic fall, especially if you're still in college. You should also remember that, while a law school may accept December LSAT scores, taking the test in December could affect your chances of admission. Many law schools use a rolling admissions system, which means that they begin making admissions decisions as early as mid-October and continue to do so until the application deadline. Applying late in this cycle could mean that fewer spots are available. Check with your potential law schools to find out their specific policies.

FEBRUARY

If you want to begin law school in the following fall, the February LSAT will be too late for most law schools. However, if you don't plan to begin law school until the *next* academic year, you can give yourself a head start on the entire admissions process by taking the LSAT in February, then spending your summer researching schools and your fall completing applications.

UPCOMING LSAT TEST DATES		
TEST DATE	**Registration Deadline**	**Late Registration Ends**
October 1, 2005	August 30	September 9
December 3, 2005	November 1	November 11
February 4, 2006	January 3	January 13
June, 2006	TBA	TBA

HOW IS THE LSAT SCORED?

LSAT scores currently range from 120 to 180. Why that range? We have no idea. The following table indicates the percentile rating of the corresponding LSAT scores between 141 and 180. This varies slightly from test to test.

This is the case because your raw score (the number of questions you answer correctly) doesn't always produce the same scaled score as previous LSATs. What actually happens is that your raw score is compared to that of everyone else who took the test on the same date you did. The LSAC looks at the scales from every other LSAT given in the past three years and "normalizes" the current scale so that it doesn't deviate widely from those scaled scores in the past.

LSAT Score	Percent Below	LSAT Score	Percent Below
180	99.9	160	82.2
179	99.9	159	79.1
178	99.9	158	76.5
177	99.8	157	72.6
176	99.7	156	68.7
175	99.6	155	65.7
174	99.5	154	61.5
173	99.3	153	57.3
172	99.0	152	53.2
171	98.5	151	49.1
170	98.1	150	44.9
169	97.5	149	41.0
168	96.7	148	37.0
167	95.7	147	33.4
166	94.6	146	29.6
165	93.2	145	26.4
164	91.4	144	23.3
163	89.7	143	20.2
162	87.3	142	17.7
161	84.9	141	15.2

A GOOD LSAT SCORE

A good score on the LSAT is the score that gets you into the law school you want to attend. Remember that a large part of the admissions game is the formula of your UGPA (undergraduate grade point average) multiplied by your LSAT score. Chances are, you are at a point in life where your UGPA is pretty much fixed (if you're reading this early in your college career, start getting very good grades pronto), so the only piece of the formula you can have an impact on is your LSAT score. We cannot emphasize enough the notion that you must prepare for this test.

A LITTLE IMPROVEMENT GOES A LONG WAY

A student who scores a 154 is in the 62nd percentile of all LSAT-takers. If that student's score was 161, however, that same student would jump to the 85th percentile. Depending upon your score, a 7-point improvement can increase your ranking by over 25 percentile points.

COMPETITIVE LSAT SCORES AROUND THE UNITED STATES

The range of LSAT scores from the 25th to 75th percentile of incoming full-time students at U.S. law schools is pretty broad. Here is a sampling.

Law School	Score 25 to 75 percentile
Widener University, School of Law, Harrisburg	149–152
Gonzaga University, School of Law	150–156
University of Pittsburgh, School of Law	158–162
Temple University, James E. Beasley School of Law	157–162
Northeastern University, School of Law	157–162
Rutgers University–Newark, School of Law	153–162
University of Florida, Levin College of Law	156–162
University of Tennessee, College of Law	155–161
Case Western Reserve University, School of Law	157–161
University of Alabama, School of Law	159–163
Southern Methodist University, School of Law	156–164
Loyola University Chicago, School of Law	159–163
Boston University, School of Law	162–165
Emory University, School of Law	161–165
University of Southern California, The Law School	163–167
George Washington University, Law School	162–166
Duke University, School of Law	162–169
University of Michigan, Law School	164–169
Stanford University, School of Law	166–172
University of Chicago, Law School	167–171
Yale University, Yale Law School	168–175

PREPARING FOR THE LSAT

No matter who you are—whether you graduated *magna cum laude* from Cornell University or you're on academic probation at Cornell College—the first thing you need to do is order a recent LSAT. One comes free with every *Official LSAT Registration Booklet*. Once you get the test, take it, but not casually over the course of two weeks. Bribe someone to be your proctor. Have them administer the test to you under strict time conditions. Follow the test booklet instructions exactly, and do it right. Your goal is to simulate an actual testing experience as much as possible. When you finish, score the test honestly. Don't give yourself a few extra points because "you'll do better on test day." The score on this practice test will provide a baseline for mapping your test preparation strategy.

If your practice LSAT score is already at a point where you've got a very high-percentage shot of getting accepted to the law school of your choice, chances are you don't need much preparation. Order a half dozen or so of the most recent LSATs from LSAC and work through them over the course of a few months, making sure you understand why you are making specific mistakes. If your college or university offers a free or very cheap prep course, consider taking it to get more tips on the test. Many of these courses are taught by pre-law advisors who will speak very intelligently about the test and are committed to helping you get the best score you can.

If, after you take a practice LSAT, your score is not what you want or need it to be, you are definitely not alone. Many academically strong candidates go into the LSAT cold because they assume that the LSAT is no more difficult than or about the same as their college courses. Frankly, many students are surprised at how poorly they do the first time they take a dry run. Think about it this way: It's better to be surprised sitting at home with a practice test than while taking the test for real.

If you've taken a practice LSAT under exam conditions and it's, say, 10 or 15 points below where you want it to be, you should probably consult an expert. Test preparation companies spend quite a bit of money and time poring over the tests and measuring the improvements of their students. We sure do. Ask around. Assess your financial situation. Talk to other people who have improved their LSAT scores and duplicate their strategies.

Whatever you decide to do, make sure you are practicing on real LSAT questions, and you take full-length practice tests under realistic testing conditions—again and again and again.

SOME ESSENTIAL, DOWN-AND-DIRTY LSAT TIPS

Slow down. Way down. The slower you go, the better you'll do. It's that simple. Any function you perform, from basic motor skills to complex intellectual problems, will be affected by the rate at which you perform that function. This goes for everything from cleaning fish to taking the LSAT. You can get 25 questions wrong and still get a scaled score of 160, which is a very good score (it's in the 84th percentile). You can get at least six questions wrong per section or, even better, you can ignore the two or three most convoluted questions per section, *still* get a few *more* questions wrong, and you'll get an excellent overall score. Your best strategy is to find the particular working speed at which you will get the most questions correct.

There is no guessing penalty. If you don't have time to finish the exam, it's imperative that you leave yourself at least 30 seconds at the end of each section in which to grab free points by bubbling in some answer to every question before time is called. Pick a letter of the day—like B—don't bubble in randomly. If you guess totally randomly, you might get every single guess right. Of course, you may also get struck by lightning in the middle of the test. The odds are about the same. *You are far more likely to miss every question if you guess without a plan.* On the other hand, if you stick with the same letter each time you guess, you will definitely be right once in a while. It's a conservative approach, but it is also your best bet for guaranteed points, which is what you want. By guessing the same letter pretty much every time as time runs out, you can pick up anywhere from two to four raw points per section. Be careful about waiting until the very last second to start filling in randomly, though, because proctors occasionally cheat students out of the last few seconds of a section.

Use process of elimination all the time. This is absolutely huge. On 75 percent of the LSAT (all the Logical Reasoning and the Reading Comprehension questions), you are *not* looking for the *right* answer, only the *best* answer. It says so right there in the instructions. Eliminating even one answer choice increases your chances of getting the question right by 20 to 25 percent. If you can cross off two or three answer choices, you are really in business. Also, very rarely will you find an answer choice that is flawless on the LSAT. Instead, you'll find four answer choices that are definitely wrong and one that is the least of five evils. You should constantly look for reasons to get rid of answer choices so you can eliminate them. This strategy will increase your odds of getting the question right, and you'll be a happier and more successful standardized test-taker. We swear.

Law School Trivia

The last president to argue a case before the United States Supreme Court was Richard Nixon (a Duke alumnus). He argued the case between his tenure as vice president and his presidency. The case was Time, Inc. v. Hill (1967), a rather complicated First Amendment case.

Attack! Attack! Attack! Read the test with an antagonistic, critical eye. Read it like it's a contract you are about to sign with the devil; look for holes and gaps in the reasoning of arguments and in the answer choices. Many LSAT questions revolve around what is wrong with a particular line of reasoning. The more you can identify what is wrong with a problem before going to the answer choices, the more successful you'll be.

Write all over your test booklet. Actively engage the exam and put your thoughts on paper. Circle words. *Physically cross out wrong answer choices you have eliminated.* Draw complete and exact diagrams for the logic games. Use the diagrams you draw.

Do the questions in whatever order you wish. Just because a logic game question is first doesn't mean you should do it first. There is *no order of difficulty* on the LSAT—unlike some other standardized tests—so you should hunt down and destroy those questions at which you are personally best. If you are doing a Reading Comprehension question, for example, or tackling an argument, and you don't know what the hell is going on, then cross off whatever you can, guess, and move on. If you have no idea how to solve a particular logic game, don't focus your energy there. Find a game you can do and milk it for points. Your mission is to gain points wherever you can. By the way, if a particular section is really throwing you, it's probably because it is the dastardly experimental section (which is often kind of sloppy and, thankfully, does not count toward your score).

CHAPTER 5
WRITING A GREAT PERSONAL STATEMENT

There is no way to avoid writing the dreaded personal statement. You'll probably need to write only one personal statement, and it will probably address the most commonly asked question: "Why do you want to obtain a law degree?" This question, in one form or another, appears on virtually every law school application and often represents your only opportunity to string more than two sentences together. Besides your grades and your LSAT score, it is the most important part of your law school application. Your answer should be about two pages long, and it should amount to something significantly more profound than "A six-figure salary really appeals to me," or "Because I watch *Law & Order* every night."

Unlike your application to undergraduate programs, the personal statement on a law school application is not the time to discuss what your trip to Europe meant to you, describe your wacky chemistry teacher, or try your hand at verse. It's a fine line. While you want to stand out, you definitely don't want to be *overly* creative here. You want to be unique, but you don't want to come across as a weirdo or a loose cannon. You want to present yourself as intelligent, professional, mature, persuasive, and concise because these are the qualities law schools seek in applicants.

THE BASICS

Here are the essentials of writing essays and personal statements.

Find your own unique angle. The admissions people read tons of really boring essays about "how great I am" and how "I think there should be justice for everyone." If you must explain why you want to obtain a law degree, strive to find an angle that is interesting and unique to you. If what you write *isn't* interesting to you, we promise that it won't be remotely interesting to an admissions officer. Also, in addition to being more effective, a unique and interesting essay will be far more enjoyable to write.

In general, avoid generalities. Again, admissions officers have to read an unbelievable number of boring essays. You will find it harder to be boring if you write about particulars. It's the details that stick in a reader's mind.

Good writing is writing that is easily understood. You want to get your point across, not bury it in words. Don't talk in circles. Your prose should be clear and direct. If an admissions officer has to struggle to figure out what you are trying to say, you'll be in trouble. Also, legal writing courses make up a significant part of most law school curriculums; if you can show that you have good writing skills, you have a serious edge.

Buy and read *The Elements of Style* by William Strunk, Jr. and E. B. White. We can't recommend it enough. In fact, we're surprised you don't have it already. This little book is a required investment for any writer (and, believe us, you'll be doing plenty of writing as a law student and a practicing attorney). You will refer to it forever, and if you do what it says, your writing will definitely improve.

Have three or four people read your personal statement and critique it. If your personal statement contains misspellings and grammatical errors, admissions officers will conclude not only that you don't know how to write but also that you aren't shrewd enough to get help. What's worse, the more time you spend with a piece of your own writing, the less likely you are to spot any errors. You get tunnel vision. Ask friends, boyfriends, girlfriends, professors, brothers, sisters—somebody—to read your essay and comment on it. Use a computer with a spellchecker. *Be especially careful about punctuation!* Another tip: Read your personal statement aloud to yourself or someone else. You will catch mistakes and awkward phrases that would have gotten past you otherwise because it sounded fine in your head.

Don't repeat information from other parts of your application. It's a waste of time and space.

Stick to the length that is requested. It's only common courtesy.

Maintain the proper tone. Your essay should be memorable without being outrageous and easy to read, without being too formal or sloppy. When in doubt, err on the formal side.

Being funny is much harder than you think. An applicant who can make an admissions officer laugh never gets lost in the shuffle. The clever part of the personal statement is passed around and read aloud. Everyone smiles and the admissions staff can't bear to toss your application into the "reject" pile. But beware! Most people think they're funny, but only a few are able to pull it off in this context. Obviously, stay away from one liners, limericks, and anything remotely off-color.

WHY DO YOU WANT TO GO TO LAW SCHOOL?

Writing about yourself often proves to be surprisingly difficult. It's certainly no cakewalk explaining who you are and why you want to go to law school, and presenting your lifetime of experiences in a mere two pages is nearly impossible. On the bright side, though, the personal statement is the only element of your application over which you have total control. It's a tremendous opportunity to introduce yourself, if you avoid the urge to communicate your entire genetic blueprint. Your goal should be much more modest.

Websites about Getting into Law School

www.PrincetonReview.com

You can access tons of information about law school and the LSAT at our site.

www.lsac.org

This site is home to the people who bring you the LSAT and the LSDAS application processing service.

www.pre-law.com

This is a confidential service designed to answer your questions about how best to prepare for and successfully apply to law school. Once registered, you become eligible for up to a full year of unlimited, personalized, high-quality, pre-law advising for one flat fee.

DON'T GET CARRIED AWAY

Although some law schools set no limit on the length of the personal statement, you shouldn't take their bait. You can be certain that your statement will be at least glanced at in its entirety, but admissions officers are human, and their massive workload at admissions time has an understandable impact on their attention spans. You should limit yourself to two or three typed, double-spaced pages. Does this make your job any easier? Not at all. In fact, practical constraints on the length of your essay demand a higher degree of efficiency and precision. Your essay needs to convey what kind of thinking, feeling human being you are, and a two-page limit allows for absolutely no fat.

MAKE YOURSELF STAND OUT

We know you know this, but you will be competing against thousands of well-qualified applicants for admission to just about any law school. Consequently, your primary task in writing your application is to separate yourself from the crowd. Particularly if you are applying directly from college or if you have been out of school for a very short time, you must do your best to see that the admissions committee cannot categorize you too broadly. Admissions committees will see innumerable applications from bright 22-year-olds with good grades. Your essay presents an opportunity to put those grades in context, to define and differentiate yourself.

WHAT MAKES A GOOD PERSONAL STATEMENT?

Like any good writing, your law school application should be clear, concise, and candid. The first two of these qualities, clarity and conciseness, are usually the products of a lot of reading, rereading, and rewriting. Without question, repeated critical revision by yourself and others is the surest way to trim and tune your prose. The third quality, candor, is the product of proper motivation. Honesty cannot be superimposed after the fact; your writing must be candid from the outset.

In writing your personal statement for law school applications, pay particularly close attention to the way your essay is structured and the fundamental message it communicates. Admissions committees will read your essay two ways: as a product of your handiwork and as a product of your mind. Don't underestimate the importance of either perspective. A well-crafted essay will impress any admissions officer, but if it does not illuminate, you will not be remembered. You will not stand out; this is bad. Conversely, a thoughtful essay that offers true insight will stand out unmistakably, but if it is not readable, it will not receive serious consideration.

THINGS TO AVOID IN YOUR PERSONAL STATEMENT

"MY LSAT SCORE ISN'T GREAT, BUT I'M JUST NOT A GOOD TEST TAKER."

If you have a low LSAT score, avoid directly discussing it in your personal statement like the plague. Law school is a test-rich environment. In fact, grades in most law-school courses are determined by a single exam at the semester's end, and as a law student, you'll spend your Novembers and Aprils in a study carrel, completely removed from society. Saying that you are not good at tests will do little to convince an admissions committee that you've got the ability to succeed in law school once accepted.

Consider also that a low LSAT score speaks for itself—all too eloquently. It doesn't need you to speak for it, too. The LSAT may be a flawed test but don't go arguing the merits of the test to admissions officers because ordinarily it is the primary factor they use to make admissions decisions. We feel for you, but you'd be barking up the wrong tree here. The attitude of most law school admissions departments is that while the LSAT may be imperfect, it is equally imperfect for all applicants. Apart from extraordinary claims of serious illness on test day, few explanations for poor performance on the LSAT will mean much to the people who read your application.

About the only situation in which a discussion of your LSAT score is necessary is if you have two (or more) LSAT scores and one is significantly better than another. If you did much better in your second sitting than in your first, or vice versa, a brief explanation couldn't hurt. However, your explanation may mean little to the committee, which may have its own hard-and-fast rules for interpreting multiple LSAT scores. Even in this scenario, however, you should avoid bringing up the LSAT in the personal statement. *Save it for an addendum.*

The obvious and preferable alternative to an explicit discussion of a weak LSAT score would be to focus on what you *are* good at. If you really are bad at standardized tests, you must be better at something else, or you wouldn't have gotten as far as you have. If you think you are a marvelous researcher, say so. If you are a wonderful writer, show it. Let your essay implicitly draw attention away from your weak points by focusing on your strengths. There is no way to convince an admissions committee that they should overlook your LSAT score. You may, however, present compelling reasons for them to look beyond it.

"MY COLLEGE GRADES WEREN'T THAT HIGH, BUT . . ."

This issue is a bit more complicated than the low LSAT score. Law school admissions committees will be more willing to listen to your interpretation of your college performance, but only within limits. Keep in mind that law schools require official transcripts for a reason. Members of the admissions committee will be aware of your academic credentials before ever getting to your essay. Just like with low LSAT scores, your safest course of action is to *save low grades for an addendum.*

Make no mistake: if your grades are unimpressive, you should offer the admissions committee something else by which to judge your abilities. Again, the best argument for looking past your college grades is evidence of achievement in another area, whether in your LSAT score, your extracurricular activities, your economic hardship as an undergraduate, or your career accomplishments.

"I'VE ALWAYS WANTED TO BE A LAWYER."

Sure you have. Many applicants seem to feel the need to point out that they really, really want to become attorneys. You will do yourself a great service by avoiding such throwaway lines. They'll do nothing for your essay but water it down. Do not convince yourself in a moment of desperation that claiming to have known that the law was your calling since age six (when—let's be honest—you really wanted to be a firefighter) will somehow move your application to the top of the pile. The admissions committee is not interested in how much you want to practice law. They want to know *why*.

"I WANT TO BECOME A LAWYER TO FIGHT INJUSTICE."

No matter how deeply you feel about battling social inequity, between us, writing it down makes you sound like a superhero on a soapbox. Moreover, though some people really do want to fight injustice, way down in the cockles of their hearts, most applicants are motivated to attend law school by less altruistic desires. Among the nearly one million practicing lawyers in the United States, there are relatively few who actually earn a living defending the indigent or protecting civil rights. Tremendously dedicated attorneys who work for peanuts and take charity cases are few and far between. We're not saying you don't want to be one of them; we're merely saying that folks in law school admissions won't *believe* you want to be one of them. They'll take your professed altruistic ambitions (and those of the hundreds of other personal statements identical to yours) with a chunk of salt.

If you can in good conscience say that you are committed to a career in the public interest, show the committee something tangible on your application and in your essay that will allow them to see your statements as more than mere assertions. If however, you cannot show that you are already a veteran in the Good Fight, don't claim to be. Law school admissions committees certainly do not regard the legal profession as a Saints vs. Sinners proposition, and neither should you. Do not be afraid of appearing morally moderate. If the truth is that you want the guarantee of the relatively good jobs a law degree practically ensures, be forthright. Nothing is as impressive to the reader of a personal statement as the ring of truth. And what's wrong with a good job, anyhow?

CHAPTER 6

RECOMMENDATIONS

The law schools to which you apply will require two or three letters of recommendation in support of your application. Some schools will allow you to submit as many letters as you like. Others make it clear that any more than the minimum number of letters of recommendation is unwelcome. If you've ever applied to a private school (or perhaps a small public school) then you know the drill.

Unlike the evaluation forms for some colleges and graduate programs, however, law school recommendation forms tend toward absolute minimalism. All but a few recommendation forms for law school applications ask a single, open-ended question. It usually goes something like, "What information about this applicant is relevant that is not to be found in other sources?" The generic quality of the forms from various law schools may be both a blessing and a curse. On the one hand, it makes it possible for those writing your recommendations to write a single letter that will suffice for all the applications you submit. This convenience will make everybody a lot happier. On the other hand, if a free-form recommendation is to make a positive impression on an admissions committee, it must convey real knowledge about you.

WHOM TO ASK

Your letters of recommendation should come from people who know you well enough to offer a truly informed assessment of your abilities. Think carefully before choosing whom to ask to do this favor for you, but, as a general rule, pick respectable people you've known for a long time. If the writers of your recommendations know you well and understand the broader experience that has brought you to your decision to attend law school, they will be able to write a letter that is specific enough to do you some good. You also want people who can and are willing to contribute to an integrated, cohesive application.

The application materials from most law schools suggest that your letters should come, whenever possible, from people in an academic setting. Some schools want at least two recommendations, both of which must be academic. Others explicitly request that the letters come from someone who has known you in a professional setting, especially if you've been out of school for a while.

HELP YOUR RECOMMENDATION WRITERS HELP YOU

Here, in essence, is the simple secret to great recommendations: Make sure the writers of your recommendations know you, your academic and professional goals, and the overall message you are trying to convey in your application. The best recommendations will fit neatly with the picture you present of yourself in your own essay, even when they make no specific reference to the issues your essay addresses. An effective law school application will present to the admissions committee a cohesive picture, not a pastiche. A great way to point your recommendation writers in the right direction and maximize their ability to contribute to your overall cause is to provide them with copies of your personal statement. Don't be bashful about amiably communicating a few "talking points" that don't appear in your personal statement, as well.

ACADEMIC REFERENCES

Most applicants will (and should) seek recommendations from current or former professors. The academic environment in law school is extremely rigorous. Admissions committees will be looking for assurance that you will be able not just to survive, but to excel. A strong recommendation from a college professor is a valuable corroboration of your ability to succeed in law school.

You want nothing less than stellar academic recommendations. While a perfunctory, lukewarm recommendation is unlikely to damage your overall application, it will obviously do nothing to bolster it. Your best bet is to choose at least

Helpful Websites

www.findlaw.com

Findlaw has the mother lode of free information about law, law schools, and legal careers.

www.ilrg.com

Mother lode honorable mention.

www.hg.org/students.html

Another honorable mention.

www.canadalawschools.ca

Pretty much everything you ever wanted to know about Canadian law schools, eh.

www.jurist.law.pitt.edu

The University of Pittsburgh School of Law's splendid "Legal News and Research" website offers a wealth of useful information.

one professor from your major field. An enthusiastic endorsement from such a professor will be taken as a sign that you are an excellent student. Second—and we hope that this goes without saying—you should choose professors who do not immediately associate your name with the letter C.

Specifics are of particular interest to admissions officers when they evaluate your recommendations. If a professor can make *specific* reference to a particular project you completed, or at least make substantive reference to your work in a particular course, the recommendation will be strengthened considerably. Make it your responsibility to enable your professors to provide specifics. Drop hints, or just lay it out for them. You might, for example, make available a paper you wrote for them of which you are particularly proud. Or you might just chat with the professor for a while to jog those dormant memories. You might feel uncomfortable tooting your own horn, but it's for the best. Unless your professors are well enough acquainted with you to be able to offer a very personal assessment of your potential, they will greatly appreciate a tangible reminder of your abilities on which to base their recommendation.

ESCAPING THE WOODWORK

If you managed to get through college without any professors noticing you, it's not the end of the world. Professors are quite talented at writing recommendations for students they barely know. Most consider it part of their job. Even seemingly unapproachable academic titans will usually be happy to dash off a quick letter for a mere student. However, these same obliging professors are masters of a sort of opaque prose style that screams to an admissions officer, "I really have no idea what to say about this kid who is, in fact, a near-total stranger to me!" Although an admissions committee will not dismiss out of hand such a recommendation, it's really not going to help you much.

REELING IN THE YEARS

Obviously, the longer it has been since you graduated, the tougher it is to obtain academic recommendations. However, if you've held on to your old papers, you may still be able to rekindle an old professor's memory of your genius by sending a decent paper or two along with your request for a recommendation (and, of course, a copy of your personal statement). You want to provide specifics any way you can.

NONACADEMIC REFERENCES

Getting the mayor, a senator, or the CEO of your company to write a recommendation helps only if you have a personal and professional connection with that person. Remember, you want the writers of your recommendations to provide specifics about your actual accomplishments. If you're having trouble finding academic recommendations, choose people from your workplace, from the community, or from any other area of your life that is important to you. If at all possible, talk to your boss or a supervisor from a previous job who knows you well (and, of course, likes you).

SEND A THANK-YOU NOTE

Always a good idea. It should be short and handwritten. Use a blue pen so the recipient knows for sure that your note is no cheap copy. As with any good thank-you note, and any good recommendation, mention a specific. (Send a thank-you note if you have an interview at a law school, too.)

CHAPTER 7
REAL LIFE WORK EXPERIENCE AND COMMUNITY SERVICE

WORK EXPERIENCE IN COLLEGE

Most law school applications will ask you to list any part-time jobs you held while you were in college and how many hours per week you worked. If you had to (or chose to) work your way through your undergraduate years, this should come as good news. A great number of law schools make it clear that they take your work commitments as a college student into consideration when evaluating your undergraduate GPA.

WORK EXPERIENCE IN REAL LIFE

All law school applications will ask you about your work experience beyond college. They will give you three or four lines on which to list such experience. Some schools will invite you to submit a resume. If you have a very good one, you should really milk this opportunity for all it's worth. Even if you don't have a marvelous resume, these few lines on the application and your resume are the only opportunities you'll have to discuss your post-college experience meaningfully—unless you choose to discuss professional experience in your personal statement as well.

The kind of job you've had is not as important as you might think. What interests the admissions committee is what you've made of that job and what it's made of you. Whatever your job was or is, you want to offer credible evidence of your competence. For example, mention in your personal statement your job advancement or any increase in your responsibility. Most importantly, though, remember your overriding goal of cohesive presentation: you want to show off your professional experience within the context of your decision to attend law school. This does not mean that you need to offer a geometric proof of how your experience in the workplace has led you inexorably to a career in the law. You need only explain truthfully how this experience influenced you and how it fits nicely into your thinking about law school.

COMMUNITY SERVICE

An overwhelming majority of law schools single out community involvement as one of several influential factors in their admissions decisions. Law schools would like to admit applicants who show a long-standing commitment to something other than their own advancement.

It is certainly understandable that law schools would wish to determine the level of such commitment before admitting an applicant, particularly since so few law students go on to practice public interest law. Be forewarned, however, that nothing—*nothing*—is so obviously bogus as an insincere statement of a commitment to public interest issues. It just reeks. Admissions committees are well aware that very few people take the time out of their lives to become involved significantly in their communities. If you aren't one of them, trying to fake it can only hurt you.

CHAPTER 8

INTERVIEWS

The odds are very good that you will never encounter an interview in the law school admissions process. Admissions offices just aren't very keen on them. They do happen occasionally, though, and if you are faced with one, here are a few tips.

Be prepared. Interviews do make impressions. Some students are admitted simply because they had great interviews; less often, students are rejected because they bombed. Being prepared is the smartest thing you can do.

Don't ask questions that are answered in the brochures you got in the mail. This means you have to read those brochures. At breakfast before the interview is an ideal time.

If there is a popular conception of the school (e.g., Harvard is overly competitive), don't ask about it. Your interviewer will have been through the same song and dance too many times. You don't want to seem off the wall by asking bizarre questions; but even more, you don't want to sound exactly like every other boring applicant before you.

Look good, feel good. Wear nice clothes. If you aren't sure what to wear, *ask the admissions staff*. Say these words: "What should I wear?" Get a respectable haircut. Don't chew gum. Clean your fingernails. Brush your teeth. Wash behind your ears. You can go back to being a slob just as soon as they let you in.

Don't worry about time. Students sometimes are told that the sign of a good interview is that it lasts longer than the time allowed for it. Forget about this. Don't worry if your interview lasts exactly as long as the secretary said it would. And don't try to stretch out the end of your interview by suddenly becoming long-winded or asking a lot of questions you don't care about.

CHAPTER 9
MONEY MATTERS

Law school is a cash cow for colleges and universities everywhere and, especially at a private school, you are going to be gouged for a pretty obscene wad of cash over the next three years. Take University of Southern California Gould School of Law, where tuition is more than $30,000 a year. If you are planning to eat, live somewhere, buy books, and (maybe) maintain health insurance, you are looking at about $47,000 per year. Multiply that by three years of law school. You should get $141,000. Now faint. Correct for inflation (USC certainly will), add things like computers and other miscellany, and you can easily spend $150,000 to earn a degree. Assume that you have to borrow every penny of that $150,000. Multiply it by 8 percent over 10 years (a common assumption of law school applicants is that they will be able to pay all their debt back in 10 years or less). Your monthly payments will be around $1,820.

On the bright side, while law school is certainly an expensive proposition, the financial rewards of practicing can be immensely lucrative. You won't be forced into bankruptcy if you finance it properly. There are tried-and-true ways to reduce your initial costs, finance the costs on the horizon, and manage the debt you'll leave school with—all without ever asking "Have you been in a serious accident recently?" in a television commercial.

LAW SCHOOL ON THE CHEAP

Private schools aren't the only law schools, and you don't have to come out of law school saddled with tens of thousands of dollars of debt. Many state schools have reputations that equal or surpass some of the top privates. It might be worth your while to spend a year establishing residency in a state with one or more good public law schools. Here's an idea: Pack up your belongings and move to a cool place like Minneapolis, Seattle, Berkeley, Austin, or Boulder. Spend a year living there. Wait tables, hang out, listen to music, walk the Earth, write the great American novel, and *then* study law.

COMPARISON SHOPPING

Here are the full-time tuition costs at law schools around the country. They are randomly paired schools in the same region (one public and one private) and are provided to help you get a feel of what law school costs are going to run you. Those schools that have the same tuition in both columns are private law schools.

Law School	In State	Out of State
University of Florida, Levin College of Law	$6,891	$24,680
University of Miami, School of Law	$29,016	$29,016
Indiana University–Bloomington, School of Law	$13,045	$25,875
University of Notre Dame, Law School	$29,740	$29,740
University of Tennessee, College of Law	$7,734	$20,472
Vanderbilt University, Law School	$31,900	$31,900
University of Iowa, College of Law	$11,510	$25,718
Drake University, Law School	$22,250	$22,250
Louisiana State University, Law Center	$10,410	$20,746
Tulane University, School of Law	$28,900	$28,900
University of California, Hastings College of Law	$21,894	$33,119
University of San Fransisco, School of Law	$28,977	$28,977
University of Texas, School of Law	$11,480	$22,620
Baylor University, School of Law	$23,247	$23,247
University of Illinois, College of Law	$14,306	$26,644
Northwestern University, School of Law	$35,896	$35,896
University of Pittsburgh, School of Law	$18,494	$27,390
University of Pennsylvania, Law School	$34,920	$34,920
University of Oregon, School of Law	$15,175	$19,075
Lewis and Clark College, Northwestern School of Law	$25,334	$25,334

LOAN REPAYMENT ASSISTANCE PROGRAMS

If you are burdened with loans, we've got more bad news. The National Association of Law Placement (NALP) shows that while salaries for law school graduates who land jobs at the big, glamorous firms have skyrocketed in the past few years, salaries of less than $55,000 are more common than salaries of $75,000–$130,000 for the general run of law school grads. There are, however, a growing number of law schools and other sources willing to pay your loans for you (it's called loan forgiveness—as if you've sinned by taking out loans) in return for your commitment to employment in public interest law.

The Skinny on Loan Repayment Assistance Programs

For a comprehensive listing of assistance programs and for other loan-forgiveness information, call Equal Justice Works at 202-466-3686, or look them up on the Web at www.napil.org.

While doing a tour of duty in public service law will put off dreams of working in a big firm or becoming the next Mark Geragos, the benefits of these programs are undeniable. Here's how just about all of them work. You commit to working for a qualified public service or public interest job. As long as your gross income does not exceed the prevailing public service salary, the programs will pay off a good percentage of your debt. Eligible loans are typically any educational debt financed through your law school, which really excludes only loan sharks and credit-card debts.

MAXIMIZE YOUR AID

A simple but oft-forgotten piece of wisdom: if you don't ask, you usually don't get. Be firm when trying to get merit money from your school. Some schools have reserves of cash that go unused. Try simply asking for more financial aid. The better your grades, of course, the more likely they are to crack open their safe of financial goodies for you. Unfortunately, grants aren't as prevalent for law students as for undergrads. Scholarships are not nearly as widely available, either. To get a general idea of availability of aid at a law school, contact the financial aid office.

PARENTAL CONTRIBUTION?!

If you are operating under the assumption that, as a tax-paying grownup who has been out of school for a number of years, you will be recognized as the self-supporting adult you are, you could be in for a surprise. Veterans of financial aid battles will not be surprised to hear that even law school financial aid offices have a difficult time recognizing when apron strings have legitimately been cut. Schools may try to take into account your parents' income in determining your eligibility for financial aid, regardless of your age or tax status. Policies vary widely. Be sure to ask the schools you are considering exactly what their policy is regarding financial independence for the purposes of financial aid.

BORROWING MONEY

It's an amusingly simple process and several companies are in the business of lending large chunks of cash specifically to law students. Your law school financial aid office can tell you how to reach them. You should explore more than one option and shop around for the lowest fees and rates.

> ***Let the Law School Pick Up the Tab for Phone Calls Whenever Possible***
>
> *A lot of schools have free telephone numbers that they don't like to publish in books like this one. If the number we have listed for a particular law school is not an 800-number, it doesn't necessarily mean that you have to pay every time you call the school. Check out the school's Internet site, or ask for the 800-number when you call the first time.*

WHO'S ELIGIBLE?

Anyone with reasonably good credit, regardless of financial need, can borrow enough money to finance law school. If you have financial need, you will probably be eligible for some types of financial aid if you meet the following basic qualifications:

- You are a United States citizen or a permanent U.S. resident.
- You are registered for Selective Service if you are a male, or you have the documentation to prove that you are exempt.
- You are not in default on student loans already.
- You don't have a horrendous credit history.
- You haven't been busted for certain drug-related crimes, including possession.

WHAT TYPES OF LOANS ARE AVAILABLE?

There are three basic types of loans: federal, private, and institutional.

Federal

The federal government funds federal loan programs. Federal loans, particularly the Stafford Loan, are usually the "first resort" for borrowers. Most federal loans are need-based, but some higher-interest loans are available regardless of financial circumstances.

TABLE OF LOANS			
NAME OF LOAN	**SOURCE**	**ELIGIBILITY**	**MAXIMUM ALLOCATION**
Subsidized Federal Stafford Student Loan (SSL, formerly GSL)	Federal, administered by participating lender	Demonstrated financial need; selective service registration; not in default on any previous student loan	$8,500/year with maximum aggregate of $65,500; aggregate includes undergraduate subsidized loans made under the same program
Unsubsidized Stafford Student Loan	Federal, administered by participating lender	Not need-based; selective service registration; not in default on any previous student loan.	$18,500/year with maximum aggregate of $138,500; aggregate includes undergraduate loans made under the same program and undergraduate and graduate loans made under the Unsubsidized and Subsidized Stafford Student Loan program
Perkins Loan (formerly NDSL)	Federal, administered by school	Demonstrated financial need; selective service registration; not in default on student loans.	$6,000/year with maximum aggregate of $40,000; aggregate includes undergraduate Perkins loans
Law Access Loan (LAL)	Access Group	Not need-based	$120,000 for most schools (up to amount certified by your school)

Private

Private loans are funded by banks, foundations, corporations, and other associations. A number of private loans are targeted to aid particular segments of the population. You may have to do some investigating to identify private loans for which you might qualify. Like always, contact your law school's financial aid office to learn more.

Institutional

The amount of loan money available and the method by which it is disbursed vary greatly from one school to another. Private schools, especially those that are older and more established, tend to have larger endowments and can offer more assistance. To find out about the resources available at a particular school, refer to its catalogue or contact—you guessed it—the financial aid office.

TABLE OF LOANS

REPAYMENT AND DEFERRAL OPTIONS	INTEREST RATE	PROS	CONS
10 years to repay; begin repayment 6 months after graduation; forbearance possible.	Variable, doesn't exceed 8.25%	Most common law school loan; interest is subsidized by the feds during school; once you get a loan, any subsequent loans are made at the same rate	None
10 years to repay; principal is deferred while in school, but interest accrues immediately; begin repayment six months after graduation; forbearance possible	Variable, doesn't exceed 8.25%	Not need based; same interest rates as Federal Stafford; once you get a loan, any subsequent loans are made at the same rate	Interest accrues immediately and is capitalized if deferred.
10 years to repay; begin repayment 9 months after graduation; forbearance possible	Fixed, 5%	Low interest rate	Low maximum allocation; primarily restricted to first- and second-year students
20 years to repay; principal repayment begins nine months after graduation.	Varies quarterly; 3-month LIBOR (London Interbank Offered Rate) Rate plus 2.75% or 3.95% determined by your credit history	High maximum allocation, not need based	Importance of credit rating in determining interest rate (for those with a poor credit history)

CHAPTER 10
CAREER MATTERS

Okay, it's a long time away, but you really ought to be thinking about your professional career beyond law school from day one, especially if your goal is to practice with a major law firm. What stands between you and a job as an "associate," the entry-level position at one of these firms, is a three-stage evaluation: first, a review of your resume, including your grades and work experience; second, an on-campus interview; and last, one or more "call-back" interviews at the firm's offices. It's a fairly intimidating ordeal, but there are a few ways to reduce the anxiety and enhance your chances of landing a great job.

Making Law Review

Every law school has something called a law review, which is an academic periodical produced and edited by law students. It contains articles about various aspects of law—mostly written by professors. While some schools sponsor more than one law review, there is generally one that is more prestigious than all the others. In order to "make" law review, you will have to finish the all-important first year at (or very, very near) the top of your class or write an article that will be judged by the existing members of the law review. You might have to do both. Making law review is probably the easiest way to guarantee yourself a job at a blue-chip firm, working for a judge, or in academia. In all honesty, it is a credential you will proudly carry for the rest of your life.

YOUR RESUME

The first thing recruiters tend to notice after your name is the name of the law school you attend. Tacky, but true. Perhaps the greatest misconception among law students, however, is that hiring decisions are based largely upon your school's prestige. All those rankings perpetuate this myth. To be sure, there are a handful of schools with reputations above all others, and students who excel at these schools are in great demand. But you are equally well situated, if not better off, applying from the top of your class at a strong, less prestigious law school class than from the bottom half of a "Top Ten" law school class.

FIRST-YEAR GRADES ARE THE WHOLE ENCHILADA

Fair or not, the first year of law school will unduly influence your legal future. It's vital that you hit the ground running because law school grades are *the* critical factor in recruitment. An even harsher reality is that *first-year grades are by far the most critical in the hiring process.* Decisions about who gets which plum summer jobs are generally handed down before students take a single second-year exam. Consequently, you're left with exactly no time to adjust to law-school life and little chance to improve your transcript if you don't come out on top as a first-year student.

WORK EXPERIENCE

If you're applying to law school right out of college, chances are your most significant work experience has been a summer job. Recruiters don't expect you to have spent these months writing Supreme Court decisions. They are generally satisfied if you have shown evidence that you worked diligently and seriously at each opportunity. Students who took a year or more off after college obviously have more opportunities to impress, but also more of a burden to demonstrate diligence and seriousness.

Work experience in the legal industry—clerkships and paralegal jobs for instance—can be excellent sources of professional development. They are fairly common positions among job applicants, though, so don't feel you have to pursue one of these routes just to show your commitment to the law. You'll make a better impression by working in an industry in which you'd like to specialize (e.g., a prospective securities lawyer summering with an investment bank).

A Couple Good Books

If you are thinking about law school, here are a few books you might find interesting:

***The Princeton Review's* Law School Essays That Made a Difference**

Check out successful essays written for an assortment of selective schools.

***Jeff Deaver,* The Complete Law School Companion: How to Excel at America's Most Demanding Post-Graduate Curriculum**

This straightforward law school survival guide has much to commend it.

THE INTERVIEWS

There are as many "right approaches" to an interview as there are interviewers. That observation provides little comfort, of course, especially if you're counting on a good interview to make up for whatever deficiencies there are on your resume. Think about the purpose of the initial 30-minute interview you are likely to have: it provides a rough sketch not only of your future office personality but also your demeanor under stress. The characteristics you demonstrate and the *impression* you give are more important than anything you say. Composure, confidence, maturity, articulation, and an ability to develop rapport are characteristics recruiters are looking for. Give them what they want.

CHAPTER 11
LAW SCHOOL 101

IS IT REALLY THAT BAD?

The first semester of law school has the well-deserved reputation of being among the greatest challenges to your intellect and stamina that you'll ever face. It is tons and tons of work and, in many ways, it's an exercise in intellectual survival. Just as the gung-ho army recruit must survive boot camp, so too must the bright-eyed law student endure the homogenizing effects of that first year.

Though complex and difficult, the subject matter in first-year law-school courses is probably no more inherently difficult than what is taught in other graduate or professional schools. The particular, private terror that is shared by roughly 40,000 1Ls every year stems more from law school's peculiar *style*. The method of instruction here unapologetically punishes students who would prefer to learn passively.

THE FIRST-YEAR CURRICULUM

The first-year curriculum in the law school you attend will almost certainly be composed of a combination of the following courses:

TORTS

The word comes from the Middle French for "injury." The Latin root of the word means "twisted." Torts are wrongful acts, excluding breaches of contract, over which you can sue people. They include battery, assault, false imprisonment, and intentional infliction of emotional distress. Torts can range from the predictable to the bizarre, from "Dog Bites Man" to "Man Bites Dog" and everything in between. The study of torts mostly involves reading cases in order to discern the legal rationale behind decisions pertaining to the extent of, and limits on, the civil liability of one party for harm done to another.

CONTRACTS

They may seem fairly self-explanatory but contractual relationships are varied and complicated, as two semesters of contracts will teach you. Again, through the study of past court cases, you will follow the largely unwritten law governing the system of conditions and obligations a contract represents, as well as the legal remedies available when contracts are breached.

CIVIL PROCEDURE

Civil procedure is the study of how you get things done in civil (as opposed to criminal) court. "Civ Pro" is the study of the often dizzyingly complex rules that govern not only who can sue whom, but also how, when, and where they can do it. This is not merely a study of legal protocol, for issues of process have a significant indirect effect on the substance of the law. Rules of civil procedure govern the conduct of both the courtroom trial and the steps that might precede it: obtaining information (discovery), making your case (pleading), pretrial motions, etc.

PROPERTY

You may never own a piece of land, but your life will inevitably and constantly be affected by property laws. Anyone interested in achieving an understanding of broader policy issues will appreciate the significance of this material. Many property courses will emphasize the transfer of property and, to varying degrees, economic analysis of property law.

CRIMINAL LAW

Even if you become a criminal prosecutor or defender, you will probably never run into most of the crimes you will be exposed to in this course. Can someone who shoots the dead body of a person he believes to be alive be charged with attempted murder? What if they were both on drugs or had really rough childhoods? Also, you'll love the convoluted exam questions, in which someone will invariably go on a nutty crime spree.

CONSTITUTIONAL LAW

"Con Law" is the closest thing to a normal class you will take in your first year. It emphasizes issues of government structure (e.g., federal power versus state power) and individual rights (e.g., personal liberties, freedom of expression, property protection). You'll spend a great deal of time studying the limits on the lawmaking power of Congress as well.

LEGAL METHODS

One of the few twentieth-century improvements on the traditional first-year curriculum that has taken hold nearly everywhere, this course travels under various aliases, such as Legal Research and Writing, or Elements of the Law. In recent years, increased recognition of the importance of legal writing skills has led over half of the U.S. law schools to require or offer a writing course after the first year. This class will be your smallest, and possibly your only, refuge from the Socratic Method. Methods courses are often taught by junior faculty and attorneys in need of extra cash and are designed to help you acquire fundamental skills in legal research, analysis, and writing. The methods course may be the least frightening you face, but it can easily consume an enormous amount of time. This is a common lament, particularly at schools where very few credits are awarded for it.

In addition to these course requirements, many law schools require 1Ls to participate in a moot-court exercise. As part of this exercise, students—sometimes working in pairs or even small groups—must prepare briefs and oral arguments for a mock trial (usually appellate). This requirement is often tied in with the methods course so that those briefs and oral arguments will be well researched—and graded.

> ***Tips for Classroom Success***
>
> *Be alert. Review material immediately before class so that it is fresh in your memory. Then review your notes from class later the same day and the week's worth of notes at the end of each week.*
>
> *Remember that there are few correct answers. The goal of a law school class is generally to analyze, understand, and attempt to resolve issues or problems.*
>
> *Learn to state and explain legal rules and principles with accuracy.*
>
> *You don't want to focus on minutiae from cases or class discussions; always try to figure out what the law is.*
>
> *Accept the ambiguity in legal analysis and class discussion; classes are intended to be thought-provoking, perplexing, and difficult.*
>
> *No one class session will make or break you. Keep in mind how each class fits within the course overall.*
>
> *Don't write down what other students say. Write down the law. Concentrate your notes on the professor's hypotheticals and emphasis in class.*
>
> *A simple but effective way of keeping yourself in touch with where the class is at any given time is to review the table of contents in the casebook.*
>
> *If you don't use a laptop, don't sit next to someone who does. The constant tapping on the keys will drive you crazy, and you may get a sense that they are writing down more than you (which is probably not true).*
>
> *If you attend class, you don't need to tape record it. There are better uses of your time than to spend hours listening to the comments of students who were just as confused as you were when you first dealt with the material in class.*

THE CASE METHOD

In the majority of your law school courses, and probably in all of your first-year courses, your only texts will be things called casebooks. The case method eschews explanation and encourages exploration. In a course that relies entirely on the casebook, you will never come across a printed list of "laws." Instead, you will learn that in many areas of law there is no such thing as a static set of rules, but only a constantly evolving system of principles. You are expected to understand the principles of law—in all of its layers and ambiguity—through a critical examination of a series of cases that were decided according to such principles. You will often feel utterly lost, groping for answers to unarticulated questions. This is not merely normal; it is intended.

In practical terms, the case method works like this: For every class meeting, you will be assigned a number of cases to read from your casebook, which is a collection of (extremely edited) written judicial decisions in actual court cases. The names won't even have been changed to protect the innocent. The cases are the written judicial opinions rendered in court cases that were decided at the appeals or Supreme Court level. (Written opinions are not generally rendered in lower courts.)

Your casebook will contain no instructions and little to no explanation. Your assignments simply will be to read the cases and be in a position to answer questions based on them. There will be no written homework assignments, just cases, cases, and more cases.

You will write, for your own benefit, summaries—or briefs—of these cases. Briefs are your attempts to summarize the issues and laws around which a particular case revolves. *By briefing, you figure out what the law is.* The idea is that, over the course of a semester, you will try to integrate the content of your case briefs and your notes from in-class lectures, discussions, or dialogues into some kind of cohesive whole.

THE SOCRATIC METHOD

As unfamiliar as the case method will be to most 1Ls, the real source of anxiety is the way the professor presents it. Socratic instruction entails directed questioning and limited lecturing. Generally, the Socratic professor invites a student to attempt a cogent summary of a case assigned for that day's class. Hopefully, it won't be you (but someday it will be). Regardless of the accuracy and thoroughness of your initial response, the professor then grills you on details overlooked or issues unresolved. Then, the professor will change the facts of the actual case at hand into a hypothetical case that may or may not have demanded a different decision by the court.

The overall goal of the Socratic Method is to forcibly improve your critical reasoning skills. If you are reasonably well-prepared, thinking about all these questions will force you beyond the immediately apparent issues in a given case to consider its broader implications. The dialogue between the effective Socratic instructor and the victim-of-the-moment will also force nonparticipating students to question their underlying assumptions of the case under discussion.

WHAT IS CLINICAL LEGAL EDUCATION?

The latest so-called innovation in legal education is ironic in that it's a return to the old emphasis on practical experience. Hands-on training in the practical skills of lawyering now travels under the name "Clinical Legal Education."

HOW IT WORKS

Generally, a clinical course focuses on developing practical lawyering skills. "Clinic" means exactly what you would expect: a working law office where second- and third-year law students counsel clients and serve human beings. (A very limited number of law schools allow first-year students to participate in legal clinics.)

Watch* The Paper Chase. *Twice.

This movie is the only one ever produced about law school that comes close to depicting the real thing. Watch it before you go to orientation. Watch it again on Thanksgiving break and laugh when you can identify your classmates.

In states that grant upper-level law students a limited right to represent clients in court, students in a law school's clinic might actually follow cases through to their resolution. Some schools have a single on-site clinic that operates something like a general law practice, dealing with cases ranging from petty crime to landlord-tenant disputes. At schools that have dedicated the most resources to their clinical programs, numerous specialized clinics deal with narrowly defined areas of law, such as employment discrimination. The opportunities to participate in such live-action programs, however, are limited.

OTHER OPTIONS

Clinical legal education is a lot more expensive than traditional instruction, which means that few law schools can accommodate more than a small percentage of their students in clinical programs. If that's the case, check out external clinical placements and simulated clinical courses. In a clinical externship, you might work with a real firm or public agency several hours a week and meet with a faculty advisor only occasionally. Though students who participate in these programs are unpaid, they will ordinarily receive academic credit. Also, placements are chosen quite carefully to ensure that you don't become a gopher.

There are also simulated clinical courses. In one of these, you'll perform all of the duties that a student in a live-action clinic would, but your clients are imaginary.

CHAPTER 12
How to Excel at Any Law School

Preparation for law school is something you should take very seriously. Law school will be one of the most interesting and rewarding experiences of your life, but it's also an important and costly investment. Your academic performance in law school will influence your career for years to come. Consider the following facts when thinking about how important it is to prepare for law school:

- The average full-time law student spends more than $125,000 to attend law school.
- The average law student graduates with over $80,000 of debt.
- The median income for law school graduates is only about $60,000.

Contact Law Preview

Law Preview

10 Cordage Park Circle, Suite 115

Plymouth, MA 02360

Phone: 888-PREP-YOU

E-mail: admin@lawpreview.com

Website: www.lawpreview.com

As you can see, most law students cannot afford to be mediocre. Money isn't everything, but when you're strapped with close to six figures of debt, money concerns will weigh heavily on your career choices. Even if money is not a concern for you, your academic performance in law school will profoundly affect your employment options after graduation and, ultimately, your legal career. Consider these additional facts:

- Students who excel in law school may have opportunities to earn up to $160,000 right out of law school.
- Only law students who excel academically have opportunities to obtain prestigious judicial clerkships, teaching positions, and distinguished government jobs.

As you can see, law students who achieve academic success enjoy better career options and have a greater ability to escape the crushing debt of law school. The point here is obvious: Your chances of achieving your goals—no matter what you want to do with your career—are far better if you succeed academically.

Now comes the hard part: How do you achieve academic success? You are going to get plenty of advice about how to excel in law school—much of it unsolicited. You certainly don't need any from us. We strongly advise, however, that you pay extra-special attention to what Don Macaulay, the president of Law Preview, has to say about surviving, and thriving, as a law student. Macaulay, like all the founders of Law Preview, graduated at the top of his law school class and worked at a top law firm before he began developing and administering Law Preview's law school prep course in 1998.

All B+s put you in the top quarter at most schools, and in the top fifth at many.

While there are many resources that claim to provide a recipe for success in law school, Law Preview is the best of the lot. They have retained some of the most talented legal scholars in the country to lecture during their week-long sessions, and they deliver what they promise—a methodology for attacking and conquering the law school experience.

We asked Macaulay a few questions we thought prospective law students might like to know the answers to:

It is often said that the "first year" of law school is the most important year. Is this true and, if so, why?

It is true. Academic success during the first year of law school can advance a successful legal career unlike success in any other year because many of the top legal employers start recruiting so early that your first-year grades are all they will see. Most prestigious law firms hire their permanent attorneys from among the ranks of the firm's "summer associates"—usually second-year law students who work for the firm during the summer between the second and third years of law school. Summer associates are generally hired during the fall semester of the second year, a time when only the first year grades are available. A student who does well during the first year, lands a desirable summer associate position, and then impresses his or her employer, is well on his or her way to a secure legal job regardless of his or her academic performance after the first year.

In addition, first-year grades often bear heavily upon a student's eligibility for law review and other prestigious scholastic activities, including other law journals and moot court. These credentials are considered the most significant signs of law school achievement, often even more than a high grade point average. Many of the top legal employers in the private and the public sectors seek out young lawyers with these credentials, and some employers will not even interview candidates who lack these honors, even after a few years of experience. As a result, a solid performance during the first year of law school can have a serious impact upon your professional opportunities available after graduation.

How does law school differ from what students experienced as undergraduates?

Many students, especially those who enjoyed academic success in college, presume that law school will be a mere continuation of their undergraduate experience, and that, by implementing those skills that brought them success in college, they will enjoy similar success in law school. This couldn't be further from the truth. Once law school begins, students often find themselves thrown into deep water. They are handed an anchor in the form of a casebook (they are told it's a life preserver), and they are expected to sink or swim. While almost nobody sinks in law school anymore, most spend all of first year just trying to keep their heads above water. In reality, virtually every student who is admitted into law school possesses the intelligence and work ethic needed to graduate. But in spite of having the tools needed to survive the experience, very few possess the know-how to truly excel and make law review at their schools.

What makes the law school experience unique is its method of instruction and its system of grading. Most professors rely on the case method as a means for illustrating legal rules and doctrines encountered in a particular area of the law. With the case method, students are asked to read a particular case or, in some instances, several cases, that the professor will use to lead a classroom discussion illustrating a particular rule of law. The assigned readings come from casebooks, which are compilations of cases for each area of law. The cases are usually edited to illustrate distinct legal rules, often with very little commentary or enlightenment by the casebook editor. The casebooks often lack anything more than a general structure, and law professors often contribute little to the limited structure. Students are asked to read and analyze hundreds of cases in a vacuum. Since each assigned case typically builds upon a legal rule illustrated in a previous case, it isn't until the end of the semester or, for some classes, the end of the year, that students begin to form an understanding of how these rules interrelate.

One of the objectives of Law Preview's law school prep course is to help students to understand the "big picture" before they begin their classes. We hire some of the most talented law professors from around the country to provide "previews" of the core first-year law school courses: Civil Procedure, Constitutional Law, Contracts, Criminal Law, Property, and Torts. During their lectures, our professors provide students with a roadmap for each subject by discussing the law's development, legal doctrines, and recurring themes and policies that students will encounter throughout the course. By providing entering law students with a conceptual framework for the material they will study, Law Preview eliminates the frustration that most of them will encounter when reading and analyzing case law in a vacuum.

What is the best way to prepare for law school, and when should you start?

When preparing for law school, students should focus on two interrelated tasks: 1) developing a strategy for academic success, and 2) getting mentally prepared for the awesome task ahead. The primary objective for most law students is to achieve the highest grades possible, and a well-defined strategy for success will help you direct your efforts most efficiently and effectively toward that goal. You must not begin law school equipped solely with some vague notion of hard work. Success requires a concrete plan that includes developing a reliable routine for classroom preparation, a proficient method of outlining, and a calculated strategy for exam-taking. The further you progress in law school without such a plan, the more time and energy you will waste struggling through your immense work load without moving discernibly closer toward achieving academic success.

You must also become mentally prepared to handle the rigors of law school. Law school can be extremely discouraging because students receive very little feedback during the school year. Classes are usually graded solely based on final exam scores. Mid-term exams and graded papers are uncommon, and classroom participation is often the only way for students to ascertain if they understand the material and are employing effective study methods. As a result, a winning attitude is critical to success in law school. Faith in yourself will help you continue to make the personal sacrifices during the first year that you need to make to succeed in law school, even when the rewards are not immediately apparent.

Incoming law students should begin preparing for law school during the summertime prior to first year, and preparation exercises should be aimed at gaining a general understanding of what law school is all about. A solid understanding of what you are expected to learn during the first year will give you the information you need to develop both your strategy for success and the confidence you need to succeed. There are several books on the market that can help in this regard, but those students who are best prepared often attend Law Preview's one-week intensive preparatory course specifically designed to teach beginning law students the strategies for academic success.

What factors contribute to academic success in law school?

Academic success means one thing in law school—exam success. The grades that you receive, particularly during the first year, will be determined almost exclusively by the scores you receive on your final exams. Occasionally, a professor may add a few points for class participation, but that is rare. In most classes, your final exam will consist of a three- or four-hour written examination at the end of the semester or—if the course is two semesters long—at the end of the year. The amount of material you must master for each final exam will simply dwarf that of any undergraduate exam you have ever taken. The hope that you can "cram" a semester's worth of information into a one-week reading period is pure fantasy and one that will surely lead to disappointing grades. The focus of your efforts from day one should be success on your final exams. Don't get bogged down in class preparation or in perfecting a course outline if it will not result in some discernible improvement in your exam performance. All of your efforts should be directed at improving your exam performance in some way. It's as simple as that.

What skills are typically tested on law school exams?

Law school exams usually test three different skills: 1) the ability to accurately identify legal issues, 2) the ability to recall the relevant law with speed, and 3) the ability to apply the law to the facts efficiently and skillfully. The proper approach for developing these skills differs, depending on the substantive area of law in question and whether your exam is open-book or closed-book.

Identifying legal issues is commonly known as issue-spotting. On most of your exams, you will be given complex, hypothetical fact patterns. From the facts you are given, you must identify the particular legal issues that need to be addressed. This is a difficult skill to perfect and can only be developed through practice. The best way to develop issue-spotting skills is by taking practice exams. For each of your classes, during the first half of the semester you should collect all of the available exams that were given by your professor in the past. Take all of these exams under simulated exam conditions—find an open classroom, get some blue books, time yourself, and take the exams with friends so that you can review them afterwards. It is also helpful for you to practice any legal problems you were given during the semester. Issue-spotting is an important skill for all lawyers to develop. Lawyers utilize this skill on a daily basis when they listen to their clients' stories and are asked to point out places where legal issues might arise.

The ability to recall the law with speed is also very important and frequently tested. On all of your exams, you will be given a series of legal problems, and for each problem you will usually be required to provide the relevant substantive law and apply it to the facts of the problem. Your ability to recall the law with speed is critical because, in most classes, you will be under time constraints to answer all of the problems. The faster you recall the law, the more problems you will complete and the more time you will have to spend on demonstrating your analytical skills. For courses with closed-book exams, this means straight memorization or the use of memory recall devices, such as mnemonics. Do not be passive about learning the law—repeatedly reviewing your outline is not enough. You must actively learn the law by studying definitions and using memory-assistance devices like flash cards. When you have become exceedingly familiar with your flash cards, rewrite them so as to test your memory in different words. This is particularly critical for courses such as Torts and Criminal Law where you must learn a series of definitions with multiple elements. For courses with open-book exams, this means developing an index for your outline that will enable you to locate the relevant law quickly. Create a cover page for your outline that lists the page number for each substantive sub-topic. This will help you get there without any undue delay.

Books About Doing Well in Law School:

Getting to Maybe: How to Excel on Law School Exams, *Professors Jeremy Paul and Michael Fischl*

This book is excellent! While many books and professors may preach "IRAC" as a way of structuring exam answers, Getting to Maybe *correctly points out that such advice does not help students first correctly identify legal issues and, more importantly, master the intricacies of legal analysis.*

Law School Confidential: A Complete Guide to the Law School Experience (Second Edition), Robert H. Miller, Esq.

Robert H. Miller, a former federal judicial clerk, Law Review editor, and graduate of University of Pennsylvania Law School, covers every aspect of the law school experience in thoughtful detail. Whether you are a college student just starting to think about law school, a student in the midst of law school applications, or someone who has already been admitted, Law School Confidential is a book you should not be without. An extensive new chapter is devoted to an exclusive one-on-one interview with Dean of Admissions Richard Geiger of the Cornell Law School, wherein closely guarded secrets of the increasingly competitive admissions process are discussed openly for the first time anywhere. In another chapter, Miller goes one-on-one with the hiring partners of two prestigious U.S. law firms about how to succeed in the hiring process, and what it takes to make it to partnership.

The final skill you need to develop is the ability to apply the law to the facts efficiently and skillfully. On your exams, once you have correctly identified the relevant issue and stated the relevant law, you must engage in a discussion of how the law applies to the facts that have been given. The ability to engage in such a discussion is best developed by taking practice exams. When you are practicing this skill, you should focus on efficiency. Try to focus on the essential facts, and do not try to engage in irrelevant discussions that will waste your energy and your professor's time.

Any final comments for our audience of aspiring law students?

The study of law is a wonderful and noble pursuit, one that I thoroughly enjoyed. Law school is not easy, however, and proper preparation can give you a firm foundation for success. I invite you to visit our website (www.lawpreview.com) and contact us with any questions (888-PREP-YOU).

CHAPTER 13
How to Use This Book

It's pretty simple.

The first part of this book provides a wealth of indispensable information covering everything you need to know about selecting and getting into the law school of your choice. There is also a great deal here about what to expect from law school and how to do well. You name it—taking the LSAT, choosing the best school for you, writing a great personal statement, interviewing, paying for it—it's all here.

The second part is the real meat and potatoes of *The Best 159 Law Schools*. It comprises portraits of 159 law schools across the United States and Canada. Each school has one of two possible types of entries. The first type of entry is a two-page descriptive profile. It contains data The Princeton Review has collected directly from law school administrators and textual descriptions of the school we have written based on our surveys of current law students. The second type of entry is a data listing, which includes all the same data that appears in the sidebars of the descriptive profiles, but does not have the student-survey driven descriptive paragraphs. For an explanation of why all schools do not appear with descriptive profiles, turn to page 59. As is customary with school guidebooks, all data, with the exception of tuition (which should be for the current year if the school reported it by our deadline), reflects figures for the academic year prior to publication unless otherwise noted on the pages. Since law school demographics vary significantly from one institution to another and some schools report data more thoroughly than others, some entries will not include all the individual data described below.

The third part of the book is where the "School Says . . ." profiles live. The "School Says . . ." profiles give extended descriptions of admissions processes, curricula, internship opportunities, and much more. This is your chance to get even more in-depth information on programs that interest you. These schools have paid us a small fee for the chance to tell you more about themselves, and the editorial responsibility is solely that of the law school. We think you'll find these profiles add lots to your picture of a school.

WHAT'S IN THE PROFILES: DATA

The Heading: The first thing you will see for each profile is (obviously) the school's name. On the facing page, you'll find the school's snail mail address, telephone number, fax number, e-mail address, and website. You can find the name of the admissions office contact person in the heading, too.

INSTITUTIONAL INFORMATION

Public/Private: Indicates whether a school is state-supported or funded by private means.

Student/Faculty Ratio: The ratio of law students to full-time faculty.

Affiliation: If the school is affiliated with a particular religion, you'll find that information here.

% Faculty Part-time: The percentage of faculty who are part-time.

% Faculty Female: The percentage of faculty who are women.

% Faculty Minority : You guessed it! The percentage of people who teach at the law school who are also members of minority groups.

Total Faculty: The number of faculty members at the law school.

Yet Another Good Book:

One L: The Turbulent True Story of a First Year at Harvard Law School, *Scott Turow*

This law school primer is equal parts illuminating and harrowing.

Survey Says: The Survey Says list appears in the sidebar of each law school's two-page descriptive profile, and up to three Survey Says items will appear on each list. As the name suggests, these items communicate results of our law student surveys. There are eleven possible Survey Says items, each explained below. Of these eleven, the three items that appear are those about which student respondents demonstrated the greatest degree of consensus. Survey Says items represent the agreement amongst students only at *that particular law school*, and are not relative to how students at other law schools felt about that particular Survey Says item.

Liberal students: Students report that their fellow law students lean to the left politically.

Conservative students: Students report that their fellow law students lean to the right politically.

Students love Hometown, State: Students are pleased with the location of their law school.

Good social life: Students report a lively social life at the law school.

Students never sleep: Students report a low average number of hours of sleep each night. Little sleep in law school is often an indication of extra-long hours of study on a daily basis.

Heavy use of Socratic Method: Students report that their professors primarily employ the traditional Socratic Method in the classroom.

Beautiful campus: Students report that their law school campus is practical and beautiful.

Great research resources: Students report that the library, computer databases, and other research tools are good.

Great judicial externship/internship/clerkship opportunities: Students rate these opportunities excellent.

Diverse opinions in classrooms: Students agree that differing points of view are tolerated in the classroom.

STUDENTS

Enrollment of Law School: The total number of students enrolled in the law school.

% Male/Female: The percentage of full-time students with an X and a Y chromosome and the percentage of students with two X chromosomes, respectively.

% Out-of-state: The percentage of full-time students who are from out-of-state. This field only applies to state schools.

% Full-time: The percentage of students who attend the school on a full-time basis.

% Minority: The percentage of full-time students who represent minority groups.

% International: The percentage of students who hail from foreign soil.

# of Countries Represented: The number of different foreign countries from which the current student body hails.

Average Age of Entering Class: On the whole, how old the 1Ls are.

ACADEMICS

Academic Experience Rating: The quality of the learning environment, on a scale of 60-99. The rating incorporates the Admissions Selectivity Rating and the average responses of law students at the school to several questions on our law student survey. In addition to the Admissions Selectivity Rating, factors include how students rate the quality of teaching and the accessibility of their professors, the school's research resources, the range of available courses, the balance of legal theory and practical lawyering skills stressed in the curriculum, the tolerance for diverse opinions in the classroom, and how intellectually challenging the course work is. This individual rating places each law school on a continuum for purposes of comparing all law schools within this edition only. If a law school receives a "low" Academic Experience Rating, it doesn't mean that the school provides a bad academic experience for its students. It simply means that the school scored

Law School Fun Fact
The least litigated amendment in the Bill of Rights is the Third Amendment, which prohibits the quartering of soldiers in private homes without consent of the owner.

lower relative to how other schools scored in our computations based on the criteria outlined above. Because this rating incorporates law student opinion data, only those law schools that appear in the section with the descriptive profiles based on student surveys receive an Academic Experience Rating.

Professors Interesting Rating: Based on law student opinion. We asked law students to rate the quality of teaching at their law schools. Because this rating incorporates law student opinion data, only those law schools that appear in the section with the descriptive profiles receive a Professors Interesting Rating.

Professors Accessible Rating: Based on law student opinion. We asked law students to rate how accessible the law faculty members at their schools are. Because this rating incorporates law student opinion data, only those law schools that appear in the section with the descriptive profiles receive a Professors Accessible Rating.

Hours of Study Per Day: From our student survey. The average number of hours students at the school report studying each day.

Academic Specialties: Different areas of law and academic programs on which the school prides itself.

Advanced Degrees Offered: Degrees available through the law school and the length of the program.

Combined Degrees Offered: Programs at this school involving the law school and some other college or degree program within the larger university, and how long it will take you to complete the joint program.

Grading System: Scoring system used by the law school. (Data listings only)

Academic Requirements: Most law schools require their students to complete some courses and/or programs that go beyond traditional legal theory, whether to broaden their understanding of and experience with the law or to develop important practical lawyering skills.

Clinical Program Required? Indicates whether clinical programs are required to complete the core curriculum.

Clinical Program Description: Programs designed to give students hands-on training and experience in the practice of some area of law. (Data listings only)

Legal Writing Course Requirement? Tells you whether there is a required course in legal writing.

Legal Writing Description: A description of any course work, required or optional, designed specifically to develop legal writing skills vital to the practice of law. (Data listings only)

Legal Methods Course Requirements? Indicates whether there is a mandatory curriculum component to cover legal methods.

Legal Methods Description: A description of any course work, required or optional, designed specifically to develop the skills vital to legal analysis. (Data listings only)

Legal Research Course Requirements? If a school requires course work specifically to develop legal research skills, this field will tell you.

Legal Research Description: A description of any course work, required or optional, designed specifically to develop legal research skills vital to the practice of law. (Data listings only)

Moot Court Requirement? Indicates whether participation in a moot court program is mandatory.

Moot Court Description: Surprise! This will describe any moot court program, mandatory or optional, designed to develop skills in legal research, writing, and oral argument. (Data listings only)

Public Interest Law Requirement? If a school requires participation on a public interest law project, we'll let you know here.

Public Interest Law Description: Programs designed to expose students to the public interest law field through clinical work, volunteer opportunities, or specialized course work. (Data listings only)

Academic Journals: This field will list any academic journals offered at the school. (Data listings only)

ADMISSIONS INFORMATION

Admissions Selectivity Rating: How competitive admission is at the law school, on a scale of 60 to 99. Several factors determine this rating, including LSAT scores and the average undergraduate GPA of entering 1L students, the percentage of applicants accepted, and the percentage of accepted applicants who enrolled in the law school. We collect this information through a survey that law school administrators complete for the Fall 2004 entering class. This individual rating places each law school on a continuum for purposes of comparing all law schools within this edition only. All law schools that appear in this edition of the guide, whether in the section with the descriptive profiles based on student surveys or in the section with school-reported statistics only, receive an Admissions Selectivity Rating. If a law school has a relatively "low" Admissions Selectivity Rating, it doesn't necessarily mean that it's easy to gain admission to the law school. (It's not "easy" to get into any ABA-approved law schools, really). It simply means that the school scored lower relative to other schools in our computations based on the criteria outlined above.

# of Applications Received: The number of people who applied to the law school's full-time JD program.

# of Applicants Accepted: The number of people who were admitted to the school's full-time class.

# of Acceptees Attending: The number of those admitted who chose to attend the school full-time.

Average LSAT/Range of LSAT: Indicates the average LSAT score of incoming 1Ls, as reported by the school. The range is the 25th to 75th percentiles of 1Ls.

Average Undergrad GPA: It's usually on a 4.0 scale.

Application Fee: How much it costs to apply to the school.

Regular Application Deadline and "Rolling": Many law schools evaluate applications and notify applicants of admission decisions on a continuous, "rolling" basis over the course of several months (ordinarily from late fall to midsummer). Obviously, if you apply to one of these schools, you want to apply early because there will be more places available at the beginning of the process.

Law School Trivia
The guarantee that each state must have an equal number of votes in the United States Senate is the only provision in the Constitution of 1787 that cannot be amended.

Regular Notification? The official date by or on which a law school will release a decision for an applicant who applied using the "regular admission" route.

Early Application Program? Whether the law school has an early application program. If you are accepted to an early decision program, you are obligated to attend that law school. If you are accepted under an early action program, you have no obligation to attend. You just get to know earlier whether you got in.

Early Application Deadline: The official date by which the law school must receive your application if you want to be considered for its early application program.

Early Application Notification: The official date on which a law school will release a decision for an applicant who applied using the "early application" route.

Transfer Students Accepted? Whether transfer students from other schools are considered for admission.

Evening Division Offered? Whether the school offers an evening program in addition to its full-time regular program. Evening division programs are almost always part-time and require four years of study (instead of three) to complete.

Part-time Accepted? Whether part-time students may enroll in the JD program on a basis other than the standard full-time.

LSDAS Accepted? A "Yes" here indicates that the school utilizes the Law School Data Assembly Service.

Applicants Also Look At: The law schools to which applicants to this school also apply. It's important. It's a reliable indicator of the overall academic quality of the applicant pool.

RESEARCH FACILITIES (DATA LISTINGS ONLY)

Research Resources Available: Online retrieval resources, subscription services, libraries, databases, etc. available for legal research.

% of JD Classrooms Wired: You got it: the percentage of dedicated law school classrooms wired for laptops and Internet access.

Computer Labs: The number of rooms full of computers that you can use for free.

School-Supported Research Centers: Indicates whether the school has on-campus, internally supported research centers.

INTERNATIONAL STUDENTS

TOEFL Required/Recommended of International Students? Indicates whether or not international students must take the TOEFL, or Test of English as a Foreign Language, in order to be admitted to the school.

Minimum TOEFL: Minimum score (paper and computer) an international student must earn on the TOEFL in order to be admitted.

FINANCIAL FACTS

Annual Tuition (Residents/Nonresidents): What it costs to go to school for an academic year. For state schools, both in-state and out-of-state tuition is listed.

Room and Board (On-/Off-campus): This is the school's estimate of what it costs to buy meals and to pay for decent living quarters for the academic year. Where available, on- and off-campus rates are listed.

Books and Supplies: Indicates how much students can expect to shell out for textbooks and other assorted supplies during the academic year.

Financial Aid Application Deadline: The last day on which students can turn in their applications for monetary assistance.

% Receiving Scholarships: The percentage of students here who received some sort of "free money" award. This figure can include grants as well.

Average Grant: Average financial aid amount awarded to students that does not have to be paid back. This figure can include scholarships as well.

Average Loan: Average amount of loan dollars accrued by students for the year.

% of Aid That Is Merit-Based: The percentage of aid not based on financial need

% Receiving Some Sort of Aid: The percentage of all the students here presently accumulating a staggering debt.

% First Year Students Receiving Some Sort of Aid: Same as above, but limited to just new JD students.

Average Total Aid Package: How much aid each student here receives on average for the year.

Average Debt: The amount of debt—or, in legal lingo, arrears—you'll likely be saddled with by the time you graduate.

Tuition Per Credit (Residents/Nonresidents): Dollar amount charged per credit hour. For state schools, both in-state and out-of-state amounts are listed when they differ.

Fees Per Credit (Residents/Nonresidents): That mysterious extra money you are required to pay the law school in addition to tuition and everything else, on a per-credit basis. If in-state and out-of-state students are charged differently, both amounts are listed.

EMPLOYMENT INFORMATION

Career Rating: How well the law school prepares its students for a successful career in law, on a scale of 60-99. The rating incorporates school-reported data and the average responses of law students at the school to a few questions on our law student survey. We ask law schools for the average starting salaries of graduating students, the percentage of graduating students who find employment after graduation, and the percentage of students who pass the bar exam the first time they take it. We ask students about how much the law program encourages practical experience; the opportunities for externships, internships, and clerkships; and how prepared to practice the law they will feel after graduating. If a school receives a "low" Career Rating, it doesn't necessarily mean that the career prospects for graduates are bad; it simply means that the school scored lower relative to how other schools scored in our computations based on the criteria outlined above. Because this rating incorporates law student opinion data, only those law schools that appear in the section with the descriptive profiles receive a Career Rating.

Job Placement Rate: Placement rate of graduates into the job market after completing of the Juris Doctor.

% employed within nine months: Percent of graduates who secured employment within nine months of graduating from law school.

Average Starting Salary: The amount of money the average graduate of this law school makes the first year out of school.

State for Bar Exam: The state for which most students from the school will take the bar exam.

Pass Rate for First-Time Bar: After three years, the percentage of students who passed the bar exam the first time they took it. It's a crucial statistic. You *don't* want to fail your state's bar.

Employers Who Frequently Hire Grads: Firms where past grads have had success finding jobs.

Prominent Alumni: Those who made it.

Grads Employed By Field:

Academia: The percentage of graduates who got jobs at law schools, universities, and think tanks.

Business/Industry: The percentage of graduates who got jobs working in business, in corporations, in consulting, etc. These jobs are sometimes law-related and sometimes not.

Government: Uncle Sam needs lawyers like you wouldn't even believe.

Judicial Clerkships: The percentage of graduates who got jobs doing research for judges.

Military: The percentage of lawyers who work to represent the Armed Forces in all kinds of legal matters, like Tom Cruise in *A Few Good Men*.

Private Practice: The percentage of graduates who got jobs in traditional law firms of various sizes or "put out a shingle" for themselves as sole practitioners.

Public Interest: The percentage of (mostly) altruistic graduates who got jobs providing legal assistance to folks who couldn't afford it otherwise and fighting the power in general.

NOTA BENE

If a 60* appears for any of a law school's ratings, it means that the school's administrators did not report by our deadline all of the statistics that rating incorporates.

Please note that we target each law school for resurveying at least every other year, which means we rewrite each law school's descriptive profile at least every other year, too. Student surveys captured via our online survey (http://survey.review.com) are considered current for the purposes of our own rating, rankings, and Survey Says items for two years.

WHAT'S IN THE PROFILES: DESCRIPTIVE TEXT

Academics, Life, and Getting In Sections: The text of the descriptive profiles is broken out into three sections: Academics, Life, and Getting In. The Academics and Life sections of each descriptive profile are driven by the student opinions collected from current law students at the school, and the quotations sprinkled throughout each of these sections come directly from the written comments students provided us with on their surveys. In the Academics section, we often discuss professors and their teaching methods, the workload, special clinical programs, the efficiency of the administration, and the helpfulness of the library staff. In the Life section, we often discuss how academically competitive the student body is, how (and if) students separate into cliques, clubs or organizations students often join and the amenities of the town in which the school is located. We don't follow a cookie-cutter formula when writing these profiles, however, relying instead on students' responses to the open-ended questions on our student survey and analysis of their aggregate responses to our multiple choice questions to drive the topics each profile focuses on. The Getting In section is based on the data we collect from law school administrators and our own additional research.

DECODING DEGREES

Many law schools offer joint or combined degree programs with other departments (or sometimes even with other schools) that you can earn along with your Juris doctor. You'll find the abbreviations for these degrees in the individual school profiles, but we thought we'd give you a little help in figuring out exactly what they are.

AMBA	Accounting Master of Business
BCL	Bachelor of Civil Law
DJUR	Doctor of Jurisprudence
DL	Doctor of Law
DLaw	Doctor of Law
EdD	Doctor of Education
HRIR	Human Resources and Industrial Relations
IMBA	International Master of Business Administration
JD	Juris Doctor
JSD	Doctor of Juridical Science
JSM	Master of the Science of Law
LLB	Bachelor of Law
LLCM	Master of Comparative Law (for international students)
LLM	Master of Law
MA	Master of Arts
MAcc	Master of Accounting
MALD	Master of Arts in Law and Diplomacy
MAM	Master of Arts Management
MM	Master of Management
MANM	Master of Nonprofit Management
MAPA	Master of Public Administration
MAUA	Master of Arts in Urban Affairs
MBA	Master of Business Administration
MCJ	Master of Criminal Justice
MCL	Master of Comparative Law
MCP	Master of Community Planning
MCRP	Master of City and Regional Planning
MDiv	Master of Divinity
ME	Master of Engineering OR Master of Education
MEd	Master of Education
MED	Master of Environmental Design
MEM	Master of Environmental Management
MFA	Master of Fine Arts
MHA	Master of Health Administration
MHSA	Master of Health Services Administration
MIA	Master of International Affairs
MIB	Master of International Business
MIP	Master of Intellectual Property
MIR	Master of Industrial Relations
MIRL	Master of Industrial and Labor Relations
MJ	Master of Jurisprudence
MJS	Master of Juridical Study (not a JD)
MLIR	Master of Labor and Industrial Relations
MLIS	Master of Library and Information Sciences
MLS	Master of Library Science
MMA	Master of Marine Affairs
MOB	Master of Organizational Behavior
MPA	Master of Public Administration
MPAFF	Master of Public Affairs
MPH	Master of Public Health
MPP	Master of Public Planning OR Master of Public Policy
MPPA	Master of Public Policy
MPPS	Master of Public Policy Sciences
MPS	Master of Professional Studies in Law
MRP	Master of Regional Planning
MS	Master of Science
MSEL	Master of Studies in Environmental Law
MSES	Master of Science in Environmental Science
MSF	Master of Science in Finance
MSFS	Master of Science in Foreign Service

MSI	Master of Science in Information
MSIA	Master of Industrial Administration
MSIE	Master of Science in International Economics
MSJ	Master of Science in Journalism
MSPH	Master of Science in Public Health
MSW	Master of Social Welfare OR Master of Social Work
MT	Master of Taxation
MTS	Master of Theological Studies
MUP	Master of Urban Planning
MUPD	Master of Urban Planning and Development
MURP	Master of Urban and Regional Planning
PharmD	Doctor of Pharmacy
PhD	Doctor of Philosophy
REES	Russian and Eastern European Studies Certificate
SJD	Doctor of Juridical Science
DVM	Doctor of Veterinary Medicine
MALIR	Master of Arts in Labor and Industrial Relations

LAW SCHOOLS RANKED BY CATEGORY

ABOUT OUR LAW SCHOOL RANKINGS

On the following few pages, you will find 11 top ten lists of ABA-approved law schools ranked according to various metrics. It must be noted, however, that none of these lists purports to rank the law schools by their overall quality. Nor should any combination of the categories we've chosen be construed as representing the raw ingredients for such a ranking. We have made no attempt to gauge the "prestige" of these schools, and we wonder whether we could accurately do so even if we tried. What we have done, however, is presented a number of lists using information from two very large databases—one of statistical information collected from law schools and another of subjective data gathered via our survey of more than 16,000 law students at 159 ABA-approved law schools. We target each law school's student body for resurveying at least every other year. This means that schools' student opinion data is considered current for the book's rankings and descriptive profiles for two years.

Ten of the ranking lists are based partly or wholly on opinions collected through our law student survey. The only schools that may appear in these lists are the 159 ABA-approved law schools from which we were able to collect a sufficient number of student surveys to accurately represent the student experience in our various ratings and descriptive profiles.

One of the rankings, "Toughest to Get Into," incorporates *only* admissions statistics reported to us by the law schools. Therefore, any ABA-approved law school appearing in this edition of the guide, whether we collected student surveys from it or not, may appear on this list.

Under the title of each list is an explanation of what criteria the ranking is based on. For explanations of many of the individual rankings components, turn to page 45.

It's worth repeating: there is no one best law school in America. There is a best law school for you. By using these rankings in conjunction with the descriptive profiles and data listings in subsequent sections of this book, we hope that you will begin to identify the attributes of a law school that are important to you, as well as the law schools that can best help you to achieve your personal and professional goals.

The top schools in each category appear in descending order.

TOUGHEST TO GET INTO

Based on the Admissions Selectivity Rating (see page 47 for explanation)

1. Yale University
2. Harvard University
3. Stanford University
4. Columbia University
5. University of Pennsylvania
6. Northwestern University
7. University of California—Berkeley
8. University of Chicago
9. University of California—Los Angeles (UCLA)
10. The University of Texas at Austin

BEST OVERALL ACADEMIC EXPERIENCE

Based on the Academic Experience Rating (see page 46 for explanation)

1. University of Chicago
2. Stanford University
3. Loyola Marymount University
4. University of Virginia
5. Georgetown University
6. Brigham Young University
7. Washington and Lee University
8. University of Michigan
9. University of Pennsylvania
10. Boston University

PROFESSORS ROCK (LEGALLY SPEAKING)

Based on the Professors Interesting and Professors Accessible Ratings (see page 47 for explanations)

1. Washington and Lee University
2. Boston University
3. Loyola Marymount University
4. Ave Maria School of Law
5. University of Kentucky
6. Samford University
7. University of Chicago
8. Chapman University
9. Mercer University
10. Wake Forest University

MOST COMPETITIVE STUDENTS

Based on law student assessments of: the number of hours they spend studying outside of class each day, the number of hours they think their fellow law students spend studying outside of class each day, the degree of competitiveness among law students at their school, and the average number of hours they sleep each night

1. Baylor University
2. St. John's University
3. Yeshiva University
4. Roger Williams University
5. St. Mary's University
6. Ohio Northern University
7. Brigham Young University
8. Suffolk University
9. Cornell University
10. The Ohio State University

BEST CAREER PROSPECTS

Based on the Career Rating (see page 49 for explanation)

1. Northwestern University
2. University of Michigan
3. University of Chicago
4. Harvard University
5. New York University
6. University of Pennsylvania
7. University of Notre Dame
8. Georgetown University
9. University of Virginia
10. University of California—Berkeley

CANDIDATES FOR HERITAGE FOUNDATION FELLOWSHIPS? (OR, STUDENTS LEAN TO THE RIGHT)

Based on student assessment of the political bent of the student body at large

1. Ave Maria School of Law
2. Regent University
3. Brigham Young University
4. University of Notre Dame
5. The University of Mississippi
6. George Mason University
7. Louisiana State University
8. University of Alabama
9. Baylor University
10. University of Idaho

CANDIDATES FOR CENTER FOR AMERICAN PROGRESS FELLOWSHIPS? (OR, STUDENTS LEAN TO THE LEFT)

Based on student assessment of the political bent of the student body at large

1. University of the District of Columbia
2. City University of New York
3. Northeastern University
4. Vermont Law School
5. Lewis & Clark College
6. American University
7. University of Oregon
8. University of California—Berkeley
9. University of New Mexico
10. New York University

BEST ENVIRONMENT FOR MINORITY STUDENTS

Based on the percentage of the student body that is from underrepresented minorities and student assessment of whether all students receive equal treatment by fellow students and the faculty, regardless of ethnicity

1. Howard University
2. University of Hawaii—Manoa
3. University of the District of Columbia
4. Florida International University
5. City University of New York
6. Loyola Marymount University
7. St. Thomas University
8. University of Southern California
9. University of New Mexico
10. University of California—Davis

MOST DIVERSE FACULTY

Based on the percentage of the law school faculty that is from a minority and student assessment of whether the faculty comprises a broadly diverse group of individuals.

1. Howard University
2. Florida International University
3. City University of New York
4. Northern Illinois University
5. University of Hawaii—Manoa
6. University of the District of Columbia
7. University of New Mexico
8. University of California—Davis
9. St. Thomas University
10. Washburn University

BEST QUALITY OF LIFE

Based on student assessment of: whether there is a strong sense of community at the school, how aesthetically pleasing the law school is, the location of the law school, the quality of the social life, classroom facilities, and the library staff.

1. University of St. Thomas
2. University of Virginia
3. Chapman University
4. Regent University
5. Stanford University
6. University of Oregon
7. Southern Methodist University
8. Vanderbilt University
9. Samford University
10. Northwestern University

MOST WELCOMING OF OLDER STUDENTS

Based on the average age of entry of law school students and student reports of how many years they spent out of college before enrolling in law school

1. William Mitchell College of Law
2. The University of Tulsa
3. University of Maine
4. University of the District of Columbia
5. Florida International University
6. Southwestern University School of Law
7. Rutgers University—Newark
8. Seattle University
9. Georgia State University
10. Lewis & Clark College

LAW SCHOOL DESCRIPTIVE PROFILES

In this section you will find the two page descriptive profile of each of 159 ABA-approved law schools. As there are currently a total of 191 ABA-approved law schools in the country, there are obviously many law schools not appearing in this section; those schools appear in the following section, "Law School Data Listings."

In order for a law school to appear in this section, we had to collect the opinions of a sufficient number of current law students at that school to fairly and responsibly represent the general law student experience there. Our descriptive profiles are driven primarily by 1) comments law students provide in response to open-ended questions on our student survey and 2) our own statistical analysis of student responses to the many multiple-choice questions on the survey. While many law students complete a survey unsolicited by us at http://survey.review.com, in the vast majority of cases we rely on law school administrators to get the word out about our survey to their students. In the ideal scenario, the law school administration emails a Princeton Review-authored E-mail to all law students with an embedded link to our survey website (again, http://survey.review.com). If for some reason there are restrictions that prevent the administration from contacting the entire law student body on behalf of an outside party, they often help us find other ways to notify students of the fact that we are seeking their opinions, like advertising in law student publications or posting on law student community websites or listservs. In almost all cases, when the administration is cooperative, we are able to collect opinions from a sufficient number of students to produce an accurate descriptive profile and ratings of its law school.

There is a group of law school administrators, however, that doesn't agree with the notion that the opinions of current law students presented in descriptive profile and rankings formats are useful to prospective law school students trying to choose the right schools to apply to and attend. Administrators at the 32 ABA-approved law schools not appearing in this section are a part of this group. They either ignored our multiple attempts to contact them in order to request their assistance in notifying their students about our survey, or they simply refused to work with us at all. And while we would like to be able to write a descriptive profile on each of these 32 schools anyway, we won't do so with minimal law student opinion. So if you are a prospective law school student and would like to read the opinions of current law students about your dream school(s), contact the missing school(s) and communicate this desire to them. (We include contact information in each of the data listings.) If you are a current law student at one of the 32 ABA-approved law schools not profiled in this section, please don't send us angry letters; instead, go to http://survey.review.com, complete a survey about your school, and tell all of your fellow students to do the same. If we collect enough current student opinion on your school in the coming year, we'll include a descriptive profile in the next edition of the guide.

SPECIAL NOTE ON THE TEXT OF EACH DESCRIPTIVE PROFILE

The Academics and Life sections of each descriptive profile are driven by the student opinions collected from current law students at the school, and the quotations sprinkled throughout each of these sections comes directly from the written comments students provided us with on their surveys. The Getting In section is based on the data we collect from law school administrators and our own additional research. Every law school with a descriptive profile has its students resurveyed and its profile rewritten at least every other year.

SPECIAL NOTE ON THE SIDEBAR STATISTICS

Explanations of what each field of data signifies may be found in the "How to Use This Book" section, which begins on page 45.

ALBANY LAW SCHOOL

INSTITUTIONAL INFORMATION

Public/private	private
Student/faculty ratio	16:1
% faculty part-time	49
% faculty female	42
% faculty minority	10
Total faculty	104

SURVEY SAYS . . .

Great research resources
Great library staff
Abundant externship/internship/clerkship opportunities

STUDENTS

Enrollment of law school	755
% male/female	51/49
% out-of-state	22
% full-time	95
% minority	18
% international	2
# of countries represented	7
Average age of entering class	25

ACADEMICS

Academic experience rating	**63**
Professors interesting rating	65
Professors accessible rating	61
Hours of study per day	4.48

Academic Specialties

Business law, civil procedure, constitutional law, criminal law, environmental law, estate planning, family & elder law, government services, health law, intellectual property law, international law, labor law, taxation.

Advanced Degrees Offered

LLM, LLM for foreign law graduates, MS in legal studies.

Combined Degrees Offered

JD, 3 yrs; JD/MBA, 3.5 to 4 yrs; JD/MPA, 3.5 to 4 yrs; JD/MSW, 3.5 to 4 yrs; JD/MRP, 3.5 to 4 yrs; JD/MPP, 3.5 to 4. yrs; LLM, 1 to 3 yrs; LLM for foreign law graduates, 1 yr.

Academic Requirements

Clinical Program Required?	No
Legal Writing Course Requirement?	Yes

Academics

Albany Law School is located in the heart of New York's capital, and thus, "there are countless opportunities to find placement with attorneys, courts, and government offices." Other practical opportunities are outstanding as well. Take the Law School Clinic for example, which provides "pro bono legal services to many types of clients." One student who worked in the program tells us that this is where "you learn how to be a lawyer. You are admitted to practice law on a limited basis and actually conduct all aspects of your cases including trials." Another student explains, "You learn how to actually write the motions you learn about in law school and do the interviews and everything else that you will be doing when you are a lawyer." However, many students at the law school grumble loudly about the drop in bar passage rates, which they attribute to the school's admitting too many students, but this will hopefully be remedied by a school movement designed to decrease class sizes continually through the 2006–2007 school year, and a new bar preparation course for graduating 3Ls.

Most students at Albany feel that the professors "truly care about their students and the future success of their students," calling them Albany Law School's "greatest assets." They tell us that along with being "accessible and helpful," the faculty is also "caring, compassionate, and very well-spoken and well-educated." As one student puts it, "Who better to learn the law than from those who wrote the law?"

The administration at Albany Law School raises the ire of almost every student with accusations of incompetence and nepotism permeating the responses we've seen. Combine that with rising tuition costs, falling bar passage rates, and reductions in amenities, and you've got one disgruntled student body. As one student puts it, "There is an extreme disconnection between most of the administration and the student body, which is why many of the students become resentful, cynical, and bitter." Another student vents, "The administration does not listen to the students at all. They host meetings for the students to voice their concerns and then do not take what they have said into consideration." Overall, students say there is "a general feeling of disinterest in student needs and wants" among the administration. One bright spot, however, seems to be the "outstanding and wonderful career planning office who, despite the institution's immense shortcomings, manage time and again to deliver jobs to students and never rest until it is done."

The library is "fantastic [and] very extensive" at Albany. "The research librarians go out of their way to help you, [and] know everything about how to access materials that aren't in the school." In the classroom, Albany has tried to update technology for the twenty-first century, but has hit some snags. There are "Internet hook-ups and electric outlets at every classroom seat," but some of the hook-ups do not work yet.

Gail Bensen, Interim Director of Admissions
80 New Scotland Avenue, Albany, NY 12208
Telephone: 518-445-2326 • Fax: 518-445-2369
E-mail: admissions@mail.als.edu • Website: www.als.edu

Life

Albany is located in the midst of the New York State government. Their "location in the state's capital provides a lot of opportunities for students." While Albany's weather is not much to write home about, students look on the bright side and say, "Gray winter months are great for studying indoors." Another great strength is the networking system at Albany, with many alumni working in the immediate area. Albany "might not be the most beautiful city in the world," says one student, "but it is well-suited for a graduate education—not too little to do that you're bored, but not too much to do that you're distracted." One added bonus is that the city itself is relatively inexpensive.

At Albany, it "is not a pressure cooker environment. Like any law school, there is plenty of work, but you don't get many of the book stealing and page cutting types." A lot of people claim, "It's high school all over again!" If you are interested in clubs at school, there are many at Albany. "There is a Republican club, a chapter of the National Lawyer's Guild, and a chapter of the Students for Choice," to name a few. Diversity at Albany is "pretty stellar, with large minority student populations." Socializing involves "beer bashes on Fridays, [which can] have a distinctly frat house feel." One student tells us, "The students themselves get along for the most part, but it is very high school cliquey! There are the nerds, the jocks, the drunks, etc." Student's overall feelings, "are united in their discontent with the administration and their appreciation for the faculty."

Getting In

Albany Law School's admitted students at the 25th percentile have an LSAT score of 150 and a GPA of 3.0. Admitted students at the 75th percentile have an LSAT score of 156 and a GPA of 3.5.

EMPLOYMENT INFORMATION

Career Rating	**73**
Job placement rate (%)	95
Average starting salary	$53,303
State for bar exam	NY
Pass rate for first-time bar	77

Employers who frequently hire grads: Private law firms, government agencies, business & industry, high-tech industry, corporations.

Prominent Alumni: Thomas Vilsack, governor of Iowa; Richard D. Parsons, chief executive officer of AOL Time Warner; Mary Donohue, lieutenant governor, New York State.

Grads employed by field (%):	
Academic	3
Business/industry	7
Government	21
Judicial clerkships	8
Military	2
Private practice	57
Public interest	2

Legal Methods Course Requirement?	Yes
Legal Research Course Requirement?	Yes
Moot Court Requirement?	No
Public Interest Law Requirement?	No

ADMISSIONS

Selectivity Rating	**75**
# applications received	2,361
# applicants accepted	732
# acceptees attending	235
Average LSAT	154
LSAT Range	151–157
Average undergrad GPA	3.3
Application fee	$50
Regular application deadline	3/15
Regular notification	rolling
Rolling notification?	Yes
Early application program?	No
Transfer students accepted?	Yes
Evening division offered?	No
Part-time accepted?	No
LSDAS accepted?	Yes

Applicants Also Look At

Hofstra University, New England School of Law, New York Law School, Pace University, St. John's University, Syracuse University, University at Buffalo—The State University of New York.

International Students

TOEFL required of international students?	No
TOEFL recommended of international students?	Yes
Minimum Paper TOEFL	600
Minimum Computer TOEFL	250

FINANCIAL FACTS

Annual tuition	$29,963
Books and supplies	$900
Tuition per credit	$980
Room & board (off-campus)	$6,400
% first-year students receiving some sort of aid	94
% receiving some sort of aid	89
% of aid that is merit-based	44
% receiving scholarships	37
Average grant	$11,700
Average loan	$29,300
Average total aid package	$34,651
Average debt	$73,500

American University
Washington College of Law

INSTITUTIONAL INFORMATION

Public/private	private
Student/faculty ratio	15:1
% faculty part-time	62
% faculty female	40
% faculty minority	13
Total faculty	211

SURVEY SAYS . . .

Great research resources
Abundant externship/internship/clerkship opportunities
Students love Washington, DC

STUDENTS

Enrollment of law school	1,485
% male/female	39/61
% out-of-state	99
% full-time	80
% minority	29
% international	1
# of countries represented	14
Average age of entering class	24

ACADEMICS

Academic experience rating	**80**
Professors interesting rating	80
Professors accessible rating	74
Hours of study per day	4.35

Academic Specialties

Commercial law, corporation securities law, environmental law, government services, human rights law, intellectual property law, international law.

Advanced Degrees Offered

LLM, international legal studies, 1 year to 1.5 years; LLM, law and government, 1 year; S/JD, 3 to 4 years.

Combined Degrees Offered

JD/MBA, JD/MA international affairs, JD/MS justice. All are 3.5 to 4-year programs.

Academic Requirements

Clinical Program Required?	No
Legal Writing Course Requirement?	No

Academics

American University's Washington College of Law is "a quality law school [with] a strong emphasis, at least philosophically, on providing legal representation to all" and a focus on "public interest and other atypical environments—not just corporate law." There is also a notable emphasis on international law, and several tremendously cool study-abroad options are available. The academic atmosphere is described as "challenging without the traditional rigidity and Socratic method." Washington College of Law's "fabulous" professors are "funny, well-respected in their fields, and really want to be teaching." One student proclaims, "I have only had one professor I have not found particularly interesting, but he was very approachable and helpful outside of the classroom." Also, "the school does a good job in hiring adjunct professors with real-world experience." The biggest complaint that students seem to have with their otherwise excellent professors is that too many are blatantly "ultra-liberal. Even moderate liberals feel stifled," sniffs one student.

The "forward thinking" administration is "sensitive to student concerns [but] communication between the administration and students could improve." And in the eyes of at least a few students, "tuition is way too high." One such student says, "There should be more opportunities for middle-class Americans to get financial aid." As at most law schools, students aren't in love with Career Services, which provides "lots of lip service but no action." A few things to keep in mind on the career-front at WCL: First, "the average salary upon graduation for WCL is misleadingly low [because] so many (very talented) WCL grads want to go into public service [and not] Big Law." Second, American University maintains "a fairly strong academic reputation, especially in DC and the Northeast."

Washington College of Law's variety of course offerings and clinical programs is outstanding. "International law course offerings are varied every semester [and] real-world working and learning experiences" are readily available, too. "Internships and externships are plentiful," and, of course, "being located in DC gives you the opportunity to work for a variety of government agencies [and] three different jurisdictions" (DC, Maryland, and Virginia). There are also "lots of opportunities to work with professors and school-related centers on special legal projects." Take, for example, The Center for Human Rights & Humanitarian Law or The War Crimes Research Office, both international resources for human rights issues. The legal writing program, which carries the highfalutin title of "Legal Rhetoric: Research & Writing," gets mixed reviews. Proponents call it "outstanding [and] excellent at preparing students for summer jobs," while critics say it's "disorganized [and] worse than a junior high English class."

The law school's "beautiful, state-of-the-art facility [boasts] absolutely amazing" classrooms. "Every seat has an electrical outlet. The wireless network is amazing." The building can be a bit "cramped," though, thanks to recent enrollment increases. The "comfortable" library is a popular destination for all manner of studiers. Students "from other local law and medical schools [are often] caught studying here."

Life

"Many interesting people [and a] large number of international students" make up the law student population. This profusion of diversity makes social interaction at WCL "much different than at most law schools." Politically, the student body is described as "very middle of the road, [and] markedly more conservative than the faculty." It's also worth noting that there are significantly more women than men at WCL.

AKIRA SHIROMA, ASSISTANT DEAN OF ADMISSIONS
4801 MASSACHUSETTS AVENUE NW, WASHINGTON, DC 20016
TELEPHONE: 202-274-4101 • FAX: 202-274-4107
E-MAIL: WCLADMIT@WCL.AMERICAN.EDU • WEBSITE: WWW.WCL.AMERICAN.EDU

Washington College of Law is a "warm and inviting" place that breeds a "laid-back" state of mind. "A small number of students are cutthroat," but most everyone is "relaxed." One student notes, "people are not highly competitive with each other, just with themselves." The social atmosphere is serious, yet "congenial [and] open." Students "always give each other practical tips for classes, share outlines, and let each other know about bar application deadlines." One student says, "Everybody is friendly and wants to share ideas," while another marvels, "Everyone smiles and holds the door for you." All this genuine niceness is accompanied by a notable "we-try-harder attitude" because American University is Washington, DC's "underdog" law school in some respects. So, in addition to all their good humor, these students are ardently focused on being and becoming "hardworking legal professionals."

Washington, DC is obviously "a fantastic place to study law." On WCL's campus alone, "there are several daily guest lectures, symposia," and, generally, "more academic activities than you could ever attend." And if lectures and symposia are your bag, believe us: the rest of this city is a policy wonk's dream. However, the law school's exact location has its shortcomings. Washington College of Law could stand to be "located a little more conveniently in the city." Still, "parking is an ongoing struggle." The administration "forbids street parking in the neighborhood." (There is a "$75 ticket each time you're caught.") Approved law student parking is very expensive and "over a mile away from the school."

Getting In

Washington College of Law boasts competitive admissions—offering a spot to only about 20 percent of its yearly applicant pool of almost 10,000. Admitted students at the 25th percentile have an LSAT score of 159 and a GPA of 3.22. Admitted students at the 75th percentile have an LSAT score of 162 and a GPA of 3.61. If you take the LSAT more than once, WCL will average your scores.

EMPLOYMENT INFORMATION

Career Rating	**83**
% employed within 9 months	97
Average starting salary	$80,300
State for bar exam	MD, NY, VA
Pass rate for first-time bar	79

Employers who frequently hire grads: Akin Gump Strauss Hauer & Feld LLP; Hogan & Hartson LLP; Jones Day; Arnold & Porter; Manhattan district attorney; United States Department of Justice.

Prominent Alumni: Honorable Robert Byrd, U.S. senator (D-W VA); Honorable Rick Lazio, former congressman (R-NY), Republican candidate, U.S. Senate.

Grads employed by field (%):	
Academic	1
Business/industry	19
Government	15
Judicial clerkships	14
Private practice	40
Public interest	11

Legal Methods Course Requirement?	Yes
Legal Research Course Requirement?	Yes
Moot Court Requirement?	No
Public Interest Law Requirement?	No

ADMISSIONS

Selectivity Rating	**84**
# applications received	9,287
# applicants accepted	2,287
# acceptees attending	460
Average LSAT	160
LSAT Range	159–162
Average undergrad GPA	3.4
Application fee	$65
Regular application deadline	3/1
Regular notification	rolling
Rolling notification?	Yes
Early application program?	No
Transfer students accepted?	Yes
Evening division offered?	Yes
Part-time accepted?	Yes
LSDAS accepted?	Yes

Applicants Also Look At

Boston University, The Catholic University of America, Fordham University, George Mason University, The George Washington University, Georgetown University, University of Maryland.

International Students

TOEFL required of international students?	No
TOEFL recommended of international students?	No

FINANCIAL FACTS

Annual tuition	$30,528
Books and supplies	$915
Tuition per credit	$1,131
Room & board	$11,305
Financial aid application deadline	3/1
% first-year students receiving some sort of aid	79
% receiving some sort of aid	81
% of aid that is merit-based	49
% receiving scholarships	30
Average grant	$9,664
Average loan	$34,514
Average total aid package	$36,735
Average debt	$98,511

ARIZONA STATE UNIVERSITY

COLLEGE OF LAW

INSTITUTIONAL INFORMATION

Public/private	public
Student/faculty ratio	10:1
% faculty part-time	29
% faculty female	23
% faculty minority	11
Total faculty	75

SURVEY SAYS . . .

Great research resources
Great library staff
Students love Tempe, AZ

STUDENTS

Enrollment of law school	594
% male/female	53/47
% out-of-state	29
% full-time	100
% minority	28
% international	2
# of countries represented	8
Average age of entering class	25

ACADEMICS

Academic experience rating	**75**
Professors interesting rating	76
Professors accessible rating	78
Hours of study per day	2.23

Academic Specialties

Certificate in Indian law; certificate in law, science, & technology; environmental law; intellectual property law; international law; legal philosophy; taxation.

Advanced Degrees Offered

JD, 3 years.

Combined Degrees Offered

JD/MBA, 4 years; JD/PhD, justice studies, amount of time varies.

Academic Requirements

Clinical Program Required?	No
Legal Writing Course Requirement?	Yes
Legal Methods Course Requirement?	Yes
Legal Research Course Requirement?	Yes
Moot Court Requirement?	Yes

Academics

The "ridiculously cheap" College of Law at Arizona State University "offers a solid academic program and incredibly low tuition for both in- and out-of-state students." ASU is said to "encourage all-around development in academics, pro bono work, community service, and student organizations." It is also the only accredited law school in the burgeoning metropolis of Phoenix, which means that "it gets a lot of attention [from the] tightly knit surrounding professional community. Speakers, adjuncts, and judges for competitions" are plentiful and "one of the state Supreme Court justices teaches a class." Once you spend three years studying law in sunny Phoenix, you too will probably find yourself wanting to become a part of the "very supportive" legal community. Luckily, "great job opportunities exist after graduation."

The "exceptionally knowledgeable and approachable" professors at ASU "are always available for questions." One student relates, "Everyone is willing to help. You can walk into the office of any faculty member to chat, and many students do." Students are split with regard to the administration. Some say that the top brass is "generally accessible: The dean holds regular lunches with outside speakers and student groups, and one of the associate deans is constantly available by e-mail." However, other students complain that the administration is "convoluted and unhelpful." They tell us that "red tape is abundant, as it is with most large public universities."

Arizona State has a lot to offer academically. "The writing instructors are fabulous." Students "regularly stop by to ask them for job-hunting and life advice." The cutting-edge Center for Law, Science, and Technology "offers a dedicated faculty [and sponsors] a steady stream of speakers drawn from across the country." Genetics and the Law is one of the major issues addressed by the center. "Indian Law is another strength," notes one student. The nationally recognized Indian Legal Program helps train Native American lawyers and furthers an understanding of the distinctions between the legal systems of Indian Nations and the United States. Students in this unique program represent more than 25 tribal nations. You will find "an amazing intellectual property program" at ASU as well.

Architecturally, "the main building is a 70s creation." The "dreary and brown" classrooms "haven't been touched in a decade or more." One student complains that classrooms are "uncomfortable [and] don't accommodate laptops very well." At the very least, another student says, "Some more light and color would help us concentrate for two hours." On the plus side, the law school is designed to create "a lot of interaction" among students: "There are quite a few mixing areas that encourage interaction and a collegial environment." Also, the "gorgeous, amazing library [is] an actual architectural landmark." One student gushes, "It's fully equipped with everything a law student could possible need, plus it's shaped like a boat and has a wall of windows that make it bright inside."

Michael Berch, Assistant Dean for Admissions
PO Box 877906, Tempe, AZ 85287-7906
Telephone: 480-965-1474 • Fax: 480-727-7930
E-mail: law.admissions@asu.edu • Website: www.law.asu.edu

Life

Something about warm, sun-drenched Phoenix "fosters a very relaxed atmosphere, [which] enhances academic excellence and emphasizes becoming a well-rounded professional." The very laid-back vibe that envelops Arizona State also promotes cohesion. Most students at ASU reportedly "get along very well." Class sizes are "small enough that you know quite a few people." One student says that the "strong social atmosphere [at ASU] is furthered by the administration's commitment to allowing students a strong say in the operations of the school." Another student notes that there are many "newly minted undergrads" are very social. There are also "a number of older students who have done interesting things," although their "social scene is a bit different." One student explains, "I've made some of my best friends in law school; there's a plethora of social activities for anything you may be interested in, whether it's a Halloween party for kids or bar hopping on Thursday nights."

The "unique, talented individuals" that make up the law student population tell us that ASU is home to "a great mix of diversity [in] gender, ethnicity, religion, [and] interests." Academically, some students "are very competitive and study for eight hours a day." There are also those with a more relaxed attitude because, as one student admits, "It's the last time for a very long time that we'll be able to have fun." This student concludes, "Regardless of why we're here, everyone is very accepting of everyone else, and that makes the school extremely inviting."

Getting In

The College of Law at ASU is fairly selective, offering a place to only about 21 percent of applicants. Admitted students at the 25th percentile have an LSAT score of 154 and a GPA of 3.2. Admitted students at the 75th percentile have an LSAT score of 163 and a GPA of 3.7. If you take the LSAT more than once, ASU averages your scores.

EMPLOYMENT INFORMATION

Career Rating	**72**
% employed within 9 months	100
Average starting salary	$62,320
State for bar exam	AZ
Pass rate for first-time bar	76

Employers who frequently hire grads: Snell & Wilmer; Brown & Bain; Bryan Cave; Gammage & Birnham; Lewis and Roca; Fennemore Craig; Jennings, Strouss, & Salmon.

Prominent Alumni: Dan Burk, Oppenheimer Wolff & Donnelly professor, UMinn Law; Ruth McGregor, vice chief justice, Arizona State Supreme Court.

Grads employed by field (%):	
Academic	3
Business/industry	14
Government	24
Judicial clerkships	10
Private practice	47
Public interest	2

Public Interest Law Requirement?	No

ADMISSIONS

Selectivity Rating	**85**
# applications received	2,987
# applicants accepted	627
# acceptees attending	211
Average LSAT	159
LSAT Range	155–162
Average undergrad GPA	3.4
Application fee	$50
Regular application deadline	2/15
Regular notification	rolling
Rolling notification?	Yes
Early application program?	No
Transfer students accepted?	Yes
Evening division offered?	No
Part-time accepted?	No
LSDAS accepted?	Yes

Applicants Also Look At

University of Arizona.

International Students

TOEFL required of international students?	Yes
Minimum Paper TOEFL	550
Minimum Computer TOEFL	213

FINANCIAL FACTS

Annual tuition (resident)	$12,379
Annual tuition (nonresident)	$20,899
Books and supplies	$1,000
Room & board (off-campus)	$1,960
Financial aid application deadline	2/15
% receiving some sort of aid	81
% receiving scholarships	43
Average grant	$4,223
Average loan	$16,120
Average total aid package	$16,965
Average debt	$46,888

Ave Maria School of Law

INSTITUTIONAL INFORMATION

Public/private	private
Student/faculty ratio	14:1
Affiliation	Roman Catholic
% faculty part-time	32
% faculty female	34
% faculty minority	8
Total faculty	38

SURVEY SAYS . . .

Average student responses from this law school to all Survey Says items were not extreme enough for us to assign it any specific Survey Says.

STUDENTS

Enrollment of law school	302
% male/female	70/30
% out-of-state	77
% full-time	100
% minority	17
% international	3
# of countries represented	4
Average age of entering class	26

ACADEMICS

Academic experience rating	**78**
Professors interesting rating	97
Professors accessible rating	97
Hours of study per day	4.65

Advanced Degrees Offered

JD program, 3 years, full-time.

Academic Requirements

Clinical Program Required?	No
Legal Writing Course Requirement?	Yes
Legal Methods Course Requirement?	Yes
Legal Research Course Requirement?	Yes
Moot Court Requirement?	No
Public Interest Law Requirement?	No

Academics

If you are looking for "something different from any other law school, consider Ave Maria School of Law. This "unique," intimate bastion of legal education opened its doors in the fall of 2000 thanks largely to the extraordinarily Catholic-oriented philanthropy of Tom Monaghan, the founder of Domino's Pizza. "Natural law theory, moral reasoning, [and Catholicism] pervade the school," as does a strong "commitment to training lawyers who will work for justice." Faith and reason are equals at Ave Maria; both are seen as necessary to obtain truth and to pursue justice. "Every class is begun with prayer, usually the Lord's Prayer or Hail Mary." In addition to torts, civil procedure, and the standard curriculum through which every law student suffers, required course work includes Jurisprudence; Law, Ethics, Public Policy; and Moral Foundations of the Law I and II (partly taught by Judge Robert Bork).

Students tell us that Ave Maria is "intellectually rigorous [and] first class in every aspect." Students also say Ave's "amazingly accomplished [and] truly caring [professors are] experts in their fields and excited about the school and the students. Their enthusiasm for their respective topics is contagious, [and] they really make you think deeply about the law and trends in law that the cases represent." These professors are also legendary for their accessibility. "They show up at student barbeques and picnics, care about our families, and are always 100 percent available," students boast. The "incredibly professional" administration is "prone to micromanaging" but otherwise "runs the school like clockwork [and] will bend over backward to help you." Ave is "really generous, too." Full and nearly full scholarships absolutely abound.

Ave Maria's facilities are "clean, modern, well-kept, and user-friendly." In the buildings "there are Internet connections at every seat in every classroom and at every seat at every table." One student swears, "It's the nicest law school facility I've seen." Everybody loves the library, where "the fusion of traditional resources and computer technology is wonderfully accomplished." Also (and this is a massive plus), "you may eat and drink in the law library and during class." Students vigorously complain about the lack of parking, though.

As a new law school, Ave Maria does have some disadvantages. Piquing the interest of law firms can be difficult. "It is difficult to attract employers when I must introduce, not only myself, but also my school," one student says. Ave Maria offers "widely available" externships and internships, but "there could be a stronger emphasis on the practical." Students feel "an advanced trial advocacy program would be greatly appreciated." Overall, though, students are happy, and they are confident that the bells and whistles are just around the corner. In the meantime, Ave Maria boasts the highest bar passage rate in Michigan—93 percent—and "an uncommon *esprit de corp*." One student asserts, "There is a sense that we are striving to do something new. Ave Maria is an amazing place to prepare to practice law."

RACHELE CONNER, ADMISSIONS COUNSELOR
3475 PLYMOUTH ROAD, ANN ARBOR, MI 48105
TELEPHONE: 734-827-8063 • FAX: 734-622-0123
E-MAIL: INFO@AVEMARIALAW.EDU • WEBSITE: WWW.AVEMARIALAW.EDU

Life

The atmosphere at this little law school is "competitive without being too stressful." Camaraderie is strong, and "people genuinely try to help each other." One student expounds, "The students are extremely competitive. They want to do well and work very hard at it. However, 'cutthroat' is simply not an appropriate description because, overwhelmingly, the students are cooperative as well."

Ave Maria is home to "the kindest people on the planet." The "genuine" students at Ave Maria "place a strong interest on family priorities." One student says, "I can't imagine a more family-friendly law school. There is a true law school community in which spouses and families are encouraged to participate. Students feel that "the culture is pretty homogeneous. Although they say, "The school is actively working to recruit minorities and people with different life experiences," for the time being Ave Maria "basically [consists of] Catholic, conservative, white males."

Not surprisingly, "many activities surround the Catholic faith" at Ave Maria. This strongly Catholic sentiment has advantages and drawbacks. On the plus side, "there is a pervasive sense that each student is important as a person," both in class and in social settings. Also, if following "the teachings of the Catholic Church" is important to you, you will have oodles of support. While Ave Maria is "way too conservative" for some students' tastes, other students are not bothered. "I'm pretty liberal and that puts me in the minority, but intelligent debate is cultivated here," asserts one student. "It gets awkward once in a while, but on the whole I'm getting a high-quality legal education in a great setting among truly concerned people." Another student agrees, "Although we are mostly conservative here, we do have very open discussion about contentious issues." As one student puts it, "Even if you're not conservative, your point of view is heard, and you are treated with respect."

Getting In

Admitted students at the 25th percentile have an LSAT score of 152 and a grade point average of 2.89. Admitted students at the 75th percentile have an LSAT score of 162 and a GPA of 3.62. Of the class of 2006, 25 percent scored in the top 13 percent on the LSAT.

ADMISSIONS

Selectivity Rating	**67**
# applications received	793
# applicants accepted	541
# acceptees attending	146
Average LSAT	156
LSAT Range	152–161
Average undergrad GPA	3.2
Application fee	$50
Regular application deadline	4/1
Regular notification	rolling
Rolling notification?	Yes
Early application program?	No
Transfer students accepted?	Yes
Evening division offered?	No
Part-time accepted?	No
LSDAS accepted?	Yes
International Students	
TOEFL required of international students?	Yes
Minimum Paper TOEFL	600
Minimum Computer TOEFL	250

FINANCIAL FACTS

Annual tuition	$27,100
Books and supplies	$850
Financial aid application deadline	6/1
% first-year students receiving some sort of aid	97
% receiving some sort of aid	97
% of aid that is merit-based	34
% receiving scholarships	78
Average grant	$18,652
Average loan	$31,646
Average total aid package	$43,361
Average debt	$56,422

EMPLOYMENT INFORMATION

Career Rating	**72**
Job placement rate (%)	83
Average starting salary	$50,800
State for bar exam	MI, CA, OR, VA, IL
Pass rate for first-time bar	82

Employers who frequently hire grads:
Federal court judges; United States Army; United States Air Force; Butzel Long, PC; Trott & Trott; Michigan Supreme Court justices; Michigan Court of Appeals Pre-trial Division.

Grads employed by field (%):

Academic	2
Business/industry	21
Government	11
Judicial clerkships	11
Military	11
Private practice	25
Public interest	2

BAYLOR UNIVERSITY
SCHOOL OF LAW

INSTITUTIONAL INFORMATION

Public/private	private
Student/faculty ratio	17:1
Affiliation	Southern Baptist
% faculty part-time	31
% faculty female	16
% faculty minority	3
Total faculty	32

SURVEY SAYS . . .

Heavy use of Socratic method
Great research resources
Great library staff
Beautiful campus

STUDENTS

Enrollment of law school	426
% male/female	54/46
% out-of-state	24
% full-time	100
% minority	11
% international	1
# of countries represented	2
Average age of entering class	22

ACADEMICS

Academic experience rating	**86**
Professors interesting rating	77
Professors accessible rating	74
Hours of study per day	5.27

Academic Specialties

Business litigation; business transactions, estate planning, and administrative practice; civil procedure; criminal law.

Combined Degrees Offered

JD/MBA, JD/M taxation, JD/MPPA. All 3.5 to 4-year programs.

Academic Requirements

Clinical Program Required?	Yes
Legal Writing Course Requirement?	Yes
Legal Methods Course Requirement?	Yes
Legal Research Course Requirement?	Yes
Moot Court Requirement?	Yes
Public Interest Law Requirement?	No

Academics

Baylor University Law School has "a strong academic reputation" and produces world-class litigators with "practical skills" galore. But be warned, Baylor lives up to its "hardcore" reputation as "the Marine Corps of law schools" thanks to "very strict" attendance policies and a "workload designed to push your limits." Students "are not allowed any rules, restatements, codes, or statutes" on exams, and "while the third year at most other law schools is cake," Baylor's unique, intense, and rigorous Practice Court Program makes the third year grueling.

Baylor's "dedicated, enthusiastic," and mostly approachable professors are "unapologetically demanding [lawyers] with plenty of real-world experience [who] rely solely on the Socratic method." Teaching is important at Baylor, and while "famous professors are cool," students agree "teaching professors are cooler." But you had better come to class prepared because, basically, "if you think classroom dialogue in *The Paper Chase* was intimidating, this isn't the school for you." It is also important to note that adjunct professors teach several courses, and many faculty members are themselves Baylor Law grads.

The law school operates on a quarter-system and offers relatively few areas of concentration. "We are required to take a lot of classes," grumbles one student. Legal writing is "outstanding," though, and "most students graduate within 30 months (taking just one summer to work)." Certainly, highfalutin legal concepts are not Baylor's strong suit. "This is definitely not the school to go to if all you want is philosophy and obscure legal theories. [But] if you want to know how to practice law, Baylor Law is your place." During a student's final year, Baylor "requires every student to endure Practice Court." The experience, "if you can survive…is hell"—and comes complete with hazing from upper-class students—but by graduation, "Baylor lawyers know enough substance and enough procedure to successfully try a case from beginning to end."

Baylor's "fabulous facilities [are] some of the best in the country. Every seat in every classroom has a power outlet for a laptop." The technology on campus, however, does not always work as advertised. "E-mail, online grade checking, and wireless networks regularly fail." Students are also disappointed with Career Services and feel it "is a joke." Furthermore, "the single most undesirable thing about Baylor" is that grades are "low—very low—which is difficult to explain to prospective employers." Baylor "absolutely does not inflate grades. In fact, it probably deflates them." Hence, "a 3.4 at Baylor is comparable to a 3.7 somewhere else." Despite such complaints, Baylor graduates are unquestionably more successful than not. More than 92 percent of Baylor graduates pass the Texas bar exam on their first try, and more than 97 percent find employment—overwhelmingly in the Lone Star State—within a few months after passing the bar.

Heather Creed, Director of Student Relations
One Bear Place #97288, Waco, TX 76798
Telephone: 254-710-1911 • Fax: 254-710-2316
E-mail: Heather_Creed@baylor.edu • Website: http://law.baylor.edu

Life

"The worst thing about Baylor Law," according to students, "is that it is in Waco, [the] armpit of Texas." On-campus "socializing is mediocre, but the students have parties themselves, [and] there are a lot of bars since it's a college town." Intramural sports are quite popular, too. Also, "Waco is only 90 miles from Austin, Dallas, and College Station." All in all, though, there are few distractions. The primary pastime of Baylor Law students is working in the "beautiful and majestic" law library in "preparation for the 'real world.'" As such, this school is not for everybody. "I advise anyone considering Baylor law to talk to alums first and listen to them," counsels one student. "If free time is what you want, go somewhere else."

"While no one preaches religion," Baylor is "an extremely conservative," private Baptist university. "We do have a few bleeding heart liberals, [but] most of the students here are white and conservative." Also, "they really need to work on diversifying the student body, the faculty, and the administration," gripes one student. Since the students largely look alike and think alike, it should not come as a surprise that everyone gets along well. "Baylor is a small school, which lends itself to a very close community." Students "affectionately call" the law school "'Waco High' because everyone knows everything about everyone else." Academic competition is strong, but "it has never been a cutthroat or hiding-books-in-the-library kind of competition."

Getting In

Small and intimate, Baylor Law School enrolls students three times a year: in the fall, spring, and summer. The sizes of entering classes are approximately 65 students in the spring, 30 in the summer, and 65 in the fall. Competition for these few precious slots is intense. To be competitive, you will need an undergraduate GPA of 3.3 and an LSAT score of 155. Note that if you take the LSAT more than once, your scores will be averaged. If your credentials are on the borderline, but you have your heart absolutely set on Baylor, don't apply in the fall, you'll have a better chance of admission when applying for the spring or summer sessions.

EMPLOYMENT INFORMATION

Career Rating	**89**
% employed within 9 months	97
Average starting salary	$72,346
State for bar exam	TX
Pass rate for first-time bar	94

Employers who frequently hire grads: Akin Gump Strauss Hauer & Feld LLP, Jenkins & Gilcrest, Thompson & Knight, Strasburger & Price, Baker & Botts, Haynes & Boone, Bracewell & Patterson, Jackson Walker, Fulbright & Jaworski, Andrews & Kurth, Winstead Sechrest.

Prominent Alumni: Leon Jaworski, special prosecutor for the Watergate trials; William Sessions, former FBI director.

Grads employed by field (%):	
Academic	1
Business/industry	6
Government	7
Judicial clerkships	7
Military	1
Private practice	77
Public interest	1

ADMISSIONS

Selectivity Rating	**91**
# applications received	2,373
# applicants accepted	301
# acceptees attending	63
Average LSAT	162
LSAT Range	159–164
Average undergrad GPA	3.9
Application fee	$40
Regular application deadline	3/1
Regular notification	rolling
Rolling notification?	Yes
Early application program?	Yes
Early application deadline	11/3
Early application notification	3/1
Transfer students accepted?	Yes
Evening division offered?	No
Part-time accepted?	No
LSDAS accepted?	Yes

Applicants Also Look At

Southern Methodist University, Texas Tech University, University of Houston, The University of Texas at Austin.

International Students

TOEFL required of international students?	No
TOEFL recommended of international students?	Yes

FINANCIAL FACTS

Annual tuition	$23,247
Books and supplies	$1,542
Fees per credit	$24
Tuition per credit	$567
Room & board (on/off-campus)	$13,191/$16,449
% first-year students receiving some sort of aid	97
% receiving some sort of aid	92
% of aid that is merit-based	100
% receiving scholarships	69
Average grant	$12,130
Average loan	$23,350
Average total aid package	$29,305
Average debt	$70,005

BOSTON COLLEGE
LAW SCHOOL

INSTITUTIONAL INFORMATION

Public/private	private
Student/faculty ratio	13:1
Affiliation	Roman Catholic
% faculty part-time	33
% faculty female	40
% faculty minority	19
Total faculty	88

SURVEY SAYS . . .

Diverse opinions accepted in classrooms
Great research resources
Great library staff
Beautiful campus

STUDENTS

Enrollment of law school	798
% male/female	49/51
% full-time	100
% minority	20
% international	2
# of countries represented	7
Average age of entering class	25

ACADEMICS

Academic experience rating	**93**
Professors interesting rating	92
Professors accessible rating	90
Hours of study per day	4.25

Academic Specialties

Business, civil procedure, commercial law, constitutional law, corporation securities law, criminal law, environmental law, human rights law, intellectual property law, international law, labor law, legal history, legal philosophy, property, taxation.

Advanced Degrees Offered

JD, 3 years.

Combined Degrees Offered

JD/MBA, 4 years; JD/MSW, 4 years; JD/MEd, 3 years.

Academic Requirements

Clinical Program Required?	No
Legal Writing Course Requirement?	Yes
Legal Methods Course Requirement?	Yes

Academics

The "knowledgeable, witty, [and] understanding" professors at Boston College (BC) Law School are said to employ a "softer Socratic method." These profs "all seem to have so much fun teaching law." They "have been in the trenches and love what they do." One 1L announces, "My overall academic experience at BC Law has been amazing." Another often-echoed sentiment is that "the professors are all energetic, and they really bring the subject matter to life." BC Law's faculty members are further described as "excellent, accessible, [and] amazingly approachable." One student asserts, "All of my professors have made an effort to know students by name, and they have been successful in this impressive feat." A few students say the administration is "relatively out of touch," but most agree that the top brass "will bend over backward to accommodate students when the inevitable chaos of life interferes with school."

BC's nationally recognized clinical programs offer "a great opportunity to actually practice in a number of areas before you get your degree." Students can obtain hands-on experience in civil and criminal litigation, immigration law, and pretty much anything else. You can even practice law in London and The Hague. Although some students say it could be bigger, public interest work is a huge deal at BC Law School. One student feels, "There is a serious and committed focus on practicing law in the public interest and devoting time to pro bono activities." The "superior" legal writing and research program for first-year students is another hit. One student explains, "At BC Law, the writing class is a full-year, five-credit class taught by a team comprised of a professor with years of experience, a full-time research librarian, and two to three students taken from the top of the preceding year's 1L class." The course can be "very slow, [but it's] just as important to your first-year as contracts or torts."

Students are torn with regard to the effectiveness of BC's Career Services Office. A handful complain that the staff is "particularly unhelpful" and say they "need to work on the art of being nice. They love to rely on the statistic that 90 percent of jobs come from networking," says one unsatisfied student, "which, of course, means that they don't have to do anything." There may be something to the networking theory, though. Other students say that many "very accomplished and well-connected [BC Law alumni] are willing to help out current students." Also, "the ties which BC Law has to the city of Boston" allegedly make for even more excellent networking connections. Naturally, many students don't need to network because the law school "draws many on-campus recruiters from the Northeast."

The facilities at BC Law are well above average. "The campus itself is gorgeous" and teeming with advanced technology. "The law library and most of the classrooms are state of the art," describes one student. Another says, "The whole campus is a wireless environment." Other students are more circumspect. "The new part of the law school is very nice, but another half of the school is in need of serious remodeling," says one. The classroom facilities are "excellent and professional for first-year classes," but 2Ls and 3Ls "end up in the older rooms."

Life

The "collegial, noncompetitive, [and] exciting" environment all help give Boston College its reputation as "the Disney World of law schools." The "happy, friendly, helpful students [are] bright, hardworking, [and] down-to-earth." They are also "smart, outgoing, [and] interesting," too. Most are from the Northeast Corridor, which can make BC

Rita Jones, Assistant Dean of Admissions and Financial Aid
885 Centre Street, Newton, MA 2459
Telephone: 617-552-4351 • Fax: 617-552-2917
E-mail: bclawadm@bc.edu • Website: www.bc.edu/law

seem "more like a regional than national law school." One student tells us, "The Kumbaya factor at BC Law is overwhelming, and it's pounded into your head from the moment you sit down at orientation. People share notes and exchange outlines, but it's not at the expense of a rigorous, high-quality educational experience." Another student explains, "We all know that we don't need to be in the top 10 percent of our class to get a job, so the incentive to be a jerk is greatly diminished." It seems "there are those people who are super-competitive," but generally, "people don't compete with each other to the point where [it] is detrimental."

BC Law is located "on a satellite campus [in] the idyllic Boston suburb of Newton, just the right distance from Boston to feel suburban while being close to the city." A handful of first-year undergraduates lives near the law school, though. "The availability of services (e.g., dining hall, shuttle buses to and from main campus, and public transportation) revolves largely around the undergraduate schedule without much regard for the needs of the law students." Nevertheless, "the social scene here is great, [and] there is always something to do on the weekends." It seems there is always something to do on the weekdays as well. "A wide variety of student organizations encourages students to get involved in anything that interests them." Both on- and off-campus "there are many social events." And, of course, there's Boston, the student capital of the world. "[Students] can be found in Boston on almost any Friday and Saturday night," one student tells us. "It's a great counterbalance to what we put ourselves through during the week, and it reminds us that yes, there is a world outside of law school."

Getting In

Admitted students at the 25th percentile have an LSAT score of 162 and a GPA of 3.43. Admitted students at the 75th percentile have an LSAT score of 166 and a GPA of 3.75. If you submit a completed application to BC Law by November 26, you will get a decision letter before Christmas, which is nice. If you take the LSAT more than once, Boston College will average your scores.

EMPLOYMENT INFORMATION

Career Rating	**94**
% employed within 9 months	97
Average starting salary	$90,477
State for bar exam	MA
Pass rate for first-time bar	92

Employers who frequently hire grads:
Bingham McCutchen, Goodwin Procter, Holland & Knight, Foley Hoag, McDermott Will & Emery, Mintz Levin, Palmer & Dodge, Ropes & Gray, Sidley Austin Brown & Wood, Skadden Arps.

Prominent Alumni: John Kerry, senator/Democratic nominee for president; Debra Yang, United States attorney, California.

Grads employed by field (%):	
Business/industry	6
Government	7
Judicial clerkships	15
Military	1
Private practice	67
Public interest	4

Legal Research Course Requirement?	Yes
Moot Court Requirement?	No
Public Interest Law Requirement?	No

ADMISSIONS

Selectivity Rating	**90**
# applications received	7,852
# applicants accepted	1,315
# acceptees attending	260
Average LSAT	164
LSAT Range	162–166
Average undergrad GPA	3.6
Application fee	$65
Regular application deadline	3/1
Regular notification	rolling
Rolling notification?	Yes
Early application program?	Yes
Early application deadline	11/1
Early application notification	12/20
Transfer students accepted?	Yes
Evening division offered?	No
Part-time accepted?	No
LSDAS accepted?	Yes

Applicants Also Look At
Boston University, Fordham University, The George Washington University, Georgetown University.

International Students

TOEFL required of international students?	Yes

FINANCIAL FACTS

Annual tuition	$33,110
Books and supplies	$840
Room & board (off-campus)	$16,315
Financial aid application deadline	3/15
% first-year students receiving some sort of aid	91
% receiving some sort of aid	85
% receiving scholarships	51
Average grant	$11,314
Average loan	$26,959
Average total aid package	$38,723
Average debt	$84,462

Boston University
School of Law

INSTITUTIONAL INFORMATION

Public/private	private
Student/faculty ratio	13:1
% faculty part-time	30
% faculty female	26
% faculty minority	6
Total faculty	92

SURVEY SAYS . . .

Diverse opinions accepted in classrooms
Great library staff
Students love Boston, MA

STUDENTS

Enrollment of law school	850
% male/female	44/52
% out-of-state	62
% full-time	100
% minority	25
% international	3
# of countries represented	13
Average age of entering class	23

ACADEMICS

Academic experience rating	**95**
Professors interesting rating	99
Professors accessible rating	95
Hours of study per day	4.66

Academic Specialties

Corporation securities law, health care, intellectual property law, international law, legal philosophy, litigation and dispute resolution, taxation.

Advanced Degrees Offered

LLM taxation, 1 yr FT, up to 4 yrs PT; LLM banking & financial law, 1 yr FT, up to 3 yrs PT; LLM American law, 1 yr FT; LLM intellectual property law, 1 yr FT.

Combined Degrees Offered

JD/MBA, JD/MBA health care management, JD/MA international relations, JD/MS mass communication, JD/MA preservation studies, JD/MPH public health, JD/MSW in law & social work, JD/MA philosophy, JD/LLM in taxation, JD/LLM in banking.

Academics

"If I had to sum up, I would say: great teachers, ugly building," assesses one student at Boston University School of Law. "The quality of the instruction is superb" at BU, where "brilliant [and] highly engaging [professors] apply the Socratic Method in a moderate way that's effective and appropriately stressful without being unduly harsh." As one student puts it, "It is not simply black letter law. We really dig deep into the law to get at why it is what it is and how it has changed (or might change in the future)." Classes are fun, too. "Some days [the class is] crying from laughing so hard." One 1L relates, "My contracts professor closes many a class with an original poem or song parody referring to a case we've just looked at. Once it was based on 'Intergalactic' by the Beastie Boys. There's nothing funnier than hearing your contracts professor say ' . . . from their album, *Hello Nasty*.'" Outside of class, professors are "so accessible that you feel like you are attending a small liberal arts school." Sometimes, the administration is "inflexible." At other times, the staff "excels at solving any problem a law student may have."

The writing program at BU is "very good, [and] the mandatory first-year moot court program is a great way to get advocacy experience with little pressure." There are "many prestigious journals. The practical skill opportunities are wonderful." Students feel that "BU has a solid reputation in the Northeast, and students are able to find jobs at the top firms in Boston and New York." One student comments, "If you are in the top 30 percent of the class after the first year, you can work at a big firm anywhere in the country." If Big Law doesn't appeal to you or if you don't have the grades, "be prepared to be self-directed in your job search." Students would like to see Career Development focus more on helping locate "government positions at both the state and federal level and clerkships," though improvements have been made in these areas over the past year, such as the addition of staff with more government experience..

"One of the best things about the school has to be [its] incredibly convenient" wireless network. Students also enjoy "a prime location in the middle of campus [and] a great view of the Boston skyline." Classrooms are chock-full of outlets, too. Otherwise, though, these are "the absolute worst facilities ever." BU's "tall concrete slab" is an "eyesore." "Some of the classrooms can be horrible settings in which to learn." Furthermore, "elevators are a nightmare," so students must frequently climb mountains of stairs. The library is "too crowded," and the bathrooms garner less than rave reviews. Students seem to be desperately waiting for a new building "which is coming soon, they say." One design critic suggests, "After thorough testing, I think it is safe to say that the concept of an ugly, uncomfortable, vertical tower that has no temperature regulation should be retired." A myriad of recent improvements under the new dean have helped to alleviate the constant 'booing' of the facilities, but the general consensus is still that BU might have "the ugliest law school in the country."

Boston University School of Law, Office of Admissions
765 Commonwealth Avenue, Boston, MA 02215
Telephone: 617-353-3100 • Fax: 617-353-0578
E-mail: bulawadm@bu.edu • Website: www.bu.edu/law

Life

The "outgoing, motivated, [and] intelligent" students at BU Law School "mostly come from Ivies or highly regarded private schools and strong state universities." Many students at BU are "straight out of college." The "very preppy and J. Crew" student population "tends to be a very homogenous bunch of people, as far as style or interests go—no crazy artistic types, no urban city kids." One disappointed student claims, "They really advertise that there is more diversity than they achieve."

"If you throw 250 kids together who were always at the top of their high school and college classes and force them to compete against one another, you can't expect a perfect harmony," comments one student. Still, most say BU is "not overly competitive," and find their classmates to be "friendly and cooperative." Of course, "the grade curve still looms." Social life "is a large mix. Students quickly form cliques during the first year and remain in them thereafter." There are "people who spend all day at the library [and those who] make a very concerted effort to balance the work with a liberal dose of fun (and booze)." Students point out that the law school is a reasonably social place for those who choose to take advantage of the opportunities available."

Boston University is located "right on the river in the heart of an exciting [and] beautiful" city. "There are a lot of young people" pretty much everywhere you go, and Beantown "has everything a big city has [while maintaining a] relatively small city, neighborhood-type feel." A student observes, "The nightlife is diverse." Plus, BU is "right by Fenway Park and tons of museums." You can even "go sailing on the Charles River." Housing is not cheap, but it's good. "As a student, you have the choice of living downtown or west of the city with all of the undergraduates from the many Boston schools."

Getting In

Admitted students at the 25th percentile have an LSAT score of 162 and a GPA of 3.45. Admitted students at the 75th percentile have an LSAT score of 165 and a GPA of 3.76.

EMPLOYMENT INFORMATION

Career Rating	**94**
% employed within 9 months	98.3
Average starting salary	$125,000
State for bar exam	MA, NY, CA
Pass rate for first-time bar	91

Prominent Alumni: Judd Gregg, U.S. senator, New Hampshire; William S. Cohen, former secretary of defense; David Kelley, executive producer; Gary F. Locke, former governor of Washington State; Honorable Sandra L. Lynch, judge, U.S. Court of Appeals, first circuit.

Grads employed by field (%):	
Academic	4
Business/industry	6
Government	8
Judicial clerkships	13
Private practice	67
Public interest	2

Academic Requirements

Clinical Program Required?	No
Legal Writing Course Requirement?	Yes
Legal Methods Course Requirement?	No
Legal Research Course Requirement?	Yes
Moot Court Requirement?	Yes
Public Interest Law Requirement?	No

ADMISSIONS

Selectivity Rating	**89**
# applications received	6,165
# applicants accepted	1,329
# acceptees attending	291
Average LSAT	164
LSAT Range	162–165
Average undergrad GPA	3.6
Application fee	$65
Regular application deadline	3/1
Regular notification	rolling
Rolling notification?	Yes
Early application program?	No
Transfer students accepted?	Yes
Evening division offered?	No
Part-time accepted?	No
LSDAS accepted?	Yes

Applicants Also Look At

Boston College, Fordham University, The George Washington University, Georgetown University, New York University, University of Michigan, University of Southern California.

International Students

TOEFL required of international students?	Yes
Minimum Paper TOEFL	600
Minimum Computer TOEFL	250

FINANCIAL FACTS

Annual tuition	$30,988
Books and supplies	$1,134
Room & board (off-campus)	$10,540
Financial aid application deadline	3/1
% first-year students receiving some sort of aid	84
% receiving some sort of aid	82
% of aid that is merit-based	3
% receiving scholarships	46
Average grant	$16,500
Average loan	$28,420
Average total aid package	$26,430
Average debt	$75,560

Brigham Young University
J. Reuben Clark Law School

INSTITUTIONAL INFORMATION

Public/private	private
Student/faculty ratio	18:1
Affiliation	Church of Jesus Christ of Latter-day Saints
% faculty part-time	54
% faculty female	31
% faculty minority	10
Total faculty	64

SURVEY SAYS . . .

Great research resources
Great library staff

STUDENTS

Enrollment of law school	489
% male/female	62/38
% full-time	100
% minority	14
% international	3
# of countries represented	10
Average age of entering class	26

ACADEMICS

Academic experience rating	**97**
Professors interesting rating	91
Professors accessible rating	81
Hours of study per day	5.42

Advanced Degrees Offered

International comparative law, 1 school year

Combined Degrees Offered

JD/MBA; JD/MPA; JD/MAcc; JD/MOB; JD/MEd, (education) each 4 years; JD/EdD (education) 5 years.

Academic Requirements

Clinical Program Required?	No
Legal Writing Course Requirement?	Yes
Legal Methods Course Requirement?	No
Legal Research Course Requirement?	Yes
Moot Court Requirement?	Yes
Public Interest Law Requirement?	No

Academics

"Fantastic instructors, excellent students, [a] friendly atmosphere, [and a] beautiful geographic location" are just a few of the strengths of Brigham Young University's J. Rueben Clark Law School. The opportunity to get "such a high-quality legal education" for a three-year total of around $20,000 is "unparalleled." Plus "generous scholarships" are just icing on the cake. BYU is a small new-ish law school founded and sponsored by The Church of Jesus Christ of Latter-day Saints that "has attracted a much more distinguished faculty than perhaps it deserves," explains one student. "Professors who otherwise might seek a career at a more prestigious school come here because of the unique opportunity to be among others of their own religion." These "capable, caring, and charismatic [professors] all have impressive resumes and are fairly approachable." They are able to make classes "very enjoyable" as well. "Our contracts professor starts every class with a five-minute humorous monologue," recounts one student. "Once he even danced across the stage singing music from *West Side Story*." Theatrics aside, the classroom emphasis is on a "broad legal education [and] ethical behavior in the practice of law. Students are taught the impact their work will have on their families and communities." Discussion is lively. Students tell us, "Classes are rich with debate and controversy, and no one is ridiculed for having a more conservative or a more liberal outlook." Research resources and facilities are great. The "excellent" classrooms at BYU feature "electrical outlets at each seat." One student says, "Technology at the school is pervasive and cutting edge." If you miss a class, don't worry, you can "listen to it online." Also, BYU is "entirely wireless," although not glitch-free (BYU's technical support can be frustrating, but rewiring of the entire building is planned for the summer of 2005). The "awesome" library "is one of the finest and most technologically advanced in the nation." This is a good thing because "the library is where you live" thanks to the "intense pace of study." Many, many students raved about the "individual assigned carrels in the library, [complete] with lockable drawers and cabinets."

In terms of time and effort, the rigorous legal writing and research program "is a killer." Students are at odds as to its effectiveness. "I have learned so much," one gushes. Others "haven't been overly impressed." Extracurricular opportunities abound. The World Family Policy Center is a big deal, as is the International Center for Law and Religion Studies. "BYU does very well at putting people in externships with judges." Students participate in "amazing" summer public service externships all over the world. The Career Services Office "places a special emphasis on encouraging first-year students to pursue volunteer legal work during their first summer." According to one student, "There is no excuse for not getting legal experience here at BYU during your summers. They practically give you 500 different opportunities on a silver platter and ask you to pick what one you want." Post-graduation employment prospects are solid. "The Mormon connection" definitely helps. "BYU has a great alumni association that provides amazing recruiting opportunities." Most grads settle "in the west. [BYU] has few connections out east except for DC and New York."

Life

It's good to keep in mind that "this is BYU in Provo, Utah, so obviously most of us here are Mormons." As such, the Church of Jesus Christ of Latter-day Saints is a ubiquitous presence: The law school at BYU has the unique position as a prestigious law school with a highly religious student and faculty community. An honor code includes dress and behavior restrictions, as well as a total ban on alcohol and tobacco. While one student

GaeLynn Kuchar, Director of Admissions
340 JRCB, Brigham Young University Law School, Provo, UT 84602
Telephone: 801-422-4277 • Fax: 801-422-0389
E-mail: kucharg@lawgate.byu.edu • Website: www.law2.byu.edu

says, "Religion is not forced on anyone, and there is no reason why a non-Latter-day Saint student would not feel welcome here," another advises, "For those who have never experienced BYU or a strong Latter-day Saints culture before, it could possibly drive them insane." Students describe their fellow students as "smart, funny, engaging, well-spoken, and interesting." They are "well-rounded and full of life experience," not to mention "highly motivated [and] success-oriented." "There is no dog-eat-dog mentality" because "we all feel like we're in over our heads together." Still, "first-year students tend to be very competitive." Yet, one student points out, "The summer after first year, it's like a totally different class comes back from summer jobs and internships." Students say, "Women at BYU law are well represented and treated fairly [but] compared to other schools, [BYU is] pretty far down the diversity scale." Although "there is a diversity of viewpoints," students "go out of their way to accommodate and show respect for dissent and differing opinions." Politically, the majority of the students range from "conservative" to "very conservative." One student declares, "I think the greatest strength comes from the kind of people the students are." "That may sound cheesy, but they don't drink or smoke, most of them are supporting families while going through school, and a disproportionate number of them have lived abroad and speak foreign languages. I think all these things help them be more mature." But not quite everybody is married. There is a "healthy" contingent of "single students [who] hang out together all the time." But social life takes an absolute backseat to academics. "People here just work really hard. If you are looking for a place to get drunk and party, this is not the school for you." When students do take a study break, they often head for the great outdoors. The campus is "within an hour of some of the best ski resorts in the world," and the area is "a rock climber's Mecca."

Getting In

First-year students are admitted only in the fall semester, and BYU's JD program is full-time only. Admitted students at the 25th percentile have an LSAT score of 161 and a GPA of 3.5. Admitted students at the 75th percentile have an LSAT score of 166 and a GPA of 3.8. If you take the LSAT more than once, BYU will average your scores. As you would expect, most applicants are members of the Mormon Church.

EMPLOYMENT INFORMATION

Career Rating	**88**
% employed within 9 months	98.7
Average starting salary	$63,399
State for bar exam	UT, CA, NV, AZ, TX
Pass rate for first-time bar	92

Employers who frequently hire grads: Alston & Bird, Baker & Mckenzie, Best Best & Krieger, Blackwell Sanders Peper Martin, Covington & Burling, Davis Polk & Wardwell, Kirkland & Ellis, Leboeuf Lamb Greene & MacRae, Milbank Tweed.

Prominent Alumni: Steve Young, former quarterback, San Francisco 49ers; Dee V. Benson, senior judge, Federal District Court, Utah.

Grads employed by field (%):	
Academic	4
Business/industry	7
Government	14
Judicial clerkships	14
Military	2
Private practice	57
Public interest	2

ADMISSIONS

Selectivity Rating	**93**
# applications received	952
# applicants accepted	247
# acceptees attending	150
Average LSAT	164
LSAT Range	161–166
Average undergrad GPA	3.7
Application fee	$60
Regular application deadline	2/2
Regular notification	rolling
Rolling notification?	Yes
Early application program?	No
Transfer students accepted?	Yes
Evening division offered?	No
Part-time accepted?	No
LSDAS accepted?	Yes

Applicants Also Look At

Georgetown University, Loyola Marymount University, University of Nevada—Las Vegas, University of Southern California, The University of Texas at Austin, University of Utah.

International Students

TOEFL required of international students?	No
TOEFL recommended?	Yes
Minimum Paper TOEFL	590
Minimum Computer TOEFL	243

FINANCIAL FACTS

Annual tuition*	$7,450
Annual tuition (non-LDS)	$11,176
Books and supplies	$1,470
Room & board (on/off-campus)	$6,100/$7,375
Financial aid application deadline	6/1
% first-year students receiving some sort of aid	86
% receiving some sort of aid	78
% of aid that is merit-based	33
% receiving scholarships	50
Average grant	$2,300
Average loan	$13,400
Average debt	$41,000

*For members of the Church of LDS

BROOKLYN LAW SCHOOL

INSTITUTIONAL INFORMATION

Public/private	private
Student/faculty ratio	18:1
% faculty part-time	49
% faculty female	38
% faculty minority	6
Total faculty	127

SURVEY SAYS . . .

Diverse opinions accepted in classrooms
Great research resources
Abundant externship/internship/clerkship opportunities
Students love Brooklyn, NY

STUDENTS

Enrollment of law school	1,518
% male/female	51/49
% out-of-state	39
% full-time	76
% minority	22
% international	1
# of countries represented	33
Average age of entering class	24

ACADEMICS

Academic experience rating	**85**
Professors interesting rating	79
Professors accessible rating	80
Hours of study per day	4.25

Academic Specialties

Center for health science & public policy, civil procedure, commercial law, constitutional law, corporation securities law, criminal law, government services, human rights law, intellectual property law, international law, law & cognition, legal history, legal philosophy, property, taxation.

Combined Degrees Offered

JD/MA political science, JD/MS planning, JD/MBA, JD/MS library/information science, JD/M urban planning, JD/MPA.

Academic Requirements

Clinical Program Required?	No
Legal Writing Course Requirement?	Yes

Academics

According to its students Brooklyn Law School is an up-and-coming and underrated law school that emphasizes public interest. The faculty is impressive and supportive, and the "clinical opportunities are first rate." Students rave about their professors, who are "former SEC commissioners, appellate judges, restatement authors, you name it." They have an "open-door policy that makes it easy to ask questions." Perhaps that is partly because BLS hires lawyers who "sincerely want to be teaching and training aspiring attorneys, [are] extremely well-respected in the community," and have experience "not just in academics, [but also] offer practical experience to boot." Public interest law and clinical programs are stressed. Located a stone's throw from the New York City court system, it is no wonder that the BLS curriculum "transfers theory into action" or that "opportunities abound" for both clinical and internship experiences. Also, it seems as though "not a day goes by where there isn't a speaker, symposium, or workshop pertaining to public interest law."

Students are split over the law school's administration, however. Some believe that it could use drastic improvement because it has trouble "dealing with the current students' problems." Many students complain that much of the staff just doesn't care. "The administration offices seem functionally detached from the school," harps one student. As at almost every law school in America, there are some students who think the Career Center "could stand to improve quite a bit" and that its staff is unhelpful unless you're in the "top 10 percent of the class." Others counter that the Career Center works diligently and is "highly motivated to help students secure a satisfying position."

Some feel the school "is taking on too many students," which, like New York City itself, means all classroom space is used to maximum efficiency, sometimes forcing students "to sit at small desks in the back of the room." Things get better with time as upper level courses have smaller class sizes. And although the first-year legal writing course has a rating of excellent, students want the opportunity to take more writing courses during their second and third years. There is also a general hankering for more "journal opportunities."

Notable recent physical plant improvements at Brooklyn Law include a "brand-new building" with Internet access and outlets for computers at every seat. The law school is making bold efforts to make the campus wireless, but students warn that there are some growing pains associated with such a leap in technology, meaning that the system crashes from time to time. The library is very nice and "has all the necessities" but can sometimes feel cramped, "especially around exam time."

Life

Brooklyn Law School is located in the gorgeous and historic Brooklyn Heights neighborhood, which is "minutes from Manhattan [and only] one subway stop from Wall Street." It is still tucked away enough that students are not "distracted by the fast pace and night life of Manhattan all the time." While the law school's closeness to public transportation helps bring students to the city that never sleeps, the downside to such an urban setting is that a "lack of a campus makes it difficult to foster a student community." Brooklyn Law has a large number of commuting students, which "really makes socializing outside of school difficult." However, the school just opened a new residence hall in Summer 2005, which helps to combat both expensive off-campus housing and the sense

Henry W. Haverstick III, Dean of Admissions and Financial Aid
250 Joralemon Street, Brooklyn, NY 11201
Telephone: 718-780-7906 • Fax: 718-780-0395
E-mail: admitq@brooklaw.edu • Website: www.brooklaw.edu

that there is little infrastructure available to students for out-of-classroom fraternizing. Still, "everyone is nice to each other and a lot of people hang out together." Plus, according to students, every couple of weeks an organization gets a keg and throws a pizza party.

While some consider the student body "too competitive," others think the "students are supportive of each other but conscious that grades are important." One wag succinctly puts it, "It's very competitive, but that's New York." An upperclassman further elucidates the atmosphere: "While I thought 1L was very stressful and competitive, everyone seemed to calm down by 2L."

Opinion is divided regarding diversity. Some students think it's great, and others say it's lacking. The truth is that it is not bad, but for a school located in a borough as cosmopolitan as Brooklyn, it could probably do better in this regard. The political views tend to lean leftward, both in the faculty and the student population. Students do appreciate the strong and wide base of wonderful alumni who "enjoy coming back here to talk to us and let us know what to expect." Because of the school's proximity to the courthouses, the school provides "very informative" symposia and speakers.

Getting In

Brooklyn Law School has an enrollment of about 1,500 students. Admitted students at the 25th percentile have an LSAT score of 158 and undergraduate GPA of 3.1. Admitted students at the 75th percentile have an LSAT score of 162 and an undergraduate GPA of 3.6. The school advises prospective students to take the LSAT in February and not in June for the upcoming year because most places will be filled by the time scores come in. The school offers an evening option and several joint degrees.

EMPLOYMENT INFORMATION

Career Rating	**87**
% employed within 9 months	98
Average starting salary	$80,104
State for bar exam	NY, NJ, CA, MA
Pass rate for first-time bar	84

Employers who frequently hire grads: Cahill Gordon; Fried, Frank, Harris, Shriver, & Jacobson; Pillsbury, Winthrop; Proskauer Rose; New York City law department.

Prominent Alumni: David Dinkins, former mayor, City of New York; Honorable Edward R. Korman, chief judge, U.S. district, EDNY; Russell Lewis, president & CEO of New York Times Company; Carlos Ortiz, general counsel, Goya Foods.

Grads employed by field (%):	
Academic	1
Business/industry	14
Government	16
Judicial clerkships	7
Private practice	55
Public interest	3

Legal Methods Course Requirement?	Yes
Legal Research Course Requirement?	Yes
Moot Court Requirement?	Yes
Public Interest Law Requirement?	No

ADMISSIONS

Selectivity Rating	**88**
# applications received	4,822
# applicants accepted	976
# acceptees attending	303
Average LSAT	162
LSAT Range	161–164
Average undergrad GPA	3.4
Application fee	$65
Regular application deadline	rolling
Regular notification	rolling
Rolling notification?	Yes
Early application program?	Yes
Early application deadline	12/1
Early application notification	12/31
Transfer students accepted?	Yes
Evening division offered?	Yes
Part-time accepted?	Yes
LSDAS accepted?	Yes

Applicants Also Look At
Fordham University,
Yeshiva University.

International Students

TOEFL required of international students?	No
TOEFL recommended of international students?	Yes

FINANCIAL FACTS

Annual tuition	$32,750
Books and supplies	$1,200
Fees per credit	$200
Tuition per credit	$24,563
Room & board (off-campus)	$13,345
Financial aid application deadline	3/29
% first-year students receiving some sort of aid	60
% receiving some sort of aid	56
% of aid that is merit-based	65
% receiving scholarships	44
Average grant	$9,600
Average loan	$28,579
Average total aid package	$33,500
Average debt	$82,075

CALIFORNIA WESTERN
CALIFORNIA WESTERN SCHOOL OF LAW

INSTITUTIONAL INFORMATION

Public/private	private
Student/faculty ratio	19:1
% faculty part-time	40
% faculty female	41
% faculty minority	14
Total faculty	85

SURVEY SAYS . . .

Diverse opinions accepted in classrooms
Great research resources
Great library staff
Students love San Diego, CA

STUDENTS

Enrollment of law school	984
% male/female	50/50
% out-of-state	44
% full-time	87
% minority	23
% international	2
# of countries represented	10
Average age of entering class	26

ACADEMICS

Academic experience rating	**73**
Professors interesting rating	70
Professors accessible rating	77
Hours of study per day	4.64

Academic Specialties

Biotech law, constitutional law, creative problem solving, criminal law, environmental law, family law, human rights law, intellectual property law, international law, labor law, taxation, telecommunications law.

Advanced Degrees Offered

JD, 2 to 3 years; MCL/LLM (master of comparative law, master of laws on comparative law), 9 months; LLM, trial advocacy, 1 year.

Combined Degrees Offered

JD/MSW juris doctor/master of social work, 4 years; JD/MBA juris doctor/master of business administration, 4 years; JD/PhD juris doctor/doctor of philosophy in political science or history, 5 years.

Academics

California Western School of Law "has an outstanding reputation in the San Diego legal community" for producing graduates with "top-notch real-world skills who can hit the ground running when they get hired." Classes are hands-on. There are three mandatory semesters of legal-skills training and oral-advocacy training. A flexible trimester system enables dedicated students to graduate in two years. Less flexible is California Western's grading curve, which contributes to "people get[ting] kicked out of school for not having the required GPA."

The "smart, witty, and extremely approachable" professors really care. "It takes really wanting to teach to be good at it, and we have some [professors] that really want to be in the trenches with the students," reports one student. Also, "everyone and everything is incredibly accessible at CWSL," gloats another student. "The professors all have an open-door policy, [and their] willingness to help with networking" is another plus. According to a few students, some professors have too much of a political agenda, though, and "need to actually teach instead of ranting and raving about their own political views," which tend to skew liberal. Students are mostly enthusiastic about the administration, describing the top brass as "responsive" and telling us that "the school genuinely cares."

Many classrooms on the school's urban campus are technologically up-to-date. Others are "cramped, too cold, [and] inadequate for computers." Sometimes, the acoustics are not great, either. Students rave about the awesome, ultra-modern library. There are "plenty of quiet study areas," and the weather "allows studying outside in the cool courtyard." Also, CWSL is "located within walking distance of all the courthouses and close to lots of law offices."

A few students call job prospects "horrendous." Others tell us that career services "is the absolute best thing about" the school. "I'm here to get a job, and they do an excellent job of encouraging and helping students to find jobs," exclaims one student. The nationally recognized CWSL internship program "allows students to get great experience and meet lawyers without the stress of begging for a job." Bottom line, "If you want to intern for a semester, the school will find you an internship," writes one student. The Institute for Criminal Defense Advocacy "is the heart of this school [and] an indispensable tool for anyone thinking of getting into criminal law." Programs include the annual Trial Skills Academy and the California Innocence Project, which helps to free wrongfully convicted people from prison. "My overall experience has been wonderful," concludes one student. "Cal Western is like a Honda. It's good, reliable, and gets you where you want to go."

Life

Some students tell us that Cal Western can be "overly competitive [and] extremely cutthroat due to the forced curve." Others say, "Competition varies." One student analogizes, "The three sections during first year were like Goldilocks. One was very competitive; one was laidback; and the third was sort of in between." Everyone agrees that academic life is "substantially less competitive after the first year."

TRACI HOWARD, DIRECTOR OF ADMISSIONS
225 CEDAR STREET, SAN DIEGO, CA 92101
TELEPHONE: 619-525-1401 • FAX: 619-615-1401
E-MAIL: ADMISSIONS@CWSL.EDU • WEBSITE: WWW.CALIFORNIAWESTERN.EDU

Socially, the school can have "a commuter-school feel." Whatever it lacks in "sense of pride and community," though, it makes up in diversity galore. "There is no stereotypical Cal Western student," declares ones student. "They come in all shapes, sizes, genders, ages, backgrounds." Another student says, "We have a great mix of people, and not just your typical law students." There are a few "California slacker dudes." You'll also find an even representation of men and women and a visible gay community.

The school's location is a double-edged sword. According to students, the "metro location is great for connecting with [the] legal community, but there is always [a] hesitation about staying too late and walking to your car." A safe escort is an option as "there are security guards available to walk you to your car if requested, [but] they stop after a four-block radius from the school." Before you walk to your car you must park it, and "parking is an incredible issue for the students" as well. You can pay "prohibitively expensive [fees] at a nearby garage [or] duke it out on the streets and hope for free or metered parking." Either way, "it's a hassle." San Diego is, however, a "gorgeous [and] exciting" city. "It's sunny for about ten months out of the year." The surfing is gnarly, and "there are so many things to do here." If you nevertheless manage to get bored, you can always "sit out in the courtyard in the middle of January and get some sun."

Getting In

About two out of every five applicants is accepted to California Western School of Law. Those aren't bad odds for the law school hopeful. An LSAT score in the mid-150's and a B+ undergraduate GPA should make you a highly competitive candidate.

EMPLOYMENT INFORMATION

Career Rating	**69**
Job placement rate (%)	88
Average starting salary	$55,000
State for bar exam	CA, NV, AZ, NY, MD
Pass rate for first-time bar	57

Employers who frequently hire grads: Multiple private, public, and nonprofit employers of all sizes from many regions nationally.

Prominent Alumni: Lisa Haile, partner at DLA Piper, Rudnick, Gray, Cary; Garland Burrell, U.S. district court judge; John Childs, partner at Sonnenschein, Nath, & Rosenthal; David Roger, district attorney, Clark County, Nevada.

Grads employed by field (%):	
Academic	2
Business/industry	14
Government	10
Judicial clerkships	2
Military	2
Private practice	65
Public interest	7

Academic Requirements

Clinical Program Required?	No
Legal Writing Course Requirement?	Yes
Legal Methods Course Requirement?	Yes
Legal Research Course Requirement?	Yes
Moot Court Requirement?	No
Public Interest Law Requirement?	No

ADMISSIONS

Selectivity Rating	**77**
# applications received	3,977
# applicants accepted	1,125
# acceptees attending	275
Average LSAT	155
LSAT Range	152–157
Average undergrad GPA	3.2
Application fee	$45
Regular application deadline	4/1
Regular notification	rolling
Rolling notification?	Yes
Early application program?	No
Transfer students accepted?	Yes
Evening division offered?	No
Part-time accepted?	Yes
LSDAS accepted?	Yes

Applicants Also Look At

University of San Diego.

International Students

TOEFL required of international students?	Yes
Minimum Paper TOEFL	600

FINANCIAL FACTS

Annual tuition	$39,500
Books and supplies	$1,088
Fees per credit	$10
Tuition per credit	$1,030
Room & board (off-campus)	$15,816
Financial aid application deadline	4/8
% first-year students receiving some sort of aid	87
% receiving some sort of aid	85
% of aid that is merit-based	11
% receiving scholarships	23
Average grant	$15,778
Average loan	$35,793
Average total aid package	$40,457
Average debt	$82,545

CAMPBELL UNIVERSITY
NORMAN ADRIAN WIGGINS SCHOOL OF LAW

INSTITUTIONAL INFORMATION

Public/private	private
Student/faculty ratio	19:1
Affiliation	Baptist
% faculty part-time	56
% faculty female	22
% faculty minority	4
Total faculty	48

SURVEY SAYS . . .

Heavy use of Socratic method
Diverse opinions accepted in classrooms

STUDENTS

Enrollment of law school	369
% male/female	53/47
% full-time	100
% minority	10
Average age of entering class	26

ACADEMICS

Academic experience rating	**79**
Professors interesting rating	85
Professors accessible rating	86
Hours of study per day	5.42

Academic Specialties

Tracks in business/transactions and trial & appellate advocacy.

Advanced Degrees Offered

JD, 3-year program, 90 semester hours.

Combined Degrees Offered

JD, MBA.

Academic Requirements

Clinical Program Required?	No
Legal Writing Course Requirement?	Yes
Legal Methods Course Requirement?	Yes
Legal Research Course Requirement?	Yes
Moot Court Requirement?	Yes
Public Interest Law Requirement?	No

Academics

Be prepared for an intense first year at the Norman Adrian Wiggins School of Law, where classroom discussion is demanding and late-night study sessions are par for the course. A 3L tells us, "The Socratic Method is employed for at least your first three terms and the core classes are beyond 'challenging' at Campbell." Another student warns, "Campbell is not for the weak hearted. You must want to be a lawyer and be determined to persevere." However, with an excellent student/teacher ratio, a respectful Christian tradition, and a helpful teaching staff, Campbell is a kinder, gentler form of legal boot camp. "While professors are demanding of students in the classroom and rigorous in their implementation of the Socratic Method, outside of class they are approachable and eager to assist and love to engage students in dialogue," according to one student. Another goes on, "The faculty is outstanding. They are always available to talk to students about anything, even if it has nothing to do with law."

In addition to course difficulty, students tell us that Campbell upholds difficult marking standards, eschewing any form of grade inflation. "There seems to exist a friendly rivalry among the faculty as to who teaches the best [and] the hardest subject, who has the best jokes; however, the competition stops short of including which professor can give the most A's." Even so, students assure us that their hard work pays off in the long run. For one thing, "Campbell's bar-passage rate has been the highest in North Carolina in 10 of the last 13 years." On top of that, students say that Campbell has an excellent reputation among local firms, ensuring excellent career placement after graduation. "Campbell is a small private law school with a big reputation within North Carolina. After graduation, prepare to live up to the high standard that graduates before you have set for Campbell Law attorneys," admonishes a 2L. Students point to the support and guidance they receive from Campbell's top-notch Career Services as a big part of why the school has such a solid placement rate.

Speaking of career preparation, students say that Campbell leaves them well prepared for the practical aspects of practicing law through various programs, such as the Professionalism Lecture Series for first-year students. "Campbell's emphasis on professionalism is quite impressive," reports a 1L. "First-year students are required to go [to the lecture series] in order to . . . further develop the skill of thinking like a lawyer." As they progress, "students get to participate on Law Review, Moot Court, Trial Teams, and any one of at least four pro bono projects," reports one student. "I believe this is why we have a reputation for being so well prepared to start our careers."

Affiliated with the Baptist Church, Campbell is committed to promoting the ethical practice of law. A student praises the school's Christian ethos: "Campbell not only provides a great legal education, but [also] something that is less and less valued in the legal world today: a solid grounding in ethics and Christian principles." Another adds this warning: "Campbell Law is a wonderful place to learn, if you don't mind a Republican-Conservative-Professed-Christian atmosphere." However, non-Baptists need not avoid Campbell. As one student confides, "Even though the school has a religious affiliation, one which I am not a part of, I feel just as welcome as every student here."

Associate Dean for Admissions
PO Box 158, 113 Main Street, Buies Creek, NC 27506
Telephone: 910-893-1754 • Fax: 910-893-1780
E-mail: admissions@law.campbell.edu • Website: www.law.campbell.edu

Life

The small town of Buies Creek, North Carolina, doesn't offer much in the form of entertainment. Take it from the 2L who tells us, "The school is pretty much in the middle of nowhere, so you have to drive 45 minutes to get to a variety of social activities. There are a few restaurants and a movie theater close by, but that's about it." Another puts it even more bluntly: "Buies Creek itself is a great place to study law because there is not much else to do." As a result, Campbell students must rely on each other for fun and diversion. Luckily, the small school atmosphere engenders an intimate, friendly feeling within the student body. "Students at this small law school get to know each other, and in a sense you live together. There is a sense of family because we all are going to represent why we went to Campbell one day," writes one student. Another adds, "Campbell encourages competitive attitudes, but not for the sake of self-aggrandizement or mere greed. People come first here; that is what matters."

Getting In

Accepted students to the class entering in fall 2004 had a median GPA of 3.35 and a median LSAT score of 156. (Note that median and average LSAT scores can differ significantly.) In addition to common law school application requirements, Campbell does what few other law schools do: prior to admission, students must also submit to a personal interview with the law school faculty. Invitations to interview are based on a student's application; most, but not all, applicants are invited to interview.

EMPLOYMENT INFORMATION

Career Rating	**76**
Job placement rate (%)	98
Average starting salary	$50,000
State for bar exam	NC, SC, VA, MD, UT
Pass rate for first-time bar	78

Employers who frequently hire grads: Small to midsize private firms.

Prominent Alumni: Elaine Marshall, North Carolina secretary of state; John Tyson, judge, North Carolina Court of Appeals; Richard Thigpen, general counsel, Carolina Panthers NFL franchise; Ann Marie Calabria, judge, North Carolina Court of Appeals; Laura Bridges, North Carolina district court judge.

Grads employed by field (%):	
Business/industry	5
Government	7
Judicial clerkships	3
Private practice	82
Public interest	3

ADMISSIONS

Selectivity Rating	**82**
# applications received	1,194
# applicants accepted	249
# acceptees attending	143
Average LSAT	155
LSAT Range	152–157
Average undergrad GPA	3.3
Application fee	$50
Regular application deadline	rolling
Regular notification	rolling
Rolling notification?	Yes
Early application program?	No
Transfer students accepted?	Yes
Evening division offered?	No
Part-time accepted?	No
LSDAS accepted?	Yes

Applicants Also Look At

Appalachian School of Law, North Carolina Central University, Regent University, Samford University, University of North Carolina at Chapel Hill, University of South Carolina, Wake Forest University MBA Program.

International Students

TOEFL required of international students?	No
TOEFL recommended of international students?	Yes

FINANCIAL FACTS

Annual tuition	$22,000
Books and supplies	$1,100
Room & board (on/off-campus)	$10,120/$12,718
Financial aid application deadline	4/15
% receiving some sort of aid	85
% receiving scholarships	37
Average grant	$3,000
Average loan	$28,900
Average debt	$86,702

CASE WESTERN RESERVE UNIVERSITY

SCHOOL OF LAW

INSTITUTIONAL INFORMATION

Public/private	private
Student/faculty ratio	14:1
% faculty female	33
% faculty minority	12
Total faculty	51

SURVEY SAYS . . .

Diverse opinions accepted in classrooms
Great library staff
Abundant externship/internship/clerkship opportunities

STUDENTS

Enrollment of law school	708
% male/female	60/40
% out-of-state	73
% full-time	97
% minority	15
% international	2
# of countries represented	16
Average age of entering class	24

ACADEMICS

Academic experience rating	**76**
Professors interesting rating	78
Professors accessible rating	70
Hours of study per day	4.83

Academic Specialties

Commercial law; constitutional law; corporation securities law; criminal law; government services; health law; human rights law; intellectual property law; international law; litigation; law, technology, and the arts; public law; taxation.

Advanced Degrees Offered

LLM, U.S. legal studies, 1 year for international lawyers.

Combined Degrees Offered

JD/MBA, management, 4 yrs; JD/MNO, nonprofit management, 4 yrs; JD/CNM, certificate in nonprofit management, 3 yrs; JD/MSSA, social work, 4 yrs; JD/MA, legal history, 4 yrs; JD/MA, bioethics, 4 yrs; JD/MD medicine, 7 yrs; JD/MPH, public health, 4 yrs.

Academics

At Case Western Reserve University, students are taught "practical lawyering skills from the first day of orientation." Students appreciate that the curriculum offered at Case allows those "who want to specialize [and] develop the skills necessary to do so," while at the same time "providing those who don't know exactly what they want to do yet with a broad range of subjects to choose from." As far as specialized concentrations go, students speak highly of the Health Law Program and "the school's commitment to improving its Intellectual Property Law Program." Furthermore, students applaud the "opportunities for dual programs [and the] heavy emphasis on technology in the learning environment."

At Case, students are proud to be taught by professors who are "nationally known" and who are "experts in their fields." One student boasts, "I was watching *Hannity and Colmes* one night and was surprised to see one of our faculty—and he was making great points!" But it is not for their ability to trade barbs on television that students laud most about their professors at Case. It is, as students say, that the "approachable and down to earth" professors treat students "with respect and encourage us as people, scholars, and aspiring lawyers." Students also tell us "professors are tremendously interesting, [and] the curriculum at Case is progressive and well-designed." The "top-notch" faculty is "always willing to go out of their way to help you with research or job searches."

Like most law schools, the administration at Case gets a mixed review from students. A few say the school has "accepted more students than the school can accommodate" and that administration should "listen to students more closely." One student says, "The administration works hard to make Case a good school with a good reputation, however, it is occasionally at the expense of the students." But some students would beg to differ, saying the "very helpful [and] completely accessible [administrators] make an effort to obtain our input on curriculum and academic matters."

Students agree that financial aid is an area where there is room for improvement. Students call the packages "weak" and the office "not helpful." One student says, "The financial aid programs sometimes seem like a lot of smoke and mirrors."

Case's law library has "a nice view of the Cleveland Botanical Gardens and lots of nooks and crannies for studying," although students are looking forward to a badly needed "complete remodeling," scheduled for winter 2005 completion. While the classrooms, too, "could look better," they are generously outfitted with "state-of-the-art wireless access, SmartBoards, and plenty of power sources for laptops," perhaps not surprisingly, given Case's emphasis on technology.

Christopher Lucak, Director of Admissions
11075 East Boulevard, Cleveland, OH 44106
Telephone: 800-756-0036 • Fax: 216-368-1042
E-mail: lawadmissions@case.edu • Website: www.law.case.edu

Life

Cleveland may have "one of the top legal communities in the country," but this is only one of the reasons students say the city has "so much to offer," making it "a great place to go to school." If culture is what you want, "within five minutes Case Law students can walk to a beautiful orchestra hall, an art museum, botanical garden, or a planetarium." According to one student, Cleveland is home to "the nation's best symphony." If an urban social scene is what you're looking for, "Case is located fifteen minutes from the bars, restaurants, and theaters of downtown Cleveland." And of course, the Case Western Reserve University campus itself offers "many exciting events and great facilities." A 1L says, "Often law students spend time listening to visiting scholars lecture at the medical and engineering schools and vice versa." Recent lecturers at Case Western include Stephen Hawking, Oliver Sacks, and Kurt Vonnegut. There was even a debate of 2004 Vice Presidential Candidates at Case. Students are "pleasantly surprised at how much entertainment, culture, and social activity is available in Cleveland." As one student puts it, "Cleveland truly rocks!"

The competition at Case Western runs a bit high, but that's just the nature of the beast. One student explains, "There seem to be two distinct groups of students, those who are social and not outwardly competitive [and] those who are extremely competitive." The latter is in the "minority [and] do not fare well in social settings." Instead, "most students are friendly and even supportive of other students." Classmates see their peers as "engaging, intelligent, and fun" and also say they're "particularly pleased with the friends" they've made.

Getting In

At Case, admitted students at the 25th percentile have an LSAT score of 157 and a GPA of 3.0. Admitted students at the 75th percentile have an LSAT score of 161 and a GPA of 3.5.

EMPLOYMENT INFORMATION

Career Rating	**85**
Job placement rate (%)	98
Average starting salary	$82,000
State for bar exam	OH, NY, CA, DC, PA
Pass rate for first-time bar	85

Employers who frequently hire grads: Jones, Day, Reavis, & Pogue; Squire, Sanders and Dempsey; Baker & Hostetler; Jenner & Block; Ernst & Young; PriceWaterhouseCoopers; Altheimer & Gray; federal government.

Prominent Alumni: Fred Gray, senior partner, civil rights attorney, represented Rosa Parks; Lincoln R. Diaz-Balart, congressman, U.S. House of Representatives.

Grads employed by field (%):	
Academic	4
Business/industry	11
Government	11
Judicial clerkships	5
Private practice	58
Public interest	5

Academic Requirements

Clinical Program Required?	No
Legal Writing Course Requirement?	Yes
Legal Methods Course Requirement?	Yes
Legal Research Course Requirement?	Yes
Moot Court Requirement?	No
Public Interest Law Requirement?	No

ADMISSIONS

Selectivity Rating	**82**
# applications received	2,851
# applicants accepted	801
# acceptees attending	228
Average LSAT	159
LSAT Range	157–161
Average undergrad GPA	3.3
Application fee	$40
Regular application deadline	4/1
Regular notification	rolling
Rolling notification?	Yes
Early application program?	Yes
Early application deadline	11/15
Early application notification	12/20
Transfer students accepted?	Yes
Evening division offered?	No
Part-time accepted?	Yes
LSDAS accepted?	Yes

International Students

TOEFL required of international students?	No
TOEFL recommended of international students?	Yes

FINANCIAL FACTS

Annual tuition	$28,200
Books and supplies	$1,200
Tuition per credit	$1,175
Room & board	$12,250
Financial aid application deadline	5/1
% first-year students receiving some sort of aid	77
% receiving some sort of aid	81
% of aid that is merit-based	100
% receiving scholarships	53
Average grant	$12,600
Average loan	$26,224
Average total aid package	$35,900
Average debt	$64,700

CHAPMAN UNIVERSITY
CHAPMAN UNIVERSITY SCHOOL OF LAW

INSTITUTIONAL INFORMATION

Public/private	private
Student/faculty ratio	18:1
Affiliation	Disciples of Christ
% faculty part-time	32
% faculty female	35
% faculty minority	12
Total faculty	26

SURVEY SAYS . . .

Beautiful campus

STUDENTS

Enrollment of law school	521
% male/female	50/50
% out-of-state	10
% full-time	91
% minority	33
% international	2
# of countries represented	4
Average age of entering class	25

ACADEMICS

Academic experience rating	**75**
Professors interesting rating	96
Professors accessible rating	93
Hours of study per day	3.97

Academic Specialties

Advocacy and resolution, environmental law, property, taxation.

Advanced Degrees Offered

JD, 3 years full-time.

Combined Degrees Offered

JD/MBA, 4 years.

Academic Requirements

Clinical Program Required?	No
Legal Writing Course Requirement?	Yes
Legal Methods Course Requirement?	Yes
Legal Research Course Requirement?	Yes
Moot Court Requirement?	No
Public Interest Law Requirement?	No

Academics

"Students are serious and proud" at Chapman University School of Law, "the premier law school in Orange County, California." Chapman is relatively new (founded in 1995), and "everyone is dedicated to making Chapman a nationally respected law school." To any visitor it is apparent that "the dean has worked hard to achieve full accreditation in record time." The campus is full of a new energetic feeling. "There is an entrepreneurial spirit." Students see themselves as "trailblazers." One member of this vanguard writes, "Chapman is full of potential. Every year since its inception, the quality of the faculty and students has improved, and this steady progression doesn't have an end in sight." Another student aggresses, "It's cool because you can feel the energy of everyone working together to make Chapman shine. Looking back in 20 years, I will be genuinely giddy to tell people that I got my JD from Chapman."

The "surprisingly personal" administration is very approachable and "tries to limit its interferences." The "remarkably helpful, friendly, available, knowledgeable, and approachable" faculty works long hours to "ensure that the students' needs are met." One student writes, "A few of the teachers actually meet individually with each student as a matter of course at least once per semester. Another declares, "Chapman offers some of the best professors you will find at any law school." Professors are democratic (with a little d), too. "We do a lot of voting in classes to determine some of the class structure."

Clinics and practical opportunities are abundant. There is the Elder Law Clinic, the Low-Income Taxpayer Clinic, and a Bankruptcy Clinic. The Claremont Institute Center for Constitutional Jurisprudence allows students to participate in trial and appellate litigation. Chapman offers a certificate program in land use and real estate law as well as a JD/MBA. Proximity to Los Angeles, Hollywood, and the Pacific Rim in general provides many clerkship opportunities. Chapman could stand to "offer more courses," though. Also, "the legal writing program is highly variable." One student observes, "Some students have a good experience and some have a very poor experience, depending on the quality of the adjunct professor." The good news is that Chapman's plan to add two full-time legal writing and research professors will hopefully alleviate this problem. Chapman's "biggest weakness" is its "newness and novelty." Low recognition makes it "difficult to walk into an interview with a hiring partner wholly unfamiliar with your law school." One student laments, "It would be helpful if Chapman's visibility outside of Southern California were improved." Improvements on this issue are just beginning as "it is becoming well known locally, but is virtually unheard of elsewhere."

The "brand new, fully modernized" law school is "absolutely beautiful." The School of Law is located in "a fantastic building" on the university campus. Students tell us that Kennedy Hall is "a perfect blend of modern technology and pleasing, classical aesthetics." You'll love the "marble-laden lobby." Furthermore, "Technology is good in the classrooms and library." There are "network connections at all the desks and study tables." "However, I have noticed a problem," writes one wry student. "The chairs are much too comfortable."

Life

Competition is negligible. "The 2Ls and 3Ls are very supportive of the 1Ls, so the student body really feels like a family." One student writes, "Except for a few ultra-competitive freaks, the students are supportive of one another." Typically, students "bend over backward" to help each other understand the material.

Tracy Simmons, Assistant Dean of Admissions and Financial Aid
One University Drive, Orange, CA 92866
Telephone: 714-628-2500 • Fax: 714-628-2501
E-mail: lawadm@chapman.edu • Website: www.chapman.edu/law

"The school is small, [and] everybody knows everybody." One student opines, "Social activities are pretty well-organized and lots of people get involved." Another comments, "If you don't like the clubs and organizations, you can easily start your own, which gives you a stake in its success. People with a little initiative can do incredibly well at Chapman." On the social front, "The Student Bar Association does a good job of organizing mixers, [and] every Thursday night is Bar Review. Other extracurricular activities leave students with the opportunity to "play football, have stupid movie nights, and do a number of things to escape the grind of school."

Chapman is "centrally located [in] sunny, beautiful Orange County, California, a booming environment" between Los Angeles and San Diego. It can be "difficult to study on a 75-degree January day." If you need a break, "beaches, Disneyland, and Catalina Island" are all nearby. "You can drive from the law school to Newport Beach in 15 minutes." If you find yourself missing the snow, "snowboarding and skiing" aren't far, either. "Coming to an open house here seals the deal," swears one student. "If you come for a visit, you will not want to leave."

Getting In

If you want to go to school in Southern California, and you think you might not make the cut at highly selective law schools like UCLA, Chapman should definitely be on your short list. A very young law school whose reputation has nowhere to go but up, you can bet that admissions competitiveness will heat up at Chapman as the word gets out about its idyllic setting and solid academic offerings. For the time being, an LSAT score between 155–158 and a B-average undergraduate GPA makes you competitive at Chapman.

EMPLOYMENT INFORMATION

Career Rating	**79**
% employed within 9 months	84
Average starting salary	$73,644
State for bar exam	CA
Pass rate for first-time bar	67

Employers who frequently hire grads:
O'Melveny & Myers, Orange County district attorney, Orange County public defender, United States district courts, Knobbe Martens, Riverside district attorney.

Prominent Alumni: Allison LeMoine-Bui, associate, Rutan & Tucker; Bryan Gadol, associate, Greenberg Traurig; Melanie Triebel, associate, O'Melveny & Myers; MD Schopper, Gilbert, & Schopper, LLP.

Grads employed by field (%):	
Academic	4
Business/industry	15
Government	11
Judicial clerkships	2
Other	2
Private practice	62
Public interest	4

ADMISSIONS

Selectivity Rating	**60***
# applications received	2,333
# applicants accepted	595
# acceptees attending	181
LSAT Range	154–158
Application fee	$60
Regular application deadline	rolling
Regular notification	rolling
Rolling notification?	Yes
Early application program?	No
Transfer students accepted?	Yes
Evening division offered?	No
Part-time accepted?	No
LSDAS accepted?	Yes

Applicants Also Look At

California Western, Loyola Marymount University, Pepperdine University, Southwestern University School of Law, University of San Diego, University of Southern California, Whittier College.

International Students

TOEFL required of international students?	Yes
Minimum Paper TOEFL	600
Minimum Computer TOEFL	250

FINANCIAL FACTS

Annual tuition	$29,800
Books and supplies	$1,000
Room & board	$11,540
Financial aid application deadline	3/2
% first-year students receiving some sort of aid	91
% receiving some sort of aid	93
% of aid that is merit-based	20
% receiving scholarships	45
Average grant	$13,050
Average loan	$27,718
Average total aid package	$29,062
Average debt	$64,456

City University of New York
School of Law at Queens College

INSTITUTIONAL INFORMATION

Public/private	public
Student/faculty ratio	12:1
% faculty part-time	30
% faculty female	51
% faculty minority	49
Total faculty	43

SURVEY SAYS . . .

Diverse opinions accepted in classrooms
Great library staff

STUDENTS

Enrollment of law school	444
% male/female	33/67
% out-of-state	35
% full-time	98
% minority	46
% international	4
# of countries represented	63
Average age of entering class	28

ACADEMICS

Academic experience rating	**64**
Professors interesting rating	66
Professors accessible rating	80
Hours of study per day	4.51

Academic Specialties

Criminal law, human rights law, civil rights law, domestic violence law, immigration law, international human rights law, labor/worker law.

Advanced Degrees Offered

JD, 3 years full-time only.

Academic Requirements

Clinical Program Required?	Yes
Legal Writing Course Requirement?	Yes
Legal Methods Course Requirement?	Yes
Legal Research Course Requirement?	Yes
Moot Court Requirement?	No
Public Interest Law Requirement?	Yes

Academics

City University of New York is a unique urban law school with a distinctive mission, which is expressed in its motto, "Law in the Service of Human Needs." While CUNY will provide a quality education in all the foundational legal topics, the school's expressed mission is "to teach students to be lawyers who will use their skills to serve the public interest," a goal that permeates every aspect of the classroom, culture, and population at CUNY. A 1L explains: "The entire focus of the school is public interest law and community service. All of the courses are taught with this in mind, and clinical programs serving low-income people in the community are required." All law students are required to participate in free legal clinics that benefit needy New Yorkers; this program not only serves the community, but it also provides CUNY students with essential real-world experience. "The amount and variety of real situations and people in the legal system I have observed and dealt with helped to shape the theoretical perspective that will guide my practice upon graduation." One student reports: "I've written several briefs, memoranda of law, and complaints in my classes; and I even got the chance to represent clients in administrative hearings as a 2L."

The school's diversity in terms of "both its students and faculty, is beyond exceptional." A 1L writes: "The faculty mirrors [the students'] diversity of ethnicity and experience. This semester, only one of my professors is a white male and three out of five are lesbian." Students describe their professors as "brilliant, committed, and on the cutting edge of liberal law." On top of that, "students, professors, and administrators get to know each other on a first-name basis and have real, one-on-one interaction." United by a common vision, the CUNY community is "a unique environment in which the dedication to students' academic and professional growth is always the priority of faculty and students alike."

"If you are set on making a lot of money and practicing big law with a firm, CUNY is not for you. If you want to become a public interest lawyer because of, and not in spite of, your legal education, this is best law school you could find." While most CUNY students feel right at home on this activist campus, a handful has difficulty living in a "political environment [that] makes John Kerry look like Pat Buchanan." One 3L grouses: "If you're anything but an ultra-progressive liberal, you will not be happy. If you want a job that pays above the poverty line, you will not be popular." In fact, a few feel that the school's mission impedes critical thinking, claiming that "it is hard to have a challenging discussion when everyone thinks alike." For better or for worse, the school's progressive reputation has an influence on the jobs that alumni are likely—and encouraged—to find. Career Services generally places students in low-paying public interest jobs and makes little effort to contact firms.

Students gripe that "there are far too many required courses" and that this "makes it virtually impossible to plan a creative or interesting schedule." While CUNY students appreciate the fact that they "are paying a third of the average tuition for a fantastic legal education," they also note that, "due to the low cost of attendance, CUNY doesn't have the same resources as some private institutions." The school's location—"in an old junior high across from a cemetery in a place aptly named Flushing"—"could stand to be improved." Students complain that the campus is hard to reach via public transit systems, there is no campus cafeteria, and there have been sightings of cockroaches and mice. But many take the undesirable facilities in stride, telling us that "CUNY doesn't need frills and thrills to prove itself as a notable law school; it has heart and soul."

Yvonne Cherena-Pacheco, Assistant Dean for Enrollment Mgmt & Director of Admissions
65-21 Main Street, Flushing, NY 11367-1358
Telephone: 718-340-4210 • Fax: 718-340-4435
E-mail: admissions@mail.law.cuny.edu • Website: www.law.cuny.edu

Life

While united by a common vision of public service, CUNY students are otherwise extremely diverse. "CUNY Law School isn't beautiful, and it isn't housed in prestigious, ivy covered buildings. It is a school full of very real people, many of whom had very real lives before they came to law school." At CUNY, "almost 2 out of 3 students are female, there is a very large GLBT community, and almost a majority are people of color." "Most of our students come from nothing, and they fight for those with nothing. We fight with our soul and hearts, and that is what makes us the best lawyers." Students "bond intensely by sharing in an endless flow of deprecating comments about the environment. In this way, we show our love for one another and our zeal for martyrdom in the public interest." This zeal manifests itself in the CUNY experience: "During any given week, there are likely to be several student-sponsored panel discussions, film screenings, special guest speakers providing education, and discussions about important events affecting international human rights or politics."

Most students regard the academic environment as respectful and report that "students, even when they disagree politically (and no matter how hard the debate), still struggle to afford each other respect and consideration." However, occasionally "the passion [students] harbor for some of their ideological issues causes them to lash out against other students with vicious and crude attacks." For the most part, the "we're-all-in-this-together" vibe is strong. "Students are all committed to helping one another out. We share ideas, class notes, outlines, and support, rather than competing for the best grades." That said, CUNY "is predominantly a commuter school" and, as a result, "lacks a campus life."

Getting In

CUNY evaluates prospective students based on their demonstrated ability and intellectual capacity to complete a rigorous legal program, using test scores, previous academic record, and, where applicable, postcollege work experience. In addition to these factors, CUNY seeks students who can bring diversity of background and experience to the campus and who express a specific interest in and affinity for the values of the program. Finally, CUNY favors New York residents or students with a particular interest in serving the New York community.

EMPLOYMENT INFORMATION

Career Rating	**61**
Job placement rate (%)	83
Average starting salary	$41,200
State for bar exam	NY
Pass rate for first-time bar	55

Employers who frequently hire grads: District attorneys' offices (Bronx, Manhattan, and Queens), legal aid society (NYC), legal services offices (NYC), Nassau County attorney's office.

Prominent Alumni: Honorable Diccia Pineda-Kirwan, judge of the civil court, Queens County; Carmen Rita Torrent, executive director, mayor's commission on women.

Grads employed by field (%):	
Academic	3
Business/industry	18
Government	20
Judicial clerkships	4
Other	1
Private practice	24
Public interest	30

ADMISSIONS

Selectivity Rating	**73**
# applications received	2,318
# applicants accepted	474
# acceptees attending	153
Average LSAT	151
LSAT Range	148–154
Average undergrad GPA	3.2
Application fee	$50
Regular application deadline	3/15
Regular notification	5/31
Rolling notification?	No
Early application program?	No
Transfer students accepted?	Yes
Evening division offered?	No
Part-time accepted?	No
LSDAS accepted?	Yes

Applicants Also Look At

Brooklyn Law School; New York Law School; New York University; Northeastern University; Rutgers, The State University of New Jersey; St. John's University.

International Students

TOEFL required of international students?	No
TOEFL recommended of international students?	Yes

FINANCIAL FACTS

Annual tuition (resident)	$7,130
Annual tuition (nonresident)	$11,880
Books and supplies	$1,400
Financial aid application deadline	5/1
% first-year students receiving some sort of aid	87
% receiving some sort of aid	93
% of aid that is merit-based:	6
% receiving scholarships	34
Average grant	$4,416
Average loan	$22,753
Average total aid package	$23,012
Average debt	$50,179

CLEVELAND STATE UNIVERSITY
CLEVELAND-MARSHALL COLLEGE OF LAW

INSTITUTIONAL INFORMATION

Public/private	public
Student/faculty ratio	13:1
% faculty part-time	36
% faculty female	38
% faculty minority	5
Total faculty	73

SURVEY SAYS . . .

Diverse opinions accepted in classrooms
Great research resources
Great library staff
Students love Cleveland, OH

STUDENTS

Enrollment of law school	747
% male/female	54/46
% out-of-state	20
% full-time	66
% minority	13
% international	1
# of countries represented	7
Average age of entering class	26

ACADEMICS

Academic experience rating	**70**
Professors interesting rating	65
Professors accessible rating	69
Hours of study per day	4.47

Academic Specialties

Business law, civil litigation and dispute resolution, criminal law, employment and labor law, tax law.

Advanced Degrees Offered

LLM, 20 to 24 credits, may be completed in 1 to 4 years.

Combined Degrees Offered

JD/MPA, master in public administration; JD/MUPDD, master in urban planning, design, and development; JD/MAES, master of arts in environmental studies; JD/MSES, master of science in environmental science; and JD/MBA. All may be completed in 4 years of full-time study.

Academic Requirements

Clinical Program Required?	No

Academics

Cleveland-Marshall College of Law, located "in the heart of one of the largest legal markets in the nation, places extraordinary emphasis on practical lawyering skills." Students tell us, "This is a place to prepare for life after school." While professors spend "an appropriate amount of time on theory, [they are] always mindful of the fact that most of us are here to learn, get our degree, and actually practice." The teaching approach is not the only practical thing about Cleveland-Marshall—the part-time program and evening classes, as well as the affordable in-state tuition, make the school itself very convenient and user-friendly.

Students at Cleveland-Marshall love the fact that their professors are "enthusiastic about law [and] go out of their way to make sure that they are accessible either at home or school." Sometimes they are the "Socratic fire-breathing dragons, the terror of 1Ls everywhere," but outside of class they're "uniformly accessible, informative, and helpful." In the whirlwind of stress that can be law school, it is comforting to know that "professors take a deep interest in their students and do anything possible to make the learning environment more bearable and less confusing." Students also praise the faculty for their diverse legal backgrounds. As one student tells us, "In my first year, I was taught by experienced trial attorneys and also professors with experience in international government and lawmaking."

Students at Cleveland-Marshall seem generally pleased with the school's administration, which they say "treats you like a professional from day one [and] bends over backward to assist with any problems or dilemmas." The school has eased the transition for new law students by "implementing a number of new seminars geared toward preparing the student for practically every facet of law school study and life." Plus, Cleveland-Marshall's career services staff is "committed to giving every student the tools and skills necessary to successfully obtain positions in the legal field." One thing many students do express concern about is their perception of the school's "strict 'C' curve," saying "it makes life more miserable and stressful than it should have to be"—although a few are optimistic that the curve will force students to work harder and be better prepared for the bar.

Cleveland-Marshall students seem generally satisfied with the facilities. The school has gone wireless and "is wiring rooms for laptops to plug into every seat of every classroom." As one student says, "Being able to do research anywhere on campus is absolutely wonderful!" Students are in love with their "to-die-for beautiful" library, which offers them "the best possible resources and research opportunities," writes one student. "Amazing, open and light, and state of the art" are just a few of the many praises students offer to this study haven. Unfortunately, not every building on campus is as "new, beautiful, and extremely functional" as the library. For instance, the "aesthetically lacking" law building is done in a "modernist bomb shelter style of architecture," which one student suggests the school "should tear down [in favor of] something more like the library." Students will be happy to hear that the law school's plan is to use a recent million dollar gift to renovate the building in keeping with the look of the library.

Melody J. Stewart, Assistant Dean for Admissions
2121 Euclid Avenue, LB 138, Cleveland, OH 44115-2214
Telephone: 866-687-2304 • Fax: 216-687-6881
E-mail: admissions@law.csuohio.edu • Website: www.law.csuohio.edu

Life

Being located in Cleveland makes it easy for students "to work at law firms downtown," while going to school. And networking opportunities abound, since the school has a good "relationship with the legal community, [and the] alumni support is great." One student exclaims, "Since many of the alumni have chosen to stay here, they offer a rich resource for current students to draw on." Not to mention the fact that "the courthouses are also nearby." Furthermore, if you choose to stick around the city after graduation, "being a Cleveland-Marshall grad in Cleveland opens a lot of doors."

While some Cleveland-Marshall students are fresh out of college, others have years of work experience behind them. The result is a mix that students consider one of the school's greatest assets. As one second-career, full-time student, explains, "Diversity in background is encouraged and appreciated at Cleveland-Marshall. This school values my previous work experience, and I never feel that law school was simply an academic extension of undergraduate work." Additionally, most students are generally "friendly and willing to help each other out, [and] no one hides books or delights in your failure, [as it] is not a cutthroat school by any means."

While the student body is "diligent most of the time, you can always find people unwinding on the weekends. There is a good balance." The SBA "continually organizes nights out or parties at school [and] schedules a social at a downtown bar at least once a month." As one student says, "For the life of me, I cannot understand why lawyers get a bad rap because we truly know how to party." Extracurricular activities are also popular at Cleveland-Marshall, where "it seems as though almost everyone [in the] very active student body" participates in at least one of the "over 25 student organizations" to choose from.

Getting In

At Cleveland-Marshall, admitted students at the 25th percentile have an LSAT score of 151 and a GPA of 3.02. Admitted students at the 75th percentile have an LSAT score of 156 and a GPA of 3.6. The Law School enrolls about 750 students, about a third of which are part-timers.

EMPLOYMENT INFORMATION

Career Rating	**71**
Job placement rate (%)	90
Average starting salary	$67,020
State for bar exam	OH, NY, MD, MA, NV
Pass rate for first-time bar	73

Employers who frequently hire grads: Jones Day; Thompson, Hine; Squire, Sanders, & Dempsey; Calfee, Halter & Griswold; Arter & Hadden; Ernst & Young; Benesch, Friedlander, Coplan, & Arnold; Hahn, Loeser, & Parks, LLP.

Prominent Alumni: Tim Russert, senior vice president, NBC News; Honorable Louis Stokes, U.S. House of Representatives, retired.

Grads employed by field (%):	
Academic	2
Business/industry	17
Government	13
Judicial clerkships	5
Military	1
Private practice	59
Public interest	3

Legal Writing Course Requirement?	Yes
Legal Methods Course Requirement?	Yes
Legal Research Course Requirement?	Yes
Moot Court Requirement?	No
Public Interest Law Requirement?	No

ADMISSIONS

Selectivity Rating	**76**
# applications received	1,912
# applicants accepted	562
# acceptees attending	248
Average LSAT	153
LSAT Range	151–156
Average undergrad GPA	3.3
Application fee	$35
Regular application deadline	5/5
Regular notification	5/5
Rolling notification?	Yes
Early application program?	No
Transfer students accepted?	Yes
Evening division offered?	Yes
Part-time accepted?	Yes
LSDAS accepted?	Yes

Applicants Also Look At

Capital University, Case Western Reserve University, The Ohio State University, The University of Akron, University of Dayton, University of Toledo.

International Students

TOEFL required of international students?	Yes

FINANCIAL FACTS

Annual tuition (resident)	$13,052
Annual tuition (nonresident)	$17,969
Books and supplies	$700
Tuition per credit (resident)	$502
Tuition per credit (nonresident)	$691
Room & board	$10,350
Financial aid application deadline	5/5
% first-year students receiving some sort of aid	90
% receiving some sort of aid	95
% of aid that is merit-based	90
% receiving scholarships	34
Average grant	$4,600
Average loan	$17,333
Average total aid package	$24,658
Average debt	$48,000

College of William & Mary

Marshall-Wythe Law School

INSTITUTIONAL INFORMATION

Public/private	public
Student/faculty ratio	16:1
% faculty part-time	57
% faculty female	38
% faculty minority	10
Total faculty	72

SURVEY SAYS . . .

Diverse opinions accepted in classrooms
Great library staff
Abundant externship/internship/clerkship opportunities

STUDENTS

Enrollment of law school	585
% male/female	56/44
% out-of-state	56
% full-time	100
% minority	13
% international	1
# of countries represented	9
Average age of entering class	23

ACADEMICS

Academic experience rating	**88**
Professors interesting rating	90
Professors accessible rating	86
Hours of study per day	4.25

Academic Specialties

Civil procedure, commercial law, constitutional law, corporation securities law, criminal law, environmental law, human rights law, intellectual property law, international law, labor law, legal history, property, taxation.

Advanced Degrees Offered

JD, 3 years; LLM in the American legal system, 1 year.

Combined Degrees Offered

JD/master of public policy, 4 years; JD/master of business administration, 4 years; JD/master of arts in American studies, 4 years.

Academic Requirements

Clinical Program Required??	No
Legal Writing Course Requirement?	Yes

Academics

The Marshall-Wythe School of Law at the College of William & Mary is proud to offer a "world-class legal education. Small classes, wildly accessible and passionate [professors,] national prominence," and generous scholarships certainly don't hurt.

Students dig the curriculum. According to students, "The law school here at William and Mary is unique in its dedication to educating 'citizen lawyers' who possess 'a thorough understanding of the practice of law [as well as of] philosophy, government, and history.'" Dual-degree programs include a JD/MBA, Law/Masters of Public Policy, and Law/MA in American Studies. Furthermore, the legal skills program combines "legal research, writing, and ethics [into an] incredibly valuable" two-year program. Students are "organized into 'firms' that take mock clients through all stages of a trial—from initial contact to appeals." Critics grouse that the program "dishes out way too much busywork." Others are more circumspect. "Legal Skills is quite a headache while going through it, but very much worthwhile once you see the difference it makes," reflects one student. "I was better prepared for practical work at my 1L job (at the Justice Department) than the 2Ls from more prestigious schools."

Students praise the "accommodating, very visible, [and] genuinely committed" administration. "The dean has weekly open lunches where students are encouraged to come and give criticism [and] to have lively conversation." Career Services provides "good summer job placement." Some students wish job opportunities were more available "outside the East Coast" but all agree that "it's fairly easy to get into a large DC law firm." In a word, William & Mary professors rock. They excel in their craft, and their accessibility is the stuff of legend. Students report, "They consistently remind us that they are available to answer questions outside of class. No door is ever closed, [and professors are] willing to converse with students regularly about anything." One student observes, "Advice is like air here." In class, professors provide "a relaxed atmosphere in which to learn." A student writes, "One professor keeps things interesting by using crazy analogies and hypotheticals and doing voices from Monty Python." Another student explains, "The professors not only teach the law, they turn to relevant questions of justice and fairness. They encourage us to think about why decisions are made and whether we think they are good decisions." Another important note is that the fairly small class sizes mean that students are called on in class frequently. The William & Mary campus is "stunning, well-maintained, [and] very technologically advanced. Fully integrated wireless [access is] available in all rooms, [and] the school has an actual working courtroom." However, students gripe bitterly about the "decidedly second-rate" law school facility, which is "straight out of a 1970s time warp." One student comments, "The heating system is actually air conditioning, except in the spring and fall." The library is "small and cramped" too, though the "excellent" library staff "will bend over backward for you." The good news is that complete renovations are underway. "The last remnants [of 70s-era construction] are being removed, and the library has several million dollars [actually 16.8] earmarked for the additional renovation that should be completed by spring 2007."

Life

"True story," swears one student. "I attended a student-only forum with the ABA's reaccredidation committee as a 1L. The committee reported back that we were probably the happiest law students they had ever encountered." Another student adds, "I don't think there could be any more of a community in a law school atmosphere than exists at

Faye Shealy, Associate Dean
Office of Admission, PO Box 8795, Williamsburg, VA 23187-8795
Telephone: 757-221-3785 • Fax: 757-221-3261
E-mail: lawadm@wm.edu • Website: www.wm.edu/law/

W&M. People care how you are." The "friendly, encouraging, driven" students are "for the most part, uninterested in the competitive jockeying for position." Also, the Honor Code "is taken very seriously, [so] there is no need to worry about cheating [or] leaving your laptop around." Some students say, "Because the school is so small, anonymity [is] tough to find" and "things can get a bit incestuous." In technical demographic terms, William & Mary is "very white and very young." Students say, "Bleeding hearts [are plentiful, as are] rabid right-wingers." One student reports, "There is also a strong military population." Another student asserts, "I'm a liberal, and most kids here are mildly conservative, but that's never been a problem. We have great discussions and realize that reasonable people can disagree."

The "quiet [and] oppressively small" surrounding hamlet of Williamsburg is "a lovely colonial town in that Jeffersonian, Southern, white-columned, intellectual way, [where] people dressed in colonial outfits walk the streets." One student notes, "The law school is a little bit isolated" from the main campus, and many students report "difficulty obtaining housing within walking distance," so it's a good idea to "bring a car if you come here."

Williamsburg is "a perfect place [to] study hard all week." Students say, "There's no dancing for 20 minutes in any direction [and] pancake houses outnumber the bars about threefold, [making the location] a little sleepy (comatose, actually)." All the bellyaching about the "sense of boredom," though, doesn't mean there aren't a few self-described "party animals." One such student reports, "We have weekly bar nights, class football games, soccer teams, hockey teams, basketball teams, etc., and there's an abundance of things to do to keep your mind off the law." One student exclaims, "I've met my best friends here. We go to class together, live together (in the graduate complex), eat together, and spend an incredible amount of time drinking together. This place is great."

Getting In

It's difficult to get admitted. Approximately 4,200 applicants seek admission to the Marshall-Wythe School of Law at the College of William & Mary in a given year. About 800 are admitted. Just over 200 actually enroll. The mean LSAT score is 162 and the mean GPA is 3.6.

EMPLOYMENT INFORMATION

Career Rating	**88**
% employed within 9 months	99
Average starting salary	$78,252
State for bar exam	VA, NY, PA, FL, DE
Pass rate for first-time bar	88

Grads employed by field (%):	
Academic	1
Business/industry	4
Government	14
Judicial clerkships	10
Military	9
Private practice	58
Public interest	4

Legal Methods Course Requirement?	Yes
Legal Research Course Requirement?	Yes
Moot Court Requirement?	No
Public Interest Law Requirement?	No

ADMISSIONS

Selectivity Rating	**88**
# applications received	4,243
# applicants accepted	848
# acceptees attending	206
Average LSAT	162
LSAT Range	160–165
Average undergrad GPA	3.6
Application fee	$40
Regular application deadline	3/1
Regular notification	3/30
Rolling notification?	No
Early application program?	No
Transfer students accepted?	Yes
Evening division offered?	No
Part-time accepted?	No
LSDAS accepted?	Yes

Applicants Also Look At

Boston College, The George Washington U., Georgetown U., U. of Virginia, Washington and Lee U.

International Students

TOEFL required of international students?	No
TOEFL recommended of international students?	Yes
Minimum Paper TOEFL	600
Minimum Computer TOEFL	250

FINANCIAL FACTS

Annual tuition (resident)	$14,160
Annual tuition (nonresident)	$24,400
Books and supplies	$1,500
Tuition per credit (resident)	$400
Tuition per credit (nonresident)	$725
Room & board	$6,300
Financial aid application deadline	2/15
% first-year students receiving some sort of aid	59
% receiving some sort of aid	56
% of aid that is merit-based	75
% receiving scholarships	25
Average grant	$4,473
Average loan	$22,582
Average total aid package	$26,991
Average debt	$61,621

Columbia University
School of Law

INSTITUTIONAL INFORMATION

Public/private	private
Student/faculty ratio	11:1
% faculty part-time	38
% faculty female	29
% faculty minority	11
Total faculty	163

SURVEY SAYS . . .

Great research resources
Abundant externship/internship/clerkship opportunities
Students love New York, NY

STUDENTS

Enrollment of law school	1,239
% male/female	55/45
% out-of-state	80
% full-time	100
% minority	29
% international	10
# of countries represented	22
Average age of entering class	24

ACADEMICS

Academic experience rating	**87**
Professors interesting rating	69
Professors accessible rating	62
Hours of study per day	4.02

Academic Specialties

Civil procedure, commercial law, constitutional law, corporation securities law, criminal law, environmental law, government services, human rights law, intellectual property law, international law, labor law, legal history, legal philosophy, property, taxation.

Advanced Degrees Offered

LLM, 1 year; JSD, 2 semesters in residence and a dissertation.

Combined Degrees Offered

JD/PhD, JD/MA, JD/MBA, JD/MFA (arts administration), JD/MS urban planning, JD/MS social work, JD/MS journalism, JD/MIA in international affairs, JD/MPA in public administration with Columbia, JD/MPA in public affairs with Woodrow Wilson School at Princeton, JD/MPH in public health.

Academics

Resources-wise, "if it exists, they've got it" at Columbia University School of Law. "Academically, this school is tough," to say the least. In the words of one current law student, "Be prepared to feel a lot dumber than you ever have before." But the humiliation is worth it, say students, for on the other side of the three-year commitment, "a Columbia degree garners much prestige and respect." To put it simply (and to which the statistics in the sidebars will attest), "Columbia's name can get you into any door [and] making an obscene amount of money" after graduating. "If you want to get a job with a top law firm, regardless of your grades or lack of social skills, this is the school for you." Solid careers are par for the course of Columbia alumni. "We pay a lot of tuition, but we get paid tons of money when we leave. It's the biggest, yet the best investment of your life."

For your many tuition dollars, you will get professors who reportedly "are all geniuses." Some, however, are "very old." One student remarks, "The fossils wandering the hallways are fascinating." Others are "brilliant but arrogant." Still, others appear "thoroughly bored with the material they are teaching you." One student gripes, "We often have professors who we can brag about outside the classroom, but we don't understand a single thing they say inside the classroom." Most professors, however, are "wonderful [and] accessible." The law school's administration is "excellent." However, the larger university's "notoriously horrible, bureaucratic, and inefficient" administration is "unbearably slow." One student makes a scary comparison, "A few hours at the housing office will make you wish for an afternoon at the DMV."

Students remark, "the legal writing 'curriculum' is the definition of insufficient." All in all, though, "Columbia provides an excellent legal education." An overwhelmingly majority of students agree, "All you have to do is show up and take advantage [of it]." Some students complain that the emphasis on legal theory is too strong. "The clinics are a wonderful chance to actually see what practicing law is like, but outside of the clinics, it is very easy to forget that you'll actually be dealing with clients once you graduate." Other students tell us there is a "nice balance of theory and practice." You just have to "seek out" practical opportunities "among the oodles of theoretical course work." Additionally, Columbia has "a very committed and involved public interest center [that] makes Ralph Nader look like a right winger."

The law school building is "practical but hideous" from the outside, "but the inside is functional and comfortable, especially the upper floors, where the professors' offices are located." The newer classrooms are "aesthetically pleasing [and] technology-equipped, [but] you can't fit a computer and a book on the desk in front of you." Students observe that "the library is old and somewhat dank" but it, too, is "functional." They also agree, "comfortable study areas" are ample.

Life

"Since there are no class rankings, [Columbia] is not competitive. Students are happy to share notes and outlines." The "interesting students" at Columbia are "accomplished, talented, and driven, [though they] generally work too hard." Students say, "The population is very diverse. We have doctors, former professors, business people, and social workers." There are also "a lot of minorities." Students come to agreement on the issue of grades, remarking that "with the classrooms filled with ridiculously smart people, you can actually slide by. Grade inflation is alive and well."

Nkonye Iwerebon, Acting Dean of Admissions
435 West 116th Street, Box A-3, New York, NY 10027
Telephone: 212-854-2670 • Fax: 212-854-1109
E-mail: admissions@law.columbia.edu • Website: www.law.columbia.edu

Columbia is "a very exciting place [that offers] unparalleled professional opportunities." According to one student, "Weekly bar events and regular firm receptions keep the alcohol and gossip flowing." There is a high visitor flow as "the law school has a constant influx of celebrity speakers and international conferences." A student explains, "One day the guest speaker can be Hillary Clinton, and the next day you have Eminem's agent." Then, it's off to "a gala dinner with Ruth Bader Ginsburg and a reception at the Waldorf-Astoria." Another student, exhausted by the embarrassment of riches around him, writes, "Conferences and receptions are almost too plentiful. When you get 25 to 30 emails a day about seminars, internship opportunities, bar nights, and group meetings, you can feel like you're not taking full advantage of everything that's going on."

The surrounding area of Morningside Heights "has a very nice residential feel to it that the rest of Manhattan doesn't have." One student writes, "The student apartments are unbelievable [but also] incredibly expensive." "The social life at school is somewhat fragmented," primarily because there is so much going on. "There are lots of cliques. A core group of students are very involved in the law school community, both intellectually and socially. But there are also plenty of students who just go do their own thing. New York is a great place for that. [It's] the most exciting, cosmopolitan, energetic city in the world."

Getting In

Admitted students at the 25th percentile have an LSAT score of 167 and a GPA of 3.5. Admitted students at the 75th percentile have an LSAT score of 173 and a GPA of 3.8. At law schools this prestigious, admission can be a crapshoot. There are too many qualified students and not enough spots in each entering class. Our advice: if your grades and LSAT scores are competitive with these numbers, apply to at least a handful of really good schools. We wish you the best.

EMPLOYMENT INFORMATION

Career Rating	**90**
% employed within 9 months	99
Average starting salary	$125,000
State for bar exam	NY, NJ, CA, FL, TX
Pass rate for first-time bar	94

Employers who frequently hire grads: Large international corporate law firms, federal judges, federal government agencies, and public interest organizations.

Prominent Alumni: Ruth Bader Ginsburg, justice/U.S. Supreme Court; George Pataki, governor/New York State; Franklin D. Roosevelt, former president of United States; Paul Robeson, performing artist/civil rights activist.

Grads employed by field (%):	
Academic	1
Business/industry	2
Government	3
Judicial clerkships	13
Private practice	78
Public interest	3

Academic Requirements

Clinical Program Required?	No
Legal Writing Course Requirement?	Yes
Legal Methods Course Requirement?	Yes
Legal Research Course Requirement?	Yes
Moot Court Requirement?	Yes
Public Interest Law Requirement?	Yes

ADMISSIONS

Selectivity Rating	**97**
# applications received	8,355
# applicants accepted	1,187
# acceptees attending	374
Average LSAT	170
LSAT Range	167–173
Average undergrad GPA	3.65
Application fee	$70
Regular application deadline	2/15
Regular notification	rolling
Rolling notification?	Yes
Early application program?	Yes
Early application deadline	11/15
Early application notification	1/1
Transfer students accepted?	Yes
Evening division offered?	No
Part-time accepted?	No
LSDAS accepted?	Yes

Applicants Also Look At

Harvard U., New York U., Stanford U., Yale U.

International Students

TOEFL required of international students?	No
TOEFL recommended of international students?	No

FINANCIAL FACTS

Annual tuition	$36,300
Books and supplies	$925
Fees per credit	$1,816
Room & board (on-campus)	$16,377
Financial aid application deadline	3/1
% first-year students receiving some sort of aid	82
% receiving some sort of aid	84
% of aid that is merit-based	35
% receiving scholarships	38
Average grant	$15,137
Average loan	$36,020
Average total aid package	$36,640
Average debt	$99,900

Cornell University
Cornell Law School

INSTITUTIONAL INFORMATION

Public/private	private
Student/faculty ratio	12:1
% faculty female	42
Total faculty	60

SURVEY SAYS . . .

Great research resources
Great library staff
Beautiful campus

STUDENTS

Enrollment of law school	585
% male/female	53/47
% out-of-state	66
% full-time	100
% minority	30
Average age of entering class	23

ACADEMICS

Academic experience rating	**83**
Professors interesting rating	73
Professors accessible rating	83
Hours of study per day	5.36

Academic Specialties

International law.

Advanced Degrees Offered

JD, 3 years; LLM, 1 year; JD/LLM in international and comparative law, 3 years; JD/Maitrise en Driot French law degree, 4 years; JSD, 2 years; JD/MLLP master of German and European law and legal practice, 4 years; JD/ DESS (French degree in global business law), 3 years.

Combined Degrees Offered

JD/MBA, JD/MPA, JD/MA, JD/PhD, JD/MRP, JD/MILR.

Academic Requirements

Clinical Program Required?	No
Legal Writing Course Requirement?	No
Legal Methods Course Requirement?	Yes
Legal Research Course Requirement?	No
Moot Court Requirement?	No

Academics

Cornell University is a small school with a big name. Thanks to this favorable combination, Cornell students enjoy a world-class education in the context of a personal, student-oriented environment. Across the board, "the professors at Cornell are top scholars in their respective fields" whose "prodigious academic accomplishments" are a significant asset to the classroom experience. What's more, most professors "are witty and make the classes worth getting up early for." Despite their impressive names and backgrounds, Cornell professors invest a lot of time and energy into their roles as teachers and mentors. A 2L insists, "The faculty is focused on teaching, not only publishing, and are clearly the greatest asset at Cornell Law School."

While Cornell boasts the high level of scholarship one would expect to find at a top school, "the close relationship between faculty and students is what sets Cornell apart from its peers." There are few lecture halls at Cornell, and "small class sizes allow professors to really get to know students." Outside of class, professors are available for academic assistance, mentorship, and advice. "It is an honor to have classes and discussions with my professors. I have never had anyone here meet my questions without enthusiasm or support," gushes one student. But don't mistake kindness for laxness. Cornell is tough, and students caution that "professors drive us hard." In fact, students are constantly scrambling to keep up with the demands of their educations. A 2L recalls that "Last year, I definitely spent more than nine hours a day studying outside of class."

It is unanimously agreed that "Cornell's strength is in its size," but there's a flip side to that coin, for students point out that Cornell's course offerings are narrower than they would likely be if the school were larger. In addition, since "the faculty is too small, we end up with way too many visiting professors." Still, for many students "small seminars with current topics make up for an otherwise small range of classes." In addition, Cornell provides a number of first-rate programs and opportunities within the law school and the greater university. In particular, many students mention the school's excellent international law program: "If you're interested in international law with a European focus, this is the place to be," advises one student. "The school is also adding to its international program by offering new classes in Asian law (e.g., Japanese law)." On top of that, Cornell students say they really benefit from their affiliation with the greater university. For example, "Cornell has a wide range of non–law school classes" for which law students are able to sign up. "A small community within a large university means that professors and students aren't stretched too thin, but we have ample opportunity for a broad curriculum if we try hard enough," is how one student puts it.

When it comes to the administration, students report that "Cornell is run like a well-oiled machine"; "everything is done quickly and efficiently." Another major benefit to a Cornell education is that the school enjoys "name recognition in NYC," and as a result, "across the board, Cornell graduates seem to get the very best jobs." Students say that "Cornell's career office is amazing—knowledgeable, accessible, and well connected. I have absolutely no complaints. I just got my dream job for the summer—and most of my classmates will say the same thing." Some students would, however, like to see more connections in public interest firms, as well as outside of New York.

Richard Geiger, Dean of Admissions
Myron Taylor Hall, Ithaca, NY 14853-4901
Telephone: 607-255-5141 • Fax: 607-255-7193
E-mail: lawadmit@postoffice.law.cornell.edu • Website: www.lawschool.cornell.edu

Life

Cornell attracts ambitious, interesting, and accomplished students who "come from all walks of life and experience." For at least one student, "My classmates are the most uniformly intelligent and ambitious group of which I've ever been a member." Despite their personal accomplishments and drive, "Students are cooperative. Everyone feels they are in this together and there is no point in trying to knock one another down."

The campus vibe is friendly and social, and "the very active student organizations provide numerous non-academic opportunities." That's good, since "students here are uniformly amiable and like spending time together" even to the exclusion of other members of the Cornell community; "The majority of law students socialize only with other law students," reports one student.

Consider yourself warned: "People are warm, weather is cold" in Ithaca, NY. Indeed, if there is one resounding complaint among Cornell students, it is that "Ithaca is an isolated college town." Students joke that the best way to improve the atmosphere at Cornell would be to "put the whole school in a bio-dome and turn up the heat and sunshine." However, one student aptly adds, "Everyone knew that before they came here. [There is] not much night life to speak of, but that's not what I am here for." Students make the best of the situation, however, informing us that "Cornell is beautiful [and] it's a great place to study for the lack of distraction."

Getting In

Admissions to Cornell is highly competitive. The Admissions Committee weighs all aspects of an applicant's background, including extracurricular and community activities, graduate work, LSAT scores, letters of recommendation, and undergraduate transcripts. Applicants are also encouraged to submit a separate document that details how their ethnic, cultural, or linguistic background will contribute to the diversity of the school community.

Public Interest Law Requirement?	No

ADMISSIONS

Selectivity Rating	**93**
# applications received	4,706
# applicants accepted	794
# acceptees attending	193
Average LSAT	167
LSAT Range	165–168
Average undergrad GPA	3.6
Application fee	$70
Regular application deadline	2/1
Regular notification	rolling
Rolling notification?	Yes
Early application program?	No
Transfer students accepted?	Yes
Evening division offered?	No
Part-time accepted?	No
LSDAS accepted?	Yes

International Students

TOEFL required of international students?	No
TOEFL recommended of international students?	No

FINANCIAL FACTS

Annual tuition	$35,230
Books and supplies	$800
Room & board	$9,500
Financial aid application deadline	3/15
% receiving some sort of aid	80
% receiving scholarships	50
Average grant	$9,275

EMPLOYMENT INFORMATION

Career Rating	**90**
% employed within 9 months	98
Average starting salary	$116,080
State for bar exam	NY
Pass rate for first-time bar	94

Grads employed by field (%):	
Academic	1
Business/industry	1
Government	2
Judicial clerkships	12
Military	1
Other	6
Private practice	73
Public interest	1

Creighton University
Creighton University School of Law

INSTITUTIONAL INFORMATION

Public/private	private
Student/faculty ratio	17:1
Affiliation	Roman Catholic
% faculty part-time	51
% faculty female	28
% faculty minority	6
Total faculty	61

SURVEY SAYS . . .

Diverse opinions accepted in classrooms
Great research resources
Great library staff

STUDENTS

Enrollment of law school	474
% male/female	56/44
% out-of-state	63
% full-time	95
% minority	9
% international	1
# of countries represented	3
Average age of entering class	23

ACADEMICS

Academic experience rating	**82**
Professors interesting rating	86
Professors accessible rating	98
Hours of study per day	4.89

Academic Specialties

Commercial law, corporation securities law, criminal law, dispute resolution, international law, taxation, trial practice.

Combined Degrees Offered

JD/MBA, JD/master of science in information management technology, JD/master of arts in international relations. These combined degrees can each be completed in 3.5 years with summer study.

Academic Requirements

Clinical Program Required?	No
Legal Writing Course Requirement?	Yes
Legal Methods Course Requirement?	No

Academics

At Creighton University School of Law, expect to hit the books. At this rigorous law program, the curriculum is challenging and "the workload is extremely heavy," especially in the first year. As one Creighton student claims, "Law school is not for the faint of heart." In addition to the massive amounts of required reading, professors expect a lot in the classroom, encouraging critical thinking and interpretation of material, not just memorization. As one student tells us, "Every professor encourages and impresses upon each student to act, think, speak, and conduct his or herself as lawyers in the classroom. At Creighton, you are an individual, not just another student."

Despite the challenges, students love going to school at Creighton. While course work is tough, professors "keep torture sessions to a minimum [and] allow the student to ask any question, no matter how dumb." Most important, professors are always willing to provide extra assistance outside the classroom. In fact, students say the level of support they receive from the faculty has a major positive impact on their performance. A student enthuses, "Those who come from a large, public undergraduate school find themselves somewhat bewildered by the care that is taken to ensure that students have what they need to be successful. I find myself working harder than I otherwise might because I feel a need to justify all the expense of time and effort that these people spend on their students." Another student raves, "The research/writing faculty and staff are always available to assist with any questions and have significantly contributed to my legal research and writing skills so far."

The faculty at Creighton brings a wide range of backgrounds and experience to the program, giving students the option of learning about many different legal fields. A student relates, "The variety in the faculty's personalities, teaching styles, professional and personal backgrounds, and areas of expertise amaze me every time I start a new class." Another agrees, "Creighton is a great school and allows each individual student a chance to excel in every area." Students say that this broad-based, practical instruction pays off in the real world. One claims, "Having clerked with students from Harvard, Washington University in St. Louis, and Nebraska, I can honestly say I was in a better position than my colleagues when it came down to the practicalities behind the practice of law. Not only was I familiar with the substantive law, I was able to apply it with vigor and gain the confidence of my employer, allowing me to pursue larger projects than my co-workers." Even so, some students feel "the school could help a little more with specialization" and either offer more course selection, or "at least a broader offering of class times."

Administration at Creighton wins rave reviews. "I could not have asked for a more accommodating and helpful administrative group," says one student. Another says, "Everybody knows your name and is interested in what is currently going on in your life and where you would like to go with your law degree." Facilities are allegedly "so comfortable" that at least one student has "been found fast asleep in numerous places at school—several times." The "wonderful" library provides "private study rooms students can reserve" and a staff who are "always willing to help you locate whatever you are looking for." On Creighton's to-do list, however, should be "getting a reliable Internet connection for the campus, [and making] professors sit down and take a PowerPoint class over the summer."

Andrea D. Bashara, Assistant Dean
2500 California Plaza, Omaha, NE 68178
Telephone: 402-280-2872 • Fax: 402-280-3161
E-mail: lawadmit@creighton.edu • Website: http://culaw2.creighton.edu

Life

Creighton's small size makes for "very strong bonds between students." A mentoring program that begins during orientation further encourages a sense of community in the student body. One student explains, "We are placed into small groups of seven or eight people with two 2Ls as our mentors. It was comforting going the first day and knowing that I would be able to talk and hang out with people from my small group." And while there is a certain amount of competitiveness, it does not "create division among the students."

While Creighton students are a hard-working crowd, they are not opposed to a little "out-of-school fun." Students say, "The Student Bar Association throws many parties, [and] there is a wide range of school activities and organizations." And who doesn't want to meet their peers "in a different environment to see what they're actually like outside of law school?" Students seem happy with what they have found. In "classrooms as well as the social spheres," one of Creighton's "most fascinating aspects [is] the diversity in the student population."

Getting In

Creighton seeks students who will bring intelligence, diversity, and accomplishment to the program. Admissions evaluate these qualities through examining a candidate's undergraduate GPA, LSAT scores, personal statement, and letters of recommendation, as well as the strength of a student's undergraduate institution. Last year, the average admitted student had a GPA of 3.5 and an LSAT score of 154.

EMPLOYMENT INFORMATION

Career Rating	**67**
% employed within 9 months	98
Average starting salary	$45,822
State for bar exam	NE, IA, MO, AZ, IL
Pass rate for first-time bar	81

Employers who frequently hire grads: McGrath North, Kutak Rock, Fraser Stryker, Baird Holm, Koley Jessen, Blackwell Sanders, Stinson Morrison, Erickson Sederstrom, Fitzgerald Schorr.

Prominent Alumni: Michael O. Johanns, United States secretary of agriculture; Bruce C. Rohde, president and CEO/chairman, ConAgra Inc.

Grads employed by field (%):

Academic	3
Business/industry	20
Government	11
Judicial clerkships	6
Military	1
Other	1
Private practice	57
Public interest	1

Legal Research Course Requirement?	Yes
Moot Court Requirement?	Yes
Public Interest Law Requirement?	No

ADMISSIONS

Selectivity Rating	**73**
# applications received	1,282
# applicants accepted	501
# acceptees attending	162
Average LSAT	154
LSAT Range	152–157
Average undergrad GPA	3.5
Application fee	$45
Regular application deadline	5/1
Regular notification	rolling
Rolling notification?	Yes
Early application program?	No
Transfer students accepted?	Yes
Evening division offered?	No
Part-time accepted?	Yes
LSDAS accepted?	Yes

Applicants Also Look At

Drake University, Gonzaga University, University of Nebraska—Lincoln.

International Students

TOEFL required of international students?	No
TOEFL recommended of international students?	Yes

FINANCIAL FACTS

Annual tuition	$21,528
Books and supplies	$1,170
Fees per credit	$64
Tuition per credit	$715
Room & board	$12,500
Financial aid application deadline	3/1
% first-year students receiving some sort of aid	90
% receiving some sort of aid	90
% of aid that is merit-based	100
% receiving scholarships	40
Average grant	$8,670
Average loan	$25,300
Average total aid package	$38,000
Average debt	$75,910

DePaul University
College of Law

INSTITUTIONAL INFORMATION

Public/private	private
Student/faculty ratio	17:1
Affiliation	Roman Catholic
% faculty part-time	41
% faculty female	40
% faculty minority	13
Total faculty	100

SURVEY SAYS . . .

Diverse opinions accepted in classrooms
Great research resources
Students love Chicago, IL

STUDENTS

Enrollment of law school	1,111
% male/female	48/52
% out-of-state	45
% full-time	70
% minority	20
% international	1
# of countries represented	5
Average age of entering class	25

ACADEMICS

Academic experience rating	**70**
Professors interesting rating	68
Professors accessible rating	63
Hours of study per day	4.17

Academic Specialties

Commercial law, criminal law, human rights law, intellectual property law, international law, taxation, family law, health law, information technology law, public interest law.

Advanced Degrees Offered

LLM in health law, 1 to 3 years; LLM in taxation, 1 to 3 years; LLM in intellectual property law, 1 to 3 years.

Combined Degrees Offered

JD/MBA, 3 to 4 years; JD/MS in public service management, 4 years; JD/MA in international studies, 4 years; JD/MA in computer science, 4 years; JD/MS in computer science, 4 years.

Academics

DePaul University College of Law is "a good place for people who want to be a lawyer but still have a life." At DePaul, there is a "focus on practical aspects of law with the correct mix of philosophical analysis, [making it] a great place to get a well-rounded legal education." Students say they are impressed with classmates' "spirit of public service," and they rave about the highly touted intellectual property and health law programs. While the students are very dedicated to their studies, "the camaraderie is great."

DePaul's faculty is, perhaps, "the school's strongest suit." One student says, "Since coming to DePaul, I've had three of the best teachers I've ever had in my life. I've learned more in a year and a half than I had in 16 prior years of schooling." DePaul professors seem to have a certain flair that keeps students engaged and stimulated. One student tells us that the "professors have been hilarious and enthusiastic about teaching"—a spirit that's "infectious." Another adds, "My civil procedure professor not only made civ pro fascinating (a major feat in itself), but also instilled a desire and love for learning the law." Maybe it's because DePaul retains professors that are "not only bright legal scholars and lawyers, [but] can actually teach." Many agree "this makes for a very stimulating and challenging classroom environment."

For the most part, students are very frustrated with the law school's administration, calling it "aggravating, ineffective, and bogged down with red tape." One student claims the administration is a "distraction from my legal education," while another calls it a "nightmare." But on the flip side, a few students maintain that "the administration is awesome [and that] they really care about us." It seems that although the administration "can be very disorganized from time to time," the administrators, in the end, "manage to keep everything together."

According to most students, DePaul's classrooms could benefit from a face-lift. One student opines that the designer must have known "nothing about acoustics [and] didn't always take line of sight into consideration." Another student agrees that the classrooms "leave some thing to be desired [and that] their odd shape and pillars sometimes make hearing/seeing difficult." A third gripes, "The classrooms are ridiculously small and uninviting with no windows and extraordinarily uncomfortable seating." Furthermore, the rumbling of Chicago's nearby elevated train can also sometimes be a little distracting. On the positive side, the College of Law's classrooms do "provide students with wireless Internet access at no cost." The library, which is "beautiful and easily navigated," deserves mentioning as well.

Life

Located in the heart of Chicago's Loop, DePaul College of Law students believe "there are strong opportunities [thanks to] the location in Chicago and a huge alumni network." The Federal and Illinois State courthouses, Lake Michigan, and scores of law firms are only a few blocks from the campus. The proximity of the L train means the school is connected to the whole city, and many students live outside the neighborhood. But the convenience of being a "commuter campus" can have its downsides—as one student laments, DePaul "does not have the sense of community I had hoped for." Even so, many students would agree that DePaul has an "excellent student atmosphere socially." A satisfied 1L says, "My section was a good mix of students right out of college and those a bit older. There were social activities if people wanted to partake, and it was a very supportive atmosphere."

Michael S. Burns, Assistant Dean & Director of Admissions
25 East Jackson Boulevard, Chicago, IL 60604
Telephone: 312-362-6831 • Fax: 312-362-5280
E-mail: lawinfo@depaul.edu • Website: www.law.depaul.edu

The students seem to get along swimmingly. "It is amazing how the students here can manage to be so pleasant under the circumstances," one student tells us. "We all work together and help each other out emotionally and academically. We don't have that extremely competitive student that every law school class supposedly has." Another student explains, "There will always be the annoying guy in your class who asks stupid questions, but for the most part students get along well with each other. I am close friends with many of my classmates. [And although] everyone is competitive by nature, and everyone wants to do his or her best, [there] isn't anyone here who would deny help to a fellow student if asked."

While the students are committed to their studies, they do enjoy a healthy social life. While a few wish there were more "community-building programs (especially during orientation) by school administration," others say, "parties and get-togethers occur throughout the year, and there are enough student organizations around to make sure everyone's got something they can enjoy or identify with." Even the learned faculty partakes in some libations as one student reveals: "This is one of the few law schools I know of where students and faculty actually grab a beer together." At DePaul there seems to be that "perfect balance of career drive and social release among the student body."

Getting In

DePaul's College of Law enrolls around 1,100 students. Full-time enrolled students at the 25th percentile have an LSAT score of 156 and a GPA of 3.1. Full-time enrolled students at the 75th percentile have an LSAT score of 161 and a GPA of 3.5. More than 25 percent of DePaul's enrollment is in the evening program.

EMPLOYMENT INFORMATION

Career Rating	**73**
% employed within 9 months	94
Average starting salary	$60,101
State for bar exam	IL
Pass rate for first-time bar	84

Employers who frequently hire grads: Bell Boyd & Lloyd, Chapman and Cutler, Hinshaw & Culbertson, Kirkland & Ellis, Vedder Price Kaufman & Kammholz, Winston & Strawn, Cook County State's Attorney's Office.

Prominent Alumni: Richard M. Daley, mayor, City of Chicago; Mary Dempsey, commissioner, Chicago Public Library System; Frank Clark, president, ComEd.

Grads employed by field (%):	
Academic	2
Business/industry	17
Government	11
Judicial clerkships	3
Other	1
Private practice	62
Public interest	4

Academic Requirements

Clinical Program Required?	No
Legal Writing Course Requirement?	Yes
Legal Methods Course Requirement?	No
Legal Research Course Requirement?	Yes
Moot Court Requirement?	No
Public Interest Law Requirement?	No

ADMISSIONS

Selectivity Rating	**81**
# applications received	4,814
# applicants accepted	1,444
# acceptees attending	364
Average LSAT	159
LSAT Range	156–161
Average undergrad GPA	3.3
Application fee	$60
Regular application deadline	3/1
Regular notification	2/1
Rolling notification?	Yes
Early application program?	No
Transfer students accepted?	Yes
Evening division offered?	Yes
Part-time accepted?	Yes
LSDAS accepted?	Yes

Applicants Also Look At

Illinois Institute of Technology, Loyola University Chicago, University of Illinois at Urbana-Champaign.

International Students

TOEFL required of international students?	Yes
Minimum Paper TOEFL	550

FINANCIAL FACTS

Annual tuition	$27,560
Books and supplies	$1,200
Fees per credit	$100
Tuition per credit	$900
Room & board	$15,223
Financial aid application deadline	3/1
% first-year students receiving some sort of aid	94
% receiving some sort of aid	90
% of aid that is merit-based	12
% receiving scholarships	48
Average grant	$7,914
Average loan	$31,507
Average total aid package	$34,606
Average debt	$78,642

DRAKE UNIVERSITY
LAW SCHOOL

INSTITUTIONAL INFORMATION

Public/private	private
Student/faculty ratio	18:1
% faculty part-time	39
% faculty female	37
% faculty minority	7
Total faculty	46

SURVEY SAYS . . .

Diverse opinions accepted in classrooms
Great research resources
Great library staff

STUDENTS

Enrollment of law school	466
% male/female	51/49
% full-time	97
% minority	10
% international	1
# of countries represented	6
Average age of entering class	25

ACADEMICS

Academic experience rating	**77**
Professors interesting rating	76
Professors accessible rating	83
Hours of study per day	3.77

Academic Specialties

Constitutional law, agricultural law, legislative practice, litigation and dispute resolution.

Advanced Degrees Offered

JD, 3 years

Combined Degrees Offered

JD/MBA, JD/MPA, JD/PharmD, JD/MA political science, JD/MS agricultural economy.

Academic Requirements

Clinical Program Required?	No
Legal Writing Course Requirement?	Yes
Legal Methods Course Requirement?	Yes
Legal Research Course Requirement?	Yes
Moot Court Requirement?	Yes
Public Interest Law Requirement?	No

Academics

If you "actually want to experience what you'll do after law school instead of sitting around during class talking about what you'll do," consider Drake University Law School. "Anyone can look up statutes or analyze case law," asserts one student. "Drake shows you how to be a lawyer." To this end, there is a "strong focus on writing, research, and practical skills." For example, Drake is the only American law school where 1L classes stop for a week, so students can watch a jury trial. Also, the Legal Clinic and "unparalleled" Trial Practicum provide "exceptional real-world" experience. Drake's location in the state capital provides "access to clerkships and internships galore." There are also occasions when "nationally recognized legal experts" such as Michael McConnell and Akil Amar fly in to "teach week long seminars." The "intense and thorough" legal writing and research program is another "jewel." It's "time-consuming and demanding" but, in the end, "Drake clerks run circles around clerks from 'top tier' schools when it comes to writing briefs."

The "amazing [professors] are experienced attorneys who have great stories and advice." They are "knowledgeable, accessible, and genuinely concerned about your progress." One student gushes, "Passion for a profession is impossible to fake. The teachers want to help and actively encourage you to come to them with questions about the course, the law school experience, or future plans after school." Drake's Career Services is not so universally beloved. Many students tell us that it "needs an overhaul, [and that] if you want a clerking job or an associate position, you better hit the pavement and find it yourself." A few also say that "financial aid is a nightmare."

Facilities-wise, the classroom building "functions perfectly well [but is] a bit dated" and can be "drafty, cold, and dark." Drake's "highly functional yet gorgeous" library, on the other hand, is "a wonderful environment to research and study in." Students brag that their library is "one of the best law libraries in the country." As an added bonus, "almost every student is provided with a carrel in the library." And Drake can hang with most schools technologically. "The entire law school is connected through a wireless network, [and] there is always a computer available. Each classroom has wireless Internet access," too.

Overall, the biggest concern of Drake students is the university's ability to channel them into employment. One declares, "Sure, we're getting a great education. We come out knowing how to write a killer brief and how to argue it properly. But can we find a job that will pay us enough to shoulder our high-dollar education?" A few grumble, "Drake needs to be able to attract more firms to campus." It doesn't help that the university has "little-to-no name recognition outside of the Midwest." One student disappointingly says, "Des Moines is Drake's largest detriment to its reputation." However, the relocation of the American Judicature Society to the Drake campus has brought numerous opportunities to the students and faculty, including an enhanced judicial internship program and higher-caliber speakers on campus, and Drake's reputation in Des Moines and Iowa is "top-notch." If you plan to stay in-state, "there's probably not a better school to attend."

Kara Blanchard, Director of Admissions and Financial Aid
2507 University Avenue, Des Moines, IA 50311
Telephone: 515-271-2782 • Fax: 515-271-1990
E-mail: lawadmit@drake.edu • Website: www.law.drake.edu

Life

The relatively small student population at Drake is "largely white [and] upper-middle-class." There is a "definite division between people who are single and straight out of college and those who have worked for a few years and are married or in long-term relationships." Depending on whom you ask, Drake has either a "competitive atmosphere" or a "friendly and warm atmosphere." Perhaps it's both. One student differentiates, "Drake students are very competitive without being cutthroat." Students "focus on doing their best, and we try to push each other to do better." Naturally, "there will always be people who insist that their notes are the Holy Grail, but they are few and soon find themselves lonely." Most students are "open, friendly to everyone, [and] willing to help when asked." A student says, "One of the reasons I chose Drake was for its sense of community. I've made many, many friends, and we all have the pleasure of suffering through law school together."

In a word, life at Drake is balanced. "The balance of academics and social life is about as good as you can expect in law school," discloses a student. "We have the top Delta Theta Phi chapter (legal fraternity) in the nation here," agrees another student. "I think the SBA and the Delts here on campus do a tremendous job encouraging us to have a life outside of law school." Strong student organizations, monthly philanthropic events, and weekly Bar Reviews contribute to the definitely "good social atmosphere, [which is] available for anyone who wishes to leave the warmth and comfort of the library." Students tell us, "The school itself is located in the middle of the city, so it's not too hard to commute, and housing is available everywhere nearby." Also, "Des Moines offers a lot more opportunities than I ever thought it could," admits a stunned out-of-towner. You should know that Gruner & Jahr's *Fast Company* magazine named Des Moines the "Hippest City in the USA" in 2003. We are not making this up.

Getting In

Admitted students at the 25th percentile have an LSAT score of 152 and a GPA of 3.0. Admitted students at the 75th percentile have an LSAT score of 157 and a GPA of 3.7.

EMPLOYMENT INFORMATION

Career Rating	**76**
Job placement rate (%)	94
Average starting salary	$50,281
State for bar exam	IA, MN, MO, IL
Pass rate for first-time bar	82

Employers who frequently hire grads: Davis, Brown, Des Moines; Nyemaster, Goode, Des Moines; Jag Corps; Blackwell Sanders, Kansas City; Shughart Thompson, Kansas City.

Prominent Alumni: Dwight D. Opperman, CEO Publishing Company; Chief Justice Louis Lavarato, Iowa Supreme Court; Robert Ray, former governor; Terry Branstad, former governor.

Grads employed by field (%):	
Academic	2
Business/industry	14
Government	9
Judicial clerkships	4
Military	3
Other	3
Private practice	62
Public interest	3

ADMISSIONS

Selectivity Rating	**74**
# applications received	1,087
# applicants accepted	477
# acceptees attending	168
Average LSAT	155
LSAT Range	153–157
Average undergrad GPA	3.4
Application fee	$40
Regular application deadline	rolling
Regular notification	rolling
Rolling notification?	Yes
Early application program?	No
Transfer students accepted?	Yes
Evening division offered?	No
Part-time accepted?	Yes
LSDAS accepted?	Yes

Applicants Also Look At

Creighton University, Hamline University, University of Iowa, William Mitchell College of Law.

International Students

TOEFL required of international students?	Yes
Minimum Paper TOEFL	560

FINANCIAL FACTS

Annual tuition	$22,250
Books and supplies	$1,100
Tuition per credit	$775
Room & board (off-campus)	$11,000
Financial aid application deadline	3/1
% first-year students receiving some sort of aid	99
% receiving some sort of aid	99
% of aid that is merit-based	74
% receiving scholarships	55
Average grant	$9,082
Average loan	$24,800
Average total aid package	$34,750
Average debt	$65,500

Duke University

Duke University School of Law

INSTITUTIONAL INFORMATION

Public/private	private
Student/faculty ratio	12:1
% faculty part-time	33
% faculty female	41
% faculty minority	4
Total faculty	90

SURVEY SAYS . . .

Diverse opinions accepted in classrooms
Great research resources
Great library staff
Abundant externship/internship/clerkship opportunities

STUDENTS

Enrollment of law school	640
% male/female	55/45
% full-time	100
% minority	23
% international	1
Average age of entering class	25

ACADEMICS

Academic experience rating	**87**
Professors interesting rating	73
Professors accessible rating	83
Hours of study per day	4

Advanced Degrees Offered

JD, 3 years; LLM, 1 year; S/JD, 1 year, for international students only.

Combined Degrees Offered

JD/MA, 3.5 years, in cultural anthropology, East Asian studies, economics, English, forestry and environmental studies, history, humanities, philosophy, public policy studies, religion, romance studies; JD/MS, 3.5 years, in electrical and computer engineering, mechanical engineering; JD/MBA, JD/MPP, JD/MEM, JD/MTS, 4 years; JD/MD, 6 years; JD/PhD, 7 years; JD/LLM in international & comparative law, 3.5 years.

Academics

Duke School of Law offers "a highly intellectual, rigorous, and stimulating learning environment" where students have the opportunity to learn from some of the brightest legal minds in the country. Besides its stellar reputation, Duke's strengths include an excellent "international focus," a variety of clinical course offerings (including business law, children's education law, and AIDS law) and the joint degree program, which offers the convenient opportunity "to pursue a joint degree with one of Duke University's other graduate programs and still graduate with your class."

According to students, the "greatest strength of Duke Law is its professors," a group they describe as "experienced, very bright, [and] stars in their field." Professors at Duke are especially popular with students for their down-to-earth congeniality. A student writes, "I quickly find that even the most-impressive-on-paper professor is engaging, interesting, fun, challenging, and surprisingly accessible." In fact, professors "eat in the building's café with the students and are always available for a chat." Combine this accessibility with a small student body, and Duke students have the opportunity to get to know their professors on a personal level. One student attests, "There are at least 10 faculty members with whom I regularly talk about everything from my son's current cold to my ambitions 10 years down the road to the import of Holmes's dissent in Lochner."

While students rave about the academic curriculum, be forewarned that Duke's program is highly academic, stressing theory and critical thought over practical skills. Duke even offers a class on law and literature. While most students appreciate the intellectual approach, some would like to see more real-world instruction. A student suggests, "There needs to be more emphasis on practical legal skills—a drafting class would be especially nice." In particular, students feel that it is difficult to "do government or public interest work" with a degree from Duke. One student complains, "The high tuition at the school, coupled with a public interest loan forgiveness program that is less than completely adequate, practically rules out any work in the public sector after graduation.

As far as career options are concerned, "the bottom line [is that] if you go to Duke, you will get a good job." One student testifies, "All the top firms from the major markets come here to recruit," while another adds, "If you want to work in DC or NYC, Career Services can get you more interviews than you can count." He qualifies, however, that "you're on your own if you want to work in Topeka or even LA." While students at most law schools complain that Career Services caters to only the top students, Duke operates an unusual program, which gives every student an equal crack at job interviews. A student explains, "Duke has a lottery system for on-campus interviews—everyone gets a shot at every firm. They do not let the firms choose which students to interview. If you are not in the top 25 percent (and 75 percent of the people are in this category), this is incredibly important!" Perhaps this helps contribute to the "noncompetitive, collaborative" vibe that so many students praise.

Life

While most students choose Duke for its excellent reputation and strong academic programs, the warm North Carolinian climate doesn't hurt either. As one student tells us, "It is sunny and beautiful in Durham much of the year [making for] an upbeat, more well-adjusted law student." Duke is not a large party school; students are mostly mature and serious about their education. As one student explains, "We have a fairly wide range of ages but mainly mid-20s (so, not everyone is straight out of undergrad), which makes the

Dennis Shields, Associate Dean for Admissions and Financial Aid
PO Box 90393, Durham, NC 27708-0393
Telephone: 919-613-7020 • Fax: 919-613-7257
E-mail: admissions@law.duke.edu • Website: http://admissions.law.duke.edu

social life a bit more laid-back." But students "do their best to create a fun social life in otherwise dismal Durham with weekly bar reviews plus a few large parties throughout the year." Students believe that "while the City of Durham might not be the hot metropolis that other locations may be, [there is still] plenty to do—you just have to look a little bit harder for it."

Students describe their peers as "diverse, bright, friendly, and engaged group of students from across the country." Indeed, the accomplished student body is one of the best aspects of a Duke education. As one student gushes, "The students are of such a high caliber that I am constantly being challenged to work harder and learn more." On top of that, Duke students find their classmates to be quite friendly. "The collegial atmosphere is what sells most people on Duke Law. The students do not just study, they are involved, excited, and extremely social." This feeling is a result of the school's size, "since the Law School community is small, it is really easy to get involved in everything from student government to community service to fund-raising for the public law interest fund." Plus, as one student divulges, "The workload is reasonable enough that we still want to see each other when we leave school." What's not so cool is that a number of students mention that Duke's environment can sometimes be inhospitable for women. One student finds professors are fair, but says, "I do not think the male students treat women equally."

Getting In

Admission to Duke Law is highly competitive. Duke looks for students with outstanding academic records and LSAT scores, coupled with a strong background in community service, graduate study, or professional work. Most admits were at the top of their undergraduate class, with the average GPA of 3.7. Applications can be submitted after October 1, and students are admitted on a rolling basis from that date forward.

EMPLOYMENT INFORMATION

Career Rating	**91**
% employed within 9 months	100
Average starting salary	$110,000
State for bar exam	NY, NC, CA, MD, VA
Pass rate for first-time bar	90

Employers who frequently hire grads:
More than 400 law firms annually offer positions to Duke law students.

Grads employed by field (%):	
Business/industry	3
Government	4
Judicial clerkships	15
Other	5
Private practice	70
Public interest	3

Academic Requirements

Clinical Program Required?	No
Legal Writing Course Requirement?	Yes
Legal Methods Course Requirement?	Yes
Legal Research Course Requirement?	Yes
Moot Court Requirement?	Yes
Public Interest Law Requirement?	No

ADMISSIONS

Selectivity Rating	**93**
# applications received	4,099
# applicants accepted	869
# acceptees attending	219
Average LSAT	168
LSAT Range	162–169
Average undergrad GPA	3.7
Application fee	$70
Regular application deadline	1/1
Regular notification	rolling
Rolling notification?	Yes
Early application program?	No
Transfer students accepted?	Yes
Evening division offered?	No
Part-time accepted?	No
LSDAS accepted?	Yes

International Students

TOEFL required of international students?	Yes
Minimum Paper TOEFL	600

FINANCIAL FACTS

Annual tuition	$33,870
Books and supplies	$1,300
Room & board (off-campus)	$8,750
Financial aid application deadline	3/15
% first-year students receiving some sort of aid	88
% receiving some sort of aid	81
% receiving scholarships	65
Average grant	$8,000
Average loan	$33,500
Average debt	$82,000

EMORY UNIVERSITY
SCHOOL OF LAW

INSTITUTIONAL INFORMATION

Public/private	private
Student/faculty ratio	14:1
Affiliation	Methodist
% faculty female	41
% faculty minority	11
Total faculty	56

SURVEY SAYS . . .

Diverse opinions accepted in classrooms

Students love Atlanta, GA

STUDENTS

Enrollment of law school	685
% male/female	49/51
% out-of-state	80
% full-time	100
% minority	22
% international	2
# of countries represented	12
Average age of entering class	22

ACADEMICS

Academic experience rating	**91**
Professors interesting rating	95
Professors accessible rating	89
Hours of study per day	4.26

Academic Specialties

Business law, comparative law, constitutional law, criminal law, environmental law, health law, human rights law, intellectual property law, international law, labor law, law & religion, legal theory, taxation, trial practice.

Advanced Degrees Offered

LLM, 1 year.

Combined Degrees Offered

JD/MBA, 4 years; JD/MTS, 4 years; JD/MDIV, 5 years; JD/MPH, 3.5 years; JD/LLM, 4 years; JD/REES, 3 years; JD/PhD religion, 5 years; JD/MA Judaic studies, 4 years.

Academic Requirements

Clinical Program Required?	No
Legal Writing Course Requirement?	Yes
Legal Methods Course Requirement?	Yes

Academics

Emory University School of Law has a lot going for it: "Strong academics, a location in a major city, strong alumni ties to the area, very bright, diverse students from all over the country, [and] most of all, a very laid-back, fun-loving atmosphere." Is it any wonder that students at Emory are happy? Professors are compared to those at a "small, liberal arts college." Students say Emory "has the faculty and research facilities that make it comparable to an Ivy League school, [with students who are] more relaxed and less competitive." There seems to be the impression among students that Emory's already good reputation is on its way up. "The law school at Emory is a star that is still rising. Emory Law School markedly improves itself each year in its facilities, technology, and most important, its faculty."

Emory students are absolutely crazy about their "dedicated, brilliant, [and] eccentric" professors, who wow them with their "phenomenally far-sighted and penetrating wisdom." These professors, with their "very impressive educational backgrounds, [have] clerked for the Supreme Court, won cases before the Supreme Court, headed up major government agencies like the EEOC, assisted other countries in creating democratic governments, and pioneered new schools of thought." But don't think they are intimidating or unapproachable—these "accessible" professors "are all real people and surprisingly cool outside of the classroom."

A little more about the classes: "Emory Law is incredibly good at providing students with practical experiences useful for 'real-world' lawyering." There is an "emphasis on legal writing and researching" that you do not see at many other schools. In addition to "the year-long intensive research, writing, and oral advocacy program" for 1Ls, Emory requires every second-year student to complete a "nationally recognized" trial techniques program." Course work is largely "corporate-oriented," but there are "a lot of programs for volunteer work [including] a very strong and well-supported public interest program in environmental law." Programs like "the Student Legal Services program, the Emory Public Interest Summer grants, and a wealth of judicial externships" provide additional opportunities for students to receive experience and credit hours. Several cool dual degree programs are available through the School of Theology as well.

Emory's facilities are a mixed bag. Students say the "campus is beautiful [and] very pleasant to walk around," and they adore the library, "a beautiful, modern and luminous facility that has the latest in modern technology." But other areas could surely stand to be updated. "Classrooms are cold and institutional," and, we hear the common area—to which students grimly refer as "the bus station" is very ugly [and] horribly outdated." Furthermore, Emory is "not very high tech, either. "Too few computers and a very slow network" frustrate many students. Fortunately, wireless networking has recently been implemented throughout the school.

Job prospects for Emory grads are nothing short of stellar thanks to a "strong alumni network [and a] very helpful" mentor program that "matches first-year students up with lawyers in Atlanta." Students say mentoring provides "opportunities to get practical experience, even in the first year" and, more important, "allows students to make contacts in the legal profession." The upshot is that job offers at large firms in the southeast are plentiful (although employment in New York, Boston, and DC can be "hard to get").

Lynell A. Cadray, Assistant Dean for Admissions
1301 Clifton Road, Atlanta, GA 30322-2770
Telephone: 404-727-6802 • Fax: 404-727-2477
E-mail: lawinfo@law.emory.edu • Website: www.law.emory.edu

Life

Emory is home to "an extremely intelligent student body," if students do say so themselves. Many report, "There is a lot of diversity, geographically and ethnically, for a school in the south," although a few wish for more "diversity—and not just racial diversity," but diversity in student ages and socioeconomic backgrounds. Politically, Emory students run the gamut. One student tells us, "I have friends who are extremely liberal (socialist) and friends who adore Dubya, Dick, and the gang. All in all, the political spectrum balances out to a fairly moderate environment."

Students say, "There is an atmosphere of collegiality and camaraderie that pervades" the school. Competition is reportedly moderate. Students report, "Our class is very driven, and everyone takes their work very seriously, but not so much that the environment is ultra-competitive." One student notes, "There are always people chilling all over the school, and it is mainly a very relaxing atmosphere that doesn't give off a very stressful vibe at all." In terms of clothing, "jeans and pajamas are the pretty standard wardrobe, which makes everything incredibly casual."

Socially, everyone seems to be thrilled to be attending a "top law school in an inexpensive city [that is] fun for young people." Emory boasts "a great location a few miles north of the city, making it easily accessible to nightlife and restaurants." You'll find "lots of great shopping," too. "Hotlanta" offers "a bar scene for every mood, [and] there is definitely a still-like-to-go-out-like-I'm-in-college crowd, but most people are more moderate." We hear "many students like to work hard during the week and then go out together on the weekends." And Atlanta, "with a population of around 4.5 million people," is a great place from which to "escape the law school fish bowl every once in a while."

Getting In

Emory receives over 4,000 applications every year for its entering class of just over 200 students. Suffice it to say, admission is competitive. The average undergraduate GPA of admitted students is 3.4. The average LSAT score is 164.

EMPLOYMENT INFORMATION

Career Rating	**87**
Job placement rate (%)	93
Average starting salary	$74,345
State for bar exam	GA, NY, NJ, FL, CA
Pass rate for first-time bar	93

Employers who frequently hire grads: Alston & Bird; Arent Fox; Arnall Golden Gregory; Arnold & Porter; Atlanta Legal Aid Society; Chadbourne & Parke; Crowell & Moring; Holland & Knight; Jones Day; Kilpatrick Stockton; King & Spalding.

Prominent Alumni: Honorable Sanford Bishop, U.S. congressman; Honorable Leah Sears, chief justice, Georgia Supreme Court.

Grads employed by field (%):	
Academic	1
Business/industry	9
Government	13
Judicial clerkships	11
Military	1
Private practice	64
Public interest	1

Legal Research Course Requirement?	Yes
Moot Court Requirement?	No
Public Interest Law Requirement?	No

ADMISSIONS

Selectivity Rating	**87**
# applications received	3,852
# applicants accepted	1,016
# acceptees attending	215
Average LSAT	164
LSAT Range	161–165
Average undergrad GPA	3.4
Application fee	$70
Regular application deadline	3/1
Regular notification	rolling
Rolling notification?	Yes
Early application program?	No
Transfer students accepted?	Yes
Evening division offered?	No
Part-time accepted?	No
LSDAS accepted?	Yes

Applicants Also Look At

Boston College, Boston University, Duke University, Fordham University, The George Washington University, Georgetown University, Vanderbilt University.

International Students

TOEFL required of international students?	Yes
Minimum Paper TOEFL	600
Minimum Computer TOEFL	250

FINANCIAL FACTS

Annual tuition	$34,700
Books and supplies	$1,852
Room & board	$13,176
Financial aid application deadline	2/15
% first-year students receiving some sort of aid	87
% receiving some sort of aid	81
% of aid that is merit-based	35
% receiving scholarships	30
Average grant	$19,739
Average loan	$32,286
Average total aid package	$37,561
Average debt	$82,556

FLORIDA INTERNATIONAL UNIVERSITY*

COLLEGE OF LAW

INSTITUTIONAL INFORMATION

Public/private	public
Student/faculty ratio	15:1
% faculty part-time	15
% faculty female	42
% faculty minority	58
Total faculty	24

SURVEY SAYS . . .

Diverse opinions accepted in classrooms
Great research resources
Great library staff

STUDENTS

Enrollment of law school	271
% male/female	54/46
% out-of-state	4
% full-time	61
% minority	50
Average age of entering class	29

ACADEMICS

Academic experience rating	**81**
Professors interesting rating	90
Professors accessible rating	80
Hours of study per day	3.31

Combined Degrees Offered

JD/MSW, master of social work, 4.5 years; JD/MPA, master of public administration, 3.5 years; JD/MIB, master of international business); 3.5 years, JD/MSPsych, master of science in psychology, 4 years; JD/MALACS, master of Latin America and Caribbean studies), 3.5 years.

Academic Requirements

Clinical Program Required?	No
Legal Writing Course Requirement?	Yes
Legal Methods Course Requirement?	Yes
Legal Research Course Requirement?	Yes
Moot Court Requirement?	No
Public Interest Law Requirement?	Yes

Academics

At the brand-new Florida International University College of Law, "students and faculty all work together to improve the college," promoting a spirit of camaraderie, conscientiousness, and cooperation on campus. Having received provisional ABA accreditation in 2004, the school is quickly building its course offerings, teaching faculty, and regional reputation. Students love "the opportunity to be a part of the foundation of a rising law school" and applaud the strides the school has made in just three years of operation. As a 2L says, "I have been very impressed by the faculty and the administration because they developed a reasonably broad range of courses, including an evening program, while at the same time keeping the college on track for provisional accreditation at the earliest possible time. I give them all an A-plus."

At FIU, "the faculty is excited about teaching in a new school," a sentiment that translates into lively and engaging academic atmosphere. Having recently recruited and hired the entire teaching staff, you won't have any old, stodgy, tenured lecturers at FIU. "Our greatest strength is definitely in our faculty," says one student. "There is no dead weight here—only live wires!" Indeed, FIU students insist that "professors are top-notch across the board." On top of that, for a public school price tag, students point to many benefits of a tiny, private school. Despite the "cheap cost," the school maintains a small student body, keeping total enrollment under 300 students. FIU students report a strong sense of campus community; most classes are reasonably sized, and students have the opportunity to build strong relationships with the school's talented teaching staff. One contented 3L says, "We have a small student body, creating a fantastic sense of collegiality."

While FIU's forward-thinking attitude is apparently unequivocally appreciated, there are a few drawbacks to studying at a newer institution. In particular, the school is awaiting completion of the permanent law school building, using a number of temporary and makeshift facilities while finishing up construction. "Sitting in a cramped class on the first floor of the university's main library four nights a week is not exactly my idea of a true law school experience," says one 3L. While the classrooms aren't exactly comfortable, FIU doesn't lack any of the important amenities, such as a functional library or ample student areas: "Although we are awaiting completion of our law building, the research facilities we currently have are sufficient." Students are also quick to point out that "it's a new law school, and most of its shortcomings, such as the facilities, are in the process of being addressed."

FIU was founded in 2000 with the mission to serve the legal needs of Florida residents and residents of South Florida in particular. During their studies, FIU students have the opportunity to "make a substantial impact on the local community" through the school's clinical program and community-service program. In fact, students are required to participate in the community-service program, through which they participate in pro bono legal work in underserved Miami communities. After graduation, this real-world experience pays off—and FIU students have something of a corner on the Miami market. By all accounts, there are "many opportunities for local employment" in surrounding Miami, and FIU students are in the unique position to influence and direct Florida law.

*Provisionally approved by the ABA.

Alma O. Miró, Director of Admissions and Financial Aid
FIU College of Law, Office of Admissions and Financial Aid, GL 475, Miami, FL 33199
Telephone: 305-348-8006 • Fax: 305-348-2965
E-mail: lawadmit@fiu.edu • Website: http://law.fiu.edu

Life

While the physical facility is still under construction, FIU has nonetheless built a strong, friendly campus community. In fact, many students say that "the greatest strength of the law school is the non-competitive, tight-knit environment that exists" between classmates. Despite the rigors of course work, FIU maintains a largely cooperative environment. According to a 1L, "People seem to have their priorities in the right place and are not neurotic about competition, which is what I hear happens in other contexts." In fact, students "tend to depend on each other for help and understanding. Whenever times are stressful or confusing, you can always count on a fellow student for help or class notes. Maybe it's because we are a newly formed law school, or maybe it's the city of Miami. Either way, it's great!"

Outside the classroom, students say they get along well with their amiable and interesting classmates. A 3L says, "I know everyone in my class pretty well, and there's not a person among them I wouldn't cross the street to say hello to if I saw them outside of school." However, many of the evening students scoff at the idea of meeting their colleagues for dinner or drinks after class: "Most of us don't have a social life, neither in school nor outside it. There are just so many hours in a day."

Getting In

Florida International University College of Law "seeks to enroll a diverse group of students who have demonstrated academic and personal achievement." In addition to a student's undergraduate transcript and LSAT scores, the Admissions Committee evaluates a student's demonstrated leadership ability, ethics, commitment to public service, and understanding of global issues.

ADMISSIONS

Selectivity Rating	**80**
# applications received	1,091
# applicants accepted	203
# acceptees attending	113
Average LSAT	154
LSAT Range	151–156
Average undergrad GPA	3.2
Application fee	$20
Regular application deadline	6/1
Regular notification	rolling
Rolling notification?	Yes
Early application program?	No
Transfer students accepted?	Yes
Evening division offered?	Yes
Part-time accepted?	Yes
LSDAS accepted?	Yes

Applicants Also Look At

Barry University, Florida State University, Nova Southeastern University, St. Thomas University, Stetson University, University of Florida, University of Miami.

International Students

TOEFL required of international students?	Yes
Minimum Paper TOEFL	550
Minimum Computer TOEFL	213

FINANCIAL FACTS

Annual tuition (resident)	$7,893
Annual tuition (nonresident)	$28,511
Books and supplies	$2,096
Fees per credit (resident)	$255
Fees per credit (nonresident)	$920
Tuition per credit (resident)	$255
Tuition per credit (nonresident)	$920
Room & board (on/off-campus)	$8,860/$9,346
Financial aid application deadline	3/1
% first-year students receiving some sort of aid	68
% receiving some sort of aid	71
% of aid that is merit-based	20
% receiving scholarships	43
Average grant	$4,602
Average loan	$16,772
Average total aid package	$18,727

Florida State University
College of Law

INSTITUTIONAL INFORMATION

Public/private	public
Student/faculty ratio	14:1

SURVEY SAYS . . .

Diverse opinions accepted in classrooms
Great research resources
Great library staff
Students love Tallahassee, FL

STUDENTS

Enrollment of law school	753
% male/female	53/47
% out-of-state	25
% full-time	100
% faculty minority	22
% international	1
Average age of entering class	24

ACADEMICS

Academic experience rating	**85**
Professors interesting rating	84
Professors accessible rating	83
Hours of study per day	4.12

Academic Specialties
Business law, environmental law, international law.

Advanced Degrees Offered
JD, minimum 88 credit hours to graduate; LLM in American law for foreign lawyers; international law certificate program; environmental, natural resources, and land use law certificate program.

Combined Degrees Offered
JD/MBA, JD/MS URP, JD/MS IA, JD/MS economics, JD/MPA, JD/MS SW, JD/MS LIS. Most programs take 4 years to complete.

Academic Requirements

Clinical Program Required?	No
Legal Writing Course Requirement?	Yes
Legal Methods Course Requirement?	Yes
Legal Research Course Requirement?	Yes
Moot Court Requirement?	No

Academics

Students at Florida State University College of Law tell us their school is a "hidden gem for good students who don't want the typical law school pressure cooker." The "bright, friendly" student body enjoys the sense of "community one would find in a small school," while benefiting from "the technological and logistical advantages one might find in a larger law school in a larger city." Strengths include the capital location, which "makes for great opportunities for clerkships or externships around town" and an esteemed environmental and land use law program. And at around $20,000 for three years' in-state tuition, the price is difficult to beat.

Most students agree that professors are "great, knowledgeable, experienced, [and] very accessible to students both in and out of class." One student tells us, "Regardless of whether I have had the professor in class or not, I know I can come to him or her with a legal question, and that he or she will take the time to help me." Another expounds that profs are "ridiculously intelligent, [some of them] extremely friendly and funny and easy to relate to despite their achievements—people you'd like to be friends with." It may be because the school hires professors who are "experts in their field, highly knowledgeable, and eager to share their experiences and expertise." As one student points out, "When you read a case and have your professor say, 'When I wrote the brief for the Supreme Court,' you know you are in the right place."

The students feel the administration overall is doing a pretty good job. The "young, energetic [staff] go out of their way to make the students feel like the school is honored to have us there." The Career Placement Office sets up "seminars or personal meetings to help students out with any job-hunting needs." Overall, administration is found to be "easily accessible and very responsive to the students."

The classrooms "are very technologically advanced" and include "wireless networking, televisions, digital blackboard equipment, [and] video recording technology." But in the past, students felt that the technology "could use a little tweaking." FSU College of Law has since invested significant staff and financial resources to improve technology. A few other things could also use improvement. "The classrooms and the library are really ugly," one student grumbles, but "they do their job well." Another would like to see "more classrooms and wider hallways." We hear that the library doubles as a hang-out spot—it may "sometimes seem more like a social gathering than a place to study, [so] you get a chance to meet all of your classmates and have opportunities to socialize with classmates outside of the law school setting."

SHARON J. BOOKER, DIRECTOR OF ADMISSIONS AND RECORDS
425 WEST JEFFERSON STREET, TALLAHASSEE, FL 32306-1601
TELEPHONE: 850-644-3787 • FAX: 850-644-7284
E-MAIL: ADMISSIONS@LAW.FSU.EDU • WEBSITE: WWW.LAW.FSU.EDU

Life

The law school is a government enthusiast's dream being only a "stone's throw away from the Capitol building and the Florida Supreme Court [in] beautiful downtown Tallahassee." There are plenty of social events, and students "often meet on the weekends to go on trips together, attend sporting events, [or just to] spend time together in large groups." And we can only imagine that year-round warm weather creates a nice backdrop for these activities.

The school helps facilitate Florida State's "real sense of camaraderie" in several ways. The SBA, for example, "makes it a point to provide opportunities for students to relax and socialize," while the school coordinates Thursday night socials that really allow everyone an opportunity to bond on more than just an academic level." And drinking is not the only thing the SBA coordinates—they "recently held a clothing drive for a local shelter, and many SBA students mentor local elementary children." Overall, the "we're-going-to-get-through-this-together" vibe seems to minimize competitiveness and give students a healthy sense of community.

FSU is "unlike most schools in which the students are in heated competition with one another; here there is a strong sense of camaraderie." One student says, "As a whole the law school is a close-knit community. I enjoy knowing students here." Although other students seem to think the community is a little too close-knit, complaining that FSU "is like a high school—students seem to hang out in cliques."

Getting In

At Florida State University College of Law, admitted students at the 25th percentile have an LSAT score of 156 and a GPA of 3.3. Admitted students at the 75th percentile have an LSAT score of 162 and a GPA of 3.7. Applications are accepted between October 1 and February 15. There is no part-time or evening program at FSU.

EMPLOYMENT INFORMATION

Career Rating	**77**
% employed within 9 months	99
Average starting salary	$54,386
State for bar exam	FL
Pass rate for first-time bar	85

Employers who frequently hire grads:
Akerman Senterfitt; Alston & Bird LLP; Arnstein & Lehr LLP; Broad & Cassel; Carlton Fields, PA; Foley & Lardner; Gray Robinson; Greenberg Traurig, LLP; Holland & Knight LLP; Hopping, Green, & Sams, P.A.; Stearns, Weaver, Miller, Weissler, Alhadeff, & Sitterson, P.A.; Steel Hector & Davis, LLP; federal and state judges; federal and state agencies.

Grads employed by field (%):	
Business/industry	6
Government	30
Judicial clerkships	7
Private practice	53
Public interest	3

Public Interest Law Requirement?	Yes

ADMISSIONS

Selectivity Rating	**86**
# applications received	4,225
# applicants accepted	828
# acceptees attending	243
Average LSAT	159
LSAT Range	156–161
Average undergrad GPA	3.4
Application fee	$30
Regular application deadline	2/15
Regular notification	rolling
Rolling notification?	Yes
Early application program?	No
Transfer students accepted?	Yes
Evening division offered?	No
Part-time accepted?	No
LSDAS accepted?	Yes

Applicants Also Look At

American University, Duke, Emory University, Stetson University, Tulane University, University of Florida, University of Georgia, University of Miami, University of North Carolina at Chapel Hill.

International Students

TOEFL required of international students?	Yes
Minimum Paper TOEFL	600

FINANCIAL FACTS

Annual tuition (resident)	$7,505
Annual tuition (nonresident)	$27,517
Books and supplies	$1,000
Room & board	$10,000
Financial aid application deadline	2/15
% first-year students receiving some sort of aid	85
% receiving some sort of aid	85
% of aid that is merit-based	40
% receiving scholarships	36
Average grant	$1,200
Average loan	$19,415
Average total aid package	
Average debt	$43,644

Fordham University
School of Law

INSTITUTIONAL INFORMATION

Public/private	private
Student/faculty ratio	17:1
Affiliation	Roman Catholic
% faculty female	37
% faculty minority	17
Total faculty	214

SURVEY SAYS . . .

Diverse opinions accepted in classrooms
Abundant externship/internship/clerkship opportunities
Students love New York, NY

STUDENTS

Enrollment of law school	1,546
% male/female	48/52
% out-of-state	41
% full-time	77
% minority	25
% international	2
# of countries represented	9
Average age of entering class	25

ACADEMICS

Academic experience rating	**86**
Professors interesting rating	82
Professors accessible rating	72
Hours of study per day	4.36

Academic Specialties

Civil procedure, commercial law, constitutional law, corporation securities law, criminal law, environmental law, government services, human rights law, intellectual property law, international law, labor law, legal history, legal philosophy, property, taxation.

Advanced Degrees Offered

JD, 3 yrs FT, 4 yrs PT; LLM, 1 yr FT.

Combined Degrees Offered

JD/MBA w/Fordham Grad School of Business, 4 yrs FT; JD/MSW w/Fordham Grad School of Social Work, 4 yrs FT; JD/MA w/the Graduate School of Arts and Science, concentration in international political economic development.

Academics

Known as "the Friendly Law School" of New York City, Fordham University is an amiable oasis within the hustle and bustle of its hometown. While the curriculum is indisputably difficult, Fordham students are guided through the myriad challenges they face with the encouragement and support of the school's accomplished faculty, who "are available, encouraging, incredibly knowledgeable of their subject matter, interesting, and personable. They take time and view students as people and individuals with whom they are working." Inside the classroom, Fordham professors are "genuinely enthusiastic about teaching" and "truly want their students to go beyond basic understanding of the law." The overall effect is an "extremely challenging intellectual environment" that is somehow "less mind-boggling" than its reputable name might suggest.

Many professors join the Fordham faculty with impressive professional experience. "I've been taught by judges, senior partners, authors, and participants on federal rule boards. One professor is actually the Chief Judge Emeritus of the United States Court of International Trade. Can't beat their backgrounds," is how one 3L puts it. Students also point out that "in addition to the already strong faculty, the school has added young, smart, and energetic people during the last few years." The teaching staff is, therefore, "a good mix of practicing lawyers and theoretical academics," creating excellent equilibrium between real-world and academic skills in the curriculum.

There is an "incredible range of courses and activities" at Fordham, and "the clinical and externship opportunities are unsurpassed and a great way to network and get valuable practical experience." Of the many special programs and courses offered at Fordham, the "Crowley Program in International Human Rights is unmatched in any other school because it gives students the opportunity to do actual hands-on human rights fieldwork in a third world country and publish a report about it." In the extracurricular arena, Fordham students get plenty of career experience in New York City and brag that "there is no more convenient location for externships, part-time work, or conducting your job search." But while "the location of the school is spectacular," students warn that "Fordham's building is not its forte" and that classroom facilities are "slightly outdated and not comparable to other schools in the same range of cost and prestige."

Upon graduation, prospects are good for Fordham grads. Located in "the center of the legal world" and "well known in the regional marketplace," the school affords direct access to a multitude of excellent career opportunities. Students maintain that "the Career Planning Center is great" and will go to great lengths to help students land a plum position. "Even if you don't get a summer job, they will help you," reports one student. "I didn't, and as a 3L, I still got into 'big law' with their help." Students who are interested in working in public interest law claim that the Career Planning Center places "too much emphasis on large law firms." However, "the Public Interest Resource Center is terrific and staffed with amazing people" who can help civic-minded students find ways to put their training to public use. Students can also turn to instructors, as "many professors will go to extraordinary lengths to help students get the best jobs." In addition to these resources, "Fordham law alumni really look out for the law students, and the network is extremely strong." As a result of all these conduits into legal careers, you will find "Fordham law students at all of the best firms in the country."

JOHN CHALMERS, ASSISTANT DEAN OF ADMISSIONS
140 WEST SIXTY-SECOND STREET, NEW YORK, NY 10023
TELEPHONE: 212-636-6810 • FAX: 212-636-7984
E-MAIL: LAWADMISSIONS@LAW.FORDHAM.EDU • WEBSITE: HTTP://LAW.FORDHAM.EDU

Life

With a prime location on the west side of Manhattan, you might think the Fordham campus would get swallowed up in the noise of the city, leaving little by way of campus culture. Not so. At Fordham, "it's like you're not even in NYC when you walk through the doors, but a small town, where you're friends with everyone." On campus, students are encouraged to socialize, and "the school offers tons of pizza, ice cream, and cupcake nights, passes out free movie tickets, and has different speakers each week on pertinent topics to keep you in touch with the real world." True to its moniker, "the Friendly Law School," students describe Fordham as an "incredibly welcoming environment." How welcoming? "The cafeteria woman, Gloria, regularly inquires how we are doing and encourages us . . . we give and get hugs from 'Mom.' It's just too good for words," enthuses a 3L.

The diverse student body at Fordham Law School reflects its urban environs. Fordham also "tends to attract older students who have worked in a variety of professional fields." By all accounts, diversity is an asset to the educational experience, and "having these diverse perspectives in the classroom have been tremendously beneficial." While differing opinions are common, contention and competition are rare. A 2L explains, "The school is very respectful of the students' diverse backgrounds, including ethnic, religious, and sexual orientations," and there is a "sense of camaraderie among students and alumni." The diversity and social opportunities on campus are further enhanced by the school's propitious location in the urban environment of New York City. A 3L attests that "the location of the school is probably one of the best in the whole country, being situated in the middle of NYC. Cultural, political, and recreational activities are all practically within walking distance."

Getting In

Fordham receives about 7,500 applications for 480 first-year seats. That means it has to be quite selective, admitting only those students with a strong academic background and a high level of achievement in their undergraduate curriculum. The middle 50 percent of applicants submitted LSAT scores between 163–167 and had an undergraduate GPA between 3.4 and 3.8.

EMPLOYMENT INFORMATION

Career Rating	**93**
% employed within 9 months	98
Average starting salary	$101,516
State for bar exam	NY, CA, FL, DC, PA
Pass rate for first-time bar	88

Employers who frequently hire grads:
Cahill Gordon & Reindel; U.S. Department of Justice; Simpson, Thacher, & Bartlett; New York legal aid; Skadden, Arps, Slate, Meagher, & Flom; AT&T; Merrill Lynch; U.S. courts.

Grads employed by field (%):	
Academic	1
Business/industry	10
Government	5
Judicial clerkships	3
Private practice	77
Public interest	2

Academic Requirements

Clinical Program Required?	No
Legal Writing Course Requirement?	Yes
Legal Methods Course Requirement?	Yes
Legal Research Course Requirement?	Yes
Moot Court Requirement?	No
Public Interest Law Requirement?	No

ADMISSIONS

Selectivity Rating	**92**
# applications received	7,598
# applicants accepted	1,467
# acceptees attending	479
Average LSAT	165
LSAT Range	163–167
Average undergrad GPA	3.7
Application fee	$65
Regular application deadline	3/1
Regular notification	rolling
Rolling notification?	Yes
Early application program?	No
Transfer students accepted?	Yes
Evening division offered?	Yes
Part-time accepted?	Yes
LSDAS accepted?	Yes

Applicants Also Look At
Boston College, Boston University, Brooklyn Law School, Columbia University, The George Washington University, New York University, Yeshiva University.

International Students

TOEFL required of international students?	No
TOEFL recommended of international students?	Yes
Minimum Paper TOEFL	650

FINANCIAL FACTS

Annual tuition	$32,750
Books and supplies	$865
Room & board	$14,645
% first-year students receiving some sort of aid	92
% receiving some sort of aid	94
% of aid that is merit-based	7
% receiving scholarships	38
Average grant	$8,846
Average loan	$18,500
Average total aid package	$19,200
Average debt	$83,789

George Mason University
School of Law

INSTITUTIONAL INFORMATION

Public/private	public
Student/faculty ratio	15:1
% faculty part-time	68
% faculty female	21
% faculty minority	4
Total faculty	117

SURVEY SAYS . . .

Great research resources
Students love Arlington, VA

STUDENTS

Enrollment of law school	723
% male/female	63/37
% out-of-state	22
% full-time	55
% faculty minority	15
% international	3
# of countries represented	17
Average age of entering class	26

ACADEMICS

Academic experience rating	**87**
Professors interesting rating	76
Professors accessible rating	72
Hours of study per day	4.24

Academic Specialties

Civil procedure, corporation securities law, criminal law, government services, intellectual property law, international business law, international law, regulatory law taxation, technology law.

Advanced Degrees Offered

LLM, a post-JD degree specializing in intellectual property or law and economics.

Academic Requirements

Clinical Program Required?	No
Legal Writing Course Requirement?	Yes
Legal Methods Course Requirement?	No
Legal Research Course Requirement?	Yes
Moot Court Requirement?	Yes
Public Interest Law Requirement?	No

Academics

Located in the suburbs of Washington, DC, George Mason University School of Law is a "young rising star" among law schools with an "extremely challenging" curriculum and "dirt cheap" in-state tuition. George Mason's "über-economic approach to learning the law," means that "First-year students are required to take a course on basic economics, [and] there is a heavy emphasis on economics in almost all required courses." Not suprisingly, students tell us GMU is "a conservative or libertarian law school."

Mason's "very rankings-conscious" administration is "extremely helpful and accessible." And the "extremely intelligent [and] dedicated [professors] exhibit serious enthusiasm in the classroom," and take an "encouraging yet challenging attitude toward students." Perhaps the faculty is so "extraordinary" because the location "provides a deep pool of accomplished professionals from which to hire professors." Some students think that the faculty is "too conservative" and "have trouble keeping their personal views to themselves," but others say "the faculty is not afraid to engage in discussions of all schools of thought."

The legal research and writing program leaves students bitterly divided. It's an eight-credit, four-semester affair that trains students comprehensively in, among other things, brief writing; oral argument; and drafting of wills, contracts, and legislation. Some students call the program "top-notch [and] outstanding." One happy legal writer says, "I have noticed a clear improvement in my writing skills. As a summer associate, I was complimented and recognized on my legal writing ability." But critics call the writing program "too time-consuming and intense," even "abysmal." They gripe that a "separate 'writing GPA' on transcripts [makes] mediocre writing grades really stand out to prospective employers." At George Mason, 3Ls teach part of the writing courses as well, and "most students resent being graded by a fellow student." Another source of mixed feelings is the fact that students are "broken into groups of 10" and graded on Mason's "2.9 curve."

After the first year, many students choose to pursue one of several specialization programs. Students single out the "excellent intellectual property specialization" for praise and say that "the school makes a serious effort" to promote it. Other specialties include technology law, international business law, regulatory law, legal and economic theory, and tax. Also notable is a semester-long "exchange program in law and economics offered with the University of Hamburg." The Career Center "works tirelessly (and cheerfully) to help students find summer employment, externships, judicial clerkships, and post-graduation employment." However, graduating from a fairly new law school means "there are a limited number of alumni in the market," so George Mason students may "have to work a little harder to get noticed."

"The facilities at George Mason are brand new, and everything is state-of-the-art," including the library. You'll find "cutting-edge" technology and "wireless Internet throughout much of the academic building." Plus, "classrooms have Internet access at every seat." Shortcomings include "the lack of space" at desks and "[bad] acoustics in the big classrooms." The law building, which "feels a bit sterile at times," "could use a bit more decor on the inside."

ANNE M. RICHARD, ASSOCIATE DEAN AND DIRECTOR OF ADMISSIONS
3301 FAIRFAX DRIVE, ARLINGTON, VA 22201
TELEPHONE: 703-993-8010 • FAX: 703-993-8088
E-MAIL: ARICHAR5@GMU.EDU • WEBSITE: WWW.LAW.GMU.EDU

Life

"There are basically two kinds of students at GMU," observes a keen 1L, "those who come for the school's conservative reputation and those who come for the cheap tuition." Overall, there is "a very good mix of students who are just out of college, students who have worked a few years, and students who are transitioning to a second career." This is a "get-down-to-business school," and students say, "Compared to our friends at surrounding law schools, the prevailing sentiment is that Mason students work harder." They continue, "The law and economics theme attracts conservative, business types" and, although "Mason is hardly diverse, the majority and minority seem to mesh well." For day students, "there is a real sense of community" because "the class sizes are small and [students] all know each other." This is less true for night students. Academically, the atmosphere is "highly competitive" but not really cutthroat. "Students are competitive because of the strict curve," explains one student, "but it never becomes so intense that someone wouldn't share notes with you if you miss a class." It seems that "the overall attitude of the student body is excitement to be part of such a rapidly up-and-coming school." GMU's location in "bucolic Arlington" is a hit with students—"so close to the pulse of Washington, DC but without the hassle of the traffic, high prices, and crime." However, "parking is not a plus." One student writes, "Law school social life is not robust, but not because Mason students are social misfits. Many are returning students who have families or other non–law school circles of friends. They simply prefer to maintain the social life they have built up outside of law school." When not in class or studying, "there are fewer social events than many would prefer," but because "Mason students work so hard, there is not much time left to devote to social activities." It's not like there is a social void, though. "The school sponsors a lot of activities" including "happy hours in the atrium, volunteer opportunities, and sports." One student sums up the end of the week scene, "It seems like every week someone is having a party or students are mingling in the atrium on a Thursday or Friday night to head to the bar or to dinner."

Getting In

In recent years, George Mason has offered admission to approximately 10 percent of the applicant pool. The average admitted student has an LSAT score of 162 and a GPA of 3.4. George Mason offers a three-year full-time as well as a four-year part-time program.

EMPLOYMENT INFORMATION

Career Rating	**84**
% employed within 9 months	99
Average starting salary	$73,947
State for bar exam	VA, MD, DC, CA, NY

Employers who frequently hire grads: Hunton & Williams; McGuirewoods LLP; Finnegan, Henderson, Farabow, Garrett, & Dunner, LLP; Shaw Pittman; Wiley, Rein, and Fielding; Sterne, Kessler, Goldstein, and Fox; Sutherland, Asbill, and Brennan.

Prominent Alumni: Richard Young, U.S. District Court judge; Leslie Alden, Fairfax County Circuit Court judge; Paul Misener, vice president of global policy for Amazon.com.

Grads employed by field (%):	
Academic	4
Business/industry	14
Government	17
Judicial clerkships	13
Military	2
Private practice	44
Public interest	6

ADMISSIONS

Selectivity Rating	**92**
# applications received	4,353
# applicants accepted	617
# acceptees attending	138
Average LSAT	164
LSAT Range	159–166
Average undergrad GPA	3.7
Application fee	$35
Regular application deadline	3/15
Regular notification	4/15
Rolling notification?	Yes
Early application program?	No
Transfer students accepted?	Yes
Evening division offered?	Yes
Part-time accepted?	Yes
LSDAS accepted?	Yes

Applicants Also Look At

American University, The Catholic University of America, College of William & Mary, The George Washington University, Georgetown University, University of Maryland, University of Richmond.

International Students

TOEFL required of international students?	Yes

FINANCIAL FACTS

Annual tuition (resident)	$10,906
Annual tuition (nonresident)	$21,532
Books and supplies	$940
Tuition per credit (resident)	$390
Tuition per credit (nonresident)	$769
Room & board (off-campus)	$15,604
Financial aid application deadline	3/1
% first-year students receiving some sort of aid	71
% receiving some sort of aid	68
% of aid that is merit-based	4
% receiving scholarships	7
Average grant	$5,000
Average loan	$17,190
Average total aid package	$17,482
Average debt	$49,152

THE GEORGE WASHINGTON UNIVERSITY
LAW SCHOOL

INSTITUTIONAL INFORMATION

Public/private	private
Student/faculty ratio	14:1
% faculty part-time	67
% faculty female	29
% faculty minority	9
Total faculty	327

SURVEY SAYS . . .

Diverse opinions accepted in classrooms
Abundant externship/internship/ clerkship opportunities
Students love Washington, DC

STUDENTS

Enrollment of law school	1,578
% male/female	52/48
% out-of-state	96
% full-time	83
% minority	30
% international	2
# of countries represented	17
Average age of entering class	24

ACADEMICS

Academic Experience rating	**87**
Professors interesting rating	89
Professors accessible rating	78
Hours of study per day	3.95

Academic Specialties

Civil procedure, commercial law, constitutional law, corporation securities law, criminal law, environmental law, government contracts, human rights law, intellectual property law, international law, labor law, legal history, legal philosophy, property, taxation.

Advanced Degrees Offered

JD, 3 years full-time; JD, 4 years part-time; master of laws, 1 to 2 years, doctor of juridical science, 3 years.

Combined Degrees Offered

JD/MBA, JD/MPA, JD/MA international affairs, JD/MA history, JD/MA women's studies, JD/MPH. All can be completed in 4 years with full-time and summer attendance.

Academics

With more than 1,500 full- and part-time students, the George Washington University Law School is one of the largest legal training grounds in the country. Its fairly mind-boggling array of resources include "an interesting range of classes" and a host of dual-degree programs. Although "the best thing about GW is its location in one of the best legal markets in the United States. " Going along with the territory is "a strong emphasis on clinical and real-world legal work" and "the only international human rights law clinic in the country." Students say "amazing opportunities abound for internships, clerkships, externships, and full-time jobs at law firms, government agencies, and nonprofit organizations,"—which is great, as "many students are interested in public-interest law, not just 'big firm' work." Without question, "if you want immediate access to high levels of government, GW is a great choice." If intellectual property is your bag, the "high-quality" IP law program is "taught by federal circuit judges" and boasts a four-week program in Munich, Europe's "Intellectual Property Capital." Also noteworthy is "an excellent Trial Advocacy program" and an evening program that "treats evening students quite well."

The "very accessible, down-to-earth" professors at GW are "nationally (even internationally) renowned, funny, and brilliant" many students tell us. "They are challenging and thought-provoking, and it is a pleasure to go to class," explains one student. "While some schools teach policy and then just expect you to know the law for the exam, the faculty here makes sure that students leave their classroom knowing how to apply the law and why." The faculty is also "diverse in interests, strengths, opinions, and styles [and represents a] wide political spectrum."

"My experience at GW has been far and above what I expected," says one student. "Our Financial Aid Office is the smoothest-run machine in all of the District of Columbia," and "the administration really wants to come through for us as students." Aesthetically, the law school and its facilities have recently undergone a "very modern" transformation. The law school "interior is filled with rich wood, glass, leather, and gold ornamentation" to the delight of students. "The entire school looks gorgeous. They have wireless Internet access throughout the entire school, state-of-the-art classrooms, nice lounge areas, and an incredible moot courtroom." One student says, "I love having wireless Internet in class and taking exams on laptops." Now, students hope for more lounges in which to study and a bigger, better library that doesn't feel "crowded." The renovations are "really nice, but there are not enough tables to do research."

Life

George Washington is home to "easygoing law school students from all different backgrounds." These "genuinely friendly and fun" future attorneys are "smart and driven, but not to the point of insanity." "You can find every type of person here, from conservative to cutthroat liberal to punk rock chick to kids from Germany. Everyone is very involved in school clubs, which is a great way to meet people." One student relates, "My conservative friends assure me that the student body is liberal, but I have never met so many Republicans in my life." It is apparent that "students are often cliquey with their section mates," but overall, "there is a lot of camaraderie." In fact, "if you miss class, at least three people will send you the notes before you even ask." Also, "nobody is focused on success at the expense of others. This is a very supportive environment." Some students may be self-described "nerds, but we can still talk baseball, politics, college

Robert V. Stanek, Associate Dean for Admissions & Financial Aid
700 Twentieth Street NW, Washington, DC 20052
Telephone: 202-994-7230 • Fax: 202-994-3597
E-mail: jdadmit@law.gwu.edu • Website: www.law.gwu.edu

football, travel, the law, and where we are going to be drinking this weekend." Overall, students at GW tell us, "We are much happier than the people I've met who attend other DC schools."

In addition, the nation's capital is a great place to attend law school. The cost of living "isn't exorbitant like New York City" (although "a lack of affordable housing" is a "big detractor"). GW "has the best location of the DC law schools," too. The "IMF is across the street, and the World Bank is two blocks away." The White House is also nearby. "Supreme Court Justices are sometimes spotted in the law school," and political big wigs "including the president and the Secretary of State" often speak on campus. One student marvels, "Activities just today ranged from a roundtable discussion with a federal judge to a reception and discussion on sports and entertainment law." Social life is swell, even if some feel it "revolves around beer." The Student Bar Association definitely has its act together. "You can count on a keg on the back patio for Thirsty Thursday and a bunch of rowdy GW students at a local bar for Bar Review after that." And "if you don't like lawyers, you can stroll over to an undergrad party, talk to med students, or go to Dupont Circle or Adams Morgan and mingle with DC residents." At GW, "we have bake sales, lockers, and live auctions with tons of beer. It's like a twisted version of middle school, and I wouldn't choose to go to law school anywhere else."

Getting In

Admission to George Washington is highly competitive. It's not quite as hard to get in here as it is at its crosstown rival, Georgetown, but it's close. You should have an LSAT score at or above the 90th percentile and an A-minus average to be seriously considered here.

EMPLOYMENT INFORMATION

Career Rating	**90**
Job placement rate (%)	98
Average starting salary	$95,850
State for bar exam	NY, MD
Pass rate for first-time bar	82

Employers who frequently hire grads:
Department of Justice; Howrey Simon; Finnegan, Henderson, et al; Akin Gump, et al; Shearman & Sterling; Arnold & Porter; Wiley, Rein & Fielding; Arent Fox; various government agencies.

Grads employed by field (%):

Business/industry	11
Government	14
Judicial clerkships	12
Military	1
Other	3
Private practice	56
Public interest	1

Academic Requirements

Clinical Program Required?	No
Legal Writing Course Requirement?	Yes
Legal Methods Course Requirement?	Yes
Legal Research Course Requirement?	Yes
Moot Court Requirement?	No
Public Interest Law Requirement?	No

ADMISSIONS

Selectivity Rating	**90**
# applications received	11,171
# applicants accepted	2,066
# acceptees attending	512
Average LSAT	165
LSAT Range	162–166
Average undergrad GPA	3.5
Application fee	$75
Regular application deadline	3/1
Regular notification	rolling
Rolling notification?	Yes
Early application program?	No
Transfer students accepted?	Yes
Evening division offered?	Yes
Part-time accepted?	Yes
LSDAS accepted?	Yes

Applicants Also Look At

American University, Boston College, Boston University, Columbia University, Fordham University, Georgetown University, New York University.

International Students

TOEFL required of international students?	No
TOEFL recommended of international students?	Yes

FINANCIAL FACTS

Annual tuition	$32,620
Books and supplies	$890
Tuition per credit	$1,147
Room & board	$10,700
% first-year students receiving some sort of aid	84
% receiving some sort of aid	85
% of aid that is merit-based	32
% receiving scholarships	40
Average grant	$13,000
Average loan	$32,000
Average total aid package	$35,000
Average debt	$86,400

Georgetown University
Law Center

INSTITUTIONAL INFORMATION

Public/private	private
Student/faculty ratio	14:1
Affiliation	Roman Catholic
% faculty female	32
% faculty minority	12
Total faculty	211

SURVEY SAYS . . .

Diverse opinions accepted in classrooms
Great research resources
Great library staff
Abundant externship/internship/clerkship opportunities

STUDENTS

Enrollment of law school	1,936
% male/female	53/47
% full-time	80
% faculty minority	23
% international	3
Average age of entering class	25

ACADEMICS

Academic experience rating	**97**
Professors interesting rating	90
Professors accessible rating	80
Hours of study per day	3.93

Academic Specialties

Alternative dispute resolution, civil procedure, clinical legal studies, commercial law, constitutional law, corporation securities law, criminal law, environmental law, government services, human rights law, intellectual property law, international law, labor law, legal history, legal philosophy, property, taxation.

Advanced Degrees Offered

SJD, LLM taxation, LLM securities and financial regulation, LLM individualized, LLM general studies & LLM international legal studies, certificate in employee benefits, certificate in international human rights law, certificate in national security law, and certificate in IIEL/WTO studies, all in conjunction with the LLM individualized, LLM general studies, or LLM international legal studies degrees.

Academics

Georgetown University Law Center is a lion among law schools—huge, prestigious and located smack in the heart of the "political center of the world." The large size at Georgetown means there are "more opportunities," such as "an incredible selection of clinics, journals, and other cocurricular as well as extracurricular activities," not to mention "a larger array of courses to select from." And "there's nothing like being a law student a few blocks from the Supreme Court and at the seat of government." The DC location makes for access to some of the country's best legal minds. As one student puts it, "In addition to the brilliant and accomplished tenured faculty, which includes former top-ranking White House officials and nationally acclaimed scholars, we also have an exquisite array of adjunct faculty members, which include judges from DC and seasoned practitioners from both the private and public interest sectors." The location and the "outstanding alumni base" make Georgetown Law an environment "excellent for networking and establishing connections with some pretty important scholars and political figures."

Students are truly "in awe of [the] impressive credentials" of Georgetown's faculty, a group that "argues cases before the Supreme Court and publishes cutting-edge material." Not to mention their "very successful—sometimes famous—careers in one legal field or the other prior to joining the faculty." More important, perhaps, professors at Georgetown "are great teachers as well." And while "the Socratic method is alive and well at Georgetown," most professors "have the humanity and sense of humor to make class interesting and nearly painless." Students appreciate their professors not just for their formidable resumes or vast knowledge, but for their dynamic presentation of the material. One student says, "Class is always engaging; I don't skip for fear I'll miss something fun or memorable." Another says, "The faculty push you to the furthest of your intellectual capacity and then pull you back into discussion with a joke." Yet another student exclaims, "Not only are they smart and accomplished, but they are just so darn nice!" Others call professors, "Accessible, easy to talk to, and interested in ensuring their students truly understand the law and do well."

Georgetown's administration gets high marks from students, mainly for the impressive feat of somehow managing to make each of its 2,000 students feel individually pampered. This "great effort put forth to make the school feel like an intimate community" manifests itself in everything from knowing students on a "first-name basis" to "providing coffee during finals" to "making sure first year students are able to take advantage of the wide range of opportunities available to them." Georgetown's Career Services is "the best." One student relays, "My career counselor was so happy for me when I got my job offer for this summer that he hugged me!"

Students log a few complaints about classes being crowded and some not so up-to-date facilities. But two new recently opened buildings—an international law facility and a "state-of-the-art workout center with an Olympic-sized swimming pool"—alleviated some of these issues. These changes should have a positive effect on the "moody" wireless network, which in the past provided only "spotty coverage through the campus."

Andrew P. Cornblatt, Assistant Dean of Admissions
600 New Jersey Avenue NW Room 589, Washington, DC 20001
Telephone: 202-662-9010 • Fax: 202-662-9439
E-mail: admis@law.georgetown.edu • Website: www.law.georgetown.edu

Life

Georgetown Law is located in the heart of the nation's capital, at the epicenter of lawmaking. "Being practically next door to DC Superior Court, the Federal Tax Court, the DC Circuit Court, and the Supreme Court makes student observation and participation at these institutions not only possible but easy," one student gloats. Additionally, Congress and the White House are within walking distance—a political junkie's fix. On the other hand, there are some frowns since the law school is separated from the main campus. And the school's location does make parking problematic, although between student housing and the Metro, it is not a crippling issue.

Students love Georgetown's "liberal" and "diverse" student body who they describe as "friendly, normal, and cool." Students feel they "seem to strike a good balance between working hard and playing hard," which is good because, "with DC being such a vibrant city, it'd be hard to sit in the library all day." Many praise the "experiences that the student body brings to the classroom, [since] so many students have been in the real world and know why they are here now!" Students do not understand why Georgetown gets a bad rep for being super competitive, saying, "For the most part, everyone is willing to study in groups, share notes and outlines, and discuss difficult concepts with other students." One student elaborates, "Anywhere you go to law school there's going to be those few people—the gunners—who are really annoying and competitive in class. At Georgetown, at least, you either have to have a sense of humor about yourself, or the professor will shoot you down—to the delight of your classmates." The size of the school "cuts down on the ability to know everyone well," but students assure us that many friends are made during one's time at Georgetown. Furthermore, "There are over 60 student organizations. And many groups organize happy hours and parties off-campus that help relieve stress and provide an opportunity to meet new people."

Getting In

Georgetown Law's admitted students at the 25th percentile have an LSAT score of 166 and a GPA of 3.4. Admitted students at the 75th percentile have an LSAT score of 170 and a GPA of 3.8. Georgetown does offer a part-time and an evening program. They also have several interesting joint-degree programs.

EMPLOYMENT INFORMATION

Career Rating	**96**
Job placement rate (%)	98
Average starting salary	$105,000
State for bar exam	NY, MD
Pass rate for first-time bar	90

Grads employed by field (%):	
Academic	2
Business/industry	6
Government	8
Judicial clerkships	9
Military	1
Other	9
Private practice	61
Public interest	4

Combined Degrees Offered

JD/MBA, JD/MPH, JD/MPP, JD/MSFS, JD/PhD government, JD/PhD or MA philosophy, JD/MAAS, JD/MAGES, JD/MALAS, JD/MAREES, JD/MASSP

Academic Requirements

Clinical Program Required?	No
Legal Writing Course Requirement?	Yes
Legal Methods Course Requirement?	Yes
Legal Research Course Requirement?	Yes
Moot Court Requirement?	No
Public Interest Law Requirement?	No

ADMISSIONS

Selectivity Rating	**94**
# applications received	11,620
# applicants accepted	2,143
# acceptees attending	453
Average LSAT	169
LSAT Range	166–170
Average undergrad GPA	3.7
Application fee	$75
Regular application deadline	2/1
Regular notification	rolling
Rolling notification?	Yes
Early application program?	Yes
Early application deadline	11/1 and 12/1
Early application notification	12/10
Transfer students accepted?	Yes
Evening division offered?	Yes
Part-time accepted?	Yes
LSDAS accepted?	Yes

International Students

TOEFL required of international students?	No
TOEFL recommended of international students?	No

FINANCIAL FACTS

Annual tuition	$33,055
Books and supplies	$875
Tuition per credit	$1,210
Room & board	$17,945
Financial aid app. deadline	3/1
% first-year students receiving some sort of aid	87
% receiving some sort of aid	86
% receiving scholarships	32
Average grant	$12,100
Average loan	$30,890
Average total aid package	$35,000
Average debt	$92,675

GEORGIA STATE UNIVERSITY
COLLEGE OF LAW

INSTITUTIONAL INFORMATION

Public/private	public
Student/faculty ratio	16:1
% faculty part-time	26
% faculty female	38
% faculty minority	18
Total faculty	72

SURVEY SAYS . . .

Diverse opinions accepted in classrooms
Great research resources
Great library staff
Abundant externship/internship/clerkship opportunities

STUDENTS

Enrollment of law school	680
% male/female	50/50
% out-of-state	13
% full-time	75
% faculty minority	20
% international	3
# of countries represented	8
Average age of entering class	27

ACADEMICS

Academic experience rating	**84**
Professors interesting rating	82
Professors accessible rating	72
Hours of study per day	4.38

Academic Specialties

Civil procedure, commercial law, corporation securities law, criminal law, environmental law, human rights law, intellectual property law, international law, taxation.

Combined Degrees Offered

JD/MBA, 4 years; JD/MPA, 4 years; JD/MA philosophy, 4 years: JD/MCRP, 4 years; JD/MHA, 4 years; JD/MSHA, 4 years.

Academic Requirements

Clinical Program Required?	No
Legal Writing Course Requirement?	Yes
Legal Methods Course Requirement?	No

Academics

If you can put up with a bureaucratic administration and some lackluster physical facilities, you can get a great education for a very low price at Georgia State University College of Law. Part of a large, public university, the College of Law—like all publicly supported institutions of higher learning—has suffered lately due to financial cutbacks. But law students at GSU still believe that their education is world class. One student puts it into perspective: "Georgia State does not have the most beautifully decorated law school facilities, but it is comfortable and doesn't interfere with academics, and tuition is definitely affordable." Another student agrees, "I believe that I have gotten a top-of-the-line education at Georgia State. There may be some lack of classroom space and the administration at the highest level is somewhat out of touch, but I am prepared for my career and my teachers have been great."

Students say they learn key critical thinking and practical skills at GSU. In the words of one student, "Never before in my life have I been taught to think so abstractly and creatively. I love the challenge and the quality education I am receiving." A large part of that quality education can be attributed to professors who "are vibrant, enthusiastic people, involved in various parts of the legal community as well as being law school professors." From the moot court program, to litigation class, to the law review, students say that the importance of applied aspects of the law are drilled into them. One student declares, "We are prepared to practice law upon graduation. GSU stresses the importance of real-world lawyering skills—litigation, negotiation, appellate advocacy—and students all feel that they "can hit the ground running after graduating."

Only twenty-three years old, Georgia State University is a fairly new law school, but students are quick to point out that "the school seems to really be building momentum as its reputation extends outside of the city limits of Atlanta." An active externship program and local contacts in the Atlanta law community are building part of that reputation. "The mentor program offered through the Career Services Office matching 1Ls with practicing attorneys was great. I found a good friend in my mentor and in the judge she worked for as well," recalls one student. Another adds, "Our students have the opportunity to extern at over 40 different agencies and courts during the school year, which makes us competitive as professionals because we have experience that a graduate from another school may not have." Students feel that as it continues to grow, the law school "needs to spend more money expanding and funding the Career Services Office to better help students in finding jobs." Students also complain that Georgia State needs to provide better and more comprehensive financial assistance to law students. One suggests the law school's "own financial aid center, separate from the other undergraduate programs and other colleges within the university. We need a real person to talk to, not a voice recording."

In addition to the low tuition costs, many students choose Georgia State because the school offers flexible schedules, joint degree programs, and other services for working or part-time students. "One strength of the program is the different 'packages' it offers. For instance, I'm enrolled in its part-time, joint-degree program," confides one older student with responsibilities outside of law school.

Dr. Cheryl Jester Jeckson, Director of Admissions
PO Box 4049, Atlanta, GA 30302-4049
Telephone: 404-651-2048 • Fax: 404-651-1244
E-mail: admissions@gsulaw.gsu.edu • Website: http://law.gsu.edu

Life

If you ask law students, they will tell you that there isn't much campus life at Georgia State University College of Law. Students explain, "We have a lot of married students, so the social atmosphere is not like that at an undergraduate school where everyone is single." On top of that, "the students live throughout metro Atlanta, making it harder to socialize." Students tell us, however, that there is a feeling of camaraderie between them, and "there are many student activities and events that are well-attended." A student explains, "People generally hang out with a few friends, but there aren't a lot of parties." Some make lasting friendships over late night study sessions. One evening student writes, "The night students have bonded together like a clan. Our Thursday night 'study groups' at the local pub are always memorable."

Speaking of night students, unlike many law schools that offer both part-time and full-time programs, Georgia State does not suffer from a major divide between daytime and evening students. One part-timer writes, "GSU has a good blend of mature, older students (like myself) and young pups right out of undergrad. Day students often take classes at night, so the part-timers have opportunities to interact with them." Students also praise the diversity within the student body. A student enthuses, "With such a broad range of ages and backgrounds, it provides for an interesting and enriching environment to learn the law."

Getting In

Undergraduate GPA and LSAT scores are the two most important factors in an admissions decision at Georgia State. The school also considers the student's personal statement and letters of recommendation when making an admissions decision. Last year, admits had a mean GPA of about 3.32 and mean LSAT scores of 158. While roughly 90 percent of applicants are residents of Georgia, no admission priority is given to state residents. The school starts accepting applications after January 1 and accepts students on a rolling basis after that date.

EMPLOYMENT INFORMATION

Career Rating	**79**
Job placement rate (%)	95
Average starting salary	$65,847
State for bar exam	GA
Pass rate for first-time bar	93

Employers who frequently hire grads: Alston & Bird; Arnall Golden & Gregory; Drew Eckl; Jones Day; Kilpatrick & Stockton; Holland & Knight; Hunton and Williams; King & Spalding.

Prominent Alumni: Dr. Claudia Adkison, higher education administrative executive assistant dean/Emory Medical; Evelyn Ann Ashley, partner, founder/Red Hot Law Group of Ashley LLC.

Grads employed by field (%):	
Business/industry	11
Government	13
Judicial clerkships	7
Other	1
Private practice	62
Public interest	6

Legal Research Course Requirement?	Yes
Moot Court Requirement?	No
Public Interest Law Requirement?	No

ADMISSIONS

Selectivity Rating	**86**
# applications received	3,610
# applicants accepted	577
# acceptees attending	234
Average LSAT	159
LSAT Range	157–160
Average undergrad GPA	3.3
Application fee	$50
Regular application deadline	3/15
Regular notification	rolling
Rolling notification?	Yes
Early application program?	No
Transfer students accepted?	Yes
Evening division offered?	Yes
Part-time accepted?	Yes
LSDAS accepted?	Yes

Applicants Also Look At

Emory University, Mercer University, University of Florida, University of Georgia.

International Students

TOEFL required of international students?	No
TOEFL recommended of international students?	Yes
Minimum Paper TOEFL	680

FINANCIAL FACTS

Annual tuition (resident)	$5,212
Annual tuition (nonresident)	$20,306
Books and supplies	$750
Fees per credit (resident)	$450
Fees per credit (nonresident)	$450
Tuition per credit (resident)	$218
Tuition per credit (nonresident)	$809
Room & board (on/off-campus)	$10,796/$10,986
Financial aid application deadline	4/1
% first-year students receiving some sort of aid	40
% receiving some sort of aid	70
% of aid that is merit-based	7
% receiving scholarships	4
Average grant	$3,542
Average loan	$14,951
Average total aid package	$15,341
Average debt	$45,326

GOLDEN GATE UNIVERSITY

SCHOOL OF LAW

INSTITUTIONAL INFORMATION

Public/private	private
Student/faculty ratio	20:1
% faculty part-time	69
% faculty female	44
% faculty minority	22
Total faculty	31

SURVEY SAYS . . .

Diverse opinions accepted in classrooms
Great library staff
Students love San Francisco, CA

STUDENTS

Enrollment of law school	853
% male/female	43/57
% out-of-state	8
% full-time	78
% minority	11
% international	1
# of countries represented	24
Average age of entering class	26

ACADEMICS

Academic experience rating	**62**
Professors interesting rating	61
Professors accessible rating	61
Hours of study per day	4.79

Academic Specialties

Business law, criminal law, environmental law, intellectual property law, international law, labor law, litigation, property, public interest law, taxation.

Advanced Degrees Offered

JD, 3 years full-time, 4 years part time; LLM, 1 year.

Combined Degrees Offered

JD/MBA, 3 to 4 years, JD/PhD, 7 years, SJD, 1 year.

Academic Requirements

Clinical Program Required?	No
Legal Writing Course Requirement?	Yes
Legal Methods Course Requirement?	No
Legal Research Course Requirement?	Yes

Academics

San Francisco's Golden Gate University School of Law provides "a solid foundation of legal theory," but places the greatest emphasis on gaining "practical lawyering skills." Strengths include the "wide range of programs (mid-year, part-time, night)" offered, as well as a "serious commitment to public interest law." Being "located within blocks of the financial district, close to the majority of the major law firms and businesses," means there are plenty of internships and externships available nearby. And that's not the only perk of GGU's location. "Due in part to the diversity of San Francisco, there is a highly diverse student population," not to mention, "the faculty is very diverse, not just ethnically, but in political views and other perspectives."

Most students agree, "The practical experience of the faculty is outstanding, [and the] knowledgeable and connected [professors] prepare students for the practice of law in the real world." Professors' experience is perceived as one of the school's "greatest strengths." Another student continues, "Many professors are practicing lawyers who share their 'war stories.' Those ideas and techniques cannot be taught out of a textbook and are the most valuable and memorable." Students are also impressed by their professors' commitment to students' education. "They are dedicated as far as time and effort" and are truly interested in "communicating an understanding of the law to students in and out of the classroom." Plus, "since it is a small law school, it is very easy to approach the professors, and there are great research opportunities available." A cool peer mentoring program that helps first-year students adjust to the law school environment is one more link in the support network. As one GGU upperclassman tells us, "The peer mentoring is an excellent idea and helped all throughout my law school experience in every way."

Students feel the administration is doing a pretty good job. They "focus on the students [and] keep the student body informed." Golden Gate has "flexibility for evening students" and offers a few joint degrees. While students complain about the school's lack of a national reputation, they do admit, "If you graduate from GGU and work in the Bay Area, you have an available network all around you in the thriving local legal system."

Golden Gate School of Law's classrooms "have outlets at every chair for laptops" and Internet connections in the lecture halls. Most students feel the library "isn't roomy enough to accommodate all the students who want to use it," and say it "could use some remodeling." On the plus side, it is "equipped with modern technology, [like] multiple computer labs [and] wireless Internet access." Library staff "is always helpful and knowledgeable."

Tracy Simmons, Assistant Dean
536 Mission Street, San Francisco, CA 94105
Telephone: 415-442-6630 • Fax: 415-442-6631
E-mail: lawadmit@ggu.edu • Website: www.ggu.edu/law/

Life

Golden Gate has a "diverse and talented student body," so diverse, it seems, that there is no "typical" student. Students come from all different ethnic and life backgrounds and even live throughout "the entire Bay Area, from Silicon Valley to the wine country." For some this commute generally means "people head off and do their own things when class is over," but others say they go out with classmates so much that sometimes it "is distracting and gets in the way of schoolwork." Overall, students have positive feelings about their "fantastic, supportive, [and] caring" peers. One student notes, "The environment is not overly competitive. People are working and studying together and other students have been willing to help me." And they can always find support from their fellow classmates outside of the law school as well. "If you have a social issue you feel strongly about, it is likely you can find other like-minded students who will join you in your efforts." In the end, your level of participation is up to you. While GGU "is pretty relaxed, you can choose to be as involved or uninvolved as you want."

The location in "the San Francisco financial center" makes it a "good place to go looking for jobs." As far as academic clubs, "there are opportunities for everyone from Future Lawyers with Social Conscious to Queer Law Students Association, and more." Furthermore, greater San Francisco offers a myriad of cultural, dining, and shopping possibilities just a cable car ride away.

Getting In

Admitted students at the 25th percentile have an LSAT score of 148 and a GPA of 2.8. Admitted students at the 75th percentile have an LSAT score of 154 and a GPA of 3.4. The average admitted student has an LSAT score of 151 and a GPA of 3.1.

EMPLOYMENT INFORMATION

Career Rating	**61**
Job placement rate (%)	60
Average starting salary	$58,000
State for bar exam	CA
Pass rate for first-time bar	32

Employers who frequently hire grads:
Small, medium, and large firms; government agencies; public interest organizations; and businesses and corporations.

Grads employed by field (%):

Academic	7
Business/industry	12
Government	11
Judicial clerkships	5
Private practice	60
Public interest	5

Moot Court Requirement?	No
Public Interest Law Requirement?	No

ADMISSIONS

Selectivity Rating	**72**
# applications received	3,318
# applicants accepted	1,262
# acceptees attending	357
Average LSAT	154
LSAT Range	151–155
Average undergrad GPA	3.2
Application fee	$60
Regular application deadline	4/15
Regular notification	rolling
Rolling notification?	Yes
Early application program?	No
Transfer students accepted?	Yes
Evening division offered?	Yes
Part-time accepted?	Yes
LSDAS accepted?	Yes

Applicants Also Look At

California Western, Chapman University, Roger Williams University, Southwestern University School of Law, Texas A&M University, Whittier College.

International Students

TOEFL required of international students?	No
TOEFL recommended of international students?	Yes
Minimum Paper TOEFL	580

FINANCIAL FACTS

Annual tuition	$26,680
Books and supplies	$870
Fees per credit	$12
Tuition per credit	$970
Room & board (off-campus)	$15,000
Financial aid application deadline	4/15
% first-year students receiving some sort of aid	80
% receiving some sort of aid	80
% of aid that is merit-based	85
% receiving scholarships	30
Average grant	$7,693
Average loan	$35,535
Average total aid package	$38,000
Average debt	$68,787

GONZAGA UNIVERSITY
SCHOOL OF LAW

INSTITUTIONAL INFORMATION

Public/private	private
Student/faculty ratio	19:1
Affiliation	Roman Catholic
% faculty part-time	41
% faculty female	41
% faculty minority	4
Total faculty	56

SURVEY SAYS . . .

Great library staff
Beautiful campus

STUDENTS

Enrollment of law school	628
% male/female	55/45
% out-of-state	51
% full-time	96
% minority	12
# of countries represented	4
Average age of entering class	26

ACADEMICS

Academic experience rating	**61**
Professors interesting rating	62
Professors accessible rating	65
Hours of study per day	4.44

Academic Specialties

Business law, environmental law, public interest law, taxation.

Combined Degrees Offered

JD/MBA, JD/MAcc, JD/MSW. All 3 to 4 years.

Academic Requirements

Clinical Program Required?	No
Legal Writing Course Requirement?	Yes
Legal Methods Course Requirement?	No
Legal Research Course Requirement?	Yes
Moot Court Requirement?	No
Public Interest Law Requirement?	Yes

Academics

"For the most part, the Catholic influence is very unobtrusive" at Gonzaga University School of Law. "It's not like a bunch of tree-hugging hippies are running around telling you that you are evil for wanting to work in the corporate world," writes one smart-aleck student. But the Jesuit influence is notable in Gonzaga's "emphasis on public service after law school." One student gushes, "The respect and support you get from Gonzaga when pursuing a career in public interest is incredible." Another comments, "This is definitely law school with a conscience." There is a strong "commitment to social justice," and community service is both a "requirement for graduation [and] a way of life for the student body." There is an "emphasis on practical experience" as well. One student asserts, "The greatest strength of the law school is that it requires two full years of legal research and writing. Everyone who graduates is an expert at it."

The "very warm" professors at Gonzaga "give their all to the cause of education." Faculty members are "more than willing to go out of their way to help you achieve your personal and professional goals." Students say, "The school wants everyone to succeed [and] really makes an effort to help you rather than weed people out." Faculty accessibility is a staple. "There is not a professor who won't meet with you. If you want the attention of professors, you can get it easily," declares one student. "If you're looking for a school in which you can stay anonymous as a student, this is not the place for you." The "self-serving administration" does not get nearly the same sort of praise as the faculty.

Student opinion diverges with regard to life after law school. Some say career prospects are great. "I got a two-year internship with the United States Attorney for the Eastern District of Washington," brags a satisfied student. "The last few years, they have hired five new interns each year, all from Gonzaga. I have a buddy doing an externship for a federal judge. Another works for the federal defender. There is an abundance of opportunity here that few other schools can match, and we are the only law school in the area." Other students say, "Career Services could use some work" because too many students end up practicing "dog bite law in some small town in Montana."

The "first-rate" facilities make Gonzaga "the nicest looking law school in the Northwest. The building is practically brand-new, so almost; everything in it is state-of-the-art." Other architecture on campus is raved about, too; the "excellent law library" boasts "all the amenities and then some [including] WiFi connections throughout the school, which is really nice." The one quibble would be that while "the school makes every attempt to have the technological resources functioning as much as possible," the network is occasionally "a bit erratic."

Susan Lee, Director of Admissions
PO Box 3528, Spokane, WA 99220
Telephone: 800-793-1710 • Fax: 509-323-3697
E-mail: admissions@lawschool.gonzaga.edu • Website: http://law.gonzaga.edu

Life

Some students say that one of Gonzaga's "greatest characteristics [is the] strong sense of community" that permeates the law school. Others say it depends. "Each class has its own personality," says one student. "Ours was one of support and camaraderie. The class behind ours is far more competitive. The class ahead of us was petty and nasty."

There is "not very much" ethnic diversity in the student population, but there is more than enough political diversity to go around. "Students range from fiery liberals to hard-line conservatives." One student notes, "You ask liberals, and they think it's the most conservative law school in the country. You ask the conservatives, and they say it's ridiculously liberal."

Life outside the classroom has much to commend it. "The opportunity to be involved as a student in the Spokane community, and the law school community is overwhelming," writes one student. "The Student Bar Association is committed to helping students be exposed to many different activities and events." Law students don't mingle much with undergraduates. "The law school is separated from the main campus by the athletic facilities, [which] contributes to attitudes of insularity on both sides." One student explains, "I'm not aware of any significant participation by either side in the activities of the other, with the sole exception of attendance at basketball games." Gonzaga basketball is huge, and attendance at games is "almost obligatory." Also, "with a handful of ski mountains within two hours and tons of state parks close by, [Gonzaga is] great for ski bums and mountain bikers."

Getting In

About two out of five applicants are accepted by Gonzaga. So competition for admission is strong, but not overwhelming. And A-minus undergraduate GPA and an LSAT in the low-to-mid 150s puts you in the same boat as the majority of accepted students.

EMPLOYMENT INFORMATION

Career Rating	72
% employed within 9 months	96.5
Average starting salary	$46,893
State for bar exam	WA
Pass rate for first-time bar	78

Employers who frequently hire grads: Various law firms in Spokane and throughout Washington and various local and state government entities hire grads.

Prominent Alumni: Christine Gregoire, governor, State of Washington; Barbara Madsen, justice, Washington Supreme Court; Mary Fairhurst, justice, Washington Supreme Court; Paul Luvera, plantiffs attorney, lead in tobacco litigation.

Grads employed by field (%):	
Academic	1
Business/industry	19
Government	19
Judicial clerkships	12
Military	3
Private practice	42
Public interest	4

ADMISSIONS

Selectivity Rating	**72**
# applications received	1,742
# applicants accepted	574
# acceptees attending	222
Average LSAT	152
LSAT Range	150–156
Average undergrad GPA	3.4
Application fee	$50
Regular application deadline	6/1
Regular notification	rolling
Rolling notification?	Yes
Early application program?	No
Transfer students accepted?	Yes
Evening division offered?	No
Part-time accepted?	Yes
LSDAS accepted?	Yes

Applicants Also Look At

Arizona State University, California Western, Lewis & Clark College, Seattle University, University of Denver, University of Washington, Willamette University.

International Students

TOEFL required of international students?	Yes
Minimum Paper TOEFL	650

FINANCIAL FACTS

Annual tuition	$24,540
Books and supplies	$1,000
Tuition per credit	$818
Room & board (off-campus)	$7,875
Financial aid application deadline	2/1
% first-year students receiving some sort of aid	100
% receiving some sort of aid	100
% of aid that is merit-based	22
% receiving scholarships	74
Average grant	$10,000
Average loan	$39,055
Average total aid package	$39,055
Average debt	$73,120

Hamline University
School of Law

INSTITUTIONAL INFORMATION

Public/private	private
Student/faculty ratio	17:1
Affiliation	Methodist
% faculty female	46
% faculty minority	13
Total faculty	39

SURVEY SAYS . . .

Diverse opinions accepted in classrooms
Great library staff
Abundant externship/internship/clerkship opportunities

STUDENTS

Enrollment of law school	714
% male/female	42/58
% out-of-state	48
% full-time	72
% minority	13
% international	1
# of countries represented	7
Average age of entering class	24

ACADEMICS

Academic experience rating	**68**
Professors interesting rating	70
Professors accessible rating	71
Hours of study per day	4.91

Academic Specialties

Alternative dispute resolution, commercial law, corporations, criminal law, government services, international law, labor law, social justice.

Advanced Degrees Offered

JD, 3 years; LLM for international lawyers, 1 year.

Combined Degrees Offered

JD/MAPA, master's of public administration, 4 years; JD/MANM, master's nonprofit management; JD/MAM, master's management; JD/MLIS, master's library & information science, 4 years; JD/MAOL, master's arts in organizational leadership, 4 years.

Academics

Hamline University School of Law is a small, relatively new law school with a special "focus on giving back to the community." Students tell us, "Through various clerkships, internships, and practicums, Hamline allows students to participate in the practical application of law while helping some of those who are most in need." Clinics include Child Advocacy and Legal Assistance for Minnesota Prisoners. Because Hamline is a "young school," it has "the flexibility of be[ing] innovative and progressive" and the freedom to "try new ideas, such as the Alternative Dispute Resolution Program." Through this much-loved program, students do mediations at local internships, an experience they say fosters success "regardless of area of practice." Another innovative and highly touted feature at Hamline is the part-time Weekend Option, "a great opportunity for nontraditional students," that allows them to work full-time while earning their JD.

The "intelligent and interesting [faculty at Hamline] bring an element of humanity to the learning environment." Students relish that their teachers "take an active interest in the individual student [and go] out of their way in order to be able to help the students." And professors are so accessible that they "even provide the students with home phone numbers to reach them in the evenings with questions." It's not all hand-holding. In the classroom, the professors are "challenging," exhibiting a "healthy dose of 'tough love' because they truly want students to become conscientious lawyers who will contribute to society in a meaningful way."

Administration at Hamline receives unusually high marks from the students. Over and over again, students emphasize, "The administration is very open, supportive, accessible, and interested in our opinions." Not only are they "responsive to our requests for changes, improvements, [and] additions," one student tells us, "but they actively seek our input." Many students at Hamline even seem to have personal relationships with the administration. One student tells us, "The staff, from the registrar to admissions to the deans, are also especially helpful. They have answered all kinds of questions from how to find a place to live to helping me find a good vet." In the words of another, "Hamline School of Law offers more help than one individual could ever need."

Probably no student has ever come to Hamline for the facilities, which are a bit "shabby." A less "cramped [library], a larger computer lab, [and] more windows in the classrooms" would be welcome additions. Students also harp on the fact that the technology is stuck somewhere in the late twentieth century, bemoaning the lack of a wireless Internet. One student speculates, perhaps Hamline has a valid excuse for these shortcomings: "Because the school places such an emphasis on public service, their graduates do not make a lot of money, and they do not generate many endowments." Fair enough.

Robin Ingli, Director of Admissions
1536 Hewitt Avenue, St. Paul, MN 55104-1284
Telephone: 800-388-3688 • Fax: 651-523-3064
E-mail: lawadm@gw.hamline.edu • Website: www.hamline.edu/law

Life

If you are looking for a "close-knit" and nurturing environment, Hamline's your place. Students tell us, "Because we are a small school, there is a sense of closeness among the student body." This intimacy was mentioned by almost every student surveyed—the consensus at Hamline seems to be that "people here care about you and want to get to know you." While there is some element of competition, it's not "stifling." The Hamline as "one big family" motif came up again and again. Sometimes implicitly: "We compete and we gossip and we get on each other's nerves, but at the end of the day, we meet at Billy's bar and know that we wouldn't have it any other way." But more often students explicitly told us, "Hamline is more than a law school—it is a (sometimes dysfunctional) family of students, professors, and administrators who learn together, laugh together, argue together, challenge each other, and then go to the inter-law-school hockey game afterward to cheer on our losing team."

Hamline offers a "good mix of traditional and nontraditional students," the latter of which "brings with them life experiences that give the classes a well-rounded and realistic flavor." Older students have even formed a very popular "Second Career Society." Hamline "holds a lot of social events to comfort 1Ls and welcome students," as well as weekly bar nights and celebratory pizza parties. Plus, students can always explore the "fantastic metropolitan area" of the Twin Cities, where "there are always plenty of choices for entertainment." As one student puts it, there is "nothing like living in the heart of the Twin Cities, but feeling like you're in a nice, quiet, residential neighborhood."

Getting In

Hamline's admitted students at the 25th percentile have an LSAT score of 150 and a GPA of 3.1. Admitted students at the 75th percentile have an LSAT score of 155 and a GPA of 3.6. Hamline enrolls about 670 students, 80 percent of them full-time.

EMPLOYMENT INFORMATION

Career Rating	**76**
Job placement rate (%)	92
Average starting salary	$49,794
State for bar exam	MN, WI, IL, NY, WA
Pass rate for first-time bar	86

Grads employed by field (%):	
Academic	1
Business/industry	19
Government	8
Judicial clerkships	18
Private practice	48
Public interest	5

Academic Requirements

Clinical Program Required?	No
Legal Writing Course Requirement?	Yes
Legal Methods Course Requirement?	No
Legal Research Course Requirement?	Yes
Moot Court Requirement?	No
Public Interest Law Requirement?	No

ADMISSIONS

Selectivity Rating	**72**
# applications received	1,306
# applicants accepted	568
# acceptees attending	233
Average LSAT	154
LSAT Range	150–158
Average undergrad GPA	3.3
Application fee	$40
Regular application deadline	rolling
Regular notification	rolling
Rolling notification?	Yes
Early application program?	No
Transfer students accepted?	Yes
Evening division offered?	Yes
Part-time accepted?	Yes
LSDAS accepted?	Yes

Applicants Also Look At

Drake University, Marquette University, University of Denver, University of Minnesota, University of St. Thomas, University of Wisconsin, William Mitchell College of Law.

International Students

TOEFL required of international students?	Yes
Minimum Paper TOEFL	600
Minimum Computer TOEFL	250

FINANCIAL FACTS

Annual tuition	$23,820
Books and supplies	$800
Tuition per credit	$945
Room & board (on/off-campus)	$9,740/$13,500
% first-year students receiving some sort of aid	95
% receiving some sort of aid	88
% of aid that is merit-based	98
% receiving scholarships	48
Average grant	$12,248
Average loan	$25,750
Average total aid package	
Average debt	$79,243

HARVARD UNIVERSITY
HARVARD LAW SCHOOL

INSTITUTIONAL INFORMATION

Public/private	private
Student/faculty ratio	11:1
% faculty part-time	18
% faculty female	30
% faculty minority	12
Total faculty	218

SURVEY SAYS . . .

Great research resources
Great library staff
Abundant externship/internship/clerkship opportunities

STUDENTS

Enrollment of law school	1,665
% male/female	56/44
% out-of-state	94
% full-time	100
% minority	30
% international	3
# of countries represented	29
Average age of entering class	24

ACADEMICS

Academic experience rating	**92**
Professors interesting rating	81
Professors accessible rating	61
Hours of study per day	3.66

Academic Specialties

Civil procedure, commercial law, constitutional law, corporation securities law, criminal law, environmental law, government services, human rights law, intellectual property law, international law, labor law, legal history, legal philosophy, property, taxation.

Advanced Degrees Offered

LLM, master of laws, 1 year; S/JD, doctor of juridical science(S/JD), course work, exam, and dissertation.

Combined Degrees Offered

JD/LLM (with Cambridge University), JD/MBA, JD/MPP, JD/MPP/ID, JD/PhD, JD/MA, JD/MALD.

Academics

Students at "the world's most famous law school have more of everything than anyone else—more smart students, more amazing faculty, more interesting classes, and more opportunities to explore whatever you want. There is a club or journal for everything." The clinical program is "incredible." Harvard Law School's large size "really does translate into exponentially more resources and opportunities than comparable schools at the top of the academic pile," explains one student. "There are tons of possibilities for finding your own way within the law, doing joint degrees, and taking odd classes." The generally Socratic classroom experience "fluctuates from enthusiastic revelry to intense intellectual debate each day." Harvard's "innovative [and] quirky" professors "border on omniscient [and] really care about teaching." One student declares, "I have former litigators, a negotiations expert, and a professor who was arrested multiple times during the Civil Rights movement. Some stress economics. One incorporates literature and Bob Dylan songs." Still other professors have "truly bizarre personalities [or are] too smart for their own good" and, as a result, "cannot communicate the material very well." Harvard's administration is "effective, attentive, [and] extremely responsive." Students are in love with their "phenomenal" new dean, a "godsend [who] has brought a new energy [and] excitement" to campus. She "is always open to meet with students about any concerns [and] committed to [creating] a more warm and fuzzy place for students." From "free coffee in the mornings [to] new lounge areas," the new dean is ringing in a "kinder, gentler, Starbucks-y Harvard." However, registration is "complicated [and] confusing as hell." As one student says, "Online course selection and a less Byzantine attitude toward all things registrar-related would help greatly." During their summers and upon getting their diplomas, HLS students have "job options out the yin-yang." Harvard's reputation "can open any door, [so] there is no way a student who graduates from HLS will have a hard time finding a job." Students say, "There is an opportunity to do anything you could imagine, [and] everyone is guaranteed a six-figure job" or a great public-interest career "regardless of GPA." Students agree, "It's kind of messed up that law firms slobber all over us just because we are at Harvard," but no one seems to be complaining. As one student admits, "It's almost fun to drop the 'H-Bomb' and garner instant credibility."

Student enthusiasm falls off a bit on the topic of facilities. We hear that "the outward appearance of some buildings is fairly depressing, [and] the entire campus has a bad retro feel to it." Students say, "Many of the facilities are in woeful need of renovation." Luckily, HLS is currently undergoing just such a facelift but, as one student puts it, "given the amount of money that Harvard Law has, you'd expect the buildings to look a little better than they do." On the other hand, students are happy that "unlike most law schools, [HLS] actually has a campus." The "gorgeous [library is] the largest law library in the world, [containing] more resources than any student could ever need." The reading room alone "extends the length of a football field," or at least it seems that way.

Life

"Other law schools told me that they weren't as 'cutthroat' as Harvard and that their students were not as 'tense' as those at Harvard," says one student. "They wanted me to know that they were 'not as bad as Harvard.' The truth is, even Harvard isn't as awful as Harvard." For the most part, students vigorously beg to differ with the portrayal of HLS in *One L*, *The Paper Chase*, and *Legally Blonde*. Competitiveness is manifestly not a problem. "The fact that HLS students don't have to worry about getting a job makes it

HARVARD LAW SCHOOL
1563 MASSACHUSETTS AVENUE, CAMBRIDGE, MA 02318
TELEPHONE: 617-495-3109
E-MAIL: JDADMISS@LAW.HARVARD.EDU • WEBSITE: WWW.LAW.HARVARD.EDU

less competitive than other law schools." Harvard is "a politically, socially, and ethnically diverse school." As one student puts it, it is "not full of dorks or elitists."

A healthy dork-and-elitist contingent does exist, though. "People study a lot (at least first year)." You'll find some "extremely cold, uninteresting, uptight" folks. But, in general, students "tend to play well with others." These "fantastically outspoken, very committed, passionate individuals [are] almost all fun, relaxed people who also happen to be really bright." One student observes,"People generally care a great deal about something, be it academics or extracurriculars, or even just how much money they hope to make some day." HLS is "shockingly fun." It's "the New York City of law schools—big, diverse, and exciting." Harvard Law students "seem to be pursuing their own individual goals." As a result, "it's hard to characterize a common experience." Ultimately, "the law school is whatever a student chooses it to be." One student exclaims, "The opportunity to meet different types of people and make future connections is amazing." An involved student notes, "There's a conservative society (The Federalist Society), a liberal society (The American Constitution Society), a shooting club, a Texas Club, a California Club," and the list goes on. There's "free food" galore. "The availability of speakers at both the law school and the university as a whole makes for difficult choices nearly every night." A harried student gushes, "In the same week, I've seen lectures by Peter Gammons (an ESPN analyst) and a debate featuring Judge Richard Posner. A few weeks ago I attended Con Law with Larry Tribe, proceeded to sit in on John Kerry's appearance on *Hardball with Chris Matthews* at the Kennedy School, and then had dinner with a group of students from my first-year section who will travel across the globe to work next year." Students who get bored can head off-campus to Cambridge and nearby Boston, both of which are "lively and swarming with students."

Getting In

Don't bet the farm on getting admitted to Harvard Law School. Note: in 2003, more than 7,000 would-be students applied. Fewer than 900 were offered admission. Admitted students at the 75th percentile have a near-perfect LSAT score of 174 and a GPA of 3.9. Admitted students at the 25th percentile have an LSAT score of 169 and a GPA of 3.7. If you take the LSAT more than once, Harvard covers all the bases by considering every reported score as well as your average.

EMPLOYMENT INFORMATION

Career Rating	**98**
Job placement rate (%)	99
Average starting salary	$107,611
State for bar exam	NY, MA
Pass rate for first-time bar	98

Employers who frequently hire grads:
Major national law firms, federal & state government, investment banks, consulting firms, law schools.

Grads employed by field (%):	
Academic	1
Business/industry	3
Government	3
Judicial clerkships	22
Private practice	67
Public interest	4

Academic Requirements

Clinical Program Required?	No
Legal Writing Course Requirement?	Yes
Legal Methods Course Requirement?	Yes
Legal Research Course Requirement?	Yes
Moot Court Requirement?	Yes
Public Interest Law Requirement?	Yes

ADMISSIONS

Selectivity Rating	**99**
# applications received	7,302
# applicants accepted	841
# acceptees attending	554
Average LSAT	171
LSAT Range	169–175
Average undergrad GPA	3.9
Application fee	$75
Regular application deadline	2/1
Regular notification	rolling
Rolling notification?	Yes
Early application program?	No
Transfer students accepted?	Yes
Evening division offered?	No
Part-time accepted?	No
LSDAS accepted?	Yes

Applicants Also Look At
Columbia University, New York University, Stanford University, Yale University.

International Students

TOEFL required of international students?	No
TOEFL recommended of international students?	No

FINANCIAL FACTS

Annual tuition	$31,250
Books and supplies	$972
Room & board	$15,252
% first-year students receiving some sort of aid	82
% receiving some sort of aid	81
% receiving scholarships	38
Average grant	$16,367
Average loan	$35,208
Average total aid package	$42,493
Average debt	$82,714

Howard University
School of Law

INSTITUTIONAL INFORMATION

Public/private	private
Student/faculty ratio	16:1
% faculty part-time	3
% faculty female	60
% faculty minority	85
Total faculty	51

SURVEY SAYS . . .

Diverse opinions accepted in classrooms
Great library staff
Students love Washington, DC

STUDENTS

Enrollment of law school	402
% male/female	40/60
% full-time	100
% minority	94
Average age of entering class	25

ACADEMICS

Academic experience rating	**79**
Professors interesting rating	87
Professors accessible rating	80
Hours of study per day	4.62

Academic Specialties

Commercial law, constitutional law, criminal law, environmental law, human rights law, intellectual property law, international law, labor law, property, taxation.

Advanced Degrees Offered

LLM, foreign lawyers only, 1 to 2 years.

Combined Degrees Offered

JD/MBA, 4 years.

Academic Requirements

Clinical Program Required?	No
Legal Writing Course Requirement?	Yes
Legal Methods Course Requirement?	Yes
Legal Research Course Requirement?	No
Moot Court Requirement?	No
Public Interest Law Requirement?	No

Academics

In the tradition of the famous civil rights lawyer Charles Hamilton Houston, Howard University promotes its "legacy for cultivating social engineers." Because Howard is an historically black institution, its students take their responsibility of serving as the next generation of minority attorneys very seriously. Reports a 3L: "Many of our professors encourage us to think beyond the rules of the law and apply it to the real world and also to analyze the implications of the law, particularly as they apply to poor and minority communities." This classroom emphasis on "strong policy and social justice responses to the law" further provides students with the experience they need to succeed in their careers post-graduation.

Howard's Washington, DC location "makes it easy to connect with professionals in a variety of fields, especially if you are going into public interest." Students find internships and jobs with the government, nonprofits, and lobby organizations. But not everyone wants to engineer society from the trenches: "Corporate law is alive and well at Howard." A 2L reports, "Students focus on getting a job more than anything, especially those highly coveted six-figure law firm positions." The Career Placement Office staff members win approval from the students for their "tireless efforts to encourage firms to recruit and hire from Howard." Students feel like they're in "the center of the recruiting universe," with plenty of "unique opportunities because of our institution's history."

Some students even feel that Howard has become too workforce-oriented and places too intense a focus on "teaching students how to be employees instead of leaders and innovators." Most, however, appreciate the "emphasis on practical experience," including clinics in criminal justice, immigration law, small business law, and alternative dispute resolution. In the classroom, students enjoy "a nontraditional dialogue approach," which allows them to get to know their professors, whom they consider "intense, dedicated, [...] absolutely brilliant, and true scholars in their respective fields." Beyond their achievements, the faculty is personally invested in the success of students. Professors "push hard" and "expect a lot," but also maintain the fine line between testing students' limits and keeping them afloat. Dean Kurt Schmoke, the former mayor of Baltimore, also racks up popularity points for his "pleasant attitude and accessibility." His reputation mitigates some gripes with the rest of the administration, whose "bureaucracy can be a little frustrating." Howard also offers "merit-based awards to the top 50 percent of the class" as a way of encouraging students to succeed.

One of the highlights of a Howard Law education is the Legal Research, Reasoning, and Writing program, which trains students in the elusive arts of navigating a law library, formulating analogical reasoning, and writing readable legalese. "Legal and scholarly writing is very important, and recruiters are constantly commenting on the quality of the writing from this law school," notes a 3L. Students looking for courses beyond the scope of the Howard curriculum may take part in a summer program in Cape Town, where they have the chance to study international trade law and visit the South Africa Parliament. Additionally, the school runs an exchange with Brigham Young University School of Law and the University of Vermont for students interested in environmental law.

On the Howard campus, you won't spot a law student without the required laptop, although some experience difficulty when they try to find a place to plug in and log on. "It's currently difficult to rely on Howard Law E-mail for communication from employ-

Reginald McGahee, Esq., Assistant Dean of Admission/Director of Admissions
2900 Van Ness Street, Suite 219, Washington, DC 20008
Telephone: 202-806-8008 • Fax: 202-806-8162
E-mail: admissions@law.howard.edu • Website: www.law.howard.edu

ers," writes a 3L. Students complain about classrooms with shabby furnishing and arctic temperatures in the winter. The brand-new library, however, earns praise for offering "lots of study space in a quiet and state-of-the-art building."

Life

A number of students describe the Howard student community as a "big extended family." Howard's "reputation attracts thousands of applicants of all races and ethnicities. Its familial atmosphere keeps them there." Another guiding philosophy at Howard, "Lifting As We Climb," means that "students who are in the top of the class are more than willing to take time to help other students who may be struggling." First-year students "don't even have to ask for help. Upperclassmen volunteer it out of love." There's no "ripping pages out of books in the library" here; everyone shares cases and invites each other to parties, "making it very easy to meet others" and creating a "community feeling I have never seen at any other educational institution."

Politically, students tend to "fall on the liberal side, for the most part," and make their opinions known both in and out of the classroom. Student organizations run the gamut, from The Scroll, a social justice law review (whose "reputation is on the rise"), to the Christian Legal Society and La Alianza, a Latino student group. The dean's lecture series addresses topics such as racial profiling, the implications of national elections, and the modern applications of historic legal decisions.

Getting In

The rolling admissions window runs from October to March for fall semester start only. Out of 2,600 applicants, roughly 450 are accepted, and 150 subsequently enroll.

EMPLOYMENT INFORMATION

Career Rating	**87**
% employed within 9 months	98
Average starting salary	$71,304

Employers who frequently hire grads:
Law firms, judicial clerkships, government.

Grads employed by field (%):

Academic	2
Business/industry	21
Government	19
Judicial clerkships	6
Private practice	46
Public interest	6

ADMISSIONS

Selectivity Rating	**79**
# applications received	2,550
# applicants accepted	421
# acceptees attending	155
Average LSAT	153
LSAT Range	148–158
Average undergrad GPA	3.3
Application fee	$60
Regular application deadline	3/31
Regular notification	rolling
Rolling notification?	Yes
Early application program?	No
Transfer students accepted?	Yes
Evening division offered?	No
Part-time accepted?	No
LSDAS accepted?	Yes

Applicants Also Look At

American University, The Catholic University of America, The George Washington University, Georgetown University, New York University, Texas Southern University, University of Maryland.

International Students

TOEFL required of international students?	Yes
Minimum Paper TOEFL	550

FINANCIAL FACTS

Annual tuition	$15,990
Books and supplies	$1,103
Fees per credit	$655
Tuition per credit	$724
Room & board	$10,169
Financial aid application deadline	3/1
% first-year students receiving some sort of aid	90
% receiving some sort of aid	95
% of aid that is merit-based	58
Average grant	$13,000
Average loan	$18,500
Average total aid package	$29,000
Average debt	$60,000

Illinois Institute of Technology
Chicago-Kent College of Law

INSTITUTIONAL INFORMATION

Public/private	private
Student/faculty ratio	6:1
% faculty part-time	61
% faculty female	30
% faculty minority	8
Total faculty	174

SURVEY SAYS . . .

Diverse opinions accepted in classrooms
Great research resources
Students love Chicago, IL

STUDENTS

Enrollment of law school	1,073
% male/female	54/46
% out-of-state	37
% full-time	75
% minority	18
% international	1
# of countries represented	18
Average age of entering class	25

ACADEMICS

Academic experience rating	**82**
Professors interesting rating	80
Professors accessible rating	80
Hours of study per day	3.91

Academic Specialties

Corporation securities law, criminal law, environmental law, financial services, human rights law, intellectual property law, international law, labor law, litigation and alternative dispute resolution, taxation, tech.

Advanced Degrees Offered

JD, 3 years full-time, 4 years part-time; LLM, 2 to 8 semesters.

Combined Degrees Offered

JD/MBA, 3.5 to 5 yrs; JD/LLM, 4 to 5 yrs; JD/MS in financial markets, 4 to 5 yrs; JD/MPA, 3.5 to 5 yrs; JD/MS in environmental management, 3.5 to 5 yrs; JD/master of public health, 3.5 yrs.

Academic Requirements

Clinical Program Required?	No
Legal Writing Course Requirement?	Yes

Academics

Chicago-Kent College of Law, part of the Illinois Institute of Technology, is "a very cutting-edge, forward-thinking place." Students praise the modern classrooms and marvel that "there seems to be a network connection on every flat surface in the school." Professors very often integrate technology into their courses through the use of "class websites, PowerPoint® presentations, E-mail, chat rooms, and online practice tests." So it follows that students "take final exams via computer," though, and not every student is impressed with all this "superior technology." Some say it's "distracting from what really matters—knowing the law." High-tech stuff aside, Chicago-Kent's impressive downtown building makes you feel as though "you're already working in a law firm." The reading room in the library is tremendously "aesthetically pleasing" and offers extraordinary views.

Academically, "the workload is intense, [and the] very impressive, accessible" professors "are all-stars." Students mention that "professors don't generally use the Socratic method, but all of them find a way to get students involved in discussions." More specifically, "They put you on the spot, thrash you a little, and then help you to understand the legal doctrines." One student says, "The professors' individual styles make the classes interesting." Another writes, "Some use a philosophical approach, others examine the minutiae of each case, and others encourage tangents and discussions."

There is a "strong emphasis on practical lawyering skills" at Chicago-Kent. Many of the "one-of-a-kind" clinics, such as the criminal law division are fee-generating with real, paying clients;" others provide free or low-cost legal services such as a public interest environmental law clinic. Acclaimed certificate programs include labor and employment and intellectual property. Judicial externships are readily available, Chicago-Kent students love to brag about what they call "one of the best legal writing programs in the country." Whereas "other law schools require a mere semester or two at the most, Kent requires five or six semesters [of] extensive" course work in legal writing. "Be prepared to work your butt off," advises one student. "When you're in it, it sucks and it's a lot of work," explains another candid student, "but when you start working and you see how much better prepared you are than associates from other schools, it's worth it."

The administration is "great on an individual, personal level." They are "approachable and open to resolving problems," and, overall, very "student-centered." One student tells us that the staff "cares a great deal about helping 1Ls adjust to the trauma that is the first semester." As far as organization is concerned, though, administration isn't always at the top of their game. Students grumble that registration is "rarely on time [and] always rushed, [while] important classes often conflict." Career Services will not win any popularity contests until it becomes "more proactive in assisting students in obtaining summer and postgraduate employment." On the plus side, Kent provides students "with a lot of current information" via an electronic newsletter and E-mail. Also, "law clerk and attorney positions are listed on a password protected job-posting system."

Life

"Chicago-Kent is a downtown school [with] no real 'campus' atmosphere." It's "mainly a commuter school." But students don't seem to miss residential life all that much. "Being in the downtown loop of Chicago right by Union Station [and] practically across the street from the Sears Tower" is not a bad place to be. Federal and state courts are "very close" as well.

Nicole Vilches, Assistant Dean for Admissions
565 West Adams Street, Chicago, IL 60661
Telephone: 312-906-5020 • Fax: 312-906-5274
E-mail: admit@kentlaw.edu • Website: www.kentlaw.edu

Students at Chicago-Kent are "quite eclectic, with a mix of classic, straight-out-of-college kids who are focused and prepared for careers as high-paying attorneys," as well as "people from different backgrounds who have already had one or more careers but have decided to study law." As a result, "classroom discussions are stimulating." Most students have "a very businesslike demeanor [and] pretty realistic notions about the practice of law." The evening students seem to think they are "much less ruthlessly competitive than Day Division students," although full-time students say it's "friendly competition," and not "cutthroat." One student writes, "Students are generally very cooperative [and] very friendly, relative harmony" is the rule. One student explains, "Students work hard and want to do well, but not at each other's expense. If I miss class or need assistance, I have never had a problem getting notes from other students."

"If you are looking for a collegial atmosphere with extracurriculars," Chicago-Kent may "not be the place for you." Although it lacks "a campus feeling, this school has great social opportunities [if] you find your niche (law review, student bar association, a clinic, etc.)." Students could probably stand to mix a bit more, since "the law reviewers hang with their like; the moot courters hang with their like; and the trial team thinks it rules the roost." Luckily, Chicago-Kent's Student Bar Association is well-organized and "spends a great deal of time and energy to promote a social atmosphere." The SBA sponsors parties at different bars and clubs including "six parties every year" where (as many students mention) "the drinks are free." Not into the bar scene? The SBA can also hook you up with "free tickets to the opera."

Getting In

With a GPA of 3.0 or higher and an LSAT score in the high 150s, you should be a competitive applicant at Chicago-Kent. The average LSAT score for entering students is 159. The average GPA is 3.4.

EMPLOYMENT INFORMATION

Career Rating	**80**
Job placement rate (%)	97
Average starting salary	$70,695
State for bar exam	IL
Pass rate for first-time bar	89

Prominent Alumni: Honorable Ilana Diamond Rovner, U.S. Court of Appeals for the 7th Circuit; Honorable Anne Burke, Illinois Appellate Court, 1st District; Tom Demetrio, Partner, Corboy & Demetrio; Barry Maram, Director of Illinois Department of Public Aid; Anita Alverez, Chief of Staff, Office of the Cook County State's Attorney.

Grads employed by field (%):	
Academic	2
Business/industry	12
Government	17
Judicial clerkships	3
Private practice	65
Public interest	1

Legal Methods Course Requirement?	No
Legal Research Course Requirement?	Yes
Moot Court Requirement?	Yes
Public Interest Law Requirement?	No

ADMISSIONS

Selectivity Rating	**81**
# applications received	3,178
# applicants accepted	987
# acceptees attending	280
Average LSAT	159
LSAT Range	157–162
Average undergrad GPA	3.4
Application fee	$60
Regular application deadline	3/1
Regular notification	rolling
Rolling notification?	Yes
Early application program?	No
Transfer students accepted?	Yes
Evening division offered?	Yes
Part-time accepted?	Yes
LSDAS accepted?	Yes

Applicants Also Look At

American University, DePaul University, The John Marshall Law School, Loyola University Chicago, Northwestern University, University of Illinois at Urbana-Champaign, University of Wisconsin.

International Students

TOEFL required of international students?	No
TOEFL recommended of international students?	No

FINANCIAL FACTS

Annual tuition	$27,450
Books and supplies	$610
Fees per credit	$245
Tuition per credit	$960
Room & board (on/off-campus)	$6,916/$13,860
Financial aid application deadline	4/15
% first-year students receiving some sort of aid	97
% receiving some sort of aid	92
% of aid that is merit-based	14
% receiving scholarships	53
Average grant	$10,634
Average loan	$32,371
Average total aid package	$34,310
Average debt	$89,917

INDIANA UNIVERSITY
SCHOOL OF LAW—BLOOMINGTON

INSTITUTIONAL INFORMATION

Public/private	public
Student/faculty ratio	14:1
% faculty part-time	1
% faculty female	33
% faculty minority	12
Total faculty	51

SURVEY SAYS . . .

Diverse opinions accepted in classrooms
Great research resources
Great library staff

STUDENTS

Enrollment of law school	637
% male/female	58/42
% out-of-state	55
% full-time	99
% minority	16
% international	1
Average age of entering class	24

ACADEMICS

Academic experience rating	**85**
Professors interesting rating	83
Professors accessible rating	75
Hours of study per day	4.45

Academic Specialties

Civil procedure, commercial law, constitutional law, corporation securities law, criminal law, environmental law, government services, human rights law, intellectual property law, international law, labor law, legal history, legal philosophy, property, taxation, telecommunications, trial & appellate advocacy.

Advanced Degrees Offered

S/JD, LLM, LLM, MCL.

Combined Degrees Offered

JD, MBA, 4 yrs; JD, master of public affairs, 4 yrs; JD, MSES, 4 yrs; JD, master of library and information science, 4 yrs; JD, MA/MS in telecommunication, 4 yrs; PhD in law and social science, 4 yrs; JD, MA of public accountancy, 4 yrs; JD, MA in journalism, 4 yrs.

Academics

Indiana University School of Law—Bloomington "places a high premium on collaboration and community." As a result, the school fosters a "supportive, positive network of colleagues—a relationship that extends into the workforce upon graduation." Furthermore, such an academic environment creates an atmosphere that is "challenging without being hostile." In fact, "the competitive spirit is very friendly—enough competition to make you the best you can be, but not so much it adds to the stress." The school helps to engender this sense of cooperation from the start with a great mentoring program for first-year students that "helps to ease the transition" into law school. Students appreciate the "variety of courses."

Students value learning from professors who are "recognized experts in their fields." One student boasts, "It's an incredible opportunity to learn from the people who shape our world." The faculty "genuinely want their students to succeed, [and] their doors are always open" for students to stop by and ask questions. There is not an "imaginary wall between students and professors" at IU—Bloomington. Rather, "it's not uncommon to catch a professor letting her students buy her a beer after the final." (Wait a minute, the student is buying?)

The administration "is excellent in addressing student concerns [and is] very receptive to suggestions," students tell us. "The dean holds town hall meetings to let us know what's going on with the school, including administrational issues like hiring, as well as answering questions about our concerns," writes one student. With regards to the administration, some complain, "Career Services could use a boost." However, there are others who counter saying that the "Career Services office is everyone's favorite whipping boy," and that, in fact, the folks running it really "do a great job."

Bookworms and the highly studious won't be disappointed at IU—Bloomington. "Our library is simply beautiful," exclaim students. "There is an abundance of natural light streaming in from the floor to ceiling windows. Long days in the library don't seem so bad when you're studying in such lovely surroundings." In addition to its aesthetic character, the library is also "one of the largest in the country, [and] the research facilities are substantial." The excellent full-time library staff also deserves some props. There are several interesting dual-degree programs offered by the school.

Patricia S. Clark, Director of Admissions
211 South Indiana Avenue, Bloomington, IN 47405-1001
Telephone: 812-855-4765 • Fax: 812-855-0555
E-mail: lawadmis@indiana.edu • Website: www.law.indiana.edu

Life

Bloomington is "one of the greatest college towns in America [and] brings stability and calm to the otherwise rigorous experience of law school." One student decrees the town "a perfect mix of culture, sports, academics, and fun," adding, "The campus is absolutely beautiful." Being at a large school can have its advantages because it offers so much to do. Students admit that the people at Indiana "love to be social and there are definitely some big parties." They say that sometimes even "professors get involved in the social atmosphere." Bloomington is "relatively liberal, accommodating of diverse cultures, offers diverse cuisine [and] great outdoor recreation." Furthermore, "the city and university seem to get along well."

At Indiana-Bloomington, students feel they are "not just a number." In fact, "there is an amazingly supportive, noncompetitive atmosphere that allows the students to both learn a lot and have fun. 'Gunners' are at a minimum." One law student opines, "Students are always willing to assist one another. Sharing outlines is a common practice. No one would ever hide a book or do anything to disadvantage anyone else." Another further elucidates, "All law schools are competitive, but I think that IU is on the low-end of the spectrum. Students work together and help each other instead of trying to sabotage grades. It really is a fabulous place to go to school." Students at the law school say there is a "great diversity [and] students with many interests." One student exclaims, "You'll find people to go to the bars with, to go to the gym with, anything you can think of!" And if that's not you're bag, "there are numerous political, social service, and networking events" to attend. "You can make friendships that will last a lifetime at IU—Bloomington."

Getting In

Admitted students at the 25th percentile have an LSAT score of 159 and a GPA of 3.0. Admitted students at the 75th percentile have an LSAT score of 164 and a GPA of 3.7.

EMPLOYMENT INFORMATION

Career Rating	**86**
% employed within 9 months	97
Average starting salary	$76,016
State for bar exam	IN, IL, NY, CA, DC
Pass rate for first-time bar	90

Employers who frequently hire grads: Arnold & Porter; Baker & Daniels; Bose McKinney; Ice Miller; Jones Day; Kirkland & Ellis; Mayer Brown; U.S. Dept of Justice; U.S. Federal Circuit & District Courts.

Prominent Alumni: Feisel Istrabadi, Iraqi Ambassador to the U.N.

Grads employed by field (%):	
Academic	4
Business/industry	9
Government	13
Judicial clerkships	9
Other	6
Private practice	56
Public interest	3

Academic Requirements

Clinical Program Required?	No
Legal Writing Course Requirement?	Yes
Legal Methods Course Requirement?	No
Legal Research Course Requirement?	Yes
Moot Court Requirement?	No
Public Interest Law Requirement?	No

ADMISSIONS

Selectivity Rating	**84**
# applications received	2,724
# applicants accepted	952
# acceptees attending	202
Average LSAT	163
LSAT Range	160–164
Average undergrad GPA	3.5
Application fee	$35
Regular application deadline	rolling
Regular notification	rolling
Rolling notification?	Yes
Early application program?	Yes
Early application deadline	11/15
Early application notification	12/15
Transfer students accepted?	Yes
Evening division offered?	No
Part-time accepted?	No
LSDAS accepted?	Yes

Applicants Also Look At

Ohio State U., U. of Illinois at Urbana-Champaign, U. of Michigan, U. of Minnesota, U. of Notre Dame, U. of Wisconsin, Vanderbilt U

International Students

TOEFL required of international students?	Yes
Minimum Paper TOEFL	600
Minimum Computer TOEFL	250

FINANCIAL FACTS

Annual tuition (resident)	$13,045
Annual tuition (nonres.)	$25,875
Books and supplies	$1,288
Room & board	$11,304
Financial aid app. deadline	4/1
% first-year students receiving some sort of aid	93
% receiving some sort of aid	93
% of aid that is merit-based	70
% receiving scholarships	72
Average grant	$6,517
Average loan	$29,000
Average total aid package	$33,000
Average debt	$64,000

INDIANA UNIVERSITY—INDIANAPOLIS
SCHOOL OF LAW

INSTITUTIONAL INFORMATION

Public/private	public
Student/faculty ratio	15:1
% faculty part-time	37
% faculty female	34
% faculty minority	1
Total faculty	69

SURVEY SAYS . . .

Great research resources
Beautiful campus
Students love Indianapolis, IN

STUDENTS

Enrollment of law school	843
% male/female	53/47
% out-of-state	18
% full-time	70
% minority	15
% international	2
# of countries represented	6
Average age of entering class	26

ACADEMICS

Academic experience rating	**76**
Professors interesting rating	69
Professors accessible rating	70
Hours of study per day	4.41

Academic Specialties

Constitutional law, criminal law, government services, health law, human rights law, intellectual property law, international law, labor law, taxation.

Combined Degrees Offered

JD/MPA, 4 years; JD/MBA, 4 years; JD/MHA, 4 years; JD/MPH, 4 years; JD/MPhil, 4 years; JD/MLS, 4 years.

Academic Requirements

Clinical Program Required?	No
Legal Writing Course Requirement?	Yes
Legal Methods Course Requirement?	Yes
Legal Research Course Requirement?	Yes
Moot Court Requirement?	No
Public Interest Law Requirement?	No

Academics

Weighing in with an enrollment of about 850 students, "rising star" Indiana University School of Law—Indianapolis is the largest law school in the Hoosier state. Students tell us IU—Indy is a "very hands-on [place where] they teach you how to be a lawyer, [by] mixing a traditional academic experience [with] practical, real-world experiences." There are definitely some very cool offerings including a program on law and state government, a curriculum in international human rights law, and study abroad opportunities in France, China, Croatia, and Argentina. IU—Indy also offers "one of the top health law concentrations in the country" and a regular smorgasbord of dual-degree programs associated with health law. Brand-new facilities and a new dean seem to be giving students the feeling IU—Indy is "a school that's really on the brink of becoming bigger and better."

The faculty and administration draw mostly rave reviews. "The dean is very accessible and interested in the students," and the "congenial" professors "go above and beyond the call of duty," making themselves "easy to approach." One student explains, "Even the most imposing in-class personalities are quite cordial (and dare I say, nice) outside of lecture. Some have had parties and cookouts at their own homes." In the classroom, some professors are "middle-of-the-road" types who "could improve" their teaching skills. Others are "excellent [and] entertaining." Legal writing is a mixed bag. Some students call it "second to none," while others find it "frustrating and baffling." Also, some students would like to see "more course offerings," especially for night students.

Law school facilities are reportedly above par. The law building is "an architectural gem," featuring a reading room with "windows from the floor to the ceiling [and] the most amazing view of downtown." Students say their school has "some of the best technological resources in the nation, [the] excellent" classrooms are wired to the gills with "laptop, Ethernet, and wireless connections." Unfortunately, "after spending all that money on the high-tech, someone forgot to get decent chalkboards." Let's not forget, "most important, [the] sweet swivel chairs [are] really comfortable."

Perhaps IU—Indy's greatest asset is the simple fact that it is "the only law school located in Indianapolis." The law school's proximity to the Indiana Government Center and the Indiana State House "well situates students to intern and clerk with all agencies, courts, and branches of government." As one student explains, "While most big cities have several law schools competing for the big city internships and clerkships, here in Indianapolis, IU—Indy has nearly a monopoly." The location also provides "easy and plentiful access to attorneys working in the community" who judge students' moot court and come to their bar nights. Scores of part-time legal positions are available as are "endless opportunities for pro bono work." Career Services "offers several seminars and networking opportunities [and is] extremely helpful and active" in helping students find jobs during school and after graduation.

Angela Espada, Associate Dean for Student Services and Admissions
530 West New York Street, Indianapolis, IN 46202-3225
Telephone: 317-274-2459 • Fax: 317-278-4780
E-mail: khmiller@iupui.edu • Website: www.indylaw.indiana.edu

Life

Students at IU—Indy are "very diverse in age, background, and ethnicity, IU—Indy is an excellent place to go if you are a nontraditional student because you are sure to find more than one or two others" like you. Students say, "People are very nice [and] always willing to help one another," but you don't have to be around very long to realize that "this is a commuter school." Most of the students "tend to have lives or families outside of law school, so there's not much of a social life." However, it is definitely possible to keep yourself busy when you aren't hitting the books. "Law school associations are constantly sponsoring parties, social events, and networking events. The events often include free food, so on any given day, you are sure to find a free lunch or dinner." Full-time day students "have more of a social life [and] seem to socialize more than evening students." Part-time students seem to feel a little neglected. "The evening program is like a red-headed stepchild," says one student, while another complains that the school is too "slanted toward the day students who don't work."

Although the administration has gone to great lengths to improve the parking situation on and near campus, it continues to range from "infuriating" to downright "horrible." A student observes, "There is also a lack of places to eat" around campus. Of course, "you could drive off-campus, but then you lose your parking place." Students are optimistic that "new bars and restaurants" should make life "more social" in the immediate future. You should also note that you cannot live very well in Indianapolis without wheels. "Nearby housing and mass transit are embarrassingly absent for such a large city."

Getting In

So long as you have an LSAT score over 150 and a GPA of 3.0 or higher, you stand a decent shot at getting admitted to IU—Indy. If your credentials are a little weaker, consider enrolling in the summer. Students who enter in the summer have an average LSAT score of about 148 and an average GPA lower than 3.0. The admissions staff will look at your best LSAT score if you take it more than once.

EMPLOYMENT INFORMATION

Career Rating	**74**
% employed within 9 months	93.9
Average starting salary	$55,000
State for bar exam	IN
Pass rate for first-time bar	79

Employers who frequently hire grads: Private law firms, Baker & Daniels, Barnes & Thornburg, Ice Miller.

Prominent Alumni: Dan Coats, former senator; Anece Baxter White, captain, U.S. Army legal advisor & ethics counselor; Rebecca Kendall, vice president/general counsel, Eli Lilly & Co.; Mark Roesler, president & CEO, CMG Worldwide, Inc.

Grads employed by field (%):	
Academic	3
Business/industry	19
Government	18
Judicial clerkships	3
Military	1
Private practice	51
Public interest	4

ADMISSIONS

Selectivity Rating	**83**
# applications received	1,820
# applicants accepted	474
# acceptees attending	286
Average LSAT	157
LSAT Range	151–158
Average undergrad GPA	3.4
Application fee	$50
Regular application deadline	3/1
Regular notification	rolling
Rolling notification?	Yes
Early application program?	No
Transfer students accepted?	Yes
Evening division offered?	Yes
Part-time accepted?	Yes
LSDAS accepted?	Yes
International Students	
TOEFL required of international students?	Yes
Minimum Paper TOEFL	550
Minimum Computer TOEFL	213

FINANCIAL FACTS

Annual tuition (resident)	$10,589
Annual tuition (nonresident)	$23,400
Books and supplies	$800
Fees per credit (resident)	$253
Fees per credit (nonresident)	$253
Tuition per credit (resident)	$342
Tuition per credit (nonresident)	$755
Room & board	$13,948
% first-year students receiving some sort of aid	59
% receiving some sort of aid	76
% of aid that is merit-based	80
% receiving scholarships	17
Average grant	$3,550
Average loan	$16,835
Average total aid package	$4,500
Average debt	$51,676

The John Marshall Law School

INSTITUTIONAL INFORMATION

Public/private	private
Student/faculty ratio	19:1
% faculty part-time	81
% faculty female	17
% faculty minority	13
Total faculty	290

SURVEY SAYS . . .

Diverse opinions accepted in classrooms
Great library staff
Students love Chicago, IL

STUDENTS

Enrollment of law school	1,329
% male/female	55/45
% out-of-state	25
% full-time	72
% minority	18
% international	1
# of countries represented	13
Average age of entering class	24

ACADEMICS

Academic Experience rating	**61**
Professors interesting rating	61
Professors accessible rating	61
Hours of study per day	4.26

Academic Specialties

Intellectual property law, international law, property, taxation.

Advanced Degrees Offered

LLM degree in taxation, intellectual property, real estate, information technology, comparative legal studies, international business and trade law. Employee benefits, 1 year full-time. MS degree in information technology.

Combined Degrees Offered

JD/MBA, JD/MPA, JD/MA, JD/LLM.

Academic Requirements

Clinical Program Required?	Yes
Legal Writing Course Requirement?	Yes
Legal Methods Course Requirement?	Yes

Academics

Smack-dab in the middle of Chicago's South Loop, the John Marshall Law School offers students a stimulating academic environment enhanced by the school's propitious location and extensive contacts in the Chicago legal community. Academically, "a few professors teach by the fear of God method (or the Socratic method). Yet despite their toughness in the classroom, they are very accessible and open to discussion about course materials, legal trends, or the latest Cubs woes," writes a 3L. In particular, many students praise the adjunct staff, which "includes federal circuit judges and prosecutors" who "bring real-world experience right into the classroom, which is a breath of fresh air." It also "enables the students to gain a real-world perspective of the law." For those wishing to specialize, students point out the strength of the "Global Legal Studies program, the Intellectual Property Law program, and the amazing LLM programs," of which John Marshall offers seven: comparative legal studies, employee benefits, information technology, intellectual property, international business and trade, real estate, and tax.

John Marshall places a great deal of emphasis on fostering professional skills in future lawyers through training in appellate advocacy, alternative dispute resolution, client counseling and negotiations. In addition, there is "great attention to legal writing," and "extracurricular activities—such as moot court, law journal, and the many symposiums held at the school—are a great benefit" to traditional studies. As a result, John Marshall graduates feel well prepared for their future careers and ready to "hit the ground running" once they receive their JD. A 2L advises, "If you are looking for legal theory, look elsewhere. At John Marshall, it is expected that you will practice upon graduation."

While they are introduced to legal skills in the classroom, the school's excellent location gives students direct access to a wide array of legal resources. Many say that "the school's location can't be beat," poised "right next door to the Chicago Bar Association and across the street from federal buildings." With so many important resources in the immediate vicinity, it's a piece of cake for students to interact directly with the Chicago legal community. "On my days off, I would take study breaks watching the 7th Circuit oral arguments. Likewise, my internship was across the street—just walking distance from campus," recalls one 3L. At the hub of the city government, John Marshall maintains "great contacts" with the right people and institutions, just in case "you want to work for a judge or get involved in politics." On top of that, "alumni relations seem to be particularly strong at JMLS."

While favorably located, students say the John Marshall campus could use a little facelift. "The facilities are somewhat mixed," explains a 2L. "It's two fairly large buildings slammed together to make one law school comprising half a city block. There's a modern side, which is remodeled and has technical resources, and there's the antiquated side, comprised of lecture halls fashioned from rooms that were distinctly not suited for lecturing." On the older side of campus there is a general grumble that it's "difficult to find a plug for your laptop," and several students mention that "it would be nice to have more student areas, a gym or workout center, and a day-care [center], especially for night students." However, the school has kept up with much of the latest classroom technology, and "wireless Internet is available throughout the school." Most important, John Marshall maintains world-class legal research facilities. Of particular note, "the library stores the reference material for the Chicago Bar Association, making it extremely resourceful compared to other institutions."

William B. Powers, Associate Dean for Admission & Student Affairs
315 South Plymouth Court, Chicago, IL 60604
Telephone: 800-537-4280 • Fax: 312-427-5136
E-mail: admission@jmls.edu • Website: www.jmls.edu

Life

Whether at work or play, there is a strong sense of camaraderie and friendship between students at the John Marshall Law School. Competition is mild, and no matter how tough things get, "everyone wants their friends to do well" in class. With a total enrollment of more than 800 students, the school nonetheless maintains a low-key, intimate environment. In fact, students say "it feels like a small town community" where "everyone knows everyone." In fact, a 2L notes, "If I bump into another student outside school, there is always a smile or an exchange of recognition, which is very comforting." Students in the part-time program report a similar sense of solidarity: "There is a great camaraderie among the evening students. We all have diverse careers and these add to the discussions in class," reports one 2L.

When they aren't hitting the books, John Marshall students are generally sociable and eager to unwind with their classmates. "When it's time to study, everyone is serious and focused, but when we can get a break, the drinks start flowing and the music starts cranking," explains a 2L. By all accounts, Chicago is an excellent backdrop for professional and personal pursuits; however, many point out that "John Marshall is located in a business area, and there is not really a lot to choose from in terms of social bars/restaurants to hang around in." In fact, students complain that it can be hard to find a decent gathering spot in and around John Marshall, as the surrounding area is not conducive, and "student lounges need to be upgraded from old rat-infested couches and lawn chair style seating on the fourth and fifth floors."

Getting In

John Marshall enrolls classes twice a year, admitting students for August and January. To apply to John Marshall, you must submit an undergraduate transcript, LSAT scores, a personal statement, and letters of recommendation. About one in three applicants is accepted.

EMPLOYMENT INFORMATION

Career Rating	**71**
Job placement rate (%)	89
Average starting salary	$64,495
State for bar exam	IL
Pass rate for first-time bar	75

Employers who frequently hire grads:
Hinshaw & Culbertson, Cook County State's Attorney, Clausen Miller, City of Chicago Law Department.

Grads employed by field (%):	
Business/industry	21
Government	12
Judicial clerkships	4
Private practice	56
Public interest	1

Legal Research Course Requirement?	Yes
Moot Court Requirement?	No
Public Interest Law Requirement?	No

ADMISSIONS

Selectivity Rating	**73**
# applications received	3,137
# applicants accepted	1,079
# acceptees attending	367
Average LSAT	154
LSAT Range	151–155
Average undergrad GPA	3.1
Application fee	$50
Regular application deadline	3/1
Regular notification	rolling
Rolling notification?	Yes
Early application program?	No
Transfer students accepted?	Yes
Evening division offered?	Yes
Part-time accepted?	Yes
LSDAS accepted?	Yes

Applicants Also Look At

DePaul University, Illinois Institute of Technology.

International Students

TOEFL required of international students?	Yes
Minimum Paper TOEFL	600

FINANCIAL FACTS

Annual tuition	$28,560
Books and supplies	$900
Tuition per credit	$952
Room & board (off-campus)	$17,620
% first-year students receiving some sort of aid	90
% receiving some sort of aid	90
% of aid that is merit-based	10
% receiving scholarships	18
Average grant	$8,400
Average loan	$9,999
Average total aid package	$18,500
Average debt	$83,053

LEWIS & CLARK COLLEGE
LEWIS & CLARK LAW SCHOOL

INSTITUTIONAL INFORMATION

Public/private	private
Student/faculty ratio	14:1
% faculty part-time	59
% faculty female	32
% faculty minority	5
Total faculty	107

SURVEY SAYS . . .

Great research resources
Great library staff
Beautiful campus
Students love Portland, OR

STUDENTS

Enrollment of law school	742
% male/female	51/49
% out-of-state	65
% full-time	72
% minority	17
% international	1
# of countries represented	11
Average age of entering class	27

ACADEMICS

Academic experience rating	**78**
Professors interesting rating	78
Professors accessible rating	79
Hours of study per day	4.61

Academic Specialties

Commercial law, corporation securities law, criminal law, environmental law, government services, intellectual property law, labor law, property, taxation.

Advanced Degrees Offered

LLM, environmental & natural resources, 1 to 1.5 years.

Academic Requirements

Clinical Program Required?	No
Legal Writing Course Requirement?	Yes
Legal Methods Course Requirement?	Yes
Legal Research Course Requirement?	Yes
Moot Court Requirement?	No
Public Interest Law Requirement?	No

Academics

At Lewis & Clark Law School, the students pride themselves on being at "one of the best environmental law programs in the country" and a place that draws "socially minded individuals who care more about changing the world than competing with their classmates." This environment breeds students that are friendly, so a "cutthroat competition is not a problem at all." But it is the environmental law program that is "deservedly, the pride of the school." It has many facets. "The strength of the environmental law program is incredible, from the environmental faculty, to the environmental clinics, to opportunities to do semester-long environmental externships and participate in national environmental conferences—all in an environmentally conscious city like Portland." In addition to the strong environmental program, many are "very excited about animal law as an emerging field of study."

Most students rave about the administration being "very understanding [of] all of life's pressures outside of law school, [as well as] willing to work with you to ensure that you do not fall [by] the wayside." It's easy to see why students like the administration when there is "student participation in almost every aspect of running the school." Furthermore, by only requiring a few classes after first year, Lewis & Clark allows students to create their own path. The Career Services Center is "very user friendly for students, [and the] resources are extensive and easy to use." Students are happy that the school is "very tied into the local legal community."

The professors at Lewis & Clark run the gamut from "typical curmudgeons who will scare you to death in the first year" to others "who want to go get a beer and 'talk shop' with you." But whichever is the case, all are "very available to the students" through their refreshing open-door policies and make an effort to get to know students "on a personal level, as well as academically." One student beams, "I have developed personal relationships with many of my professors, and they are my constant mentors and confidants."

The law library at Lewis & Clark is "very beautiful and a good place to spend three years of your life." Students enjoy the library's "several group study rooms, as well as areas where there are more comfortable lounge chairs and sofas." One student even admits that he has "found the perfect 'nap couch.'" As far as computer services go, L&C "has campus-wide wireless Internet, making portable computing a campus norm." One student writes, "Even a wayward Mac user like me hasn't had any big problems."

Lewis & Clark Law School, Admissions Office
10015 SW Terwilliger Boulevard, Portland, OR 97219
Telephone: 503-768-6613 • Fax: 503-768-6793
E-mail: lawadmss@lclark.edu • Website: http://law.lclark.edu

Life

Many students claim that the best part of Lewis & Clark "is that it is located in Portland, Oregon." They note, "The setting is pure paradise. There are trees everywhere," and a state park "nearly surrounds the campus," which lends a lot to a "very relaxing atmosphere." The scenery provides "a great study-break option" to the rigors of law school life. Such a relaxing setting undoubtedly contributes to the "laid-back attitude of the student body, [and a] casual, supportive environment." On the competitiveness factor, there is "nothing cutthroat about this place." It's not that there isn't competition; it's that it exists within the parameters of a "friendly environment." Students grumble that Portland does not provide many parking alternatives.

The student population could be more diverse, but students assure us that students are coming in wider varieties each year. Furthermore, the school tends to have "an older population, lots of married people with kids. The population can vary from year to year, but it tends toward people who have already established themselves" in life. Overall, however, students describe their peers as "a close-knit group, really friendly, and always willing to help each other out. It is such a demanding environment, and it is comforting to know that you have the support of your classmates." That being said, "the campus (and city) does definitely lean to the left, so if you're a conservative on some issues, you feel out of place sometimes." The students at Lewis & Clark like to have their fun, too. "On an average week, there is usually at least one social event planned." A student explains to us, "The student body is small and mixes enough that there is a healthy amount of social life without it being distracting."

Getting In

At Lewis & Clark, admitted students at the 25th percentile have an LSAT score of 157 and a GPA of 3.1. Admitted students at the 75th percentile have an LSAT score of 163 and a GPA of 3.6. The school enrolls about 700 students. Part-time and evening programs are available.

EMPLOYMENT INFORMATION

Career Rating	**71**
Job placement rate (%)	92
Average starting salary	$50,568
State for bar exam	OR, CA, WA
Pass rate for first-time bar	73

Employers who frequently hire grads: Numerous small and midsize firms; state government (Oregon, Washington, Idaho, Alaska); Multnomah, Washington, and Clackamas Countiese.

Prominent Alumni: Earl Blumenauer, U.S. representative; Heidi Heitkamp, former attorney general and 2000 gubernatorial nominee; Honorable Robert E. Jones, U.S. District Court for the district of Oregon.

Grads employed by field (%):	
Academic	1
Business/industry	12
Government	18
Judicial clerkships	14
Private practice	44
Public interest	11

ADMISSIONS

Selectivity Rating	**81**
# applications received	2,479
# applicants accepted	903
# acceptees attending	236
Average LSAT	160
LSAT Range	158–164
Average undergrad GPA	3.2
Application fee	$50
Regular application deadline	3/1
Regular notification	rolling
Rolling notification?	Yes
Early application program?	No
Transfer students accepted?	Yes
Evening division offered?	Yes
Part-time accepted?	Yes
LSDAS accepted?	Yes

Applicants Also Look At

Seattle University, University of California—-Davis, University of Colorado, University of Minnesota, University of Oregon, University of Washington, Willamette University.

International Students

TOEFL required of international students?	No
TOEFL recommended of international students?	Yes
Minimum Paper TOEFL	600
Minimum Computer TOEFL	250

FINANCIAL FACTS

Annual tuition	$25,334
Books and supplies	$800
Room & board (off-campus)	$14,400
Financial aid application deadline	3/1
% first-year students receiving some sort of aid	93
% receiving some sort of aid	92
% of aid that is merit-based	19
% receiving scholarships	40
Average grant	$9,359
Average loan	$28,628
Average total aid package	$39,734
Average debt	$75,696

Louisiana State University
Paul M. Hebert Law Center

INSTITUTIONAL INFORMATION

Public/private	public
Student/faculty ratio	16:1
% faculty part-time	37
% faculty female	15
% faculty minority	8
Total faculty	75

SURVEY SAYS . . .

Great research resources
Great library staff

STUDENTS

Enrollment of law school	657
% male/female	49/51
% out-of-state	14
% full-time	100
% minority	22
% international	1
# of countries represented	6

ACADEMICS

Academic experience rating	**79**
Professors interesting rating	84
Professors accessible rating	75
Hours of study per day	3.74

Academic Specialties

Civil procedure, commercial law, constitutional law, corporation securities law, criminal law, environmental law, government services, human rights law, intellectual property law, international law, labor law, legal history, legal philosophy, property, taxation.

Advanced Degrees Offered

Master of laws (LLM), 1 year; master of civil law (MCL), 1 year.

Combined Degrees Offered

Master's in public in administrations (JD), 3 years; master's of business administration (JD), 4 years.

Academic Requirements

Clinical Program Required?	Yes
Legal Writing Course Requirement?	Yes
Legal Methods Course Requirement?	Yes

Academics

At Louisiana State University Paul M. Hebert Law Center, students get a strong background in both civil and common law, preparing them to practice throughout the nation, as well as internationally. It is the only law school in the U.S. that awards to graduates the JD and BCL simultaneously. The BCL recognizes students' unique training in civil law in addition to common law, which is taught at all other law schools. Students say the curriculum is challenging, but that faculty and staff go out of their way to promote cooperation and teamwork, rather than grade grubbing and rivalry. A student tells us, "The students are strongly encouraged to help each other out, and not to be competitive." Another adds, "LSU does a good job in making a family-type atmosphere for the 1Ls by providing lots of student activities." On top of that, students say their professors are always available for extra assistance when the going gets rough. "The faculty are very accessible outside of the classroom and are willing to take the time outside of class to help you understand concepts that give you grief," writes one student.

While students agree that LSU professors are generally obliging and helpful outside the classroom, they say that some of them are disappointing in the lecture hall. A student explains, "There are so many different professors—some excellent and some who couldn't teach their way out of a paper sack." Another agrees, "The professors I've had thus far are either hit or miss. Most of the miss comes with the size of their ego and their unreasonable expectation of knowledge in your first year (specifically the first month). Most of the hit comes with professors that probably remember what it was like before they started practicing law 20 to 30-some-odd years or so ago." Even so, most students say that the good far outweigh the bad. "While every school has those select terrible professors, I can honestly say I've only had two out of my 20 different professors who I thought were not outstanding," writes one such student. Students also point to the diversity within the teaching staff as part of what makes their education at LSU unique. In the words of one happy student, such diversity "gives students the opportunity to learn to look at things from other perspectives."

The curriculum at LSU is broad-based, with a "heavy emphasis on speaking and writing," as well as a focus on promoting real-world skills. In particular, LSU offers extensive litigation training and practice. Throughout their three years of academics, LSU law students participate in national trial and appellate training programs under the guidance of their competent and experienced professors. Students would like to see, however, the practical curriculum go further. One such student suggests that LSU should "create some clinical programs that offer students worthwhile practical skills in trial advocacy and transactional legal work." In a similar vein, students say the Career Services Office could be more helpful in creating "organizations that further career opportunities and foster networking." Even though they think it could stand a few improvements, students know that LSU has a "strong reputation in the state of Louisiana," which is where most graduating students choose to practice.

Michele Forbes, Director of Student Affairs and Registrar
202 Law Center, Baton Rouge, LA 70803
Telephone: 225-578-8646 • Fax: 225-578-8647
E-mail: admissions@law.lsu.edu • Website: www.law.lsu.edu

The administration at LSU takes an active interest in student life and internalizes student concerns. "Chancellor Costonis impresses me with his sincere desire to raise the academic standards at LSU dramatically," writes one student. Another adds, "The administration is extremely helpful and flexible with students, and seems sincerely devoted to improving your life at the law school." While students have complained in the past of the Law Center's poor classroom facilities and lacking technology, millions of dollars in renovation over the last year now have one satisfied student declaring, "facilities and technology are excellent now that renovations are complete or nearing completion."

Life

If you didn't have enough fun in college, you might want to check out LSU. A student tells us, "Even though there's a strong sense of professionalism here because it's a professional school, the 'party vein' from our rather notorious undergrad still runs quite deep among the student body at the law school." Another adds, "The student government rents out Fred's in Tigerland, and we party like undergrads; this kind of social activity helps in creating a real sense of community at the law center." Partying aside, students report, "The school environment is very pleasant, the students get along well, and the staff are very helpful to everyone."

Getting In

The Paul M. Hebert Law Center bases acceptance on an admissions index calculated by adding ten times the undergraduate GPA (10 x GPA) together with the average LSAT score. Although GPA and LSAT scores are the most important aspects of an application to LSU, the school also considers the student's letters of recommendation, verbal and written skills, extracurricular activities, caliber of undergraduate institution, and work experience. The average GPA for last year's entering class was 3.4 and the average LSAT score was 154. Multiple LSAT scores are averaged.

EMPLOYMENT INFORMATION

Career Rating	**72**
Job placement rate (%)	89
Average starting salary	$48,935
State for bar exam	LA
Pass rate for first-time bar	89

Employers who frequently hire grads:
Adams & Reese, Baker & Hostetler, Breazeale Sachse & Wilson, Phelps Dunbar, McGinchey Stafford Lang, Taylor Porter Brooks & Phillips, Stone Pigman, Vinson & Elkins, Chaffe Mccall Phillips Toler & Sarpy, Cook Yancey King & Galloway, Correro Fishman Haygood Phelps Weiss, Courtenay Forstall Hunter & Fontana, Cox & Smith, Crawford & Lewis.

Grads employed by field (%):	
Academics	2
Business/industry	3
Government	7
Judicial clerkships	21
Military	2
Private practice	59
Other	6

Legal Research Course Requirement?	No
Moot Court Requirement?	No
Public Interest Law Requirement?	No

ADMISSIONS

Selectivity Rating	**79**
# applications received	1,846
# applicants accepted	473
# acceptees attending	212
Average LSAT	154
LSAT Range	151–158
Average undergrad GPA	3.5
Application fee	$25
Regular application deadline	2/3
Regular notification	2/3
Rolling notification?	Yes
Early application program?	No
Transfer students accepted?	Yes
Evening division offered?	No
Part-time accepted?	No
LSDAS accepted?	Yes

Applicants Also Look At

Loyola University New Orleans, Tulane University, University of Mississippi.

International Students

TOEFL required of international students?	Yes
Minimum Paper TOEFL	600
Minimum Computer TOEFL	250

FINANCIAL FACTS

Annual tuition (resident)	$10,410
Annual tuition (nonresident)	$20,746
Books and supplies	$1,500
Room & board (on/off-campus)	$10,550/$18,950
Financial aid application deadline	3/4
% receiving scholarships	44
Average grant	$4,479
Average loan	$18,040
Average debt	$51,304

LOYOLA MARYMOUNT UNIVERSITY
LOYOLA LAW SCHOOL

INSTITUTIONAL INFORMATION

Public/private	private
Student/faculty ratio	16:1
% faculty part-time	44
% faculty female	37
% faculty minority	17
Total faculty	126

SURVEY SAYS . . .

Diverse opinions accepted in classrooms
Great research resources
Abundant externship/internship/clerkship opportunities

STUDENTS

Enrollment of law school	1,331
% male/female	52/48
% full-time	75
% minority	39
% international	1
Average age of entering class	24

ACADEMICS

Academic experience rating	**98**
Professors interesting rating	98
Professors accessible rating	96
Hours of study per day	4.3

Academic Specialties

Cancer rights law, civil procedure, commercial law, constitutional law, corporation securities law, criminal law, election law, environmental law, entertainment law, government services, human rights law, intellectual property law, international law, labor law, legal history, legal philosophy, mediation, property, taxation.

Advanced Degrees Offered

LLM in taxation, 1 year full-time, 3 years full-time; LLM in American law and international legal practice, 1 year full-time, 3 years part-time.

Combined Degrees Offered

JD/MBA, 4 years.

Academic Requirements

Clinical Program Required?	No
Legal Writing Course Requirement?	No

Academics

Whether dropping the names of celebrity alumni or discussing the high quality of their academic program, Loyola Marymount students sing the praises of their small Southern Californian school. While you will get a rigorous legal education at Loyola, don't expect to attend an endless series of boring lectures. The school's "brilliant [and] accessible" teaching staff draws praises for being able to "communicate the complex clearly." "They're also a damn funny lot, which goes a long way when you're slogging through a 14-week course on civil procedure." On top of that, the teaching staff is generally described as "wonderful and supportive," always willing to lend academic or personal support. A 1L recounts, "All of the professors really care about their students; I even had a criminal law professor that would bring cookies and brownies in for the class."

Loyola has built a reputation for producing renowned litigators. "The school places a strong emphasis on practical application, skills classes, and real-world experience. Loyola is known throughout the Los Angeles region for producing top-notch litigators (among them Mark Geragos, Robert Shapiro, and Gloria Allred), and the school maintains a "great reputation among employers in the Southern California area," as well as "a large alumni network of successful and respected lawyers in California." As a result, "the bulk of Loyola lawyers end up working somewhere in L.A." A few note that because Loyola's national reputation does not mirror its strong regional reputation, it is sometimes more difficult to find a job in another state. At Loyola, "students have abundant opportunities to acquire practical researching, writing, and courtroom skills through extensive connections to the judicial system, a well-respected law review, and excellent trial and appellate advocacy programs, as well as numerous practical skills courses." "The trial advocacy program, particularly the Hobbs Program, enables students at Loyola to complete a trial advocacy course and then do an externship at the district attorney's office for school credit. This program enables the student to get courtroom experience by handling preliminary hearing and misdemeanor jury trials." A 3L tells us that for students set on working on Law Review, "Law Review is a write-on, and if you complete your paper for the competition, your chances of getting on are very, very good. With three Law Reviews, there are a lot of positions for staffers." Loyola also offers unique opportunities for study abroad. A 2L boasts, "I've been to Costa Rica and China through Loyola…I not only met people from other countries, but have made lasting friendships (and connections) all over the country."

While enjoying the sunny California weather, lucky Loyola students attend classes in a building designed by the famous architect Frank O. Gehry, a facility that one student describes as "almost like an Escher painting." An added benefit to the building is its location: It is set apart from the main undergraduate campus. This location fosters "a good sense of togetherness with an enclosed campus." "Loyola's small campus means that you can have lunch with your professors any day you want, get your Con Law taught by the dean who clerked in the Supreme Court, all while being in the heart of one of the biggest legal cities in the country." While intimate and beautiful, Loyola has some drawbacks: "The classrooms are aesthetically different (à la industrial/loft chic), but have terrible acoustics. The professors complain about it incessantly." On top of that, students gripe that the wireless Internet network is often down. Improvements are in the making, though: The school recently constructed a new facility "designed specifically for trial advocacy and has several 'courtrooms' set up with video, Internet, and computer capability, all state of the art."

Life

"The students are an incredibly diverse population" at Loyola. Even though "Loyola is a Jesuit institution," students report that "there is no forced emphasis with regard to

Sonel Shropshire, Assistant Dean of Admissions
919 Albany Street, Los Angeles, CA 90015
Telephone: 213-736-1180 • Fax: 213-736-6523
E-mail: admissions@lls.edu • Website: www.lls.edu

religion." A 2L writes, "My class consists of students of every nationality, religion, and political affiliation." Students boast about the "true sense of community the students have with one another," noting that "no one hides books in the library; everyone is willing to share outlines; and diverse opinions are tolerated." As a result of its diversity, "Loyola has an organization for almost every interest, from Bioethics to East Asian Law Society to OutLaw: Gay/Straight Alliance and everything in between." On this active campus, "there is something for everyone—and if not, the Student Bar Association is supportive and encouraging of starting a new organization." "From inviting distinguished speakers to debate on controversial issues to providing hot chocolate with marshmallows during finals week, the student organizations always have ways for students to become more involved in the school and the community."

While it may be surprising to hear that a bunch of future litigators are actually friendly folks, Loyola students insist that their classmates are outgoing, supportive, and social. "You always have someone to catch happy hour with." "Professors, librarians, your fellow students, and even alumni come back to hang out." That said, because Loyola is located in the business district of downtown L.A., it tends to be a "commuter school" with an on-campus vibe that is more academic than social. A 3L explains, "In the first year, there are many social activities as the different sections start to bond. As the years progress, the large scale social activities shift into smaller-scale social activities." Many students say they take advantage of the school's excellent location "in the heart of downtown Los Angeles, so close to all sorts of employment opportunities, cultural places of interest, and an extremely diverse community." Loyola students, a "well-rounded and socially comfortable" bunch, often end up going out to "some of the top nightclubs in L.A." Finally, because Loyola "is not a suburban environment," but rather "in the middle of the hubbub," students warn that the neighborhood is "not the safest place."

Getting In

To be considered for admission to Loyola Law School, students must submit undergraduate transcripts, LSAT scores, and a personal statement, as well as a secondary written statement in response to a question presented in the application materials. Students also must submit three letters of recommendation, of which at least one should be from an academic source.

EMPLOYMENT INFORMATION

Career Rating	**82**
Job placement rate (%)	95
Average starting salary	$75,612
State for bar exam	CA

Employers who frequently hire grads: O'Melveny & Myers; Los Angeles district attorney; Skadden, Arps, Slate, Meagher, & Flom; Paul Hastings; Jones, Day, Reavis, & Pogue; Shephard, Mullin, Richter, & Hampton; Foley & Lardner.

Prominent Alumni: Gloria Allred, trial attorney; Larry Feldman, trial attorney; Mark Geragos, trial attorney; Robert Shapiro, trial attorney.

Grads employed by field (%):	
Academic	2
Business/industry	16
Government	6
Judicial clerkships	1
Military	1
Private practice	68
Public interest	6

Legal Methods Course Requirement?	Yes
Legal Research Course Requirement?	No
Moot Court Requirement?	No
Public Interest Law Requirement?	Yes

ADMISSIONS

Selectivity Rating	**87**
# applications received	4,582
# applicants accepted	932
# acceptees attending	343
Average LSAT	161
LSAT Range	159–164
Average undergrad GPA	3.3
Application fee	$50
Regular application deadline	rolling
Regular notification	rolling
Rolling notification?	Yes
Early application program?	No
Transfer students accepted?	Yes
Evening division offered?	Yes
Part-time accepted?	Yes
LSDAS accepted?	Yes

International Students

TOEFL required of international students?	Yes
Minimum Paper TOEFL	600
Minimum Computer TOEFL	250

FINANCIAL FACTS

Annual tuition	$29,550
Books and supplies	$1,080
Room & board (off-campus)	$10,510
Financial aid application deadline	3/2
Average grant	$26,523
Average loan	$31,497
Average debt	$85,930

LOYOLA UNIVERSITY CHICAGO
SCHOOL OF LAW

INSTITUTIONAL INFORMATION

Public/private	private
Student/faculty ratio	15:1
Affiliation	Roman Catholic
% faculty part-time	76
% faculty female	44
% faculty minority	7
Total faculty	121

SURVEY SAYS . . .

Diverse opinions accepted in classrooms

Students love Chicago, IL

STUDENTS

Enrollment of law school	859
% male/female	48/52
% out-of-state	41
% full-time	70
% minority	21
% international	1
# of countries represented	15
Average age of entering class	24

ACADEMICS

Academic experience rating	**84**
Professors interesting rating	81
Professors accessible rating	79
Hours of study per day	3.97

Academic Specialties

Child and family law, corporation securities law, health law, intellectual property law, international law, labor law, taxation.

Advanced Degrees Offered

MJ health law, MJ child law, MJ business law, 22 semester hours; LLM health law, LLM child law, LLM tax law, 24 semester hours; S/JD health law, 2 years full-time.

Combined Degrees Offered

JD/MBA, JD/MSW, JD/MA political science. All 4 years.

Academic Requirements

Clinical Program Required?	No
Legal Writing Course Requirement?	Yes
Legal Methods Course Requirement?	No

Academics

Loyola University Chicago School of Law is blessed with a magnificent location, a "very collegial" environment, and "great job placement" across the Midwest. An annual bar-passage rate for first-time testers of around 90 percent is just gravy. Loyola's "tough, dedicated" professors are "truly into teaching" and apparently engaging enough to "really cut into the desire to play Free Cell" on your laptop during class. Students tell us that professors "believe in the Jesuit tradition," meaning they demonstrate "compassion [and] humanity" to their students and place "an emphasis on public service." Although "there is a small minority of professors that seem totally inept, great professors" abound at Loyola. "Many have been the best I've ever had," testifies one student. "Professor Kaufman is by far the greatest civil procedure and business organizations professor to walk the planet."

"Classroom and research facilities are wonderful, [although they] could be modernized a little." Loyola "has become more computer-friendly," but some say it's still "lacking in the area of technology [and] has a long way to go." The library houses "an endless number of resources" and plenty of quiet places to study. We hear that "even alumni consistently take advantage of Loyola's library."

Loyola offers a "broad range of educational opportunities [and] a remarkable variety of classes"—impressive when you consider the school's modest size. Several dual-degree programs are available, as are a host of certificate programs. Other highlights include an outstanding tax certificate program, which "gives students an opportunity to kind of 'major'" in taxation; a Health Law Institute of "great variety and depth;" and highly ranked Institutes for Health Law and Child Law. On top of that, Loyola is home to "one of the best trial advocacy programs in the country." Also noteworthy are the study abroad programs—Loyola even has its own campus in Rome. And, finally, let's not forget the "wide range of extracurricular activities—everything from moot court to negotiation teams to various clinics, externships, and fellowships."

Prospects for gaining professional experience and getting a real job are "fantastic." Students note, "Loyola has a great reputation in the Chicago area [and] being in such a large market [means] there are so many opportunities." It doesn't hurt that Loyola's alumni network is "extensive, especially in Chicago." One student declares, "I get the distinct sense that Loyola alums are very loyal to their school and that my degree will be a valuable asset when applying at Chicago-area law firms."

Life

"This school has the most communal feeling I have ever experienced," exclaims one student. "You don't see a whole lot of a 'rah-rah' attitude toward the school, [but] the student body is unbelievably friendly, outgoing, and fun. I never thought that I would have this much fun in law school." The consensus among students is that from the first-year orientation period onward, "the social aspect is amazing." Of course, "there are people who just show up, go to class, and go home, [and] there is always that jerk in the back row [but] the overall feel is laid back." There is "a genuine camaraderie, [which] permeates throughout the school." Don't get us wrong, "students are competitive," and you'll still "get clobbered by the workload." Plus, "exams are brutal." There's also "the stress of the mandatory grading curve." Most students "study in groups, look out for each other," and share a common "we're-all-in-this-together mentality."

OFFICE OF ADMISSION AND FINANCIAL ASSISTANCE
25 EAST PEARSON, 14TH FLOOR, CHICAGO, IL 60611
TELEPHONE: 312-915-7170 • FAX: 312-915-7906
E-MAIL: LAW-ADMISSIONS@LUC.EDU • WEBSITE: WWW.LUC.EDU/SCHOOLS/LAW

"Chicago is a wonderful city to live in," and Loyola's downtown location "affords the opportunity to experience city life fully while being a member of a smaller community." The law school is "perfectly positioned between the North Side residential neighborhoods and the Loop." Basically, "there is everything you need within three blocks—at least "everything but affordable housing." Students agree that while "downtown Chicago is a great place to learn, it's an even better place not to learn." After class, you can "unwind on the Magnificent Mile," relax at one of dozens of bars and restaurants, or participate in one of the many "organized student social activities," which happen "at least once per week" and are reportedly "packed."

While students would like to see more ethnic diversity, they admit there's no lack of variety when it comes to political viewpoints. "There are people who are on polar ends of the spectrum (Fox News meets Al Franken), and they're given equal time by professors." Students' frequent debates "make class discussions very interesting, and sometimes a bit heated!" But ultimately, "despite their widely differing opinions, students treat each other with respect."

Getting In

Enrollment is about 850 students. Admitted students at the 25th percentile have an LSAT score of 159 and a GPA of 3.17. Admitted students at the 75th percentile have an LSAT score of 161 and a GPA of 3.58. It's a little bit easier to get admitted to Loyola if you are a part-time or evening student.

EMPLOYMENT INFORMATION

Career Rating	**88**
% employed within 9 months	95
Average starting salary	$72,004
State for bar exam	IL
Pass rate for first-time bar	94

Prominent Alumni: Lisa Madigan, attorney general, Illinois; Henry Hyde, U.S. senator; Philip Corboy, attorney, personal injury; Jeff Jacobs, former president, Harpo Entertainment; Mary Ann McMorrow, chief justice, Illinois Supreme Court.

Grads employed by field (%):	
Academic	2
Business/industry	17
Government	13
Judicial clerkships	8
Private practice	55
Public interest	6

Legal Research Course Requirement?	Yes
Moot Court Requirement?	Yes
Public Interest Law Requirement?	No

ADMISSIONS

Selectivity Rating	**87**
# applications received	2,459
# applicants accepted	555
# acceptees attending	175
Average LSAT	161
LSAT Range	159–162
Average undergrad GPA	3.5
Application fee	$50
Regular application deadline	4/1
Regular notification	rolling
Rolling notification?	Yes
Early application program?	Yes
Transfer students accepted?	Yes
Evening division offered?	Yes
Part-time accepted?	Yes
LSDAS accepted?	Yes

Applicants Also Look At

American University, Boston University, DePaul University, The George Washington University, Illinois Institute of Technology, Northwestern University, University of Illinois at Urbana-Champaign.

International Students

TOEFL required of international students?	Yes
Minimum Paper TOEFL	650
Minimum Computer TOEFL	280

FINANCIAL FACTS

Annual tuition	$29,900
Books and supplies	$950
Tuition per credit	$995
Room & board (off-campus)	$12,900
Financial aid application deadline	3/1
% first-year students receiving some sort of aid	47
% receiving some sort of aid	85
% of aid that is merit-based	41
% receiving scholarships	85
Average grant	$7,000
Average loan	$18,500
Average total aid package	$24,200
Average debt	$64,500

LOYOLA UNIVERSITY NEW ORLEANS
SCHOOL OF LAW

INSTITUTIONAL INFORMATION

Public/private	private
Student/faculty ratio	17:1
Affiliation	Roman Catholic
% faculty part-time	29
% faculty female	22
% faculty minority	16
Total faculty	58

SURVEY SAYS . . .

Diverse opinions accepted in classrooms
Students love New Orleans, LA

STUDENTS

Enrollment of law school	803
% male/female	48/52
% out-of-state	35
% full-time	79
% minority	20
% international	1
# of countries represented	5
Average age of entering class	25

ACADEMICS

Academic experience rating	**71**
Professors interesting rating	70
Professors accessible rating	78
Hours of study per day	4.05

Academic Specialties

International law, pubic interest law.

Combined Degrees Offered

JD/MBA, JD/master's of religious studies, JD/master's of communications, JD/master's of public administration, JD/master's of urban and regional planning. All combined degree programs add an additional year to the JD program.

Academic Requirements

Clinical Program Required?	No
Legal Writing Course Requirement?	Yes
Legal Methods Course Requirement?	Yes
Legal Research Course Requirement?	Yes
Moot Court Requirement?	Yes

Academics

Loyola University New Orleans School of Law "balances theory and academia with practical skill-building courses that will be invaluable in the real world." Students may groan about the "rigorous" writing and oral appellate advocacy programs and the "mandatory moot court experience," but, in the end, admit these programs are "really beneficial to developing the skills necessary to be a lawyer." It pays off for the school, too, since Loyola's moot court teams "have consistently performed phenomenally" around the world. "Loyola's commitment to public service [means] practical skills opportunities [for] the pro bono project and the public interest law group." Loyola offers an evening program, which students say is "comprehensive and flexible." A certificate program in international law and "excellent summer abroad programs" are also noteworthy. Attending law school in Louisiana is "unique" because Louisiana is the only civil law state; all other U.S. states have a common law tradition. But since "civil law is what most countries use," understanding it "will help many who wish to engage in international law," counsels one student. "Don't forget that while Louisiana is a civil law island in America's common law ocean, America, Britain, and Australia are common law islands in a civil law world."

Students say the Jesuit spirit pervades and distinguishes their school. One student proclaims, "From day one, Loyola emphasized honesty, professional ethics, and responsibility to the community. This law school produces scholars, judges, and community activists, not the kind of attorneys that are the subject matter of lawyer jokes." We hear that professors are "extremely informed, erudite, and well-spoken, but still approachable." Students agree, "Most have the right mix of academic and real-world experience." There is no doubt that "the work is challenging, but the professors take time to guarantee that every student gains a proper understanding of the material." Another student says, "They want you to excel. Isn't that a unique concept?"

The "excellent" Office of Career Services has "many resources" and is "always very helpful." Loyola's "local reputation and connections to New Orleans job market" are solid. The alumni base is "local, strong, large, and very eager to hire" newly minted Loyola grads. "When you say you go to school in New Orleans everyone assumes Tulane, but Loyola is a good school if you plan to stay in the area," explains one student. "Tulane grads leave while there are a lot of Loyola alumni in the area, and they hire from their alma mater."

The large problem at Loyola is the facilities, which "could stand to be updated." Students grumble, "The building itself [is terrible]. The temperature is never right, [and] the "eating facilities offered at Loyola are slight." The classrooms are "dark, antiquated, and not up-to-date." Students feel "more technology" would be an improvement, but "the library really needs the most help." Fortunately, the School of Law has recently broken ground on a 12,000 square foot addition with an expected completion date of June 2006. The new state-of-the-art classrooms and additional space for student organizations should give students something to look forward to.

K. Michele Allison-Davis, Dean of Admissions
7214 Saint Charle's Avenue, Box 904, New Orleans, LA 70118
Telephone: 504-861-5575 • Fax: 504-861-5772
E-mail: ladmit@loyno.edu • Website: http://law.loyno.edu

Life

"Camaraderie is very high" at Loyola, it is "a place where you can make friends easily and feel secure that your peers aren't trying to screw you." Another student elaborates, "While there is healthy competition, students are generally pretty friendly and not overly aggressive or hostile." A 1L observes, "I find that most students get along and help each other out. We all want to succeed, but yet we want to see our classmates succeed as well." There is "a significant divide" between common law students and civil law students. The "controversy and disputes over which curriculum is the most difficult" are never-ending. Most Loyola students are from the Pelican State, and many "already know each other from high school and college, which can be a little daunting for the 'outsider'." A few suggest, "Loyola could try to recruit more graduates from out-of-state universities."

"An appropriate balance of rigor and fun" exists. Students say, "There are many opportunities to meet people in the legal community through activities or school-sponsored events. If you take advantage, many doors will be opened to you." When they are not networking, Loyola students are socializing with one another. Students say that the Student Bar Association "sponsors several events to help us meet other law students, [and] every other Friday, [they] hold a TGIF party at a different bar and pay for our drinks." The law school "has a great location in uptown New Orleans, which is not congested with people but is very close to the city life." The French Quarter is nearby and, as you may have heard, "New Orleans has a pretty festive atmosphere." At a place where students get "three days off for Mardi Gras, it's easy to let loose [and to] remember that there are other things in life besides school."

Getting In

Admitted students at the 25th percentile have an LSAT score of 151 and a GPA of 3.2. Admitted students at the 75th percentile have an LSAT score of 158 and a GPA of 3.7.

EMPLOYMENT INFORMATION

Career Rating	**81**
% employed within 9 months	100
State for bar exam	LA, TX, FL, GA, MS
Pass rate for first-time bar	62

Employers who frequently hire grads: Private firms, the judiciary, government agencies.

Prominent Alumni: Pascal Calogero, chief justice, Louisiana Supreme Court; Moon Landrieu, secretary of HUD, mayor of New Orleans, etc.; Carl Stewart, U.S. Court of Appeals, fifth circuit; Theodore M. Frois, general counsel, Exxon Mobil International; Robert L. Wilkie, special assistant to the president, NSA.

Grads employed by field (%):	
Academic	4
Business/industry	8
Government	9
Judicial clerkships	11
Military	1
Other	8
Private practice	58

Public Interest Law Requirement?	Yes

ADMISSIONS

Selectivity Rating	**76**
# applications received	1,746
# applicants accepted	593
# acceptees attending	215
Average LSAT	154
LSAT Range	151–156
Average undergrad GPA	3.4
Application fee	$40
Regular application deadline	rolling
Regular notification	rolling
Rolling notification?	Yes
Early application program?	No
Transfer students accepted?	Yes
Evening division offered?	Yes
Part-time accepted?	Yes
LSDAS accepted?	Yes

Applicants Also Look At

Florida Coastal School of Law, Florida State University, Louisiana State University, Southern University, Tulane University, University of Miami, University of Mississippi.

International Students

TOEFL required of international students?	No
TOEFL recommended of international students?	Yes
Minimum Paper TOEFL	580
Minimum Computer TOEFL	237

FINANCIAL FACTS

Annual tuition	$27,993
Books and supplies	$1,240
Fees per credit	$806
Tuition per credit	$836
Room & board	$8,826
% first-year students receiving some sort of aid	81
% receiving some sort of aid	85
% of aid that is merit-based	23
% receiving scholarships	52
Average grant	$11,698
Average loan	$28,552
Average total aid package	$40,250
Average debt	$81,973

Mercer University
Walter F. George School of Law

INSTITUTIONAL INFORMATION

Public/private	private
Student/faculty ratio	14:1
Affiliation	Baptist
% faculty part-time	45
% faculty female	30
% faculty minority	10
Total faculty	62

SURVEY SAYS . . .

Great research resources
Great library staff
Beautiful campus

STUDENTS

Enrollment of law school	424
% male/female	54/46
% out-of-state	35
% full-time	99
% minority	13
% international	1
# of countries represented	3
Average age of entering class	24

ACADEMICS

Academic Experience rating	**89**
Professors interesting rating	87
Professors accessible rating	98
Hours of study per day	4.98

Academic Specialties

Civil procedure, commercial law, constitutional law, corporation securities law, criminal law, environmental law, government services, intellectual property law, international law, Internet law, labor law, legal history, legal writing certificate program, professionalist ethics, property, taxation, trial advocacy.

Advanced Degrees Offered

JD, 3 years.

Combined Degrees Offered

JD/MBA, 4 years.

Academic Requirements

Clinical Program Required?	No
Legal Writing Course Requirement?	Yes
Legal Methods Course Requirement?	Yes

Academics

Mercer University offers a rigorous legal education in an intimate, Southern atmosphere. While students say the curriculum is challenging, they can always get extra help from their accessible instructors. One student testifies, "Mercer Law's faculty prides itself on its open-door policy. This is no empty boast. The professors at Mercer Law are always available for questions and, in fact, encourage extra-class discussion." In fact, another continues, "Some professors have even come in on the weekend to help students who were having difficulty." With a total enrollment of just over 400, the average class size at Mercer is small. In the last two years, advanced legal seminars may have as few as 8 students in them. As a result, students get a great deal of personal attention from their professors. One satisfied student writes, "This small atmosphere allows for a great deal of interaction with faculty members, which increases our opportunity to learn to be professionals and lawyers that work well with one another."

Like professors, administrators stay in close contact with students, many of whom they know by first-name. Students praise the fact that "the administration has been extremely supportive of minorities." They also tell us that the higher-ups try to "get the minority students actively involved in recruiting efforts and sufficiently fund minority programs." In fact, a student notes, "There are many students, including myself, who came to Mercer because they have an extremely well-endowed scholarship fund."

While the intimate environment draws praises all around, there are a few disadvantages to the school's small size. Students tell us that the course offerings are slim, as there are not enough faculty members to offer some of the highly specialized classes you might find in larger law programs. One student elaborates, "As a result of the small size, there are limited course offerings in many specialties. This does not pose a problem in terms of learning, but it limits the number of alumni in certain specialties." Another confers, "Because of its smaller student body, many people outside the South are not familiar with the quality legal education provided here." Even so, most students feel that the positive aspects of a small school environment far outweigh the drawbacks. This is especially true with regard to the school's legal writing certificate program, which students claim is one of Mercer's greatest strengths.

Across the board, students rave about the beautiful Mercer campus, the top-of-the-line facilities, and the quaint small-town environment. A student glows, "The school has achieved a rare balance between a beautiful, traditional building on the outside and up-to-date technology inside." Indeed, Mercer is equipped with all the latest technology and research tools. "Our facilities are first-rate, with Internet access in nearly every classroom," gushes one student. Another adds, "Most classrooms are wired for student use of laptops. Many rooms have wireless Internet. Students are also permitted, but not required, to take their exams on computer. The computer lab has enough computers available for student use. I have never seen anyone waiting to use a computer."

Marilyn E. Sutton, Assistant Dean of Admissions and Financial Aid
1021 Georgia Avenue, Macon, GA 31207
Telephone: 478-301-2605 • Fax: 478-301-2989
E-mail: Martin_sv@mercer.edu • Website: www.law.mercer.edu

Life

Even though the school brings some activity to campus, it should be known that "Macon is a sleepy Southern town" that doesn't offer much by way of nightlife. Most students say they like the calmness of Macon because it is easy to focus on their studies. They are also quick to point out that "Atlanta is only 85 miles away" and that the city offers a wealth of entertainment activities for the weekend. But even without the distractions of Atlanta, Mercer students still unwind when they can. "Socially, everybody is willing to get together and have fun on the weekends. Study hard, play hard!" is how one student puts it. Another tells us, "Thursday nights are the generally accepted everybody's-going-out night." Still, another elaborates, "Thursday night is happy hour(s) at CJ's or Loco's, and Phi Alpha Delta has weekly 'bar reviews' where they review the bar and not the law."

During such revelry, students say they get to know each other well and that "the atmosphere and relationships among students is one of the greatest strengths about Mercer. It is small enough that you know most everyone in your class, but big enough that you get differing ideas and opinions." Students report, "There is a competitive, yet extremely collegial atmosphere in both the classroom and on the intramural fields!" While everyone works hard, a student reassures us, "There is certainly a competitive spirit among students, but students do not strive to succeed at the expense of other students."

Getting In

Most future lawyers enter Mercer a year or two after finishing their undergraduate studies, though the ages of students span from 19 to 45. Mercer admits students with a strong academic background and desire to study law. Last year's incoming class had a median LSAT score of 156 and the median GPA of 3.4.

EMPLOYMENT INFORMATION

Career Rating	**80**
% employed within 9 months	98.5
Average starting salary	$56,230
State for bar exam	GA
Pass rate for first-time bar	94

Employers who frequently hire grads: King & Spalding, Atlanta; McKenna, Long, and Aldridge, Atlanta; Moore, Ingram, Johnson & Steele, Marietta; Martin Snow, LLP, Macon; Alston & Bird, Atlanta; James, Bates, Pope, and Spivey, Macon.

Prominent Alumni: Griffin Bell, former attorney general; Cathy Cox, secretary of state, Georgia; John Oxendine, insurance commissioner, Georgia.

Grads employed by field (%):	
Academic	1
Business/industry	6
Government	10
Judicial clerkships	10
Military	2
Private practice	64
Public interest	7

Legal Research Course Requirement?	Yes
Moot Court Requirement?	Yes
Public Interest Law Requirement?	No

ADMISSIONS

Selectivity Rating	**81**
# applications received	1,630
# applicants accepted	375
# acceptees attending	143
Average LSAT	156
LSAT Range	154–158
Average undergrad GPA	3.4
Application fee	$50
Regular application deadline	3/15
Regular notification	rolling
Rolling notification?	Yes
Early application program?	No
Transfer students accepted?	Yes
Evening division offered?	No
Part-time accepted?	Yes
LSDAS accepted?	Yes

Applicants Also Look At

Emory University, Florida State University, Georgia State University, Samford University, University of Georgia, University of South Carolina, Wake Forest University.

International Students

TOEFL required of international students?	No
TOEFL recommended of international students?	Yes
Minimum Paper TOEFL	600

FINANCIAL FACTS

Annual tuition	$25,450
Books and supplies	$1,000
Tuition per credit	$1,060
Room & board	$12,000
Financial aid application deadline	4/1
% first-year students receiving some sort of aid	80
% receiving some sort of aid	80
% of aid that is merit-based	20
% receiving scholarships	30
Average grant	$16,000
Average loan	$29,000
Average total aid package	$33,000
Average debt	$67,529

MICHIGAN STATE UNIVERSITY
COLLEGE OF LAW

INSTITUTIONAL INFORMATION

Public/private	private
Student/faculty ratio	20:1
% faculty part-time	40
% faculty female	30
% faculty minority	2
Total faculty	30

SURVEY SAYS . . .

Great research resources
Great library staff
Beautiful campus
Students love East Lansing, MI

STUDENTS

Enrollment of law school	656
% male/female	58/42
% out-of-state	14
% full-time	78
% minority	19
% international	3
# of countries represented	4
Average age of entering class	28

ACADEMICS

Academic Experience rating	**65**
Professors interesting rating	71
Professors accessible rating	75
Hours of study per day	4.85

Academic Specialties

International law, taxation.

Combined Degrees Offered

JD/MBA, 4 years; JD/MPA, 4 years; JD/MLIR, 4 years; JD/JDMS, 4 years; JD/MA, 4 years.

Academic Requirements

Clinical Program Required?	Yes
Legal Writing Course Requirement?	No
Legal Methods Course Requirement?	Yes
Legal Research Course Requirement?	No
Moot Court Requirement?	No
Public Interest Law Requirement?	No

Academics

Known for a century as the Detroit College of Law, Michigan State University College of Law has been reborn with a new name, a mutually beneficial affiliation with Michigan State, and a "positive, up-and-coming attitude." A 2L writes, "Instead of seeming chaotic, the school and the students have embraced these changes and used them as a springboard for advancing new ideas, fostering ownership of the curriculum, and creating an infectious enthusiasm for the school." Two things haven't changed, though: the private-school price tag and the fourth-tier ranking. In an ongoing effort to lure top students and continue the school's transformation, the administration is doling out merit-based scholarships and flashy laptops. Some students call the recruitment efforts "bait-and-switch tactics," warning that as few as one in five scholarship recipients see their funding renewed for the second year. Most students, however, focus on the numerous improvements they see and consider MSU Law to be "a top-tier school that doesn't know it's a top-tier school."

This "best-kept secret" status may not last long, as everyone loves to talk about the school's state-of-the-art moot court, considered to be "easily one of the best in the nation." The "technologically sophisticated" renovations mean that the school now features plenty of flat screens, microphones, presentation equipment, and other "computer gadgets possessed by only a few of the most progressive courts." In the words of a 2L, "I can plug my computer in anywhere I sit." All administrative offices and classrooms are housed in a single impressive building, complete with relatively reliable wireless Internet access. "The building is conducive to learning and gives us a sense of pride. It's what a graduate school should look like." Recently, the deans transformed the hallways into a political art show, and this "makes walking to class entertaining and interesting." The library also facilitates scholarship, with "amazingly helpful and knowledgeable Lexis and Westlaw representatives on staff."

Professors are divided into those who "follow the Socratic method strictly" and a newer group of instructors described by students as "extremely laid back." One from this latter group shows a *South Park* episode on the first day of contracts to explain "that every time we take action as a lawyer, we risk bringing Janet Reno in a fuzzy bunny suit to our clients' homes. I've been fully impressed with the weight of my duty ever since." Professor Jack Apol, who ran for the Michigan legislature, "managed to make criminal law fun and interesting without disrespecting the subject matter or the victims of the many crimes that we studied." Nearly all instructors are "willing to involve themselves as mentors to various student organizations, providing useful legal insight as well as friendly career advice." They draw on impressive backgrounds as "the heads of corporate law departments for large successful law firms, as well as former federal judges and prosecutors." Politically, "the faculty range from the radical liberal to merely liberal." Rare issues arise around "brilliant and well-published" professors who were educated at "first-tier schools" and sometimes "show contempt for MSU students." Overall, students praise their professors for "promoting individual thought and challenging our answers"; they just wish for a few more of them to reduce the student-to-faculty ratio.

MSU Law is geared toward "entrepreneurial go-getters who want to get into a courtroom, practice the law, and make a real difference" rather than "high-brow ivory-towered theoreticians." Students appreciate "opportunities for dual-degree programs and advanced specialization for all law students" through connections with other MSU departments. The well-known Fieger Trial Practice Institute gives select students the ben-

368 Law College Building, East Lansing, MI 48824-1300
Telephone: 517-432-0222 • Fax: 517-432-0098
E-mail: law@msu.edu • Website: www.dcl.edu

efit of "unique instruction in trial practice." Everyone loves their clinic classes, which get students arguing cases early in their law school careers: "You can be in trial by the end of your first week." Many students intend to work on behalf of local people, like the 2L who is "interested in helping the American worker earn an honest living in a steady, safe, and satisfying job." Others opt to work for the government or in private practice. While the school's East Lansing location provides some opportunities for government work in the capital, many students want to see more done to "market the school's name to law firms not just in Michigan, but also in other states."

Life

Typically, students at MSU Law are "committed to making a difference in our society." Most graduates plan to stay in the state after graduation, furthering the collegial alumnae network. Recently formed interest groups—including the Native American Law Students Association, the Society for Mental Health Law, Older Wiser Law Students (OWLS), the Family Law Society, the Triangle Bar Association, and the Student Animal Legal Defense Fund—promote professional bonding and fuel the school's progressive reputation. Students express "excitement about the changes that have occurred and the school's association with a Big 10 university."

Students report a "virtual lack of pretension and mean-spirited competition" and note that most opt to "get through the hell together." Many live in the graduate dorm right across from the law school and work to cultivate the kind of atmosphere in which study groups "drink a glass of wine over a civil procedure sample exam question." Most "recognize the importance of social life in law school" and "make strong efforts to include everyone in activities and events."

Getting In

Although the application deadline is officially April 15, the Admissions Committee recommends submitting materials earlier (as the school has rolling admissions). Letters of recommendation may not be required, but it's a good idea to submit them anyway. All applicants are automatically considered for merit-based and trustee scholarships, so there's no need to do anything extra to apply for these.

EMPLOYMENT INFORMATION

Career Rating	**74**
% employed within 9 months	91.1
Average starting salary	$60,000
State for bar exam	MI
Pass rate for first-time bar	76

Employers who frequently hire grads:
Clark Hill, PLC; Dykema Gossett PLLC; Kitch, Drutchas, Wagner, & Kenney, PC; Secrest, Wardle, Lynch, Hampton; Truex & Morley; Michigan Court of Appeals; Oakland County prosecutor's office; Plunkett & Cooney, PC; Blue Cross Blue Shield of Michigan; Deloitte and Touche, LLP; Ford Motor Company; General Motors Legal Staff; Pepsi.

Grads employed by field (%):	
Academic	3
Business/industry	10
Government	17
Judicial clerkships	6
Military	3
Private practice	42
Public interest	2

ADMISSIONS

Selectivity Rating	**65**
# applications received	1,055
# applicants accepted	701
# acceptees attending	210
Average LSAT	154
LSAT Range	150–158
Average undergrad GPA	3.2
Application fee	$50
Regular application deadline	4/15
Regular notification	rolling
Rolling notification?	Yes
Early application program?	No
Transfer students accepted?	Yes
Evening division offered?	Yes
Part-time accepted?	Yes
LSDAS accepted?	Yes

Applicants Also Look At

Boston College, Roger Williams University.

International Students

TOEFL required of international students?	Yes
Minimum Paper TOEFL	600

FINANCIAL FACTS

Annual tuition	$20,244
Books and supplies	$872
Fees per credit	$566
Room & board	$6,931
Financial aid application deadline	6/30
% first-year students receiving some sort of aid	73
% receiving some sort of aid	80
% of aid that is merit-based	7
Average grant	$17,000
Average loan	$15,539
Average debt	$59,381

Mississippi College
School of Law

INSTITUTIONAL INFORMATION

Public/private	private
Student/faculty ratio	22:1
Affiliation	Southern Baptist
% faculty part-time	23
% faculty female	33
% faculty minority	4
Total faculty	42

SURVEY SAYS . . .

Diverse opinions accepted in classrooms

STUDENTS

Enrollment of law school	434
% male/female	65/35
% out-of-state	45
% full-time	100
% minority	9
Average age of entering class	25

ACADEMICS

Academic Experience rating	**73**
Professors interesting rating	85
Professors accessible rating	91
Hours of study per day	4.02

Academic Specialties

Certificate program in civil law studies.

Advanced Degrees Offered

JD, 3 years.

Combined Degrees Offered

JD/MBA; JD, 3 years; MBA, 1 year.

Academic Requirements

Clinical Program Required?	No
Legal Writing Course Requirement?	Yes
Legal Methods Course Requirement?	Yes
Legal Research Course Requirement?	Yes
Moot Court Requirement?	Yes
Public Interest Law Requirement?	No

Academics

Mississippi College School of Law is, according to its students, "one of the best-kept secrets of the South." While that may be the case today, MC is "beginning to earn the solid reputation that it deserves," and it may not be long before the law school starts to gain more prominent stature. Students say that the school distinguishes itself through its serious commitment to superior teaching. "For a relatively new school," one student opines, "MC has established strong roots by paying primary attention to the quality of its teachers." Another student adds that "the greatest strengths of Mississippi College School of Law are the support the faculty gives the students and the respect and friendship among all of the students." While the faculty is extremely friendly and supportive, students warn that the program is challenging, and especially demanding on first-year students. "The Socratic method is in full force during first-year classes," one student reports. "Of course, it's intimidating at first, but as the year has passed, 1Ls have warmed up to it and now appreciate it." Another adds, "I feel I am getting a top-notch legal education here due to the presence of some great teachers and a surprisingly challenging program. It is academically quite rigorous. I had a 4.0 undergrad [GPA] and a 161 LSAT, but still I have had to work my butt off to excel here."

The school makes every effort to prepare students for the bar exam and their careers through practical instruction, externships, and clinical programs. One of only two law schools in the Magnolia State, Mississippi College is the better-situated to make these sorts of real-world opportunities available to students. "Being located in Jackson, Mississippi, all students have abundant opportunities to clerk and have access to a wonderful adjunct teaching staff," writes one student. In addition, the bar-passage rate at the school is high, hovering around 85 percent annually.

In addition to the stellar faculty, students say that the administration is deeply engaged in the community, working hard to listen to student needs and improve the student quality of life. In particular, students are impressed with the school's new dean. "We have a new, enthusiastic dean after years of interim deans. He is very excited and motivated. I think he will have a huge positive impact on our school," writes one enthusiastic student. Many other administrators get special mention from students. For example, a student raves, "Our admissions director is a model of hospitality and professionalism; the same for our Career Services director. They both go way out of their way for their students."

Life

As the capital of the state, Jackson affords many lifestyle amenities. Its relatively small size and an air of Southern hospitality make it a pleasant place to live. "If you want to focus on school, the slow pace of Jackson, compared with the rest of the nation, is a great place to do it," advises one student. But even though it takes a slow pace, make no mistake: Jackson isn't the boonies. Jackson "is a great town for married couples, but there is a good social scene for those who like to get out on Friday nights." On campus, students say that their classmates are friendly and social, and that most people have no trouble making friends. In the words of one student, "Everyone has their social groups, but I don't feel like anyone is . . . an outcast, either. There are groups who go out and party together, others who gather for BBQs, others who go to church together, or hunting."

Patricia H. Evans, Dean of Admissions
151 East Griffith Street, Jackson, MS 39201
Telephone: 601-925-7150 • Fax: 601-925-7166
E-mail: hweaver@mc.edu • Website: www.law.mc.edu

While a student tells us that Mississippi College School of Law is "much more competitive than my undergraduate experience," many students also point out that most people are cheerful, open, and affable. Most students hail from Mississippi, and the political opinions on campus are generally reflective of those of the Deep South overall. For example, a student tells us, "As a Christian school, assemblies are likely to have prayer, but I have found that to be true of every institution here in Jackson. This is the Bible Belt, and there is an assumption that you are Christian, though one is not made to feel unwelcome otherwise." Another attests, "MCSOL, like the state in which it is located (and indeed the whole area), is populated by people with very conservative attitudes." Students say, however, that there is some diversity within the student community and that different viewpoints can be illuminating." "As a good old-fashioned tax-and-spend liberal," one student explains, "I have had some interesting experiences here. I believe I will look back on this time as a great learning experience culturally, though. I have made some true friends among people whose political outlook is completely opposite mine, and that kind of exposure and experience is fairly rare."

Getting In

Mississippi College School of Law evaluates candidates on personal and academic achievement, with the LSAT score and undergraduate GPA being the most heavily weighted factors. Standards may change annually. The previous year's entering class had a mean LSAT score of 150 and a median GPA of 3.13. The application deadline is May 1 for fall admission.

EMPLOYMENT INFORMATION

Career Rating	**76**
% employed within 9 months	94
Average starting salary	$53,981
State for bar exam	MS, AL, TN, SC, KS
Pass rate for first-time bar	84

Employers who frequently hire grads:
International law firms, law firms from multiple states, Mississippi law firms, state government.

Grads employed by field (%):	
Academic	2
Business/industry	4
Government	10
Judicial clerkships	11
Private practice	67

ADMISSIONS

Selectivity Rating	**70**
# applications received	1,136
# applicants accepted	403
# acceptees attending	183
Average LSAT	151
LSAT Range	148–153
Average undergrad GPA	3.3
Application fee	$50
Regular application deadline	rolling
Regular notification	rolling
Rolling notification?	Yes
Early application program?	No
Transfer students accepted?	Yes
Evening division offered?	No
Part-time accepted?	No
LSDAS accepted?	Yes

Applicants Also Look At

Louisiana State University, Samford University, University of Alabama, University of Memphis, University of Mississippi.

International Students

TOEFL required of international students?	No
TOEFL recommended of international students?	No

FINANCIAL FACTS

Annual tuition	$18,030
Books and supplies	$900
Tuition per credit	$601
Room & board (off-campus)	$9,000
Financial aid application deadline	5/1
% first-year students receiving some sort of aid	85
% receiving some sort of aid	80
% of aid that is merit-based	25
% receiving scholarships	25
Average grant	$9,000
Average loan	$18,500
Average total aid package	$27,000
Average debt	$58,000

NEW ENGLAND SCHOOL OF LAW

INSTITUTIONAL INFORMATION

Public/private	private
Student/faculty ratio	20:1
% faculty part-time	66
% faculty female	37
% faculty minority	14
Total faculty	108

SURVEY SAYS . . .

Diverse opinions accepted in classrooms
Great library staff
Students love Boston, MA

STUDENTS

Enrollment of law school	1,101
% male/female	45/55
% out-of-state	66
% full-time	67
% minority	13
% international	2
# of countries represented	9
Average age of entering class	26

ACADEMICS

Academic Experience rating	**67**
Professors interesting rating	81
Professors accessible rating	77
Hours of study per day	4.42

Academic Specialties

Taxation.

Advanced Degrees Offered

JD degree, 3 to 4 years; LLM degree, 1 year.

Academic Requirements

Clinical Program Required?	No
Legal Writing Course Requirement?	Yes
Legal Methods Course Requirement?	Yes
Legal Research Course Requirement?	Yes
Moot Court Requirement?	Yes
Public Interest Law Requirement?	Yes

Academics

New England School of Law is a small, independent institution with an excellent teaching faculty, "pretty low" tuition, and a prime location in downtown Boston.

While it may not have much name recognition, it's a great value. One student likens NESL to a Honda, saying it's "not too flashy, but you'll get a ton of reliable mileage out of it." And it's "more valuable than some of [the] higher-priced models out there."

While students say their "incredible [professors] provide the perfect balance between theory and practice," they are particularly taken with the practical aspects of the NESL education. "Our professors are truly training us to practice law, not just theorize about it," says one student. "In addition to the standard oral arguments and advocacy requirements of Legal Research and Writing, our civil procedure professors put us through exercises of the litigation procedure (filing complaints, answers, and motions, drafting interrogatories)." Students have ample opportunity for hands-on experience in the surrounding Boston legal community, since "all students are strongly encouraged to participate in multiple clinics, and the school has a fantastic honors judicial internship program." Since "NESL is centrally located in Boston," the school is able to "offer a wide variety of clinical opportunities, internships, and clerkships." One student beams, "Although only in my first year, I have already secured a summer internship at a legal aid center."

At NESL, "there is a good mix of personalities among the faculty," some friendly and encouraging, others a bit more intense. A student shares this story: "On the first day of Torts class, my professor came into class, introduced herself, and immediately began grilling the class on the most basic tort-battery. It was a memorable, albeit frightening experience." But it isn't all torture sessions, and most professors "balance Socratic method with traditional lecture." In fact, a student insists, "On the first day of class my first year, I could tell that my professors wanted to teach rather than intimidate." But whatever their classroom style, NESL's "approachable and supportive [professors are] extremely helpful [and] very accessible if you have questions or concerns."

While students agree that they are receiving a great education, NESL's weak reputation in the Boston area seriously affects their job placement rates after graduation. One student laments, "We have been a school for almost a hundred years and not many know what or who we are." Another confides, "I know people on Law Review who are 0/100 in applying for positions this year. It is a shame because the education is exceptional." Students say the problem is confounded by the fact that Boston is a "tough city [to look for a job] because of all the other law schools" in the area.

Students also lament the outdated facilities and lack of modern technology on the NESL campus. Many students say that "classrooms need to be updated [because] technology here is dismal." One student suggests "that students who are not in the top ten of their class (and [they] don't mean 10 percent) are at a serious disadvantage." Also, the school itself needs to expand because the hallways are so small and get easily jammed because of the growing student population." Students agree that "technological capabilities are the school's weakest area." However, a newly upgraded student E-mail system and administrative software system along with a hired chief information officer and additional technology support staff serve as a reflection of the school's effort to address the technology needs on campus.

MICHELLE L'ETOILE, DIRECTOR OF ADMISSIONS
154 STUART STREET, BOSTON, MA 02116
TELEPHONE: 617-422-7210 • FAX: 617-457-3033
E-MAIL: ADMIT@ADMIN.NESL.EDU • WEBSITE: WWW.NESL.EDU

Life

Because NESL is small, students "get to know each other really well in the first year," making for a more "cooperative" than "competitive" atmosphere. Students say their "very community-minded [peers] really come together [and that] everyone helps each other." But others seem to think the school is maybe a little too "tight-knit" and that combined with a young student body, that can sometimes create a "cliquish" or "high-school" environment.

Students love NESL's "fantastic" central Boston locale. "You can't beat the location—near the T, the Common, food, and Downtown Crossing." Students say that the vibe on campus is fun and social and that "there's always a lot to do around the school." There are many opportunities to get involved in extracurricular clubs, activities, and speakers. "For a small school, New England has quite a number of groups that cater to most students on a range of interests, from the Republicans Club to Children's Law and Social Activities. They do a great job in engaging most of the students."

Getting In

New England School of Law seeks candidates who demonstrate intelligence, previous academic achievement, professional experience, and motivation to study the law. NESL evaluates candidates based on their undergraduate GPA, LSAT scores, personal statement, and letters of recommendation, reviewing almost 3,500 applications annually for roughly 380 places in the program. The majority of accepted students' LSAT scores range from 149 to 154. The school will not consider students with a GPA lower than 2.0.

EMPLOYMENT INFORMATION

Career Rating	**70**
% employed within 9 months	89.3
Average starting salary	$52,910
State for bar exam	MA, NY, CT, PA, NJ
Pass rate for first-time bar	72

Prominent Alumni: Leonard P. Zakim, NE Anti-Defamation League, namesake, Boston Bridge; Honorable Susan J. Crawford, chief justice, U.S. Court of Appeals for Armed Forces; Honorable John R. Simpson, former head of the U.S. Secret Service; Honorable Karyn F. Scheier, chief justice of the MA Land Court; Wendy J. Murphy, victim advocacy and research group.

Grads employed by field (%):	
Academic	2
Business/industry	15
Government	19
Judicial clerkships	6
Military	1
Other	4
Private practice	48
Public interest	5

ADMISSIONS

Selectivity Rating	**68**
# applications received	3,467
# applicants accepted	1,317
# acceptees attending	394
Average LSAT	151
LSAT Range	149–153
Average undergrad GPA	3.1
Application fee	$50
Regular application deadline	3/15
Regular notification	rolling
Rolling notification?	Yes
Early application program?	No
Transfer students accepted?	Yes
Evening division offered?	Yes
Part-time accepted?	Yes
LSDAS accepted?	Yes

Applicants Also Look At

Franklin Pierce Law Center, New York Law School, Northeastern University, Roger Williams University, Suffolk University, Syracuse University, Western New England College.

International Students

TOEFL required of international students?	Yes
Minimum Paper TOEFL	600
Minimum Computer TOEFL	250

FINANCIAL FACTS

Annual tuition	$22,410
Books and supplies	$1,150
Tuition per credit	$930
Room & board (off-campus)	$14,180
Financial aid application deadline	4/20
% first-year students receiving some sort of aid	83
% receiving some sort of aid	84
% of aid that is merit-based	74
% receiving scholarships	38
Average grant	$7,615
Average loan	$25,962
Average total aid package	$28,744
Average debt	$73,231

NEW YORK UNIVERSITY
SCHOOL OF LAW

INSTITUTIONAL INFORMATION

Public/private	private
Student/faculty ratio	11:1
% faculty part-time	36
% faculty female	30
% faculty minority	12
Total faculty	197

SURVEY SAYS . . .

Students love New York, NY

STUDENTS

Enrollment of law school	1,310
% male/female	53/47
% full-time	100
% minority	25
% international	4

ACADEMICS

Academic Experience rating	**88**
Professors interesting rating	79
Professors accessible rating	64
Hours of study per day	3.71

Academic Specialties

Clinical programs, commercial law, constitutional law, corporate law, criminal law, environmental law, human rights law, international law, labor law, legal history, legal philosophy, public interest, taxation, trade regulation.

Advanced Degrees Offered

LLM, JSD.

Combined Degrees Offered

JD/LLM, JD/MBA, JD/MUP, JD/MSW, JD/MA, JD/PhD, JD/MPA with Woodrow Wilson School of Public and Informational Affairs at Princeton University; JD/MPA with John F. Kennedy School of Government at Harvard Law School.

Academic Requirements

Clinical Program Required?	No
Legal Writing Course Requirement?	Yes
Legal Methods Course Requirement?	No
Legal Research Course Requirement?	No

Academics

A fixture in the city and a mirror to its culture, New York University is a large, famous, diverse, and cosmopolitan law school, boasting a distinguished faculty and strong scholarly community. With many well-known names on the faculty, you may be surprised to learn that "most professors are incredibly accessible and wonderful teachers." In the words of a 3L, "The faculty here has, on the whole, been outstanding. That applies not only to my classroom experience, but also the atmosphere of accessibility that is an essential part of the school."

There are a wide variety of course offerings at NYU, and "picking classes for upcoming semesters is pretty fun because there are usually some well-known names, sometimes judges." Of particular note, NYU offers a wide range of "international course offerings" as well as a staggering array of colloquia, seminars, institutes, centers, and special programs, such as the lauded Global Public Service Law Project.

Although many NYU alumni end up in top private law firms across the country, "NYU students are generally very down to earth and extremely dedicated to public service." A 3L attests that "the public interest reputation is well-deserved, and I think it has a lot to do with the atmosphere and civic culture of NYU Law." The school's progressive vision is promoted through coursework, extracurriculars, and special programs. For example, the Public Interest Law Center "guarantees $4,000 worth of funding if you elect to partake in a public interest internship over the 1L summer and $5,000 for a 2L summer," a program that "shows just how dedicated NYU is to placing students in public interest jobs." "Even though I've ultimately chosen to take a private job," one 3L shares, "I appreciate the promotion of the idea that everyone in the profession still has obligations to the public interest."

While the educational experience is undeniably first rate, NYU occasionally falls short in meeting the needs of every one of its 1,300-plus students. At this large school, classes are assigned by lottery, and "almost every class, even basic classes, such as evidence and criminal procedure, have waiting lists, sometimes with 70 people waiting to get in." Students also say that the presence of big name faculty can also be a double-edged sword, as some professors can make students feel "like teaching is not important to them" and can occasionally "brush off" students in favor of professional or academic projects. Still, for one of the most prestigious law schools in the country, "it is amazing how much NYU gives back to the student in terms of career counseling, placement, access to professors, and the overall classroom experience."

The academic program at NYU places a great deal of emphasis on legal theory. Outside of the classroom, however, "NYU provides you with opportunities to do every kind of practical work imaginable," and, on top of that, "all the journals are great." The school's host of "incredibly interesting" extracurricular activities include public service-oriented clinics such as "PREP: Prisoners Rights and Education Project, which takes students into area women's correctional facilities to serve as teachers for a law clerk class." This program and others help students apply legal theory to the real world situations they will encounter as practicing attorneys. "You can come out of school feeling like a third-year associate if you are diligent," reports one 2L. And on that note, NYU students have little trouble securing the most coveted jobs after graduation. As one 2L succinctly puts it, "Career services are great here. We all get awesome jobs pretty much no matter what."

40 WASHINGTON SQUARE SOUTH, NEW YORK, NY 10012
TELEPHONE: 212-998-6060 • FAX: 212-995-4527
E-MAIL: LAW.MOREINFO@NYU.EDU • WEBSITE: WWW.LAW.NYU.EDU

Life

When it comes to life at New York University, the first two words of the name say it all. In terms of location for work, culture, or socializing, "it really doesn't get much better than the Village in NYC." As one 2L puts it, "The neighborhood is awesome, especially if you choose to live in the dorms (most people do, and they're not bad)." With so many students choosing to reside in campus housing, "there is a big sense of community." While law students certainly enjoy their favorable location for off-campus social pursuits, they always take the time to socialize on campus. In fact, there is a "social event every week with free alcohol and two huge parties a year."

Overall, NYU students describe their classmates as highly intelligent, diligent, and accomplished. "I was amazed when I first got here at how bright and motivated my colleagues were," notes a 2L. When it comes to the competitive atmosphere on campus, however, NYU students send mixed messages. On the one hand, some say, "Competition is almost nonexistent. People share outlines and notes. They are courteous in the library and at workstations." On the other hand, some students describe their classmates as "greedy, self-interested, competitive jerks," who are "just as cutthroat and competitive as anywhere else."

Getting In

You want to go to NYU? So do a lot of other smart people. NYU bases admissions decisions on the intellectual potential, academic achievement, character, community involvement, and work experience of each applicant, but with an average LSAT score of a near-perfect 170 for each incoming class, we would suggest that if you want to attend NYU School of Law, you prepare for the test. A lot. There is an extensive scholarship program for highly qualified applicants.

Moot Court Requirement?	No
Public Interest Law Requirement?	No

ADMISSIONS

Selectivity Rating	**94**
# applications received	8,220
# applicants accepted	1,628
# acceptees attending	440
Average LSAT	170
LSAT Range	167–172
Average undergrad GPA	3.7
Application fee	$75
Regular application deadline	2/1
Regular notification	4/30
Rolling notification?	No
Early application program?	Yes
Early application deadline	10/15
Early application notification	12/30
Transfer students accepted?	Yes
Evening division offered?	No
Part-time accepted?	No
LSDAS accepted?	Yes

International Students

TOEFL required of international students?	No
TOEFL recommended of international students?	No

FINANCIAL FACTS

Annual tuition	$35,710
Books and supplies	$890
Room & board	$17,980
Financial aid application deadline	4/15

EMPLOYMENT INFORMATION

Career Rating	**97**
Job placement rate (%)	100
State for bar exam	NY
Pass rate for first-time bar	97

Employers who frequently hire grads:
Private law firms, public interest organizations, government agencies, corporations, and public accounting firms.

Grads employed by field (%):	
Business/industry	3
Government	3
Judicial clerkships	14
Private practice	70
Public interest	10

NORTHEASTERN UNIVERSITY
SCHOOL OF LAW

INSTITUTIONAL INFORMATION

Public/private	private
Student/faculty ratio	19:1
% faculty part-time	59
% faculty female	50
% faculty minority	13
Total faculty	78

SURVEY SAYS . . .

Great library staff
Abundant externship/internship/clerkship opportunities
Students love Boston, MA

STUDENTS

Enrollment of law school	619
% male/female	39/61
% full-time	100
% minority	27
% international	1
# of countries represented	2
Average age of entering class	25

ACADEMICS

Academic Experience rating	**84**
Professors interesting rating	88
Professors accessible rating	88
Hours of study per day	4.71

Academic Specialties

Civil procedure, commercial law, constitutional law, corporation securities law, criminal law, environmental law, human rights law, intellectual property law, international law, labor law, property, taxation.

Combined Degrees Offered

JD/MBA, JD/MBA/MS in accountancy, JD/MPH.

Academic Requirements

Clinical Program Required?	No
Legal Writing Course Requirement?	Yes
Legal Methods Course Requirement?	Yes
Legal Research Course Requirement?	No
Moot Court Requirement?	No
Public Interest Law Requirement?	Yes

Academics

A "commitment to progressive lawyering and the co-op internship model" are the hallmarks of Northeastern University School of Law, "a fantastic school, grounded in experiential learning." Northeastern is "a truly unique school" in many ways. For starters, there is no law journal, and a pass/fail grading system utilizes written evaluations instead of traditional grades. "We don't have ranking or grade-point averages," explains one student. "This really works to help students gauge how well they are doing. We have a very cooperative learning experience." On the other hand, while "the school has a great reputation in the Boston legal market," some students grumble that employment prospects in other cities seem dim because "no one wants to read a huge packet of written evaluations." However, most students absolutely rave about the "unparalleled commitment to public interest law." One student says, "If you are committed to practicing law while working toward social justice, then this is the place to be."

Students say their "dedicated, brilliant, and passionate [professors are] super-approachable" experts in their fields who "explain things very clearly [and are] very dedicated to public interest." Faculty members also "really take the time to write personalized evaluations for each student." Northeastern's administration either "welcomes student voices and opinions" or has "very little commitment to the overall health and well being of law students," depending on whom you ask.

"In terms of the facilities, we're like the Red Sox," suggests one student. "We need a new building, but I'd sure miss the old one." We're not sure how much other students would miss, though. Almost all agree, "The building could stand to get a facelift," describing it as "leaky and old (it's all cinder blocks) [with] notoriously uncomfortable [classrooms that] are alternately tropical or arctic." Without question, "the law school building needs an overhaul." One student assures us, though, "We're in the process of expanding and renovating the classroom and library facilities. When the new building opens, it will make a huge difference in terms of the facilities."

It is no doubt that Northeastern's crown jewel is its hands-on Cooperative Legal Education program. After completing a mostly traditional 1L curriculum, 2Ls and 3Ls rotate every three months between working as full-time, paid legal interns and attending classes. All students must complete four co-op quarters in order to graduate. This valuable program "is a fantastic opportunity to get twice as much hands-on experience as you would get at other schools." It also "allows you to discover your passion for a specific area of the law [and] see what may fit for after graduation." One 2L declares, "After next summer I will have completed three internships, one with a judge, one with in-house counsel at a large computer company, and one with a large law firm." Another student agrees, "The co-op office has amazing connections all over the country. We get into amazing internships sitting next to Harvard kids all the time." Another student adds, "If you want real-world legal experience and to be four internships ahead of all of the other graduating law students, Northeastern is ideal." Still another gushes, "Some schools turn out graduates who are exactly the same in terms of classes, experiences, and ideas. At Northeastern, the 180 (or so) students who graduate each year have had 180 different law school experiences, since each of us works in four unique co-ops over the course of the three years. Who cares if the classrooms are bad if the quality of the education is so good?"

M. J. Knoll-Finn, Assistant Dean and Director of Admissions
400 Huntington Avenue, Boston, MA 02115
Telephone: 617-373-2395 • Fax: 617-373-8865
E-mail: lawadmissions@neu.edu • Website: www.slaw.neu.edu

Life

"The unique grading system provides for [an] extremely cooperative atmosphere." One student notes, "There is not an overwhelming sense of competition that stifles your ability to concentrate on functioning and thinking like a lawyer." Another explains, "Everyone truly works together. Without grades, we have no reason to compete with each other." It is important to note that "though the typical complaints are here (law school is [tough], after all), people are generally eager and happy to be here."

"The students are incredibly unique" at Northeastern, and they don't mind telling you so. "The level of diversity, activism, and intelligence at this school is simply amazing." Note, though, that it's all pretty much exclusively of the "progressive" variety. While "there are some conservative and libertarian types, we are very liberal here," discloses one student. "The more progressive students essentially dominate the school."

Socially, "there is some cliquishness—like middle school, but friendlier." One student confides, "Because of the co-op program, it is hard to feel a strong sense of community with your classmates." Another writes, "After first year, you will never see half of your class until graduation day." Yet another confers, "You won't know classmates' names because you probably never had the chance to meet them." Hence, Northeastern can be "a bit of a commuter law school." Geographically speaking, "the community ultimately revolves around e-mail exchanges because half the school at any time is somewhere else in the country." On the plus side, "Boston is a fantastic place to live," and the campus "is within walking distance or a T ride away from" live music, all manner of sports, fabulous food, and "everything exciting in town."

Getting In

Thanks to the public-interest bent, Northeastern's student body is in some ways self-selecting. Admitted students at the 25th percentile have an LSAT score of 161 and a GPA of 3.18. Admitted students at the 75th percentile have an LSAT score of 165 and a GPA of 3.62. It's full-time or nothing at Northeastern. The nature of the co-op program makes it next to impossible to accommodate part-time or evening students.

EMPLOYMENT INFORMATION

Career Rating	**84**
% employed within 9 months	90
Average starting salary	$70,000
State for bar exam	MA, NY, CA
Pass rate for first-time bar	80

Employers who frequently hire grads:
Mintz, Levin, Cohen, Ferris, Glovsky, & Popeo, PC; Goodwin Proctor, LLP; Massachusetts Superior Court and Appeals Court; Greater Boston Legal Services; Securities and Exchange Commission; Health Law Advocates; The Legal Aid Society, Criminal Division; Brigham McCutcheon, LLP; U.S. Court of Appeals.

Grads employed by field (%):	
Academic	2
Business/industry	10
Government	16
Judicial clerkships	18
Private practice	37
Public interest	17

ADMISSIONS

Selectivity Rating	**85**
# applications received	3,843
# applicants accepted	885
# acceptees attending	221
Average LSAT	160
LSAT Range	157–162
Average undergrad GPA	3.5
Application fee	$75
Regular application deadline	3/1
Regular notification	4/15
Rolling notification?	Yes
Early application program?	Yes
Early application deadline	11/15
Early application notification	1/15
Transfer students accepted?	Yes
Evening division offered?	No
Part-time accepted?	No
LSDAS accepted?	Yes

Applicants Also Look At

American University, Boston College, Boston University, Fordham University, The George Washington University, New England School of Law, Suffolk University.

International Students

TOEFL required of international students?	Yes
Minimum Paper TOEFL	600
Minimum Computer TOEFL	250

FINANCIAL FACTS

Annual tuition	$31,170
Books and supplies	$1,200
Room & board	$13,275
Financial aid application deadline	2/15
% first-year students receiving some sort of aid	82
% receiving some sort of aid	86
% of aid that is merit-based	25
% receiving scholarships	62
Average grant	$9,110
Average loan	$30,105
Average total aid package	$36,555
Average debt	$79,267

NORTHERN ILLINOIS UNIVERSITY
COLLEGE OF LAW

INSTITUTIONAL INFORMATION

Public/private	public
Student/faculty ratio	17:1
% faculty part-time	24
% faculty female	33
% faculty minority	45
Total faculty	33

SURVEY SAYS . . .

Diverse opinions accepted in classrooms
Great library staff

STUDENTS

Enrollment of law school	324
% male/female	46/54
% out-of-state	21
% full-time	97
% minority	27
% international	1
Average age of entering class	27

ACADEMICS

Academic Experience rating	**62**
Professors interesting rating	61
Professors accessible rating	65
Hours of study per day	3.5

Academic Specialties

Alternative dispute resolution, civil procedure, commercial law, constitutional law, corporation securities law, criminal law, environmental law, government services, human rights law, intellectual property law, international law, labor law, legal history, property, public interest, taxation.

Combined Degrees Offered

JD/MBA and JD/MPA are our dual programs; other dual degrees have and can be done upon review of student requests. Normally these programs are completed in 4 to 5 years.

Academic Requirements

Clinical Program Required?	No
Legal Writing Course Requirement?	Yes
Legal Methods Course Requirement?	No

Academics

For future Chicago lawyers, Northern Illinois University College of Law offers a lot of bang for your buck. With an excellent teaching staff and a strong reputation, students say that NIU is nothing short of a bargain. In the words of one student, "facilities-aside, NIU is a great school, especially considering annual tuition is less than $10,000." Another chimes in, "Most of our graduates have significantly less debt than other law school grads across the country. The secret to some of this is the wide availability of graduate/research assistantships. In exchange for a full tuition waiver and a monthly stipend, working 20 hours a week is a very good deal."

Despite the affordability, NIU professors take a personal interest in students and offer the kind of personal attention typical to a small, private school. Students insist, "It's important to all the faculty at NIU that you're not just a social security number," and tell us that, "all classes at NIU are small and generally close-knit." A student praises, "I cannot say enough good things about the faculty at NIU. They are a diverse and open group, and go beyond any expectations I had when I arrived." Even the administration takes a personal interest in the student body. A student shares this story: "In the beginning of my first year, I noticed the assistant dean of student affairs, Dean Mandell, sitting in on some of our classes periodically. A few months later, a group of us were sitting outside eating lunch. Dean Mandell approached us to say 'hi' and see how things were going. Surprisingly, he was calling us by name even though none of us had met with him before. Apparently, when he was sitting in on our classes, he was doing so in an effort to learn each of our names, so he could address us personally."

For the most part, students give high marks to their professors, saying the quality of the teaching staff is strong and always improving. Students also like the academic and idealistic atmosphere at NIU, where social responsibility and pro bono work are encouraged. A student tells us, "NIU-COL is a place where students and faculty still view the law as a service profession. We are not all third-generation tax lawyers consumed with the idea of making yet more money." While the professors take a strong intellectual approach to law, students say they also get a lot of practical instruction at NIU. For example, a student shares, "There are some excellent externships available to 3Ls. The Elder Law and Domestic Violence Clinic I would strongly recommend. It is hard work, but you learn so much of it is worth it." Another adds, "The Legal Research program is excellent."

Unfortunately, the facilities at NIU leave something to be desired. With a low tuition price and state budget cuts, NIU has not had the resources to update classrooms or libraries, leaving them in a sorry state of disrepair. A student tells us, "Lecture halls and classrooms are either freezing cold (to the point where students are wearing coats and scarves indoors) or ridiculously hot (to the point where students are sweating even when wearing sleeveless shirts and shorts). Bathrooms are seldom clean and almost always smell like there is a plumbing problem." Another student tells us, "Our library features plastic tarps in a few places to prevent water damage from the leaks in the roof when it rains."

Judith L. Malen, Director of Admissions & Financial Aid
Swen Parson Hall, College of Law, Room 276, De Kalb, IL 60115
Telephone: 815-753-8559 • Fax: 815-753-4501
E-mail: lawadm@niu.edu • Website: http://law.niu.edu

Life

Located in the small, suburban town of DeKalb, students say the campus atmosphere at NIU is pleasant and mellow, but near a large city and its many professional opportunities. A student tells us, "DeKalb is close enough to Chicago to get the benefits of the city and suburbs, but the tuition is well under what would be paid in a downtown Chicago law school." NIU maintains a mellow and friendly campus environment in a pleasant suburban setting. Campus organizations are plentiful, and students say they enjoy socializing together outside the classroom. Students tell us, "The SBA often sponsors socials at local bars and various events that are a lot of fun and a nice break from studying." By all accounts, the NIU student body is a nice blend of diverse interests and backgrounds. A student elaborates, "The students range from fresh out of school to successful business people coming back to further their careers. Each class offers a broad range of opinions and life experiences." Another student chimes in, "The diversity here shows the school's dedication to adding color to a very colorless profession." When not catching up on their homework, NIU students say the social life at law school is surprisingly fun. A student shares, "Two great dance parties and two active fraternity chapters as well as other organizations make for active student bodies." Another student adds, "Students at the law school are very personable, and it is very hard not to make friends."

Getting In

Northern Illinois University seeks students whose LSAT scores and undergraduate performance suggest that they would excel in the field of law. In 2003, the average LSAT score for matriculants was 155 and the average undergraduate GPA was 3.2. For students who have taken the LSAT more than once, NIU will average their scores. Applicants are encouraged to apply before the May 15 priority deadline.

EMPLOYMENT INFORMATION

Career Rating	**66**
Job placement rate (%)	94
Average starting salary	$43,807
State for bar exam	IL, WI, FL, TX
Pass rate for first-time bar	85

Employers who frequently hire grads:
State's attorneys, public defenders, Illinois attorney general, private firms.

Prominent Alumni: Kathleen Zellner, won reversals of 7 murder convictions by use of DNA evidence; Cheryl Niro, top 10 female lawyers (Illinois) and former president of IBA; Dr. Kenneth Chessick, firm specializes in medical negligence litigation.

Grads employed by field (%):	
Academic	3
Business/industry	9
Government	26
Judicial clerkships	3
Military	1
Private practice	53
Public interest	5

Legal Research Course Requirement?	Yes
Moot Court Requirement?	Yes
Public Interest Law Requirement?	No

ADMISSIONS

Selectivity Rating	**79**
# applications received	1,504
# applicants accepted	396
# acceptees attending	105
Average LSAT	156
LSAT Range	153–158
Average undergrad GPA	3.3
Application fee	$50
Regular application deadline	rolling
Regular notification	rolling
Rolling notification?	Yes
Early application program?	No
Transfer students accepted?	Yes
Evening division offered?	No
Part-time accepted?	Yes
LSDAS accepted?	Yes

International Students

TOEFL required of international students?	Yes
Minimum Paper TOEFL	550
Minimum Computer TOEFL	250

FINANCIAL FACTS

Annual tuition (resident)	$8,346
Annual tuition (nonresident)	$16,692
Books and supplies	$1,500
Fees per credit (resident)	$65
Fees per credit (nonresident)	$65
Tuition per credit (resident)	$348
Tuition per credit (nonresident)	$696
Room & board (on/off-campus)	$5,950/$6,850
Financial aid application deadline	3/1
% first-year students receiving some sort of aid	85
% receiving some sort of aid	80
% receiving scholarships	22
Average grant	$8,346
Average loan	$17,500
Average total aid package	$21,300
Average debt	$44,132

NORTHERN KENTUCKY UNIVERSITY
SALMON P. CHASE COLLEGE OF LAW

INSTITUTIONAL INFORMATION

Public/private	public
Student/faculty ratio	15:1
% faculty part-time	44
% faculty female	37
% faculty minority	5
Total faculty	63

SURVEY SAYS . . .

Heavy use of Socratic method
Diverse opinions accepted in classrooms
Great research resources
Great library staff

STUDENTS

Enrollment of law school	580
% male/female	57/43
% out-of-state	30
% full-time	52
% minority	6
Average age of entering class	27

ACADEMICS

Academic Experience rating	**78**
Professors interesting rating	80
Professors accessible rating	85
Hours of study per day	3.93

Combined Degrees Offered

JD/MBA, 4 years full-time.

Academic Requirements

Clinical Program Required?	No
Legal Writing Course Requirement?	Yes
Legal Methods Course Requirement?	Yes
Legal Research Course Requirement?	Yes
Moot Court Requirement?	No
Public Interest Law Requirement?	No

Academics

At Northern Kentucky University Salmon P. Chase College of Law, an unwavering commitment to quality teaching fosters a stimulating and engaging learning atmosphere. Recruiting and retaining superior teachers is a priority at Chase, and the school "has gone out of its way to get good professors, especially in the last few years." As a result, "classes are rich and rewarding." The "student-oriented [professors] create an atmosphere that is comfortable but challenging." In the classroom, critical thinking skills and student participation are emphasized, and professors make lectures engaging with their humor, enthusiasm, and intelligence. While material can be difficult and dry, Chase professors take a lighthearted approach to instruction. A 1L explains, "The majority of our professors use humor to keep us involved and challenge us to work through difficult theories instead of just giving us the answers or letting us off the hook." One professor even "came up with lyrics to a country song during property class to help us understand fees."

In addition to traditional course work in legal theory, students appreciate Chase's "good, structured curriculum geared toward preparing students for the bar." This excellent program has allowed Chase to claim the "highest first-time bar-passage rate in Kentucky" (with a 79 percent average). In addition, "Chase's emphasis on practical experience is found in such classes as interview and negotiation, trial ad, and externships. These classes/externships are offered on a regular basis [and] prepare the student for immediate success in the courtroom or the boardroom." "Chase's practical teaching methods and adherence to the principles of the ever-evolving legal world allow a student to learn how to practice law and not simply what the law is historically." This applied experience also plays out positively in career placement, as "Chase has a great local reputation for turning out lawyers who are capable of hitting the ground running."

Described by weary students as "exhausting and exhilarating," the Chase experience is extremely competitive. Students warn that "the work load is obscene," and they are further challenged by the school's Draconian grading policies. A 3L explains, "Unlike most law schools, Chase has what is known as a C curve. On every exam the majority of the class will get a C. While this is at times harsh, it really helps to push students. When you get an A, you know that it really means something. Also, this curve has helped to improve our bar-passage rating by making students work harder." Ultimately, "Chase is about helping people succeed"; to that end, "the faculty really go out of their way for students." One student reports, "My writing professor is not only a good lawyer and writer, but also a personable and kind individual. He seems genuinely concerned about my education and about me personally." According to another, "The faculty are always willing to have students to their offices to answer questions or help in finding jobs." On top of that, "there is a very personal relationship between the deans and the students," and the administration is active in establishing programs to help students adjust to and succeed in law school. In particular, "Chase truly works on transitioning students into their first classes." First-years can "enroll in a summer program designed to introduce them to the law school process. In addition, there is a required course, Introduction to Legal Studies, for all first-years, which builds on the summer program. This made the first day of law school a lot less intimidating."

Chase's supportive atmosphere is particularly evident in the remarks of evening program participants. While part-time students at other law schools often feel overlooked or misunderstood, Chase is "accommodating for students who work full-time, have children, or have been out of the classroom for a long time." One night student reports, "As a part-time student with a more than full-time job, my professors value my experience. I find they incor-

Ashley Folger Gray, Acting Director of Admissions
Nunn Hall, Room 550, Highland Heights, KY 41099
Telephone: 859-572-6476 • Fax: 859-572-6081
E-mail: folger@nku.edu • Website: www.nku.edu/~chase

porate our expertise in their questioning, which means they have taken the time to get to know us." Indeed, night students say that "there are a large number of older students with real-world work and life experience attending classes [along] with traditional students."

Life

There is a noticeable divide between the day and evening programs at Chase. While full-time students describe the campus as friendly and social, evening students tend to keep to themselves. A day student comments, "Most of our class has genuinely become friends with each other, and we hang out together whenever we get free time." Among full-timers, participation in clubs, campus events, and student parties is common. On the other hand, students in the evening program usually work full time, so "relations among students outside the classroom are minimal (with exception of study groups)." While they may not socialize together, evening students maintain a generally noncompetitive and supportive atmosphere in the classroom. One shares, "because the majority of my class is composed of nontraditional students, social relationships are nonexistent. Academic relationships, however, are much stronger than any I've seen."

On that note, all Chase students agree that the academic environment is collegial and supportive. "Although there is a definite competitive atmosphere due to the bell curve, students are not as cutthroat as they may be at other schools." Students write that the school's "strongest fault is the lack of diversity within our faculty and our students." A 2L laments, "The law school could improve on its diversity retention." The school does, however, maintain fairly active student communities, and "there are groups for every type of student: law fraternities, the Black Lawyers' Society, the Christian Legal Society, the Public Interest Group. You can find support almost everywhere you turn."

Getting In

In 2004, Chase matriculated 228 students with an average LSAT score of 154 and an average undergraduate GPA of 3.22. Chase principally considers LSAT scores, undergraduate GPA, letters of recommendation, and the personal statement in making admissions decisions. Chase looks for students with a broad liberal arts education and strong writing and verbal skills. While the school does not prefer any specific course of undergraduate study, political science, finance, and psychology were the most common undergraduate majors represented in the entering class.

EMPLOYMENT INFORMATION

Career Rating	**73**
% employed within 9 months	90
Average starting salary	$55,917
State for bar exam	KY, OH
Pass rate for first-time bar	79

Employers who frequently hire grads: Fidelity Investments; Proctor & Gamble; Dinsmore & Shohl; Kentucky Department of Public Advocacy; Freund, Freeze, & Arnold.

Prominent Alumni: Congressman Steve Chabot, United States representative, first district of Ohio; Honorable Daniel T. Guidugli, judge, Kentucky Court of Appeals.

Grads employed by field (%):	
Academic	3
Business/industry	24
Government	12
Judicial clerkships	7
Military	1
Private practice	44
Public interest	9

ADMISSIONS

Selectivity Rating	**75**
# applications received	681
# applicants accepted	252
# acceptees attending	108
Average LSAT	154
LSAT Range	152–157
Average undergrad GPA	3.3
Application fee	$30
Regular application deadline	3/1
Regular notification	rolling
Rolling notification?	Yes
Early application program?	No
Transfer students accepted?	Yes
Evening division offered?	Yes
Part-time accepted?	Yes
LSDAS accepted?	Yes

Applicants Also Look At

University of Cincinnati, University of Dayton, University of Kentucky, University of Louisville.

International Students

TOEFL required of international students?	Yes

FINANCIAL FACTS

Annual tuition (resident)	$9,240
Annual tuition (nonresident)	$20,184
Books and supplies	$2,600
Tuition per credit (resident)	$385
Tuition per credit (nonresident)	$841
Room & board	$10,500
Financial aid application deadline	3/1
% receiving some sort of aid	84
% of aid that is merit-based	8
% receiving scholarships	20
Average grant	$9,375
Average loan	$16,759
Average total aid package	$18,949
Average debt	$53,485

NORTHWESTERN UNIVERSITY
SCHOOL OF LAW

INSTITUTIONAL INFORMATION

Public/private	private
Student/faculty ratio	12:1
% faculty part-time	35
% faculty female	39
% faculty minority	8
Total faculty	154

SURVEY SAYS . . .

Diverse opinions accepted in classrooms
Great research resources
Students love Chicago, IL

STUDENTS

Enrollment of law school	771
% male/female	52/48
% out-of-state	80
% full-time	100
% minority	31
% international	3
# of countries represented	10
Average age of entering class	25

ACADEMICS

Academic Experience rating	**94**
Professors interesting rating	83
Professors accessible rating	84
Hours of study per day	4.01

Academic Specialties

Civil litigation, corporation securities law, human rights law, international law, taxation, health law, law and social policy.

Advanced Degrees Offered

JD, 3 years; LLM, 1 year; SJD, 5 years; LLM in taxation, 1 year; LLM in human rights, 1 year; JD for international lawyers, 2 years.

Combined Degrees Offered

JD/MBA, 3 years; JD/PhD, 6 years; JD/MA, 4 years; MSJ/MSL, 2 years; LLM/certificate in management, 1 year.

Academic Requirements

Clinical Program Required?	No
Legal Writing Course Requirement?	Yes

Academics

Northwestern University's "kinder, gentler" School of Law "has one foot firmly planted in the professional world and the other well-rooted in the academic world. Like at any top school, there is a heavy emphasis on the theoretical"; however, there are also "world-class clinics, [a] great litigation focus," and internship and externship opportunities galore. Plus, "you get actual legal experience" to boot: "The school does a fabulous job of providing opportunities for students to work in legal clinics, state attorney's offices, and judges' chambers." One student comments on how Northwestern students are blessed in this regard: "What other law students do you know of that have spent time in the courtroom defending death-row inmates or working with start-up companies to help them succeed?" Given that example, the diversity of available work experiences certainly does seem remarkable. Back on campus, the legal writing program, featuring workshops, panel discussions, and industry colloquiums is "simply unparalleled." NU's intense three-year JD/MBA program reportedly "offers access to two of the best graduate schools in the country." One satisfied customer crows, "Whether I practice law first or go straight back to business, I am confident that I have the decision-making framework and management skills to be successful in either arena."

The "extremely intelligent professors [at Northwestern] seem pleased to be here teaching." Students say, "Everyone is famous for something but completely humble and approachable." A few students comment that their professors "are a very talented bunch, teaching-wise, but sometimes lack work experience." But don't worry, any potential weakness there has been fortified. Each semester, the school brings in a substantial number of adjuncts from the Chicago legal community to teach specialized classes, and students report, "Many of the adjuncts are great at providing practical instruction and showing their passion for teaching. They have been helpful in hunting down job leads and making contacts." Some students complain that "layers of bureaucracy" abound within the administration, while others say administrators (including the dean) are accessible and contend that Northwestern "definitely has a vision and a plan." More than a few students have noted that this plan appears to include larger first-year classes. Some worry, "This population explosion has had a detrimental effect on class selection, on-campus interviews, and facilities overall (e.g., having to share lockers)."

Thanks to the school's first-rate national reputation, Northwestern law students are extremely confident about their job prospects. "Many doors are open to me as an NU student that simply wouldn't be if I had attended other schools," professes one student. "The Chicago firms just love NU students" and if you have "decent grades, it's really easy to get a job coming out of Northwestern." One student proudly informs us that "law firm interview spots are awarded by lottery and not by the firms pre-screening resumes." In addition, NU's loan repayment assistance program "actually makes a career in the public interest possible."

Northwestern's "absolutely gorgeous [facilities are] modern with comfortable seating and, perhaps most important, wireless access to the Internet." The wireless is "sometimes a little spotty, [though, and] the fight over electrical outlets can be a real challenge." In addition, some complain about climate control: "The classrooms are over–air conditioned in the summer and over-heated in the winter." One student explains, "The school is continuously upgrading facilities, but they could stand to pick up the pace."

Don Rebstock, Associate Dean of Enrollment
357 East Chicago Avenue, Chicago, IL 60611
Telephone: 312-503-8465 • Fax: 312-503-0178
E-mail: nulawadm@law.northwestern.edu • Website: www.law.northwestern.edu

Life

The "very, very smart" students at NU reportedly have "strong ethical sensibilities." They come equipped with real-world know-how, too—almost all incoming 1L students are at least a year out of undergrad with prior work experience. Naturally, with this being law school and all, "there are times when everyone feels stressed." Nevertheless, students maintain that competition is nil. In fact, Northwestern is "anti-competitive." One student writes, "The students here get along amazingly well and have zero problems sharing notes, outlines, and whatever else may be helpful." Another student even disclosed, "Instead of ripping pages out of library books, people put Post-It notes in the books to show each other where to look."

Socially, NU is "very much like college." There is a "balance between a quality education and quality of life, [and] students here really know how to have fun." One student declares, "We have huge turnouts for Bar Review each week, plus there are always a variety of lunchtime chats with free lunches and club sponsored events." One student applauds the Wigmore Follies, at which "students and professors get involved in producing, directing, and acting in a hilarious, satirical look at life at Northwestern Law." The beer and scotch reportedly flow freely at this popular annual end-of-the-year revue.

The law school is located "in a really nice and centrally located part of Chicago—a haven in a big city." Michigan Avenue's "Magnificent Mile of shopping" is practically next door, as is Lake Michigan. It's a "swanky" area, though, and nearby restaurants can be a bit costly. But you can always live and eat elsewhere because, students say, "It's easy to get around Chicago without a car."

Getting In

It's tough to get admitted at NU. The average LSAT score for students admitted in the fall of 2003 was 169. The average GPA of admitted students is 3.6. Also, note that Northwestern is committed to admitting students who have a few years of work experience under their belts. The average age of entering 1Ls is 25. If you take the LSAT more than once, Northwestern uses your highest score.

EMPLOYMENT INFORMATION

Career Rating	**99**
% employed within 9 months	99
Average starting salary	$125,000
State for bar exam	IL
Pass rate for first-time bar	98

Employers who frequently hire grads: Skadden Arps, Cravath, Swain, & Moore; Sidley & Austin; Kirkland & Ellis; Latham & Watkins; Jones, Day, Reavis, & Pogue; Katten, Muchin, & Zavis; Morrison & Foerster; Winston & Strawn.

Prominent Alumni: John Paul Stevens, Supreme Court justice; Arthur Goldberg, Supreme Court justice; Donald Washburn, chairman & president of Northwest Airliines.

Grads employed by field (%):	
Academic	1
Business/industry	5
Government	3
Judicial clerkships	16
Private practice	73
Public interest	2

Legal Methods Course Requirement?	No
Legal Research Course Requirement?	Yes
Moot Court Requirement?	Yes
Public Interest Law Requirement?	Yes

ADMISSIONS

Selectivity Rating	**96**
# applications received	4,802
# applicants accepted	774
# acceptees attending	244
Average LSAT	169
LSAT Range	166–170
Average undergrad GPA	3.7
Application fee	$80
Regular application deadline	2/15
Regular notification	rolling
Rolling notification?	Yes
Early application program?	Yes
Early application deadline	12/1
Early application notification	12/31
Transfer students accepted?	Yes
Evening division offered?	No
Part-time accepted?	No
LSDAS accepted?	Yes

Applicants Also Look At

Columbia University, Georgetown University, Harvard University, New York University, University of California—Berkeley, University of Chicago, University of Pennsylvania.

International Students

TOEFL required of international students?	No
TOEFL recommended of international students?	No

FINANCIAL FACTS

Annual tuition	$35,896
Books and supplies	$7,998
Room & board	$12,078
Financial aid application deadline	2/15
% first-year students receiving some sort of aid	80
% receiving some sort of aid	80
% of aid that is merit-based	50
% receiving scholarships	45
Average grant	$15,000
Average loan	$30,000
Average total aid package	$45,000
Average debt	$95,000

NOVA SOUTHEASTERN UNIVERSITY
SHEPARD BROAD SCHOOL OF LAW

INSTITUTIONAL INFORMATION

Public/private	private
Student/faculty ratio	15:3
% faculty part-time	48
% faculty female	41
% faculty minority	16
Total faculty	116

SURVEY SAYS . . .

Diverse opinions accepted in classrooms
Great research resources
Students love Fort Lauderdale, FL

STUDENTS

Enrollment of law school	963
% male/female	50/50
% full-time	80
% minority	30
% international	1
# of countries represented	8
Average age of entering class	24

ACADEMICS

Academic Experience rating	**71**
Professors interesting rating	70
Professors accessible rating	77
Hours of study per day	4.51

Academic Specialties

Civil procedure, commercial law, constitutional law, corporation securities law, criminal law, environmental law, government services, human rights law, intellectual property law, international law, labor law, legal history, property, taxation.

Combined Degrees Offered

JD/MBA; JD/MS, psychology; JD/MS, dispute resolution; JD/MS, computer; JD/MURP.

Academic Requirements

Clinical Program Required?	No
Legal Writing Course Requirement?	Yes
Legal Methods Course Requirement?	No
Legal Research Course Requirement?	Yes

Academics

The law meets modern technology at Nova Southeastern University Law Center. Widely regarded as one of the most highly connected (in terms of technological capabilities) law schools in the country, Nova prides itself on being the frontrunner in getting technological advances into the classroom. "It is nice to be able to listen to a lecture while sitting at home with the flu," a student tells us. And streaming media is just one way "the school tries to ensure the success of its students." However, a few students do not see such high-tech capabilities as all positive. For a school that touts itself as being the most wired in the nation, it is also the most vulnerable with viruses and probably [has] the most distracted students in the classroom. "Many of my peers IM & web surf when they ought to be taking notes," writes one student. Practical learning is valued at Nova, as "every law student who wants to do a clinic is guaranteed a place in one of the many clinics offered." The clinical program "provides students different opportunities to practice in a certain area during their third year." Inside the classroom, the "Socratic Method is used in a way that the students are taught and not just harassed." Complaints about the curriculum center on a two required semester sequence of classes called "Lawyering Skills and Values," which, according to one student finishing up his legal education, "were of little use and made it difficult to take all core, bar, and recommended general classes and still put together a coherent specialization." It appears as though the faculty and administration are taking such student reactions to the class into consideration, as the number of required semesters of it has recently been reduced from four to two semesters. Students are also concerned about bar-passage rates and would like to see more required (and available) courses geared toward the bar exam. For example, they would like the school to require "two semesters of the basic classes like contracts and torts instead of just one."

The faculty earns high marks among students. Professors at Nova Southeastern "actively engage the student body to critically analyze current social and political issues with an eye for any legal ramifications that may stem from there." This sort of attitude fosters an "academic fervor within the institution, and the frequent exchange of ideas helps broaden the student's collective intellectual experience." Additionally, the law center "employs a lot of specialists who come on-board with very practical and real-life legal experiences, [such as the] local law firm senior partners [who] teach fourth-semester legal writing." With that sort of combination, it is hardly any wonder the students feel that they "receive an excellent legal education."

Also receiving high marks from students is the administration. Many students rave that the "administration strives for excellence, seeking out dedicated and spirited professors, including adjunct professors who bring with them brilliance and a solid sense of reality." Both the administration and the faculty "really care about each individual student who enters the law center. I am consistently amazed at how they go out of their way to help us all. They make a challenging experience (law school) just that much easier through their caring and supportive attitudes," writes one law student.

Beth Hall, Director of Admissions
3305 College Avenue, Fort Lauderdale, FL 33314
Telephone: 954-262-6117 • Fax: 954-262-3844
E-mail: admission@nsu.law.nova.edu • Website: www.nsulaw.nova.edu

Life

If you like cold and bleak winters, Nova Southeastern is not the place for you. "NSU is located close to downtown Ft. Lauderdale and Miami, so if you need to find something fun to do, it's always there!" Students declare, "We can play golf all year. We can go to the beaches all year. The social opportunities around school are vast, although you run the risk of always seeing the same people." Other students explain, "Nova is its location. It is in the center of the three most populous counties in the state of Florida, which provides for many competitive jobs within many fields of law." South Florida also has a pretty pleasant climate to unwind in.

Around campus, "students are afforded the opportunity to voice their opinions, regardless of how disagreeable others may find it." There always seems to be "some ongoing debate going on via the E-mail system. It is pretty much an open forum on politics, gender issues, sexuality, ethnicity, parking lot issues. Any and everything is debated among the student body." Although the traditional law school competitiveness exists between classmates, "Everyone at NSU wants to learn, and most of the students are willing to help each other out in any way possible." Student organizations abound at Nova Southeastern. "We even have a Celtic American law student association!" cheers one student.

Getting In

Admission at Nova Southeastern is not particularly competitive, with a little more than a third of all applicants being offered admission. Admitted students at the 75th percentile have an LSAT score of 152 and a GPA of 3.3.

EMPLOYMENT INFORMATION

Career Rating	**67**
% employed within 9 months	83
Average starting salary	$53,270
State for bar exam	FL
Pass rate for first-time bar	58

Employers who frequently hire grads: Private law firms, local and state agencies, state attorney's office, public defender offices.

Prominent Alumni: Melanie G. May, judge; Ilene Lieberman, Broward County mayor; Ellyn Setnor Bogdanoff, Florida House of Representatives; Jay Spechler, judge; Israel Reyes, judge.

Grads employed by field (%):

Academic	2
Business/industry	12
Government	14
Judicial clerkships	3
Military	1
Other	3
Private practice	58
Public interest	7

Moot Court Requirement?	Yes
Public Interest Law Requirement?	No

ADMISSIONS

Selectivity Rating	**70**
# applications received	2,908
# applicants accepted	746
# acceptees attending	359
Average LSAT	149
LSAT Range	147–152
Average undergrad GPA	3.0
Application fee	$50
Regular application deadline	3/1
Regular notification	3/1
Rolling notification?	Yes
Early application program?	No
Transfer students accepted?	Yes
Evening division offered?	Yes
Part-time accepted?	Yes
LSDAS accepted?	Yes

Applicants Also Look At

Florida Coastal School of Law, Florida International University, Florida State University, St. Thomas University, Stetson University, University of Florida, University of Miami.

International Students

TOEFL required of international students?	Yes
Minimum Paper TOEFL	550
Minimum Computer TOEFL	213

FINANCIAL FACTS

Annual tuition	$23,873
Books and supplies	$3,800
Room & board (on/off-campus)	$9,000/$13,000
Financial aid application deadline	4/15
% first-year students receiving some sort of aid	84
% receiving some sort of aid	89
% of aid that is merit-based	10
% receiving scholarships	10
Average grant	$17,115
Average loan	$26,773
Average total aid package	$27,474
Average debt	$85,000

Ohio Northern University
Claude W. Pettit College of Law

INSTITUTIONAL INFORMATION

Public/private	private
Student/faculty ratio	12:1
Affiliation	Methodist
% faculty part-time	25
% faculty female	30
% faculty minority	3
Total faculty	30

SURVEY SAYS . . .

Great research resources
Great library staff

STUDENTS

Enrollment of law school	310
% male/female	52/48
% out-of-state	65
% full-time	100
% minority	11
% international	1
# of countries represented	4
Average age of entering class	25

ACADEMICS

Academic Experience rating	**66**
Professors interesting rating	67
Professors accessible rating	78
Hours of study per day	5.5

Academic Specialties

Capital punishment, civil procedure, commercial law, constitutional law, corporation securities law, criminal law, environmental law, human rights law, intellectual property law, international law, labor law, legal history, legal philosophy, property, taxation.

Advanced Degrees Offered

JD, 3 years.

Academic Requirements

Clinical Program Required?	No
Legal Writing Course Requirement?	Yes
Legal Methods Course Requirement?	Yes
Legal Research Course Requirement?	Yes
Moot Court Requirement?	No

Academics

At the small Claude W. Pettit College of Law, no one is a face in the crowd, so you can forget about sitting in the back row and remaining unnoticed. Thanks to small class sizes, "there is a high degree of accountability in the classroom," and students are expected to keep up with a hefty workload; a 2L warns, "You really have to be on your game for class every day." Students also feel the need to be on the ball outside the classroom. "I didn't realize when I came here that I would have to walk around with clever things to say in case a professor happened to be near when I was roaming the building. You never know when a professor will approach you in the hall or lounge to talk about anything from what you discussed in class to something they remembered about your application essay," reports one student. Indeed, at many other law schools, the top ten percent of the class eats up most of the attention of faculty and staff, but at ONU, "the dean knows not only who is number one in the class, but also who is fiftieth and who is last."

The intimate environment at ONU makes for a lively and competitive atmosphere. But "while there is competition, you get personal attention every step of the way." The school promotes an open-door policy for professors, and students tell us that "the faculty is always around and usually more than willing to help out, answer questions, or shoot the breeze." A 2L adds, "They are there to help you not only with legal concepts, but also how to go about starting your legal career." On that note, students say they get excellent career preparation through the clinical programs, for even though ONU is located in a tiny, rural town, "the clinic/externship program is one of the best," placing many students in jobs in the nearby city of Lima. So "if you want a placement somewhere, they can make it happen." On top of that, the school operates "tons of extracurriculars," such as moot court and Law Review, which are described as top-notch and highly competitive. However, ONU doesn't just cater to overachievers. "Our programs differ in ways that allow each student to maximize their potential," reports one 2L. For example, the school runs "extra help sessions taught by teaching assistants" and "the summer starter program, intended for those with lower LSAT scores."

The school has been receiving increasing prominence of late, and the administration is eager to keep the ball rolling. Explains a 2L, "As for the goals of the university, the school seems to be moving toward increasing the quality of the students and faculty and generally ensuring a better reputation for the future." Some feel that the higher-ups are now too focused on building status at the expense of building personal bonds with students, leading some students to report that "the relationship between the administration and students feels like it gets chillier every year."

Located in the tiny town of Ada, Pettit's pleasant campus is an excellent place to study, offering little distraction for the serious law student. Some campus buildings need to be renovated, according to students who also point out that classrooms are old and limited in outlets for laptops Others feel, however, that the school hits the mark in all the important areas: "The building could use some sprucing up," a 2L writes, "but what it lacks in looks it makes up for in having wireless everywhere and being a comfortable place to learn." On top of that, students praise the research facilities and staff: "The librarians are hands on, holding workshops that complement the research assignments."

Life

You might be surprised to learn that many students say ONU's location "in the middle of a cornfield" is among the school's greatest assets because for the overburdened law

LINDA K. ENGLISH, ASSISTANT DEAN AND DIRECTOR OF LAW ADMISSIONS
OHIO NORTHERN UNIVERSITY, PETTIT COLLEGE, ADA, OH 45810-1599
TELEPHONE: 877-452-9668 • FAX: 419-772-3042
E-MAIL: LAW-ADMISSIONS@ONU.EDU • WEBSITE: WWW.LAW.ONU.EDU

student, Ada is free of distractions and is "conducive to studying." In addition, "the actual location of the school is in a small town setting but only 10 minutes from the next city. You are right between Columbus, Dayton, and Toledo, so you can go wherever you wish to have fun" if you have a car, that is. The small-town environment "lacks the diversity of a big city," a condition that is mirrored by the campus population, but students insist that there is nonetheless some variety among the student population. "Despite our cultural diversity being rather low due to the area of the university," reports one 2L, "we have a great deal of different life experiences."

On campus the atmosphere is active, social, and friendly. "Our student body is very outgoing," writes one student. "This allows for many different organizations to be successful and for different events to be more enjoyable." Outside of class, it's easy to make friends among interesting and amiable classmates: "Throughout your time in law school you will make closer friends than you could possibly imagine, not only with people in your section, but the whole school," reports a typical student. With such a small number of students, however, "the rumor mill is endless." As is the case at many law schools, "it's like high school, but you can drink now without hiding it from your parents."

Getting In

No surprises here. Undergraduate GPA and LSAT scores are the most heavily weighted factors for admission; however, the Admissions Committee will also consider factors such as graduate work, work experience that may have enhanced a student's communication and analytical skills, or a history of overcoming racial or ethnic barriers. Successful applicants usually submit an undergraduate GPA above 3.0 and LSAT scores above 150.

EMPLOYMENT INFORMATION

Career Rating	**90**
Job placement rate (%)	94
State for bar exam	OH, FL, PA, NC, MD
Pass rate for first-time bar	93

Prominent Alumni: Michael DeWine, U.S. senator; Gregory Frost, U.S. district judge, Southern Ohio; Benjamin Brafman, senior partner at Brafman & Ross, New York City; Greg Miller, U.S. attorney for Northwest Florida.

Grads employed by field (%):	
Academic	2
Judicial clerkships	6
Military	3
Other	3
Public interest	3

Public Interest Law Requirement?	No

ADMISSIONS

Selectivity Rating	**74**
# applications received	1,538
# applicants accepted	422
# acceptees attending	121
Average LSAT	153
LSAT Range	150–156
Average undergrad GPA	3.3
Application fee	$40
Regular application deadline	rolling
Regular notification	rolling
Rolling notification?	Yes
Early application program?	No
Transfer students accepted?	Yes
Evening division offered?	No
Part-time accepted?	No
LSDAS accepted?	Yes

Applicants Also Look At

Capital University, Case Western Reserve University, Duquesne University, The Ohio State University, University of Cincinnati, University of Dayton, University of Pittsburgh, University of Toledo, Widener University.

International Students

TOEFL required of international students?	Yes
Minimum Paper TOEFL	550

FINANCIAL FACTS

Annual tuition	$22,640
Books and supplies	$900
Room & board (on/off-campus)	$6,570/$7,830
Financial aid application deadline	4/5
% first-year students receiving some sort of aid	97
% receiving some sort of aid	97
% of aid that is merit-based	23
% receiving scholarships	51
Average grant	$11,133
Average loan	$25,140
Average total aid package	$31,023
Average debt	$70,000

Ohio State University
Michael E. Moritz College of Law

INSTITUTIONAL INFORMATION

Public/private	public
Student/faculty ratio	14:1
% faculty part-time	18
% faculty female	37
% faculty minority	16
Total faculty	67

SURVEY SAYS . . .

Diverse opinions accepted in classrooms
Great research resources
Great library staff

STUDENTS

Enrollment of law school	660
% male/female	49/51
% out-of-state	33
% full-time	100
% minority	19
% international	2
# of countries represented	3
Average age of entering class	23

ACADEMICS

Academic Experience rating	**80**
Professors interesting rating	80
Professors accessible rating	73
Hours of study per day	4.34

Academic Specialties

Alternative dispute resolution, commercial law, criminal law, environmental law, international law, legal philosophy.

Combined Degrees Offered

JD/MBA, 4 years; JD/MHA, 4 years; JD/MPA, 4 years; JD/MD, JD/over 80 different individually designed, 4 to 5 years.

Academic Requirements

Clinical Program Required?	No
Legal Writing Course Requirement?	Yes
Legal Methods Course Requirement?	Yes
Legal Research Course Requirement?	Yes
Moot Court Requirement?	No

Academics

Students graduate from the Ohio State University Michael E. Mortiz College of Law with a strong legal education and excellent career prospects but without the crushing debt typical to top-tier law schools. "The faculty is composed of some of the top legal scholars in the country," and students report that "many of our professors are prolific writers and are widely known in the academic and legal communities." The value, then, of an Ohio State legal education is "exposure to top professors at a public school price." While the college's accomplished faculty brings prestige to the school and expertise to the classroom, students say that it is their "caring and student-focused" attitudes that really stand out. "Across the board," one 3L attests, "the faculty at Ohio State is approachable and dedicated to teaching students. Students always come before publishing and other personal endeavors." Adds another student, "The professors here are outstanding and care about the students 150 percent. They will put forth the effort for you not only in the classroom, but in your career preparation and job searching as well."

With about 145 courses offered annually, Ohio State students can choose from "an incredible number of classes in a number of interesting areas." While first-year course work is prescribed, as it is at most law schools, the final two years are largely elective, and students can design their own course of study within a legal specialty. Many first-year classes are limited in terms of enrollment, which students see as a benefit, and as "the law school is attached to a great university," there are "so many opportunities" academically and socially that students at unaffiliated law schools may not enjoy. Of particular strength is the college's "focus and reputation for alternative dispute resolution [ADR]," which attracts many lawyers with an interest in public service. In fact, Ohio State has a history as a fairly liberal and social justice–oriented school. A 2L explains, "Because of the lower cost, we are exposed to a less cynical side of lawyering. We can come out and actually help someone, rather than pay off debt."

The Ohio State academic experience focuses largely on legal scholarship; however, the school also offers a variety of opportunities for students to put their theory to work. From the first year on, "the school offers a fair number of practicum courses," including a variety of upper-level classes, many of which enroll no more than 20 students at a time. In addition, the school operates a number of legal clinics and student-published legal reviews. Not everyone, however, feels the school goes far enough in promoting practical lawyering skills and feel that the school needs "to balance all this ADR and constitutional and rights course work with material that lawyers actually practice."

Despite such complaints, most Ohio State students easily find jobs in the area since the college has "a great regional reputation as the best law school in Ohio." In addition, "the law school is always looking to improve," and, as a result, students say their national reputation is on an upward trajectory.

The administration maintains a very considerate, student-friendly attitude. In fact, the administration is so solicitous that some complain they "could use a little more backbone" and are "too nice and too concerned about student opinions." While they report general satisfaction with the higher-ups, some students are sorely disappointed in the fact that the "university recently backed away from supporting its GLBT students and allies in favor of avoiding a legal battle with the Christian Legal Society." A 3L advises, "If you want a school that doesn't use your tuition/public money to discriminate,

Sarbeth J. Fleming, Assistant Director
55 West Twelfth Avenue, Columbus, OH 43210
Telephone: 614-292-8810 • Fax: 614-292-1492
E-mail: lawadmit@osu.edu • Website: http://moritzlaw.osu.edu

rethink applying to OSU. They refuse to take a stand on this and have allowed 'sincere religious beliefs' to trump their own nondiscrimination policy."

Life

By all accounts, "the student body and the faculty at Ohio State is quite diverse," both ethnically and culturally. A 3L details, "The male-female ratio is about even, there are large numbers of racial minorities, there are substantial numbers of gays and lesbians, and minorities excel in all areas at OSU." Despite the ethnic and cultural diversity, students say that there is a surprising uniformity in age and opinion. "A huge percentage of students come straight to Moritz directly out of Ohio State undergrad," notes one student. "This leads to 'group think' on a lot of issues. I'm not talking about racial or ethnic diversity—that seems pretty good. I'm talking diversity of ideas, which makes for a better learning environment." In fact, many say that the school's political environment leans largely to the left and that "a liberal viewpoint is always eagerly welcomed."

While some conservatives may moan about the school's liberal bias, most students agree that, for the most part, Ohio State is "a cohesive and welcoming community" and that competitiveness is kept to a minimum. In general, life at Ohio State is pleasant, laid-back, and casual, and students appreciate the slower pace of their midwestern environs. In the words of one 3L, "Columbus is a great city to live in as a student because there's a low cost of living and the pace of life is not hectic." If you are looking for bright lights and big city, though, Columbus is not the place: "There's not a lot of variety to Columbus. Enough to keep you busy, but not a lot of variety," reports a 2L.

Getting In

Ohio State University admits students who have demonstrated ability to succeed in a rigorous legal program. In particular, the admissions committee carefully evaluates a student's undergraduate record, examining grades, grade trends, rigor of the course work and major curriculum, reputation of the undergraduate institution, and recommendations from academic faculty. About 42 percent of entering students in fall 2004 were residents of a state other than Ohio.

Public Interest Law Requirement?	No

ADMISSIONS

Selectivity Rating	**85**
# applications received	2,386
# applicants accepted	645
# acceptees attending	246
Average LSAT	160
LSAT Range	156–163
Average undergrad GPA	3.6
Application fee	$60
Regular application deadline	3/1
Regular notification	rolling
Rolling notification?	Yes
Early application program?	No
Transfer students accepted?	Yes
Evening division offered?	No
Part-time accepted?	No
LSDAS accepted?	Yes

International Students

TOEFL required of international students?	Yes
Minimum Paper TOEFL	600

FINANCIAL FACTS

Annual tuition (resident)	$14,372
Books and supplies	$2,020
Room & board	$8,184
Financial aid application deadline	3/1
% first-year students receiving some sort of aid	65
% receiving some sort of aid	70
% of aid that is merit-based	2
Average grant	$2,135
Average debt	$50,000

EMPLOYMENT INFORMATION

Career Rating	**75**
Job placement rate (%)	94
Average starting salary	$63,700
State for bar exam	OH
Pass rate for first-time bar	90

Grads employed by field (%):	
Academic	1
Business/industry	8
Government	12
Judicial clerkships	12
Military	1
Other	10
Private practice	50
Public interest	5

OKLAHOMA CITY UNIVERSITY
SCHOOL OF LAW

INSTITUTIONAL INFORMATION

Public/private	private
Student/faculty ratio	18:1
Affiliation	Methodist
% faculty part-time	28
% faculty female	42
% faculty minority	6
Total faculty	55

SURVEY SAYS . . .

Diverse opinions accepted in classrooms
Great library staff

STUDENTS

Enrollment of law school	684
% male/female	58/42
% out-of-state	52
% full-time	72
% minority	18
# of countries represented	11
Average age of entering class	28

ACADEMICS

Academic Experience rating	**64**
Professors interesting rating	75
Professors accessible rating	71
Hours of study per day	4.72

Academic Specialties

Certificate in business law, certificate in public law.

Combined Degrees Offered

JD/MBA, 4 years.

Academic Requirements

Clinical Program Required?	No
Legal Writing Course Requirement?	Yes
Legal Methods Course Requirement?	No
Legal Research Course Requirement?	Yes
Moot Court Requirement?	No
Public Interest Law Requirement?	No

Academics

A first-year at Oklahoma City University School of Law writes, "I was nervous about going to a school that did not have a better academic reputation on the national level, but quickly I realized that OCU Law is very competitive with respect to its curriculum and professors." In particular, "if you are going to practice in Oklahoma, OCU Law has a stellar reputation within the community and surrounding states." Students interested in dispute resolution and Native American law find top programs here that are backed by "an unmatched Legal Research and Writing department." Some students, particularly those in the part-time evening program, complain about sparse course options. Furthermore, a few gripe that "the first three semesters are largely mandatory courses." That said, "the school is working on obtaining adjunct professors to teach some of the more popular courses requested by the students," and students are optimistic about having a wider range of course options in the future.

The professors at OCU "range from the typical Ivy-League eggheads to those who worked their way through law school." Students value the "intellectual energy" and practical experiences of their instructors, most of whom can "make even the driest theoretical concept interesting." Take the property professor who "got on top of a desk and shouted, 'Never, never, never change a legal description of a property!'" Professors toss around "fun terms, like 'playground justice,'" and come up with "offbeat hypos that really stick in your memory." A 1L writes, "The classroom environment is open. Free discussions, dissenting opinions, and intellectual dialogs between students are welcomed." Above all, the faculty show they care. "We actually had a professor e-mail 1Ls on driving techniques in the snow because he knew that many of us had never been in those conditions." But don't mistake kind-hearted professors for pushovers. Small classes mean there's nowhere to hide when the Socratic grilling gets going, and "high grades must be truly earned."

When it comes to the administration, "the doors are open at every level." The school's "personal touch" means that faculty and administration members "remember your name even when you are not one of those students who is president of almost every organization." The monthly Dean's Forum "allows students to have lunch with the dean and discuss any matter freely and openly."

While the law library—described as "amazing on the outside, but run-down on the inside"—could use some updating, students write that "the beautiful, historic atmosphere of the building makes the somewhat outdated technology more bearable." Although they've seen some upgrades in recent years, less-generous respondents call the campus "Stone Age" and the elusive wireless signal "an absolute joke." Students sit in "broken, squeaky chairs" and take exams on paper. Some students find themselves "studying at Starbucks, OU Law School, or the public library, simply because [OCU] facilities aren't comfortable in many ways."

Job placement worries keep some OCU students up at night. The relatively low first-time Oklahoma bar-passage rate (60 percent), the area's depressed job market—which keeps "salary potential for OCU law students below national average"—and competition with University of Oklahoma grads make launching a career an all-too-difficult task for OCU grads. Come graduation time, a large percentage face that sinking feeling of having substantial debt and no job offer. Some like to fault the "unhelpful" career placement staff, which needs "to do a better job of promoting us to the judges." Students can keep their chins up, though, since there are many factors that mediate this bleak picture. Because the

Tamara Martinez-Anderson, Assistant Dean for Admissions
PO Box 61310, Oklahoma City, OK 73146-1310
Telephone: 405-521-5354 • Fax: 405-521-5814
E-mail: lawadmit@okcu.edu • Website: www.okcu.edu/law

school is located just five minutes from the state capitol building, it remains "very connected to the government and local business." Students are able to build personal networks over their three years, thanks to the "high priority placed on community involvement through internships, externships, and volunteer opportunities." Students can also tap into the "very large and loyal alumni base in Oklahoma" once they've graduated.

Life

Law students at OCU refuse to give up their social lives just because they're pending professionals. "People here party more than the students at my undergraduate institution," admits one student, but this is sometimes to the chagrin of the studious types. The class size is "small enough to make it possible to be friends with your entire cohort"; there are a "plethora [of] clubs for everyone's tastes"; and the student body "organizes numerous activities for the whole school or just your class." "If you want to engage in any type of social activity, there is always something going on." As a result, "lots of people find great friends and relationships." The varied student body includes people of all ages, many of whom come from outside of Oklahoma; this diversity fosters "a welcoming and rich environment," according to a nontraditional student.

The convivial social environment carries over to the academic realm, in which students collaborate rather than compete with one another. "Even though we are pitted against each other in the curve, it is not cutthroat here," writes a 3L. The overriding "atmosphere of teamwork and togetherness" keeps morale high and study groups well attended. The campus may be "a beautiful oasis" in the middle of a "rough" neighborhood, but the cost of living is low, and the friendly campus security force "will always walk you to your vehicle without complaint, or even give you a ride to your off-campus apartment."

Getting In

OCU will accept applications until August 1, but nearly all applications are submitted by April 1. Requisite admissions criteria include LSAT scores, undergraduate GPA, personal statement, and letters of recommendation. If you are looking to study law in Oklahoma, then Oklahoma City University, like the University of Tulsa, is a good backup law school to the University of Oklahoma. It's also a good alternative to Texas schools like Southern Methodist University, Texas Tech University, and Texas Wesleyan University.

EMPLOYMENT INFORMATION

Career Rating	**66**
% employed within 9 months	74
Average starting salary	$49,500
State for bar exam	MO, OK, TX
Pass rate for first-time bar	60

Employers who frequently hire grads:
Small to midsize law firms, government agencies.

Grads employed by field (%):	
Academic	2
Business/industry	18
Government	22
Military	3
Other	6
Private practice	51

ADMISSIONS

Selectivity Rating	**64**
# applications received	1,602
# applicants accepted	769
# acceptees attending	247
Average LSAT	150
LSAT Range	139–169
Average undergrad GPA	3.0
Application fee	$50
Regular application deadline	8/1
Regular notification	rolling
Rolling notification?	Yes
Early application program?	No
Transfer students accepted?	Yes
Evening division offered?	Yes
Part-time accepted?	Yes
LSDAS accepted?	Yes

Applicants Also Look At

Florida Coastal School of Law, Texas A&M University, Texas Southern University, Texas Wesleyan University, Thomas M. Cooley Law School, University of Oklahoma, The University of Tulsa.

International Students

TOEFL required of international students?	Yes
Minimum Paper TOEFL	560
Minimum Computer TOEFL	220

FINANCIAL FACTS

Annual tuition	$24,750
Books and supplies	$1,120
Fees per credit	$13
Tuition per credit	$825
Room & board (on/off-campus)	$5,550/$6,700
Financial aid application deadline	3/1
% first-year students receiving some sort of aid	89
% receiving some sort of aid	90
% of aid that is merit-based	8
% receiving scholarships	23
Average grant	$10,360
Average loan	$25,000
Average debt	$75,000

PACE UNIVERSITY
SCHOOL OF LAW

INSTITUTIONAL INFORMATION

Public/private	private
Student/faculty ratio	16:1
% faculty part-time	52
% faculty female	37
% faculty minority	5
Total faculty	75

SURVEY SAYS . . .

Diverse opinions accepted in classrooms
Great library staff
Abundant externship/internship/clerkship opportunities

STUDENTS

Enrollment of law school	774
% male/female	38/62
% out-of-state	38
% full-time	68
% minority	17
% international	3
# of countries represented	13
Average age of entering class	26

ACADEMICS

Academic Experience rating	**78**
Professors interesting rating	82
Professors accessible rating	90
Hours of study per day	4.72

Academic Specialties

Civil procedure, commercial law, constitutional law, corporation securities law, criminal law, environmental law, government services, health law & policy, human rights law, intellectual property law, international law, labor law, legal history, property, taxation.

Advanced Degrees Offered

S/JD in environmental law; LLM in environmental law; LLM in comparative legal studies.

Combined Degrees Offered

JD/MBA w/Pace U.; JD/MPA w/Pace U.; JD/MEM w/Yale U.; JD/MS w/Bard College; JD/MA w/Sarah Lawrence College; JD/MPH w/New York Medical College.

Academics

Pace University School of Law offers "a very intimate community [and] a broad range" of opportunities for "hands-on, real-world" experience. The "amazing" environmental program is one of "the best in the country" and includes an Environmental Litigation Clinic. Pace offers an environmental law certificate, "so a lot of the people who come here specifically want to use their degrees to go out and make some part of the world better," explains one student. Other concentrations include intellectual property law and land use law. Pace's New York State Judicial Institute "serves as the educational stomping ground for New York's judicial minds [and] allows students to interact with judges from all over." The Energy Project and the Women's Justice Center are also noteworthy.

Pace Law's location—"minutes away from federal courthouses in White Plains [and roughly] between New York City and Stamford, Connecticut—results in endless opportunities for students," especially when it comes to externships and clinics. Proximity to NYC also means Pace brings in a lot of guest speakers and "important lecturers." Since Pace is "the only law school in Westchester County, [they have a] monopoly on Westchester resources (including DA's office, private law firms, corporations, Federal Court, state and local courts, etc.)." If you get tired of New York, you can take advantage of Pace's "extensive" international programs, which give students the opportunity to travel abroad for externships in Brazil and London.

Students at Pace Law School tell us that their "motivated, enthusiastic [professors are] genuinely eager to teach the material." They "have a way of making even the most mundane issue interesting and applicable to our lives," say students. "Their enthusiasm is contagious." Beyond the classroom, the faculty is "very approachable and willing to spend additional time with students." The administration is "always available [and] definitely student-oriented," although, like lots of places, the red tape can be "ridiculous."

The "small, beautiful, [and] secluded" Pace campus is "kind of a potpourri of buildings [with] a lot of old growth trees and grassy areas to lounge on during nice days." The "very high-tech" classroom building is, by all accounts, "more than decent." Wireless connections are "just about everywhere," which is good because "basically everyone brings their laptops to class." Other parts of the campus are "stuck in a 1970s nightmare," though. The library boasts "the best environmental law collection in the country," but it is "a monolithic, catastrophic exercise in bad architecture." Students report, "It's made of metal and glass, so if you sit on the third floor, you can hear someone typing in the basement stacks."

Cathy M. Alexander, Director of Admissions
78 North Broadway, White Plains, NY 10603
Telephone: 914-422-4210 • Fax: 914-989-8714
E-mail: admissions@law.pace.edu • Website: www.law.pace.edu

Life

Though Pace has a considerable out-of-state population and on-campus housing, students say many classmates are "locals [who have been] embedded in the area" with jobs and pre-existing groups of friends. They "drive in for class and then drive home," which can be "detracting from social life." Lots of students are "married or engaged [as well,] so it's not exactly a meat market." If you choose to be social, though, it is doable. "Student organizations are extremely active at Pace." The Barrister's Guild is a popular "student-run networking club [that] provides business cards for students [and sets up] private dinners with area lawyers and a networking golf tournament." Students comment, "Whether it's skiing with environmental attorneys or dinner with the NYC mayor's office, [the Guild] creates unique networking opportunities for students." It should also be noted, "At least one organization has a gathering at a local tavern each week."

Pace is on the small side, so the classroom atmosphere is "close-knit." One student says, "We see the same faces in every class." Another student observes, "There is no crazy competitive feeling." Yet another student continues, "It's definitely a plus that the school isn't competitive. People tend to share outlines and work together for exams with a minimum of blackmail." Politically, Pace students lean left, with a sizable contingent of "crunchy, sandal-wearing recyclers." But that doesn't mean there aren't a few "Dubya lovahs" hanging around.

The "relaxing" area surrounding the law school has "a great suburban feel," if you are into that sort of thing. There are "pubs, clubs, a movie theater, and malls." One student professes, "I would rather study for finals on the tree-lined streets of Westchester than in the cab-filled streets of New York City." On that note, Gotham "is always nice to visit [and] only 35 minutes away."

Getting In

Admitted students at the 25th percentile have an LSAT score of 152 and a GPA of 3.0. Admitted students at the 75th percentile have an LSAT score of 156 and a GPA of 3.6.

EMPLOYMENT INFORMATION

Career Rating	**81**
% employed within 9 months	88.7
Average starting salary	$69,923
State for bar exam	NY, CT, NJ, PA, DC

Employers who frequently hire grads: Large law firms, large corporations, government and public interest offices.

Prominent Alumni: Michael Finnegan, managing director, J.P. Morgan; Robert F. Kennedy Jr., Co-Director, Pace Environmental Litigation Clinic and Chief Prosecuting Attorney for Riverkeeper; Peter Sacripanti, Managing Partner, McDermott Will and Emery; Judith Lockhart, managing partner, Carter, Ledyard & Milburn.

Grads employed by field (%):

Academic	1
Business/industry	22
Government	14
Judicial clerkships	5
Private practice	44
Public interest	2

Academic Requirements

Clinical Program Required?	No
Legal Writing Course Requirement?	Yes
Legal Methods Course Requirement?	Yes
Legal Research Course Requirement?	No
Moot Court Requirement?	Yes
Public Interest Law Requirement?	No

ADMISSIONS

Selectivity Rating	**77**
# applications received	2,626
# applicants accepted	723
# acceptees attending	179
Average LSAT	155
LSAT Range	154–157
Average undergrad GPA	3.3
Application fee	$60
Regular application deadline	3/1
Regular notification	rolling
Rolling notification?	Yes
Early application program?	Yes
Early application deadline	11/1
Early application notification	12/15
Transfer students accepted?	Yes
Evening division offered?	Yes
Part-time accepted?	Yes
LSDAS accepted?	Yes

Applicants Also Look At

American U., Brooklyn Law School, Fordham U., Hofstra U., New York Law School, Seton Hall U., St. John's U.

International Students

TOEFL required of international students?	Yes
Minimum Paper TOEFL	600
Minimum Computer TOEFL	250

FINANCIAL FACTS

Annual tuition	$31,158
Books and supplies	$1,000
Fees per credit	$90
Room & board (on/off-campus)	$10,970/$13,800
Financial aid app. deadline	2/1
% first-year students receiving some sort of aid	86
% receiving some sort of aid	84
% of aid that is merit-based	65
% receiving scholarships	34
Average grant	$10,600
Average loan	$22,621
Average total aid package	$33,221
Average debt	$70,780

PEPPERDINE UNIVERSITY
SCHOOL OF LAW

INSTITUTIONAL INFORMATION

Public/private	private
Student/faculty ratio	19:1
% faculty part-time	49
% faculty female	35
% faculty minority	5
Total faculty	91

SURVEY SAYS . . .

Beautiful campus
Students love Malibu, CA

STUDENTS

Enrollment of law school	720
% male/female	49/51
% out-of-state	44
% full-time	100
% minority	17
% international	1
# of countries represented	5
Average age of entering class	23

ACADEMICS

Academic Experience rating	**81**
Professors interesting rating	84
Professors accessible rating	97
Hours of study per day	3.96

Academic Specialties

Commercial law, corporation securities law, dispute resolution, intellectual property law, international law, taxation.

Advanced Degrees Offered

LLM in dispute resolution.

Combined Degrees Offered

JD/MBA, 4 years; JD/MDR, 3 to 4 years; JD/MPP, 4 years; JD/MDiv, 5 years.

Academic Requirements

Clinical Program Required?	Yes
Legal Writing Course Requirement?	Yes
Legal Methods Course Requirement?	No
Legal Research Course Requirement?	Yes
Moot Court Requirement?	Yes
Public Interest Law Requirement?	No

Academics

One of the premiere law schools in the Southern California region, Pepperdine University offers an intense legal education on a laid-back Malibu campus. Students at Pepperdine say the curriculum is rigorous, especially in the first year. Luckily, the faculty is "accessible [and] supportive." In the words of one newbie, "Professors expect a lot academically, but go out of their way to support students personally and academically." Many students praise the collegial atmosphere at Pepperdine and "its sense of strong community and friendship." One enthuses, "My experience at Pepperdine has been incredible. The administration sets a tone of cooperativeness among themselves, the faculty, and the students make Pepperdine a very positive place to be. Because of that, I consider several members of the faculty and administration to be close personal friends." One student even confides, "I think of one of my teachers as a surrogate grandpa. I go to him for advice on far more things than class help!"

Experiential learning is an important part of the Pepperdine curriculum. Students say that Pepperdine "does not bog its students down in ridiculous theoretical courses," but instead provides a "practical education." Indeed, Pepperdine offers extensive hands-on extracurricular opportunities like the "to-die-for" externship program in the Los Angeles area, the excellent moot court program, and the "outstanding" and a highly acclaimed Dispute Resolution curriculum. Students rave about the school's "amazing" London campus, where an excellent "International Entertainment Law Program with a focus on film and music" is offered. According to its students, Pepperdine "is one of the top schools in the nation for those that want to get into the entertainment industry."

As far as postgraduation employment, experiences vary. One proud student whose goal was to work in entertainment "was able to extern at one of the top five Hollywood Talent Agencies, [and so] secured a job for after law school." But as at almost every school, some students complain that Career Services should try a bit harder to "improve its job placement after graduation." Another source of concern among students is Pepperdine's bar-passage rate, which is not particularly impressive at about 60 percent for first-time test takers.

Facilities at Pepperdine are "decent." Students feel "the classrooms are standard, the campus has wireless Internet, [and there] are usually outlets for laptops," but some students gripe, "The computers are broken more [often] than they are working." Students also say, "The entire law building needs more light and windows." There is "a tremendous view of the Pacific Ocean, [yet ironically,] none of the classrooms have windows." One student tells us, "The interior of the law school can best be described as 'brown.'" But is that really a big deal when you are situated in a "resortlike ocean setting"?

SHANNON PHILLIPS, DIRECTOR OF ADMISSIONS
24255 PACIFIC COAST HIGHWAY, MALIBU, CA 90263
TELEPHONE: 310-506-4631 • FAX: 310-506-7668
E-MAIL: SOLADMIS@PEPPERDINE.EDU • WEBSITE: HTTP://LAW.PEPPERDINE.EDU

Life

Students at Pepperdine wish there was more "in the way of racial diversity" and would like to see more students with "real work or life experience under their belts." One student says, "Some classrooms are similar to a 4-H club meeting in Arkansas." On the plus side, student relations are "close" and laid-back. "The school environment is not overly competitive at all. Everyone is always willing to help each other—no book stealing going on here!"

With a campus perched in the Malibu hills and overlooking the Pacific Ocean, it's no wonder Pepperdine students are in love with their school's "gorgeous" vistas. One student jokes, "Bury yourself deep in the library, away from any windows, because the views from campus are too stunning, and you'll find yourself on the beach instead of in the books." Another says, "Did I mention that the ocean is, like, right across the street?" Students report, "Many first-years live on campus (across the street from the school), the rest are spread out in all directions." As a result, the campus community is friendly but somewhat disjointed. A student admits, "The social atmosphere here is good, but being so close to LA, most students don't hang around campus but go into the city for social activities." Also worth noting—maybe because of the SoCal setting, the small campus, or the high percentage of students who are "straight out of undergrad"—Pepperdine can have a "gossipy 90210 episode" feel at times. But all and all, whether "you're looking for a tight-knit community, [or] you want to work on your own away from the stress of other law students, you're bound to find what you want at Pepperdine."

Getting In

Pepperdine University School of Law evaluates candidates based on the strength of their undergraduate GPA and LSAT scores. In addition, Pepperdine considers a student's letters of recommendation, personal statement, and undergraduate institution, as well as any graduate work. In particular, Pepperdine looks for students who have solid reasons for pursuing a legal education, display a strong sense of ethics, and have had unique life or work experience. Applications are due March 1.

ADMISSIONS

Selectivity Rating	**83**
# applications received	3,456
# applicants accepted	879
# acceptees attending	250
Average LSAT	159
LSAT Range	157–161
Average undergrad GPA	3.5
Application fee	$50
Regular application deadline	3/1
Regular notification	rolling
Rolling notification?	Yes
Early application program?	No
Transfer students accepted?	Yes
Evening division offered?	No
Part-time accepted?	No
LSDAS accepted?	Yes

Applicants Also Look At

Loyola Marymount University, University of San Diego.

International Students

TOEFL required of international students?	No
TOEFL recommended of international students?	No

FINANCIAL FACTS

Annual tuition	$29,690
Books and supplies	$700
Tuition per credit	$1,090
Room & board	$18,990
Financial aid application deadline	4/1

EMPLOYMENT INFORMATION

Career Rating	**82**
Job placement rate (%)	94
Average starting salary	$83,389
State for bar exam	CA
Pass rate for first-time bar	74

Grads employed by field (%):	
Academic	1
Business/industry	16
Government	10
Judicial clerkships	4
Other	2
Private practice	66
Public interest	1

Quinnipiac University
School of Law

INSTITUTIONAL INFORMATION

Public/private	private
Student/faculty ratio	15:1
% faculty part-time	47
% faculty female	34
% faculty minority	4
Total faculty	68

SURVEY SAYS . . .

Great research resources
Beautiful campus

STUDENTS

Enrollment of law school	653
% male/female	53/47
% out-of-state	49
% full-time	74
% minority	7
% international	1
# of countries represented	3
Average age of entering class	25

ACADEMICS

Academic Experience rating	**74**
Professors interesting rating	75
Professors accessible rating	79
Hours of study per day	4.2

Academic Specialties

Civil advocacy & dispute resolution, criminal law, intellectual property law, taxation, health law, family & juvenile law.

Advanced Degrees Offered

JD, 3 years full-time, 4 years part-time.

Combined Degrees Offered

JD/MBA, 4 years.

Academic Requirements

Clinical Program Required?	No
Legal Writing Course Requirement?	Yes
Legal Methods Course Requirement?	No
Legal Research Course Requirement?	Yes
Moot Court Requirement?	No
Public Interest Law Requirement?	No

Academics

"Before I decided to go to Quinnipiac Law, I had never heard of the school," writes a 1L, but many students actively seek out the QUSL health law program. "Given that my career goal is to work in the health policy field, Quinnipiac was a perfect fit," writes a 3L. Other popular concentrations include tax law, criminal law, family law, intelectual property, civil advocacy, and dispute resolution. The school runs a traditional full-time day program and also offers part-time night classes. Both groups of students would like to see more higher-level courses offered in various practice areas. Night students in particular would like "more offerings outside of required areas." Because of their role as part of a "small law program on a much larger undergraduate campus," Quinnipiac students can broaden their scope through joint-degree opportunities, including a joint JD-MBA program.

Quinnipiac tends to focus on the practical rather than the theoretical facets of law. "If you want to learn to practice law, come to Quinnipiac." Most students embrace this "trade school is trade school" attitude, but some agree with one student who suggests that the school could "offer more theory based courses and move away from traditional law school teaching styles, including the one exam equals your grade for the course method."

The question keeping many up at night is whether graduates will have a place to exercise their professional filing skills after their three years here. Three main concerns fuel the job-market fear: grade deflation, significantly less than adequate career services, and the debt that accompanies a Quinnipiac diploma. "Get rid of the curve!" begs a 2L, who emerged from her first year expressing concern about the law school's rigor in grading, supported in part by the school's suggested median grade of C-plus or B-minus for required first-year courses, and suggested median grade of B-minus or B for upper-level core electives. Students also seem to feel that the Career Placement office "caters only to the students ranked one through ten." Though it does arrange "a wide variety of externships with local corporations and government organizations," many students "resort to sending cold resumes to area law firms as graduation approaches." Pressure mounts in the face of the "slightly outrageous price" of tuition at Quinnipiac, which ranks among the more costly law schools in the nation. Some get uneasy if they spend "too much time thinking about the expense of the lavish end-of-semester parties with white tablecloths and snappily attired wait staff."

The high cost of tuition also has its benefits, though. Quinnipiac has "arguably the most beautiful campus in New England." Furthermore, "computers are available ad nauseam. Students don't need to buy laptops or even printer paper." The library, complete with comfortable study areas and a helpful research staff, is deemed "a great place to work." Classrooms, on the other hand, are kept at meat-locker temperatures year-round, and the wireless service is patchy. If students ever want to escape their slice of New England paradise, the summer program at Trinity College in Dublin is said to be "a total blast."

Praised for their "mentorship, thoughtful conversation, and candidness," Quinnipiac professors know the names and career aspirations of their students and get involved in law school life. "Every year at our public interest auction, there is one professor who offers a home-cooked dinner for the winner and three guests." In the classroom, instructors "command respect" while maintaining a "peer relationship." A 1L writes, "Our contracts professor stays until all hours of the night to meet with students to go over outlines."

Edwin Wilkes, Executive Dean of Law School Enrollment Services
275 Mount Carmel Avenue, Hamden, CT 06518-1948
Telephone: 203-582-3400 • Fax: 203-582-3339
E-mail: ladm@quinnipiac.edu • Website: http://law.quinnipiac.edu

Some students call for a "move away from traditional law school teaching styles, including the method where one exam equals your grade for the course." Certain professors employ an "interactive and Socratic style"; others sound more like "talking textbooks"; and a handful actually "insult students in front of their peers." Administrators dispel initial law school intimidation with their professional, courteous, and "surprisingly approachable" ways. Dean Saxton in particular earns praise for improving the school's image and ranking.

Life

"The classroom environment tends to be more light-hearted at night," and evening classmates consider themselves a generally more supportive group. One of the day students writes of the "fierce competition" that she witnessed during her first year. A third-year student assures, however, that after the first year, "students will have found the classmates whom they feel they can trust and pretty much stick to that group." Given the small class size, everyone knows everyone else, a phenomenon that sometimes fosters a "high-school atmosphere" with the requisite rumor mill.

Some students are reportedly "more interested in playing stupid drinking games and watching television" than in debating legal issues during off-hours. Quinnipiac students, hailing mostly from the East Coast, like to raise their glasses at weekly club-sponsored events as well as at neighborhood and New Haven bars. As an alternative, many students also like to recharge by spending some quality time in nature. Fortunately for them, there is a picturesque state park right across the street.

Getting In

Quinnipiac fills its 200 seats from a pool of roughly 2,500 applicants annually. Those who don't have a 3.0 GPA still have a shot at acceptance, but applicants with LSAT scores lower than 150 would only rarely be competitive for admission. Although the school operates on a rolling admissions system, the priority application deadline is March 1st. Therefore, early application is strongly advised. Students may take day classes on a part-time basis by special arrangement and even switch their enrollment status between terms. January entry is also available.

EMPLOYMENT INFORMATION

Career Rating	**75**
% employed within 9 months	98
Average starting salary	$56,460
State for bar exam	CT, NY, NJ, MA, RI
Pass rate for first-time bar	76

Employers who frequently hire grads:
QUSL graduates are hired by law firms, corporations, public defender offices, prosecutor offices, and various government and public interest organizations.

Grads employed by field (%):	
Academic	2
Business/industry	21
Government	20
Judicial clerkships	7
Military	1
Other	6
Private practice	42
Public interest	1

ADMISSIONS

Selectivity Rating	**76**
# applications received	2,132
# applicants accepted	546
# acceptees attending	154
Average LSAT	154
LSAT Range	152–156
Average undergrad GPA	3.2
Application fee	$40
Regular application deadline	rolling
Regular notification	rolling
Rolling notification?	Yes
Early application program?	No
Transfer students accepted?	Yes
Evening division offered?	Yes
Part-time accepted?	Yes
LSDAS accepted?	Yes

International Students

TOEFL required of international students?	No
TOEFL recommended of international students?	Yes

FINANCIAL FACTS

Annual tuition	$29,640
Books and supplies	$1,200
Fees per credit	$30
Tuition per credit	$1,035
Room & board (off-campus)	$8,200
Financial aid application deadline	4/15
% first-year students receiving some sort of aid	96
% receiving some sort of aid	93
% of aid that is merit-based	90
% receiving scholarships	70
Average grant	$9,792
Average loan	$27,626
Average total aid package	$32,403
Average debt	$68,052

Regent University
School of Law

INSTITUTIONAL INFORMATION

Public/private	private
Student/faculty ratio	20:1
Affiliation	Nondenominational
% faculty female	17
% faculty minority	17
Total faculty	24

SURVEY SAYS . . .

Beautiful campus

STUDENTS

Enrollment of law school	511
% male/female	52/48
% full-time	86
% minority	14
% international	1
# of countries represented	4
Average age of entering class	25

ACADEMICS

Academic Experience rating	**82**
Professors interesting rating	94
Professors accessible rating	87
Hours of study per day	5.05

Combined Degrees Offered

JD/MBA, 4 years; JD/master of government,4 years; JD/MA in management, 4 years; JD/MA in counseling, 4 years; JD/MA in communication, 4 years; JD/MA in divinity, 4 years.

Academic Requirements

Clinical Program Required?	No
Legal Writing Course Requirement?	Yes
Legal Methods Course Requirement?	Yes
Legal Research Course Requirement?	Yes
Moot Court Requirement?	Yes
Public Interest Law Requirement?	No

Academics

If you have a "passion for ethical Christian lawyering" and want to "approach the law from a biblical worldview," Regent University School of Law should be on your short list. At Regent Law, one of very few Christian law schools, "God is acknowledged in everything." The curriculum reportedly "emphasizes learning how to be a lawyer without compromising your spiritual convictions." One student stresses, "I was pleased to find that the incorporation of Christian principles in the law profession did not turn out to be Sunday School with a little bit of law mixed in. By mixing the wisdom of centuries of legal philosophers with the pragmatic strengths of more recent scholarship, Regent is regaining the moral underpinnings that promise to revitalize respect for and integrity in the law." Another highlight is the small class sizes. "Although some 1L classes are larger," one student notes, Regent "tries to keep most classes smaller than 60 students." Regent boasts some interesting summer opportunities: A study-abroad program in Strasbourg, France, focuses on international law and human rights, and the Summer Program in Christian Jurisprudence explores the biblical foundations of law and legal institutions. The alumni network "is still in its formative stages," but it is getting better every year. "Career placement is one of the areas that Regent University has improved in most since my time here," relates one student.

Members of the "dedicated and caring faculty [at Regent] come from the top law schools in the country (e.g., Harvard, Yale, Chicago) and provide a unique and distinctive approach to the law." Some professors have a tendency to "rework your opinion in class so that it agrees with their own, [which is] an annoying obstacle." This quibble aside, Regent Law's professors "are the perfect blend of humor, knowledge of the law, and Godly experience." One student testifies, "They are tough on you in the classroom but show a genuine concern for students." One delighted student notes, "Each professor has gone out of their way to be available to go over our finals individually." But students warn, "Fail at your own risk because this school does its best to support the success of all of its students." Students did not have too much to say about the administration, except that "management of the day-to-day administrative details could be improved."

The "brand-new and state-of-the-art" facilities at Regent Law "have got to be the best in the nation!" at least, according to one student. "The grounds are always manicured and the buildings are spotless," maintains another. "The campus is a beautiful place," replete with Georgian architecture, and "the law school building takes your breath away." Students don't hog the beloved resources either, as "the library is a resource for the entire legal community" in Virginia Beach. "We have plenty of computers available and a great student center," brags one student. Classrooms are chock-a-block with the latest gadgets and technology, and wireless access is readily available, providing "Lexis-Nexis wherever you go."

Bonnie Creef, Director of Admissions and Financial Aid
1000 Regent University Drive, Virginia Beach, VA 23464
Telephone: 757-226-4584 • Fax: 757-226-4139
E-mail: lawschool@regent.edu • Website: www.regent.edu/law

Life

The most salient feature of Regent Law is its manifest Christianity. "This is a very religious school," agree all on its roll call. Though "some students are very devout while some students are middle of the road," in general, "the atmosphere is staunchly conservative, and the Bible is regularly integrated in every aspect of the law school experience from actual classroom preaching to biblical retreats." The average age at entry is 25, and many students are married with children. The students' common belief system seems to fortify the sense of community at Regent U, where everyone "strives for excellence and upholds the highest integrity."

"Regent has an incredible atmosphere [in which] students are really appreciated, really cared for, and genuinely loved," writes a satisfied student. "There is a camaraderie that comes from all of us facing the challenge together," bespeaks another. "Regent wants to see you succeed, not just in the legal realm, but in every area of your life." Others say, "Students share resources, outlines, tips, and notes, [and] although there is natural competition," no one is "one-upping other students." A wistful 3L recalls, "My best memory is when I was struggling to grasp the concept of future interests. The number-one student in the class who is now slated for a Supreme Court clerkship spent three hours diagramming and explaining future interests to me. I barely knew him, but that is the congenial support found here at Regent." Another student adds, "The greatest strength of Regent University is that the faculty and students are here because they really want to be in this school, at this time. They aren't here because it is Daddy's alma mater or to make big names for themselves. They are here to teach and to learn the law with other people who believe in an absolute truth. It is this perspective that makes my school unique."

Getting In

Admitted students at the 25th percentile have an LSAT score of 150 and a GPA of 2.9. Admitted students at the 75th percentile have an LSAT score of 155 and a GPA of 3.5. If you take the LSAT more than once, Regent Law will average your scores.

EMPLOYMENT INFORMATION

Career Rating	**61**
% employed within 9 months	83.5
Average starting salary	$41,411
State for bar exam	VA, NC, TX, CA, FL
Pass rate for first-time bar	61

Employers who frequently hire grads: American Center for Law and Justice; Just Law International; U.S. Air Force Jag Corps; U.S. Army Jag Corps; Alliance Defense Fund; Williams Mullen; Virginia Beach Public Defender; Lexis-Nexis.

Prominent Alumni: Robert F. McDonnell, Virginia House of Delegates; April Wood Berg, North Carolina District Court judge; Ron Pahl, Oregon Circuit Court judge.

Grads employed by field (%):	
Academic	6
Business/industry	20
Government	15
Judicial clerkships	7
Military	4
Private practice	42
Public interest	6

ADMISSIONS

Selectivity Rating	**72**
# applications received	734
# applicants accepted	309
# acceptees attending	188
Average LSAT	153
LSAT Range	150–155
Average undergrad GPA	3.2
Application fee	$40
Regular application deadline	6/1
Regular notification	rolling
Rolling notification?	Yes
Early application program?	No
Transfer students accepted?	Yes
Evening division offered?	No
Part-time accepted?	Yes
LSDAS accepted?	Yes

Applicants Also Look At

Appalachian School of Law, Florida Coastal School of Law, University of Richmond, Yale University.

International Students

TOEFL required of international students?	Yes
Minimum Paper TOEFL	600
Minimum Computer TOEFL	250

FINANCIAL FACTS

Annual tuition	$22,785
Books and supplies	$1,372
Fees per credit	$56
Tuition per credit	$735
Room & board (off-campus)	$6,138
Financial aid application deadline	6/1
% first-year students receiving some sort of aid	94
% receiving some sort of aid	92
% of aid that is merit-based	13
% receiving scholarships	70
Average grant	$7,011
Average loan	$23,956
Average total aid package	$30,807
Average debt	$62,854

Roger Williams University
Ralph R. Papitto School of Law

INSTITUTIONAL INFORMATION

Public/private	private
Student/faculty ratio	21:1
% faculty part-time	31
% faculty female	44
% faculty minority	5
Total faculty	59

SURVEY SAYS . . .

Great research resources
Great library staff
Beautiful campus

STUDENTS

Enrollment of law school	630
% male/female	47/53
% out-of-state	72
% full-time	76
% minority	15
# of countries represented	3
Average age of entering class	28

ACADEMICS

Academic Experience rating	**75**
Professors interesting rating	86
Professors accessible rating	79
Hours of study per day	5.71

Academic Specialties

Commercial law, constitutional law, corporation securities law, criminal law, environmental law, intellectual property law, international law, labor law, maritime law, public interest law.

Advanced Degrees Offered

JD, 3 years full-time.

Combined Degrees Offered

JD/MCP master's of community planning, 4 years; JD/MMA master's marine affairs, 3.5 years; JD/MS master's of science in labor relations & human resources, 4 years; JD/MCJ master's of criminal justice, 3.5 years.

Academic Requirements

Clinical Program Required?	No
Legal Writing Course Requirement?	No
Legal Methods Course Requirement?	Yes

Academics

A decidedly optimistic spirit permeates the atmosphere of the Ralph R. Papitto School of Law. At this young law school, students applaud the cooperative spirit, school pride, and dedication to excellence demonstrated by the entire community, noting that "everyone at the school—staff and students—seem dedicated to making Roger Williams as good as it can possibly be." With a dedicated and responsive administrative staff "willing to listen to new ideas and . . . open to suggestions," students at Roger Williams feel they have the unique opportunity to help shape their school's future. As a result, Papitto is constantly improving: "Every year brings new challenges, better qualified students, and further experienced professors," explains a 2L.

Over its short history, Roger Williams has focused on building a superior academic program. A 2L reports, "The administrators of Roger Williams were extremely smart in their hiring; they knew that the only way to take a fledgling law school and move it quickly up through the ranks was to hire the best faculty." As a result of these efforts, "The diverse backgrounds that the professors bring, the different teaching skills, and the rigorous expectations this young law school demands of its student body will lead it to great dimensions."

Papitto students must be primed to give their all in the classroom. A 3L explains, "The faculty are among the best and they don't take 'pass' for an answer. Preparedness is expected, and we're being grilled and graded as if we were at Harvard." But students insist that they are amply rewarded for their efforts: "The law school is extremely challenging, and the professors coax more from me than I ever believed I could give," reports one 2L. In addition, students reassure us that professors are dedicated to promoting academic success. By most accounts, professors are readily available to meet with struggling students, and "the smaller size and availability of the faculty allows for great communication and interactions outside the classroom." In addition, the school has instituted a number of programs to help students succeed academically, like the "excellent orientation program and seminar series continuing into the school year to teach and reinforce skills vital to 1L success."

Roger Williams is the only law school in the state of Rhode Island, a happy privilege that pays off in many ways. For example, "the local judiciary [including the Chief Justice of the Rhode Island Supreme Court] and legal community are highly involved with the school and frequently attend functions here." In fact, "the moot court competition involves arguing before the RI Supreme Court." In addition, "internship opportunities abound because RWU has an exclusive franchise in the state." "I was able to work for a federal judge over the summer between my 1L and 2L years," recalls one 2L. When it comes to extracurriculars and externships, many students point out that "Roger Williams has an excellent public service focus" that likewise exerts a strong influence in the Rhode Island community; one student reports that "the Feinstein Institute for public service is the best thing about this school! They are amazing and have a huge range of placements available." After graduation, career prospects are good for Roger Williams' alumni, especially if they plan to practice in Rhode Island. After a recent revamp, "the new Career Services department is outstanding!" While things already look good for RWU grads, students are convinced that their prospects improve with every passing year. As one enthusiastic 2L explains, "As more and more employers see the excellent caliber of students RWU turns out year after year, the school will continue to garner respect in the legal community."

Michael Boylen, Director of Admissions
10 Metacom Avenue, Bristol, RI 02809
Telephone: 401-254-4555 • Fax: 401-254-4516
E-mail: admissions@law.rwu.edu • Website: http://law.rwu.edu

Life

Situated in Bristol, "Roger Williams is located in one of the most scenic locations in the country, Rhode Island's East Bay." "From my classroom I can see the bay and the sailboats out on a sunny day," reports one student. On campus "there are many clubs and organizations that make it a priority to put together different activities; anything from study groups and sports to parties and balls." Students say a decidedly social atmosphere pervades the campus, and students appreciate it. A 1L reasons, "I'd much rather spend three intensive years with classmates who can kick back and drink a beer on a Thursday night than with a competitive group of straight-A stress cases."

Thanks to an "extremely proactive admissions staff," Papitto attracts a "really interesting, fun student body" from all across the nation. By most accounts, "the students are by and large quite friendly and outgoing," and "there really isn't a competitive atmosphere, despite the brutal curve." But don't expect much by way of ethnic diversity: "Where are the minorities? I feel like I'm the only one sometimes, and usually I am," writes one 2L. Adds another, "My only complaint is the school is lily white."

Getting In

LSAT scores and undergraduate GPA are generally considered to be the two most important factors in an application to Papitto. However, the school also considers graduate work, work experience, extracurricular activities, undergraduate curriculum, community involvement, and life experiences. A B-minus undergraduate GPA and an LSAT score above the 50th percentile puts you in the running here, although it certainly doesn't guarantee admission.

EMPLOYMENT INFORMATION

Career Rating	**70**
Job placement rate (%)	80
Average starting salary	$47,912
State for bar exam	RI, CT, MA, PA, NJ
Pass rate for first-time bar	75

Employers who frequently hire grads: Rhode Island courts, small New England firms.

Prominent Alumni: Kenneth K. McKay, chief of staff of Rhode Island Governor Carcieri; John M. Sutherland III, vice president of finance/CFO of Women's & Infants' Hospital; Cindy DeMarco, assistant general counsel, FBI; Betty Ann Waters, attorney, freed wrongly accused brother after 18 years.

Grads employed by field (%):	
Academic	3
Business/industry	11
Government	11
Judicial clerkships	14
Other	1
Private practice	51
Public interest	9

Legal Research Course Requirement?	No
Moot Court Requirement?	No
Public Interest Law Requirement?	Yes

ADMISSIONS

Selectivity Rating	**71**
# applications received	1,618
# applicants accepted	643
# acceptees attending	248
Average LSAT	153
LSAT Range	150–155
Average undergrad GPA	3.2
Application fee	$60
Regular application deadline	rolling
Regular notification	rolling
Rolling notification?	Yes
Early application program?	No
Transfer students accepted?	Yes
Evening division offered?	No
Part-time accepted?	No
LSDAS accepted?	Yes

Applicants Also Look At

Northeastern University School of Law, Quinnipiac University, Suffolk University, Vermont Law School, Western New England College.

International Students

TOEFL required of international students?	Yes
Minimum Paper TOEFL	600
Minimum Computer TOEFL	250

FINANCIAL FACTS

Annual tuition	$24,940
Books and supplies	$1,100
Fees per credit	$150
Tuition per credit	$860
Financial aid application deadline	3/15
% first-year students receiving some sort of aid	99
% receiving some sort of aid	94
% of aid that is merit-based	14
% receiving scholarships	42
Average grant	$11,465
Average loan	$32,795
Average total aid package	$41,034
Average debt	$54,138

Rutgers University—Camden
School of Law

INSTITUTIONAL INFORMATION

Public/private	public
Student/faculty ratio	5:1
% faculty part-time	58
% faculty female	31
% faculty minority	9
Total faculty	116

SURVEY SAYS . . .

Diverse opinions accepted in classrooms
Great research resources
Great library staff
Abundant externship/internship/clerkship opportunities

STUDENTS

Enrollment of law school	770
% male/female	61/39
% out-of-state	40
% full-time	75
% minority	16
% international	1
# of countries represented	7
Average age of entering class	25

ACADEMICS

Academic Experience rating	**89**
Professors interesting rating	88
Professors accessible rating	85
Hours of study per day	4.23

Academic Specialties

Commercial law, constitutional law, corporation securities law, criminal law, environmental law, family law, health law, international law, labor law, taxation.

Advanced Degrees Offered

JD, 3 yrs full-time, 4 yrs part-time.

Combined Degrees Offered

JD/MBA, 4 yrs; JD/MPA public administration, 4 yrs; JD/MSW social work, 4 yrs; JD/MS public policy, 3.5 yrs; JD/MCRP city and regional planning, 4 yrs; JD/MD and JD/DO University of Medicine and Dentistry of New Jersey; JD/MPA public administration in health care management and policy, 4 yrs.

Academic Requirements

Clinical Program Required?	No

Academics

If going to law school gives you the jitters, your fears will quickly be assuaged at Rutgers University—Camden School of Law. Sure, just like other prestigious JD programs, Rutgers will treat you to a dose of the "Socratic thunderstorm approach," and there is the typical "never-ending workload" throughout the first year. But Rutgers maintains a remarkably friendly and supportive academic environment. Students insist that "first-year classes don't intimidate you," as "there's no fear of speaking your mind in class, and diversity in thinking is highly encouraged." Outside the classroom, Rutgers professors are personable, to say the least: "Every Wednesday afternoon, there's a veritable party in our torts professor's office during his office hours. So many students go to discuss both academic and non-textbook-related topics that there aren't enough chairs and people sit on the floor," recalls one 2L. In fact, "it's common for professors to take students out to lunch, to conferences, and even to show up at student-sponsored pub crawls." The administration draws similar praise from students, who believe it "tries to be very open door and available for anything we could possibly need." A 1L jokes, "I came to Rutgers expecting to witness students getting 'burned' by professors every day in class. Instead the only burn I got was on the roof of my mouth while eating pizza with the dean."

Students are impressed with the caliber of the Rutgers faculty, describing them as "knowledgeable and passionate about their subjects" and able pedagogues to boot. In the lecture hall, "the faculty is as intelligent as they are witty. Anecdotes from the real-world experiences are common in the classroom and make some of the drudgery more interesting." Many also point out the strength of the adjunct staff, who "come from varied fields, providing a unique and practical perspective to current topics." Indeed, a practical approach is emphasized at Rutgers, and classes may even include "spontaneous field-trips to the federal court house across the street from the campus just so we can view real-world motions to dismiss, jury selection, and final arguments." The school's active alumni network is also called upon to contribute to the JD experience, and students tell us that "in many courses, alumni return to give lectures on the practical aspects of the subject, and they have been willing to assist any student that has a question."

Among the greatest perks of Rutgers—Camden is its low tuition, offering a "fantastic and highly respected education at a very reasonable price." As a result, students do not experience the financial anxiety common to law students today. "Due to a scholarship and a summer internship at a Philadelphia law firm," reports one 2L, "I will graduate with a top-rate legal education and virtually no debt. That combination is hard to beat, and I expect it will free up my career options considerably." The downside to a low-cost education is that "because of prior decreases in state funds, the law school's physical facilities are limited," and many complain that the classrooms lack ample outlets for laptops. Many are quick to point out, however, that "the school has just received funding to build a new building," which will be available to future classes in 2007.

The school takes advantage of the resources in the surrounding community to instruct students in the playing out of law in the real world. "The federal courthouse is literally around the corner, the county courthouse a couple of blocks," and Rutgers students "have tremendous access to the judges in the area and several teach as adjuncts." Students also praise the fact that "the law school is very involved in the community through its pro bono clinics."

Rutgers is "located close to Philly, Trenton, and New York, so there are plenty of job opportunities." On that note, "Career Services are always on the job helping students get

ASSISTANT DIRECTOR MAUREEN O'BOYLE, ASSISTANT DIRECTOR OF ADMISSIONS
406 PENN STREET, THIRD FLOOR, CAMDEN, NJ 08102
TELEPHONE: 800-466-7561 • FAX: 856-225-6537
E-MAIL: ADMISSIONS@CAMLAW.RUTGERS.EDU • WEBSITE: WWW-CAMDEN.RUTGERS.EDU/

placed for both summer and permanent positions. They also expose students to the different options available to attorneys by having guests come to the law school to provide experiences in different areas." Rutgers is somewhat unique among law schools in that almost half of the graduating class takes judicial clerkship positions, more students than those who take positions in private practice.

Life

Attracting students from all across the nation and the world, the Rutgers student body is "extremely diverse in all aspects, including gender, socioeconomics, age, and interests." On this multicultural campus "there is an organization for just about any interest a person may have, [and] the SBA and other clubs do a great job of providing numerous social functions nearly every week." A 2L explains that "the environment is positive and students are involved with the school. Whether it be moot court, law journals, or politics, students are engaged in society and provide for a very strong sense of community." Off-campus "people are always looking to get together to study or to just go out socially," though most prefer hanging out in Philly to hitting the bars in the surrounding town of Camden. While some describe Camden as "the pit of despair," others tell us that "the waterfront on both sides of the Delaware River is beautiful." In addition, many appreciate the fact that "Philadelphia is exactly a mile away and provides for plenty of social opportunities."

Students warn that there are "a handful of students who are hell bent on getting a certain GPA." Most, however, value kindness and cooperation over competition. A 3L explains, "My school is both cooperative and competitive. Students here care deeply about being successful, but everyone is quick to lend a hand to bring someone else along for the ride." Indeed, many students praise the fact that "you can always find a good conversation outside after class."

Getting In

Rutgers—Camden recently began an experimental recruitment program, soliciting prospective law students based on their performance on the GRE or GMAT, rather than the LSAT. Therefore, there are a number of current law students who were previously pursuing advanced degrees in other subject areas. For all other prospective students, the admissions process is standard fare: Rutgers admits students who have demonstrated a high level of academic achievement, as well as strong standardized test scores.

EMPLOYMENT INFORMATION

Career Rating	**85**
Job placement rate (%)	96
Average starting salary	$76,000
State for bar exam	NJ, NY, PA, CA, TX
Pass rate for first-time bar	81

Employers who frequently hire grads: All major Philadelphia, New Jersey, and Delaware law firms hire grads, as do numerous prestigious firms from New York City, DC, California, and other major metropolitan areas.

Prominent Alumni: Honorable James Florio, former governor/U.S. congressman; Honorable Joseph Rodriguez, U.S. federal district judge.

Grads employed by field (%):	
Business/industry	14
Government	7
Judicial clerkships	41
Military	1
Other	1
Private practice	35
Public interest	1

Legal Writing Course Requirement?	Yes
Legal Methods Course Requirement?	Yes
Legal Research Course Requirement?	No
Moot Court Requirement?	Yes
Public Interest Law Requirement?	No

ADMISSIONS

Selectivity Rating	**89**
# applications received	2,554
# applicants accepted	544
# acceptees attending	252
Average LSAT	162
LSAT Range	159–163
Average undergrad GPA	3.4
Application fee	$50
Regular application deadline	rolling
Regular notification	rolling
Rolling notification?	Yes
Early application program?	No
Transfer students accepted?	Yes
Evening division offered?	Yes
Part-time accepted?	Yes
LSDAS accepted?	Yes

Applicants Also Look At

Fordham U.; The George Washington U.; Rutgers U.; Temple U.; U. of California—Los Angeles; U. of Maryland; U. of Pennsylvania.

International Students

TOEFL required of international students?	Yes
Minimum Paper TOEFL	600
Minimum Computer TOEFL	250

FINANCIAL FACTS

Annual tuition (resident)	$15,012
Annual tuition (nonres.)	$22,043
Books and supplies	$1,000
Fees per credit (resident)	$45
Fees per credit (nonresident)	$45
Tuition per credit (resident)	$621
Tuition per credit (nonres.)	$918
Room & board (on/off-campus)	$5,910/$8,000
Financial aid app. deadline	4/1
% first-year students receiving some sort of aid	92
% receiving some sort of aid	92
% of aid that is merit-based	25
% receiving scholarships	30
Average grant	$5,000
Average loan	$23,000
Average total aid package	$23,000
Average debt	$69,000

Rutgers University—Newark

School of Law

INSTITUTIONAL INFORMATION

Public/private	public
Student/faculty ratio	17:1
% faculty part-time	56
% faculty female	37
% faculty minority	19
Total faculty	64

SURVEY SAYS . . .

Diverse opinions accepted in classrooms
Great research resources
Great library staff
Abundant externship/internship/clerkship opportunities
Beautiful campus

STUDENTS

Enrollment of law school	825
% male/female	56/44
% out-of-state	29
% full-time	70
% minority	34
% international	2
# of countries represented	24
Average age of entering class	27

ACADEMICS

Academic Experience rating	**81**
Professors interesting rating	76
Professors accessible rating	67
Hours of study per day	3.68

Academic Specialties

Civil procedure, commercial law, constitutional law, corporation securities law, criminal law, environmental law, global affairs, government services, human rights law, intellectual property law, international business, international law, labor law, legal history, legal philosophy, property, taxation.

Combined Degrees Offered

JD/MBA, 4 yrs; JD/MD, 6 yrs; JD/PhD jurisprudence, 5 yrs; JD/MA criminal justice, 4 yrs; JD/MCRP city/regional planning, 4 yrs; JD/MSW, 4 yrs.

Academic Requirements

Clinical Program Required?	No

Academics

Students at Rutgers University Newark School of Law agree that the school has a tremendous clinical program "both in terms of various areas in which to work and the quality of work" available. "Rutgers is a clinical factory! Basically, there is a functional law firm in the building, [staffed] solely [by] students, that handles issues from constitutional law practice to business law matters." Many students like how the clinical program both "provides a valuable service to the community at large" and allows students to "work side by side with experienced attorneys on real legal issues." Those impatient to get their hands dirty with the law, then, should be happy at Rutgers—Newark because "the first time you step into a courtroom does not have to be after graduation." Take the Constitutional Litigation Clinic, for example. A student involved tells us that the clinic "has been involved in many cases that has shifted case law appreciably. In working in the clinic, I have felt that I have really been a part of policy-making in this country." Students are proud to attend a school where public interest is a priority. Another area at Rutgers that garners high praise is the writing program, which "is very intensive and prepares students for real-time lawyering very well." Furthermore, "the school allows for a great deal of academic freedom," since there are "no required classes after first year," allowing students to choose their own path.

At Rutgers law school, students relish that the "faculty are receptive to student views and appreciate insights students offer." One student writes, "There is a general sense that if you have an opinion, you should express it openly and articulately, but most important, you should do so unapologetically." Professors are inspiring because they are "impassioned and genuine in their love of teaching and of law." Students are not only impressed by the faculty member's passion in the classroom, but also by their humanity outside of it. One student reports that professors "let us know that they want to get to know us on a personal, as well as academic, level. They go out of their way to attend networking events that are held for the students." Students say, "Overall the professors are engaged and passionate about the law and their areas of expertise. The viewpoints run the entire spectrum." Opinion is evenly split about the administration, with some students describing it as "very helpful and supportive," while others complain that it "moves at a glacial speed when responding to students' concerns."

The classrooms at Rutgers—Newark are "modern and up-to-date technologically." Students report, "Every seat in the library and most of the seats in the classrooms are wired for power and data, and there is also a wireless network," which make studying and research a whole lot easier for everyone.

Anita Walton, Assistant Dean for Admissions
Center for Law and Justice, 123 Washington Street, Newark, NJ 07102
Telephone: 973-353-5554 • Fax: 973-353-3459
E-mail: geddis@andromeda.rutgers.edu • Website: http://law.newark.rutgers.edu

Life

Without hellacious traffic, Newark is about a 30-minute car ride to and from New York City, and because it is so close to New York, opportunities for work and play abound. On the local front, Newark seems to be an "up-and-coming city" with various social and cultural events of its own. While "the parking situation stinks," students agree, "That is not the law school's fault in particular." Some students also believe that "Rutgers also benefits from having McGovern's Bar conveniently [located] across the street to lubricate social interaction."

Structured social events include "a public interest auction and a Jazz for Justice Night, as well as the Barrister's Ball." Students tell us, "We work hard, but we still have a good time." For things to do around town, there's "the Newark Museum, the Ironbound section of Newark, the NJ Performing Arts Center, and the Newark Bears baseball team."

Students are also very proud of how diverse their student body is. The school has "done a great job in making sure that our classrooms are filled with students of all races, socioeconomic backgrounds, and cultures, and this truly adds to the learning experience." The school "is an extremely diverse law school both ethnically and with the career goals of its students." While there is competition between classmates, "the students are generally cordial, approachable and willing to assist other students. By and large, it is a great learning environment that provides students with a mentally stimulating forum."

Getting In

Admission to Rutgers—Newark is not easy, but it is not impossible, either. About one out of every five applicants is accepted, and the chances of acceptance are much better if one's LSAT score is north of 160. Last year, admitted students at the 75th percentile had an LSAT score of 161 and a GPA of 3.5.

EMPLOYMENT INFORMATION

Career Rating	**85**
% employed within 9 months	94
Average starting salary	$64,067
State for bar exam	NJ, NY, PA
Pass rate for first-time bar	72

Employers who frequently hire grads:
Federal judges, New Jersey State court judges, large NJ and NY law firms, medium NJ firms, NY and NJ corporations, legal services.

Prominent Alumni: Robert Menendez, U.S. congressman; Jaynee LaVecchia, New Jersey State Supreme Court justice; Ida Castro, New Jersey commissioner of personnel.

Grads employed by field (%):	
Academic	1
Business/industry	15
Government	5
Judicial clerkships	31
Military	1
Other	2
Private practice	43
Public interest	2

Legal Writing Course Requirement?	Yes
Legal Methods Course Requirement?	Yes
Legal Research Course Requirement?	Yes
Moot Court Requirement?	Yes
Public Interest Law Requirement?	No

ADMISSIONS

Selectivity Rating	**89**
# applications received	3,536
# applicants accepted	728
# acceptees attending	285
Average LSAT	159
LSAT Range	153–162
Average undergrad GPA	3.3
Application fee	$50
Regular application deadline	3/15
Regular notification	rolling
Rolling notification?	Yes
Early application program?	No
Transfer students accepted?	Yes
Evening division offered?	Yes
Part-time accepted?	Yes
LSDAS accepted?	Yes

Applicants Also Look At

American U.; Boston U.; Fordham U.; The George Washington U.; Rutgers, The State U. of New Jersey—Camden; Seton Hall U.; Yeshiva U.

International Students

TOEFL required of international students?	No
TOEFL recommended of international students?	No

FINANCIAL FACTS

Annual tuition (resident)	$15,012
Annual tuition (nonres.)	$22,043
Books and supplies	$4,172
Fees per credit (resident)	$712
Fees per credit (nonresident)	$712
Tuition per credit (resident)	$621
Tuition per credit (nonres.)	$918
Room & board (on/off-campus)	$8,951/$11,399
Financial aid application deadline	3/1
% receiving some sort of aid	90
% of aid that is merit-based	13
% receiving scholarships	53
Average grant	$3,449
Average loan	$19,213
Average total aid package	$21,001
Average debt	$45,286

ST. JOHN'S UNIVERSITY
SCHOOL OF LAW

INSTITUTIONAL INFORMATION

Public/private	private
Student/faculty ratio	16:1

SURVEY SAYS . . .

Great research resources
Abundant externship/internship/clerkship opportunities

STUDENTS

Enrollment of law school	292
% male/female	54/46
% full-time	81
% minority	27
Average age of entering class	23

ACADEMICS

Academic Experience rating	**67**
Professors interesting rating	61
Professors accessible rating	61
Hours of study per day	3.5

Advanced Degrees Offered

JD, 3 years; LLM in bankruptcy, 1 year full-time, 2 to 3 years part-time.

Combined Degrees Offered

JD/MBA; JD/MA (MS); BA (BS)/JD.

Academic Requirements

Clinical Program Required?	No
Legal Writing Course Requirement?	Yes
Legal Methods Course Requirement?	Yes
Legal Research Course Requirement?	Yes
Moot Court Requirement?	Yes
Public Interest Law Requirement?	No

Academics

Located in Jamaica, Queens, St. John's University is a fine place to get a strong, traditional legal education while benefiting from the many practical and professional opportunities available in the New York metropolitan area. With an emphasis on legal theory and the fundamentals of law, students say that "St. John's is old-fashioned, but in good ways." For example, "professors' continued reliance on the Socratic method is challenging, to be sure, but also stimulating and a great incentive to always read carefully!" The faculty comprises some of the country's top legal scholars, many of whom have published extensively or still hold prestigious positions as practicing attorneys or judges. In addition to their backgrounds, there is a lot of diversity within the teaching staff and many are "still very much involved in their fields and are very well known." What's more, students feel they have ample opportunity to learn from these great minds, as the school does not experience the scheduling hassles and class waitlists common to other law schools. Case in point: A part-time student tells us that "I am an evening student and they take care of us by having all professors rotate to the evening. We don't get gypped by going at night." While students mainly applaud the school's academic program, some feel that St. John's could benefit from "more classes about research and writing, which is the most important skill a lawyer can have."

Even so, there is no lack of practical opportunities at St. John's. Its hometown is a goldmine for the motivated student, and the school operates a number of applied learning programs, such as the Domestic Violence Litigation Clinic, Elder Law Clinic, and Immigration Rights Clinic. In addition, St. John's operates criminal, judicial, and civil law externships.

On campus, "the law school facilities are excellent, [...] clean, convenient, and efficiently designed." The building is "immaculate" and "features wireless Internet throughout, a great library, and plenty of room for students to study and socialize. In that vein, students report that "the library is generally a nice, quiet place to study, and the research librarians are very helpful."

If you are planning to practice in New York City, St. John's is an excellent place to do it, as the school has a strong regional reputation and extensive contacts in the legal community. In particular, St. John's alumni are a fantastic resource to students, as they are "extremely loyal and enthusiastic about giving St. John's students and alums opportunities in a cross-section of legal specialties." "The alumni are by far the greatest strength," reports one student. "Many are professors, full-time and adjunct, and all are perpetually upbeat, helpful with any academic concerns and pursuits." Not only do they teach at the school, many alumni "go above and beyond the call in trying to match students up with challenging and exciting employment opportunities."

Life

Like its hometown, "the law school is diverse," both ethnically and culturally. While they hail from a variety of backgrounds, St. John's students are generally friendly and non-competitive. In fact, many report that "the greatest strength of the law school is by far the close sense of community." "St. John's students tend to see each other as teammates rather than adversaries," writes a 1L. "One good example of the kind of atmosphere here was the Tsunami Relief Poker Tournament. The students and faculty raised more than $4,000 in one night through this poker tournament, and all proceeds went to tsunami victims."

Robert M. Harrison, Assistant Dean for Admissions
8000 Utopia Parkway, Queens, NY 11439
Telephone: 718-990-6474 • Fax: 718-990-2526
E-mail: lawinfo@stjohns.edu • Website: www.law.stjohns.edu

While St. John's is well-located for jobs and externships, many students disparage the neighborhood surrounding the campus. One wiseacre student cracks, "Located in the heart of Jamaica, Queens, there is a chance that your car will not be where you parked it when you return from class." And if you want to leave your ride at home, think again; students complain that getting to Jamaica is "a hassle if you commute by public transportation." On top of that, Jamaica isn't exactly law school–friendly: "There is only one bar worth going to after class and only on school-sponsored nights," gripes a 3L. It should come as no surprise, then, that few students attend St. John's for the campus life. In fact, "almost everyone is a commuter student, so the building clears out after classes end."

Getting In

St. John's University receives more than 4,000 applications annually for about 300 first-year spots. In addition to LSAT scores and undergraduate GPA, which are heavily weighted, St. John's considers factors that could be beneficial to the study of law and to the school community, such as graduate work, extracurricular activities, community service, work experience, or personal obstacles a student may have overcome before or during their undergraduate studies.

ADMISSIONS

Selectivity Rating	**84**
# applications received	4,177
# applicants accepted	1,035
# acceptees attending	292
Average LSAT	160
LSAT Range	158–163
Average undergrad GPA	3.4
Application fee	$60
Regular application deadline	4/1
Regular notification	rolling
Rolling notification?	Yes
Early application program?	No
Transfer students accepted?	Yes
Evening division offered?	Yes
Part-time accepted?	Yes
LSDAS accepted?	Yes
International Students	
TOEFL required of international students?	No
TOEFL recommended of international students?	Yes
Minimum Paper TOEFL	600
Minimum Computer TOEFL	250

FINANCIAL FACTS

Annual tuition	$30,500
Books and supplies	$1,000
Tuition per credit	$1,050
Room & board	$8,500
Average grant	$6,904
Average loan	$16,911
Average total aid package	$18,500
Average debt	$53,619

EMPLOYMENT INFORMATION

Career Rating	**89**
% employed within 9 months	97
State for bar exam	NY
Pass rate for first-time bar	87

Employers who frequently hire grads:
Private law firms, corporations, governmental agencies.

St. Mary's University
School of Law

INSTITUTIONAL INFORMATION

Public/private	private
Student/faculty ratio	18:1
Affiliation	Roman Catholic
% faculty part-time	53
% faculty female	35
% faculty minority	22
Total faculty	95

SURVEY SAYS . . .

Diverse opinions accepted in classrooms
Great research resources
Great library staff

STUDENTS

Enrollment of law school	793
% male/female	52/48
% out-of-state	11
% full-time	100
% minority	30
% international	2
# of countries represented	8
Average age of entering class	24

ACADEMICS

Academic Experience rating	**72**
Professors interesting rating	72
Professors accessible rating	84
Hours of study per day	5.1

Academic Specialties

Constitutional law, criminal law, human rights law, international law.

Advanced Degrees Offered

LLM in international and comparative law for U.S. educated graduates, 1 yr; LLM in American legal studies for foreign educated graduates, 1 yr.

Combined Degrees Offered

JD/MBA accounting, JD/MA economics, JD/MA international relations with a concentration in justice administration, JD/MA public administration, JD/MA English language and literature, JD/MA theology, JD/MS computer science, JD/MS industrial engineering, JD/MBA business administration, JD/MA communication studies. All 3.5 to 4 years total.

Academics

"Unfortunately, heart is not a criterion by which law schools are judged. If it were, St. Mary's would be at the top of the list," writes a 3L. Although the bar-passage rate at St. Mary's (80 percent for first-time test-takers) is on par with that of other schools in the southwest region, many students express concern over what they perceive to be a particularly "low bar-passage rate," worrying that "the negative emphasis on the school's low bar-passage rate will become a self-fulfilling prophecy." Many, however, feel confident that the current administration has "taken the necessary steps to get the passage rate back up to where it was very soon." They put their trust in dean Bill Piatt, who frequents student lounges and "seems more like a friend than a superior." A 1L praises, "Expect to see great things from this school as long as he's around." A practical bent characterizes the legal education at St. Mary's, an institution "with a strong dedication to creating practicing attorneys." Students would rather not take "useless survey classes," preferring instead course work that focuses on bar preparation and other practical skills. Indeed, St. Mary's already offers students ways to gain real-world experience. An emphasis on "clinical programs," "clerkships, internships, and writing and research" produces graduates ready for the working world, although a 3L cautions that "few obtain summer clerkship positions after their second year." Students see the importance of the legal writing requirement; they just wish they weren't "rushed through the material." They also ask for "a wider range of elective courses for students who may not intend to practice law in the traditional sense." Second-year students spend significant time in mock trial and moot court; this program "helps first-years realize there is something to strive for besides two more years of boring repetition."

"The faculty are extremely dedicated to providing the best education possible for their students. However, because the school does not have the resources or the reputation to attract the most sought-after professors, the quality of education is not comparable to that of most other upper-tier Texas schools." Nonetheless, students characterize their professors as "very accessible," "helpful," and "absolutely excellent." Instructors also earn praise for their effective teaching techniques. A 2L comments dryly, "They understand that the Socratic Method was a great teaching tool . . . in 300 B.C." To jazz things up, one torts professor "handcuffed two students together to demonstrate false imprisonment," and others "play short movie clips and project photos to accompany cases." These antics succeed in "pulling students easily into debate over the subject matter." A few instructors come from "strictly academic backgrounds with little experience in the practice of law," but most are "outstanding lecturers, prolific legal writers, and incredible achievers in their fields," according to a 3L. No matter how engaging the class, it's the GPA that matters, and the only topic as contentious as bar passage at St. Mary's is grades. "The mandatory curve is the devil and needs to go!" At minimum, students would like to see the curve raised slightly—"so that grades more accurately reflect achievement"—or even abandoned after the first year. "Among 1Ls, we all know that because of the forced curve, 20 percent of us will not be here next year." Many students take advantage of "the awesome tutoring program in place to help 1Ls" survive the difficult year.

In terms of facilities and technology, "St. Mary's is like being stuck in the original Star Trek when all the other schools have upgraded to the Next Generation." Students sometimes come crashing to the ground during lecture because of sub-par classroom seating. In contrast, "the library facilities are expansive and modern, and for the few of us who use them every day, the staff knows us by name." Students find "comfortable places to study, as well as small meeting rooms, so you can get together with friends to review tough cases." The functional wireless network allows students to "sit outside in the sun work-

Director of Admissions, Assistant Dean and Director of Admissions
One Camino Santa Maria, San Antonio, TX 78228-8601
Telephone: 866-639-5831 • Fax: 210-431-4202
E-mail: lawadmissions@stmarytx.edu • Website: www.law.stmarytx.edu/law

ing on [their] computers and then send something to the printer from the courtyard." "St. Mary's is San Antonio's law school, and the local bar association may as well be a second alumni association." The active student bar association cultivates strong ties with alumni, "allowing students to network with potential employers throughout law school." These connections compensate for a less-than-effective Career Services office: "Options and opportunities seem to be clandestine topics with our career advisors," writes a 3L. Students note that many local positions require bilingual proficiency, an advantage for the school's many Spanish-speaking students.

Life

The student population shows diversity, "not just ethnically, but also in age and previous occupation." Students are split into four sections upon arrival, and they tend to "become very close with those in [their] groups," sometimes not even learning "who else is in the class until the end of the first year." A 2L describes the school as having an "air of collegiality and a growing community that trades textbooks and gives notes to each other." The overall "lackadaisical, mañana-style attitude" keeps stress levels low on the law school scale. The only time that the "great camaraderie and support among classmates" cracks seems to be during intramural athletic competition. Students find easy "access to both the social events and student organizations." In increasing numbers, students are joining the law journal, which "ranked the fourth most-cited among federal and state cases this past year." Although St. Mary's is a Catholic institution, students report that they "never feel pressure to alter [their] religious beliefs." Indeed, the school's religious affiliation doesn't seem to have as great an impact on social life as does the workload. While some students manage to find time "to go out three nights a week," many—especially first-years—find that "social life is relative to the amount of free time a 1L has: none."

Getting In

Falling well below the mean LSAT score (154) or GPA (3.05) doesn't necessarily result in rejection at St. Mary's. The committee carefully considers intangibles, such as maturity derived from previous career experience, the ability to overcome challenges, and cultural competence. They are looking for rigorous undergraduate course work and an inclination toward public service. Best to get applications in soon after the Admissions Office starts accepting them in November.

EMPLOYMENT INFORMATION

Career Rating	**68**
Job placement rate (%)	74
Average starting salary	$55,000
State for bar exam	TX, FL, MO, OK, NM
Pass rate for first-time bar	80

Employers who frequently hire grads: Small and midsize firms, government agencies, courts, district attorney offices, business (banking/financial).

Prominent Alumni: John Cornyn, United States senator from Texas; Charles Gonzalez, congressman; Alma L. Lopez, chief justice of the Texas Court of Appeals; Thomas Mummert, U.S. magistrate judge.

Grads employed by field (%):	
Academic	2
Business/industry	3
Government	17
Judicial clerkships	6
Private practice	70
Public interest	2

Academic Requirements

Clinical Program Required?	No
Legal Writing Course Requirement?	Yes
Legal Methods Course Requirement?	Yes
Legal Research Course Requirement?	Yes
Moot Court Requirement?	No
Public Interest Law Requirement?	No

ADMISSIONS

Selectivity Rating	**75**
# applications received	2,170
# applicants accepted	685
# acceptees attending	295
Average LSAT	154
LSAT Range	152–156
Average undergrad GPA	3.1
Application fee	$55
Regular application deadline	3/1
Regular notification	5/1
Rolling notification?	Yes
Early application program?	No
Transfer students accepted?	Yes
Evening division offered?	No
Part-time accepted?	No
LSDAS accepted?	Yes

Applicants Also Look At

Baylor University, Southern Methodist University, Texas A&M University, Texas Tech University, Texas Wesleyan University, University of Houston, The University of Texas at Austin.

International Students

TOEFL required of international students?	Yes

FINANCIAL FACTS

Annual tuition	$21,390
Books and supplies	$1,100
Tuition per credit	$667
Room & board (on/off-campus)	$6,500/$7,230
Financial aid application deadline	3/31
% first-year students receiving some sort of aid	93
% receiving some sort of aid	90
% of aid that is merit-based	13
% receiving scholarships	40
Average grant	$3,003
Average loan	$28,573
Average total aid package	$26,911
Average debt	$84,365

St. Thomas University
School of Law

INSTITUTIONAL INFORMATION

Public/private	private
Student/faculty ratio	27:1
Affiliation	Roman Catholic
% faculty part-time	68
% faculty female	42
% faculty minority	25
Total faculty	69

SURVEY SAYS . . .

Heavy use of Socratic method
Diverse opinions accepted in classrooms
Great library staff
Abundant externship/internship/clerkship opportunities

STUDENTS

Enrollment of law school	721
% male/female	55/45
% out-of-state	29
% full-time	100
% minority	42
% international	1
# of countries represented	5
Average age of entering class	25

ACADEMICS

Academic Experience rating	**71**
Professors interesting rating	80
Professors accessible rating	89
Hours of study per day	4.71

Academic Specialties

Human rights law, international law, taxation.

Advanced Degrees Offered

Online LLM in international tax, 2 years; LLM in intercultural human rights, 1 year.

Combined Degrees Offered

JD/MS in marriage & family counseling, 3 years; JD/MS in sports administration, 3 years; JD/MBA in accounting, 3 years; JD/MBA in international business, 3 years; JD/BA 3+3 program, 6 years.

Academic Requirements

Clinical Program Required?	No

Academics

Markedly Catholic, St. Thomas University School of Law is "a hidden gem [that] produces some of the best lawyers Miami-Dade and Broward counties have to offer." Students tell us that you'll get heaping helpings of "law with a conscience" at this university. They are also very proud of the school's "dedication to creating lawyers who are ethical in their work [and who] make an effort to better the world case by case." St. Thomas's "small size" is a good thing, too. "Students, faculty, and staff get to interact in an amicable environment that enhances relationships and stimulates improvement." The weakness, students say, is St. Thomas's lack of name recognition. "The school is so young and not that many people, even locally, know about it."

There are one or two "not-so-great professors," but the vast majority of the faculty is pretty much "amazing." While many professors "happily employ the Socratic Method [and] challenge students to scrutinize each legal opinion to determine whether they agree with the court's reasoning," the curriculum is largely "geared toward black letter law [the principles of law generally accepted as indubitable or indisputable] in an effort to prepare students for the bar." Members of the faculty "teach a wide variety of subjects [and have] practical experience" galore. They are "completely approachable" as well. "Every professor, tenured and adjunct alike, is willing to spend inordinate amounts of time with the students." The "very kind [and] sincerely concerned" administration maintains an "open-door policy" and impresses students to no end. The dean is particularly "fantastic." A wistful 3L says, "Dean Bob Butterworth, Florida's Attorney General for 16 years, has brought flair to St. Thomas School of Law, and his impact has been felt immediately. The dean and the faculty give off a sense of energy and determination to take the school to new heights." However, we have found that no law school has a perfectly-run administration, and St. Thomas is no exception. "The incompetence" of the business and financial aid offices is "unbearable."

Lawyering skills are easy to come by at St. Thomas. In fact, you won't be able to avoid acquiring them. The school actually "requires that every student attain legal experience prior to graduation." Clinical externships are "readily available." The clinics in immigration and bankruptcy are "practical." Out of the classroom, "internships for credit and experience" with area judges and the state's attorney offices are abundant. Two lucky students get to clerk in Tallahassee for the Supreme Court of Florida. There is also a popular summer-in-Spain study abroad program. The excellent Career Services office has a "motivated and upbeat" staff that helps students obtain more real-world experience.

The facilities of the school are "adequate" but could use some improvements. "They give you enough to get your work done but are not so luxurious that you are distracted," reflects one student. "The wireless network is wonderful, [but] classrooms could have more outlets for the students to use laptops." The library is "nice, [but it is] too small, [and there are] not enough resources" within it.

DIRECTOR FOR ADMISSIONS
16401 NORTHWEST THIRTY-SEVENTH AVENUE, MIAMI GARDENS, FL 33054
TELEPHONE: 305-623-2310 • FAX: 305-623-2357
E-MAIL: ADMITME@STU.EDU • WEBSITE: WWW.STU.EDU

Life

According to its students, "St. Thomas is very diverse." It may well be the most diverse law school in the country. You will find individuals "of all ages, ethnicities, [and] walks of life." Students "come from all over the United States and foreign countries," too. The school also "has a very good mix of liberals, conservatives, and in-between." The academic environment is "highly competitive." Outside the classroom, though, "the camaraderie among students at STU is unusual"—in a good way. Upperclassmen "help out the newbies," and everyone gets along swimmingly.

Socially, "everyone knows everyone else. The student body is small enough that you know most everybody on a first-name and familiar basis." One student explains, "The breezeway of the law school is the social hub. From early morning until late at night, there are people sitting at the tables surrounded by their books and laptops, or with their study groups, or sometimes just chatting with whoever happens to walk by." The intimacy that develops over the months and years "allows students to form long-lasting friendships and important career contacts." On the other hand, "gossip gets out of hand at times," too. Beyond the bounds of the law school, "the Student Bar Association and other student organizations constantly plan social events geared at bringing the community together."

The cosmopolitan, international city of Miami is "a great place to learn, study, and practice the law." Plus, you may have heard, "the weather is nice." If you are so inclined, "you can study on the beach the majority of the year." Students at St. Thomas tell us, "The school itself is not in the greatest neighborhood." Nevertheless, you can "feel completely safe on campus at any hour of the day or night."

Getting In

The admissions statistics are pretty forgiving at St. Thomas University School of Law. Admitted students at the 25th percentile have an LSAT score of 148 and a GPA of 2.6. Admitted students at the 75th percentile have an LSAT score of 153 and a GPA of 3.3. Students with an interest of practicing law in South Florida should consider applying at St. Thomas. If you were a B student in college and scored a 150 or higher on your LSAT, the odds are in your favor.

EMPLOYMENT INFORMATION

Career Rating	**70**
Job placement rate (%)	86
Average starting salary	$50,000
State for bar exam	FL, NY, GA
Pass rate for first-time bar	54

Employers who frequently hire grads: Private law firms of all sizes; government agencies, including the U.S. Department of Justice, the Florida State attorney's office, public interest organizations & corporations.

Prominent Alumni: Mikki Canton, Esq, partner, Gunster, Yoakley, & Stewart; Honorable Samuel J. Slom, eleventh judicial circuit; Honorable Don Thomas Hall, DeSoto County Court judge.

Grads employed by field (%):	
Business/industry	11
Government	19
Judicial clerkships	1
Private practice	57
Public interest	12

Legal Writing Course Requirement?	Yes
Legal Methods Course Requirement?	Yes
Legal Research Course Requirement?	Yes
Moot Court Requirement?	Yes
Public Interest Law Requirement?	Yes

ADMISSIONS

Selectivity Rating	**66**
# applications received	2,115
# applicants accepted	789
# acceptees attending	275
Average LSAT	150
LSAT Range	148–153
Average undergrad GPA	3.0
Application fee	$45
Regular application deadline	rolling
Regular notification	rolling
Rolling notification?	No
Early application program?	No
Transfer students accepted?	Yes
Evening division offered?	No
Part-time accepted?	No
LSDAS accepted?	Yes

Applicants Also Look At

Nova Southeastern University, University of Miami.

International Students

TOEFL required of international students?	No
TOEFL recommended of international students?	Yes
Minimum Paper TOEFL	550

FINANCIAL FACTS

Annual tuition	$23,560
Books and supplies	$1,140
Room & board (on/off-campus)	$8,950/$9,675
Financial aid application deadline	5/1
% first-year students receiving some sort of aid	95
% receiving some sort of aid	98
% of aid that is merit-based	15
% receiving scholarships	39
Average grant	$11,000
Average loan	$26,000
Average total aid package	$29,000
Average debt	$85,500

Samford University
Cumberland School of Law

INSTITUTIONAL INFORMATION

Public/private	private
Student/faculty ratio	20:1
Affiliation	Southern Baptist
% faculty part-time	51
% faculty female	18
% faculty minority	9
Total faculty	45

SURVEY SAYS . . .

Great research resources
Beautiful campus
Students love Birmingham, AL

STUDENTS

Enrollment of law school	540
% male/female	62/38
% out-of-state	52
% full-time	99
% minority	8
Average age of entering class	24

ACADEMICS

Academic Experience rating	**89**
Professors interesting rating	92
Professors accessible rating	99
Hours of study per day	4.76

Academic Specialties

Trial advocacy, practical lawyering skills.

Advanced Degrees Offered

Master of comparative law.

Combined Degrees Offered

JD/master of accountancy, JD/MBA, JD/MDivinity, JD/master of public administration, JD/master of public health, JD/MS in environmental management. All 3.5- to 4-year programs except the JD/MDivinity, which is a 5-year program.

Academic Requirements

Clinical Program Required?	No
Legal Writing Course Requirement?	Yes
Legal Methods Course Requirement?	Yes
Legal Research Course Requirement?	Yes
Moot Court Requirement?	No

Academics

Samford University Cumberland School of Law offers its students "the classic law school experience," including classes taught using the Socratic Method, an emphasis on critical thinking skills and ethical dilemmas, and, of course, a lot of homework. Students at Cumberland love the challenging curriculum. One explains, "Most professors teach using the Socratic Method, which I believe is a great tool for developing lawyers. If you cannot speak intelligently in front of your peers, you have no business speaking before a judge or jury." Another student adds, "The professors are highly qualified, intelligent, and engaging. In class, we do so much more than discuss black letter law—we wrestle with its effects and implications on our lives and on society."

Students say their professors are accomplished, brilliant, and friendly, each offering a unique professional and educational background to the program. Students say, "Our professors bring their experience as judges, attorneys, civic leaders, and students from the most prestigious law schools in the country. This provides for a wide range of testing and classroom philosophies." Among the faculty's many accomplishments, students inform us, "Two notable professors are active in developing a new state constitution for Alabama." Despite their prestigious responsibilities, professors come across to their students as down-to-earth and friendly, always willing to provide extra assistance and guidance outside the classroom. In the words of one student, "The school is very academically challenging, but the faculty is always willing to help when you are struggling." Another insists, "They want you to know and really understand the topics, and they love to answer your questions."

Above all else, Samford is known for training tough trial lawyers through extensive course work and clinics. Students praise "Lawyering and Legal Reasoning," a first-year class that "teaches practical skills, following a mock case from the complaint and discovery phases to appellate." The trial program also includes "an in-school trial competition, as well as three different Alternative Dispute Resolution competitions each semester and during the summer." A student recounts, "Cumberland's trial program was the deciding factor for me when applying to law school. Most of my family members are litigators, so I wanted to continue in their footsteps. With the prestige and reputation Cumberland has received here in the South, it was an easy decision." Another adds, "The trial advocacy courses are excellent, and the opportunities for Moot Court competitions abound. If you want to be a trial lawyer, this is the place to go to school." One student admits, however, "The focus on litigation is a blessing and a curse, depending on what you want to do when you graduate." In that vein, some students think the curriculum is too broad-based, discouraging students from taking classes in a legal specialty. One student explains, "Specialization in distinct areas of the law is not emphasized here. Although most employers agree that specialization is not necessary or expected, those who positively know their niche before enrolling tend to get frustrated." Even so, Cumberland students are very successful after graduation. "Cumberland has a very high standard for academics, and, therefore, an extremely high bar-passage rate," one student observes.

Located in Alabama, students claim that Samford is "the epitome of Southern hospitality." By almost all accounts, the administration is extremely friendly and helpful, working tirelessly to meet student needs and improve the school's educational offerings. "The administration is very capable, outgoing, and accessible," raves one student. Plus, they are involved academically, too. Students love to point out that "Cumberland's Dean, Judge John Carroll, actually teaches classes, including first-year writing classes."

M. Giselle Gauthier, Director of Admissions
800 Lakeshore Drive, Birmingham, AL 35229
Telephone: 205-726-2702 • Fax: 205-726-2057
E-mail: law.admissions@samford.edu • Website: http://cumberland.samford.edu

Life

Students say that Samford is an ideal law school environment, boasting a modern and beautiful campus while providing all the culture and amenities of urban Birmingham. One student describes a campus that "sits on top of a hill overlooking part of Birmingham, a city with large rolling hills at the foot of the Appalachians."

Like the faculty and administration, the student body is generally friendly, keeping competitiveness at bay. A student explains, "The students really care about each other and help each other, but at the same time the competitive atmosphere still exists." Most students say their classmates are collegial and that they maintain friendships with their peers. On campus, the library seems to be a focal point, though for different reasons to different types of students. "During the day, the library is the 'truck stop' of the law school, meaning all the 1Ls congregate to exchange war stories. It can be fun, but also very loud if you are actually trying to study," writes one student.

As far as off-campus diversions go, students say, "We often hang out in downtown Birmingham, and other times we enjoy parties at different classmates' houses. I have been surprised that law school has been so much fun." Another adds, "Students enjoy getting together outside of class for numerous activities. Groups play intramural sports, attend movies, hang out at local clubs, pretty much everything imaginable."

Getting In

The Cumberland School of Law evaluates applicants based on their LSAT scores and undergraduate GPA, as well as their personal statement and letters of recommendation. The school also considers the quality of the applicant's undergraduate institution and course of study, as well as any graduate work, unique extracurricular activities, or professional experience. The Office of Admissions warns that the quality of the applicant pool varies from year to year.

EMPLOYMENT INFORMATION

Career Rating	**79**
% employed within 9 months	97.3
Average starting salary	$54,377
State for bar exam	AL, FL, TN, GA, VA
Pass rate for first-time bar	86

Employers who frequently hire grads: Bradley, Arant, Rose & White; Burr & Forman; Balch & Bingham; Adams Reese; Cabaniss, Johnston, Gardner, Dumas, & O'Neal; Sirote & Permutt; Alabama Attorney General's Office.

Prominent Alumni: Cordell Hull, founder of United Nations; Howell E. Jackson, U.S. Supreme Court; Horace H. Lurton, U.S. Supreme Court.

Grads employed by field (%):	
Academic	1
Business/industry	6
Government	11
Judicial clerkships	6
Private practice	69
Public interest	2

Public Interest Law Requirement?	No

ADMISSIONS

Selectivity Rating	**79**
# applications received	1,397
# applicants accepted	386
# acceptees attending	174
Average LSAT	155
LSAT Range	154–157
Average undergrad GPA	3.2
Application fee	$50
Regular application deadline	rolling
Regular notification	rolling
Rolling notification?	Yes
Early application program?	No
Transfer students accepted?	Yes
Evening division offered?	No
Part-time accepted?	Yes
LSDAS accepted?	Yes

Applicants Also Look At

Mercer University, University of Alabama, University of Memphis, University of Mississippi, University of South Carolina, University of Tennessee.

International Students

TOEFL required of international students?	Yes
Minimum Paper TOEFL	550
Minimum Computer TOEFL	213

FINANCIAL FACTS

Annual tuition	$24,708
Books and supplies	$1,380
Fees per credit	$20
Tuition per credit	$824
Room & board (off-campus)	$10,530
Financial aid application deadline	3/1
% first-year students receiving some sort of aid	86
% receiving some sort of aid	87
% receiving scholarships	35
Average grant	$3,634
Average loan	$32,664
Average total aid package	$41,000
Average debt	$81,706

Santa Clara University
School of Law

INSTITUTIONAL INFORMATION

Public/private	private
Student/faculty ratio	19:1
Affiliation	Roman Catholic
% faculty part-time	39
% faculty female	45
% faculty minority	12
Total faculty	94

SURVEY SAYS . . .

Great library staff
Beautiful campus
Students love Santa Clara, CA

STUDENTS

Enrollment of law school	940
% male/female	50/50
% full-time	77
% minority	41
# of countries represented	7
Average age of entering class	26

ACADEMICS

Academic Experience rating	**70**
Professors interesting rating	64
Professors accessible rating	70
Hours of study per day	4.41

Academic Specialties

Intellectual property law, international law, public interest law.

Advanced Degrees Offered

LLM in U.S. law for foreign lawyers, LLM in international and comparative law, LLM in intellectual property law.

Combined Degrees Offered

JD/MBA, 3.5 to 4 years, JD/MST, 3.5 to 4 years.

Academic Requirements

Clinical Program Required?	No
Legal Writing Course Requirement?	Yes
Legal Methods Course Requirement?	No
Legal Research Course Requirement?	Yes
Moot Court Requirement?	Yes
Public Interest Law Requirement?	No

Academics

Santa Clara University School of Law is a small Catholic school in the heart of Silicon Valley with "a lot of resources, amazing overseas summer programs, [and] in-depth clinical programs for public interest law." Students say, it's "a great place for techies." One student proclaims, "High tech law [is huge, and] Santa Clara is a great school for people interested in intellectual property law, particularly patent law." Students say, "The school has strong ties with the community of Silicon Valley IP lawyers who teach a number of upper-level seminars." The Jesuit Catholic tradition also ensures a "focus on human rights and social justice." The Alexander Community Law Center is a free clinic that "provides excellent opportunities to gain practical legal experience."

Students are mostly enthusiastic about the faculty. Although some feel that the faculty "needs new blood," most testify, "The professors are the greatest strength of Santa Clara." They also tell us, "The faculty have good credentials and strike a good balance between theory and practice. They are available in and outside of class." One student gushes, "I have had some incredibly knowledgeable and enthusiastic professors who make a seemingly boring topic interesting and exciting." Furthermore, the "extremely exciting and dedicated [visiting professors] clearly invoke enthusiasm and eagerness in the students" as well. Santa Clara's "extremely flexible, focused, and attentive [administration] will work with you to deal with whatever issue you are facing." As far as registration is concerned, "There are plenty of courses [at SCU, but] the popular ones fill up quick." Also, many respondents agree, "The legal writing program is notoriously bad," some calling it a joke, and others, "a waste of time." In addition, "the mandatory grade curve" is a source of persistent dissatisfaction.

Career prospects are promising for Santa Clara graduates, "particularly close to home." One proud student professes, "Our academic reputation is strong in the Bay Area. There is a great willingness for Santa Clara alums to help other students coming out of Santa Clara." Patent law students have it especially good. "Big firms don't do a lot of hiring from SCU," though. Even worse, "SCU grads are competing for jobs against graduates of Stanford, Boalt, and Hastings, which makes it tough." Career Services could "use some improvements," complain many students who worry that only those at the very top of the class are well placed. One student contributes that the staff is "nice, but doesn't seem effective."

Santa Clara's "small, bright, pretty, well-maintained, comfortable, and well-equipped" campus boasts "perfectly manicured lawns, flowerbeds everywhere, and palm trees lining the entrance." One student notes, "SCU takes its high-tech reputation seriously and has equipped its campus accordingly." The wireless classrooms "couldn't be better" (though students say there are too few of them). "Research facilities are very high-tech." Another student writes, "There is an Internet connection at every seat, [which makes for] a bunch of clicking from laptops in class." On the study front, the "nice and well-stocked library is too small" to fit these students' needs, it seems. Students are calling for more quiet space, more comfy chairs, and more Internet connections. When exams roll around, "it becomes unbearably busy and noisy."

Jeanette J. Leach, Assistant Dean for Admissions and Diversity Services
500 El Camino Real, Santa Clara, CA 95053
Telephone: 408-554-4800 • Fax: 408-554-7897
E-mail: lawadmissions@scu.edu • Website: www.scu.edu/law

Life

"SCU has one of the most diverse class compositions of any law school," shares one impressed student. "It is really amazing to see the wide range of ethnicities." The mega-diverse law student population at SCU is a "uniformly friendly and nice" bunch. There are a few "whiny students who complain a lot, [and others are] intellectually shallow," but these types are the exception. Despite all the ethnic diversity, most of the students are "still rich kids from LA." Luckily, "SCU does not have a high-pressure atmosphere." While the students at Santa Clara are smart and competitive, they aren't "mean and vicious."

When students are not hitting the books, they can take advantage of "a plethora of clubs and student activities happening at any given time." In the event that available clubs don't cut it, "students are very good about organizing activities on their own." Social activity tends to "stay mostly within your year," writes one student who seems displeased by this fact. The school's "location in the heart of Silicon Valley is very convenient," professionally but not socially. The "tragically boring city" of Santa Clara is "pretty dead [and] lacks of access to nightlife." Some students aren't impressed. "If you call getting drunk at a sleazy dive local bar across the street from campus a 'social life,'" relays one sarcastic student, "then woo-hoo!" Students want you to know that the Bay Area is not right next door, though the location does have its perks, far away from the nightlife of San Francisco. "If you want to be close to San Francisco, go to school close to San Francisco," advises one student. "Santa Clara is about an hour away in light traffic."

Getting In

Admitted students at the 25th percentile have an LSAT score of 156 and a GPA of 3.2. Admitted students at the 75th percentile have an LSAT score of 161 and a GPA of 3.5.

EMPLOYMENT INFORMATION

Career Rating	**90**
Job placement rate (%)	96
Average starting salary	$106,296
State for bar exam	CA
Pass rate for first-time bar	69

Employers who frequently hire grads:
Cooley, Godward; Bingham McCutchen; Reed Smith Crosby Heafey; Morrison & Foerster; Ropers Majeski; Fenwick & West; Wilson Sonsini; Skadden Arps; Miller Morton.

Grads employed by field (%):	
Academic	2
Business/industry	18
Government	13
Judicial clerkships	1
Military	1
Other	7
Private practice	56
Public interest	2

ADMISSIONS

Selectivity Rating	**79**
# applications received	4,538
# applicants accepted	1,194
# acceptees attending	309
Average LSAT	156
LSAT Range	156–161
Average undergrad GPA	3.2
Application fee	$75
Regular application deadline	2/1
Regular notification	rolling
Rolling notification?	Yes
Early application program?	Yes
Early application deadline	11/1
Early application notification	12/15
Transfer students accepted?	Yes
Evening division offered?	Yes
Part-time accepted?	Yes
LSDAS accepted?	Yes

Applicants Also Look At

Pepperdine University, University of California—Hastings, University of San Diego, University of San Francisco.

International Students

TOEFL required of international students?	No
TOEFL recommended of international students?	Yes

FINANCIAL FACTS

Annual tuition	$30,750
Books and supplies	$1,367
Fees per credit	$958
Tuition per credit	$1,025
Room & board	$11,696
Financial aid application deadline	3/1
% first-year students receiving some sort of aid	78
% receiving some sort of aid	79
% of aid that is merit-based	59
% receiving scholarships	28
Average grant	$11,400
Average loan	$28,943
Average total aid package	$40,343
Average debt	$77,743

Seattle University
School of Law

INSTITUTIONAL INFORMATION

Public/private	private
Student/faculty ratio	16:1
Affiliation	Roman Catholic
% faculty part-time	38
% faculty female	42
% faculty minority	17
Total faculty	96

SURVEY SAYS . . .

Great research resources
Great library staff
Beautiful campus

STUDENTS

Enrollment of law school	1,102
% male/female	45/55
% out-of-state	21
% full-time	77
% minority	21
% international	1
# of countries represented	13
Average age of entering class	28

ACADEMICS

Academic Experience rating	**81**
Professors interesting rating	79
Professors accessible rating	76
Hours of study per day	4.71

Academic Specialties

Commercial law, constitutional law, corporation securities law, criminal law, environmental law, estate planning, health law and real estate, human rights law, intellectual property law, international law, labor law, legal writing, poverty law, property, taxation.

Advanced Degrees Offered

School of Law: JD and LLM degrees in 3 yrs & 3.5 yrs. Seattle U.: MBA, MSN, EdD, MAS in psychology or applied economy, MS in software engineering, finance & international business, master's in public administration.

Combined Degrees Offered

JD/MBA, JD/master of intnl. business, JD/MS in finance & JD/master of professional accounting.

Academics

Jesuit-affiliated Seattle University School of Law offers "a vast amount of opportunities for students to get practical, hands-on experience, [and] a commitment to giving back to the community." SU also boasts an "outstanding evening program. The evening students carry diverse backgrounds from various industries that add to the learning environment." Students rave about the "excellent legal writing program, [known as] one of the school's biggest assets." One student explains, "Although the Seattle U legal writing criteria are more demanding than most law schools; the skill level and education I will receive because of it far outweighs the extra time it requires." Another comments, "Employers have commented to me that Seattle U students are better equipped to handle the pressures of writing motions, memos, and briefs. One student verifies this by saying, "My writing skills improved dramatically. I was a strong writer before I came to law school, but I'm pretty damn amazing now. Seattle U Law is exceptional at giving students options," enthuses one future lawyer. The school "offers a strong blend of classroom theory and policy with practical experience through labs, externships, and clinics" in all areas of the law. "The Jesuit influence comes through in SU's elaborate public interest focus in the community," writes one student. Another specifies that there are "lots of opportunities related to social justice, public interest law, and poverty law" at SU. Students cite "the excellence of our Access to Justice Institute" as a great strength, as it provides "a street-front clinic staffed by approximately 80 students [that] serves low-income clients." When the time comes to find a real job, "the alumni base is large, [at least] for those seeking to practice in the Northwest." Still, the general sentiment is that the "Career Services department leaves something to be desired," though the staff's personalities are almost universally appreciated, ("The staff with Career Services rock!"), and the school appears to be working to improve its placement services.

The "amazingly approachable [professors] have practical experience and true enthusiasm for their subjects [and are] deeply committed to their students." A student says, "I enjoyed walking into my first day of classes and finding my professors to be a Southern gentleman, an eccentric Northwesterner, and an erudite clarinet player." But those aren't the only kinds of profs you'll see at SU; "dreadlocked, tongue-pierced" professors are also found on campus. In addition, "the best legal minds in Seattle teach as adjunct professors." Just one major teaching complaint resounds: "The professors need to stop cramming their political views down our throats." Kind words toward administrators were difficult to come by. Students say the "standoffish [administration] could use some friendlier faces." They continue, "Paperwork gets lost, [and] the student handbook looks like it was slapped together at Kinko's." To top it off, classes are difficult to get into. One student gripes, "It would be great if they could arrange to have enough professors to teach the most popular classes."

The "fairly new" facilities at SU are "stunningly beautiful and sophisticated." Classes are large but classrooms are ample, with Internet connections at each seat and wireless access throughout the school. The "sprawling, four-floor [library] has a lot of study rooms, too, but it's almost impossible to reserve one without planning way ahead." Fortunately, "The librarians will assist with any research request, even if it's just to explain (again) where to locate some source." Seattle U also boasts a convenient—though gritty—urban location "close to downtown Seattle."

Carol Cochran, Director of Admissions
901 Twelfth Avenue, Sullivan Hall, PO Box 222000, Seattle, WA 98122-1090
Telephone: 206-398-4200 • Fax: 206-398-4058
E-mail: lawadmis@seattleu.edu • Website: www.law.seattleu.edu

Life

"SU really embraces the differences in people, [and its] commitment to diversity" is noteworthy. "I have never been a part of a more diverse student body," gushes one student. This "very eclectic" crowd of students represents "many different ages and experiences." One student observes that there are "lots of women, minorities, and gays." Students are "black, white, hip, geeky"—you name it. There are "people straight out of undergrad [as well as] older people who work full-time and have families." Politically, "the student body leans left." One student explains, "It's the cause of much whining by Federalist Society members who feel their political sentiments are drowned out. It makes for interesting debate on hot legal issues of the day, which has become entertaining sport at SU." The laid-back attitude of the Pacific Northwest is evident in the student population. "Some people are overly competitive, [but] cutthroat attitudes [are] strongly discouraged." Generally, "students are very respectful of each other, [and] cooperation and support" reign supreme. There are a lot of students at SU, and while "most students seem to get along, it's hard to feel the sense of community."

Despite the size of the student body, social life is thriving at Seattle U, particularly among day students. In fact, "there are far too many social activities." Students say, "Social events are planned in abundance and students excitedly attend—from karaoke nights to political debates." One student promises, "You'll never ever be bored. If you are, you aren't checking your E-mail." It helps that "Seattle is such a [great] town." There are "off-campus recreational and social opportunities" galore—the entire Pacific Coast is "an outdoor recreation haven." One student athlete reports, "The Olympic and Cascade Mountains [are close by,] and there are a number of year-round adult sports leagues (including at least three soccer leagues), so it's easy to find a sanity break away from campus." Another student explains, "Students actually have lives outside of law school, kayaking, mountain climbing, skiing, practicing yoga, or simply raising a family."

Getting In

Admitted students at the 25th percentile have an LSAT score of 153 and a GPA of 3.1. Admitted students at the 75th percentile have an LSAT score of 160 and a GPA of 3.6. If you take the LSAT more than once, Seattle U considers your highest score (though you should do your best to explain away any lower scores).

EMPLOYMENT INFORMATION

Career Rating	**74**
Job placement rate (%)	100
Average starting salary	$61,000
State for bar exam	WA, CA, OR, TX, IL
Pass rate for first-time bar	68

Employers who frequently hire grads: Perkins Coie, Lane Powell Spears Lubersky, King County Prosecuting Attorney, Washington State Attorney General, Williams Kastner & Gibbs, Foster Pepper Shefelman, Preston Gates & Ellis.

Prominent Alumni: Judge Ralph Beistline, federal district court judge; Judge Charles Johnson, Washington State Supreme Court.

Grads employed by field (%):	
Academic	2
Business/industry	33
Government	18
Judicial clerkships	6
Private practice	35
Public interest	4

Academic Requirements

Clinical Program Required?	No
Legal Writing Course Requirement?	Yes
Legal Methods Course Requirement?	No
Legal Research Course Requirement?	Yes
Moot Court Requirement?	No
Public Interest Law Requirement?	No

ADMISSIONS

Selectivity Rating	**80**
# applications received	2,920
# applicants accepted	818
# acceptees attending	342
Average LSAT	156
LSAT Range	153–160
Average undergrad GPA	3.4
Application fee	$50
Regular application deadline	4/1
Regular notification	rolling
Rolling notification?	Yes
Early application program?	No
Transfer students accepted?	Yes
Evening division offered?	Yes
Part-time accepted?	Yes
LSDAS accepted?	Yes

Applicants Also Look At

Gonzaga University, Lewis & Clark College, Santa Clara University, University of Oregon, University of San Francisco, University of Washington.

International Students

TOEFL required of international students?	Yes
Minimum Computer TOEFL	250

FINANCIAL FACTS

Annual tuition	$25,980
Books and supplies	$903
Tuition per credit	$866
Room & board (off-campus)	$14,983
Financial aid application deadline	3/1
% first-year students receiving some sort of aid	98
% receiving some sort of aid	99
% of aid that is merit-based	42
% receiving scholarships	45
Average grant	$5,900
Average loan	$27,694
Average total aid package	$31,364
Average debt	$69,231

Seton Hall University
School of Law

INSTITUTIONAL INFORMATION

Public/private	private
Student/faculty ratio	17:1
Affiliation	Roman Catholic
% faculty part-time	58
% faculty female	36
% faculty minority	16
Total faculty	145

SURVEY SAYS . . .

Diverse opinions accepted in classrooms
Great research resources
Great library staff

STUDENTS

Enrollment of law school	1,234
% male/female	56/44
% out-of-state	30
% full-time	70
% minority	17
% international	3
# of countries represented	19
Average age of entering class	25

ACADEMICS

Academic Experience rating	**74**
Professors interesting rating	73
Professors accessible rating	70
Hours of study per day	3.86

Academic Specialties

Intellectual property law, health law.

Advanced Degrees Offered

JD, 3 years full-time, 4 years part-time; LLM, 1 year full-time, 2 years part-time; MSJ, 1 year full-time, 2 years part-time.

Combined Degrees Offered

JD/MD, 6 years; MD/MSJ, 5 years; JD/MBA, 4 years; JD/MADIR international relations, 4 years.

Academic Requirements

Clinical Program Required?	No
Legal Writing Course Requirement?	Yes
Legal Methods Course Requirement?	No
Legal Research Course Requirement?	Yes

Academics

As part of its mission statement, Seton Hall aspires to treat all individuals with dignity, justice, and compassion. In line with that philosophy, students at this large, New Jersey law school receive a rigorous legal education in the context of a nurturing and student-centered environment. By almost all accounts, the accomplished faculty is the school's greatest strength, bringing expertise, passion, and enthusiasm to the classroom. At Seton Hall, you will be taught by "great legal minds" and "leading experts in the fields of criminal procedure, property, and evidence, among others." Faculty brings more than impressive credentials to the table, though: "Professors view teaching as their first priority, so even though they have other responsibilities around the community, they are teachers ahead of anything. I can't stress how much of a relief this is as a first-year who is just learning the ropes," one student notes. Adds another, "From standing on tables barefoot, to portraying unilateral contracts using an analogy to *The Wizard of Oz*, to wearing a cheese-head throughout a lecture, to 'Porno Wednesday' in criminal law, the professors have demonstrated their mastery of presenting legal theory in a highly entertaining manner."

The student-centered approach extends well beyond the lecture hall, and "professors can relate to a broad spectrum of individuals and can comfortably talk about anything ranging from the First Amendment to last night's Yankees–Red Sox game." Students love the surprisingly individualized attention they receive from the faculty and are quick to share anecdotes about their outgoing professors: "I have had professors make phone calls and e-mails on my behalf several times regarding jobs and internships," reports a 1L. A 2L recounts that "one professor called me at home on Thanksgiving night to answer a question I had that did not relate to school."

The Seton Hall administration demonstrates a "sincere interest in the students." In particular, "Seton Hall Law takes student evaluations very seriously and employs rigorous screening procedures for hiring new faculty members and in promoting current ones." Outside the classroom "the deans go out of their way to counsel 1Ls in making the transition into law school less painful" and work hard to maintain a number of special, student-friendly programs. Attentive to detail, the deans provide "those little touches that set the school apart from others." For example, "on the first day of orientation, Seton Hall gives you a key chain with the dean's home and cell phone numbers," and "if you are sick, they'll send a car to pick you up at school and drive you to the health center." Unfailingly friendly, students say they "feel very welcome approaching almost all administrators," and a 3L tells us, "Dean Patrick Hobbs is as good looking as a movie star, runs a great school, and can often be seen chatting with students well into the night." There are, however, some general grumbles that the administration can be inefficient in responding to individual students' concerns. In particular, many students complain that "Financial Aid takes their time in processing and delivering the loan checks to the students," which can lead to some damaging financial issues for struggling students.

The Seton Hall campus and facilities are first-rate. "The building is relatively new, so the classrooms are big and clean, with outlets for pretty much every seat. The library is great and the staff is really helpful," comments one 2L. Located in Newark, New Jersey, the campus isn't set in the Garden of Eden, but it is nonetheless a propitious place for the ambitious law student. A 3L explains, "While Newark is not pretty, the district and circuit courts, as well as the U.S. Attorney's Office and Federal Defender, are all within a 10- to 15-minute (entirely safe) walk from school. The school's contacts with those offices are excellent." While Seton Hall focuses more on the theoretical aspects of legal educa-

Ms. Gisele Joachim, Assistant Dean of Admissions and Financial Aid
One Newark Center, Newark, NJ 7102
Telephone: 888-415-7271 • Fax: 973-642-8876
E-mail: admitme@shu.edu • Website: http://law.shu.edu

tion, the clinical and externship opportunities in the surrounding area are nothing to sneeze at. A case in point: "The clinical program offered at Seton Hall Law is excellent. I participated in the Immigration clinic, and I found it to be the most rewarding experience of my academic career." On top of that, Seton Hall has a "good reputation in the tri-state area" and "has really great ties in New Jersey." Additionally, many are pleased to report that "each year we have more New York firms coming to campus to recruit students, as well as more firms participating in the resume drop. I've talked to alums from a few years back and they're really impressed with the response that many of us have gotten from NY firms."

Life

Seton Hall is home to a lively academic and intellectual atmosphere. After class, "Seton Hall Law provides many interesting seminars or presentations where prominent guests are featured or professors present lectures on practical aspects of law." On top of that, "the student government does a good job in holding social events for the students, as well as public service activities to help the community." However, given the fact that most students commute, the feeling of a campus community is not particularly strong. A 3L elaborates, "The school certainly suffers from the fact that most students commute to it from NYC and elsewhere in NJ. Let's face it: No one wants to live in Newark."

While Seton Hall is a historically Catholic institution, students hail from all backgrounds, cultures, and walks of life. A 1L elaborates, "It is a Catholic school, but there isn't a huge religious vibe. I have friends here who are Mormon, Jewish, Sikh, and agnostic." In fact, a 2L reports that the "law school has a fully supported gay and lesbian student group that functions well and is a leadership group within the school."

Getting In

Admissions to Seton Hall are competitive. Every year, the school receives almost 3,000 applications for about 310 first-year seats. Admissions decisions are based primarily on the strength of a candidate's undergraduate record and test scores; however, the admissions committee may take other factors into consideration, such as graduate education or work experience.

EMPLOYMENT INFORMATION

Career Rating	**75**
Job placement rate (%)	95
Average starting salary	$53,003
State for bar exam	NJ, NY
Pass rate for first-time bar	84

Employers who frequently hire grads:
Graduates are frequently hired by the most prestigious firms in the United States, all national and state government agencies, public interest organizations, and state and federal judges nationwide.

Prominent Alumni: Anthony Principi, former secretary of veterans affairs; Christopher Christie, U.S. attorney for the State of New Jersey.

Grads employed by field (%):	
Academic	1
Business/industry	12
Government	6
Judicial clerkships	38
Military	1
Private practice	41
Public interest	1

Moot Court Requirement?	Yes
Public Interest Law Requirement?	No

ADMISSIONS

Selectivity Rating	**83**
# applications received	2,883
# applicants accepted	702
# acceptees attending	189
Average LSAT	160
LSAT Range	158–162
Average undergrad GPA	3.3
Application fee	$65
Regular application deadline	4/1
Regular notification	rolling
Rolling notification?	Yes
Early application program?	No
Transfer students accepted?	Yes
Evening division offered?	Yes
Part-time accepted?	Yes
LSDAS accepted?	Yes

Applicants Also Look At

Brooklyn Law School; Fordham University; New York Law School; Rutgers, The State University of New Jersey—Newark; St. John's University.

International Students

TOEFL required of international students?	No
TOEFL recommended of international students?	Yes
Minimum Paper TOEFL	600
Minimum Computer TOEFL	250

FINANCIAL FACTS

Annual tuition	$29,760
Books and supplies	$1,100
Tuition per credit	$992
Room & board (off-campus)	$11,100
Financial aid application deadline	4/1
% first-year students receiving some sort of aid	88
% receiving some sort of aid	88
% of aid that is merit-based	16
Average grant	$12,725
Average loan	$34,500
Average total aid package	$47,225
Average debt	$81,500

SOUTH TEXAS COLLEGE OF LAW

INSTITUTIONAL INFORMATION

Public/private	private
Student/faculty ratio	20:1
% faculty part-time	42
% faculty female	25
% faculty minority	8
Total faculty	104

SURVEY SAYS . . .

Diverse opinions accepted in classrooms
Great research resources
Great library staff

STUDENTS

Enrollment of law school	1,254
% male/female	54/46
% out-of-state	7
% full-time	76
% minority	20
# of countries represented	1
Average age of entering class	27

ACADEMICS

Academic Experience rating	**75**
Professors interesting rating	74
Professors accessible rating	73
Hours of study per day	3.79

Academic Specialties

Advocacy.

Academic Requirements

Clinical Program Required?	No
Legal Writing Course Requirement?	Yes
Legal Methods Course Requirement?	Yes
Legal Research Course Requirement?	Yes
Moot Court Requirement?	No
Public Interest Law Requirement?	No

Academics

"From where do the best advocates come?" A slew of them come from South Texas College of Law, where "theory is only taught when it is needed. The rest is practical lawyering skills." The moot court teams are, reportedly, simply legendary. Students get to see their school's name appear "as the national champion time and time again." One student brags, "Every student who graduates from South Texas is fully prepared to walk into any courtroom in the country and competently represent the interests of any client." Another student agrees, "The training that we get prepares us for the real world. I am being groomed to stand in a courtroom and represent my clients by talking to a judge, rather than to talk on a phone and write letters crammed with legalese."

Students tell us, "South Texas is steeped in a tradition of excellent teaching." The faculty is "passionate about the material, down to earth, [and] funny." One student writes, "Most professors have actually practiced for a number of years. Their practical experience and personal anecdotes contribute greatly to the learning experience." And if you attend STCL, according to students, you will be "able to walk into any professor's office and have them know your name." The administration is "very responsive" but sometimes "insists on treating students like children." Many students moan, "Communication between the school and the students is extremely poor." The "inflexible" registrar comes in for harsh criticism. There are lots of courses, but the registration system is "outdated." Note also that "STCL will never be accused of grade inflation." The "steep curve (at or below B-minus) causes problems" for the less academically ambitious.

Opportunities to gain practical experience are excellent. "You are given the opportunity to participate in a wide variety of clinics and clerkships," writes one student. And career prospects are solid in Houston. "We have the luxury of being downtown in the state's largest city [and the fourth largest in the nation]. There are more attorneys than anywhere else in Texas, and this leads to great job opportunities," claims one student. "We are a local law school," explains another student. "Our roots are in Houston, and if someone is interested in practicing here, then South Texas is a great choice." However, there is still the complaint that statewide and national exposure could improve."

South Texas is "located in a building comprising one city block [which] also houses the First and fourteenth State Courts of Appeals." It boasts "the best law library in the state of Texas [and a] fantastic" library staff. The "brand-new [library] has floor-to-ceiling window panels that overlook the city, making for awesome views day or night." Another plus is that every seat in the place has access to the Internet," and study rooms are "unlimited." Not surprisingly, the local legal community frequently uses the college's library. The "overall building, [however,] needs a good bath."

Life

The great thing about South Texas College of Law, say students, is that "everyone has a chance regardless of family background." "I know that my success is based on my achievement," asserts one meritocratic student. "Even though giving some people a chance may lower the school's ranking in [*U.S. News & World Report*], it's the right thing to do and it provides an environment more reflective of the real world." The student population is "similar to the demographics of Houston [and] highly diverse [in terms of] gender, ethnicity, and age." The college has many part-time and evening students as well.

This place is "competitive. Cutthroat is a kind term," suggests one student. "There are

Alicia K. Cramer, Assistant Dean of Admissions
1303 San Jacinto Street, Houston, TX 77002-7000
Telephone: 713-646-1810 • Fax: 713-646-2906
E-mail: admissions@stcl.edu • Website: www.stcl.edu

numerous examples of people unwilling to share notes or study together because they are afraid this will give other people an edge." Another notes, "There are people who return casebooks and digests to the wrong place," too.

"Despite the competition, camaraderie is high," asserts one evenhanded student. "Although you may have 100 people in some classes with popular professors, it is not uncommon to know 25 to 50 percent of those people." One student observes, "There seems to be a group of people for everyone to hang out with." Another student continues, "It is very common to have groups of tightly knit students who spend time with each other, [and] within organizations like Law Review and Board of Advocates, the members become like a family." However, there is not an overwhelming common social experience. The "incredibly active" Student Bar Association gives it the old college try, though. "Free kegs on the terrace of the library" are the centerpieces of popular student get-togethers. If you like sports, the college's "decent [location] in a rejuvenated part of downtown" is near Minute Maid Park, home of the Astros, and the Toyota Center, where the Rockets play.

Getting In

For the most part, solid undergraduate grades and LSAT scores are necessary to gain admittance to South Texas College of Law, but the college is known to take a chance on otherwise promising applicants who didn't have stellar grades in college. Admitted students in the 25th percentile had an LSAT score of 151 and an undergraduate GPA of 3.1. Admitted students in the 75th percentile had an LSAT score of 157 and an undergraduate GPA of 3.5.

EMPLOYMENT INFORMATION

Career Rating	**78**
Job placement rate (%)	84
Average starting salary	$73,673
State for bar exam	TX
Pass rate for first-time bar	65

Employers who frequently hire grads:
Private law firms, corporations, and government entities.

Grads employed by field (%):	
Business/industry	10
Government	11
Judicial clerkships	4
Other	2
Private practice	72
Public interest	1

ADMISSIONS

Selectivity Rating	**76**
# applications received	2,710
# applicants accepted	869
# acceptees attending	333
Average LSAT	154
LSAT Range	151–157
Average undergrad GPA	3.3
Application fee	$50
Regular application deadline	2/25
Regular notification	5/25
Rolling notification?	No
Early application program?	No
Transfer students accepted?	Yes
Evening division offered?	Yes
Part-time accepted?	Yes
LSDAS accepted?	Yes

Applicants Also Look At

Southern Methodist University, St. Mary's University, Texas Tech University, University of Houston, The University of Texas at Austin.

International Students

TOEFL required of international students?	No
TOEFL recommended of international students?	No

FINANCIAL FACTS

Annual tuition	$19,170
Books and supplies	$962
Room & board (off-campus)	$7,834
Financial aid application deadline	5/1
% first-year students receiving some sort of aid	84
% receiving some sort of aid	91
% of aid that is merit-based	3
% receiving scholarships	73
Average grant	$3,302
Average loan	$23,795
Average total aid package	$28,251
Average debt	$73,745

SOUTHERN ILLINOIS UNIVERSITY
SCHOOL OF LAW

INSTITUTIONAL INFORMATION

Public/private	public
Student/faculty ratio	14:1
% faculty part-time	30
% faculty female	47
% faculty minority	10
Total faculty	47

SURVEY SAYS . . .

Diverse opinions accepted in classrooms
Great research resources
Great library staff

STUDENTS

Enrollment of law school	390
% male/female	64/36
% out-of-state	33
% full-time	99
% minority	6
Average age of entering class	25

ACADEMICS

Academic Experience rating	**66**
Professors interesting rating	63
Professors accessible rating	86
Hours of study per day	4.45

Advanced Degrees Offered

JD, 3 years; MLS, 2 years; LLM, 2 years.

Combined Degrees Offered

JD/MD, 6 years; JD/MBA, 4 years; JD/MPA, 4 years; JD/MAcc, 4 years; JD/MSW; JD/MSEd; JD/PhD.

Academic Requirements

Clinical Program Required?	No
Legal Writing Course Requirement?	No
Legal Methods Course Requirement?	Yes
Legal Research Course Requirement?	No
Moot Court Requirement?	No
Public Interest Law Requirement?	No

Academics

Southern Illinois University School of Law is a very small and very affordable bastion of legal education that is "small enough to make students comfortable, yet large enough to provide a quality education." The school is characterized by a relaxed and "friendly atmosphere." One student says, "To me, it is nice to have an informal atmosphere to discuss the issues presented. It seems to lend itself more to learning than to memorizing." Another plus is the fact that SIU is "the only law school in the area." One student explains, "We are the legal hub of the region. All of the federal and state judges from the region focus their attentions on us and utilize our resources."

Most agree, "Hands down, the greatest strength of SIU is the professors, not only because of their knowledge and teaching ability, but also because or their desire to get to know the students." Professors stimulate discussion, "providing encouragement in- and outside of the classroom." A satisfied student promises, "There is never a time that a professor won't see you, help you, or just stop to chat." Another writes, "The teachers are so willing to help students on a one-on-one basis," attesting to the faculty's level of accessibility. "They want to help you get through law school [and] make you a better lawyer." The "open-door policy" by which the faculty abides extends to the approachable administration as well. One student confirms, "Because of the small size of the law school, you're just as likely to get a 'hello' from the dean as you are from your torts professor." Furthermore, a student notes, "If you have problems, [the top brass] will almost always drop what they are doing to help."

While some insist that the law school "needs to offer more classes, [including those] that address issues of race, gender, ability, or sexuality in the law," and a comparative legal studies class, students at SIU have a solid curriculum and a respectable array of clinics and practical opportunities. The legal writing course at SIU covers client interviewing, client counseling, advocacy, and negotiation in addition to meat-and-potatoes writing and research. Students in the externship program work for local judges and a host of other government capacities. There is also a pro bono family law clinic, a traditional Alternative Dispute Resolution Clinic (in which students mediate small claims, landlord-tenant disputes, and the occasional juvenile case), and the unique Illinois Agriculture Mediation Program, which offers dispute resolution services to farmers in Illinois. Also, a host of dual-degree programs includes a JD/MD, a JD/PhD in political science, and the ever-popular JD/MBA.

As far as facilities are concerned, SIU does an adequate job of providing students with the necessary resources. "The library is excellent," and all law students enjoy 24/7 library access, which is a tremendously underrated and rare perk. The law school building "was overhauled just five years ago." Nevertheless, students tell us they could use a little more breathing room.

Michael Ruiz, Director of Admissions
SIU School of Law Welcome Center, 1209 West Chautauqua, Mailcode 6811,
Carbondale, IL 62901
Telephone: 618-453-8858 • Fax: 618-453-8921
E-mail: lawadmit@siu.edu • Website: www.law.siu.edu

Life

Everyone is "motivated to do well," of course, and SIU students may "want to beat each other for the top grade." Nevertheless, most students are "not cutthroat competitive." A 3L says, "I have found that the students are supportive of each other academically and socially."

The general consensus is that "the law school needs a more diverse student body." Students say that in addition to a lack of ethnic diversity, "women make up much less than half of the class." Although there are more than 20,000 students enrolled in the university, fewer than 400 students are enrolled in the law school, which makes for a strong "overall sense of community" within the tiny subpopulation of future attorneys. The Student Bar Association plays a pretty huge role in the social scene at SIU. "Law school activities are what you make them," says one student. "If you don't get involved then people are not going to pressure you into it, but there are plenty of student organizations for everyone."

The "semi-urban" surrounding town of Carbondale is a neat little berg full of interesting shops, ethnic restaurants galore, and more than a few one-way streets. Carbondale is surrounded by "rural outlying areas" for miles in every direction. Naturally, "median incomes in the area are much lower than, say, New York City. However, the cost of living is virtually nothing in comparison." The beautiful wooded campus is peaceful and "surrounded by nature's beauty, with a lake minutes away, [and] trees abound." For the outdoor enthusiast, the area offers hiking trails, mountain biking, and bluffs for repelling.

Getting In

Admitted students at the 25th percentile have an LSAT score of 150 and a GPA of 3.1. Admitted students at the 75th percentile have an LSAT score of 155 and a GPA of 3.6. The average age of entry is 26.

EMPLOYMENT INFORMATION

Career Rating	**62**
% employed within 9 months	83
Average starting salary	$42,387
State for bar exam	IL, MO
Pass rate for first-time bar	84

Employers who frequently hire grads: Various Illinois state's attorney's offices, various large and many small law firms, various public interest organizations.

Prominent Alumni: Gordon Fischer, chairperson of the Iowa Democratic party; Tim Eaton, partner, Ungaretti & Harris; William Birkett, associate general counsel, INS, Washington, DC; Lisa Joley, general counsel, Anheuser-Busch.

Grads employed by field (%):	
Academic	1
Business/industry	2
Government	31
Private practice	56
Public interest	6

ADMISSIONS

Selectivity Rating	**73**
# applications received	754
# applicants accepted	291
# acceptees attending	129
Average LSAT	153
LSAT Range	151–156
Average undergrad GPA	3.4
Application fee	$50
Regular application deadline	3/1
Regular notification	rolling
Rolling notification?	Yes
Early application program?	No
Transfer students accepted?	Yes
Evening division offered?	No
Part-time accepted?	No
LSDAS accepted?	Yes

Applicants Also Look At

Northern Illinois University.

International Students

TOEFL required of international students?	Yes
Minimum Paper TOEFL	600

FINANCIAL FACTS

Annual tuition (resident)	$7,590
Annual tuition (nonresident)	$22,770
Books and supplies	$1,080
Room & board	$6,682
Financial aid application deadline	4/1
% first-year students receiving some sort of aid	100
% receiving some sort of aid	86
% receiving scholarships	46
Average grant	$3,100
Average loan	$19,170
Average total aid package	$19,170
Average debt	$45,623

Southern Methodist University
Dedman School of Law

INSTITUTIONAL INFORMATION

Public/private	private
Student/faculty ratio	16:1
Affiliation	Methodist
% faculty female	33
% faculty minority	15

SURVEY SAYS . . .

Beautiful campus
Students love Dallas, TX

STUDENTS

Enrollment of law school	861
% male/female	50/50
% full-time	61
% minority	27
# of countries represented	14
Average age of entering class	27

ACADEMICS

Academic Experience rating	**73**
Professors interesting rating	91
Professors accessible rating	81
Hours of study per day	4.27

Advanced Degrees Offered

LLM taxation, 1 year; LLM general, 1 year; LLM comparative & international law, 1 year.

Combined Degrees Offered

JD/MBA, 4 years; JD/MA, 4 years.

Academic Requirements

Clinical Program Required?	No
Legal Writing Course Requirement?	Yes
Legal Methods Course Requirement?	No
Legal Research Course Requirement?	Yes
Moot Court Requirement?	Yes
Public Interest Law Requirement?	Yes

Academics

Small classes are the norm on the "small, beautiful campus" of Southern Methodist University's Dedman School of Law, where "you can learn from some of the best professors in the country in a close-knit community." SMU reportedly has "a great reputation around Dallas," for a good reason: upward of 90 percent of SMU's graduates pass the Texas bar exam on their first try, while the Lone Star State average hovers around 80 percent. A unique JD/MA program allows students to study economics as well as law, and about 25 to 35 students have the opportunity each summer to study abroad in Oxford.

Most students say that their professors "meld the Socratic Method with cooperative engagement [and are] eager to share their knowledge, experience, and friendship." One student comments, "All in all, I believe SMU has the best lineup of professors in the state. Several of the 1L classes are taught by professors who are regarded throughout the state as the authorities on the subject matter they teach." Another student opines, "The professors are some of the most interesting and intelligent people I have ever met. I have only had one or two that I would not recommend to a friend." Though some feel, "For such a small school, dealing with administration is way more trouble than it should be," most say the "friendly and helpful [administration] has a great vision for the school and is leading things in the right direction." One particularly proud student adds, "They always make time for the students, and I have felt like a part of the SMU family since my first day of class."

Employment prospects for SMU law graduates are generally promising. "We realize that with a degree from SMU Law we will all get great offers," brags one student. Another informs us that "SMU is a fantastic school for corporate law, especially big firm practice." If this is what you're looking for, you'll probably leave a satisfied customer, like this student: "I could not have chosen a better school! I am certain that when I start my job with a large Dallas firm next fall that I will be able to perform with confidence based on the practical education that I learned at SMU!" Indeed, one student summed up SMU's fortes as "contacts in Dallas, reputation in Texas, and strength in corporate law." The flip side of the coin is that students seeking out a degree in public interest law may find less support in this environment. We hear a few complaints about a strict "B-curve," which reportedly "makes it harder to compete for jobs." One student gripes, "Not all of us want to practice in Dallas. It would be nice if they would network with firms that are outside the Dallas–Forth Worth Metroplex." Ultimately, "if you want to work in Dallas, SMU is the school. But if you want to go elsewhere, you'll have to work hard."

Students are happy with the facilities, especially the library, which is considered "top-notch" by most. The existence of the wireless network in the library draws accolades, though some groan that it "should work better and should be in all of the classrooms." Though some whine about the classrooms, one student speaks for the majority saying, "The school has invested a lot of money to make the facilities nice and upgrade the library and classrooms to the highest degree of technology, while maintaining the Jeffersonian appeal."

Virginia Keehan, Assistant Dean and Director of Admissions
PO Box 750110, Dallas, TX 75275-0110
Telephone: 214-768-2550 • Fax: 214-768-2549
E-mail: lawadmit@mail.smu.edu • Website: www.law.smu.edu

Life

"My classmates are gregarious, fun, interesting people," contributes one student, while another describes them as "bright and engaging." But while some feel that the student body is "diverse in terms of age, experiences, and socioeconomic status," many disagree. "I would like to see more people who bring something different to the table," remarks one student, "whether it be racial background, significant life experiences, or simply not [hailing] from Texas." The law school offers over $5 million in scholarship aid as well as five clinics for the underprivileged, but students relentlessly dog SMU for being "the country club law school." These "affluent and overwhelmingly conservative" students repeatedly describe themselves as "rich white kids." One student observes, "Our law school garage looks like a joke. Where else are you going to find 22-year-olds who own Land Rovers, BMWs, and Hummers?"

Students tell us that while SMU fosters "a very competitive atmosphere, students are still very encouraging and helpful to one another." They are "collegial yet serious-minded; there is a realization that there is no reason to be uptight and competitive," resulting in "lots of studying followed by lots of playing." Many students contend, "There is a high spirit of community here at the law school, and socializing is encouraged by the faculty and school itself." They continue, "We have happy hour every week," and among students, "there is tremendous involvement with the school and with each other." Other students regret that "there is no sense of community. Since almost everyone has previously lived in Dallas, they tend to stay in their pre-law school groups." Whatever the case, everyone agrees that Dallas is "one of the liveliest cities in the South." Another notes, "You can't beat a school located smack-dab in the middle of Highland Park, five minutes from downtown." Oh, and "the weather is beautiful," too.

Getting In

The median LSAT score for admitted students is 163. The median GPA of admitted students is 3.75. Admitted students at the 25th percentile have an LSAT score of 156. Admitted students at the 75th percentile have an LSAT score of 164. In fall of 2004, SMU Law began offering an evening law program.

ADMISSIONS

Selectivity Rating	**60***
# applications received	2,650
# applicants accepted	405
# acceptees attending	175
LSAT Range	156–164
Application fee	$50
Regular application deadline	2/15
Regular notification	4/30
Rolling notification?	Yes
Early application program?	Yes
Early application deadline	12/1
Early application notification	1/31
Transfer students accepted?	Yes
Evening division offered?	Yes
Part-time accepted?	Yes
LSDAS accepted?	Yes

Applicants Also Look At

Baylor University, University of Houston, The University of Texas at Austin.

International Students

TOEFL required of international students?	No
TOEFL recommended of international students?	No

FINANCIAL FACTS

Annual tuition	$26,860
Books and supplies	$1,800
Fees per credit	$95
Tuition per credit	$917
Financial aid application deadline	6/1
% of aid that is merit-based	100
Average grant	$17,000
Average loan	$21,500

EMPLOYMENT INFORMATION

Career Rating	**85**
% employed within 9 months	96
Average starting salary	$78,000
State for bar exam	TX
Pass rate for first-time bar	88

Employers who frequently hire grads: Akin Gump Strauss Hauer & Feld LLP, Baker Botts, Haynes and Boone, Jones Day Reavis & Pogue, Vinson & Elkins, Dallas County district attorney's office.

Prominent Alumni: Michael Boone, Haynes & Boone; Harriett Miers, White House counsel; Felis Tsai, chairman, Cathay Life Insurance; Bill Hutchison, president, Hutchison Oil & Gas.

Grads employed by field (%):

Academic	2
Business/industry	12
Government	8
Judicial clerkships	5
Military	1
Private practice	67
Public interest	2

SOUTHWESTERN UNIVERSITY
SCHOOL OF LAW

INSTITUTIONAL INFORMATION

Public/private	private
Student/faculty ratio	16:1
% faculty part-time	27
% faculty female	32
% faculty minority	20
Total faculty	76

SURVEY SAYS . . .

Diverse opinions accepted in classrooms
Great research resources
Great library staff
Beautiful campus

STUDENTS

Enrollment of law school	979
% male/female	49/51
% out-of-state	15
% full-time	71
% minority	34
% international	2
# of countries represented	19
Average age of entering class	27

ACADEMICS

Academic Experience rating	**75**
Professors interesting rating	71
Professors accessible rating	75
Hours of study per day	3.64

Academic Specialties

Civil procedure, commercial law, constitutional law, corporation securities law, criminal law, environmental law, entertainment & media law, government services, human rights law, intellectual property law, international law, labor law, legal history, legal philosophy, property, taxation.

Advanced Degrees Offered

Besides the JD degree, Southwestern offers the only LLM in entertainment and media law, which can can be completed in 1 year full-time and 2 years part-time.

Academic Requirements

Clinical Program Required?	No

Academics

Housed in a spectacular art deco building, boasting a diverse student body, and maintaining deep ties within the entertainment industry, Southwestern University School of Law is the quintessential Southern California institution. Students praise their enthusiastic teachers, calling them "fun, funny, and very good at teaching." In addition to "making the material interesting," Southwestern profs also establish meaningful bonds with their students. "The relationships I have formed with select faculty members," says one student, "have made my overall academic experience particularly memorable." Another students adds, "The faculty is readily available and sincerely interested in involving themselves in the lives of their students and helping them achieve their goals."

Southwestern offers a number of strong practical programs and externship opportunities, allowing students to gain important professional experience outside of the classroom. Southwestern's nationally recognized moot court program is an especially "rewarding experience." Students relish the opportunity it offers to "really get to know faculty members [and] fellow students [while being] part of a team that works toward a common goal—making our school look good." Being located in LA means Southwestern has strong ties in the entertainment industry, offering additional classes and externships for students who are interested in entertainment or intellectual property law. Students find "The externship program is a fabulous way for students to gain experience in a field that otherwise would prove very difficult [to enter]."

In addition to offering the only LLM in Entertainment and Media Law in the country, Southwestern offers a number of flexible JD degree options, including a three-year, full-time day program, a four-year part-time evening program, and a four-year part-time day program. Students also have the option of pursuing an accelerated JD over the course of two years. While some law schools have trouble balancing the needs of diverse student groups, students in the part-time and evening programs say they are pleased with the attention and resources available to them. One nontraditional student who worked for years and has a family says, "By providing qualified students with the opportunity to attend law school part-time, Southwestern is embracing both a need by applicants that most schools ignore and a need by firms for new lawyers with more real-life experience under their belt." Another student reports, "The school has made an effort to provide the PLEAS (Part-time Legal Education At Southwestern) students with separate luncheons and programs in an effort to help us feel supported." Southwestern also offers overseas programs in England, Argentina, Mexico, and Canada.

Despite their excellent education and solid placement rate, Southwestern students feel that they are at a disadvantage after graduation because the school's tough grading policies may make them less appealing to future employers. The mandatory grading curve is "a killer in the highly competitive legal environment of Los Angeles."

Anne Wilson, Director of Admissions
675 South Westmoreland Avenue, Los Angeles, CA 90005
Telephone: 213-738-6717 • Fax: 213-383-1688
E-mail: admissions@swlaw.edu • Website: www.swlaw.edu

"Southwestern has the most incredible campus with state-of-the art everything." Most impressive is the art-deco Bullocks Wilshire Building, which is "eye candy and totally cool," in addition to being a Los Angeles Historic-Cultural Monument that is listed in the National Register of Historic Places. "So beautiful I could cry," says one student. The "outstanding" library also scores high marks. Of this "fabulous resource," students say, "It feels good to study there." While "the classrooms are new and technologically advanced, [they] are not hooked up to the Internet, so you can't search the web or check e-mail during classes." Is that really a valid complaint?

Life

Located in downtown Los Angeles, Southwestern is surrounded by some of the world's best shopping, dining, and nightlife. Too bad students are usually in the library. One student estimates how much studying goes on at Southwestern, "I think the average time for first-years is 3 to 4 hours a night." Maybe it's because of the curve, but students are "very competitive." Still the overall vibe on campus is friendly. As one student puts it, "Southwestern's community atmosphere makes students feel as if they are part of a small family." Given its location, it is no surprise that Southwestern is home to "a very liberal student body."

Getting In

Southwestern is proud of its diverse student body and seeks students who will add their own unique experience to the campus community. In addition to a completed application, students must submit LSAT scores, letters of recommendation, and a personal statement. Students applying for the two-year JD program must also interview with a faculty member. Most admits submit LSAT scores between 155–159 and had an undergraduate GPA of 3.2 or higher.

EMPLOYMENT INFORMATION

Career Rating	**81**
Job placement rate (%)	97
Average starting salary	$82,000
State for bar exam	CA, NY, NV, WA, FL
Pass rate for first-time bar	71

Employers who frequently hire grads: Gibson, Dunn, & Crutcher; Lewis Brisbois Bisgaard & Smith; O'Melveny & Meyers; Sedgwick, Detert, Moran, & Arnold.

Prominent Alumni: Tom Bradley, LA mayor for 20 years; Stanley Mosk, longest serving California Supreme Court justice; Honorable Vaino Spencer, first African American female judge in California & third in the United States.

Grads employed by field (%):	
Academic	1
Business/industry	11
Government	8
Judicial clerkships	1
Military	1
Other	12
Private practice	63
Public interest	3

Legal Writing Course Requirement?	Yes
Legal Methods Course Requirement?	Yes
Legal Research Course Requirement?	Yes
Moot Court Requirement?	Yes
Public Interest Law Requirement?	No

ADMISSIONS

Selectivity Rating	**81**
# applications received	3,316
# applicants accepted	818
# acceptees attending	267
Average LSAT	157
LSAT Range	152–158
Average undergrad GPA	3.4
Application fee	$50
Regular application deadline	6/30
Regular notification	rolling
Rolling notification?	Yes
Early application program?	No
Transfer students accepted?	Yes
Evening division offered?	Yes
Part-time accepted?	Yes
LSDAS accepted?	Yes

Applicants Also Look At

Loyola Marymount University, Pepperdine University, University of California—Hastings, University of California—Los Angeles, University of San Diego, University of Southern California.

International Students

TOEFL required of international students?	No
TOEFL recommended of international students?	No

FINANCIAL FACTS

Annual tuition	$28,500
Books and supplies	$1,200
Tuition per credit	$950
Room & board (off-campus)	$16,200
Financial aid application deadline	6/2
% first-year students receiving some sort of aid	85
% receiving some sort of aid	93
% receiving scholarships	26
Average grant	$6,528
Average loan	$27,967
Average total aid package	$30,610
Average debt	$79,802

THE STATE UNIVERSITY OF NEW YORK
UNIVERSITY AT BUFFALO LAW SCHOOL

INSTITUTIONAL INFORMATION

Public/private	public
Student/faculty ratio	14:1
% faculty part-time	51
% faculty female	36
% faculty minority	7
Total faculty	110

SURVEY SAYS . . .

Diverse opinions accepted in classrooms
Great research resources
Great library staff

STUDENTS

Enrollment of law school	734
% male/female	47/53
% out-of-state	3
% full-time	99
% minority	18
% international	6
# of countries represented	17
Average age of entering class	25

ACADEMICS

Academic Experience rating	**72**
Professors interesting rating	71
Professors accessible rating	63
Hours of study per day	3.66

Academic Specialties

Affordable housing/community economic development, civil litigation, corporation securities law, criminal law, environmental law, family law, government services, health law, human rights law, intellectual property law, international law, labor law, law/social justice.

Advanced Degrees Offered

LLM in criminal law, 1 yr; LLM general for International Students, 1 yr.

Combined Degrees Offered

JD/MSW, 4 yrs; JD/MBA, 4 yrs; JD/MPH, 4 yrs; JD/MLS, 4 yrs; JD/MA applied economics, 3.5 yrs; JD/MA, 4 yrs; JD/PhD, 5 to 6 yrs.

Academic Requirements

Clinical Program Required? No

Academics

Described by its students as "one of the best educational values going," University at Buffalo Law School offers a high quality academic program for a low, public-school price tag. But more than its affordability, its laid-back, student-centered attitude is what separates Buffalo from other institutions. For example, while other law schools talk about being noncompetitive, SUNY lives up to its claim. In fact, "students are not ranked and there is no GPA," which "promotes a healthy working environment where students help each other instead of try to beat one another." Unlike most legal programs, which require students to follow an extensive prescribed curriculum, "UB is great because they allow you to pick whatever class you want during your final two years and you have a lot of opportunities for hands-on experience." In this and many other ways, UB treats law students like the able-minded adults they are, allowing students to take an active role in designing their own educations.

Despite the large measure of autonomy they are afforded, law students do receive a great deal of encouragement and support from the administration and teaching staff, who promote cooperation and participation both in and out of the classroom. "The Socratic Method is used in classes, but not in a threatening way," explains a 1L. "Professors try to make sure that everyone is involved in every class discussion, and everyone has a chance to voice their opinion." Professors further distinguish themselves through their casual, down-to-earth attitude; "the professors are top-notch, but still aren't afraid to wear jeans."

While many students appreciate the liberal, relaxed atmosphere at UB, others feel the academic experience could use more structure. One student is "disturbed by the excessive amount of flexibility professors are given in determining the curriculum for first-year classes. In my constitutional law class, we spent half the semester on equal protection, while I learned nothing about the full faith and credit clause." Students also feel that UB could do more to promote practical skills and bar preparation. Even so, students who are willing to take the initiative have many opportunities for gaining practical experience through the school's many journals, clinics, mock trial programs, and the "bridge classes" offered over the semester break.

"The Career Services officers give me about two hours a week of their time to help me find the summer job of my dreams," writes one satisfied 1L. Just keep in mind that "the vast majority of UB law graduates work in Buffalo, Rochester, or Syracuse, NY." While the academic program at UB is strong, many feel that the school's national recruitment and reputation is still lagging behind where it should be. A student close to graduating insists that "The school needs to stop catering to the local area . . . and start looking at creating a national name and reputation." On the bright side, UB students aren't nearly as hard-pressed as those from other schools to make six figures at a "big law" job as soon as they graduate, since the average UB student's total law school debt load doesn't even approach the national average of $80,000. On the contrary, "the better students coming out of UB can compete with almost anyone in the country for jobs and clerkships. And we pay a third or a fourth of the tuition that some of our fellow law students are paying."

Lillie V. Wiley-Upshaw, Associate Dean for Admissions and Financial Aid
309 O'Brian Hall, Buffalo, NY 14260
Telephone: 716-645-2907 • Fax: 716-645-6676
E-mail: law-admissions@buffalo.edu • Website: www.law.buffalo.edu

Life

The students at UB Law School are "a nice mix. Some are bright minds who want to excel, many just want to do well, and others are great drinking partners for the weekend—but practically none are the stereotypical page-ripping, social-phobic, arrogant malcontents that you just want to muzzle." For the party crew, law school at UB is surprisingly fulfilling and fun. However, many lament that UB's social activities tend to revolve around drinking, leaving "almost no options for students with young children or singles not into the bar scene." A 2L complains, "People can be very nice and are not competitive, but at the same time there are a fair number of immature people. There are probably more frat types than there are type A's here."

Although there are 18 percent students of color, many say the school community would still benefit from more diversity. "As a minority student, I've encountered barriers that white students wouldn't," writes one. There is however, a working courtroom on the first floor of O'Brian Hall. Set in the suburbs, "the law school would be better suited downtown, in proximity to the courts, government offices, and many law firms." On the plus side, "the suburb of Amherst supports a higher standard of living and is a comfortable place to live and study."

Getting In

UB enrolls about 250 new students each year, evaluating applicants based on both qualitative and quantitative factors. In particular, the Admissions Committee seeks students whose academic backgrounds suggest a high probability for scholastic achievement in law school, who have demonstrated excellence in work or community activities, or who display potential for substantial contribution to the law after graduation.

EMPLOYMENT INFORMATION

Career Rating	**75**
Job placement rate (%)	98
Average starting salary	$50,107
State for bar exam	NY, PA, NJ, IL, MD
Pass rate for first-time bar	80

Employers who frequently hire grads: Dechert; Leboeuf Lamb; Hodgson Russ; Dewey Ballantine; Nixon Peabody; New York County district attorney's office; Kings County district attorney.

Prominent Alumni: Honorable Julio Fuentes, U.S. Court of Appeals, third circuit; Herald Price Fahringer, constitutional lawyer; Honorable Paul Friedman, U.S. District Judge for the U.S. District Court.

Grads employed by field (%):	
Academic	7
Business/industry	17
Government	6
Judicial clerkships	3
Military	4
Other	1
Private practice	57
Public interest	5

Legal Writing Course Requirement?	Yes
Legal Methods Course Requirement?	No
Legal Research Course Requirement?	Yes
Moot Court Requirement?	No
Public Interest Law Requirement?	No

ADMISSIONS

Selectivity Rating	**78**
# applications received	1,444
# applicants accepted	517
# acceptees attending	246
Average LSAT	155
LSAT Range	152–158
Average undergrad GPA	3.4
Application fee	$50
Regular application deadline	3/15
Regular notification	rolling
Rolling notification?	Yes
Early application program?	No
Transfer students accepted?	Yes
Evening division offered?	No
Part-time accepted?	No
LSDAS accepted?	Yes

Applicants Also Look At

Albany Law School, American U., Brooklyn Law School, Hofstra U., New York Law School, St. John's U., Syracuse U.

International Students

TOEFL required of international students?	Yes
Minimum Paper TOEFL	650
Minimum Computer TOEFL	280

FINANCIAL FACTS

Annual tuition (resident)	$12,170
Annual tuition (nonres.)	$18,270
Books and supplies	$2,860
Fees per credit	$51
Tuition per credit (resident)	$507
Tuition per credit (nonres.)	$761
Room & board	$11,636
Financial aid application deadline	3/1
% first-year students receiving some sort of aid	92
% receiving some sort of aid	87
% of aid that is merit-based	48
% receiving scholarships	60
Average grant	$2,950
Average loan	$18,500
Average total aid package	$18,500
Average debt	$48,756

Stanford University
School of Law

INSTITUTIONAL INFORMATION

Public/private	private
Student/faculty ratio	12:1
% faculty female	30
% faculty minority	19
Total faculty	43

SURVEY SAYS . . .

Diverse opinions accepted in classrooms
Great research resources
Great library staff
Abundant externship/internship/ clerkship opportunities

STUDENTS

Enrollment of law school	514
% male/female	53/47
% full-time	100
% minority	34
Average age of entering class	24

ACADEMICS

Academic Experience rating	**99**
Professors interesting rating	93
Professors accessible rating	82
Hours of study per day	4.04

Academic Specialties

Civil procedure, commercial law, constitutional law, corporation securities law, criminal law, environmental law, government services, human rights law, intellectual property law, international law, labor law, legal history, legal philosophy, property, taxation. We offer courses on the above topics, but no specializations/concentrations.

Advanced Degrees Offered

MLS, 1 year; JSM, 1 year; LLM 1 year; JSD, 2 years.

Combined Degrees Offered

JD/MBA, 4 years; JD/MA, 4 years.

Academic Requirements

Clinical Program Required?	No
Legal Writing Course Requirement?	Yes
Legal Methods Course Requirement?	No

Academics

Stanford University School of Law is a serious institution with a sunny disposition. One student describes it as "brilliant, yet not stuffy." While you're no doubt familiar with its stellar reputation and world-class faculty, what you may not know is how much of an intimate and down-to-earth place Stanford can be. Students love the fact that the even the most renowned professors take time to connect with students on a personal level. "Maybe the most amazing thing about Stanford (and there are many) is the accessibility of the faculty," says one student. "Really big-name, authoritative, Hollywood-type professors are happy to talk to you about all kinds of things, legal and otherwise." Another student shares this illustrative story: "The day before my 1L criminal law final, I sent my professor three panicky e-mails in the space of a few hours. Instead of ignoring my clearly hysterical state, this amazingly distinguished professor looked up my phone number and called me to answer my questions and talk me through my anxieties. That's the kind of hand-holding and personal attention you get at an elite law school that is smaller than most public kindergartens!" The administration is similarly nurturing, and the dean of students, who is described as "the mother hen of SLS, sends out encouraging e-mails and offers a shoulder to cry on."

Students rave and sometimes even gloat about the school's posh facilities. One student tells us, "We basically go to school at an executive country club: $900 chairs fill the classrooms and library!" Another student adds, "The classrooms were all just remodeled and the physical facilities are amazing. There is wireless access in every classroom and even in the courtyards. The academic buildings were just renovated, so the library is beautiful, light, and airy. [Plus] the classrooms are also really big and comfortable."

While some students like their upper-crust environs, some say the school's money and reputation come with other negative aspects. For example, some students feel that Stanford is too deeply entrenched in its relationship with local corporate law firms, who influence courses, externship options, and placement after graduation. As a result, students say it can be "a struggle" to find a public interest position and say, "There is a need for a broader range of curricular offerings in public interest areas."

But in general, career placement isn't much of an anxiety for Stanford grads. "It's pretty hard [not to get a job at a large firm] coming out of Stanford. In the fall, there are literally hundreds of firms that come to campus to interview, and there are only around 170 students each year, so it's a pretty good market." Another student swears, "If you want a job paying $125K, you will absolutely, without-a-doubt get one. Even the caboose of our class will get an amazing job. So what's to be stressed about?" And that's not all. Stanford also "places a huge number of its graduates in plumb clerkships." Although the school has a nearly perfect job placement rate, some students complain that the Career Services department is too California-centric. One student agrees, "I wish Stanford's Career Services department was a bit stronger on non–San Francisco or –New York job placement. I wanted to work in the Pacific Northwest, but I pretty much had to do all the work for myself." Students also complain about the lack of overseas opportunities. A student explains, "If you want to study abroad (even at an ABA-accredited program), you've got to pay your own way and graduate late." Maybe Stanford just has trouble cutting the apron strings?

Office of Admissions
559 Nathan Abbott Way, Stanford, CA 94305-8610
Telephone: 650-723-4985 • Fax: 650-723-0838
E-mail: admissions@law.stanford.edu • Website: www.law.stanford.edu

Life

Students at Stanford say that they are genuinely happy at their school, where friendly people, Frisbee®, and a mellow attitude prevail. The school's California location gets great reviews for its sunny weather and its proximity to San Francisco, Santa Cruz, and other California landmarks. "The great thing about SLS is that we live in serene paradise during the weekdays but can get our urban fix in one of the country's best cities in less than 30 minutes of driving." Another student asserts, "It's impossible to be stressed here since the sky is always blue and you can wear flip-flops 360 days a year."

"Given our Bay Area location," says one student, "it is surprising to no one that the politics of the student body skews leftward." But even so, this "hardcore conservative" goes on to say, "I have never felt as though my viewpoints were not appreciated." It's no wonder students have a high level of respect for their fellow classmates. As one student divulges, "At the first barbecue, you meet people and ask them what they've done, and you get responses like 'I used to run Hewlett-Packard,' and 'I invaded Sri Lanka.' It's insane." Among these "incredibly brilliant, super cool [students,] there's a real feel of camaraderie, not competition," making for a "happy and relaxed atmosphere." Parties "are very high school–like," but in a good way. "Everyone's invited, everyone shows up, and everyone hangs out. I love it."

Getting In

With a less than 10 percent acceptance rate, admission to Stanford is highly competitive. Most entering students were in the top 5 percent of their undergraduate class. The median LSAT score of the entering class is usually around 168, with a median GPA of about 3.8.

EMPLOYMENT INFORMATION

Career Rating	**91**
% employed within 9 months	97.4
State for bar exam	CA
Pass rate for first-time bar	91

Prominent Alumni: Justice Sandra Day O'Connor, U.S. Supreme Court; Justice William Rehnquist, U.S. Supreme Court; Warren Christopher, former secretary of state; Cheryl D. Mills, former deputy counsel to President Clinton.

Grads employed by field (%):	
Business/industry	4
Government	2
Judicial clerkships	27
Private practice	64
Public interest	3

Legal Research Course Requirement?	Yes
Moot Court Requirement?	No
Public Interest Law Requirement?	No

ADMISSIONS

Selectivity Rating	**98**
# applications received	5,040
# applicants accepted	390
# acceptees attending	166
Average LSAT	169
LSAT Range	166–172
Average undergrad GPA	3.8
Application fee	$75
Regular application deadline	2/1
Regular notification	4/30
Rolling notification?	Yes
Early application program?	No
Transfer students accepted?	Yes
Evening division offered?	No
Part-time accepted?	No
LSDAS accepted?	Yes

International Students

TOEFL required of international students?	No
TOEFL recommended of international students?	Yes

FINANCIAL FACTS

Annual tuition	$33,870
Books and supplies	$1,500
Room & board (on/off-campus)	$13,900/$19,054
Financial aid application deadline	3/15
% first-year students receiving some sort of aid	80
% receiving some sort of aid	80
% receiving scholarships	43
Average grant	$15,198
Average loan	$34,000
Average debt	$92,560

SUFFOLK UNIVERSITY
LAW SCHOOL

INSTITUTIONAL INFORMATION

Public/private	private
Student/faculty ratio	18:1
% faculty part-time	42
% faculty female	50
% faculty minority	12
Total faculty	160

SURVEY SAYS . . .

Great research resources
Beautiful campus
Students love Boston, MA

STUDENTS

Enrollment of law school	1,665
% male/female	48/52
% out-of-state	46
% full-time	60
% minority	17
% international	6
# of countries represented	19
Average age of entering class	25

ACADEMICS

Academic Experience rating	**79**
Professors interesting rating	75
Professors accessible rating	70
Hours of study per day	4.47

Academic Specialties

Civil procedure, civil litigation, commercial law, constitutional law, corporation securities law, criminal law, environmental law, financial services, government services, health care and biotechnology, human rights law, intellectual property law, international law, labor law, legal history, legal philosophy, property.

Advanced Degrees Offered

JD, 3 years full-time, 4 years part-time.

Combined Degrees Offered

JD/MBA, JD/MPA, JD/MSIE, JD/MSF, JD/MSCJ, LLM global technology. All offered 3 years full-time, 5 years part-time.

Academic Requirements

Clinical Program Required? No

Academics

Located across the street from Boston Common, Suffolk University Law School is truly at the heart of Boston's legal community. Suffolk students love their propitious location, because, as one student explains, the school "benefits significantly from its location in the hub of Boston and its proximity to the state house. The school is frequented by judges and some of the most important people in the Boston legal scene." Students are also appreciative of the local "excellent network of alumni who, already in the first year, have made themselves accessible to us. They offer advice and also will be useful in securing jobs." Students will also need that career advice, it seems, for while everyone agrees that the location is ideal, some students wish that the school wasn't so myopic when it comes to career placement and instruction. "Career Services has a difficult time providing assistance for places outside of Massachusetts, and the professors almost exclusively refer to Massachusetts law. For those of us who do not plan to practice in Massachusetts, it would be helpful if the school offered a more diverse curriculum and support system." Another student agrees, "The school needs to spread themselves out further than Boston and appeal to more students on a country-wide scale."

Students are impressed by Suffolk's first-rate facilities, bragging that they compose "the most modern law school in New England." One student gushes, "The building and classrooms are brand-new and unbelievably technologically advanced. There are always plenty of study carrels, study rooms, and sitting areas to accommodate everybody's individual study habits and needs." On top of that, students say they get real use out of technology in the classroom, from passing virtual notes to each other via the Internet connection to their instructors' use of PowerPoint presentations. "Professors use technology in the classroom on a daily basis, and it is a great asset to the learning experience," writes one student.

With the largest student body of any Massachusetts law school, its not surprising many students feel that "classes need to be smaller" at Suffolk. Though students generally spend more time in the lecture hall than in small group discussion, they tell us that they receive excellent instruction from top-notch faculty. "The quality of education at Suffolk Law School is equal to that of top law schools around the country. Suffolk combines legal theory with practical experience, which gives it a fabulous reputation in New England and New York," writes one student. In fact, another student tells us, "Suffolk attracts great professors who are leaders in their fields because they can teach a class in addition to maintaining their practice" in Boston or other nearby cities.

Academically, students say Suffolk is challenging and that classes are highly competitive, especially in the first year. A student tells us that there is "an emphasis on rigorous classes that will make you pass the bar whether you like it or not. You end up with fewer classes [with titles like] 'Children, the Law, and Winnie the Pooh,' and more [with titles] along the lines of 'Evidence, Advanced Evidence, and Evidence until you Bleed.'" Still, students insist that professors are not out to get you and that "there isn't a sense of cut-throat competition." On top of that, Suffolk students reassure us that when the going gets rough, they can get extra academic support from faculty and staff. For example, a student explains, "The academic support program (ASP) is excellent and very accommodating. Suffolk's ASP runs a 'pre-law school' event, keeps tabs on those who they identify as possible 'strugglers,' and also offers a broad range of support programs to make the transition from undergrad or the workforce." In addition, most professors are "always willing to help a student out, whether it is to explain something or just to talk"

Gail Ellis, Dean of Admissions
120 Tremont Street, Boston, MA 02108-4977
Telephone: 617-573-8144 • Fax: 617-523-1367
E-mail: lawadm@suffolk.edu • Website: www.law.suffolk.edu

outside of class. There are a few dissenting voices when it comes to professorial quality, however, as some students say that it isn't that rare to run into professors who "are on a power-trip and only care about publishing their new book (and then force the students to buy the book)."

Life

Boston isn't just a great town for law. Boston is also a great town for dining, shopping, barhopping, and taking trips around New England. As Suffolk is located "right in the center of the mix of downtown Boston, kitty-cornered from the Boston Common," there is never a lack of things to do. On campus, students say, "There's a very strong social scene, especially toward Friday and Saturday," and many like blowing off steam with classmates. In the words of one, "Whether it is renting out a bar for the night or going on ski trips, we find a way to do things as a school." Many Suffolk students hail from the surrounding area, yet they bring some diversity of background and experience to the program. "Racial diversity is somewhat poorly addressed at the school" writes one student, but "perhaps that lack of racial diversity is balanced nicely by the broad range of economic backgrounds, especially those from a blue-collared working class background," he concludes. The school's outreach efforts to enhance diversity have resulted in an increase in the percentage of minority students within the last year.

Getting In

Suffolk considers a student's undergraduate performance, LSAT scores, personal statement, and letters of recommendation when making an admissions decision. In the previous year, the median LSAT score was 157 and the median GPA was 3.3. Students come to Suffolk from more than 200 undergraduate colleges.

EMPLOYMENT INFORMATION

Career Rating	**72**
% employed within 9 months	89
Average starting salary	$62,320
State for bar exam	MA, NH, RI, NY, FL
Pass rate for first-time bar	82

Employers who frequently hire grads:
Suffolk alumni practice in numerous large, medium, and small law firms in Boston. Many practice in the public sector, work in all levels of government service, and serve on the judiciary.

Grads employed by field (%):	
Academic	3
Business/industry	24
Government	13
Judicial clerkships	8
Military	2
Other	2
Private practice	47
Public interest	1

Legal Writing Course Requirement?	Yes
Legal Methods Course Requirement?	Yes
Legal Research Course Requirement?	Yes
Moot Court Requirement?	Yes
Public Interest Law Requirement?	No

ADMISSIONS

Selectivity Rating	**79**
# applications received	3,300
# applicants accepted	1,200
# acceptees attending	550
Average LSAT	157
LSAT Range	154–159
Average undergrad GPA	3.3
Application fee	$60
Regular application deadline	3/1
Regular notification	rolling
Rolling notification?	Yes
Early application program?	No
Transfer students accepted?	Yes
Evening division offered?	Yes
Part-time accepted?	Yes
LSDAS accepted?	Yes

International Students

TOEFL required of international students?	Yes
Minimum Paper TOEFL	600
Minimum Computer TOEFL	250

FINANCIAL FACTS

Annual tuition	$29,900
Books and supplies	$900
Tuition per credit	$1,000
Room & board (off-campus)	$14,205
Financial aid application deadline	3/1
% first-year students receiving some sort of aid	85
% receiving some sort of aid	85
% of aid that is merit-based	36
% receiving scholarships	41
Average grant	$4,956
Average loan	$27,362
Average total aid package	$30,133
Average debt	$80,340

Syracuse University
College of Law

INSTITUTIONAL INFORMATION

Public/private	private
Student/faculty ratio	16:1
% faculty female	33
% faculty minority	12
Total faculty	47

SURVEY SAYS . . .

Diverse opinions accepted in classrooms
Great library staff
Beautiful campus

STUDENTS

Enrollment of law school	792
% male/female	54/46
% full-time	99
% minority	18
% international	4
# of countries represented	6
Average age of entering class	24

ACADEMICS

Academic Experience rating	**61**
Professors interesting rating	61
Professors accessible rating	61
Hours of study per day	4.44

Academic Specialties

Commercial law, constitutional law, corporation securities law, criminal law, environmental law, family law, government services, human rights law, indigeneous law, intellectual property law, international law, labor law, legal history, national security and counterterrorism, taxation, technology law.

Combined Degrees Offered

JD/MPA public administration; JD/MS accounting, library science, communication, news/magazine, media; JD/MBA business administration; JD/MA economics, history, international relations; JD/MS in education, disability studies; JD/MSW social work; JD/MS or JD/PhD in environmental studies; JD/MS engineering & computer science; JD/MA, political science, English, philosophy.

Academics

At Syracuse University College of Law, students have the opportunity to pursue a highly specialized legal education in one of a wide range of areas. With a large student body and extensive teaching staff, "course selection is truly excellent," and "once you get into your second and third years, many opportunities for specialization and exploration open up." In addition, the "affiliation with Syracuse University makes for some unique joint degree and study opportunities," allowing JD students to pursue master's degrees concurrently in communications, international relations, disability studies, public administration, or accounting, among other disciplines. According to one 3L, "The public administration program, which is very highly regarded, is quite popular, as are JD/MBA and JD/IR programs. A relatively high percentage of students pursue this amazing opportunity because the law school will actually shave a semester's worth of credits off of a joint-degree law student's degree requirements."

Despite the varied academic paths, there is no easy route through law school at Syracuse. The curriculum is challenging and students warn that "five-credit classes will break you." However, most appreciate the rigorous training, telling us that "professors are tough, but in a good way." In fact, the school's "committed, talented instructors" are able teachers who "are not merely experts in their respective fields. Their commitment to clearly conveying complex information to students is obvious." In addition to their skill as lecturers, professors are "very accessible and willing to help" struggling students outside the classroom.

In addition to the standard legal curriculum, Syracuse offers several applied learning programs, like trial practice, moot court, and a number of clinics, including the Family Law and Social Policy center and the Global Law and Practice center. In addition, the school operates summer abroad programs in London and Zimbabwe and participates in International Moot Court competitions, in which Syracuse has done quite well in the past. A 2L raves, "We have a great trial advocacy program and excellent clinical legal education opportunities. I loved practicing law my second year!" Practical approaches to law are also emphasized in the curriculum, and there are "some great practitioners in upper classes," though some feel that additional adjuncts would be a benefit to the learning experience.

Located on the same grounds as the greater university, the Syracuse campus is attractive, safe, and modern. After recent remodeling, classroom facilities are "nice and shiny with some good technology" and have all the nice touches, like "the soft swivel chairs in the classrooms that make life a little more comfortable." While doling out compliments, students admit that "the one glaring deficiency of the school, which overall is quiet nice, is the library, which feels cramped and lacks adequate study space for students"; also, "the materials are limited, as are the computer facilities right in the library."

Syracuse has been going through many changes in recent years as the school attempts to build up its national reputation. Students specifically applaud the Syracuse administration for making efforts to improve the school's career placement opportunities. Among other measures, "the school has been making attempts to improve its academic reputation by instituting an upper-class grading curve, stricter attendance policies, and mandating the use of laptops." Many feel the changes have been a step in the right direction. However, some feel "the school lacks direction and focus in achieving its overall mission" and that "the administration does not seem to care about its existing students;

Nikki S. Laubenstein, Director of Admissions
Office of Admissions and Financial Aid; Suite 340, Syracuse, NY 13244
Telephone: 315-443-1962 • Fax: 315-443-9568
E-mail: admissions@law.syr.edu • Website: www.law.syr.edu

rather, it is focused on the quality of students it can enroll in the future." A 2L reassures us, however, that despite occasional misunderstandings, "in the end everything seems to come together as it should."

Life

Generally speaking, Syracuse students are a fairly homogenous bunch. While the school's sizable student body ensures that there is a little something for everyone, the school is home to "a large population of preppies in khakis and polo shirts with their collars up from the suburbs of major cities." However, everyone is able to find a niche on this active campus, and there are a wide range of campus clubs and interest groups. When it comes to socializing, the class is likewise diverse, depending on your definition of "diverse"; students report that "as far as social life is concerned, there are people who party and there are people who don't."

While the new grading policies have created some additional stress for Syracuse students, they have not generated unwanted or nasty competition between classmates. By most accounts "students are competitive, but not to a point where you can't handle it." What's more, the faculty and administration do as much as possible to keep backstabbing at bay. A 2L explains, "The competitive nature of most law schools is not as evident at Syracuse, and any instances of extreme competition (i.e., hiding books) have been immediately reprimanded and corrected by the school."

Getting In

In addition to the numbers that go into your admissions index, the Admissions Committee closely analyzes a student's undergraduate transcript, considering difficulty of the course of study, caliber of the school attended, and course selection. Syracuse may also consider other subjective information about you, like graduate study or work experience, as well as commitment to the study of law. A B-plus undergraduate average and a LSAT score in the mid-150s makes you competitive at Syracuse.

EMPLOYMENT INFORMATION

Career Rating	72
Job placement rate (%)	93
Average starting salary	$51,300
State for bar exam	NY, NJ, CA, PA, CT
Pass rate for first-time bar	84

Prominent Alumni: Joseph R. Biden, Jr., U.S. senator; Theodore A. McKee, federal appeals court judge; Donald T. MacNaughton, partner, White and Case.

Grads employed by field (%):	
Academic	2
Business/industry	12
Government	13
Judicial clerkships	17
Military	1
Other	2
Private practice	49
Public interest	4

Academic Requirements

Clinical Program Required?	No
Legal Writing Course Requirement?	Yes
Legal Methods Course Requirement?	Yes
Legal Research Course Requirement?	Yes
Moot Court Requirement?	No
Public Interest Law Requirement?	No

ADMISSIONS

Selectivity Rating	77
# applications received	3,212
# applicants accepted	783
# acceptees attending	250
Average LSAT	154
LSAT Range	152–156
Average undergrad GPA	3.4
Application fee	$60
Regular application deadline	4/1
Regular notification	rolling
Rolling notification?	Yes
Early application program?	No
Transfer students accepted?	Yes
Evening division offered?	No
Part-time accepted?	Yes
LSDAS accepted?	Yes

International Students

TOEFL required of international students?	Yes
Minimum Paper TOEFL	600
Minimum Computer TOEFL	250

FINANCIAL FACTS

Annual tuition	$32,820
Books and supplies	$1,140
Tuition per credit	$1,436
Room & board	$11,268
Financial aid application deadline	2/15
Average grant	$8,400
Average loan	$26,300
Average debt	$76,700

TEMPLE UNIVERSITY
BEASLEY SCHOOL OF LAW

INSTITUTIONAL INFORMATION

Public/private	public
Student/faculty ratio	16:1
% faculty female	36
% faculty minority	23
Total faculty	61

SURVEY SAYS . . .

Diverse opinions accepted in classrooms
Great library staff

STUDENTS

Enrollment of law school	1,053
% male/female	51/49
% out-of-state	30
% full-time	76
% minority	21
% international	1
Average age of entering class	25

ACADEMICS

Academic Experience rating	**80**
Professors interesting rating	82
Professors accessible rating	76
Hours of study per day	3.92

Academic Specialties

Commercial law, constitutional law, corporation securities law, criminal law, environmental law, government services, human rights law, intellectual property law, international law, public interest, taxation, trial advocacy.

Advanced Degrees Offered

JD, 3 years full-time, 4 years part-time; LLM in trial advocacy, 1 year; LLM in taxation, 1 semester to 1 year; LLM in transnational law, 1 semester to 1 year; graduate teaching fellowships, 2 years; LLM for graduates of foreign law schools, 1 year.

Combined Degrees Offered

JD/MBA, approximately 4 years; JD/LLM degree programs in taxation and transnational law, 3.5 years; JD individually designed joint degrees.

Academics

Temple University's James E. Beasley School of Law exemplifies the "urban public law school experience [and offers] an excellent law school education at a veritable bargain"—at least for Pennsylvania residents. "Courses are rigorous," although in terms of legal writing, "the quality of instruction is not as consistent as it could be, [and] the range of courses could improve, especially for core curriculum courses." The "flat-out fantastic" (and "very liberal") professors "truly care about their students, and they know how to teach." Professors "have very interesting backgrounds" and are able to strike "a good balance between teaching with the Socratic Method and providing a meaningful experience in the classroom by reciting entertaining war stories." One student says, "The dedication of the faculty is without peer. You can put all the flat screens and fancy audio equipment in any classrooms you want, but the bottom line is, the faculty makes the law school." One student concedes, "There's always a few you love to hate," but almost across the board, "Temple's students are lucky to have it so good." Many students tell us, "The administration is very accessible and friendly. Secretaries, administrators, and professors know who you are, what your interests are, and are willing to talk to you about law and life." A few complain that the administration "takes forever to get things done."

Temple's facilities are a mixed bag. Many students have not-so-kind words about the building's exterior, expressing, "The outside of the law school itself is hideous, [though] they are actively renovating both buildings." Students say, "Once you get past the correctional facility look of the building, the inside of Temple law school is just the opposite. Much of the school is newly renovated, and the entire building is Internet accessible." Students are calling for "more and better computers" in the library, which "was just redone, and it's way nicer than last year." Students agree, "The library resources, print and electronic, are good, and the staff is knowledgeable and helpful."

Real-world know-how is easily acquired at Temple thanks to an immense amount of "very hands-on, practical experience that truly prepares the student for practice upon graduation." The shining illustration of Temple's focus "on educating and preparing real-life lawyers" is the Trial Advocacy program, which is "perhaps the best in the country." One of the program's fans attests, "The trial ad faculty is animated, interesting, and entertaining. If you want to be a trial lawyer, there is no question that Temple is the place for you. Period." When the time comes to get a real job, "the school has a wonderful reputation in the Philadelphia legal community." Students gripe that Temple could be "more ambitious" in recruiting firms from outside Philadelphia for on-campus interviews, though. But, overall, "if you want a cheap, quality law school education, go to Temple. If you're planning on staying in the Philadelphia area, you can't beat it."

JOHANNE L. JOHNSTON, DIRECTOR OF ADMISSIONS AND FINANCIAL AID
1719 NORTH BROAD STREET, PHILADELPHIA, PA 19122
TELEPHONE: 800-560-1428 • FAX: 215-204-9319
E-MAIL: LAWADMIS@TEMPLE.EDU • WEBSITE: WWW.TEMPLE.EDU/LAWSCHOOL

Life

"Philadelphia is a fantastic city for a law school student," and Temple boasts a great location. Of course, "if you venture too far afield in North Philly, you take your life in your own hands." You'll have few problems as long as you stay near the law school, though. "Living in Philly is so much cheaper than other university cities (New York, Boston, and the Bay Area)." One student swears, "You can rent an entire house here for $500. That won't get you a recycling bin in Boston." The food is good, too. "There are a million lunch trucks that sell cheap food from Chinese to Greek to Korean to Middle Eastern to Mexican."

"Students are very social, [and] this is an urban school, so there are many things to do." However, "because this is also a large evening student and commuter school, there isn't a strong feeling of community." Ultimately, "social life is there for anyone who wants it. There are all kinds of clubs, sporting events, parties, and the ever-important happy hours."

"My fellow students, on the whole, are an interesting, diverse, and intelligent group," remarks one among them. More specifically, students are diverse in terms of "age, race, and political views, [and] Temple is a particularly welcoming place if you have been out of school for several years." As a result of all this diversity, "it is quite staggering to sit in class and listen to all of the opinions." Another student suggests, "People are mostly paying for school themselves without Mommy and Daddy's support, so people take their work seriously." Competition is not unheard of, but, on the whole, "Temple is a very friendly place—from faculty to students to security guards to food truck operators. It is a nice place to be." One student explains, "We all know that law school can be miserable. Nobody seems to feel that we need to make it more miserable for each other."

Getting In

The admissions department at Temple takes a variety of factors into consideration. LSAT scores for the middle 50 percent of an entering Temple Law class range from 157 to 162. The GPA for the middle 50 percent is between a 3.1 and a 3.6. If you take the LSAT more than once in any three-year period, Temple will average your scores.

EMPLOYMENT INFORMATION

Career Rating	**84**
Job placement rate (%)	93
Average starting salary	$68,000
State for bar exam	PA
Pass rate for first-time bar	88

Employers who frequently hire grads:
District attorney, public defender, national law firms, state and federal judges, nonprofit legal organizations.

Grads employed by field (%):	
Academic	2
Business/industry	18
Government	14
Judicial clerkships	10
Private practice	49
Public interest	7

Academic Requirements

Clinical Program Required?	No
Legal Writing Course Requirement?	Yes
Legal Methods Course Requirement?	Yes
Legal Research Course Requirement?	Yes
Moot Court Requirement?	No
Public Interest Law Requirement?	No

ADMISSIONS

Selectivity Rating	**83**
# applications received	4,152
# applicants accepted	1,149
# acceptees attending	331
Average LSAT	160
LSAT Range	157–162
Average undergrad GPA	3.4
Application fee	$60
Regular application deadline	3/1
Regular notification	rolling
Rolling notification?	Yes
Early application program?	No
Transfer students accepted?	Yes
Evening division offered?	Yes
Part-time accepted?	Yes
LSDAS accepted?	Yes

International Students

TOEFL required of international students?	No
TOEFL recommended of international students?	Yes

FINANCIAL FACTS

Annual tuition (resident)	$12,802
Annual tuition (nonresident)	$22,290
Books and supplies	$1,500
Tuition per credit (resident)	$495
Tuition per credit (nonresident)	$911
Room & board	$10,262
Financial aid application deadline	3/1
% first-year students receiving some sort of aid	85
% receiving some sort of aid	81
% of aid that is merit-based	87
% receiving scholarships	35
Average grant	$5,926
Average loan	$22,549
Average total aid package	$24,132
Average debt	$62,461

TEXAS TECH UNIVERSITY

SCHOOL OF LAW

INSTITUTIONAL INFORMATION

Public/private	public
Student/faculty ratio	20:1
% faculty part-time	29
% faculty female	27
% faculty minority	19
Total faculty	52

SURVEY SAYS . . .

Diverse opinions accepted in classrooms
Great research resources
Great library staff

STUDENTS

Enrollment of law school	683
% male/female	51/49
% out-of-state	9
% full-time	100
% minority	17
% international	1
# of countries represented	114
Average age of entering class	25

ACADEMICS

Academic Experience rating	**76**
Professors interesting rating	71
Professors accessible rating	88
Hours of study per day	4.64

Academic Specialties

Civil procedure, commercial law, constitutional law, corporation securities law, criminal law, environmental law, government services, human rights law, intellectual property law, international law, labor law, law & bioterrorism, law & science, legal history, legal philosophy, property, taxation, water law.

Combined Degrees Offered

JD/MBA, 3 years; JD/MPA, 3.5 years; JD/MS, agriculture and applied science, 3 to 3.5 years, JD/MS, accounting (taxation), 3 to 3.5 years; JD/MS, environmental toxicology, 3 to 4 year; JD/FFP, personal financial planning, 3 to 3.5 years; JD/MS, biotechnology, 3 to 4 years; JD/MS soil science/horticulture/entomology, 3 to 4 years.

Academics

Described by its students as a "litigator factory," Texas Tech University takes a decidedly practical approach to the study of law, teaching students the basics of theory while providing rigorous training in research, writing, and courtroom technique. Many students choose Texas Tech because of its "emphasis on the practical side of law." In the state of Texas, the school has a "great reputation for turning out law students who are ready to practice law from day one." Indeed, practical skills are emphasized throughout the curriculum; in the classroom, students are introduced to "skills in client counseling, negotiating, and courtroom argument." Outside of the classroom, the school offers top-notch "clinical programs, strong moot court teams, and a required year-long legal research and writing course" as well as "opportunities to study abroad." The school is currently building a new, state-of-the-art mock courtroom to further promote its clinical programs.

While Texas Tech students appreciate the strength of their legal education, they caution that law school is no picnic. TTU students compare first-year classes to "boot camp," and a 1L tells us, "Everyone I know spends at least five to six hours a day studying; and if a day is missed to go out, then they make it up on the weekend." While the material and workload are decidedly challenging, the enthusiasm of the "incredibly awesome" teaching staff inspires students to achieve. A 3L tells us, "We have a lot of young professors who have a passion for the law and for teaching." In the words of a 1L: "Their great attitude and great sense of humor help you forget you're studying ridiculously dull topics." On top of that, students report that "the professors are willing to work with anyone who is having difficulties," and there is a campus-wide open-door policy for faculty and administrators. A 3L attests, "I have great relationships with all of my professors. . . . We truly have a law school family."

Administrators are generally described as "extremely helpful to students." A 1L praises, "Professors and administration alike bend over backward to make sure you are understanding the concepts and learning to think like a lawyer." Another commends, "The administration—from the deans down to the secretaries—love what they do, and it shows; they strive to help each and every one of us." Texas Tech also has "regular peer tutoring offered to help us 1Ls survive our first semester," as well as a Mentor Program for first- and second-year students. Indeed, "you are not just a number at Texas Tech." With about 230 students per class, the school can offer small class sizes. But the school's size also leads to some limitations; for example, some students write that "the range of topics of study needs to be much broader." On top of that, students report that the high number of required courses leaves "no wiggle room to explore fields of law that aren't on the bar exam," leaving little room to specialize. That said, many report that the Texas Tech administration members have listened to these concerns and "have employed new professors and are adding courses to their curriculum."

Out in the real world, TTU students find that their education leaves them well prepared for their future practice; the school consistently "turns out young lawyers who are not overwhelmed by the large disconnect between classroom and workplace legal skills." Many see the benefits of their education as early as their first internship placement. A 3L enthuses, "from the time you start your first summer clerkship, you are ready to go." When it comes to career placement, students report that Texas Tech has a pretty single-minded "focus on criminal practice and finding jobs in high-paying firms." While some would like to see an expansion of the practice fields open to graduates as well as a more solid national reputation and recruiting, most note that "Texas Tech enjoys prestige

DONNA WILLIAMS, ADMISSIONS COUNSELOR
TEXAS TECH UNIVERSITY SCHOOL OF LAW, 1802 HARTFORD AVENUE, LUBBOCK, TX 79409
TELEPHONE: 806-742-3990 • FAX: 806-742-1629
E-MAIL: DONNA.WILLIAMS@TTU.EDU • WEBSITE: WWW.LAW.TTU.EDU

within the state of Texas" and that consequently, postgraduation in-state career prospects are auspicious. A 3L confirms, "I have received offers from law firms located throughout the state of Texas and have even considered a position with the Federal Bureau of Investigation after being accepted as an honors intern last summer."

Life

Located in the West Texas town of Lubbock, TTU's student population provides a little slice of the Lone Star State. A Dallas native exclaims, "I have never seen so many cowboy boots in all my life!" By most accounts, there is a distinctly Texan flavor to the politics and culture on campus, which most describe as unequivocally conservative and fairly religious. A 2L warns: "If you have one liberal bone in your body, be prepared to be an outcast here." According to many, the student body is largely lacking in ethnic, economic, and philosophical diversity. One student confides, "Diversity is said to be a priority here, but I haven't seen it yet, and there doesn't seem to be much support for it in the administration."

In addition to their conservative politics, Texans are famous for their upbeat, cheerful, and welcoming natures. A content 1L praises, "The whole law school, from the administration to the students, reflects the friendly, caring West Texas atmosphere." And "while competition is encouraged, so are relationships and understanding." Students find one another "very willing to lend a helping hand or even a shoulder to cry on when it's needed." On campus, students say that "Tech has a great balance of academic, social, and community service. There is always something to do." As far as off-campus life is concerned, "Lubbock actually has a pretty good nightlife." Although it "isn't a hub of cosmopolitan splendor," it nevertheless "is very favorable to the law student." "Before you know it, this place grows on you."

Getting In

Texas Tech evaluates students based on their previous academic performance, LSAT scores, letters of recommendation, and personal statements. While no specific pre-law curriculum is required, the admissions committee favors students who have a background in public speaking, reading and writing skills, an understanding of public institutions and government, and the ability to think creatively and critically.

EMPLOYMENT INFORMATION

Career Rating	**84**
% employed within 9 months	98
Average starting salary	$70,200
State for bar exam	TX, NM
Pass rate for first-time bar	84

Employers who frequently hire grads: Jones, Day Reavis, & Pogue; Thompson & Knight; Haynes & Boone; Thompson & Coe; Cousins & Irons; Strasburger & Price; Cooper & Aldous.

Prominent Alumni: Karen Tandy, administrator of the Drug Enforcement Administration; David Bridges, Dallas Court of Appeals; Glenn West, Weil, Gotshal, & Manges.

Grads employed by field (%):	
Business/industry	7
Government	17
Judicial clerkships	5
Private practice	70
Public interest	1

Academic Requirements

Clinical Program Required?	No
Legal Writing Course Requirement?	Yes
Legal Methods Course Requirement?	Yes
Legal Research Course Requirement?	Yes
Moot Court Requirement?	No
Public Interest Law Requirement?	No

ADMISSIONS

Selectivity Rating	**78**
# applications received	1,550
# applicants accepted	504
# acceptees attending	244
Average LSAT	154
LSAT Range	150–157
Average undergrad GPA	3.5
Application fee	$50
Regular application deadline	2/1
Regular notification	rolling
Rolling notification?	Yes
Early application program?	Yes
Early application deadline	11/1
Early application notification	1/15
Transfer students accepted?	Yes
Evening division offered?	No
Part-time accepted?	No
LSDAS accepted?	Yes

Applicants Also Look At

Baylor University, Southern Methodist University, University of Houston, The University of Texas at Austin.

International Students

TOEFL required of international students?	Yes
Minimum Paper TOEFL	550
Minimum Computer TOEFL	213

FINANCIAL FACTS

Annual tuition (resident)	$8,216
Annual tuition (nonresident)	$14,092
Books and supplies	$914
Room & board	$11,282
% first-year students receiving some sort of aid	74
% receiving some sort of aid	74
% of aid that is merit-based	23
% receiving scholarships	67
Average grant	$5,508
Average loan	$13,035
Average total aid package	$15,547
Average debt	$48,519

Texas Wesleyan University
School of Law

INSTITUTIONAL INFORMATION

Public/private	private
Student/faculty ratio	24:1
Affiliation	Methodist
% faculty part-time	35
% faculty female	46
% faculty minority	10
Total faculty	29

SURVEY SAYS . . .

Diverse opinions accepted in classrooms
Great library staff
Students love Fort Worth, TX

STUDENTS

Enrollment of law school	710
% male/female	54/46
% out-of-state	7
% full-time	65
% minority	21
# of countries represented	7
Average age of entering class	25

ACADEMICS

Academic Experience rating	**71**
Professors interesting rating	75
Professors accessible rating	87
Hours of study per day	4

Academic Specialties

Business planning/estate planning & probate, criminal law, family law, intellectual property law, labor law, specialty areas.

Advanced Degrees Offered

JD, 3 years full-time, 4 years part-time.

Academic Requirements

Clinical Program Required?	No
Legal Writing Course Requirement?	Yes
Legal Methods Course Requirement?	Yes
Legal Research Course Requirement?	Yes
Moot Court Requirement?	No
Public Interest Law Requirement?	Yes

Academics

Whether fresh out of college or starting on a new career path, students feel stimulated and supported at Texas Wesleyan University School of Law. At this friendly Fort Worth school, professors are described as "dynamic and engaging," "immensely knowledgeable," and "easily accessible." "They have even been known to show up at small study groups at the request of their students." One 3L reports, "Never in my educational experience have I had so many people go out of their way to help me succeed. The professors are always available outside of class, and the administration is surprisingly willing to take any step necessary to help students both personally and professionally." Another student writes, "I feel more comfortable approaching my law professors than I did any of my undergraduate professors." With a total enrollment of only 700 students, the campus community is close-knit, and the administrators receive praise for being "helpful with questions, even if they are only minor problems."

Through clinics and course work, Texas Wesleyan students report that they are well prepared for the bar exam. The school boasts a "competitive bar-passage rate" (82 percent for first-time test-takers), which is comparable to—if not better than—many top Texas schools. In addition, the course work at Texas Wesleyan aims to prepare students for professional practice. A student explains, "Professors are genuinely interested not only in our successful completion of the program, but also in our bar exam performance and—more important—our professional competence." For a small school, "the courses offered are fairly broad," and students receive a comprehensive education. Students warn, however, that "no one subject has an extensive array of topics available under it for study," and some "would like to see a wider variety of course offerings, such as courses dealing with sexual orientation, gender, and civil rights."

One feature that distinguishes Texas Wesleyan from other law schools is its excellent evening and part-time programs, which offer "flexibility for full-time professionals who want to earn a law degree." Evening students (who account for 34 percent of the school's enrollment) have access to the full range of course offerings, and "night and weekend classes are all taught by top-tier faculty." A satisfied student attests, "Working full-time while attending school at night is difficult, but the school's flexible scheduling enables me to choose the classes I want and grants me access to all the support personnel I need to take care of administrative and other needs that come up." Many nontraditional students "have day jobs, spouses, children, and an embedded social group outside of school." For the most part, they "feel included in most of the extracurricular activities offered by the school and find the faculty to be particularly sensitive" to students with jobs and families. Even still, some wish the school offered more "activities geared toward our lifestyles."

Many note that the downtown Fort Worth "location is one of the school's greatest strengths." Situated across the street from the Tarrant County Bar Association, Texas Wesleyan is just "a step away from the legal community." While students are also in close proximity to the multitude of resources in neighboring Dallas, Fort Worth receives kudos for offering "a casual and friendly environment that affords greater access to local judges and lawyers." Established in 1989, Texas Wesleyan is steadily building its reputation in the greater Fort Worth area. A student explains, "Since we're a very young law school, we lack the academic reputation and alumni establishment of most other schools in our region." Students write, however, that their excellent education is starting to make an impression on the local community, and "more people are getting big firm jobs every

Lynda L. Culver, Director of Admissions Operations
1515 Commerce Street, Fort Worth, TX 76102
Telephone: 800-733-9529 • Fax: 817-212-4002
E-mail: lawadmissions@law.txwes.edu • Website: http://law.txwes.edu

year." As the school grows in age and reputation, enrollment, too, is slightly increasing. As a result, "Texas Wesleyan School of Law has definitely outgrown its current building," and many point out that "the library facility is very poor." The school is "in the process of a major renovation and expansion," and this promises to assuage students who complain that the school is "busting at the seams."

Life

Students at Texas Wesleyan write that their legal education is profoundly enhanced by the diversity of the student body. With its excellent part-time program, it's no surprise that the school attracts "people from all walks of life." One student confirms, "The diversity of the student body is a plus. I have been in classes with actors, parents of seven, recent college grads, candle makers, and police officers, and they all bring unique perspectives that could potentially not be found at other institutions."

The diversity at Texas Wesleyan breeds classroom debate and doesn't result in competition or contention. In fact, Texas Wesleyan students generally describe their classmates as "mature and mostly respectful, friendly, [and] helpful." A first-year writes, "I can always count on 2Ls and 3Ls for the inside scoop. Everyone wants the 1Ls to succeed and is always more than willing to help out." Students report that social life on campus is slightly lacking, since there isn't much to do in downtown Fort Worth. In addition to some safety issues in the vicinity, students gripe that "there are very few places within walking distance to eat or socialize" and that the only food options come from "vending machines that operate on a part-time basis."

Getting In

Admission to the school becomes slightly more competitive every year. In 2004, Texas Wesleyan received 2,097 applications, of which the school accepted roughly a third to fill 269 seats. In addition to a completed application and LSAT scores, applicants are required to submit two letters of recommendation and a personal statement. Texas Wesleyan welcomes students of different ages and backgrounds, and the school looks beyond test scores and grades when making admissions decisions.

ADMISSIONS

Selectivity Rating	**72**
# applications received	2,097
# applicants accepted	698
# acceptees attending	269
Average LSAT	153
LSAT Range	151–156
Average undergrad GPA	3.2
Application fee	$55
Regular application deadline	3/31
Regular notification	rolling
Rolling notification?	Yes
Early application program?	No
Transfer students accepted?	Yes
Evening division offered?	Yes
Part-time accepted?	Yes
LSDAS accepted?	Yes

Applicants Also Look At

Baylor University, South Texas College of Law, Southern Methodist University, Texas A&M University, Texas Tech University, The University of Texas at Austin.

International Students

TOEFL required of international students?	No
TOEFL recommended of international students?	No

FINANCIAL FACTS

Annual tuition	$19,860
Books and supplies	$1,500
Fees per credit	$560
Tuition per credit	$670
Average grant	$5,000
Average loan	$20,000
Average debt	$55,000

EMPLOYMENT INFORMATION

Career Rating	**65**
% employed within 9 months	83.9
Average starting salary	$45,000
State for bar exam	TX
Pass rate for first-time bar	82

Employers who frequently hire grads:
Mid- to small size private practice firms, district attorney's offices, government agencies, various corporations and businesses.

Grads employed by field (%):

Academic	2
Business/industry	19
Government	16
Judicial clerkships	2
Private practice	59

THOMAS JEFFERSON SCHOOL OF LAW

INSTITUTIONAL INFORMATION

Public/private	private
Student/faculty ratio	30:1
% faculty part-time	47
% faculty female	45
% faculty minority	6
Total faculty	60

SURVEY SAYS . . .

Diverse opinions accepted in classrooms
Students love San Diego, CA

STUDENTS

Enrollment of law school	838
% male/female	58/42
% out-of-state	65
% full-time	73
% minority	17
% international	1
# of countries represented	3
Average age of entering class	24

ACADEMICS

Academic Experience rating	**66**
Professors interesting rating	76
Professors accessible rating	90
Hours of study per day	4.12

Academic Specialties

Constitutional law, criminal law, entertainment law, environmental law, international law, intellectual property.

Advanced Degrees Offered

JD, 3 years full-time; JD, 4 years part-time.

Academic Requirements

Clinical Program Required?	No
Legal Writing Course Requirement?	Yes
Legal Methods Course Requirement?	No
Legal Research Course Requirement?	No
Moot Court Requirement?	No
Public Interest Law Requirement?	No

Academics

Students at Thomas Jefferson School of Law characterize their experience by the school's practical approach to legal education, the close-knit community of students and teachers, and friendly, accessible professors, all against the backdrop of sunny San Diego. Students agree, "The overall academic experience is positive [and that] the atmosphere is very supportive, which includes professors and my fellow classmates." In order to train future lawyers through a series of foundation courses and experiential learning programs, the school maintains active moot court and mock trial programs, a highly competitive law review, and a number of field programs and externships in addition to traditional course work. One student explains, "Thomas Jefferson is the school you come to if you want to gain a working and less historic knowledge of the law. Although legal theory plays a large and important role in the curriculum, the faculty is more concerned with providing students with a knowledge base that more appropriately prepares us for the legal 'real world.'" Another student confidently contributes, "Overall, I believe I received a first-rate legal education, and the school's strong emphasis on developing my practical skills has certainly enhanced my resume far beyond those of my peers from other schools." While most students appreciate the applicability of their course work, some would like to see a greater emphasis on basic philosophy and theory of law. One student confides, "I feel that some of my professors teach us the skills to pass the bar, but not to really understand the law." Another complains, "There is a woeful lack of American legal history taught."

Overall, students feel that "TJSL's cozy atmosphere is nurturing and allows students as well as professors to interact with each other frequently, allowing a healthy exchange of ideas to circulate throughout the campus." The teaching staff gets high marks from students, who describe the faculty as "an amazing group of well-respected powerful people, active in the community locally and nationally." Consistent with the school's educational mission, many teachers "have practiced in their respective fields, so they provide real-life insight into what they teach." TJSL students love the fact that "the school's professors are easy to approach and more than willing to spend time with you outside of class." One student shares this story: "The accessibility of the faculty is outstanding. On one occasion, I e-mailed my professor a copy of my midterm and asked for his comments. In less than an hour he had e-mailed back my midterm with elaborate explanations of how I could improve." Still, some students wish they were taught only by those professors who offer the best of both worlds. "The school could strive for experienced professors (not just experienced lawyers who have no idea how to teach first year students)," says one conscientious student.

Along those lines, students worry about the school's rapid growth, watching the classrooms and parking lots burst at the seams with each year's incoming class. Students say, "Every year the average entering student GPA and LSAT scores rise," and with that, so do the class sizes. Students fret that, "the classrooms are ridiculously crowded," and that the campus is "a little on the small side and needs desperately to expand." Still, "the school is committed to constantly upgrading the technical as well as academic areas of the school," starting with fall 2004 they have reduced the size of the entering class by 100 students to eliminate overcrowding. Many feel that, with time, TJSL will catch up to itself.

Jennifer Keller, Assistant Dean
2121 San Diego Avenue, San Diego, CA 92110
Telephone: 619-297-9700 • Fax: 619-294-4713
E-mail: adm@tjsl.edu • Website: www.tjsl.edu

Life

Students at Thomas Jefferson concur, "The location couldn't be more perfect than San Diego. I love calling friends in law school on the East Coast in January and find them snowed in while I'm going surfing." Another raves, "Who can beat studying on the beach in the middle of winter?!" Students say, "It is easy to make friends because everyone is so outgoing, [and that] there is no shortage of formal and informal social activities, including parties, sporting events, volunteer work, forums, and club meetings and activities" One student even told us, "I had more fun in law school than I ever had in undergrad." Students also claim to be "active in the local community" and report that "there is a highly vocal liberal slant that predominates" within the student body.

Over 25 percent of JD students at Thomas Jefferson are enrolled in the four-year part-time program, taking some of their classes in the evening. Though the average age of entering students is 24, the part-timers tend to be "serious, mature guys and gals who have worked for years, usually still work, and often have families." There is hope for both sets of students to exist in harmony, though. Students say, "From the first day, the school has facilitated social interaction among students, including students of all ages and backgrounds." In addition, students say the school strives for unity, maintaining "an attitude suggesting we are all in this together working for common goals—to learn, do well academically, get experience, and help build our school's reputation."

Getting In

The only prerequisite for applicants to Thomas Jefferson School of Law is a bachelor's degree from an accredited college and recent LSAT scores. TJSL admits students who display a strong aptitude for the study and practice of law, a strong undergraduate record, and competitive performance on the LSAT. First-year students who score over 150 on the LSAT are eligible for LSAT scholarships, the amount of which varies depending on their score. Students who score 160–180 on their LSAT receive a renewable full-tuition scholarship.

EMPLOYMENT INFORMATION

Career Rating	**69**
% employed within 9 months	91
Average starting salary	$55,269
State for bar exam	CA, NV, TX, CO, NJ
Pass rate for first-time bar	67

Employers who frequently hire grads: Various private law firms throughout California, Nevada, and Arizona, and government agencies, such as the attorney general, district attorney, and city attorney.

Prominent Alumni: Bonnie Dumanis, San Diego district attorney; Duncan Hunter, member of congress; Stephen Cornman, faculty, Georgetown University; Mattias Luukkonen, Baker, & McKenzie.

Grads employed by field (%):	
Academic	1
Business/industry	22
Government	5
Judicial clerkships	7
Private practice	54
Public interest	1

ADMISSIONS

Selectivity Rating	**66**
# applications received	3,206
# applicants accepted	1,206
# acceptees attending	288
Average LSAT	150
LSAT Range	147–157
Average undergrad GPA	3.0
Application fee	$35
Regular application deadline	rolling
Regular notification	rolling
Rolling notification?	Yes
Early application program?	No
Transfer students accepted?	Yes
Evening division offered?	Yes
Part-time accepted?	Yes
LSDAS accepted?	Yes

Applicants Also Look At

California Western, Southwestern University School of Law, University of the Pacific, University of San Diego, Whittier College.

International Students

TOEFL required of international students?	Yes

FINANCIAL FACTS

Annual tuition	$24,600
Books and supplies	$1,792
Fees per credit	$150
Tuition per credit	$15,450
Room & board	$11,100
Financial aid application deadline	4/25
% first-year students receiving some sort of aid	94
% receiving some sort of aid	92
% of aid that is merit-based	15
% receiving scholarships	40
Average grant	$10,394
Average loan	$27,607
Average total aid package	$30,078
Average debt	$99,000

TULANE UNIVERSITY
LAW SCHOOL

INSTITUTIONAL INFORMATION

Public/private	private
Student/faculty ratio	19:1
% faculty female	24
% faculty minority	12
Total faculty	50

SURVEY SAYS . . .

Great research resources
Beautiful campus

STUDENTS

Enrollment of law school	985
% male/female	50/50
% out-of-state	84
% full-time	100
% minority	22
% international	3
# of countries represented	78
Average age of entering class	24

ACADEMICS

Academic Experience rating	**85**
Professors interesting rating	80
Professors accessible rating	76
Hours of study per day	4.64

Academic Specialties

Admiralty & maritime law, civil law, environmental law, intellectual property law, international law, public interest law, sports law.

Advanced Degrees Offered

PhD, 3 years, including LLM year; master of laws, 1 year FT; master of laws in admiralty, 1 year FT, 2 years PT; master of laws in energy and environment, 1 year FT, 2 years PT; master of laws in international and comparative law, 1 year FT; master of laws in American business law.

Combined Degrees Offered

JD/BA or JD/BS, 6 yrs; JD/MBA, 4 yrs; JD/MHA, 4 yrs; JD/MSPH, 4 yrs; LLM/MSPH, 2 yrs; JD/MSW, 4 to 4.5 yrs; JD/MA (international affairs, Latin American Studies, etc.), 3 to 4 yrs; JD/MACCT, 3.5 to 4 yrs; JD/MS in international development, 3 to 3.5 yrs.

Academics

A "wonderful academic experience [and an] impressive array of courses" are available at "grossly underrated" Tulane University Law School. A host of specialties includes sports law, reputed to be among the best programs at Tulane, and a top-notch environmental law program. "Other strengths are specialized programs in admiralty," adds another student, who wonders, "Is there even an equivalent to Tulane Law School" in this regard? Also, because Louisiana's legal system is somewhat different than every other state's system, Tulane provides "interesting opportunities for comparative law [that are] not available at most American law schools." Popular with students is "a very practice-oriented advocacy program." A strong international orientation gives students "substantial exposure to international professors and study abroad opportunities." Dual-degree programs are available in international affairs and Latin American studies. Beyond course work, "the Tulane experience offers extracurricular organizations, journals, clinics, and lectures to satisfy just about every student's particular interest." Though academic opportunities abound, some students wish for "more grants for public interest law, less focus on corporate law." In addition, we are told, "The legal research and writing program leaves a lot to be desired." There is the occasional professor whom students suggest that you "avoid like the plague," but for the most part, the professors are "brilliant, engaging, and available. Two of my professors helped to write the texts that we are using," claims a proud student. Some professors are "so excited about their work that they can make *Pennoyer v. Neff* more tantalizing than a plate of crawfish étouffée from Felix's in the French Quarter. That's hard to do!" In the classrooms, "spirited discussions" are the norm; professors "explain their subjects clearly and thoroughly [and] provide a unique balance of legal theory and practical application." Outside of class, "the professors are always walking down the halls and talking with students." One student recounts a particularly fond social interaction with a professor: "One of the most memorable experiences of my first year occurred at a party our professor hosted for us at the end of the first semester. He had forgotten his keys in his house, with his wife out of town. He was afraid that the beer would get warm, so he picked up a rock and threw it through the window to let us all in." Student opinion on the administration is mixed. A representative from one side of the fence writes, "I have never been around a more organized group of individuals," while a critic rages, "The Office of Student Affairs should be renamed the Office for Students We Like/Care About." Almost everyone is "particularly pleased [with the] quick and results-oriented" Financial Aid Office, but the Career Development Office receives harsh reviews. While "the school is very well-recruited by the entire country," "Improve career development" seems to be a common request amongst students; "more communication about job resources and networking skills would be a good start" suggests another. The school appears to be working on addressing this concern by making improvements to the career services office staff and enhancing outreach efforts. Student offers a more subdued deduction, "Tulane is your prototypical lower-end, top-tier school. The reputation means something, but you will not get a job simply based on that reputation as compared to an Ivy."

Tulane is "not only beautiful, but [also the] incredibly well-designed" law school building "is exceptional, and the reading room is gorgeous," according to students. The accolades continue: "The classrooms are all great and relatively new, [and] the library is big and comfy [with] myriad volumes and great computer facilities." The campus also has a wireless network, so students can stay connected outside the hallowed halls. Nevertheless, some students complain that "it's too cold, [that] the water fountains don't work, [and that the school] is too modern in appearance," whereas a "timeless look would have been more aesthetically pleasing." Hey, you can't please everybody.

Kirsten Nobbe, Admission Coordinator
Weinmann Hall, 6329 Freret Street, New Orleans, LA 70118
Telephone: 504-865-5930 • Fax: 504-865-6710
E-mail: admissions@law.tulane.edu • Website: www.law.tulane.edu

Life

Tulane's law students describe themselves as "dedicated, low-key, [and] pretty relaxed," and they come from all across the nation "to have a good time and earn a well-respected degree." Ethnically and geographically, Tulane's student population "is a microcosm of the nation." In addition to strong ethnic diversity, Tulane is home to both extreme liberals and conservatives. Fortunately, students say, Tulane's academic environment "allows for tolerance of all view points regardless of agreement."

The "fabulous spring and fall weather" in New Orleans is a real plus, and students tell us that the Big Easy is "an ideal environment for the study of law." One student swears, "New Orleans really does provide many activities that do not focus on drinking. Honestly. No, seriously! Stop laughing." It should come as no surprise, though, that "the social scene is heavily focused on drinking." Suffice it to say, "Bourbon Street is a great stress reliever." There's also Jazz Fest, the Sugar Bowl, and Mardi Gras—"something that should be experienced at least once." This is made very possible at Tulane because classes are cancelled for the massive bacchanal. "Future 1Ls beware: this city can suck you in," warns one student. Another offers a helpful tip: "Students need to contain themselves because there is fun to be had nearly every day of the week." In addition to Bourbon Street festivities, "there are tons of parties sponsored by various student organizations." Furthermore, "Tulane provides many opportunities for social interaction," like when the administration "rolls kegs out into the courtyard" at the end of the first week of classes "so students can blow off steam and talk." There are also "bar reviews at least once a month, crawfish boils, [and other] opportunities to party on the school's dime." All in all, "Tulane is just a blast."

Getting In

It's not easy to get into Tulane, but it's not an impossible crapshoot either. Admitted students at the 25th percentile have an LSAT score of 158 and a GPA of 3.3. Admitted students at the 75th percentile have an LSAT score of 163 and a GPA of 3.7. If you take the LSAT more than once, Tulane will average your scores. It's also worth noting that students from all over the country enroll at Tulane. The top five states represented in recent 1L classes are Louisiana, New York, Texas, Florida, and California.

EMPLOYMENT INFORMATION

Career Rating	**87**
% employed within 9 months	95
Average starting salary	$87,000
State for bar exam	NY, LA, TX, FL, DC
Pass rate for first-time bar	93

Employers who frequently hire grads: Fulbright & Jaworski; Skadden Arps, Arnold, & Porter; White & Case; Mayer Brown & Platt; Cleary Gottlieb; Schulte Roth; McGlinchey, Adams, & Reese.

Prominent Alumni: Robert Livingston, U.S. politics; David Vitter, U.S. politics; John Minor Wisdom, judiciary; William Suter, U.S. Supreme Court clerk; William Pryor, Alabama attorney general.

Grads employed by field (%):

Academic	1
Business/industry	11
Government	12
Judicial clerkships	10
Military	2
Private practice	56
Public interest	4

Academic Requirements

Clinical Program Required?	No
Legal Writing Course Requirement?	Yes
Legal Methods Course Requirement?	No
Legal Research Course Requirement?	Yes
Moot Court Requirement?	Yes
Public Interest Law Requirement?	Yes

ADMISSIONS

Selectivity Rating	**85**
# applications received	4,087
# applicants accepted	1,055
# acceptees attending	300
Average LSAT	161
LSAT Range	158–163
Average undergrad GPA	3.5
Application fee	$60
Regular application deadline	rolling
Regular notification	rolling
Rolling notification?	Yes
Early application program?	No
Transfer students accepted?	Yes
Evening division offered?	No
Part-time accepted?	No
LSDAS accepted?	Yes

Applicants Also Look At

American U., Boston U., Emory U., The George Washington U., Georgetown U., U. of Miami, The U. of Texas at Austin.

International Students

TOEFL required of international students?	No
TOEFL recommended of international students?	No

FINANCIAL FACTS

Annual tuition	$28,900
Books and supplies	$1,200
Fees per credit	$231
Tuition per credit	$2,890
Room & board	$9,090
Financial aid application deadline	3/15
% first-year students receiving some sort of aid	87
% receiving some sort of aid	87
% of aid that is merit-based	67
% receiving scholarships	60
Average grant	$10,000
Average loan	$26,837
Average total aid package	$28,000
Average debt	$85,000

UNIVERSITY OF AKRON
SCHOOL OF LAW

INSTITUTIONAL INFORMATION

Public/private	public
Student/faculty ratio	16:1
% faculty part-time	48
% faculty female	41
% faculty minority	7
Total faculty	56

SURVEY SAYS . . .

Diverse opinions accepted in classrooms
Great research resources

STUDENTS

Enrollment of law school	569
% male/female	64/36
% out-of-state	21
% full-time	62
% minority	9
% international	1
# of countries represented	2
Average age of entering class	26

ACADEMICS

Academic Experience rating	**76**
Professors interesting rating	72
Professors accessible rating	68
Hours of study per day	4.17

Academic Specialties

Business law, criminal law, intellectual property law, international law, litigation, taxation.

Advanced Degrees Offered

LLM in intellectual property.

Combined Degrees Offered

JD/master in business administration, JD/master of science and management in human resources; JD/master in taxation; JD/master of applied politics; JD/master in public administration.

Academic Requirements

Clinical Program Required?	No
Legal Writing Course Requirement?	Yes
Legal Methods Course Requirement?	Yes

Academics

At the University of Akron, quality teaching is taken seriously. While students praise their professors' expertise and experience, they are most impressed with their charismatic classroom demeanor. A student glows, "beside being extremely talented lawyers, the professors are exceptional teachers [and] their passion, irrepressible enthusiasm, and care for the law is infectious!" Another joins in, "Even when I was about to study an area of the law which did not interest me, I was able to have fun because the teachers know how to make the material interesting." In fact, one student tells us, "I sincerely believe each of my professors could moonlight as a standup comedian." As far as political topics and discussion are concerned, some students say, "The professors are almost all liberal and antiwar and don't hesitate to let it show." While some conservative students dislike the liberal slant, most agree that the atmosphere is tolerant, supportive, and open-minded. A student reassures, "I have never seen any incidents where other views were not tolerated simply because the professor disagreed." In fact, students say the general attitude at Akron is supportive and friendly, and students are encouraged to speak their mind. One claims, "Akron is such a diverse city and all those different people are represented in our school. The sharing of ideas and knowledge is respected and encouraged; we are constantly enlightened by each other." On that note, students say that despite the pressures of law school, "the students are friendly—no backbiting or ugly competitiveness, [creating] a real 'we're-all-in-it-together' kind of atmosphere."

While course work provides a strong foundation in the theory of law, students say that they also get a lot of great hands-on experience at the University of Akron. One student maintains, "U of Akron students, for whatever reason, tend to bridge the gap well between practice and theory. This is evidenced by the excellence of the trial advocacy and moot court teams." In addition, students praise the externship programs and the Appellate Review Clinic (legal clinic), which "offers an opportunity for students to aid indigent clients with questions and write appellate briefs." Some students would like to see the practical models go even further. One students suggests, "I would also like to see a mock clerk of courts where we as students (for a course) role play as facilitators in the various departments and offices to gain hands-on experience on where, when, how to file court documents."

Akron offers courses in a wide range of legal specialties, including business, labor and employment, public interest, and international studies. However, the school is particularly well known for its strong intellectual property program, including the Center for Intellectual Property Law, which boasts a number of nationally recognized faculty members and more than 20 IP-related courses. One student enthuses, "The IP symposium each spring brings the best minds in intellectual property to the campus from all over the world and creates great networking opportunities." In addition, Akron students have the option of pursuing one of four joint degree programs: JD/Master of Business Administration, JD/Master of Public Administration, JD/MS in Taxation, and JD/Master of Science in Management and Human Relations.

While most students agree that the administration is competent and that the "university is quite well run," some gripe that administrators "give you little to no access to them and are almost always unwilling to help." Another echoes, "Although some people in the dean's office are helpful, others act like they're doing you a favor by talking to you." In addition, students lament that the administration "has been less than helpful in the past few years in the area of addressing and resolving student concerns about diversity, class rankings, and the lack of Career Services."

LAURI S. FILE, ASSISTANT DEAN OF ADMISSIONS, FINANCIAL AID, STUDENT SERVICES
THE UNIVERSITY OF AKRON SCHOOL OF LAW, 150 UNIVERSITY AVENUE, AKRON, OH 44325-2901
TELEPHONE: 800-425-7668 • FAX: 330-258-2343
E-MAIL: LAWADMISSIONS@UAKRON.EDU • WEBSITE: WWW.UAKRON.EDU/LAW

Life

Campus life is laid-back and friendly at the University of Akron. Students say that they "all get along and socialize together often, [and] the student lounge is usually filled with groups of students sharing meals, ideas, and laughs." Students warn, however, that there is a bit of a dichotomy between the full-time day students and the part-time evening students. In the words of one moonlighter, "The only area that I see could be improved would be the deference given to day students as opposed to evening students. The evening students bring a wealth of real-world experience to the classroom that sometimes remains untapped by the professors and administration who remain in the traditional day-student atmosphere." Another adds, "The day students tend to have more of a social life (within the law school community), whereas many of the night students prefer to get in and get out." However, students say, no matter who you are, there are "a lot of student organizations that offer many socializing opportunities." While "there is no pressure to participate, the groups are very welcoming to those students who do wish to participate."

Getting In

With more than 2,000 applications for fewer than 200 seats, admission to Akron is competitive. Akron looks for students whose academic record suggests that they would be successful law students, with a median GPA for matriculants of 3.22. LSAT scores are also heavily considered in an admissions decision—last year, the average accepted student scored a 157. As the school is deeply involved in the local community, it also seeks out students who have experience or background that suggests they will make a positive impact on the community through legal practice. Therefore, unique work or volunteer experience; an interesting and challenging personal background; and letters of recommendation are also strongly weighed.

EMPLOYMENT INFORMATION

Career Rating	**74**
% employed within 9 months	95
Average starting salary	$56,561
State for bar exam	OH, PA, FL, NY, CA
Pass rate for first-time bar	82

Employers who frequently hire grads: Buckingham, Doolittle, & Burroughs; Brouse & Mcdowell; Roetzel & Andress; Squire, Sanders & Dempsey; Sughrue Mion; Jones Day.

Prominent Alumni: Deborah Cook, judge, U.S. Court of Appeals, sixth circuit; Rochelle Seide, partner, Arent Fox; John Vasuta, General Counsel, Bridgestone Firestone.

Grads employed by field (%):	
Academic	8
Business/industry	20
Government	15
Judicial clerkships	6
Military	1
Other	2
Private practice	44
Public interest	4

Legal Research Course Requirement?	Yes
Moot Court Requirement?	No
Public Interest Law Requirement?	No

ADMISSIONS

Selectivity Rating	**83**
# applications received	1,928
# applicants accepted	366
# acceptees attending	106
Average LSAT	158
LSAT Range	156–161
Average undergrad GPA	3.3
Regular application deadline	rolling
Regular notification	rolling
Rolling notification?	Yes
Early application program?	No
Transfer students accepted?	Yes
Evening division offered?	Yes
Part-time accepted?	Yes
LSDAS accepted?	Yes

Applicants Also Look At

Capital University, Case Western Reserve University, Cleveland State University, Ohio Northern University, The Ohio State University, University of Dayton, University of Toledo.

International Students

TOEFL required of international students?	Yes
Minimum Paper TOEFL	600
Minimum Computer TOEFL	250

FINANCIAL FACTS

Annual tuition (resident)	$11,079
Annual tuition (nonresident)	$18,515
Books and supplies	$900
Fees per credit (resident)	$67
Fees per credit (nonresident)	$67
Tuition per credit (resident)	$369
Tuition per credit (nonresident)	$617
Room & board	$13,134
Financial aid application deadline	3/1
% first-year students receiving some sort of aid	90
% receiving some sort of aid	95
% of aid that is merit-based	99
% receiving scholarships	33
Average grant	$7,877
Average loan	$23,574
Average total aid package	$26,030
Average debt	$34,136

The University of Alabama
School of Law

INSTITUTIONAL INFORMATION

Public/private	public
Student/faculty ratio	12:1
% faculty part-time	45
% faculty female	21
% faculty minority	6
Total faculty	105

SURVEY SAYS . . .

Diverse opinions accepted in classrooms

Abundant externship/internship/clerkship opportunities

STUDENTS

Enrollment of law school	536
% male/female	63/37
% full-time	100
% minority	9
Average age of entering class	25

ACADEMICS

Academic Experience rating	**86**
Professors interesting rating	81
Professors accessible rating	82
Hours of study per day	4.01

Advanced Degrees Offered

LLM in taxation, 2 years part-time; LLM in international graduate program, 1 year.

Combined Degrees Offered

JD/MBA, 4 years.

Academic Requirements

Clinical Program Required?	No
Legal Writing Course Requirement?	Yes
Legal Methods Course Requirement?	No
Legal Research Course Requirement?	Yes
Moot Court Requirement?	Yes
Public Interest Law Requirement?	No

Academics

We have to agree that "it is hard not to like a law school that gives you a first-tier degree for only a little more than you would pay at a community college." The University of Alabama School of Law does just that, and offers a "wide variety of clinics, externships, and judicial clerkships," not to mention "a trial advocacy program that provides simulated court room experience [and] gives future litigators a chance to find out if they have what it takes." One student praises the many "opportunities to gain experience through the school's five legal clinics." Another student adds, "The presence of the Public Interest Institute gives students an opportunity to do volunteer work."

Although some students complain that UA Law "could improve by offering a wider range of classes," most students speak glowingly of the administration. One student says, "The administration is serious about having quality people and training them to be quality lawyers [and the] southern hospitality" of the top brass is "a welcome change from most large university undergraduate experiences." Another student adds, "The Dean is incredible and is the main reason why the Law School has made great improvements in faculty and facilities [even though] the state's budget, especially its higher education budget, has been in the toilet." Students rave about their professors, who "have great legal minds, seem to legitimately care about the students, [and] encourage a lot of student interaction." One student notes, "If you make an effort to get to know them, then they will take the same interest in you." Another student claims, "Professors are very accessible, even in the middle of the night"; indeed, students tell us that they are taught by "some of the best faculty that you will find at a public university." Several students note that the professors "lean to the left." One student adds that although the school culture is conservative, "the professors do not reflect the politics of the students."

The Career Services office "strongly caters to those from the state of Alabama," where UA Law enjoys an excellent reputation and plenty of "name-brand recognition." One student reports, "Alabama is the natural choice for students interested in practicing in the state. Alabama grads are very partial to other Alabama grads when it comes to hiring, and many of the most powerful people in the state are alums." Employment prospects are also good throughout the region; however, it's tough "to find jobs outside of Alabama and the Southeast."

A few students complain about the school's facilities, one citing a "1970s dinosaur-looking building," which another student says "can feel like a dark dungeon sometimes." However, most students qualify their gripes with the acknowledgment that things are improving. One student says, "The law school seems to be constantly upgrading its facilities," including a new wing slated to open in December 2006. The library and research facilities are reportedly above par. One student boasts, "We have great staff that will help you find what you need. If it's not in our library, which is not often the case, the library staff will help you find it online." Technology could definitely improve. Students point to the "cheap, crappy" copiers that the school needs to replace and say, that there should be "more laptop plugs in the classrooms."

Life

Most of the students "are from Alabama originally and many social groups carry over from undergrad, and even high school, [so] out-of-staters may feel shut out." There are "lots of Southern sorority and fraternity types." Typical UA Law students are "fairly conservative Protestant"; therefore, racial and ethnic diversity is generally lacking. "We have

Claude Reeves, Assistant Dean
PO Box 870382, Tuscaloosa, AL 35487
Telephone: 205-348-5440 • Fax: 205-348-3917
E-mail: admissions@law.ua.edu • Website: www.law.ua.edu

a good number of international students but can't seem to attract a lot of American students of color," says one student.

Students are "competitive in the sense that they know good grades mean a good job." Like at all law schools, "stress is a constant factor," but here "it is mostly self-induced and not something that people try to exploit in each other." Students tell us that "there's a great sense of community in the law school and the town in general [and] the traditions of the university and the law school instill a unique common bond of pride and extracurricular involvement in the alumni." Eventually, "the school becomes somewhat of an adopted family. Even when you do not like it, you are still obligated to love it."

Outside the law school confines, "students genuinely enjoy socializing with each other." One student notes that while, "Tuscaloosa is not very cosmopolitan," it is "a great college town replete with plenty of nightlife, college football, and other sports, and a very warm town-gown relationship, [and that] it's a great place to be if you're young and want to have a full social life." Another student declares, "People don't shy away from having a good time with fellow students and enjoying the atmosphere and tradition of the University of Alabama. Hardly a week goes by without some sort of social event. The week building up to homecoming is unbelievable, as the law school has become part of the homecoming tradition." In the fall, "Alabama football is as good as it gets," and the quasi-religious devotion to the Crimson Tide extends fervently to the law school, which has its own section for football games.

Getting In

This law school is one of the toughest in the Southeast to get into. The acceptance rate here is about 24 percent. The median LSAT score of admitted students is 163. The median GPA is 3.5. Alabama natives make up roughly 80 percent of the student body. If you take the LSAT more than once, the admissions committee will consider all your scores.

ADMISSIONS

Selectivity Rating	**88**
# applications received	1,339
# applicants accepted	318
# acceptees attending	171
Average LSAT	161
LSAT Range	159–163
Average undergrad GPA	3.4
Application fee	$35
Regular application deadline	3/1
Regular notification	rolling
Rolling notification?	Yes
Early application program?	No
Transfer students accepted?	Yes
Evening division offered?	No
Part-time accepted?	No
LSDAS accepted?	Yes
International Students	
TOEFL required of international students?	Yes

FINANCIAL FACTS

Annual tuition (resident)	$8,130
Annual tuition (nonresident)	$16,802
Books and supplies	$1,168
Room & board (on/off-campus)	$7,098/$7,310
% receiving scholarships	35
Average grant	$5,208

EMPLOYMENT INFORMATION

Career Rating	**80**
Job placement rate (%)	97
Average starting salary	$61,664
State for bar exam	AL, GA, MS, TN, FL
Pass rate for first-time bar	96

Employers who frequently hire grads:
Private practices, government agencies, public interest agencies.

Grads employed by field (%):	
Academic	1
Business/industry	8
Government	5
Judicial clerkships	10
Military	6
Other	2
Private practice	63
Public interest	5

UNIVERSITY OF ARIZONA
JAMES E. ROGERS COLLEGE OF LAW

INSTITUTIONAL INFORMATION

Public/private	public
Student/faculty ratio	13:1
% faculty part-time	60
% faculty female	42
% faculty minority	20
Total faculty	85

SURVEY SAYS . . .

Diverse opinions accepted in classrooms, Great library staff, Abundant externship/internship/clerkship opportunities

STUDENTS

Enrollment of law school	475
% male/female	50/50
% out-of-state	27
% full-time	100
% minority	29
% international	1
# of countries represented	6
Average age of entering class	25

ACADEMICS

Academic Experience rating	**90**
Professors interesting rating	90
Professors accessible rating	89
Hours of study per day	4.28

Academic Specialties

Commercial law, constitutional law, corporation securities law, criminal law, environmental law, human rights law, Indian law, intellectual property law, international indigenous peoples rights and policy, international law, international trade law, legal history, legal philosophy, property, taxation.

Advanced Degrees Offered

JD, LLM in international trade law, LLM in indigenous peoples law & policy.

Combined Degrees Offered

JD/PhD in philsophy, psychology, or economics, JD/MBA, JD/MPA, JD/MA in American Indian studies, JD/MA in economics, JD/MA in women's studies, JD/MA in Latin American studies, JD/MS in management/finance.

Academics

James E. Rogers College of Law at the University of Arizona boasts "a stellar reputation in the southwest; low, low prices;" and programs galore "offering real-world experience and any internship you can dream up." Many clinics "focus on regional fields of expertise" such as immigration law and indigenous peoples law. In general, the University of Arizona is "a noble place [for] future public interest lawyers, child advocates, and public defenders. The goal is to give a five-star education while charging as little as possible, so that we can take the low-paying, white-hat jobs when we get out." In addition, "the trial advocacy program at Arizona is awesome!" A student gloats, "I have tried four bench trials, two evidentiary hearings, and one jury trial. I now have more trial experience than most law students and even many lawyers." The judicial externship program is fantastic, and the legal writing program is popular. Not only is all this enjoyable for students, it's also effective: 96 percent of UA's grads pass the Arizona bar on their first try.

Though students have a "very demanding workload, laughter is a common component in many classes, particularly the smaller ones where the professors and students are able to learn each others' quirks." On the whole, Arizona's professors are "passionate about their subjects, [and] concerned about creating good lawyers." There are some "very influential professors in trial practice, evidence," and contracts. UA is home to a few "worn-out" or otherwise "very bad" faculty members as well. But don't worry. "There has only been one class where I considered gouging my eye out," divulges one student. Also, if you are politically conservative, note that "the faculty is dominated by extremely left-wing people who do not tolerate differences of opinion." One student notes, "The administration is excellent, and they have worked hard to create a good atmosphere at the school." Another student adds, "They really go out of their way to make sure you're doing well academically, socially, and emotionally." Plus, the universally venerated dean of the law school is "an amazing leader and professor."

Career Services reportedly focuses on the "production of quality lawyers for the public sector." Some students do not love this approach. "While it's a great thing for those who are interested in that arena, they tend to encourage only the top 10 percent to go for private firm work," gripes one student. Of course, "all the top firms in Arizona and Nevada interview here, as well as a number of excellent firms from Texas, California, New Mexico, and Colorado."

The facilities, while serviceable, "are not the nicest." The building, "clearly built in the 1970s, is reminiscent of a bomb shelter." Also, "the library is a little cramped." Besides the look, what may seem to be "outdated buildings, the feeling inside the building and classrooms is not that way at all, [and] the campus is really nice." Students note, "It would be nice if the bathrooms were redone a bit, [but] the classrooms generally have up-to-date technology and relatively comfortable furniture." One of the favored features is "wireless Internet access everywhere."

Life

"We live in Tucson, paradise on earth," explains one student. "Tucson is rated one as of the healthiest cities in the Unites States, [and] it's always—and I mean always—sunny here." It's "incredibly hot as well" (like "100 degrees at the end of October"), but the near-constant sunshine "does wonders for the soul." You'll love it "in January when it is 70 degrees, and you are surrounded by mountain vistas."

"The social scene is as active as you want it to be," according to Arizona law students.

Terry Sue Holpert, Assistant Dean for Admissions
PO Box 210176, College of Law, University of Arizona, Tucson, AZ 85721-0176
Telephone: 520-621-3477 • Fax: 520-621-9140
E-mail: admissions@law.arizona.edu • Website: www.law.arizona.edu

"There is a social event at least two-to-three times a week, [and] there are numerous clubs, activities, and charitable organizations." Students comment on the abound activities: "From Thursday night bar review to activities with med students and MBA students, there is always something to do, [including] tailgates during football season, Barrister Ball (law school prom), Halloween Carnival," and a softball tournament. Arizona also has many "camping trips, skiing/snowboarding trips, Mexico trips, and Vegas trips." Some students complain of "lousy shopping, few good restaurants, [and] bars filled with undergrads." On the plus side, reasons one student, "We would beat any other law school in a drinking contest."

UA students enjoy a "very chilled out environment—shorts and flip-flops everyday." The law school is "very sequestered from the rest of the university," which helps create a strong sense of community. "Wherever you go, be it a library, computer lab, copy center, or Career Services, you will probably find friends." One student explains, "It is academically challenging but not overly competitive. The thing that has really overwhelmed me is the friendly, welcoming atmosphere that seems to permeate the entire school." Students at UA run the gamut. "There are lots of students here who are nontraditional, and the school accommodates them [as well as] the rah-rah law school kids." Students describe themselves as "smart people who, for the most part, aren't intellectual snobs." One student has a pointed message for readers: "The students here are second to none (that includes you, Harvard)."

Getting In

The mean LSAT score at the University of Arizona is 162. Admitted students at the 25th percentile have an LSAT score of 160 and a GPA of 3.3. Admitted students at the 75th percentile have an LSAT score of 166 and a GPA of 3.73. Roughly 30 percent are members of an ethnic minority.

EMPLOYMENT INFORMATION

Career Rating	**79**
Job placement rate (%)	93
Average starting salary	$62,000
State for bar exam	AZ, CA, WA, NV, DC
Pass rate for first-time bar	98

Employers who frequently hire grads: Snell & Wilmer, Quarles & Brady Streich Lang, Bryan Cave, Gibson Dunn & Crutcher, Squire Sanders, Jennings Strouss & Salmon, O'Melveny & Myers, Fennemore Craig.

Prominent Alumni: Morris K. Udall, former congressman; Stewart Udall, former congressman and secretary of interior; Dennis DeConcini, former senator.

Grads employed by field (%):	
Academic	5
Business/industry	7
Government	25
Judicial clerkships	19
Military	2
Private practice	42
Public interest	2

Academic Requirements

Clinical Program Required?	No
Legal Writing Course Requirement?	Yes
Legal Methods Course Requirement?	No
Legal Research Course Requirement?	Yes
Moot Court Requirement?	No
Public Interest Law Requirement?	No

ADMISSIONS

Selectivity Rating	**89**
# applications received	2,589
# applicants accepted	455
# acceptees attending	153
Average LSAT	162
LSAT Range	160–166
Average undergrad GPA	3.5
Application fee	$50
Regular application deadline	2/15
Regular notification	rolling
Rolling notification?	Yes
Early application program?	No
Transfer students accepted?	Yes
Evening division offered?	No
Part-time accepted?	No
LSDAS accepted?	Yes

Applicants Also Look At

Arizona State U., U. of California, Davis, U. of California—-Hastings, U. of California—-Los Angeles, U. of San Diego, U. of Southern California, The U. of Texas at Austin.

International Students

TOEFL required of international students?	Yes

FINANCIAL FACTS

Annual tuition (resident)	$12,598
Annual tuition (nonresident)	$21,578
Books and supplies	$750
Room & board (on/off-campus)	$8,864/$12,688
Financial aid application deadline	3/1
% first-year students receiving some sort of aid	80
% receiving some sort of aid	78
% of aid that is merit-based	43
% receiving scholarships	78
Average grant	$3,400
Average loan	$13,500
Average total aid package	$18,000
Average debt	$40,022

UNIVERSITY OF ARKANSAS—FAYETTEVILLE
SCHOOL OF LAW

INSTITUTIONAL INFORMATION

Public/private	public
Student/faculty ratio	13:1
% faculty part-time	31
% faculty female	33
% faculty minority	16
Total faculty	34

SURVEY SAYS . . .

Diverse opinions accepted in classrooms
Students love Fayetteville, AR

STUDENTS

Enrollment of law school	474
% male/female	54/46
% out-of-state	21
% full-time	100
% minority	21
% international	1
# of countries represented	4
Average age of entering class	25

ACADEMICS

Academic Experience rating	**70**
Professors interesting rating	74
Professors accessible rating	79
Hours of study per day	3.5

Advanced Degrees Offered

LLM in agricultural law, 1 academic year.

Combined Degrees Offered

JD/MBA, 3.5 years; JD/MPA, 3 years; LLM/MS, 1.5 years.

Academic Requirements

Clinical Program Required?	No
Legal Writing Course Requirement?	Yes
Legal Methods Course Requirement?	No
Legal Research Course Requirement?	No
Moot Court Requirement?	Yes
Public Interest Law Requirement?	No

Academics

While many public law schools are large and impersonal, students at the University of Arkansas—Fayetteville School of Law say their school has many of the perks you would expect to find at one of the nation's top private institutions but for a much lower price. Students say their "highly accessible" professors often "stay after class to answer questions," and most of them have "open-door [policies]." Professors are not only just friendly, but also skillful teachers who are armed with a "wide variety of educational methods [that they use to] encourage students to enjoy the study of law and the legal profession." A few students, however, find the faculty a bit lofty. One student claims, "All of the professors are infinitely more intelligent than all of the students. And they make sure we know it."

Students say that the school "has a very strong clinic program," which offers "excellent opportunities to practice law as a student." In addition, the school's reputation is well-established in the local legal community, giving students access to excellent clinical opportunities, externships, and—perhaps most important—jobs after graduation. One student says, "Our Board of Advocates program, a student-run competition program, is particularly excellent and a valued resource. The attorneys in the community are generous with their time and more than willing to help students grow into skilled lawyers." Another student adds, "With the law school located near the home office of the Bentonville-based Wal-Mart, the opportunities for great paying, highly diversified jobs are very high."

Students say that like the professors, administrators at UA are friendly and helpful; therefore, they take the time to get to know students as individuals. This helps contribute to the "feeling of family" students' experience. One student reports, "The deans all know me by my first name, not because I'm a goodie-goodie or the demon seed of the law school; just because they're good like that." Another student says, "The administration is wonderful. They genuinely care about the students and will do anything they can to help you out when you need it."

Facilities at the law school reflect the low tuition price. In the past, students have expressed concern about the appearance of the law school and the size of the library. In particular, students have complained that the library "is too small and slightly outdated." Luckily, an $11 million building expansion project is underway.

James K. Miller, Associate Dean for Students
University of Arkansas School of Law, Fayetteville, AR 72701
Telephone: 479-575-3102 • Fax: 479-575-3937
E-mail: jkmiller@uark.edu • Website: http://law.uark.edu

Life

With only about 150 students per class, the University of Arkansas is a small but active community that offers a wide variety of legal clubs, extracurricular activities, plus "a lot of activities outside of the law school to increase peer bonding." Students tell us that "the law school has great social functions that further the sense of community and fun among the students." For example, the weekly Bar Review is a social function where students "receive free beer for a few hours" and are then provided with safe rides to their homes. Other activities include "powder puff football, cookouts, [and hanging out in] rented-out clubs." One student adds, "Fayetteville is a wonderful place to live and work. It is the nearly impossible combination of small/peaceful and lively/fun. It is also amazingly beautiful."

"While there is a bit of competitiveness [at UA], it does not rise to a nasty level. [There is] a real sense of overall friendship within the class sections." Students say that the overall "atmosphere of the law school is very friendly." But there are some fractures in this happy community. In particular, students point out that social circles have a tendency to ethnically and racially divide.

Getting In

The majority of admitted students have LSAT scores that range from 150 to 159 and have an undergraduate GPA between 3.1 and 3.7. Most students (about 70 percent) are Arkansas state residents; however, the student body represents more than 30 states nationally and more than 100 undergraduate institutions.

ADMISSIONS

Selectivity Rating	**80**
# applications received	1,282
# applicants accepted	331
# acceptees attending	162
Average LSAT	155
LSAT Range	150–159
Average undergrad GPA	3.4
Regular application deadline	rolling
Regular notification	rolling
Rolling notification?	Yes
Early application program?	No
Transfer students accepted?	Yes
Evening division offered?	No
Part-time accepted?	No
LSDAS accepted?	Yes

International Students

TOEFL required of international students?	Yes
Minimum Paper TOEFL	550
Minimum Computer TOEFL	213

FINANCIAL FACTS

Annual tuition (resident)	$7,620
Annual tuition (nonresident)	$16,200
Books and supplies	$6,881
Room & board	$5,926
Financial aid application deadline	4/1
% first-year students receiving some sort of aid	74
% receiving some sort of aid	74
% of aid that is merit-based	65
% receiving scholarships	32
Average grant	$4,810
Average loan	$18,500
Average debt	$49,985

EMPLOYMENT INFORMATION

Career Rating	**73**
% employed within 9 months	92.6
Average starting salary	$48,500
State for bar exam	AR, TN, MO, OK, TX
Pass rate for first-time bar	82

Employers who frequently hire grads: The majority of our grads go into small firms.

Prominent Alumni: George W. Haley, former ambassador to Gambia; Philip S. Anderson, former ABA president; Morris S. Arnold, judge, eighth circuit; Rodney Slater, former U.S. secretary of transportation; Thomas A. Mars, senior vice president, general counsel, & secretary, Wal-Mart, Inc.

Grads employed by field (%):	
Academic	4
Business/industry	10
Government	1
Judicial clerkships	7
Private practice	64
Public interest	14

University of Arkansas—Little Rock
William H. Bowen School of Law

INSTITUTIONAL INFORMATION

Public/private	public
Student/faculty ratio	17:1
% faculty part-time	38
% faculty female	38
% faculty minority	8
Total faculty	48

SURVEY SAYS . . .

Diverse opinions accepted in classrooms
Great research resources
Great library staff

STUDENTS

Enrollment of law school	450
% male/female	51/49
% out-of-state	15
% full-time	70
% minority	10
# of countries represented	2
Average age of entering class	27

ACADEMICS

Academic Experience rating	**69**
Professors interesting rating	67
Professors accessible rating	72
Hours of study per day	4.07

Academic Specialties

Civil procedure, commercial law, constitutional law, corporation securities law, criminal law, environmental law, international law, labor law, legal history, property, taxation.

Combined Degrees Offered

JD/MBA, JD/MPA, JD/MPH. All combined degrees last approximately 3.5 years.

Academic Requirements

Clinical Program Required?	No
Legal Writing Course Requirement?	Yes
Legal Methods Course Requirement?	No
Legal Research Course Requirement?	Yes
Moot Court Requirement?	No
Public Interest Law Requirement?	No

Academics

The University of Arkansas—Little Rock William H. Bowen School of Law boasts small classes, a great student-faculty ratio, and a pleasant price tag. "We are not a big school, so you can make a lot of connections with a lot of people, [which is] definitely an advantage." Students believe that, "overall, the teachers here are fabulous." A few professors "have their heads in an academic cloud, [but most] really do everything they can to get you to understand the material." Professors have "great personalities [and] a wide range of backgrounds and experiences." They "find ways to use humor in [class] to make us learn." They are "brilliant, helpful, [and, if anything,] too nice." One malcontent student gripes, "I was hoping for a more *Paper Chase*–like atmosphere." Accessibility is another faculty specialty, and students find that professors' "doors are always open. This school places much emphasis on professors being available to the students." Indeed, professors "will stay as long after class as you need them to in order to answer questions." It seems that both "in and out of the classroom, [there is] quite a bit of student-professor interaction."

At UALR, "you will actually find an administration that cares more about students than anything else." The school is very "approachable and efficient, [and there is] rarely an issue that they are afraid to tackle." There is much emphasis on the students doing well. "Every member of the administration and faculty has let it be known that this law school is built for your success," says one student. "This is a law school that attempts to make every student an attorney." Of course, there are a few negatives. Being a modestly-sized school means UALR "doesn't have the variety of classes that larger schools have." At the very least, students say, "The school could offer courses more often [and stop offering] scarce elective courses at overlapping times."

Much emphasis is placed on practical skills. UALR "prepares [students] for how to practice law and be a lawyer." The school's location is "a key asset" to this end, as state capital Little Rock provides "unique opportunities [to] work in state government and the judiciary system." The location also allows students "to become familiar with the local bar." Students tell us, "The legal community is very involved with the school, [and] there are many excellent opportunities for clerkships with a wide variety of courts, firms, and organizations."

The facilities are uneven. Students say, "The inside of the building is beautiful, especially the law library, [which] serves not only the students but [also] the whole legal community of Little Rock." One student boasts, "We have two computer labs, wireless Internet throughout the library, and an exhaustive collection of legal reference materials." But the "somewhat dated [classrooms] often feel crowded, lack electrical outlets for laptop users, [and] do not have wireless Internet." Also, "the acoustics in the classrooms make it very difficult to hear sometimes," and one student suggests microphones in classrooms.

Jean Probasco, Director of Admissions
1201 McMath Avenue, Little Rock, AR 72202-5142
Telephone: 501-324-9903 • Fax: 501-324-9433
E-mail: lawadm@ualr.edu • Website: www.ualr.edu/~lawschool

Life

Minority enrollment is "very low" at UALR, especially considering Little Rock's sizeable African American population. Geographic diversity is on the rise, though. "UALR is growing because of out-of-state scholarships, which allow the student body to be comprised of a widely geographically diverse student body." At UALR "there is a big divide between the day and night students, as well as a divide within the individual classes based on age." The "just-out-of-college [and] recently-out-of-college [crowds] tend to stick together," while the older students form their own group. Students are further "divided along political lines between conservatives and liberals." Still, overall there is a "generally friendly atmosphere."

Academic competition is "noticeable" but not excessive. "Everyone is really willing to help each other," describes one cooperative student. "The classroom is similar to a group of friends just trying to work through the material together as a team. This attitude is present throughout the whole school from the 3Ls down to the 1Ls."

UALR is well-situated in Little Rock, "a great city" according to students. The school is "very close" to the city's popular River Market District. "Every Thursday night after classes, we usually make it a point to get together outside of school and relieve some stress," relates one student. The law school is also only five minutes or so from most of Arkansas's largest law firms and the headquarters of many of its corporations. The state capitol and several museums are nearby as well.

Getting In

Admitted students at the 25th percentile have an LSAT score of 150 and a GPA of 3.0. Admitted students at the 75th percentile have an LSAT score of 157 and a GPA of 3.6. If you apply online at UALR, you don't have to pay an application fee.

EMPLOYMENT INFORMATION

Career Rating	**63**
Job placement rate (%)	87
Average starting salary	$46,206
State for bar exam	AR, TN, TX, GA, FL
Pass rate for first-time bar	82

Employers who frequently hire grads: Wright, Lindsey, & Jennings; Friday, Eldredge, & Clark; Mitchell, Williams, Selig, Gates, & Woodyard; State Supreme Court.

Prominent Alumni: Vic Snyder, member, U.S. congress; Annabelle Clinton-Imber, State Supreme Court; Andrea Layton Roaf, State Court of Appeals; H. E. "Bud" Cummins, U.S. attorney.

Grads employed by field (%):	
Academic	1
Business/industry	11
Government	13
Judicial clerkships	17
Other	3
Private practice	55

ADMISSIONS

Selectivity Rating	**74**
# applications received	654
# applicants accepted	271
# acceptees attending	177
Average LSAT	153
LSAT Range	150–157
Average undergrad GPA	3.3
Regular application deadline	4/15
Regular notification	rolling
Rolling notification?	Yes
Early application program?	No
Transfer students accepted?	Yes
Evening division offered?	Yes
Part-time accepted?	Yes
LSDAS accepted?	Yes

Applicants Also Look At

Mercer University, University of Arkansas—Fayetteville, The University of Tulsa.

International Students

TOEFL required of international students?	No
TOEFL recommended of international students?	Yes

FINANCIAL FACTS

Annual tuition (resident)	$7,680
Annual tuition (nonresident)	$16,500
Books and supplies	$1,000
Fees per credit (resident)	$18
Fees per credit (nonresident)	$18
Tuition per credit (resident)	$256
Tuition per credit (nonresident)	$550
Room & board (off-campus)	$9,476
% first-year students receiving some sort of aid	77
% receiving some sort of aid	68
% of aid that is merit-based	11
% receiving scholarships	30
Average grant	$5,830
Average loan	$15,118
Average total aid package	$14,780
Average debt	$26,000

University of California—Berkeley
Boalt Hall School of Law

INSTITUTIONAL INFORMATION

Public/private	public
Student/faculty ratio	14:1
% faculty part-time	49
% faculty female	32
% faculty minority	10
Total faculty	166

SURVEY SAYS . . .

Great library staff
Abundant externship/internship/clerkship opportunities
Students love Berkeley, CA

STUDENTS

Enrollment of law school	880
% male/female	39/61
% out-of-state	33
% full-time	100
% minority	37
# of countries represented	22
Average age of entering class	25

ACADEMICS

Academic Experience rating	**92**
Professors interesting rating	87
Professors accessible rating	84
Hours of study per day	3.86

Academic Specialties

Business law & economics, comparative legal studies, corporation securities law, environmental law, intellectual property law, international law, law & technology, social justice.

Advanced Degrees Offered

LLM, JSD (PhD in jurisprudence & social policy)

Combined Degrees Offered

JD/MA & JD/PhD economics, JD/MBA School of Bus., JD/MA Asian studies, JD/MA international area studies, JD/MCP Dept. of City & Regional Planning, JD/MJ Grad. School of Journalism, JD/MPP School of Public Policy, JD/MSW School of Social Welfare, JD/MA & JD/PhD information management systems, JD/PhD history (legal history), JD/MS energy & resources group.

Academics

California public institutions of higher education have in recent years suffered some substantial and well-publicized cuts in state funding. Despite the effects that these cuts have had on all of the schools in the University of California system, students at renowned Boalt Hall insist that their law school continues to uphold its well-earned, long-standing reputation for academic excellence. In particular, students praise the unwavering commitment and quality of the school's faculty and staff. A 2L tells us, "Coming from an economically flush private undergrad, I was not expecting that a public university in economically beleaguered California would have a staff that is as accessible, knowledgeable, helpful, and cheerful as the one here at Boalt." A 3L adds, "For a large public school in a state beset with serious financial issues, I believe that Boalt does an excellent job of focusing on providing the best teaching possible in a world of limited funds." While Boalt's academic excellence has not diminished in the face of such fiscal adversity, tuition and fees are on the rise. In fact, Boalt's price tag has nearly doubled in the past four years, making it roughly "comparable to other top schools," particularly if you are not a California resident. The good news for nonresident students is that they may establish residency (if they take certain steps) after their first year, meaning that they would be eligible for the much lower resident rates in their second and third years.

In addition to cost hikes, students also warn us that the aging facilities could use some improvements. "If only the school had more money to improve facilities!" is a common refrain, but one 3L notes that despite all this, "a number of real improvements have been made since I started—more classrooms have outlets for each student [laptop]. In addition, the computer labs are all great." Besides, "People don't come to Boalt because it's shiny, new, or pretty. They come because it is a great institution with tremendously helpful faculty and a very cool, friendly, and mellow student body."

As a part of the world-renowned University of California—Berkeley, Boalt benefits in many ways. In particular, Boalt offers a number of joint-degree programs in conjunction with other graduate schools within the university. "One of the greatest, and least known, strengths is that Boalt houses an interdisciplinary PhD program (Jurisprudence and Social Policy). This program allows for a broad range of courses and faculty that are not necessarily found in other law schools." In general, students say the law school sustains an intellectual vibe. One 3L looks back and muses, "Academically, I understand why Berkeley is a top-ten school. When you can have a semester composed of four constitutional law classes with some of the country's paramount scholars, the experience of law school transcends the vocational and becomes more akin to the scholarship of a true graduate school experience."

While academically superior, Boalt distinguishes itself from some of its peer schools by promoting a casual, non-competitive atmosphere, even in the classroom. According to one 2L, "Boalt's faculty and administration make a concerted effort to keep students sane and happy. Relaxation is nearly a rule, and the general ethos is one in which hyperachievers are a curiosity." Students point to Boalt's unconventional grading system (which awards pass, fail, or honors, rather than letter grades) as particularly responsible for the lack of cutthroat grade-grubbing. A 3L posits that "although it's rough for 60 percent of the class to get merely a pass, it actually makes students focus less on grades. Also, because our grades can't be reduced to a GPA, employers have to look more closely at how we've done in other areas."

UC—Berkeley is well known for its liberal politics, and the law school is no exception. When considering Boalt Hall, keep this in mind: "If you consider yourself moderate any-

Edward Tom, Director of Admissions
5 Boalt Hall, Berkeley, CA 94720-7200
Telephone: 510-642-2274 • Fax: 510-643-6222
E-mail: admissions@law.berkeley.edu • Website: www.law.berkeley.edu

where else, be prepared to be labeled a crazy right-winger at Boalt. Some professors are not afraid to make it very clear where they stand politically (very liberal) and you might have to take that into consideration when writing exams." Most students seem to be in the right place for their politics, however, as they praise the school's lively, liberal atmosphere and commitment to philanthropy. "I applaud the social-justice activities and events that occur daily on campus," writes one 2L. Another adds, "The student body is very active in social and political causes, and there is a general sense that Boalt students don't just see their law degree as a ticket to a prestigious firm." Even so, students say it is close to a piece of cake to land a plumb job after graduation from Boalt. "I'm a third-year student, and by September most of my friends already had job offers from incredibly prestigious law firms," is how one student puts it. Another 2L puts it this way: "Almost every Boalt student [who] wants such a job will be earning $125,000-plus right after graduation."

Life

While Boalt students spend a lot of time praising their school's location, academic programs, prestige, and mellow atmosphere, they spend much more time praising each other. "My classmates are one of the greatest strengths of this school. I am constantly impressed that people so intellectually capable can also be as collegial and humble as they are," beams one 2L. Boalt values diversity and students say their classmates run the gamut. "The Berkeley community—students and faculty alike—remains true to type: quirky, eccentric, diverse, and incredibly intelligent," writes one student. After class, students enjoy "cocktail and snack parties in the school's courtyard, amazing speakers, and the rotating 'Bar Review' pub night." Students also say that making friends at Boalt should be easy. Why? Because, as one first-year student puts it, "There's a niche for every interest a person could have and the social and academic outlets to enhance those interests."

Getting In

Good luck. Boalt Hall receives between 5,000–8,000 applications annually for fewer than 300 first-year spots. The average GPA for enrolled students is 3.8, and the average LSAT score is 164, but the LSAT range is quite broad. Boalt Hall also prides itself on considering more than just an applicant's grades and test scores, reviewing extracurricular activities, achievements, and the overcoming of obstacles when making an admissions decision.

EMPLOYMENT INFORMATION

Career Rating	**95**
Job placement rate (%)	99
Average starting salary	$100,000
State for bar exam	CA
Pass rate for first-time bar	89

Employers who frequently hire grads:
Nearly 450 employers recruit at Boalt Hall each fall, including national firms, multinational corporations, public interest groups, and governmental agencies.

Grads employed by field (%):	
Academic	2
Business/industry	3
Government	8
Judicial clerkships	17
Other	1
Private practice	62
Public interest	7

Academic Requirements

Clinical Program Required?	No
Legal Writing Course Requirement?	Yes
Legal Methods Course Requirement?	Yes
Legal Research Course Requirement?	Yes
Moot Court Requirement?	Yes
Public Interest Law Requirement?	No

ADMISSIONS

Selectivity Rating	**96**
# applications received	7,706
# applicants accepted	771
# acceptees attending	270
Average LSAT	164
LSAT Range	161–168
Average undergrad GPA	3.8
Application fee	$75
Regular application deadline	2/1
Regular notification	4/1
Rolling notification?	Yes
Early application program?	No
Transfer students accepted?	Yes
Evening division offered?	No
Part-time accepted?	No
LSDAS accepted?	Yes

Applicants Also Look At

Columbia U., Georgetown U., N.Y.U., Stanford U., U. of California—Hastings, U. of California—Los Angeles, U. of Southern California.

International Students

TOEFL required of international students?	Yes
Minimum Paper TOEFL	570
Minimum Computer TOEFL	230

FINANCIAL FACTS

Annual tuition (resident)	$21,532
Annual tuition (nonresident)	$33,776
Books and supplies	$1,300
Room & board	$13,330
Financial aid ap. deadline	3/2
% first-year students receiving some sort of aid	90
% receiving some sort of aid	94
% of aid that is merit-based	1
% receiving scholarships	80
Average grant	$10,102
Average loan	$24,210
Average total aid package	$31,958
Average debt	$56,005

UNIVERSITY OF CALIFORNIA—DAVIS
SCHOOL OF LAW

INSTITUTIONAL INFORMATION

Public/private	public
Student/faculty ratio	15:1
% faculty part-time	32
% faculty female	35
% faculty minority	33
Total faculty	60

SURVEY SAYS . . .

Diverse opinions accepted in classrooms
Great research resources
Great library staff
Abundant externship/internship/clerkship opportunities

STUDENTS

Enrollment of law school	563
% male/female	43/57
% full-time	100
% minority	38
# of countries represented	4
Average age of entering class	25

ACADEMICS

Academic Experience rating	**90**
Professors interesting rating	89
Professors accessible rating	85
Hours of study per day	4.47

Academic Specialties

Criminal law, environmental law, human rights law, intellectual property law, international law, social justice, taxation.

Advanced Degrees Offered

LLM, 1 year.

Combined Degrees Offered

JD/MBA, 4 yrs; JD/MA; JD/MS, 4 yrs.

Academic Requirements

Clinical Program Required?	No
Legal Writing Course Requirement?	Yes
Legal Methods Course Requirement?	Yes
Legal Research Course Requirement?	Yes
Moot Court Requirement?	No
Public Interest Law Requirement?	No

Academics

At King Hall, the "fantastic" School of Law at UC—Davis, you will find a "relaxed environment, friendly professors, [and] a collegial atmosphere." One student explains, "The school as a whole is rather gentle on the 1Ls, abandoning the typical 'shock-and-awe' routine for a more nurturing atmosphere." From the "very supportive" administration on down, "you get the feeling that they are happy to have you there and would like you to stay." Another student says, "The reading is really reasonable, so you have time to hang out with people during lunch rather than worry about getting your reading done." Yet another agrees, "Davis is the exact opposite of the *Paper Chase* law school. The faculty works diligently to build confidence and analytical skills in students rather than to send students screaming from the room." In the classrooms the students are very involved, "All the professors refer to us as future lawyers and ask hypotheticals based on what we would do as counsel, so whatever theory we learn is applied," says a student. The faculty is described as an "outstanding, accessible, [and] eclectic bunch—from former California Supreme Court justices to former New York actresses." Many students say their professors "clearly love teaching [and] make not-so-interesting subjects seem really interesting."

Clinical opportunities are abundant. "Students at the Civil Rights Clinic seem to be arguing before the Ninth Circuit every other week." Some students say Career Services is "extremely encouraging and adept." Others say Career Services is "inept." Other gripes include a lack of specializations and course offerings and a "boring" legal research and writing component.

You don't go to King Hall for the facilities. The "dated" buildings at UC—Davis are "pretty heinous [and] were designed for a population significantly smaller than we have currently." The classrooms, while "adequate, aren't always in great shape." Students say, "Hallways get crowded, and computer labs are sometimes full." The "cramped" library is "not lacking for resources" though, and its staff is "friendly and knowledgeable." Also, "there is an electrical socket at every seat and a very fast wireless network, which works great in the library and on the lawn." Basically, "the building needs to be modernized, renovated, and expanded." Luckily, "the law school building is slated for a major expansion in the next couple of years." Students would like to inform future architects of the school that they "need more bathrooms!" In the meantime, "don't be fooled by King Hall's uninspiring classroom facilities," urges one student. "Behind the institutional-looking exterior, this is a fabulous school and a great bargain in the increasingly costly universe of law schools. Top-notch faculty and a non-competitive atmosphere make it worth coming to this cow town to study law."

Life

Ethnically, UC—Davis is "incredibly diverse." Politically, a "monolithic liberalism" pervades. Even so, students "are very respectful of opposite points of view and usually continue the debate after class is over." Most students "focus on law as a noble, public-service oriented profession," rather than as an opportunity to make the big bucks. Students emphasize, "Law school is more than a job or earning potential—it's about engaging in an honorable profession, a service profession."

The social atmosphere is excellent, and "the quality of life is so high that many of the 3Ls never want to leave." Students note, "King Hall is small; everyone knows everyone;

Sharon L. Pinkney, Director of Admission
King Hall School of Law, 400 Mrak Hall Drive, Davis, CA 95616-5201
Telephone: 530-752-6477
E-mail: lawadmissions@ucdavis.edu • Website: www.law.ucdavis.edu

and as a result students and faculty are able to get to know each other on both a personal and professional level." The "super-friendly and involved" students are supportive of each other, and "there is no pressure among students to be the best through unsavory methods." One satisfied customer exclaims, "All life experiences should be as fun and rewarding as law school at Davis." Outside of law school, "there are parties, but it is by no means a party school." For athletic recreation, "King Hall students play softball every fall on Friday afternoons." If sports aren't your style, "the law student association has a weekly list of activities going on during lunch and after hours, including the bar scene, speakers, and student organizations." There is also interaction with the surrounding legal community as "local firms sponsor parties (and provide free beer) [while] professors have get-togethers. But there's no real pressure to participate," and it's fairly easy to "balance partying with studying."

The "small, Birkenstocky/granola" town that surrounds UC—Davis is "replete with bicycle lanes and coffee houses and undergrads." "I'd compare it to a displaced Midwest college town, except with San Francisco to the West and Tahoe to the East," illustrates one student. "Coming from Berkeley and Silicon Valley, it was great to learn how to slow down and start smiling and saying 'hi' to everyone." The city of Davis "is very community-oriented, and the residents are extremely friendly," which makes for a "great" atmosphere "to study a stressful subject." For those who are "looking to get away from the distractions of city-life, this is a great place to be." Davis is also "very livable for students with families." But be warned: "It can be a bit hard to find housing if you don't start early."

Getting In

Getting into UC—Davis is pretty difficult. Admitted students at the 25th percentile have an LSAT score of 158 and a GPA of 3.4. Admitted students at the 75th percentile have an LSAT score of 163 and a GPA of 3.7. If you take the LSAT more than once, your scores will be averaged. Although UC—Davis is a public school, California residency is not an admission factor. (Of course, it is a tuition factor.)

EMPLOYMENT INFORMATION

Career Rating	**83**
Job placement rate (%)	95
Average starting salary	$74,041
State for bar exam	CA
Pass rate for first-time bar	76

Employers who frequently hire grads:
State of California, private law firms, district attorneys, public defenders, public interest entities.

Grads employed by field (%):	
Business/industry	8
Government	7
Judicial clerkships	11
Private practice	60
Public interest	13

ADMISSIONS

Selectivity Rating	**88**
# applications received	4,439
# applicants accepted	843
# acceptees attending	194
Average LSAT	162
LSAT Range	160–164
Average undergrad GPA	3.5
Application fee	$75
Regular application deadline	2/1
Regular notification	rolling
Rolling notification?	Yes
Early application program?	No
Transfer students accepted?	Yes
Evening division offered?	No
Part-time accepted?	No
LSDAS accepted?	Yes

International Students

TOEFL required of international students?	Yes
Minimum Paper TOEFL	600
Minimum Computer TOEFL	250

FINANCIAL FACTS

Annual tuition (resident)	$21,224
Annual tuition (nonresident)	$33,469
Books and supplies	$977
Room & board (off-campus)	$9,458
Financial aid application deadline	3/2
% first-year students receiving some sort of aid	88
% receiving some sort of aid	95
% of aid that is merit-based	1
% receiving scholarships	83
Average grant	$5,850
Average loan	$19,936
Average total aid package	$29,064
Average debt	$54,081

UNIVERSITY OF CALIFORNIA—HASTINGS
COLLEGE OF LAW

INSTITUTIONAL INFORMATION

Public/private	public
Student/faculty ratio	21:1
% faculty part-time	60
% faculty female	11
% faculty minority	10
Total faculty	137

SURVEY SAYS . . .

Diverse opinions accepted in classrooms
Great library staff
Abundant externship/internship/clerkship opportunities

STUDENTS

Enrollment of law school	1,244
% male/female	45/55
% out-of-state	9
% full-time	100
% minority	34
% international	1
# of countries represented	4
Average age of entering class	24

ACADEMICS

Academic Experience rating	**82**
Professors interesting rating	78
Professors accessible rating	70
Hours of study per day	4.11

Academic Specialties

Civil litigation, family law, international law, public interest law, taxation.

Advanced Degrees Offered

JD, 3 years.

Combined Degrees Offered

JD/MBA, 4 to 5 years.

Academic Requirements

Clinical Program Required?	No
Legal Writing Course Requirement?	Yes
Legal Methods Course Requirement?	No
Legal Research Course Requirement?	Yes
Moot Court Requirement?	Yes
Public Interest Law Requirement?	No

Academics

The University of California—Hastings College of Law "is in the business of making lawyers, not theorists," students report. To that end, "clinical programs and externships are strongly recommended" by the faculty and administration. Since the school is located in San Francisco, which is also home to the California State Supreme Court and the United States Ninth Circuit Court of Appeals, "the externship program offers opportunities for 'mini-clerkships' that are profoundly rewarding and intellectually stimulating." Students often find themselves "working with top-notch judges on heavy-duty cases." Additionally, if you are interested in public interest law, there "is a lot of support for that type of career path, both in clinical program opportunities and the presence of other students and faculty who are interested in it." To further inspire minds, the college "brings in several speakers over the course of the year to talk about current controversial cases and topics." Back inside the classroom, "despite the fear of getting that dreaded C, Hastings academics are top-notch." Speaking of the dreaded C, the grading curve is "ridiculously strict," some students gripe. Despite that, most students agree that Hastings does not deserve its reputation as being cutthroat and ultra-competitive, and the students are mainly collegial.

Students like the attention law professors give them. The instructors "really care about teaching and the students. Most have already built their careers and reputation and research prior to coming to Hastings and are here primarily to teach students." Students also seem to appreciate that their teachers emphasize "the law as it is practiced." One satisfied student exclaims, "I have a former prosecutor for crim, a former plaintiff's attorney and arbitrator for torts, [and] one of the authors of the Federal Rules for procedure!" The professors "may be tough [at Hastings,] but they temper it with their brilliance and their genuine concern for their students."

Unlike the faculty, the administration receives mixed reviews. On the one hand, some students claim that "there needs to be improvement in administration-student relations, [and that] a lot of decisions are made without student input, even though there is a great student government setup." On the other hand, some see things differently and explain, "The administration tries to work with the students—sometimes successfully and sometimes not." To increase successful interactions between students and administrators, the student government has initiated "a town hall [meeting] twice a semester where the deans talk to the students and answer questions." Most students are satisfied with the Career Services office. "They have tons of resources, a great mock interview program, and all the one-on-one time a law student could wish for," one student boasts.

The facilities at the law school are getting a bit long in the tooth, but they are, according to students, "perfectly adequate." Case in point, while the "library is ugly [and] needs new paint and décor, [it] has all the essentials." One giant step forward students note is that Hastings has "completely gone high-speed wireless in every classroom!"

Akira Shiroma, Director of Admissions
200 McAllister Street #214, San Francisco, CA 94102
Telephone: 415-565-4623 • Fax: 415-565-4863
E-mail: admiss@uchastings.edu • Website: www.uchastings.edu

Life

Hastings College of Law is located in the gorgeous city of San Francisco. Moreover, it's "smack-dab in the middle of a legal community. The district courthouse, the state courthouse, the Ninth Circuit courthouse, and city hall are all located within a five minute walk of campus. This means that we get access to some of the most important appellate and trial cases going on in the country today," one student explains. Yet although the courts are nearby, students tell us that the neighborhood, known as the Tenderloin, is where you "run into unpleasant people sometimes" (other than lawyers, we assume). This is San Francisco, though, a large city with solid public transportation, vibrant nightlife, and tons of outdoor recreation space, so there is always plenty to do.

Hastings does not have a large, traditional campus. One student explains, "Even though Hastings does not have the benefits and perks that come with having an undergraduate 'campus' like other UC [law schools] do (sports events, intermingling of law students with nonlaw students, etc.), student groups are very active and provide lots of opportunity for social events and law-related volunteer work or political activism." If you're looking to blow off some steam, there's the Beer on the Beach, during which the college rolls out some kegs twice a month and students mingle on the law school grounds, or there's "'Bar Review,' which is an off-campus informal get-together for all." Competitiveness is healthy, but not out of hand, according to students. "Outlines are passed around like hotcakes—if you're willing to share something yourself." Another student adds, "Nobody steals books out of the library, so others can't use them. Yes, the grade curve does try to pit us against each other, but it doesn't succeed." Most agree that their fellow classmates are "bright and diverse and will make great colleagues and friends."

Getting In

It's tough getting admitted to Hastings. About one out of every five applicants makes the cut, and successful applicants generally have LSAT scores above 160 and at least an A-minus undergraduate GPA. Hastings is a full-time only institution, and it enrolls about 1,250 students.

EMPLOYMENT INFORMATION

Career Rating	**90**
% employed within 9 months	92
Average starting salary	$88,741
State for bar exam	CA
Pass rate for first-time bar	84

Employers who frequently hire grads: Major San Francisco and Los Angeles large and midsize law firms.

Prominent Alumni: Marvin Baxter, associate justice, California Supreme Court; Willie Brown, former mayor, San Francisco; Joseph Cotchett, founding partner, Cotchett Pitre & Simon; Robert Matsui, congressman, fifth district of California.

Grads employed by field (%):	
Business/industry	8
Government	11
Judicial clerkships	4
Private practice	68
Public interest	6

ADMISSIONS

Selectivity Rating	**89**
# applications received	6,915
# applicants accepted	1,410
# acceptees attending	427
Average LSAT	163
LSAT Range	160–165
Average undergrad GPA	3.5
Application fee	$75
Regular application deadline	3/1
Regular notification	5/30
Rolling notification?	Yes
Early application program?	Yes
Early application deadline	11/15
Early application notification	12/31
Transfer students accepted?	Yes
Evening division offered?	No
Part-time accepted?	No
LSDAS accepted?	Yes

International Students

TOEFL required of international students?	No
TOEFL recommended of international students?	No

FINANCIAL FACTS

Annual tuition (resident)	$21,894
Annual tuition (nonresident)	$33,119
Books and supplies	$863
Room & board	$18,167
Financial aid application deadline	3/1
% first-year students receiving some sort of aid	83
% receiving some sort of aid	85
% of aid that is merit-based	1
% receiving scholarships	74
Average grant	$4,503
Average loan	$21,946
Average total aid package	$25,445
Average debt	$55,024

UNIVERSITY OF CALIFORNIA—LOS ANGELES
SCHOOL OF LAW

INSTITUTIONAL INFORMATION

Public/private	public
Student/faculty ratio	12:1
% faculty part-time	32
% faculty female	31
% faculty minority	12
Total faculty	145

SURVEY SAYS . . .

Great research resources
Great library staff
Students love Los Angeles, CA

STUDENTS

Enrollment of law school	943
% male/female	52/48
% out-of-state	27
% full-time	100
% minority	12
% international	3
# of countries represented	3
Average age of entering class	25

ACADEMICS

Academic Experience rating	**94**
Professors interesting rating	85
Professors accessible rating	80
Hours of study per day	3.71

Academic Specialties

Civil procedure, constitutional law, corporate law, corporation securities law, criminal law, critical race studies, environmental law, human rights law, intellectual property law, international law, labor law, property, public interest, public policy, taxation, tax law.

Advanced Degrees Offered

JD degree, 1-year advanced degree program for appro. 12 foreign scholars who complete courses in their areas of interest & prepare a research project in consultation with a faculty member. Also the doctor of juridical science (S/JD) degree program.

Combined Degrees Offered

JD/MA (African American studies), JD/MA (American Indian studies), JD/MBA, JD/MPH, JD/MA public policy, JD/MSW social welfare, and JD/MA urban planning.

Academics

UCLA School of Law has plenty going for it, and the great academic reputation and sunny locale are just the beginning. Students say attending UCLA Law is "intellectual nirvana." There's "not much cynicism [but] lots of idealism," and an emphasis on public service law. The impressive "commitment to public interest lawyering influences many students," not just those planning to go into the public sector. Other concentrations that receive kudos from students are entertainment law, corporate law, and even animal law. We also hear that UCLA is "the only law school with a critical race concentration." Plenty of opportunities for hands-on learning are available, including "really great externship programs which allow students to work for a judge, government agency, or nonprofit legal organization for a full semester's worth of credits." On that note, "the number and variety of clinical programs" also deserves a mention. Students at UCLA Law work hard, in part due to the mandatory curve, which "is brutal for first-year classes." Many grumble that their curved grades will give "a tainted impression to potential employers."

Students say their professors are "of the highest caliber" and yet are never "lofty and inaccessible." They tell us, "The best part of the school [is] the outstanding faculty who love to teach and are respected, published academics. You don't often get both in the same person." Students love to learn from professors who are "brilliant, energetic, and engaging." The environment is one that "encourages discussions [and] fosters open intelligent conversation in and outside the classroom."

The "superbly organized administrators welcome students' questions and opinions." One student reports, "You get the feeling that they care, at least a little, and want to make your life easier." The administration also receives praise for "making law school, especially the first year, as friendly as possible." They also provide support for new students with "pizza and pep talks at crucial stress times like finals and after the first-year grades come out, so [students] won't feel discouraged by the pressure of competition."

UCLA's law library "is a masterpiece." It has "lots of room, comfy chairs, and conference rooms" and is equipped with "a ton of resources [including] a very helpful staff." Students say it's "nice to have the law school on the main campus, so we have access to the other libraries as well." Furthermore, "Internet connections at every desk" are pretty sweet, too.

Life

Located in the "attractive and safe" Westwood area of Los Angeles, UCLA Law is bustling with activity. "There are always lots of academic and social extracurricular activities going on—and that's just at the law school! If one ventures out into the general UCLA environment, there is even more to do!" Students are not slow to mention the "perfect weather year-round." Classmates agree that grades are important, but there isn't "cutthroat competitiveness." In fact, "people share notes freely and are always willing to help each other out. People are also very laid-back considering the work demands and even during finals things never get too tense."

KARMAN HSU, ASSISTANT DIRECTOR OF ADMISSIONS
PO BOX 951445, LOS ANGELES, CA 90095-1445
TELEPHONE: 310-825-4041 • FAX: 310-825-9450
E-MAIL: ADMISSIONS@LAW.UCLA.EDU • WEBSITE: WWW.LAW.UCLA.EDU

It seems there's no "typical" UCLA student, but instead an "extraordinarily diverse" student population with people coming from "a broad range of backgrounds." Socially, "You have the social butterflies at one end and then you have the introverted nerdy types at the other end." But pretty much everyone is "very smart." Politically, students lean toward the left, which can be "a bit stifling if you have a different viewpoint." But there are tales of "great debates in the hallways outside of class by people who have radically different opinions, but are good friends." Overall, students "interact well with each other [and] are all tolerated and welcomed."

After hours, "people are fairly friendly and like to get together to go out." We hear that Thursday night Bar Reviews are popular for drinking and socializing with fellow law students." One student explains, "I've found some of my greatest friends and the best social activities in law school. It's just like undergraduate partying, but the people are more mature and more intelligent." If the bar scene isn't your cup of tea, there are "tons of student groups that always have some sort of interesting activity going on." Law students are often "invited to events sponsored by the UCLA medical and business graduate schools," so bring some business cards.

Getting In

At UCLA Law, admitted students at the 25th percentile have an LSAT score of 162 and a GPA of 3.5. Admitted students at the 75th percentile have an LSAT score of 168 and a GPA of 3.8. UCLA offers a number of joint degrees. It is a full-time only institution.

EMPLOYMENT INFORMATION

Career Rating	**93**
% employed within 9 months	99
Average starting salary	$93,585
State for bar exam	CA, NY, NV
Pass rate for first-time bar	87

Employers who frequently hire grads: Leading employers from law firms, corporations, government agencies, and public interest organizations visit annually and recruit for their offices.

Prominent Alumni: Honorable Henry Waxman, U.S. House of Representatives, twenty-ninth district; Nelson Rising, president/CEO, Catellus Development Corporation.

Grads employed by field (%):	
Academic	1
Business/industry	4
Government	5
Judicial clerkships	9
Military	1
Private practice	72
Public interest	7

Academic Requirements

Clinical Program Required?	No
Legal Writing Course Requirement?	Yes
Legal Methods Course Requirement?	Yes
Legal Research Course Requirement?	No
Moot Court Requirement?	No
Public Interest Law Requirement?	No

ADMISSIONS

Selectivity Rating	**95**
# applications received	7,260
# applicants accepted	987
# acceptees attending	308
Average LSAT	166
LSAT Range	163–168
Average undergrad GPA	3.66
Application fee	$75
Regular application deadline	2/1
Regular notification	5/15
Rolling notification?	Yes
Early application program?	No
Transfer students accepted?	Yes
Evening division offered?	No
Part-time accepted?	No
LSDAS accepted?	Yes

Applicants Also Look At

Columbia U., Georgetown U., N.Y.U., Stanford U., U. of California—Berkeley, U. of Southern California.

International Students

TOEFL required of international students?	No
TOEFL recommended of international students?	No

FINANCIAL FACTS

Annual tuition (resident)	$22,123
Annual tuition (nonresident)	$33,168
Books and supplies	$1,758
Room & board (off-campus)	$12,084
Financial aid application deadline	3/2
% first-year students receiving some sort of aid	85
% receiving some sort of aid	87
% of aid that is merit-based	4
% receiving scholarships	66
Average grant	$6,440
Average loan	$28,000
Average total aid package	$37,473
Average debt	$61,000

UNIVERSITY OF CHICAGO
LAW SCHOOL

INSTITUTIONAL INFORMATION

Public/private	private
Student/faculty ratio	10:1
% faculty part-time	60
% faculty female	20
% faculty minority	10
Total faculty	50

SURVEY SAYS . . .

Heavy use of Socratic method
Diverse opinions accepted in classrooms
Great library staff
Abundant externship/internship/clerkship opportunities

STUDENTS

Enrollment of law school	596
% male/female	56/44
% full-time	100
% minority	32
% international	2
Average age of entering class	24

ACADEMICS

Academic Experience rating	**99**
Professors interesting rating	99
Professors accessible rating	88
Hours of study per day	4.2

Advanced Degrees Offered

LLM, 1 year; JSD, up to 5 years; MComp; DComp.

Combined Degrees Offered

JD/MBA, 4 years; JD/PhD history; JD/PhD business; JD/PhD economics; JD/AM public policy, 4 years; JD/AM international relations, 4 years.

Academic Requirements

Clinical Program Required?	No
Legal Writing Course Requirement?	Yes
Legal Methods Course Requirement?	Yes
Legal Research Course Requirement?	Yes
Moot Court Requirement?	Yes
Public Interest Law Requirement?	No

Academics

The University of Chicago Law School is a theoretical hothouse "where Socrates meets *The Matrix*." If you want black-letter law (principles of law that seem to be beyond dispute), stay far away. Students "are exposed to a wide range of ideas and forced to critically examine their own ideas." Students say, "There's a clear emphasis on learning how to think about the law, not just to learn the cases." Other than a host of impressive clinics (that students must "lottery into"), "very, very few practical courses [are] offered." Students love it. "I can't imagine a better legal education anywhere," gushes a very representative member of this "vibrant intellectual community." He continues, "I'm learning so much it hurts." The compliments do not end there; "The seriousness with which students and faculty treat the academic enterprise is like nothing I've ever encountered before," writes one amazed student. "You always have to be thinking. Rote regurgitation of views—even the professors'—gets you nothing." Chicago is a school where egos are crushed and rebuilt daily: "The school makes you feel dumb every day, but when you are working as a summer associate, you realize how much you've really learned."

The "small, intimate teaching cabal [of] quirky, lovable, and inspiring" professors is a veritable Who's Who of academic superstars. They can seem "intimidating," but they are "invested in engaging with students." In class, faculty members encourage vigorous debate and "constantly challenge us to cast away our intellectual complacency." One student writes of the professors, "Each and every one of them finds a way to make the class discussion both meaningful and interesting." Considering their start status, what's really amazing about professors is how "ridiculously accessible" they are. The students also praise "the open-door policies of almost all faculty members, [which] mean[s] that learning is not confined to the classroom, and conversation is not confined to the Socratic Method."

The efficient and friendly administration is well-liked. Many students cannot imagine a more helpful and accessible administrative staff." Career Services does a good job, too. "The job search could not be any easier. Students have no trouble getting jobs at top firms in whatever city they choose." Certainly, "the name opens doors." One student promises, "If you come to UC, you are pretty much guaranteed a job that pays you $125,000 per year." If you want a judicial clerkship, you can do that, too. If you'd rather help people in need, Chicago "is also rolling out the world's most generous loan repayment program, [which] will revolutionize the public interest job market and make it accessible to more people.

"The floating-cube-of-glass design [of the] cold and uncomfortable" law school facilities makes the law school quite possibly "the ugliest building on the entire campus." However, the recent remodeling efforts have one student claiming, "the newly renovated classrooms are a dream come true—a far cry from the old hard cement floors, Spartan wood chairs and musty blackboards. Plus, we now have wireless access in all the classrooms." Some students view the Spartan facilities as a plus. "We want to attract people with our spiffy ideas, rather than our interior decoration," argues one student.

Life

At the law school, you will reportedly interact with the "smartest [and] most intellectually engaged" people you've ever met. "Someone once said that they chose the University of Chicago because, compared to other schools they visited, Chicago had the fewest students playing solitaire during class," discloses one student. "There is something to that. People aren't here just to punch their tickets; they are genuinely interested in the ideas themselves." Another student explains, "Chicago is like the ultimate *Revenge of the Nerds*. The smart ones

Ann Perry, Assistant Dean for Admissions
1111 East Sixtieth Street, Chicago, IL 60637
Telephone: 773-702-9484 • Fax: 773-834-0942
E-mail: admissions@law.uchicago.edu • Website: www.law.uchicago.edu

are considered cool, and it's really unusual that someone will completely blow off work, even if they pretend to." Students at Chicago are "probably more bookwormish than average," but, they'll have you know, "they are also really fun, hilarious, and interesting." The atmosphere is very collegial and intellectually diverse. "There is no political correctness." One student explains, "As long as you have something smart to say, you'll be respected." You'll find "honest-to-goodness conservatives [and] people who once ran away to join the circus." One student writes, "Chicago has a reputation as a conservative place, but as a liberal, I'm not the least bit uncomfortable here. If you're dogmatic about your political or social views (liberal or conservative), you may have a hard time. But if you're open-minded, Chicago will provide intellectual stimulation far beyond what most people think possible. Chicago is small," and socially, it "has a strong feeling of community." One student observes, "We get kids from many different backgrounds," adding, "because so many people here are not from the Midwest, everyone comes to school looking for friends." Plus, since "almost everyone gets a good job," students are laid-back. "There is definitely pressure to get good grades, especially first year, but since everyone's grades remain hush-hush, you end up competing against yourself more than anyone else," relates one student. "The school is an intense place, but we bring it on ourselves." The law school is located in the Hyde Park section of the city. Students tell us that "Hyde Park's reputation [as] a bad neighborhood [is] blown way out of proportion. It's not dangerous; it's just boring." One student writes, "My biggest gripe is that I wish the school had a better location." The setting notwithstanding, there is plenty to do. "The lunchtime lectures are always packed, [and] Coffee Mess and Wine Mess are institutions [where students] mingle with professors and classmates [over] free coffee and donuts" or discount booze. "I hate that Chicago Law pays the price for the undergraduate reputation," protests one student. "People do party and do have fun here. A lot of very normal, very successful people go out." Other students are more cynical. "The school needs to find a way to have more purely social activities," they say. "Almost everything involves thinking, and some days that should be off limits."

Getting In

So you'd like to get admitted to the law school? Well, good luck. To be competitive, you should have an LSAT score that falls in the middle 160s and a very solid GPA (the higher above 3.5, the better). Early decision is a great idea. If you have your Chicago application 100 percent completed by December 1, the school will tell you yes, no, or maybe by the end of December.

EMPLOYMENT INFORMATION

Career Rating	**98**
% employed within 9 months	99
Average starting salary	$125,000
State for bar exam	IL
Pass rate for first-time bar	98

Employers who frequently hire grads:
Cravath Swain & Moore, Latham & Watkins, Gibson Dunn & Crutcher, Sidley & Austin, Kirkland & Ellis, Skadden Arps Slate Meagher & Flom.

Grads employed by field (%):

Business/industry	2
Government	3
Judicial clerkships	21
Other	1
Private practice	68
Public interest	4

ADMISSIONS

Selectivity Rating	**96**
# applications received	4,737
# applicants accepted	750
# acceptees attending	192
Average LSAT	170
LSAT Range	167–171
Average undergrad GPA	3.6
Application fee	$65
Regular application deadline	2/1
Regular notification	rolling
Rolling notification?	Yes
Early application program?	Yes
Early application deadline	12/1
Early application notification	12/31
Transfer students accepted?	Yes
Evening division offered?	No
Part-time accepted?	No
LSDAS accepted?	Yes

Applicants Also Look At

Columbia University, Harvard University, New York University, Stanford University, University of Pennsylvania, University of Virginia.

International Students

TOEFL required of international students?	Yes
Minimum Paper TOEFL	600

FINANCIAL FACTS

Annual tuition	$34,419
Books and supplies	$1,575
Room & board	$12,825
Financial aid application deadline	3/1
% first-year students receiving some sort of aid	90
% receiving some sort of aid	82
% of aid that is merit-based	50
% receiving scholarships	45
Average grant	$11,000
Average debt	$102,000

UNIVERSITY OF CINCINNATI
COLLEGE OF LAW

INSTITUTIONAL INFORMATION

Public/private	public
Student/faculty ratio	13:1
% faculty part-time	46
% faculty female	48
% faculty minority	21
Total faculty	24

SURVEY SAYS . . .

Diverse opinions accepted in classrooms
Great research resources
Great library staff

STUDENTS

Enrollment of law school	360
% male/female	51/49
% out-of-state	35
% full-time	100
% minority	16
% international	1
# of countries represented	3
Average age of entering class	25

ACADEMICS

Academic Experience rating	**77**
Professors interesting rating	72
Professors accessible rating	80
Hours of study per day	4.08

Academic Specialties

Criminal law, human rights law, intellectual property law, taxation, corporate, law and pyschiatry.

Advanced Degrees Offered

JD, 3 years; JD/MBA; JD/MA in women's studies; JD/MCP community planning, JD/MSW.

Combined Degrees Offered

JD/MBA, 4 years; JD/MCP, 4.5 years; JD/MA in women's studies, 4 years, JD/MSW, 4 years.

Academic Requirements

Clinical Program Required?	No
Legal Writing Course Requirement?	Yes
Legal Methods Course Requirement?	No
Legal Research Course Requirement?	Yes

Academics

The University of Cincinnati College of Law offers "a small school environment with all of the resources and academic enrichment expected from a large law school." The students like the "academic focus on practical aspects of the law, [the] attention to the bar exam, [and the] opportunities for internships." One highly touted program at the college is the Urban Morgan Institute for Human Rights, which, according to the college's website was "the first endowed institute at an American law school devoted to the study of international human rights law." One student boasts, "It offers an invaluable and intensive examination of international human rights law by affording students the opportunity to work with the *Human Rights Quarterly*, to access reputable scholars, and to work in the international field." Another student recalls, "Last summer, my classmates spent time with internationally known human rights actors in such places as Sierra Leone, Belfast, Denmark, and Bosnia, to name a few." The college's small enrollment allows for "more individualized attention for students" and builds camaraderie.

Most students say the faculty have been "approachable, helpful, and genuinely interested in students' adjustment, curiosity, and achievement [and] have made even somewhat mundane classes exciting and interesting," others feel some of the professors could use improvement. Students grumble that "a bunch of the top-notch professors have left recently," but say that the administration has "brought in several new profs who are also great." However, all the students value the intimate class setting, "which provides an opportunity to build relationships with faculty," and almost every student can "get to know at least one professor well." The administration is a mixed bag, with some students claiming that it is "very open and acceptable," while others contend the contrary: it's "not always receptive to student concerns [and] slow to respond."

According to students, the facilities could use some serious improvement. "The building and its decor evokes not-so-fond memories of the past: the windowless building resembles a Cold War fallout shelter, and the classrooms are a lasting tribute to the style-impaired 1970s," moans one student. "The orange-carpeted chairs, the lack of outlets in the classrooms, the fact that the Lebanon [Ohio] State penitentiary has more windows (really, I've been there for a crim law field trip!) is really depressing," another carps. The library is not "very conducive to studying [because of the] poor acoustics and the occasional loud mouths." That's a shame, since "the library staff are extremely helpful and the resources are organized and presented in such a way to make researching easy."

Life

The college is located on the "corner of campus," an area one calls "an intellectual oasis in the middle of a sea of [car] tow-zones." However, people think the area will be much improved, once new parking facilities are completed and the "community finishes renovating the street we are on." Students do revel in the fact that their tuition is relatively low and that they won't be bogged down by student loan debt before starting their careers. All in all, the "expense is minimal compared to value of education received."

Al Watson, Assistant Dean and Director of Admissions and Financial Aid
PO Box 210040, Cincinnati, OH 45221
Telephone: 513-556-6805 • Fax: 513-556-2391
E-mail: admissions@law.uc.edu • Website: www.law.uc.edu

"Students get along well" at the college, and "there is a very active SBA, which organizes happy hours and parties every couple weeks." Furthermore, "student clubs provide plenty of opportunities for students to interact and develop their interests." Moreover, students enjoy time together in "intramural sports, theme parties, and fantasy sports leagues." As far as intensity goes, "while extremely competitive, [classmates] make a conscientious effort to keep the environment from being cutthroat." A student writes, "We don't allow things like stealing books from the library, and generally outlines are shared liberally among the students. Upper-levels attempt to reach out to first years to provide outlines and support through the rougher periods of the 1L year." One student explains it well: "There are always a few 'sore losers' in the bunch, but with such a small class, you can't afford to alienate people by being overly competitive and unfriendly. We spend our days together. We spend our evenings and weekends together, too. If law school is going to be enjoyable for you at UC, you have to have your priorities straight, and that means understanding that no one is out to get you, and everyone is going to support you when you need it."

Getting In

Admission to the University of Cincinnati College of Law is competitive, though not overly so. Don't be deceived by the relatively high acceptance rate because much of the weeding out is done by the students themselves in their choosing to apply in the first place. A good score on the LSAT and a solid, though not extraordinary, undergraduate GPA should make an applicant competitive. The university offers many various joint degrees and is a full-time only institution.

EMPLOYMENT INFORMATION

Career Rating	**76**
Job placement rate (%)	94
Average starting salary	$57,086
State for bar exam	OH
Pass rate for first-time bar	87

Employers who frequently hire grads: All major law firms in Cincinnati and other Ohio cities as well as other Midwestern cities.

Prominent Alumni: Bob Taft, governor of Ohio; Cris Collinsworth, Fox Sports; Charles Luken, mayor of Cincinnati; Billy Martin, Washington, DC-based high-profile case attorney.

Grads employed by field (%):	
Academic	4
Business/industry	14
Government	11
Judicial clerkships	10
Private practice	57
Public interest	4

Moot Court Requirement?	No
Public Interest Law Requirement?	No

ADMISSIONS

Selectivity Rating	**83**
# applications received	1,178
# applicants accepted	397
# acceptees attending	135
Average LSAT	160
LSAT Range	157–162
Average undergrad GPA	3.5
Application fee	$35
Regular application deadline	4/1
Regular notification	rolling
Rolling notification?	Yes
Early application program?	No
Transfer students accepted?	Yes
Evening division offered?	No
Part-time accepted?	No
LSDAS accepted?	Yes

Applicants Also Look At

Case Western Reserve University, The George Washington University, Georgetown University, Northern Kentucky University, The Ohio State University, University of Dayton, University of Toledo.

International Students

TOEFL required of international students?	Yes

FINANCIAL FACTS

Annual tuition (resident)	$12,236
Annual tuition (nonresident)	$23,138
Books and supplies	$4,991
Room & board	$7,113
Financial aid application deadline	4/1
% first-year students receiving some sort of aid	80
% receiving some sort of aid	75
% receiving scholarships	65
Average grant	$5,500
Average loan	$14,500
Average total aid package	$20,000
Average debt	$45,542

UNIVERSITY OF COLORADO
SCHOOL OF LAW

INSTITUTIONAL INFORMATION

Public/private	public
Student/faculty ratio	13:1
% faculty part-time	46
% faculty female	32
% faculty minority	14
Total faculty	81

SURVEY SAYS . . .

Diverse opinions accepted in classrooms
Great library staff
Students love Boulder, CO

STUDENTS

Enrollment of law school	502
% male/female	49/51
% out-of-state	14
% full-time	100
% minority	20
Average age of entering class	25

ACADEMICS

Academic Experience rating	**77**
Professors interesting rating	80
Professors accessible rating	73
Hours of study per day	4.57

Academic Specialties

Commercial law, constitutional law, criminal law, environmental law, government services, human rights law, intellectual property law, international law, labor law, property, taxation.

Advanced Degrees Offered

JD, 3 years.

Combined Degrees Offered

JD/MBA, 4 years; JD/MPA, 4 years; JD/master of science and technology, 4 years; JD/master of environmental law, 4 years; tax emphasis, 3 years; environmental policy certificate, 3 years.

Academic Requirements

Clinical Program Required?	No
Legal Writing Course Requirement?	Yes
Legal Methods Course Requirement?	Yes

Academics

Students say that the University of Colorado School of Law's greatest strengths are the "Ivy League-quality" professors and the "laid-back" attitude that pervades the school. The "friendly [and] casual" professors at CU Law are a "smart and impressive bunch." While a few rotten apples are "hostile and elitist, nearly all are interesting and accomplished, [and] there are some true gems" to be found. One student tells us, "Although professors use the Socratic Method, most have developed some way to make it a lot less intimidating than what many students expect." Additionally, though "professors demand a lot from their students," they are "approachable [and] available to help." One student comments, "Professors love to talk about law one-on-one with students." The "hard-working [and] super-helpful [administration] is always willing to answer students' (or applicants') questions" as well. "There is no area in the administration that does not involve the students." A 1L says, "I have no problem going to any of the deans to tell them my concerns." At CU it is apparent "the faculty and staff work hard to make sure that students get the resources and support they need to succeed in law school."

CU Law's clinical programs are "excellent, though underemphasized." Environmental law is a big deal. The Natural Resources Litigation Clinic, for example, plays a significant part in litigation involving the protection of public lands. Students in the Indian Law Clinic represent low-income Native American clients with specific Indian law–related problems. The Entrepreneurial Law Clinic helps indigent entrepreneurs realize their commercial dreams. Also, a whopping three law journals give "more people that excellent opportunity."

Student opinion on Career Services is mixed. On the plus side, "the office really encourages judicial externships and clerkships." Furthermore, CU grads regularly get fabulous jobs. "People here don't worry about debt or jobs," gloats one content student. "Most of us will graduate with minimal-to-no debt, and there are jobs-a-plenty up and down the Front Range." Detractors grouse, however, that "CU graduates should be much more competitive in the Denver job market." If you want to work outside the state, "you're handed a pamphlet or two and sent out the door." One student opines, "This is a quality school, but be prepared to work hard to obtain a job."

Students unanimously cry out for a new building, since the one they have now is "tiny, hideously filthy, [and] literally falling apart as it stands." Fortunately, groundbreaking ceremonies for the new Wolf Law Building were held in November 2004. This will allow the existing law school to move into the new facility by the expected date of August 2006. The $46 million Wolf Law Building is being designed to achieve certification under the United States Green Building Council's LEED (Leadership in Energy and Environmental Design) rating system for environmental sustainability. Students are confident that "once UC builds the new building, it will quite simply be the epitome of a perfect law school."

Carol Nelson-Douglas, Assistant Dean for Admissions and Financial Aid
403 UCB, Boulder, CO 80309-0403
Telephone: 303-492-7203 • Fax: 303-492-2542
E-mail: lawadmin@colorado.edu • Website: www.colorado.edu/law

Life

"I thought law school would be full of socially awkward dweebs," admits one student, who instead found "a cast of witty, smart, party die-hards." Students at CU Law describe themselves as "very laid-back and collegial, [though they] certainly work hard" when hard work is required. These students are "intense, brilliant, and focused." They are "casual, down-to-earth, [and] friendly," too. Because the atmosphere of Boulder has a way of rubbing off on students, "this is a granola-eating, Teva-wearing, beard-growing kind of school."

Boulder is "far too expensive" but, being a premier college party town, it offers excellent social opportunities. "There are a lot of beer-guzzlers," even at the law school. Whether you like to drink or not, though, "most people here are able to enjoy life and do the things they enjoy." According to one student, "We at CU Law are really good about achieving balance in [our] lives. Everybody goes skiing one afternoon a week. We go to football games, parties, and happy hour to balance out studying." The location, not too far from the urban appeal of Denver, is another plus. CU Law is also close to an endless array of "recreational activities in the mountains." One student says, "Combine the great people and the beautiful scenery, and it doesn't get better than this. I've never had so much fun."

Getting In

Incoming students at the 25th percentile have an LSAT score of 160 and a GPA of 3.4. Incoming students at the 75th percentile have an LSAT score of 164 and a GPA of 3.7. CU Law does give some preference to applicants who are Colorado residents. This school is full-time only.

EMPLOYMENT INFORMATION

Career Rating	**75**
Job placement rate (%)	93
Average starting salary	$58,832
State for bar exam	CO
Pass rate for first-time bar	89

Employers who frequently hire grads: Arnold & Porter, Davis Graham & Stubbs, Faegre & Benson, Hogan & Hartson, Holland & Hart, Holme Roberts & Owen, Kutak Rock, Otten Johnson, Rothgerber, Sherman & Howard.

Prominent Alumni: Wiley B. Rutledge, associate justice, U.S. Supreme Court; Luis D. Rovira, chief justice (retired), Colorado Supreme Court.

Grads employed by field (%):	
Academic	4
Business/industry	10
Government	10
Judicial clerkships	16
Military	1
Private practice	52
Public interest	7

Legal Research Course Requirement?	Yes
Moot Court Requirement?	No
Public Interest Law Requirement?	No

ADMISSIONS

Selectivity Rating	**86**
# applications received	2,899
# applicants accepted	679
# acceptees attending	166
Average LSAT	161
LSAT Range	159–164
Average undergrad GPA	3.6
Application fee	$65
Regular application deadline	2/15
Regular notification	5/31
Rolling notification?	No
Early application program?	No
Transfer students accepted?	Yes
Evening division offered?	No
Part-time accepted?	No
LSDAS accepted?	Yes

Applicants Also Look At

Boston College, The George Washington University, Georgetown University, The University of Texas at Austin, University of California—Berkeley, University of California—Hastings, University of Denver.

International Students

TOEFL required of international students?	No
TOEFL recommended of international students?	No

FINANCIAL FACTS

Annual tuition (resident)	$9,554
Annual tuition (nonresident)	$25,146
Books and supplies	$1,187
Room & board (on/off-campus)	$7,564/$7,236
Financial aid application deadline	3/1
% first-year students receiving some sort of aid	83
% receiving some sort of aid	86
% of aid that is merit-based	2
% receiving scholarships	53
Average grant	$2,818
Average loan	$17,529
Average total aid package	$19,377
Average debt	$52,515

University of Connecticut
School of Law

INSTITUTIONAL INFORMATION

Public/private	public
Student/faculty ratio	12:1
% faculty part-time	59
% faculty female	29
% faculty minority	11
Total faculty	126

SURVEY SAYS . . .

Diverse opinions accepted in classrooms
Great research resources
Great library staff
Beautiful campus

STUDENTS

Enrollment of law school	687
% male/female	50/50
% out-of-state	33
% full-time	67
% minority	21
% international	1
# of countries represented	8
Average age of entering class	25

ACADEMICS

Academic Experience rating	**88**
Professors interesting rating	83
Professors accessible rating	67
Hours of study per day	4.05

Academic Specialties

Commercial law, constitutional law, corporation securities law, criminal law, environmental law, government services, human rights law, intellectual property law, international law, labor law, legal history, legal philosophy, property, taxation.

Advanced Degrees Offered

JD, 3 to 4 yrs; LLM, U.S. legal studies, 1 yr; LLM, insurance, 1 yr.

Combined Degrees Offered

JD/MA public policy studies, JD/MBA, JD/MLS, JD/MPA, JD/MSW, JD/MPH, JD/LLM insurance law.

Academic Requirements

Clinical Program Required?	No
Legal Writing Course Requirement?	No

Academics

The strengths of the University of Connecticut School of Law are excellent resources and clinics, a diverse student population, small classes and a beautiful campus. Super-cheap in-state tuition is another plus. As one student who has spent too much time thinking like a lawyer puts it, "Low cost + proximity to Boston and New York + good reputation = great value." Professors at the school, however, run the gamut but most, by student accounts, are excellent. You'll find "some of the most brilliant legal minds in the United States, [and these professors] are always willing to laugh with the class and make students involved and interested in the discussions." Most students are enthusiastic about the administration, saying the top brass "bends over backward for the students." In the words of one, "they really treat us like the paying customers we are."

The legal research and writing component "that all first-year students go through" at the school is called the Lawyering Process Program. Students tell us it's phenomenal and that it lives up to its highfalutin name. "The first half, writing and research, is pretty basic, but the second half of the class incorporates small group simulations of client meetings and negotiations. Students are videotaped and provided with a great deal of feedback. It is a great learning experience."

Career Services is serviceable, but some students wish the school "could do more to attract out-of-state employers to campus." Many students have no complaints with regard to job prospects, though, citing "a strong alumni network" and the fact that "plenty of people are getting work in New York and Boston."

"A quaint residential neighborhood in the West End of Hartford" provides the setting for what is "probably the most physically beautiful law school in the country." It's pretty close to a "gothic paradise." One student discloses,. "We've dubbed it Hogwart's School of Law." Most of the classrooms "have been renovated on the inside [with] all the modern bells and whistles." These classrooms have Internet access all over the place, "ergonomic seating, pleasant decor, and decent acoustics. [They] really make you believe you're in law school and that some day you might actually be doing this for real." Though students say, "The older ones, which have yet to be refurbished, are hot, [have] awkward seating arrangements, [and are] just miserable all around." The chairs in these classrooms are not the best either as students say, "Your butt goes numb within 20 minutes." The large and generally unbelievable library boasts an incredibly helpful staff. "If they don't have it, they can get it." And if they can't get it, "there are a couple other fantastic libraries in the area."

Karen DeMeola, Assistant Dean for Admissions and Student Finance
45 Elizabeth Street, Hartford, CT 06105
Telephone: 860-570-5100 • Fax: 860-570-5153
E-mail: admit@law.uconn.edu • Website: www.law.uconn.edu

Life

While students report that theirs is an ethnically diverse campus, "The majority of students tend to be from Pennsylvania to Massachusetts and all states in between." Also, most of the students "come straight out of college and lack any real-life experience." Students observe, "There is a healthy air of competition to do better than the next guy, [but] students are extremely friendly [and they] cooperate with one another on projects when it is allowed." Overall, there is "a wonderful sense of community. People volunteer notes to you when you've missed class [and] step in and save you when the professor catches you unprepared in a Socratic dialogue."

"Hartford [is] a pit [and] a depressing area, [but the] fun-loving" students are nevertheless able to keep themselves adequately busy when they aren't studying. "There are many—perhaps too many—opportunities to meet people at a number of social functions and more clubs than you can shake a stick at," explains one student. "If you have an interest, the school probably has a club with a name to match." Students and student groups are very active. "From informal Wednesday nights out at the local bars to a group of guys who have organized Softball Sunday, there are plenty of opportunities to socialize." The era of "school-funded boozing" has been scaled back recently, but students are unfazed. "We keep the local bars in business," boasts one. "You will never meet a group of law students who work as hard in the classroom and have as much fun on the weekends as you will at UConn."

Getting In

Getting in to the University of Connecticut School of Law is no cakewalk. About one in six applicants makes the cut. Those who get in do so with LSAT scores right around 160 and B-plus/A-minus undergraduate GPAs. The school gives special consideration to residents of Connecticut. You will also get special consideration if you are a resident of a New England state that does not have a state-funded law school.

EMPLOYMENT INFORMATION

Career Rating	**85**
Job placement rate (%)	96
Average starting salary	$85,000
State for bar exam	CT, NY, MA, IL, CA
Pass rate for first-time bar	86

Grads employed by field (%):	
Academic	1
Business/industry	16
Government	9
Judicial clerkships	19
Military	2
Private practice	49
Public interest	4

Legal Methods Course Requirement?	Yes
Legal Research Course Requirement?	Yes
Moot Court Requirement?	Yes
Public Interest Law Requirement?	No

ADMISSIONS

Selectivity Rating	**89**
# applications received	2,965
# applicants accepted	488
# acceptees attending	190
Average LSAT	162
LSAT Range	160–164
Average undergrad GPA	3.3
Application fee	$30
Regular application deadline	3/1
Regular notification	rolling
Rolling notification?	Yes
Early application program?	No
Transfer students accepted?	Yes
Evening division offered?	Yes
Part-time accepted?	Yes
LSDAS accepted?	Yes

Applicants Also Look At

American U., Boston College, Boston U., Fordham U., George Mason U., Tulane U., U. of California—Hastings.

International Students

TOEFL required of international students?	Yes

FINANCIAL FACTS

Annual tuition (resident)	$14,632
Annual tuition (nonresident)	$30,860
Books and supplies	$1,054
Fees per credit (resident)	$614
Fees per credit (nonresident)	$614
Tuition per credit (resident)	$512
Tuition per credit (nonresident)	$1,079
Room & board (off-campus)	$10,350
Financial aid application deadline	3/1
% first-year students receiving some sort of aid	92
% receiving some sort of aid	93
% of aid that is merit-based	14
% receiving scholarships	72
Average grant	$6,833
Average loan	$19,113
Average total aid package	$24,040
Average debt	$50,859

UNIVERSITY OF DENVER
STURM COLLEGE OF LAW

INSTITUTIONAL INFORMATION

Public/private	private
Student/faculty ratio	17:1
% faculty female	30
% faculty minority	16
Total faculty	61

SURVEY SAYS . . .

Great research resources
Beautiful campus
Students love Denver, CO

STUDENTS

Enrollment of law school	1,192
% male/female	49/51
% out-of-state	60
% full-time	73
% minority	24
% international	2
Average age of entering class	26

ACADEMICS

Academic Experience rating	**81**
Professors interesting rating	74
Professors accessible rating	71
Hours of study per day	4

Academic Specialties

Civil procedure, corporation securities law, environmental law, human rights law, international law, taxation.

Advanced Degrees Offered

LLM American and comparative law, 1 year; LLM taxation, 1 year; LLM natural resources, 1 year.

Combined Degrees Offered

Business, geography, history, international management, international studies, legal administration, mass communications, professional psychology, psychology, social work, sociology.

Academic Requirements

Clinical Program Required?	No
Legal Writing Course Requirement?	Yes
Legal Methods Course Requirement?	Yes

Academics

In fall 2003, the Sturm College of Law of the University of Denver "unveiled its new law school building, [a] beautiful [and commodious] wonder of glass, brick, marble, and arched windows that look west to the Rocky Mountains." This "high-tech" facility is "well thought out," all the way down to "ultra-comfy classroom chairs" that recline ("a little"). It doesn't end there. "Private study rooms [are] everywhere." Every classroom seat is Internet-ready—"perfect for instant messaging during class"—and there is a ubiquitous wireless network. "The library resources are superb." Despite all the cutting-edge technology (not to mention DU Law's designation as the first certified "green" law school in the United States), the building still "feels like a law school." One student sums up the positive aspects: "It still has that old world charm and rustic smell that any good law school should have, but all of the state-of-the-art facilities that any good law student could want."

Students tell us, "The great legal minds" on the DU Law faculty are "excited to teach, engaging, and approachable." They are "truly devoted people who put students first [and who] care about the students becoming excellent attorneys." Adjunct faculty members are "terrific," too, which is a rare phenomenon. "In the right class [and] with the right professor, [though,] this can be every bit as good as any law school out there."

Students are divided on the administration's performance. Some applaud the "responsive, creative, results-oriented, [and] extremely user-friendly" top brass. However, many students tell us, "Finding help is a chore, [and] E-mails are not answered." Particularly in the financial aid and work study offices. Every semester, "required classes all begin and end at the same time," and many students complain about having to deal with the main campus's financial aid office. Evening students often feel slighted because many offices are closed by the time they get to school, although the Student Affairs office does hold evening hours a few times a month.

"DU Law has a strong emphasis on preparing practicing attorneys." A host of specializations includes transportation law and international legal studies; dual-degree programs include computer science. "Real-life experience is offered in excess" at DU, and students have "every opportunity to learn and apply legal skills before graduation." Take the "amazing" clinical program, which "is run like a real law firm." One student says of it, "All of the clinical advisers are superb, [and] there are many, many practice areas to choose from." Clerkships are abundant as well. "The assistant dean works tirelessly trying to encourage students to apply for judicial clerkships and personally assists all students wishing to submit applications." Also unique to DU are several law in Spanish courses that are, not shockingly, taught in Spanish. When the time comes to find a real job, Career Services is solid, and "DU has a great reputation in Colorado," especially in Denver. Because many professors "worked at downtown firms at some point, and many adjunct faculty are currently at those firms, DU has a great connection with the employers students will be seeking out."

KAREN HIGGANBOTHAM, ASSOCIATE DIRECTOR OF ADMISSIONS
2255 EAST EVANS AVENUE, DENVER, CO 80208
TELEPHONE: 303-871-6135 • FAX: 303-871-6992
E-MAIL: ADMISSIONS@LAW.DU.EDU • WEBSITE: WWW.LAW.DU.EDU

Life

"Recent efforts on the part of the administration have led to a much more diverse student body," at least in terms of ethnicity. Politically, "everyone is pretty open to other opinions, and no one really pushes their personal view." Students believe "there are some very competitive students but for the most part," students at DU Law are "extremely friendly [and] not too competitive." First-year students "band together" in their sections, which "can be good or bad, depending on whether you're 'in' or not." If you are "in," it can feel like "one big sorority/fraternity," according to a 1L. If you are "out," it can be "somewhat difficult to meet people." Ultimately, "student social life is a product of the students and what they want from school," explains one seasoned student. "The students who come directly from undergraduate work and have less life experience are more likely to be social." If you are not a social butterfly for whatever reason, don't worry, it's very easy to do your own thing "and not worry about what everyone else is doing."

"Denver is a laid-back place, and the university echoes that." While you will find that "law school is hectic everywhere," DU students tell us that they are blessed with "a very reasonable amount of time to pursue a social life." One student notes, "In general, the social aspect is available if you want it." Another candid student says, "We like to drink together." Furthermore, "there are constant activities and the school has an environment very conducive to group studying and interaction." DU Law sponsors "many social events." To name just a few, "the Student Bar Association and Student Affairs are both very good about offering a wide variety of social programs from happy hours to networking with DU alumni." Plus "just one hour away, [there are] great" skiing and snowboarding.

Getting In

Admitted students at the 25th percentile have an LSAT score of 152 and a GPA of 2.9. Admitted students at the 75th percentile have an LSAT score of 161 and a GPA of 3.5.

EMPLOYMENT INFORMATION

Career Rating	**75**
% employed within 9 months	99
Average starting salary	$50,000
State for bar exam	CO
Pass rate for first-time bar	83

Employers who frequently hire grads:
Small, medium, and large law firms; government agencies; corporations; nonprofit organizations.

Grads employed by field (%):	
Academic	2
Business/industry	25
Government	18
Judicial clerkships	7
Private practice	45
Public interest	3

Legal Research Course Requirement?	Yes
Moot Court Requirement?	No
Public Interest Law Requirement?	Yes

ADMISSIONS

Selectivity Rating	**84**
# applications received	3,699
# applicants accepted	822
# acceptees attending	246
Average LSAT	160
LSAT Range	153–162
Average undergrad GPA	3.1
Application fee	$60
Regular application deadline	5/30
Regular notification	rolling
Rolling notification?	Yes
Early application program?	No
Transfer students accepted?	Yes
Evening division offered?	Yes
Part-time accepted?	Yes
LSDAS accepted?	Yes

International Students

TOEFL required of international students?	Yes
Minimum Paper TOEFL	580
Minimum Computer TOEFL	213

FINANCIAL FACTS

Annual tuition	$27,466
Books and supplies	$1,187
Tuition per credit	$886
Room & board	$8,622
Financial aid application deadline	3/30
% first-year students receiving some sort of aid	96
% receiving some sort of aid	95
% of aid that is merit-based	33
% receiving scholarships	28
Average grant	$11,500
Average loan	$19,000
Average total aid package	$31,500
Average debt	$82,000

UNIVERSITY OF THE DISTRICT OF COLUMBIA*

DAVID A. CLARKE SCHOOL OF LAW

INSTITUTIONAL INFORMATION

Public/private	public
Student/faculty ratio	12:1

SURVEY SAYS . . .

Diverse opinions accepted in classrooms
Abundant externship/internship/clerkship opportunities
Students love Washington, DC

STUDENTS

Enrollment of law school	220
% male/female	37/63
% full-time	100
% minority	53

ACADEMICS

Academic Experience rating	**74**
Professors interesting rating	90
Professors accessible rating	96
Hours of study per day	5.57

Academic Specialties

Public interest law.

Advanced Degrees Offered

JD, 3 years.

Academic Requirements

Clinical Program Required?	Yes
Legal Writing Course Requirement?	Yes
Legal Methods Course Requirement?	No
Legal Research Course Requirement?	No
Moot Court Requirement?	Yes
Public Interest Law Requirement?	Yes

Academics

"An up-and-coming school with an emphasis on public interest and public service," the David A. Clarke School of Law was founded with the mission to train students from groups underrepresented at the bar to become skilled and ethical public advocates and private attorneys. This unique mission is carried out through the school's extensive clinical programs, which include, among others, an Immigrant Law Program, an HIV Law Clinic, and a Housing and Consumer Law Clinic. At these free legal centers, students advise on real, ongoing legal cases under the supervision of a practicing attorney, representing clients in the DC area who would otherwise be unable to afford legal counsel. While these clinics provide a meaningful service to the DC community, they also offer important, hands-on legal experience to the UDC student body. As a result, UDC "students and alumni enter the legal field extremely well-prepared for practical application of their legal skills." A 3L boasts, "Due to the public interest and practice focus of the school, my classmates and I will graduate with a full résumé of legal experience as we enter the workplace." Adds another, "The school trains you to be a 'street lawyer'—an advocate for the people, focusing on the disenfranchised."

While the extensive clinical training is a distinguishing characteristic of UDC, students tell us that the traditional academic program is excellent, describing their course work as "challenging and stimulating." Professors are "competent and very knowledgeable about their subject areas" and are likewise "exceptional pedagogues." In addition, UDC teachers bring important, practical experience to the classroom, as most "are experts in their field, having practiced (or are still practicing) in that area." As diversity is a cornerstone of the educational experience at UDC, students also note with pleasure that the variety of background within the teaching staff is particularly strong at their school.

When slogging through the first-year workload, UDC students appreciate the fact that their professors are "very accessible and truly want to see you succeed." On top of that, the school maintains relatively small class sizes, which foster bonds between faculty and students. "It's rigorous, but the best part about it is that you truly develop a one-on-one relationship with the faculty and staff," comments a 2L. In fact, professors treat students like colleagues and, after class, "they are not above going to the dive bar across the street to share a beer with you." Administrators, likewise, are reputed to be "always available and extremely helpful," so much so that students claim "it's a bit of a shock when, after the first month, the deans all know you by name."

While students praise the quality of their education, some worry that "as a provisionally accredited school, we underestimate ourselves and look at things from the position of underdog." However, they have great faith in the strength of the UDC program and feel that continued improvements will soon impact the school's reputation. A 3L explains, "I think this school is a diamond in the rough and will see national recognition and accolades when it gets final ABA accreditation." Students also feel the school's growing pains in its physical structure, saying that "the facilities are not always the best, having been inherited from the under-funded undergraduate school." However, they are quick to remind us that "things get better every year" at UDC. Furthermore, philanthropic UDC students say "it's not about the edifice; it's about the individuals who are trained to make a difference in the lives of people." While the classrooms may be antiquated, UDC has given students a "great new law library."

*Provisionally approved by the ABA.

Vivian Canty, Assistant Dean of Admissions
4200 Connecticut Avenue NW, Washington, DC 20008
Telephone: 202-274-7336 • Fax: 202-274-5583
E-mail: vcanty@udc.edu • Website: www.law.udc.edu

Life

Located in a residential neighborhood in Washington, DC, the UDC campus is just a short bus ride away from Capitol Hill, local and federal courts, and the many public and private agencies located downtown. Reflecting the multicultural population of the surrounding city, UDC "is a very diverse and accepting school for people of all races, religions, genders, and sexual orientations." Underrepresented minorities comprise about half of the student body.

While they hail from varied backgrounds, "students work cooperatively and respect each other's opinions." "Despite our diverse backgrounds, there is no one I'd feel uncomfortable walking up to and striking up a conversation with," writes a 1L. While seriously studious, students are only moderately competitive with each other. "The environment is like a family of brothers and sisters: competitive, but always supportive!" In fact, "if a classmate misses a class for whatever reason (even if they were out too late at the bar the night before), there are always other students willing to share their notes for the missed class."

Getting In

About half of UDC law students are underrepresented minorities, and the school seeks to admit students who represent a broad spectrum of society, culture, age, ethnicity, and gender. Because of the school's commitment to diversity and underrepresented communities, both academic and non-academic criteria are weighed heavily in an admissions decision. In particular, a demonstrated commitment to public service is a great asset to an application.

EMPLOYMENT INFORMATION

Career Rating	**61**
% employed within 9 months	84
State for bar exam	MD, DC, VA, CA, FL

Employers who frequently hire grads:
Local and federal government agencies, legal services providers, litigation-oriented law firms, public interest law firms and organizations, judicial clerkships, business and industry.

Grads employed by field (%):	
Academic	4
Business/industry	19
Government	11
Judicial clerkships	7
Private practice	37
Public interest	22

ADMISSIONS

Selectivity Rating	**71**
# applications received	1,172
# applicants accepted	248
# acceptees attending	81
Average LSAT	151
LSAT Range	148–154
Average undergrad GPA	3.1
Application fee	$35
Regular application deadline	3/15
Regular notification	rolling
Rolling notification?	Yes
Early application program?	No
Transfer students accepted?	Yes
Evening division offered?	No
Part-time accepted?	No
LSDAS accepted?	Yes

Applicants Also Look At

American University, The Catholic University of America, City University of New York, George Mason University, Howard University, University of Baltimore, University of Maryland.

International Students

TOEFL required of international students?	Yes

FINANCIAL FACTS

Annual tuition (resident)	$7,000
Annual tuition (nonresident)	$14,000
Books and supplies	$4,500
Financial aid application deadline	4/30
Average grant	$4,500
Average loan	$21,000
Average debt	$57,300

UNIVERSITY OF FLORIDA
LEVIN COLLEGE OF LAW

INSTITUTIONAL INFORMATION

Public/private	public
Student/faculty ratio	14:1
% faculty female	42
% faculty minority	13
Total faculty	86

SURVEY SAYS . . .

Diverse opinions accepted in classrooms, Abundant externship/internship/clerkship opportunities, Students love Gainesville, FL, Good social life

STUDENTS

Enrollment of law school	1,166
% male/female	53/47
% out-of-state	9
% full-time	100
% minority	21
% international	2
# of countries represented	2
Average age of entering class	25

ACADEMICS

Academic Experience rating	**63**
Professors interesting rating	62
Professors accessible rating	61
Hours of study per day	4.09

Academic Specialties

Children & family law, environmental law, estates & trusts practice, intellectual property law, international law, taxation.

Advanced Degrees Offered

LLM in taxation, LLM in comparative law, S/JD in taxation.

Combined Degrees Offered

JD/MA urban & regional planning, JD/MBA, JD/MA/PhD pol. sci., JD/MA sociology, JD/MA/PhD history, JD/MA accounting, JD/MA/PhD mass communication, JD/PhD psych., JD/MA forest resources & conservation, JD/PhD educational leadership, JD/MA exercise & sport science, JD/MD, JD/MA med. sciences, JD/MA environ. eng., JD/MA Latin American studies, JD/MA health administration, JD/MA anthro., JD building construction, JD/MA real estate, JD/MA urban & regional planning, JD/PharmD.

Academics

The University of Florida Levin College of Law is said to be "the best" law school in the state and "one of the best in the South." Also, the outrageously cheap in-state tuition "is hard to beat." Academic strengths include a nationally recognized tax law program and scores of joint-degree programs—from standards like accounting and business administration, to more unique offerings like sport sciences and environmental engineering. Study-abroad programs send UF students to Cape Town, South Africa, for international comparative law; Montpellier, France, for international business; and San Jose, Costa Rica, for environmental law.

Many students tell us that one of UF's greatest strengths is its "excellent professors who are seemingly at the top of their profession." One student professes that "the faculty are godly in their expertise, yet human in their compassionate approach in instruction." (The school's writing and legal skills instructors were singled out as "superb.") Professors in all departments here "respect us and hold us to the highest standards" and are "extremely available out of class for questions concerning their class or any matter you may wish to discuss." Some appear to have "left-wing agendas" and most "are tough," but one UF student tells us, "I've laughed in almost every class this year. Professors are interested in developing you into an ethical lawyer who is a tribute to the profession." Going beyond the classroom, "there is a collegial atmosphere here that encourages communication between students, faculty, and administration. And all three groups participate in social events outside the law school."

Students approve of the classes offered here, too: "I cannot think of a law school which emphasizes practical lawyering more than UF. We have excellent tax, intellectual property, elder law, and environmental programs." Students only wish there were "greater variety in course offerings. I know there is more out there, but I see the same courses semester after semester."

Students and faculty alike speak highly of the $25-million-dollar expansion project that resulted in "brand-new classrooms with state-of-the-art technology." "They're gorgeous and definitely worth the hassle of construction," says one student. Another believes that now "the quality of the law school's physical appearance matches the quality of education a student receives here. They are spacious, bright, and ready to take us into the future." In the final phase, "the old library is being gutted and rebuilt" in a move that will double its size. "If the new classroom buildings are any indication, the new library should be great as well."

Some students here griped of having to use a makeshift library in the meantime, but as one student told us, "For a school undergoing a complete facelift, the faculty, students, and staff have done remarkably well in maintaining a high quality of education and an extremely professional environment. As these construction projects continue to resolve, the facilities are becoming among the best in the country."

J. Michael Patrick, Assistant Dean for Admissions
PO Box 117622, Gainesville, FL 32611
Telephone: 352-392-2087 • Fax: 352-392-4087
E-mail: admissions@law.ufl.edu • Website: www.law.ufl.edu

Life

There are more than 1,150 students at the UF College of Law. They are "for the most part in their early twenties" and from Florida. Although one in five is a student of color, some complain of a homogenous student body. "The school is not as diverse as it could be," one student says. "There should be more diversity on the faculty, too." Socially, UF is home to the usual suspects. "There are those who party every night and those who live in the library, afraid someone might get ahead of them." Students report a very "Greek" feel to the social environment. "People get along well and socialize a lot" but, with so many students, there are bound to be "lots of cliques." One student says, "If you find one you like, you're grand. But even if not, nearly everyone is friendly and nice." Students seem to experience competitiveness in varying degrees at UF, as some say there is zilch, while others call it "cutthroat." But "despite the obvious underlying competitiveness of law school, students are always willing to help each other out. This is what helps to form "a strong bond between UF law students that carries on well after graduation" and create "great opportunities to form a strong alumni network."

The University of Florida is located in Gainesville, "a big college town where there is not much" to do. (Except study, of course.) Beyond the standard undergraduate fare, "Gainesville has nothing to offer." For students seeking a more urban vibe, "the nearest city is Orlando, which is an hour-and-a-half away." Gainesville does have its merits, though. The weather is mostly good, particularly if you can avoid the sweltering heat in the summer. Perhaps most important, "it is cheap to live here."

Getting In

Accepting less than one in every six candidates, admission to Levin is tough. About 80 percent of the student body are residents of the state of Florida, but there is no cap on the percentage of the student body who can come from out of state, so your nonresident status is not a strike against you in the admissions process.

EMPLOYMENT INFORMATION

Career Rating	**74**
% employed within 9 months	90
Average starting salary	$55,242
State for bar exam	FL
Pass rate for first-time bar	91

Employers who frequently hire grads: Foley & Lardner, King & Spalding, Holland & Knight, Troutman Sanders, Steel Hector & Davis, Gunster Yoakley, Powell Goldstein, Lowndes Drosdick.

Prominent Alumni: Martha Barnett, partner, Holland & Knight LLP, ABA president 2000; W. Reece Smith Jr., senior member, Carlton, Fields, ABA president 1980; Harry Lee Anstead.

Grads employed by field (%):	
Academic	1
Business/industry	5
Government	25
Judicial clerkships	6
Other	6
Private practice	54
Public interest	3

Academic Requirements

Clinical Program Required?	No
Legal Writing Course Requirement?	Yes
Legal Methods Course Requirement?	Yes
Legal Research Course Requirement?	Yes
Moot Court Requirement?	No
Public Interest Law Requirement?	No

ADMISSIONS

Selectivity Rating	**88**
# applications received	3,183
# applicants accepted	503
# acceptees attending	195
Average LSAT	159
LSAT Range	156–162
Average undergrad GPA	3.7
Application fee	$30
Regular application deadline	1/15
Regular notification	4/1
Rolling notification?	Yes
Early application program?	No
Transfer students accepted?	Yes
Evening division offered?	No
Part-time accepted?	No
LSDAS accepted?	Yes

Applicants Also Look At

American U., Florida State U., Georgetown U., Stetson U., U. of Miami

International Students

TOEFL required of international students?	Yes
Minimum Paper TOEFL	550
Minimum Computer TOEFL	213

FINANCIAL FACTS

Annual tuition (resident)	$6,891
Annual tuition (nonres.)	$24,680
Books and supplies	$3,760
Tuition per credit (resident)	$230
Tuition per credit (nonres.)	$883
Room & board (on/off-campus)	$6,570/$7,040
Financial aid application deadline	3/15
% first-year students receiving some sort of aid	80
% receiving some sort of aid	89
% of aid that is merit-based	8
% receiving scholarships	30
Average grant	$4,453
Average loan	$14,800
Average total aid package	$15,317
Average debt	$43,663

UNIVERSITY OF GEORGIA
SCHOOL OF LAW

INSTITUTIONAL INFORMATION

Public/private	public
Student/faculty ratio	17:1
% faculty part-time	26
% faculty female	17
% faculty minority	2
Total faculty	84

SURVEY SAYS . . .

Diverse opinions accepted in classrooms
Great research resources
Students love Athens, GA

STUDENTS

Enrollment of law school	698
% male/female	52/48
% out-of-state	23
% full-time	100
% minority	24
% international	1
# of countries represented	3
Average age of entering class	25

ACADEMICS

Academic Experience rating	**88**
Professors interesting rating	87
Professors accessible rating	83
Hours of study per day	4.43

Academic Specialties

Commercial law, constitutional law, criminal law, environmental law, government services, intellectual property, international law, labor law, taxation.

Advanced Degrees Offered

LLM, 1 year.

Combined Degrees Offered

JD/master of business administration, 4 years; JD/master of historic preservation, 4 years; JD/master of public administration, 4 years; JD/MA, various fields, 4 years.

Academic Requirements

Clinical Program Required?	No
Legal Writing Course Requirement?	No
Legal Methods Course Requirement?	No

Academics

The University of Georgia School of Law's loyal students say the strong alumni network and the supportive community make it one of "the best educational values around." Students receive excellent training through a curriculum of "rigorous academics." UGA professors are knowledgeable, friendly, and accomplished; they hail from a wide range of professional backgrounds. "The UGA law faculty includes former Supreme Court clerks and partners from major law firms, and each brings a great deal of expertise and enthusiasm to the classroom." The classroom experience is intense and dynamic. One student says, "The tough Socratic Method makes for tough students. The good professors are demanding, and the results are rewarding." Another tells us, "You walk into a class expecting to be bored to tears and walk out laughing and excited about something you couldn't have even explained to anyone five minutes [before]." Most professors "are highly dedicated, easily accessible, and interested in students' concerns and progress." Students enjoy the "personalized attention" they get from professors who "seem to genuinely care" about them. Plus, "small class size[s] and nice students make going to class pleasant."

While students at many state schools complain about their classrooms and facilities, Georgia students enjoy a newly renovated building and excellent resources. "The library and classrooms are quite technologically advanced, and the entire law school has wireless Internet access," students tell us. In the newly renovated law library, "one wall is a two-story glass atrium that opens onto a view of magnolia trees and fountains." Plus, it is "so expansive that lawyers from Atlanta (over an hour away) frequently come to do research." You know things are pretty good when the only suggestion a student can think of is for the school to put "a Starbucks in the library."

At the University of Georgia, "there are many programs outside of class, [including a] huge variety of spectacular [clinical programs]." When it comes time to leave class for good, UGA students don't have a difficult time finding a job, thanks to their "wonderful" alumni network. "Most graduates stay in Georgia, so if you want to practice in-state, there is no better choice than UGA," explains one student. "But our grads also practice all over the country and the state, and they are always willing to give a Law Dawg a leg up."

Another student says, "Georgia grads like to hire other Georgia grads. [UGA's] incredible cooperative atmosphere [could be the reason that] Georgia alums are so loyal to the school."

Life

Students at UGA are absolutely crazy about their classmates, who are not only "incredibly smart, talented, and hard-working [but] also kind, friendly people." The "brilliant and socially astute" law students come "from diverse backgrounds and prestigious undergraduate institutions and careers." One student adds, "The social climate at Georgia Law is ideal, and the school environment is relatively stress free (for law school!)." Although there is some "healthy competition," there is, of course, "no book hiding or note hoarding—everybody is very helpful." A 40-something, single mother of two raves, "Everyone here has been incredibly welcoming, generous, and accommodating."

Dr. Giles Kennedy, Director of Law Admissions
225 Herty Drive, Athens, GA 30602-6012
Telephone: 706-542-7060 • Fax: 706-542-5556
E-mail: ugajd@jd.lawsch.uga.edu • Website: www.uga.edu

The campus is very active and social, boasting a variety of clubs, student groups, and social events. There's even "a talent show each year [where] the whole law school comes together (including the faculty) to have fun together." Georgia students also have a heart: "Students are passionate, energetic, involved in the whole gamut of political, social, legal, religious, charitable, and other activities." Another student adds, "I've been impressed with the number and quality of my fellow students who intend to use their great education from Georgia Law to serve their communities."

Off-campus, "Athens is a short, beautiful one-block walk away." A quintessential college town, "Athens tends to be a fairly diverse, open-minded place, so there really is something for everyone here." You'll find "dozens of restaurants and coffee shops available, all with student-friendly prices, [as well as] southern charm, warm weather, and fun things to do downtown." There are plenty of bands to see, since Athens has a tradition of "overflowing with great rock and roll." (Famous acts hailing from Athens include R.E.M. and the B-52s.)

Getting In

Admission to the University of Georgia is selective. UGA seeks students with a strong academic background who can add diversity of experience to the class. In 2003, the entering class at the University of Georgia had an average LSAT score of 162 and an average undergraduate GPA of 3.6.

EMPLOYMENT INFORMATION

Career Rating	**78**
Job placement rate (%)	99
Average starting salary	$54,799
State for bar exam	GA
Pass rate for first-time bar	92

Grads employed by field (%):	
Business/industry	8
Government	12
Judicial clerkships	11
Military	3
Private practice	62
Public interest	3

Legal Research Course Requirement?	Yes
Moot Court Requirement?	No
Public Interest Law Requirement?	No

ADMISSIONS

Selectivity Rating	**89**
# applications received	2,701
# applicants accepted	598
# acceptees attending	257
Average LSAT	162
LSAT Range	158–164
Average undergrad GPA	3.6
Application fee	$30
Regular application deadline	2/15
Regular notification	rolling
Rolling notification?	Yes
Early application program?	No
Transfer students accepted?	Yes
Evening division offered?	No
Part-time accepted?	No
LSDAS accepted?	Yes

Applicants Also Look At

Duke University, Emory University, Georgia State University, Mercer University, University of Tennessee, University of Virginia, Vanderbilt University.

International Students

TOEFL required of international students?	No
TOEFL recommended of international students?	No

FINANCIAL FACTS

Annual tuition (resident)	$7,978
Annual tuition (nonresident)	$25,084
Books and supplies	$1,000
Room & board (on/off-campus)	$16,724/$18,166
Financial aid application deadline	3/1
% first-year students receiving some sort of aid	91
% receiving some sort of aid	89
% of aid that is merit-based	20
% receiving scholarships	36
Average grant	$2,000
Average loan	$12,500
Average debt	$34,000

UNIVERSITY OF HAWAII—MANOA
WILLIAM S. RICHARDSON SCHOOL OF LAW

INSTITUTIONAL INFORMATION

Public/private	public
Student/faculty ratio	15:1
% faculty female	43
% faculty minority	41
Total faculty	38

SURVEY SAYS . . .

Diverse opinions accepted in classrooms
Great library staff
Abundant externship/internship/clerkship opportunities
Students love Honolulu, HI

STUDENTS

Enrollment of law school	330
% male/female	45/55
% out-of-state	27
% full-time	100
% minority	61
% international	2
# of countries represented	5
Average age of entering class	25

ACADEMICS

Academic Experience rating	**87**
Professors interesting rating	89
Professors accessible rating	90
Hours of study per day	4.45

Academic Specialties

Environmental law, international law.

Advanced Degrees Offered

JD, 3 years.

Combined Degrees Offered

JD/environmental law, 3 yrs; JD/Pacific Asian legal studies, 3 yrs; JD/grad. ocean policy; JD/MA; JD/MBA; JD/MS; JD/MSW; JD/PhD.

Academic Requirements

Clinical Program Required?	Yes
Legal Writing Course Requirement?	Yes
Legal Methods Course Requirement?	Yes
Legal Research Course Requirement?	Yes
Moot Court Requirement?	No
Public Interest Law Requirement?	Yes

Academics

Located just 15 minutes from the beach and looking out at the famous Diamond Head (a famous geologic formation on the island of Oahu), it's a wonder that students make it to class on a regular basis instead of cutting out for fun in the sun. The fact that they do attend classes is a testament to the strength of their professors, whose teaching ability, friendliness, and expertise draw rave reviews from students. In fact, students insist that Hawaii's best and brightest teach at their school, rivaling the quality of the professors at the nation's top institutions. One student declares, "During our last ABA review, one of the team members commented that he had just witnessed the best example of teaching he had ever seen in his 20 years of experience!"

So don't choose the University of Hawaii if you are looking for that "Life's a Beach" atmosphere. The curriculum is rigorous, and the professors expect a lot from students. As one student puts it, "I had never been to Hawaii before and expected 'surf law' to be the focus. Not true. You will work hard here, but the teaching atmosphere is much more 'user friendly' than what most 1Ls expect." Indeed, students say their professors are always willing to lend a hand and keep their office doors wide open. The professors are also noted for their political involvement, philanthropy, and activism, especially for Hawaii and Hawaiian causes. One student tells us, "This school focuses on social justice and using law to be an advocate to those in need." You want diverse points of view in the classroom? You got it. According to one student, "I am a 1L and I have no white male professors. If that's not diverse, I don't know what is." Additionally, the school offers course work that is particularly pertinent to international and multiethnic students, as well as a special Asian Pacific law curriculum.

"Being the only law school in the state of Hawaii means the best opportunities in the state are offered to Richardson students first." It also means many alumni are now practicing lawyers in the area. "The administration goes out of its way to help us network with lawyers in the community," writes one student. "As a 1L I have had many chances to meet and talk with a variety of lawyers. For example, we have a Launch-a-Lawyer program that pairs students with a lawyer in the community, and through this I already have a volunteer job for winter break!" On that note, students say the administration takes a personal interest in the success of every student at UH. "The administration is extremely helpful and approachable and courts the students' input/involvement with a monthly 'Dean's Forum' open to all students to discuss school priorities and policies. Students' opinions are encouraged in the process of reviewing current policies and administrative decisions such as hiring new professors, academic requirements, and grading policies," explains one student.

Laurie Tochiki, Assistant Dean
2515 Dole Street, Honolulu, HI 96822
Telephone: 808-956-3000 • Fax: 808-956-3813
E-mail: lawadm@hawaii.edu • Website: www.hawaii.edu/law

Life

Students say it is all about location at the University of Hawaii. "Not too many law students get to spend all weekend reading at the beach instead of being cooped up and freezing in the library," brags one student. The extremely friendly environment adds to the overall sense of well-being at Richardson. One student tells us, "We have a 'big brother/big sister' program in which the 2Ls are assigned to the new 1Ls to help them through their first year. By doing this we all tend to come closer as a student body instead of just being together as a class." Additionally, "the school offers various activities that cover a wide range of interests, including Hispanic Law Students' Association, Christian Legal Society, Law Review, Pacific-Asian Legal Studies Organization, flag football team, and hula halau."

Students are "competitive in a cooperative way." While everyone works hard, cutthroat competition is not encouraged, and students are happy to see their classmates succeed. "In fact," one student notes, "most people share their notes, outlines, and checklists. We help each other prepare for oral arguments and proofread each other's papers. It's a giant group hug."

Getting In

Admission to the University of Hawaii William S. Richardson School of Law is competitive. The school looks for students with a strong academic record and competitive LSAT scores, as well as important personal qualities, such as a background in law, a unique personal history, or an interest in Hawaiian or Pacific issues. The majority of admits (about 50 percent) majored in the social sciences, with a somewhat equal distribution of students from other fields. In the most recent entering class, the median LSAT score was 159, which was a few points higher than scores from the previous year.

EMPLOYMENT INFORMATION

Career Rating	**70**
% employed within 9 months	96
Average starting salary	$45,000
State for bar exam	HI, CA, WA, OR, NY
Pass rate for first-time bar	91

Employers who frequently hire grads: Hawaii State judiciary, office of the prosecuting attorney, public defender's office, Ashford & Wriston, Bays Deaver et al, Cades Schutte, Carlsmith Ball, Goodsill Anderson Quinn & Stifel.

Prominent Alumni: John Waihee, former governor of Hawaii; Jack Fritz, speaker, House of Congress; Mari Matsuda, professor, Georgetown University Law Center.

Grads employed by field (%):	
Academic	4
Business/industry	8
Government	20
Judicial clerkships	38
Private practice	22
Public interest	1
Other	7

ADMISSIONS

Selectivity Rating	**87**
# applications received	1,080
# applicants accepted	230
# acceptees attending	100
Average LSAT	160
LSAT Range	154–160
Average undergrad GPA	3.4
Application fee	$60
Regular application deadline	3/1
Regular notification	4/15
Rolling notification?	No
Early application program?	No
Transfer students accepted?	Yes
Evening division offered?	No
Part-time accepted?	No
LSDAS accepted?	Yes

Applicants Also Look At

Santa Clara University, University of California—-Berkeley, University of California—-Hastings, University of California—-Los Angeles, University of San Diego.

International Students

TOEFL required of international students?	Yes
Minimum Paper TOEFL	600
Minimum Computer TOEFL	250

FINANCIAL FACTS

Annual tuition (resident)	$11,529
Annual tuition (nonresident)	$19,689
Books and supplies	$800
Financial aid application deadline	3/1
Average grant	$5,400
Average loan	$11,885
Average total aid package	$5,400
Average debt	$43,276

UNIVERSITY OF HOUSTON
LAW CENTER

INSTITUTIONAL INFORMATION

Public/private	public
Student/faculty ratio	17:1
% faculty part-time	32
% faculty female	31
% faculty minority	11
Total faculty	104

SURVEY SAYS . . .

Diverse opinions accepted in classrooms
Abundant externship/internship/clerkship opportunities

STUDENTS

Enrollment of law school	1,094
% male/female	50/50
% out-of-state	16
% full-time	82
% minority	20
% international	1
# of countries represented	16
Average age of entering class	25

ACADEMICS

Academic Experience rating	**74**
Professors interesting rating	74
Professors accessible rating	66
Hours of study per day	4.21

Academic Specialties

Advocacy, commercial law, consumer law, clinical programs, criminal law, energy, environmental law, health, higher education, intellectual property law, international law, taxation.

Advanced Degrees Offered

LLM, 24 credit hours, health, intellectual property, tax, energy & natural resources, international law.

Combined Degrees Offered

JD/MBA, 4 yrs; JD/MPH, 3.5 yrs; JD/MA history, 4 yrs; JD/MD, 6 yrs; JD/PhD in medical humanities, 5 yrs; JD/MSW, 4 yrs; JD/PhD in criminal justice.

Academic Requirements

Clinical Program Required?	No
Legal Writing Course Requirement?	Yes

Academics

If you are looking for "an incredible legal education at a fantastic value," it's difficult to beat the University of Houston Law Center. Equally tough to beat is its bar-passage rate of 90 percent for first-time test-takers. As one satisfied student reports, "I have had the same opportunities at the University of Houston Law Center as my friends have had at other top schools (internship with a federal district judge, clerkships at the top Houston firms, etc.). And I pay less than a third of what they pay at their schools in tuition and living expenses."

UH's "brilliant [and] clearly dedicated [professors] are distinguished and they can teach, [qualities that] don't always go hand and hand," one student observes. "They don't teach us the law, they teach us to think like lawyers—a skill far more difficult to master than memorizing a code of law," says another. Furthermore, "not a single teacher has the same style, [which] makes law school exciting." The professors "really care about your education and career, [too, and] you can always stop by their office to ask advice." One student praises the professors more, "Though they retain the innate ability to scare the heck out of 1Ls, they make up for it by meeting up with us on Friday nights for a few beers and some chitchat."

Students are divided over the effectiveness of the administration. Some say the "approachable, responsive [administration] actively seeks ways of improving the school and the experience for the students." Meanwhile, others carp that the administration is "poorly organized and often incompetent." One student-critic says, "Somewhere, there's a junior high school that's missing its vice-principal.

"Many areas of specialization" are available. Several are noteworthy. "The Intellectual Property and Litigation Skills departments are first-rate, as are the interscholastic mock trial and moot court teams." Health law is huge and the Health Law and Policy Institute is home to "some of the greatest faculty in the nation," and UH is as good a place as any to get a JD/MPH (in conjunction with UT Health Science Center).

Students at UH really hate the "gloomy concrete tomb" that houses their law school. "The building is old, but not in an Ivy-League nostalgic sort of way," describes one student, "more like in a run-down prison sort of way." Though "the UH librarians are very eager to help," some students choose to go to the "absolutely stunning library" at nearby South Texas College of Law. UH's campus wide wireless Internet network, however, draws rave reviews. "Wireless is cool," exclaims one student. "It's very much a 21st century campus." Career Services "does a respectable job. Graduates fall naturally into the large Houston firms, where there are lots of alums. If you want to practice law in Houston, an exceptional legal market, this is the place to be."

Life

Most everyone at UH is from Texas, but "there are students from all over, [with] varying backgrounds, beliefs, and religions." Politically, you will find "some ultra-liberal agitators [as well as] some ultra-conservative types, [but] most students tend toward the middle-of-the-road." Academically, there is a contingent of "catty [students who] take themselves far too seriously and are unreasonably competitive," but most students at UH perceive a more "collaborative [and] laid-back atmosphere [overall, in which] outlines are readily shared." One student explains, "In this school, there is a lot of love. Sure, you have the snobs who think they are better than everyone else, and the loner who kind

Sondra R. Tennessee, Assistant Dean for Admissions
100 Law Center, Houston, TX 77204-6060
Telephone: 713-743-2280 • Fax: 713-743-2194
E-mail: lawadmissions@uh.edu • Website: www.law.uh.edu

of smells, but in general there is a real community." Socially, "the student body is mixed." On the one hand are recent college graduates who "party, drink, socialize, [and] treat law school as an extension of undergrad." There are also students who graduated less than recently and who treat law school as work."

"Houston, the nation's fourth largest city, is young and growing, and it has an entrepreneurial spirit unmatched by nearly any city in the country." Also, the "extreme humidity" can seem unmatched at times. Students tell us that UH's location "is both wonderful and terrible. It's wonderful because it's located in the center of one of the nation's strongest legal communities, [thus giving students the] distinct advantage of easy access to a wide legal market" while they are in school. The location of UH is "terrible" because it's in a bad neighborhood. "Walking across the campus at night is a really bad idea." Also, students claim, "parking is atrocious. "We'd all gladly pay double for a guaranteed parking spot," one exasperated student claims. On the plus side, the campus boasts "a state-of-the-art fitness center with every sports venue imaginable, including a rock-climbing wall."

Getting In

Numbers-wise, it is no small feat to get admitted to the University of Houston Law Center. The average LSAT score for entering students is 158. The average GPA for entering students is 3.45. As a state school, UH must maintain a population of 80 percent in-state students. So many applicants from the Lone Star state apply, though, that admission is usually no more competitive for out-of-staters.

EMPLOYMENT INFORMATION

Career Rating	**83**
Job placement rate (%)	90
Average starting salary	$74,755
State for bar exam	TX
Pass rate for first-time bar	90

Employers who frequently hire grads: Baker & Botts; Locke, Liddel & Sapp; Fulbright & Jaworski; Vinson & Elkins; Bracewell & Giuliani; Harris County district attorney; Weil Gotshal & Manges.

Prominent Alumni: Richard Haynes, litigation; John O'Quinn, litigation; Star Jones, TV personality; Charles Matthews, VP and General Counsel, Exxon Mobil; Philip Zelikow, Exec. Dir. of the 9/11 Commission.

Grads employed by field (%):	
Academic	3
Business/industry	16
Government	3
Judicial clerkships	5
Private practice	70
Public interest	3

Legal Methods Course Requirement?	Yes
Legal Research Course Requirement?	Yes
Moot Court Requirement?	Yes
Public Interest Law Requirement?	No

ADMISSIONS

Selectivity Rating	**85**
# applications received	3,575
# applicants accepted	810
# acceptees attending	270
Average LSAT	159
LSAT Range	158–161
Average undergrad GPA	3.5
Application fee	$70
Regular application deadline	2/15
Regular notification	5/15
Rolling notification?	Yes
Early application program?	Yes
Early application deadline	11/1
Early application notification	2/15
Transfer students accepted?	Yes
Evening division offered?	Yes
Part-time accepted?	Yes
LSDAS accepted?	Yes

Applicants Also Look At

Baylor U., Southern Methodist U., Texas Tech U., The U. of Texas at Austin.

International Students

TOEFL required of international students?	Yes
Minimum Paper TOEFL	600
Minimum Computer TOEFL	250

FINANCIAL FACTS

Annual tuition (resident)	$9,450
Annual tuition (nonres.)	$16,230
Books and supplies	$1,050
Fees per credit (resident)	$1,540
Fees per credit (nonres.)	$1,540
Tuition per credit (resident)	$315
Tuition per credit (nonresident)	$541
Room & board (on/off-campus)	$6,512/$8,600
Financial aid application deadline	4/1
% receiving some sort of aid	82
% of aid that is merit-based	26
% receiving scholarships	47
Average grant	$3,000
Average loan	$18,500
Average total aid package	$20,678
Average debt	$49,640

University of Idaho
College of Law

INSTITUTIONAL INFORMATION

Public/private	public
Student/faculty ratio	15:1
% faculty part-time	5
% faculty female	33
% faculty minority	8
Total faculty	24

SURVEY SAYS . . .

Diverse opinions accepted in classrooms
Great library staff

STUDENTS

Enrollment of law school	302
% male/female	59/41
% out-of-state	40
% full-time	100
% minority	9
Average age of entering class	27

ACADEMICS

Academic Experience rating	**63**
Professors interesting rating	63
Professors accessible rating	62
Hours of study per day	4.73

Academic Specialties

Environmental law, advocacy and dispute resolution, business and entrepreneurship, environmental and natural resources.

Combined Degrees Offered

Concurrent JD/MS in environmental science, 4 years; concurrent JD/master of accountancy, 7 semesters; JD/MES, 8 semesters.

Academic Requirements

Clinical Program Required?	No
Legal Writing Course Requirement?	Yes
Legal Methods Course Requirement?	No
Legal Research Course Requirement?	Yes
Moot Court Requirement?	Yes
Public Interest Law Requirement?	No

Academics

At the University of Idaho College of Law, students experience the personal attention and friendly atmosphere of a small private college, while paying the low tuition reflective of this state institution. While students praise the quality of the teaching at UI, what really impresses them is the individual attention they receive from their professors both in and out of the classroom. One student elaborates, "The school is very small and intimate. I was able to engage one-on-one with all of my professors and the administration. Also, due to the size, students are able to interact on a very personal level creating a less stressful or competitive atmosphere." In addition, students love the fact that school places, "a very strong emphasis on ethical issues and how to responsibly apply the law as officers of the court." One attests, "We are trained as advocates instead of as hired guns." On that note, students say they are well trained for practice in the real world, praising UI's active externship programs, legal clinics, and the "wonderful "semester in practice" program for third-year students."

The only law school in the state, UI is the number one training ground for future Idaho lawyers. "If you want to get a legal education that will allow you to be placed anywhere in the state, come here," enthuses a student. Another student adds, "Since Idaho has a small population and only one law school, the opportunities to work in the legal field over summers were tremendous." However, many students feel that their location in the small town of Moscow is a detriment to their employment prospects in more metropolitan areas, such as Boise. A student explains, "Moscow is an excellent place to be if you love the outdoors—camping, fishing, hunting, hiking, and biking. However, there is almost no chance for legal employment within the surrounding community." Students also complain that their job prospects are limited by the school's draconian grading policies. One student laments, "The law school does not participate in grade inflation, which many schools across the country do. Competing with a student at another school with the equivalent grades (except theirs appear higher) gives them an unfair advantage." Another student echoes, "Our grading system is highly under-inflated. This grade deflation makes competing with graduates of other law schools difficult."

With low tuition and limited resources, the UI College of Law has been unable to spend a lot of money building new facilities or improving classrooms. Students tell us that UI's "cramped [and] aging [building is] aesthetically unpleasing." Fortunately, wireless access is now available throughout the building, and the school does try to create a nice environment for the student population through some small, personal touches. For example, "UI assigns every student a study carrel where they can place all of their books and belongings. This is also a guaranteed spot where they can study." Despite limited resources, students say the UI administrators do their best for the school and are constantly trying to improve courses, facilities, and other programs. A student insists, "Overall, the administration is good, . . . bringing in more class opportunities from practicing lawyers and is also developing more opportunities to specialize in business and natural resource law." Another student agrees, "The University of Idaho is making improvements every day. The faculty is caring, and the student population is fun."

Stephen M. Perez, Director of Admissions/Student Services
Sixth & Rayburn Streets, Moscow, ID 83844-2321
Telephone: 208-885-2300 • Fax: 208-885-5709
E-mail: lawadmit@uidaho.edu • Website: www.uidaho.edu/law

Life

At University of Idaho College of Law, the campus atmosphere is cooperative and friendly. While surrounding Moscow lacks more traditional forms of entertainment and nightlife, students say that it is easy to make friends in class and that there is an active campus social scene. A student details, "You can be as involved socially as you want. There are many, many clubs and student organizations; there are always groups of students in the law school discussing one thing or another. There are many opportunities to get involved in social, political, or career-related activities."

UI students tend to come from similar backgrounds and many say the student population is lacking in diversity. Or, more bluntly put, "The law school's student body is a very conservative group. The ratio of minorities to whites is extremely low, as is the ratio of women to men." It is good to keep in mind that UI students are a fairly serious group, eschewing the "work hard, play hard" credo found at most law schools. The sizeable Mormon population means that many students do not drink. A student testifies, "At some events (such as the Barrister's Ball or the Karaoke Party), they have to sell 'non-drinking' tickets and 'drinking' tickets. Additionally, they agree not to serve alcohol from 7 to 9. Only at 9:00 is alcohol served at which point some of the party leaves."

Getting In

University of Idaho places a great deal of importance on a prospective student's personal qualities, including life experience and desire to be a lawyer. As such, the school carefully reviews an applicant's personal statement in addition to LSAT scores, undergraduate GPA, and recommendations. In 2004, the entering class had an average GPA of 3.4 and a median LSAT score of 156. About 60 percent of all of them are in-state residents.

EMPLOYMENT INFORMATION

Career Rating	**73**
% employed within 9 months	96
Average starting salary	$46,822
State for bar exam	ID, WA, UT, OR, NV
Pass rate for first-time bar	80

Employers who frequently hire grads: Employers with offices in Idaho, Washington, Oregon, Utah, Nevada.

Prominent Alumni: Linda Copple Trout, justice & former chief justice, Idaho Supreme Court; Frank A. Shrontz, former CEO Boeing Co.; Dennis E. Wheeler, president, Coeur: The Precious Metals Co.; James A. McClure, former United States senator.

Grads employed by field (%):	
Academic	6
Business/industry	4
Government	21
Judicial clerkships	26
Private practice	41
Public interest	1

ADMISSIONS

Selectivity Rating	**80**
# applications received	948
# applicants accepted	270
# acceptees attending	114
Average LSAT	156
LSAT Range	153–158
Average undergrad GPA	3.4
Application fee	$50
Regular application deadline	2/15
Regular notification	4/1
Rolling notification?	Yes
Early application program?	No
Transfer students accepted?	Yes
Evening division offered?	No
Part-time accepted?	No
LSDAS accepted?	Yes

Applicants Also Look At

Gonzaga University, Lewis & Clark College, Seattle University, University of Nevada—-Las Vegas, University of Utah, University of Wyoming, Willamette University.

International Students

TOEFL required of international students?	Yes
Minimum Paper TOEFL	560
Minimum Computer TOEFL	280

FINANCIAL FACTS

Annual tuition (resident)	$7,572
Annual tuition (nonresident)	$8,020
Books and supplies	$1,286
Room & board	$6,802
Financial aid application deadline	2/15
% first-year students receiving some sort of aid	75
% receiving some sort of aid	90
% of aid that is merit-based	38
% receiving scholarships	35
Average grant	$3,000
Average loan	$15,500
Average total aid package	$18,500
Average debt	$50,934

UNIVERSITY OF ILLINOIS
COLLEGE OF LAW

INSTITUTIONAL INFORMATION

Public/private	public
Student/faculty ratio	14:1
% faculty part-time	35
% faculty female	28
% faculty minority	11
Total faculty	71

SURVEY SAYS . . .

Diverse opinions accepted in classrooms
Great research resources
Great library staff

STUDENTS

Enrollment of law school	679
% male/female	58/42
% full-time	100
% minority	32
# of countries represented	12
Average age of entering class	25

ACADEMICS

Academic Experience rating	**89**
Professors interesting rating	85
Professors accessible rating	92
Hours of study per day	4.52

Academic Specialties

Civil procedure, commercial law, constitutional law, corporation securities law, criminal law, environmental law, government services, human rights law, intellectual property law, international law, labor law, legal history, legal philosophy, property, taxation.

Advanced Degrees Offered

JD, 3 years; LLM, 1 year.

Combined Degrees Offered

JD/MBA, JD/PhD Ed, JD/DVM, JD/MD, JD/MUP, master's in urban planning, JD/MHRIR, master's in human resources and industrial relations, JD/MED, master's in education, JD/MSChem, master's in chemistry, JD/MSJourn, master's in journalism, JD/MCS, master's in computer science, JD/MSNRES, master's in natural resources & enviromental sciences.

Academics

"You'll definitely get the bang for your buck" at the University of Illinois College of Law, "a jewel amid the cornfields [that boasts] the best mix of academic excellence, social interaction, and human decency for the best price available." Tuition is especially affordable for in-state students. The "tireless [administration] is also very accessible" and extraordinarily popular among students. "The new dean is extremely supportive of the students and does a wonderful job of building community."

Students at the U of I tell us emphatically that "the faculty is the school's greatest strength." The "tough but not unreasonable" professors are "prolific writers [who are] clearly brilliant and accomplished." Students say the professors "are, for the most part fantastic, both in and out of the classroom [and] always able to clarify concepts that are confusing. More significant, they are completely available [and] genuinely interested in teaching and working with students." The professors make an effort to be reached in that they "have open-door policies and are available for discussions with students about class, a job, or just life in general." First-year students tell us that their professors "bring a lot of energy to the courses." The primary complaint that students have with regard to the faculty is "keeping the good professors around. "One student explains, "There's not much reason for them to stay in central Illinois. The school really needs to make an effort to not let the good ones get away."

Graduates enjoy "a great employment rate" thanks to an aggressive Career Services office. Many students find well-paying jobs at large firms in Chicago and St. Louis. "If you do well here, nothing in Chicago will be off limits." However, students complain that the college "needs to broaden its resources [and] expand beyond the Midwestern market." Until that happens, "it is difficult to get much traction" on either coast "when searching for jobs in Champaign."

The facilities at the U of I "are good" in that large chunks "are wired," and the research resources of the library are as abundant as you'll find anywhere. Overall, though, the "rather Spartan [College of Law] could use some serious help." Suffice it to say, the "incredibly ugly and cheap-looking [building] does not give anyone goose bumps for the grand study of the law." One student writes, "There are no windows in any of the rooms." It's like going to school in a casino." Students note, "Sometimes seats are scarce [in the] crowded" classrooms, as well as in the "cramped" library. Also, wear layers because "there also seems to be a bit of a temperature control problem" no matter what the season.

Life

If they do say so themselves, the students at the U of I are "very amiable, non-competitive, [and] very intellectually minded," yet "not stuck on themselves." These are the "brightest [and] most fun" people—"all the cool, smart kids." Students at the U of I are also "a bit neurotic [and] love to hear their own voices." The student population is pretty diverse. There is also a laid-back atmosphere on campus. "Everybody really cares about you. They want you to succeed, and it's almost difficult not to."

Paul D. Pless, Assistant Dean for Admissions and Financial Aid
504 East Pennsylvania Avenue, Room 201, MC-594, Champaign, IL 61820
Telephone: 217-244-6415 • Fax: 217-244-1478
E-mail: admissions@law.uiuc.edu • Website: www.law.uiuc.edu

"The school truly is a community because of its manageable size. Lunches with the dean" are common, and there are "endless other ways to connect with the other students and, more important, the faculty." One content student writes, "The cafeteria has good food and, best of all, they carry Starbucks coffee." Students also say, "Although U of I is located in the corn fields of Illinois, it is impossible to feel isolated" because the administration "is constantly bringing in lecturers, symposiums, and guest speakers." In addition, the College of Law sponsors "a weekly happy hour, [at which] professors and administrators act as the celebrity bartenders."

Life outside the classroom has many positive aspects. "It is great to be on a Big Ten campus and be able to devote yourself to the study of law full-time," and surprising though it seems, "there is actually a lot to do in Urbana-Champaign." There are "great bars, coffeehouses, [and] centers for the arts." There is also "a progressive music scene." Unfortunately, "The availability of any remotely interesting cuisine is limited," though, and the college is "too near the experimental farms, which tend to make the place smell." Some students gripe that "social life can seem dominated by a frat/sorority type atmosphere," even at the law school level. "The town is basically designed for college students, so it gets a little dullsville at times." Many students would "prefer to be in a larger city," with Chicago being the example of choice. "Socially, we do the best we can with the town we're in," asserts one student. "That means we drink a lot [and] go en masse to football and basketball games."

Getting In

The average LSAT score for admitted students is 163. The median GPA is 3.42. Those numbers are serious but not forbidding. Note also that, while it's substantially cheaper for Illinois residents to attend the college, residency in the Land of Lincoln will not get you one iota of special treatment from the admissions office.

EMPLOYMENT INFORMATION

Career Rating	**89**
% employed within 9 months	99.5
Average starting salary	$75,072
State for bar exam	IL, CA, DC, NY, MO
Pass rate for first-time bar	97

Employers who frequently hire grads:
Brinks Hofer Gilson & Lione, Bell Boyd & Lloyd, Foley & Lardner, City of Chicago Law Department, Cook County state's attorney, Deloitte Touche, Gardner Carton & Douglas, Husch & Eppenberger, Jenner & Block, Jones Day, Kirkland & Ellis, KMZ Rosenman, Latham & Watkins, Sidley Austin Brown & Wood, McGuire & Woods, McAndrews Held & Malloy.

Grads employed by field (%):	
Academic	3
Business/industry	12
Government	9
Judicial clerkships	13
Military	2
Private practice	58
Public interest	3

Academic Requirements

Clinical Program Required?	No
Legal Writing Course Requirement?	Yes
Legal Methods Course Requirement?	No
Legal Research Course Requirement?	Yes
Moot Court Requirement?	No
Public Interest Law Requirement?	No

ADMISSIONS

Selectivity Rating	**88**
# applications received	2,930
# applicants accepted	676
# acceptees attending	228
Average LSAT	163
LSAT Range	160–166
Average undergrad GPA	3.4
Application fee	$40
Regular application deadline	3/15
Regular notification	rolling
Rolling notification?	Yes
Early application program?	Yes
Early application deadline	11/1
Early application notification	12/15
Transfer students accepted?	Yes
Evening division offered?	No
Part-time accepted?	No
LSDAS accepted?	Yes

Applicants Also Look At

Indiana U., Northwestern U., U. of Chicago, U. of Iowa, U. of Michigan, U. of Wisconsin, Washington U.

International Students

TOEFL required of international students?	Yes
Minimum Paper TOEFL	600
Minimum Computer TOEFL	250

FINANCIAL FACTS

Annual tuition (resident)	$14,306
Annual tuition (nonresident)	$26,644
Books and supplies	$3,020
Room & board	$8,532
Financial aid application deadline	3/15
% first-year students receiving some sort of aid	99
% receiving some sort of aid	99
% of aid that is merit-based	100
% receiving scholarships	58
Average grant	$4,300
Average loan	$21,556
Average debt	$56,867

UNIVERSITY OF IOWA
COLLEGE OF LAW

INSTITUTIONAL INFORMATION

Public/private	public
Student/faculty ratio	13:1
% faculty part-time	13
% faculty female	38
% faculty minority	8
Total faculty	64

SURVEY SAYS . . .

Diverse opinions accepted in classrooms
Great research resources
Great library staff

STUDENTS

Enrollment of law school	712
% male/female	52/48
% out-of-state	37
% full-time	100
% minority	16
% international	1
Average age of entering class	24

ACADEMICS

Academic Experience rating	**83**
Professors interesting rating	80
Professors accessible rating	77
Hours of study per day	4.65

Academic Specialties

Constitutional law, corporation securities law, human rights law, intellectual property law, international law, legal history, property.

Advanced Degrees Offered

LLM in international and comparative law, 24 hours of academic credit and a thesis.

Combined Degrees Offered

JD/MBA, 4 years; JD/MA, 4 years; JD/MHA, 4 years; JD/MSW, 4 years; JD/MPH, 4 years; JD/MS, 4 years; JD/MD, 6 years.

Academic Requirements

Clinical Program Required?	No
Legal Writing Course Requirement?	Yes
Legal Methods Course Requirement?	Yes

Academics

At the University of Iowa's affordable College of Law, you will find "a broad range of courses [and a] friendly and accessible [administration, which is] unusual in a large university setting." One witty student draws the analogy, "Iowa's administration is like your mother on prom night: extremely overprotective and nervous that everything 'goes well' for you." The faculty is "truly outstanding, both professionally and personally." These professors "don't mess around." They have "a wide array of backgrounds and specialties, [and] they know their stuff." It is no doubt "the professors are really the best asset to Iowa." One happy student proclaims, "I think that the University of Iowa is underrated. The faculty and the level of support we receive are second to none."

The one thing that really sets Iowa apart is its "emphasis on legal writing." The "rigorous writing program" is simply awesome. "All of our graduates definitely have the skills we need to attack writing projects," brags one student. "We have an in-house writing center staffed by well-trained writers, including several lawyers pursuing degrees in creative writing at the University of Iowa's famous Writers' Workshop. They are really helpful as we learn how to write like lawyers." Also, "the law journals are among the best in the country," and the strong curriculum in international and comparative law is noteworthy.

The biggest complaint we hear is that Iowa "focuses too much on theory and not enough on practical application of the law." Toward the sunset of her law school years, one student gripes, "The emphasis on writing is great and the academics are strong, but it would have been nice to actually have the opportunity to apply what we are learning." Another student says, "We have a great reputation for theoretical law but need to work on incorporating some practicality into our curriculum." Exacerbating this problem is the fact that "internships and externships are by lottery only." Students also complain, "It's difficult to find a job outside the Midwest." So long as you are willing to work in the Midwest, though, you shouldn't have trouble finding work with a law degree from Iowa.

The facilities are a mixed bag. The "marvelous, never-ending [library] rocks." One student explains, "We have a lot of resources available; we have great hours for night owls like myself; and we have librarians that are always helpful." There is "enough room to provide all 2L and 3L students their own study space with a locked bookcase, [which is] very handy." Also, "videotaping of all classes helps" (in case you miss class), and "library carrels are wired for Internet usage." Overall, though, lack of technology is a problem. "Our school is like a dithering, old grandma trying to turn on a computer," analogizes one student. "She's just clueless as to where to begin. The school's techno-phobia borders on lunacy."

Life

You won't find a profusion of diversity at U of I. "Iowa is a very white state, and it's hard to draw people of different ethnicities to our law school," explains one student. "We have some foreign exchange students (and a particularly high number from Germany)." Another student relates, "The most shocking thing to me is how many married 23-year-olds there are at this school." One student in-the-know advises, "Single students: be prepared."

Jan Barnes, Admissions Coordinator
Melrose at Byington Streets, Iowa City, IA 52242
Telephone: 319-335-9095 • Fax: 319-335-9019
E-mail: law-admissions@uiowa.edu • Website: www.law.uiowa.edu

The "incredibly smart and witty [law students at Iowa are] high-achieving but anti-competitive." Students say, "This has to be the most laid-back place to study law. The students are much more interested in learning about and from each other than unnecessary competition." The general consensus on students is pretty tame: "Aside from the occasional gunners, the students here are focused and serious, yet have fairly good values in place." One student relates, "With approximately 200 students per class, we all know each other and have a great time together," Another student says, "People are very friendly and respectful of differing opinions." There are enough extracurricular activities to keep anyone busy. "From keg races to study groups there are plenty of social activities for everyone. The law school has its own flag football and basketball leagues. Professors routinely host students for barbecues, and they actively help students start new groups."

Beyond the law school community, Iowa City is a "great, low-stress, perfect [college town with] a great cultural atmosphere." One student notes, "There is always something to do." Another student finds the pluses of the surrounding town, "Compared to living in a major city and paying major city tuition coupled with the expenses of life, Iowa is dirt cheap," too. Parking is a problem, though, and the "cold, harsh" winters are tough to deal with. Also, the bar scene isn't necessarily the greatest. "The law school is in the heart of an undergraduate campus, so most of the crowd at the bars are testosterone-pumped undergraduates." The major complaint is that "the closest 'cool' city is Chicago, which is a good three-hour drive."

Getting In

Each entering class is comprised of approximately 70 percent Iowa residents. Admitted students at the 25th percentile have an LSAT score of 158 and a GPA of 3.3. Admitted students at the 75th percentile have an LSAT score of 164 and a GPA of 3.8. If you take the LSAT more than once, Iowa will average your scores. If there is a really huge difference in your scores, the admissions committee may use the higher score.

EMPLOYMENT INFORMATION

Career Rating	**77**
Job placement rate (%)	99
Average starting salary	$67,524
State for bar exam	IA, IL, MN, MO, AZ
Pass rate for first-time bar	89

Employers who frequently hire grads: National law firms, government agencies, state and federal judges.

Prominent Alumni: Norman B. Coleman, U.S. senator, Minnesota; James D. Ericson, president, Northwestern Mutual Life Ins. Co.; John J. Bouma, chairman, Snell & Wilmer, Phoenix; Justice Ronald T. Moon, chief justice, Hawaii Supreme Court, Honolulu.

Grads employed by field (%):	
Academic	1
Business/industry	15
Government	5
Judicial clerkships	8
Military	2
Other	7
Private practice	59
Public interest	3

Legal Research Course Requirement?	Yes
Moot Court Requirement?	Yes
Public Interest Law Requirement?	No

ADMISSIONS

Selectivity Rating	**85**
# applications received	1,601
# applicants accepted	475
# acceptees attending	218
Average LSAT	160
LSAT Range	157–163
Average undergrad GPA	3.5
Application fee	$60
Regular application deadline	3/15
Regular notification	rolling
Rolling notification?	Yes
Early application program?	No
Transfer students accepted?	Yes
Evening division offered?	No
Part-time accepted?	No
LSDAS accepted?	Yes

Applicants Also Look At

Drake University, The George Washington University, Georgetown University, Indiana University, University of Illinois at Urbana-Champaign, University of Minnesota, University of Wisconsin.

International Students

TOEFL required of international students?	Yes
Minimum Paper TOEFL	580
Minimum Computer TOEFL	237

FINANCIAL FACTS

Annual tuition (resident)	$11,510
Annual tuition (nonresident)	$25,718
Books and supplies	$2,230
Room & board (off-campus)	$6,350
Financial aid application deadline	1/1
% first-year students receiving some sort of aid	96
% receiving some sort of aid	96
% of aid that is merit-based	7
% receiving scholarships	44
Average grant	$11,510
Average loan	$19,871
Average total aid package	$24,263
Average debt	$58,036

UNIVERSITY OF KANSAS
SCHOOL OF LAW

INSTITUTIONAL INFORMATION

Public/private	public
Student/faculty ratio	15:1
% faculty part-time	35
% faculty female	32
% faculty minority	8
Total faculty	60

SURVEY SAYS . . .

Diverse opinions accepted in classrooms
Great library staff
Students love Lawrence, KS

STUDENTS

Enrollment of law school	524
% male/female	56/44
% out-of-state	27
% full-time	100
% minority	21
# of countries represented	2
Average age of entering class	23

ACADEMICS

Academic Experience rating	**83**
Professors interesting rating	86
Professors accessible rating	89
Hours of study per day	3.89

Academic Specialties

Commercial law, constitutional law, corporation securities law, criminal law, environmental law, elder law certificate, intellectual property law, international law, media law and policy, Native American law certificate, property, taxation.

Advanced Degrees Offered

JD with an accelerated degree option so students can complete it in 26 months instead of 3 years.

Combined Degrees Offered

JD/master of business administration, JD/MA in economics, JD/master of public administration, JD/MA in philosophy, JD/master of social welfare, JD/master of urban planning, JD/master of health services administration, JD/master of indigenous nations studies. All combined degree programs are 4 years.

Academics

Students at the University of Kansas School of Law can't stop bragging about their "unique, diverse, [and] deeply talented" faculty. "The commitment to teaching is phenomenal, [and these] highly motivated [professors are] always accessible." Faculty offices are located "along the perimeter [of the library,] allowing for constant and meaningful interaction with students." One stern student says, "The dean has made it abundantly clear that if you are teaching at KU Law, you are there to further the students' interests, not your own. An open-door policy is the norm, not an exception, [and] the professors play valuable mentoring roles to the students, creating relationships with students that last into their professional careers." The "challenging" classroom experience is "rigid yet relaxed." Students say, "Professors expect students to be on top of material and understand assignments but use discussion and debate as means to delve into topics." Outside of class, professors "often invite groups of students out for drinks, social events, and even dinner with their families."

KU has a hands-on approach to the law. "While schools across the country focus so much on legal theory, the University of Kansas has made it a top priority for the professors to emphasize the practicality of law," explains one student. "When you become a lawyer," says another, "you are required to assist people with their legal needs on a day-to-day basis, and KU graduates will be better prepared than many other graduates across the country." Certificate programs at KU include elder law, environmental law, communications law, tax law, and tribal law. "Opportunities for practical experience abound," including many clinical programs and an "outstanding" number of clerkship and internship opportunities. "The clinical programs are by far the greatest strength of the school," gloats a 3L. "I decided to go into criminal law after my participation in the judicial clerkship clinic the summer after my first year."

Job prospects are solid. "The Career Services staff is interested in helping you whether you are a top-ten-percent student wanting the big-firm job or you are a bottom 25 percent student interested in a different area." These days, though, "it seems like a ton of employers visit during interview season."

KU's green, rolling campus "is one of the most beautiful in the country." Unfortunately, the "ultra-modern concrete block of a building" that is the School of Law facility is "outdated and not all that accessible." The facilities are "well-designed and highly functional [but] hideously ugly." One student laments, "I'd give the facility an F." Although "the classrooms are almost all wired and multimedia ready, [there simply] aren't enough computers with Internet access." Still it remains that "the biggest problem is the lack of space. Study rooms are very limited, and students often must seek options outside of the law school if they desire to study as a group."

Carrie English, Director of Admissions
1535 West Fifteenth Street, Lawrence, KS 66045-7577
Telephone: 785-864-4378 • Fax: 785-864-5054
E-mail: admitlaw@ku.edu • Website: www.law.ku.edu

Life

"KU has a wonderful student body that works very hard to excel." Students "keep their competitive ambitions hidden below the surface and are mostly collegial toward one another. Great camaraderie [is the norm in this] open, friendly, and encouraging atmosphere." The student population is "very close-knit, sometimes annoyingly so." Students say, "KU law has everything, positive and negative, that comes with being a small academic community. On the positive side, you will make friends who will stay with you for the rest of your life. On the negative side, everyone knows everyone else, and at times it can feel like junior high all over again in terms of the gossip and cliquiness."

The "generally liberal [students can be] a little obnoxious, [but they are] very open-minded [with regard to] different political and social opinions." Ethnic diversity is respectable. "KU law has a large number of minority students and has made a concerted effort in the last few years to maintain a large percentage of minority law students."

"Winters here are gray, cold, and boring, [but] Lawrence is a great college town, relatively inexpensive, [and] only 40 minutes from Kansas City." One student comments, "The school and other student groups bring in a large number of speakers, [and] in the last two years the law school hosted Justices Scalia and Thomas, *New York Times* Supreme Court correspondent Linda Greenhouse, and Janet Reno—to name but a few." After hours, "organized social events are a great way to meet your classmates, [and KU Law's] happy hours every Thursday at a different bar make the semesters more bearable."

Getting In

Admitted students at the 25th percentile have an LSAT score of 154 and a GPA of 3.1. Admitted students at the 75th percentile have an LSAT score of 160 and a GPA of 3.7. Note that KU Law offers an accelerated summer-starter class.

EMPLOYMENT INFORMATION

Career Rating	**74**
Job placement rate (%)	85
Average starting salary	$55,785
State for bar exam	KS, MO, CA, CO, TX
Pass rate for first-time bar	91

Employers who frequently hire grads: Baker, Sterchi, Cowden, & Rice, Blackwell, Sanders, Peper, Martin, Bryan Cave, Hinkle Elkouri, Husch & Eppenberger, Kutak Rock, Lathrop & Gage, Foulson Siefkin, Stinson Morrison Hecker, Shook Hardy & Bacon.

Prominent Alumni: Carla Stovall, attorney general of Kansas; Sam Brownback, United States senate; Mary Beck Briscoe, tenth circuit judge.

Grads employed by field (%):	
Academic	2
Business/industry	19
Government	19
Judicial clerkships	7
Military	2
Other	1
Private practice	48
Public interest	2

Academic Requirements

Clinical Program Required?	No
Legal Writing Course Requirement?	Yes
Legal Methods Course Requirement?	Yes
Legal Research Course Requirement?	Yes
Moot Court Requirement?	No
Public Interest Law Requirement?	No

ADMISSIONS

Selectivity Rating	**81**
# applications received	1,238
# applicants accepted	313
# acceptees attending	167
Average LSAT	155
LSAT Range	153–160
Average undergrad GPA	3.5
Application fee	$50
Regular application deadline	3/15
Regular notification	rolling
Rolling notification?	Yes
Early application program?	No
Transfer students accepted?	Yes
Evening division offered?	No
Part-time accepted?	No
LSDAS accepted?	Yes

Applicants Also Look At

Baylor U., Loyola U. Chicago, Pepperdine U., U. of Missouri—Kansas City, U. of Missouri—Columbia, U. of Wisconsin, Washburn U.

International Students

TOEFL required of international students?	Yes
Minimum Paper TOEFL	600
Minimum Computer TOEFL	250

FINANCIAL FACTS

Annual tuition (resident)	$9,889
Annual tuition (nonresident)	$18,858
Books and supplies	$700
Room & board	$7,226
Financial aid application deadline	3/15
% first-year students receiving some sort of aid	80
% receiving some sort of aid	82
% of aid that is merit-based	85
% receiving scholarships	67
Average grant	$2,777
Average loan	$17,281
Average total aid package	$18,500
Average debt	$59,648

UNIVERSITY OF KENTUCKY
COLLEGE OF LAW

INSTITUTIONAL INFORMATION

Public/private	public
Student/faculty ratio	16:1
% faculty female	31
% faculty minority	4
Total faculty	29

SURVEY SAYS . . .

Diverse opinions accepted in classrooms
Great library staff

STUDENTS

Enrollment of law school	420
% male/female	56/44
% out-of-state	18
% full-time	100
% minority	8
% international	1
# of countries represented	5
Average age of entering class	23

ACADEMICS

Academic Experience rating	**88**
Professors interesting rating	97
Professors accessible rating	95
Hours of study per day	4.28

Academic Specialties

Advocacy, civil procedure, commercial law, constitutional law, corporation securities law, criminal law, environmental law, human rights law, intellectual property law, international law, labor law, property, taxation.

Advanced Degrees Offered

JD only. No LLM or master's of law programs offered.

Combined Degrees Offered

JD/MPA, 4 years, JD/MBA, 4 years, JD/master's in diplomacy and international commerce, 4 years.

Academic Requirements

Clinical Program Required?	No
Legal Writing Course Requirement?	Yes
Legal Methods Course Requirement?	No

Academics

While academic life at the University of Kentucky College of Law is best described as "rigorous, the down-to-earth, [and] very committed" faculty makes the daily grind of law school much more agreeable. "Most of the professors really know what they teach and try their best to help you figure it out." They are "extremely articulate and know the subject matter very well." Students say, "Many [professors] incorporate humor into the driest of subjects." One student explains, "Like fingerprints, no two are alike." Some professors "rely heavily on the Socratic Method while others prefer a more lecture-oriented format. It's refreshing to have a mixture of both." It's good to know that professors at UK are "always accessible," as well. As one student says, "They are people that I respect, both as academics and as friends."

Administrators at UK are "personable, encouraging, [and] accessible." A 3L relates, "I have found that the administration not only cares, but listens to their students," Furthermore, "Students are included in all-important faculty committees and have a voice regarding changes in the law school."

The UK College of Law curriculum "is fairly bare bones." While it's "loaded with business-related courses, some other areas suffer." If environmental law is your bag, the college is home to a Mineral Law Center and UK Law publishes the Journal of Natural Resources and Environmental Law. Also noteworthy is the fact that the Kentucky Law Journal is the 10th oldest law review published by an American law school. A host of externship, internship, and clinical programs includes the Prison Externship, which allows students to counsel inmates at the Federal Correctional Institute in Lexington on civil and criminal matters. UK Law also offers a JD/MBA dual-degree program and a JD/MPA in public administration. When the time comes to get a real job, "the school is very well connected in the legal community in Kentucky." Practicing law beyond the borders of the Bluegrass State is definitely possible; graduates frequently find jobs in Georgia, Ohio, and Washington, DC.

The facilities are so-so. "Some of the classrooms are state-of-the-art [and include] plasma-screen monitors, Internet cameras, document cameras, microphones, and power outlets for every student." Unfortunately, the building housing these classrooms "is somewhat dilapidated, [and resembles] 1960s, Soviet-style architecture." In other words, students "need a new building badly." One light-hearted student says, "Our library has ugly orange carpet, but it makes for a good laugh." Maybe because "the *Brady Bunch* home comes to mind."

DRUSILLA V. BAKERT, ASSOCIATE DEAN
209 LAW BUILDING, LEXINGTON, KY 40506-0048
TELEPHONE: 859-257-6770 • FAX: 859-323-1061
E-MAIL: DBAKERT@UKY.EDU • WEBSITE: WWW.UKY.EDU/LAW

Life

"The students as a whole are very sharp. Many viewpoints are represented, and people from different camps interact freely." One student tells us, "You are bound to find someone at UK who shares your beliefs, although there will be just as many who won't." Students say, "Quite a range of diversity exists in ethnicity, age, and family status." Since the law school is "relatively small, you tend to recognize everyone." People at UK are "easygoing, generally friendly, [and] don't take themselves too seriously." One student observes, "Random people I don't even know say 'hi' to me in the halls. If you are a nice, friendly person, you can be accepted by pretty much any group" at this school. It's the type of place where "people hold the doors open for each other and share notes." The academic atmosphere is "healthily competitive, [meaning] students may compete for grades, but they will not stab each other in the back." It seems "a generally congenial and cooperative attitude prevails."

Outside the classroom, "Lexington, Kentucky, is an inexpensive and peaceful place, [something that really] helps out when law school becomes overwhelming." The social life at UK Law is "fun [and] active." There are "many student-sponsored get-togethers, [and] there's almost always a happy hour going on somewhere a couple of nights a week." Students note, "The SBA is very active in planning student body social events—everything from tailgating to the Barrister's Ball." Of course, college basketball reigns absolutely supreme at the university, and law students get as excited about Wildcat hoops as anybody else.

Getting In

Admitted students at the 25th percentile have an LSAT score of 156 and a GPA of 3.3. Admitted students at the 75th percentile have an LSAT score of 162 and a GPA of 3.8. With an LSAT score of 152 and a GPA of 3.4, your odds of getting admitted would be "possible," according to the UK Law admissions staff. With an LSAT score of 163 and a GPA of 3.0, your odds of gaining admission would be "probable."

EMPLOYMENT INFORMATION

Career Rating	**78**
% employed within 9 months	98.5
Average starting salary	$55,000
State for bar exam	KY
Pass rate for first-time bar	87

Employers who frequently hire grads: All Kentucky legal employers; major firms in Cincinnati, Nashville, West Virginia, DC, NYC, and Atlanta. Through job fairs students also have access to employers nationwide.

Prominent Alumni: Mitch McConnell, U.S. senator; Hal Rodgers, U.S. representative; Jim Rogers, CEO Cinergy Corp; Steve Bright, national public interest attorney.

Grads employed by field (%):	
Academic	1
Business/industry	7
Government	12
Judicial clerkships	18
Private practice	59
Public interest	3

Legal Research Course Requirement?	Yes
Moot Court Requirement?	Yes
Public Interest Law Requirement?	No

ADMISSIONS

Selectivity Rating	**84**
# applications received	1,273
# applicants accepted	397
# acceptees attending	144
Average LSAT	160
LSAT Range	156–162
Average undergrad GPA	3.6
Application fee	$50
Regular application deadline	3/1
Regular notification	rolling
Rolling notification?	Yes
Early application program?	No
Transfer students accepted?	Yes
Evening division offered?	No
Part-time accepted?	No
LSDAS accepted?	Yes

Applicants Also Look At

Indiana University, Northern Kentucky University, University of Cincinnati, University of Georgia, University of Louisville, University of Tennessee, Vanderbilt University.

International Students

TOEFL required of international students?	Yes
Minimum Paper TOEFL	650
Minimum Computer TOEFL	280

FINANCIAL FACTS

Annual tuition (resident)	$10,890
Annual tuition (nonresident)	$20,591
Books and supplies	$800
Room & board	$9,300
Financial aid application deadline	4/1
% first-year students receiving some sort of aid	75
% receiving some sort of aid	75
% receiving scholarships	54
Average grant	$4,000
Average loan	$18,500
Average total aid package	$22,500
Average debt	$38,380

University of Maine
School of Law

INSTITUTIONAL INFORMATION

Public/private	public
Student/faculty ratio	19:1
% faculty female	44
Total faculty	18

SURVEY SAYS . . .

Diverse opinions accepted in classrooms

Students love Portland, ME

STUDENTS

Enrollment of law school	278
% male/female	44/56
% out-of-state	34
% full-time	97
% minority	6
% international	1
Average age of entering class	28

ACADEMICS

Academic Experience rating	**68**
Professors interesting rating	79
Professors accessible rating	85
Hours of study per day	4.39

Advanced Degrees Offered

JD, 3 years.

Combined Degrees Offered

JD/MA in community planning & development, health policy management, and public policy & management; JD/MBA.

Academic Requirements

Clinical Program Required?	No
Legal Writing Course Requirement?	Yes
Legal Methods Course Requirement?	No
Legal Research Course Requirement?	No
Moot Court Requirement?	Yes
Public Interest Law Requirement?	No

Academics

1Ls may spend most of their first year at the University of Maine School of Law in a single classroom "incredibly restricted by physical space," but they say that "what Maine lacks in state-of-the-art facilities it more than makes up for in faculty strength and availability." A mere 18 professors comprise the Maine law faculty, meaning "it's easy to become close with your peers, faculty, and the administration." A 3L tells us, "I have close working and personal relationships with several faculty members, which is exactly why I chose a small law school. That kind of access has vastly enhanced my academic experience." Students repeatedly give props to professors for "the way they treat us, always ready and willing to answer questions, offer advice, and talk with us about more than just the classes they teach." Instructors generate an environment where "the amount of humor and laughter during each class is amazing, and the mutual respect for everyone's ideas is clearly evident." Socratic tactics are "supported by a combination of articles, book reviews, cases, trial transcripts, and other materials. They work to create a functional use of the law, rather than a memorization of rules and procedural elements."

Some of the school's unique course offerings center on the Ocean and Coastal Law Program and its affiliated Marine Law Institute, the only marine policy think-tank associated with a law school in the Northeast. Some students combine their JD with a master's in public policy and management, community planning and development, or health policy and management. The academic vibe combines a desire to serve people in a practical way with an intellectual commitment to the best of the profession's principles. "Pursuit of knowledge and truth is stressed," reflects a 1L, "a refreshing recentering of values in an educational society where we sometimes lose track of what really is important: justice."

Arguably, the one person with the biggest impact on the University of Maine School of Law is the architect. The building looks like a "post-modern fortress of justice" to some, "the Death Star" to others. "Third-world, dismal, silly,—take your pick, there's no escaping the backdrop. A 2L assures us that "most people have a good sense of humor about it," like the student who marvels that walking amid the 70s décor "kind of feels like going back in time." Somewhat anachronistically, wireless coverage does function at times, though outlets can be hard to come by.

Students take pride in their work beyond grades or career prospects: "Even though our tiny school doesn't have a well-known reputation outside the state, the professors do not hold back on expectations for excellence," comments one student. The legal writing program and clinic experiences are singled out as highlight of academic life. For example, the Cumberland Legal Aid Clinic allows 3Ls to put their learning into practice under faculty supervision in "a uniquely great program" that provides legal services to the poor.

Students make a point of hinting at the offbeat nature of academic life at Maine Law. "Don't come for fancy facilities or super-specialized course offerings. Do come if you want to be a part of a very small, truly interesting student body," is how one student articulates a common sentiment. And they're eager to cultivate this original environment of theirs. An ambitious 2L writes, "We need more money for a physically larger school, a sophisticated computer lab, more scholarships, and a larger career counseling staff to expand our knowledge and contacts beyond northern New England." Already students see the school's reputation on the rise and assure prospective applicants: "Attending Maine doesn't mean you have to stay in Maine. You will graduate prepared to enter any

ELAINE M. BOURNE, DIRECTOR OF ADMISSIONS
246 DEERING AVENUE, PORTLAND, ME 04102
TELEPHONE: 207-780-4341 • FAX: 207-780-4239
E-MAIL: MAINELAW@USM.MAINE.EDU • WEBSITE: HTTP://MAINELAW.MAINE.EDU/

legal environment." Currently, students get the sense that "there aren't a whole lot of potential employers with open arms for us." However, students emphasize, "The legal community in the area is so involved in the law school." If you come here, start collecting business cards early.

Life

Maine Law runs like one long outdoor leadership and team-building retreat that just happens to be a law school. With just more than 90 students per class, the school is "large enough to have a unique student body, but small enough to get to know almost everyone personally." The overall vibe resembles that of "a small liberal arts college, given the number of students from New England's many liberal arts schools." Most people have taken a nice long academic vacation between undergrad and law school, however. "Your average 1L has seen something of the world and the workplace." People demonstrate "a healthy attitude about competition and genuinely support each other in job searches and tryouts for moot court." Many students agree that "you will not find snobbishness or cutthroat, uncomfortable competition" in this "extremely friendly and collaborative" setting. They have achieved a "friendly rivalry of intelligent peers that inspires rather than intimidates." The semester wraps up with a party with entertainment provided by the 1Ls. (An upperclassman swears, "It's not hazing!") Barhopping ranks high among popular diversions, and no Maine student would allow anything to interfere with their "outdoor-loving lifestyle." The school integrates well with the community in Portland, a city that "gives us everything we need to succeed." On a small supportive campus in a small supportive city, "You realize how special the intimacy and closeness of a school can be."

Getting In

Though the deadline doesn't come until March 1, decisions are already being made in January: Get in early. Students applying from Massachusetts, New Hampshire, Rhode Island, Vermont, or Canada pay tuition a little less than normal out-of-state rates.

EMPLOYMENT INFORMATION

Career Rating	**71**
Job placement rate (%)	94
Average starting salary	$48,263
State for bar exam	ME
Pass rate for first-time bar	69

Employers who frequently hire grads:
Maine/New England law firms and corporations, federal and state government, federal and state courts.

Grads employed by field (%):	
Academic	2
Business/industry	13
Government	9
Judicial clerkships	25
Other	4
Private practice	43
Public interest	4

ADMISSIONS

Selectivity Rating	**77**
# applications received	765
# applicants accepted	271
# acceptees attending	85
Average LSAT	156
LSAT Range	153–158
Average undergrad GPA	3.4
Application fee	$50
Regular application deadline	3/1
Regular notification	rolling
Rolling notification?	Yes
Early application program?	No
Transfer students accepted?	Yes
Evening division offered?	No
Part-time accepted?	Yes
LSDAS accepted?	Yes

International Students

TOEFL required of international students?	Yes

FINANCIAL FACTS

Annual tuition (resident)	$13,350
Annual tuition (nonresident)	$21,750
Books and supplies	$1,050
Fees per credit (resident)	$570
Fees per credit (nonresident)	$570
Tuition per credit (resident)	$445
Tuition per credit (nonresident)	$725
Room & board	$9,351
Financial aid application deadline	2/15
% receiving some sort of aid	87
% of aid that is merit-based	20
% receiving scholarships	37
Average grant	$3,500
Average loan	$21,017
Average debt	$63,051

UNIVERSITY OF MARYLAND
SCHOOL OF LAW

INSTITUTIONAL INFORMATION

Public/private	public
Student/faculty ratio	11:1
% faculty part-time	46
% faculty female	39
% faculty minority	14
Total faculty	122

SURVEY SAYS . . .

Great research resources
Abundant externship/internship/clerkship opportunities
Beautiful campus

STUDENTS

Enrollment of law school	772
% male/female	43/57
% out-of-state	35
% full-time	78
% minority	25
% international	1
# of countries represented	47
Average age of entering class	26

ACADEMICS

Academic Experience rating	**86**
Professors interesting rating	72
Professors accessible rating	82
Hours of study per day	3.85

Academic Specialties

Civil procedure, commercial law, constitutional law, corporation securities law, criminal law, environmental law, intellectual property law, international law, labor law, legal philosophy, taxation.

Advanced Degrees Offered

JD, 3 yrs FT day, 4 yrs evening.

Combined Degrees Offered

JD/PhD public policy, JD/MA public policy, JD/MBA, JD/MA public management, JD/MA criminal justice, JD/MSW, JD/MA liberal education, JD/MA community planning, JD/PharmD pharmacy, JD/MPH, JD/MS risk assessment & environmental law.

Academic Requirements

Clinical Program Required? Yes

Academics

"The aesthetics of your law school are one of the intangibles that you don't necessarily consider when you apply to law school," observes a sage student at the University of Maryland School of Law. "However, during 1L, when you spend hours upon hours at school and in the library, you don't want to be in a school that resembles a run-down middle school." Truer words were never spoken. The swanky, "brand-spanking-new, clean, modern, welcoming, [and otherwise] gorgeous" building at Maryland Law is "fabulous." One student gushes, "Now that our school has moved into a new building, our classroom and research resources are incredible." In addition to "a plethora of power outlets [and] Internet hookups at practically every seat in the entire school, the new building has comfortable seating areas [and a] beautiful secluded courtyard meant to allow students to congregate, relax, socialize, and study."

Maryland's "incredibly diverse group of professors works hard to get students to participate." A few are "not passionate people, [but most] are happy to help students work through legal theories, case work, and paper topics." Students continue to rave about their professors saying, "They often go out of their way to be helpful in other areas and to truly befriend their students. The clinical faculty, in particular, is extremely available to their students."

The "ambitious [dean is] very personable, surprisingly hip, and well respected." Despite "a few stodgy souls, [the administration is] helpful and pleasant." One panic-prone student writes, "Quite often, I have gone to them to act as financial advisors, guidance counselors, and stress relievers. This is the only place where I can see all those positive attributes you hear about when people talk about good customer service. The administration is really involved in the needs of the students." We should warn you, however, that the Dean of Student Affairs "is notorious for making this terrible honor code speech at orientation that leaves the incoming students quaking in their boots."

The "outstanding" clinical programs at UM provide plenty of "real-world" experience that absolutely run the gamut from AIDS litigation to elder law to appellate advocacy to rights of low-income workers. "The practical training we receive is fantastic," relates one student. "I am in my second year with the clinic program, and I think it is the best experience in law school." Furthermore, "The health law program is particularly wonderful." The legal writing program comes in for a few complaints, though. Also, Maryland Law needs "more hard-core black-letter law and fewer specialized electives." Career Services "is useless," but career prospects are pretty good. "Anyone who wants to stay in Baltimore will be able to find a job. If you want to leave the area, it's a lot more difficult."

Life

"There aren't too many weirdos," but there are students with "frighteningly bright, over-achiever-law-student brains." There is also a sufficient number of "wonderful, interesting, down-to-earth people," too. Students say, "Despite the competition for grades, there is a great sense of community and kinship." However, "it is amazing how uptight and cutthroat people become around exams."

Patricia Scott, Director of Admissions and Financial Aid
500 West Baltimore Street, Baltimore, MD 21201
Telephone: 410-706-3492 • Fax: 410-706-1793
E-mail: admissions@law.umaryland.edu • Website: www.law.umaryland.edu

"Overall, the school has a good social life." Students agree, "The school really supports student organizations and encourages students to get involved. The dean does a great job of holding town meetings to keep everyone up-to-date." Between participating students, "there is a strong, collegial bond." One student writes, "Maryland Law tries extremely hard to bring the law school community together and foster collegiality and camaraderie among its students; I definitely feel like I know the majority of my class, as well as the classes below me." Social highlights include "faculty follies, advocacy group–sponsored events, and Legally Sound, our a cappella group." There are "frequent bar outings [and] you won't go many days without a happy hour sponsored by some organization." It is important to note that "many people commute, [and] scheduling is all over the map." Also, "Maryland has seven professional schools on a single campus, but the only people [the law students] ever see are other stressed-out law students." One student suggests, "I'd like to see a stressed-out dental student once in a while just for variety."

Maryland Law has an "excellent location in the heart of Baltimore, very close to the business sector and to the courts." One student says, "There are several major regions of Baltimore with places to hang out—including the fabulous Inner Harbor—so there is truly always something to do, often within walking distance." Students notice, "Baltimore doesn't have that many cultural attractions, [though, and the campus is] surrounded by a fairly scary neighborhood where robberies and muggings happen a little too frequently." On the plus side, "if your interests lie in Washington, DC, it is less than an hour away."

Getting In

Admitted students at the 25th percentile have an LSAT score of 156 and a GPA of 3.3. Admitted students at the 75th percentile have an LSAT score of 162 and a GPA of 3.7. With an LSAT score of 156 and a GPA of 3.34, you would stand roughly a 10 percent chance of getting admitted. With an LSAT of 162 and a GPA of 3.5, you would have a 77 percent chance. If you take the LSAT more than once, Maryland Law will average your scores. Note also that nonresident enrollment constitutes about 25 percent of the student body. However, it should not be any harder to get admitted if you are from out-of-state.

EMPLOYMENT INFORMATION

Career Rating	**77**
% employed within 9 months	98
Average starting salary	$54,187
State for bar exam	MD
Pass rate for first-time bar	79

Employers who frequently hire grads:
U.S. Department of Justice; Dickstein, Shapiro, & Morin, LLP; Environmental Protection Agency; Arnold & Porter; Piper Rudnicks.

Prominent Alumni: Christine A. Edwards, partner, Winston & Strawn; Benjamin R. Civiletti, former U.S. attorney general; Alvin Krongard, executive director, CIA.

Grads employed by field (%):	
Academic	7
Business/industry	14
Government	16
Judicial clerkships	19
Military	6
Private practice	32
Public interest	6

Legal Writing Course Requirement?	Yes
Legal Methods Course Requirement?	Yes
Legal Research Course Requirement?	Yes
Moot Court Requirement?	Yes
Public Interest Law Requirement?	Yes

ADMISSIONS

Selectivity Rating	**90**
# applications received	3,782
# applicants accepted	438
# acceptees attending	221
Average LSAT	160
LSAT Range	156–162
Average undergrad GPA	3.5
Application fee	$60
Regular application deadline	rolling
Regular notification	rolling
Rolling notification?	Yes
Early application program?	No
Transfer students accepted?	Yes
Evening division offered?	Yes
Part-time accepted?	Yes
LSDAS accepted?	Yes

Applicants Also Look At

American U., George Mason U., The George Washington U., Georgetown U.

International Students

TOEFL required of international students?	No
TOEFL recommended of international students?	Yes
Minimum Paper TOEFL	600
Minimum Computer TOEFL	250

FINANCIAL FACTS

Annual tuition (resident)	$15,590
Annual tuition (nonres.)	$26,869
Books and supplies	$1,500
Fees per credit (resident)	$228
Fees per credit (nonresident)	$228
Tuition per credit (resident)	$494
Tuition per credit (nonres.)	$938
Room & board (on/off-campus)	$16,413/$20,351
Financial aid app. deadline	3/1
% first-year students receiving some sort of aid	89
% receiving some sort of aid	83
% of aid that is merit based	5
% receiving scholarships	59
Average grant	$4,466
Average loan	$21,024
Average total aid package	$35,000
Average debt	$65,500

UNIVERSITY OF MEMPHIS
CECIL C. HUMPHREYS SCHOOL OF LAW

INSTITUTIONAL INFORMATION

Public/private	public
Student/faculty ratio	16.5:1
% faculty part-time	17
% faculty female	36
% faculty minority	9
Total faculty	24

SURVEY SAYS . . .

Diverse opinions accepted in classrooms

STUDENTS

Enrollment of law school	443
% male/female	51/49
% out-of-state	6
% full-time	95
% minority	11
# of countries represented	1
Average age of entering class	26

ACADEMICS

Academic Experience rating	**83**
Professors interesting rating	89
Professors accessible rating	90
Hours of study per day	3.93

Academic Specialties

Civil procedure, commercial law, constitutional law, corporate law, criminal law, environmental law, intellectual property law, international law, labor law, property, taxation.

Advanced Degrees Offered

JD, 6 semesters.

Combined Degrees Offered

JD/MBA, 4 years, 8 semesters.

Academic Requirements

Clinical Program Required?	No
Legal Writing Course Requirement?	No
Legal Methods Course Requirement?	Yes
Legal Research Course Requirement?	Yes
Moot Court Requirement?	No
Public Interest Law Requirement?	No

Academics

With little exception, students say that the greatest strength of the Cecil C. Humphreys School of Law is its "practical curriculum, which prepares you both for the bar and for practice.'" While students do receive solid training in legal history and theory, they appreciate the "focus on preparing students for what lies ahead, whether it be the bar exam, upper division courses, or working in the 'real world.'" A student sums it up this way: "If you want to win in the courtroom or draft an unbeatable contract, this school could be for you."

In the classroom, professors blend academic material with practical know-how. A student elaborates, "They are distinguished academics in their own right, but all (or almost all) have spent time in the 'real world' as well, [meaning that they] strive to strike a balance between the case law from the books and experiences they have had while practicing. They continue to promote independent thinking and hone our skills for arguing all sides of every matter."

Outside of standard course work, the school operates a competitive law review and moot court program, as well as legal clinics in areas such as elder law, domestic violence, and child advocacy. Students praise the legal writing program, describing it as "demanding and highly effective at drilling home the basics of legal research, reasoning, and writing." On top of that, students take advantage of the school's hometown, where there are many employment and internship options for Humphreys students. A student tells us, "The Memphis legal community is vast and provides students with a broad spectrum of opportunities for legal experience while matriculating."

Does all the practical preparation pay off? Students say the proof is in the pudding. Memphis has "the highest bar-passage rate in the state of Tennessee." On top of that, students point out the school's excellent job placement rate, which hovers around 95 percent each year. "The job placement statistics are excellent because it is the only law school in Memphis, and the legal community recognizes the quality of graduates in comparison with other schools in Tennessee and the mid-South," writes one proud student. Another student tell us, "The Career and Alumni Services office ensures that Memphis law students have exposure to legal opportunities outside the Memphis community, so that Memphis graduates can realistically enter practice anywhere in the country and not only compete, but excel!"

Amid glowing reviews, the only consistent complaint from the student body is that "the school's classroom facilities are poor and terribly outdated." One student writes, "If the University of Memphis School of Law had a new building, the law school would offer one of the best public legal educations in the country." Students are quick to point out, however, that "by 2006 we will have a brand-new building located downtown overlooking the Mississippi River and that facility should remedy the few pitfalls we have right now." Plus, most students feel "the University of Memphis makes up for these minor shortcomings with an excellent faculty and reasonable tuition rates." In fact, some indignant students do not think future lawyers should waste time worrying about Internet connections and air conditioning systems. In the words of one such student, "If you want practical teaching that prepares you for the 'real world,' then this is the place for you. If you want plush classrooms and an accommodating administration, then consider going back to college; this school caters to future lawyers, not career students."

DR. SUE ANN MCCLELLAN, ASSISTANT DEAN FOR ADMISSIONS
207 HUMPHREYS LAW SCHOOL, MEMPHIS, TN 38152-3140
TELEPHONE: 901-678-5403 • FAX: 901-678-5210
E-MAIL: LAWADMISSIONS@MAIL.LAW.MEMPHIS.EDU • WEBSITE: WWW.LAW.MEMPHIS.EDU

Life

Memphis is an ideal place for work and play. Students say there is "a friendly atmosphere" on campus and that the surrounding town offers a wide variety of restaurants, bars, clubs, and other entertainment options. One student tells us, "As a student at the Cecil C. Humphreys School of Law, I have found an overwhelming sense of camaraderie among the students. While law school is a competitive environment in and of itself, the students here manage to maintain social relationships and help each other out." Another student adds, "Memphis is a great place to meet and keep friends throughout law school and beyond." In fact, "the law students are very social, especially considering that almost all of them commute to campus." When they aren't hitting the books, students at Memphis like to blow off steam at parties and bars. One student satirizes the life at Memphis: "The social life consists of karaoke-themed Bar Reviews and college-type keg parties. The Student Bar Association's biggest decision at every meeting is the theme for next semester's t-shirt."

Getting In

Strong LSAT scores and a competitive undergraduate GPA are the two most important factors in any application to the University of Memphis Cecil C. Humphreys School of Law. When making an admissions decision, Memphis also considers a candidate's personal background, work or volunteer experience, recommendations, and personal statement. For last year's entering class, the average LSAT score was 156 and the average GPA was 3.3. As at all law schools, acceptable LSAT scores cannot be more than 60 months old, and multiple scores in that time period will be averaged. Tennessee residents comprise the large majority of applicants and admitted students.

EMPLOYMENT INFORMATION

Career Rating	**79**
% employed within 9 months	98
Average starting salary	$57,053
State for bar exam	TN
Pass rate for first-time bar	89

Employers who frequently hire grads: Major area and regional law firms, Tenn. attorney general, public defender's office, Tennessee Supreme Court & Court of Appeals, major area corporate legal departments, city & county government.

Prominent Alumni: John Wilder, speaker of the Tennessee House; Honorable David S. Kennedy, Chief Bankruptcy Judge, U.S. Bankruptcy Court, Western District of TN.

Grads employed by field (%):	
Business/industry	6
Government	9
Judicial clerkships	7
Military	1
Private practice	74
Public interest	3

ADMISSIONS

Selectivity Rating	**80**
# applications received	1,220
# applicants accepted	314
# acceptees attending	137
Average LSAT	156
LSAT Range	154–159
Average undergrad GPA	3.3
Application fee	$25
Regular application deadline	3/1
Regular notification	4/15
Rolling notification?	Yes
Early application program?	No
Transfer students accepted?	Yes
Evening division offered?	No
Part-time accepted?	Yes
LSDAS accepted?	Yes

Applicants Also Look At

Georgia State University, Mercer University, Mississippi College, Samford University, University of Mississippi, University of Tennessee, Vanderbilt University.

International Students

TOEFL required of international students?	Yes
Minimum Paper TOEFL	600
Minimum Computer TOEFL	263

FINANCIAL FACTS

Annual tuition (resident)	$8,198
Annual tuition (nonresident)	$22,958
Books and supplies	$1,400
Fees per credit (resident)	$6
Fees per credit (nonresident)	$6
Tuition per credit (resident)	$397
Tuition per credit (nonresident)	$1,068
Room & board	$5,780
Financial aid application deadline	4/1
% first-year students receiving some sort of aid	79
% receiving some sort of aid	82
% of aid that is merit-based	11
% receiving scholarships	25
Average grant	$5,000
Average loan	$17,037
Average total aid package	$16,597
Average debt	$55,167

University of Miami
School of Law

INSTITUTIONAL INFORMATION

Public/private	private
Student/faculty ratio	22:1
% faculty part-time	57
% faculty female	31
% faculty minority	18
Total faculty	150

SURVEY SAYS . . .

Students love Coral Gables, FL

STUDENTS

Enrollment of law school	1,186
% male/female	54/46
% full-time	97
% minority	25
% international	5
# of countries represented	13
Average age of entering class	24

ACADEMICS

Academic Experience rating	**72**
Professors interesting rating	72
Professors accessible rating	64
Hours of study per day	4.48

Academic Specialties

Civil procedure, commercial law, constitutional law, corporation securities law, criminal law, environmental law, government services, human rights law, intellectual property law, international law, labor law, property, taxation.

Advanced Degrees Offered

LLM degrees in comparative law, for graduates of foreign law schools; estate planning; Inter-American law; international law; ocean and coastal law; real property development; taxation. LLM programs can be completed in 1 year full-time.

Combined Degrees Offered

JD/MBA, JD/MPH master's in public health, JD/MS in marine affairs, JD/LLM in taxation. Each program takes approximately 3.5 years to complete.

Academics

The University of Miami School of Law has a lot going for it: an ideal location, a "very diverse [student body, a] community feel, [and a] distinguished" faculty who sport "great tans." Being located in Miami, "one of America's most vibrant and culturally intricate cities," means UM attracts a diverse student body. It gives these students a chance to attend law school "in the middle of a tropical paradise," just a stone's throw away from the beach. Maybe it's the sunshine, or the students' "accepting nature [that lends to the] laid-back atmosphere," either way, the people at UM are "friendly and social." Being the biggest law school in the area means that "the majority of the more prestigious law firms are filled with UM grads, [and there are] a lot of internship, clerkship, and fellowship opportunities for students."

Professors at UM are "top-notch." One student raves, "I can't imagine a better collection of faculty." Another student says, "They all have great credentials and seem to really care about the subjects they are teaching." Most professors are "fervent advocates of the Socratic Method," but don't worry, "they employ it in a good-spirited fashion. Thus, the intimidation factor dissolves, rendering a useful educational tool." Professors are also "willing to get quite involved in helping to shape and plan your career." Students are divided with regard to the administration. Some students say, "There isn't a ton of red tape," while others point to "poor channels of communication" and insist that the staff is "inflexible."

The grading curve at UM is reportedly "much lower than at other schools, [which] has a negative effect on our employment opportunities." Some students say that the Career Planning Center "is great if you are proactive." Other students "complain of the center's lack of resources and commitment to student employment, especially postgraduation." Whatever the case, students do not want to forgo options to gain practical experience. UM is a really big fish locally, and a "very strong alumni base in Miami [means] you can clerk for a judge one semester and for a solo personal-injury lawyer another summer, once in public interest and again with a large corporate firm, and do a clinical placement at any number of federal or state agencies."

Miami's once sub-par facilities have been completely updated in recent years. The law school complex is now completely wireless, a new server is in the process of being installed, and the library is adequate, with the "excellent" undergrad library nearby. "All classrooms open onto the courtyard with a fountain [where students] gather and mingle." But, all in all, students feel, "The actual building isn't so pretty." One UM student visualizes, "When I imagined going to law school, I thought of large, cathedral classrooms with wood paneling on the walls and libraries with book shelves to the heavens. The library and classrooms of Miami, however, look more like the inside of a CVS. I suppose Victorian styling does not comport with typical Miami decor, but come on!"

Life

There are some "nutty overachievers" at UM, but overall "students aren't very competitive." One student notes, "Everyone is willing to share outlines, [and] the school has a fairly relaxed atmosphere." While many students cite UM's diversity as a strength, students disagree as to exactly how diverse the student body is. Some students say you'll find an "astounding and wonderful [array of diversity in terms of] educational and socioeconomic background." Still, others say, "While the student body is diverse ethni-

THERESE LAMBERT, DIRECTOR OF STUDENT RECRUITING
PO BOX 248087, CORAL GABLES, FL 33124-8087
TELEPHONE: 305-284-6746 • FAX: 305-284-3084
E-MAIL: ADMISSIONS@LAW.MIAMI.EDU • WEBSITE: WWW.LAW.MIAMI.EDU

cally and religiously, it's not diverse economically." Overall, though, UM is "a tolerant and, indeed, culturally curious school." One student writes, "It is very gay-friendly," as well.

The UM law school is actually "set up to encourage interaction." The "gorgeous [courtyard] within the law school campus provides a great area to socialize or study." This area, known as "The Bricks, affords students a chance to interact with other students, faculty, and staff." Students say, "The Bricks is the central place for hanging out on campus between classes. It's impossible to walk through without spotting someone you know." Outside the law school, "the students are a very social group." There are frequent "social gatherings [at which students and faculty] come together to drink beer and eat chicken wings." It seems "the school offers more events than a person could attend." One popular event is the "annual Dean's Cup, in which the law students compete in athletics and games against the med school."

Students agree, "You cannot beat the setting of the law school." They continue, "Suntan U [is] located in one of the best neighborhoods [of] one of the most beautiful cities in the world." One well-tanned student boasts, "I live five minutes away from South Beach." Far and away, the number one complaint about campus life is the "inadequacy of parking."

Getting In

Admitted students at the 25th percentile have an LSAT score of 150 and a GPA of 3.2. Admitted students at the 75th percentile have an LSAT score of 160 and a GPA of 3.6. If you take the LSAT more than once, UM will usually average your scores. If you can show a huge difference between two scores, though, the admissions committee may consider only your higher score.

EMPLOYMENT INFORMATION

Career Rating	**82**
Job placement rate (%)	90
Average starting salary	$70,000
State for bar exam	FL, NY, IL, GA, NC
Pass rate for first-time bar	84

Employers who frequently hire grads: Holland & Knight; Greenberg Traurig; Hunton & Williams; Steel Hector and Davis; White & Case; Weil, Gotshal, & Manges; Morgan Lewis & Bockius; Carlton, Fields; Shutts & Bowen.

Prominent Alumni: Patricia Ireland, former president of NOW; Alex Penelas, mayor of Miami Dade County; Roy Black, prominent criminal defense attorney, legal expert.

Grads employed by field (%):	
Academic	1
Business/industry	7
Government	19
Judicial clerkships	4
Private practice	67
Public interest	2

Academic Requirements

Clinical Program Required?	No
Legal Writing Course Requirement?	Yes
Legal Methods Course Requirement?	Yes
Legal Research Course Requirement?	Yes
Moot Court Requirement?	Yes
Public Interest Law Requirement?	No

ADMISSIONS

Selectivity Rating	**78**
# applications received	5,131
# applicants accepted	1,768
# acceptees attending	429
Average LSAT	157
LSAT Range	155–160
Average undergrad GPA	3.4
Application fee	$50
Regular application deadline	2/3
Regular notification	rolling
Rolling notification?	Yes
Early application program?	No
Transfer students accepted?	Yes
Evening division offered?	No
Part-time accepted?	Yes
LSDAS accepted?	Yes

Applicants Also Look At

American U., Florida State U., The George Washington U., Georgetown U., Nova Southeastern U., Tulane U., U. of Florida.

International Students

TOEFL required of international students?	Yes
Minimum Paper TOEFL	600
Minimum Computer TOEFL	250

FINANCIAL FACTS

Annual tuition	$29,016
Books and supplies	$1,000
Tuition per credit	$1,266
Room & board (off-campus)	$9,835
Financial aid application deadline	3/1
% first-year students receiving some sort of aid	89
% receiving some sort of aid	83
% of aid that is merit-based	17
% receiving scholarships	33
Average grant	$13,727
Average loan	$31,095
Average total aid package	$34,277
Average debt	$85,846

UNIVERSITY OF MICHIGAN
LAW SCHOOL

INSTITUTIONAL INFORMATION

Public/private	public
Student/faculty ratio	16:1
% faculty part-time	25
% faculty female	32
% faculty minority	7
Total faculty	114

SURVEY SAYS . . .

Great research resources
Great library staff
Beautiful campus

STUDENTS

Enrollment of law school	1,182
% male/female	56/44
% full-time	100
% minority	25
% international	2
# of countries represented	24
Average age of entering class	24

ACADEMICS

Academic Experience rating	**96**
Professors interesting rating	89
Professors accessible rating	78
Hours of study per day	4.42

Academic Specialties

Civil procedure, commercial law, constitutional law, corporation securities law, criminal law, environmental law, gov. services, human rights law, intellectual property law, international law, labor law, legal history, legal philosophy, property, taxation.

Advanced Degrees Offered

LLM, MCL, and S/JD.

Combined Degrees Offered

JD/MBA; JD/PhD economics; JD/AM modern Middle Eastern & North African studies; JD/master of public policy; JD/master of science in natural resources; JD/master of health services administration (MHSA); JD/AM Russian & East European studies; JD/AM world politics; JD/MSW; JD/MSI, master of science in information; JD/master's in public health (MPH); JD/MA Japanese studies; JD/master of urban planning (MUP).

Academics

The large and "very expensive" University of Michigan Law School is "two standard deviations or more above the norm," according to one student's estimate. At this school you will find "a rich tradition, a stellar faculty, [and] a broad range" of classes, though some students gripe that the school sacrifices core courses "for various interest-group courses." On the plus side, students may take courses in any of Michigan's "world-class" graduate schools. "There are a lot of opportunities to do clinics and externships" as well.

Michigan's "entertaining [professors are] floating orbs of brilliance and insight, brain ninjas at the top of their legal specialties who are the experts in their respective fields." There are "quite a number of venerable fossils, [but even they] run tight classes [and] present dry topics with a great sense of humor and in a way that challenges traditional ways of thinking." Some students express that politically, these professors "do not have a large diversity in political views," but they go to great lengths "to ensure that other viewpoints are encouraged in class." Despite their "heavy-weight champion" status, faculty members "hold review sessions often [and] maintain a remarkable degree of accessibility." Students promise, "You will have an amazingly intense academic experience here." The workload is "heavy (especially Civ Pro!)" and theory-laden, but manageable. Students say classes fly by, and "each class is an amazing interactive performance. The intellectual interchange in classroom discussion is awesome."

Michigan JDs have no trouble finding work. "The reputation is amazing," writes one student. "With a Michigan degree, you are employable from Hawaii to Maine [and] grads are around the globe, doing everything from practicing corporate law to drafting constitutions." To be sure, graduates "have their pick of top jobs in the Midwest." Career Services "has done whatever it takes to help me get my dream jobs," relates one happy student. Others are not so elated. "It's pretty much expected that you'll make $125,000 per year or else go into public interest. If you want to do anything else, you're on your own." Note that Michigan provides "a good loan forgiveness program" for students willing to pursue public interest law. The "useful legal practice program here is taught by full professors [who] spend enormous amounts of time and energy going through drafts of student papers and giving written and verbal feedback." The top brass "can be a bit paternalistic at times." One student observes, "The administration doesn't fix problems so much as it placates students. But complaining is silly. Students are ridiculously well taken care of." Reviews of the Financial Aid Office run the gamut, from "downright incompetent [to] very helpful."

Michigan's "old, dark, gorgeous [facilities provide an] inspiring, monastery-like sanctuary" for the studies of future attorneys. "The law exudes from the collegiate gothic architecture." One architecturally minded student describes these buildings having "soaring arches [with] a counterpoint in humorous stained glass etchings that depict common law crimes." Furthermore, "The magnificent reading room" is especially cool. The "well-aged, stately [classrooms have] lots of wood paneling and gold-leaf painting." Some are "cavernous, [and many] don't have enough laptop outlets." Technology is generally abundant, though, including "school-wide wireless Internet."

Life

"A day does not go by that I am not amazed by my brilliant classmates," declares one impressed student. These mostly "upper-class twenty-somethings [are] intellectual with-

Sarah C. Zearfoss, Assistant Dean and Director of Admissions
726 Oakland Avenue, Ann Arbor, MI 48104
Telephone: 734-764-0537 • Fax: 734-647-3218
E-mail: law.jd.admissions@umich.edu • Website: www.law.umich.edu

out being snobby [and are] incredibly down-to-earth." One student says, "We don't take ourselves too seriously." With regard to the student body, students say this one is "definitely one of the coolest"—and least modest—"among its peer schools." Politically, "it's definitely a more liberal school, but conservatives are alive and well here." The occasional "self-righteous activists" are ever-present, too.

The academic atmosphere is "very un-cutthroat. Everyone wants to do well, but it is never adversarial or competitive. Any competition is against yourself." For the most part, "a very close-knit, supportive environment" pervades. Of course, "the gunners are here as well [and,] like at most law schools, there are uptight students, [but they are] socially frowned upon by the rest of the students."

"While Michigan students do work very hard, opportunities for involvement in extracurriculars are almost overwhelming." Students agree, "Ann Arbor is a great college town [and] an easy place to be in school [because] it's not very expensive, and it's not at all stressful." It's "beautiful in the fall [and] quite cold" in the winter. Students say Ann Arbor is "perfect for hanging out, going over to someone's house for dinner, and going for long walks." And don't forget, "the football is fantastic" as well. "The great thing about Michigan is that you can choose to be an amused or even annoyed observer of life at a Big Ten school, or you can go down to the stadium and worship with the masses." Many students wish Ann Arbor "could move to a warmer place," though. One student thinks, "The fact that it's not near a hip urban center is kind of a drawback." But, all in all, "the social environment here is good." One gregarious law student writes, "It is a lot of fun to go to undergrad bars," and it is not uncommon for students to "go out Thursday through Saturday nights." Usually, "people enjoy themselves for the first two-thirds of the semester, then buckle down for finals."

Getting In

Good luck! The average LSAT for admitted students is a 167. The average GPA is 3.6. Those numbers are stellar for averages. Michigan residency is only a minor factor in the admissions process. In-state students constitute only about 25 percent of each incoming class.

EMPLOYMENT INFORMATION

Career Rating	**99**
% employed within 9 months	99
Average starting salary	$125,000
State for bar exam	NY, IL, CA, MI, MA

Grads employed by field (%):	
Academic	1
Business/industry	4
Government	6
Judicial clerkships	22
Private practice	61
Public interest	6

Academic Requirements

Clinical Program Required?	No
Legal Writing Course Requirement?	Yes
Legal Methods Course Requirement?	Yes
Legal Research Course Requirement?	Yes
Moot Court Requirement?	No
Public Interest Law Requirement?	No

ADMISSIONS

Selectivity Rating	**94**
# applications received	5,523
# applicants accepted	1,098
# acceptees attending	381
Average LSAT	167
LSAT Range	164–169
Average undergrad GPA	3.6
Application fee	$60
Regular application deadline	2/15
Regular notification	rolling
Rolling notification?	Yes
Early application program?	Yes
Early application deadline	11/15
Early application notification	12/15
Transfer students accepted?	Yes
Evening division offered?	No
Part-time accepted?	No
LSDAS accepted?	Yes

Applicants Also Look At

Columbia U., Georgetown U., Harvard U., N.Y.U., U. of California—Berkeley, U. of Chicago, U. of Pennsylvania.

International Students

TOEFL required of international students?	No
TOEFL recommended of international students?	No

FINANCIAL FACTS

Annual tuition (resident)	$29,171
Annual tuition (nonresident)	$34,171
Books and supplies	$5,400
Room & board	$9,415
% first-year students receiving some sort of aid	95
% receiving some sort of aid	84
% of aid that is merit-based	34
% receiving scholarships	40
Average grant	$11,746
Average loan	$33,206
Average total aid package	$37,805
Average debt	$68,856

UNIVERSITY OF MINNESOTA
LAW SCHOOL

INSTITUTIONAL INFORMATION

Public/private	public
Student/faculty ratio	14:1
% faculty part-time	53
% faculty female	41
% faculty minority	12
Total faculty	124

SURVEY SAYS . . .

Diverse opinions accepted in classrooms
Great research resources
Great library staff
Abundant externship/internship/clerkship opportunities

STUDENTS

Enrollment of law school	817
% male/female	55/45
% out-of-state	56
% full-time	100
% minority	16
% international	2
# of countries represented	23
Average age of entering class	25

ACADEMICS

Academic Experience rating	**90**
Professors interesting rating	84
Professors accessible rating	74
Hours of study per day	5.05

Advanced Degrees Offered

LLM for foreign lawyers, 1 year.

Combined Degrees Offered

JD/MBA, 4 years; JD/MPA, 4 years; JD/MA; JD/MD; JD/MPP, 4 years; JD/MURP, 4 years; JD/MS, 4 years; JD/PhD; JD/MP; JD/MBT; JD/MBS; JD/MPH.

Academic Requirements

Clinical Program Required?	No
Legal Writing Course Requirement?	Yes
Legal Methods Course Requirement?	No
Legal Research Course Requirement?	Yes
Moot Court Requirement?	No

Academics

Students agree that one of the greatest strengths of the University of Minnesota is its "hands-on, practical learning environments." The clinical programs are "awe-inspiring in their depth and breadth, [and they] are a great way to get involved in the Minnesota legal experience." If a student wishes to represent clients while going to law school, they should have no problem doing that at Minnesota. One student shares the value of his experience: "I have clerked at two governmental agencies (EEOC and NLRB) for credit under the careful supervision of faculty. I also have participated in a judicial externship program where I was able to clerk for a prestigious judge for a summer for credit. Our clinic programs enable students to have direct contact with clients." In addition to the wonderful clinical programs, Minnesota offers a very broad array of classes to choose from. Furthermore, Minnesota "places strong emphasis on the importance of legal writing and has three years of legal writing requirements." Students feel they are well prepared for real legal work after graduating from Minnesota.

A majority of students enjoy learning from the professors at the University of Minnesota. They explain, "While academically challenging, the professors are generally personable and friendly people, and they want you to learn the law and engage in the material." Furthermore, most students see the faculty as "accessible and always willing to meet one-on-one with a student who may be struggling." However, there are a few that think some professors spend too much time on research projects and not enough time in the classroom. A more prominent concern, however, is faculty retention. "The faculty is extremely bright. Many faculty are up-and-coming stars—the law schools up the food chain are always trying to steal them away," which is a disconcerting trend for the law students at Minnesota.

Most of the student body seems satisfied with the job Minnesota's administration has done with what they have to work with. They seem "quite in touch with, and responsive to, the students' law school experience. From easing the incoming student into the law school program—preparing students for taking final examinations—to career counseling, (and everything in between), the administration does a great job of anticipating and addressing the students' needs." Furthermore, "each year students start more groups around issues and activities relevant to the interests of the current student body. The administration and other funding sources are amenable to this."

"The school's crown jewel [is the library, one of the] largest law libraries in the country." Students rave that there are "computer research stations throughout the library [and that] you can research electronically on your laptop via the wireless network from anywhere in the law school." Also, the library being open 24/7 "is nice when you are facing a deadline." The law school building itself is less than inspiring, but it serves its purpose well.

Life

The University of Minnesota is located in the "tundra of the nation." Despite the climate, "students enjoy both the scenic beauty of the state, as well as cultural, historic, and political activity" of Minneapolis. Besides, as far as the cold goes, "some students find hibernating in the library helpful for their studies." One student seems to have figured out why Minnesota has established such a good reputation. She writes, "No wonder why this is such a good school. I mean, since you pretty much have to stay inside for all but a few minutes, you might as well study." Another plus students point out is that the law

COLLINS B. BYRD, JR., DIRECTOR OF ADMISSIONS
290 MONDALE HALL, 229 NINETEENTH AVENUE SOUTH, MINNEAPOLIS, MN 55455
TELEPHONE: 612-625-3487 • FAX: 612-626-1874
E-MAIL: UMNLSADM@UMN.EDU • WEBSITE: WWW.LAW.UMN.EDU

school is "well-situated because it is near the rest of the University of Minnesota, thus providing access to additional resources," such as other school libraries and recreational facilities.

Students say their classmates "are really friendly and helpful and not" cutthroat. The concept of "Minnesota Nice" seems to permeate the school. "I'm truly amazed at how friendly everyone is. People make jokes that law school is like high school, but everyone is a lot nicer than they were in high school!" gushes one student. Some have made very close friends at Minnesota. But it's not as though the student body lacks a desire for achievement. On the contrary, the law school "fosters a healthy dose of student competitiveness, but you don't have to worry about a classmate giving you the wrong notes or turning off your alarm clock on test day." As far as extracurricular activities go, "you can be as involved as you want to." There are "tons of student groups and social gatherings." There's a hockey team, a broomball team, and an intramural football team to complement the more academically oriented groups. The biggest hit currently on campus in the student activity arena, however, is a "group called TORT (theater of the relatively talentless)," which allegedly puts on musicals.

Getting In

Minnesota's admitted students at the 25th percentile have an LSAT score of 160 and a GPA of 3.48. Admitted students at the 75th percentile have an LSAT score of 166 and a GPA of 3.81. Minnesota is a public institution and enrolls about 800 students. The law school does not offer a part-time or evening program.

EMPLOYMENT INFORMATION

Career Rating	**90**
Job placement rate (%)	99
Average starting salary	$75,000
State for bar exam	MN, WI, CA, NY, IL
Pass rate for first-time bar	98

Employers who frequently hire grads: Gibson Dunn, Fried Frank, Dorsey & Whitney, Dewey Ballantine, Sidley & Austin, Mayer Brown.

Prominent Alumni: Walter Mondale, former vice president of U.S.; James Blanchard, former governor, Minnesota; Michael Hatch, Minnesota attorney general; Kathleen Blatz, chief justice, Minnesota Supreme Court.

Grads employed by field (%):	
Business/industry	13
Government	10
Judicial clerkships	15
Private practice	52
Public interest	3
Other	3

Public Interest Law Requirement?	No

ADMISSIONS

Selectivity Rating	**88**
# applications received	2,509
# applicants accepted	716
# acceptees attending	270
Average LSAT	163
LSAT Range	160–166
Average undergrad GPA	3.7
Application fee	$65
Regular application deadline	3/1
Regular notification	4/1
Rolling notification?	Yes
Early application program?	Yes
Early application deadline	11/30
Early application notification	1/15
Transfer students accepted?	Yes
Evening division offered?	No
Part-time accepted?	No
LSDAS accepted?	Yes

Applicants Also Look At

The George Washington University, Georgetown University, Northwestern University, University of Iowa, University of Michigan, University of Wisconsin, William Mitchell College of Law.

International Students

TOEFL required of international students?	Yes
Minimum Paper TOEFL	630
Minimum Computer TOEFL	267

FINANCIAL FACTS

Annual tuition (resident)	$17,948
Annual tuition (nonresident)	$28,042
Books and supplies	$1,666
Room & board	$12,930
Financial aid application deadline	2/1
% first-year students receiving some sort of aid	95
% receiving some sort of aid	91
% of aid that is merit-based	5
% receiving scholarships	51
Average grant	$7,500
Average loan	$21,178
Average debt	$58,860

UNIVERSITY OF MISSISSIPPI
LAMAR HALL

INSTITUTIONAL INFORMATION

Public/private	public
Student/faculty ratio	22:1
% faculty part-time	18
% faculty female	31
% faculty minority	9
Total faculty	32

SURVEY SAYS . . .

Diverse opinions accepted in classrooms
Students love University, MS

STUDENTS

Enrollment of law school	581
% male/female	56/44
% out-of-state	9
% full-time	100
% minority	10
# of countries represented	2
Average age of entering class	24

ACADEMICS

Academic Experience rating	**78**
Professors interesting rating	77
Professors accessible rating	77
Hours of study per day	3.46

Academic Specialties

Commercial law, corporation securities law, criminal law, environmental law, international law, remote sensing and space law, taxation.

Combined Degrees Offered

JD/MBA: 4 years.

Academic Requirements

Clinical Program Required?	No
Legal Writing Course Requirement?	Yes
Legal Methods Course Requirement?	Yes
Legal Research Course Requirement?	Yes
Moot Court Requirement?	Yes
Public Interest Law Requirement?	No

Academics

Set in the small town of Oxford, the University of Mississippi School of Law provides a strong but affordable education to future southern lawyers. For a "wooden nickel" tuition, students receive a balanced training in both the practical and theoretical aspects of the law, plus personalized attention from "accessible" professors. "The professors at Ole Miss are interested in helping students find work, helping with extracurricular activities, or just listening to students voice their problems, even on a personal level," says one student. "I know that I can go up to the fifth floor (where all the professors' offices are) and find someone with their door open to listen to me about almost anything." At Ole Miss, "It just seems that everyone here treats you with respect and really wants you to do well."

One major source of student anxiety is the strict grading curve for 1Ls, which means that those seeking highly competitive law jobs—especially out-of-state—will have to put in a lot of work early. Though about 25 percent of grads obtain jobs outside of Mississippi, many students feel resigned to take jobs in-state, where the law school is well-known and respected, rather than try to explain a low GPA to unforgiving out-of-state firms. Despite the curve, one student reassures, "The job placement rate brought me here above other schools that have a 'higher' ranking nationally. It is all about getting a job, and that will happen if you come to Ole Miss."

While the surrounding town and general campus environment get high marks, students complain that the law school building is "old and uninviting, [even,] a nightmare straight out of the disco era." But luckily, "a new one is being planned and should be finished in a few years." In the meantime, the building does have its perks, like "ample" research facilities and classrooms that are "equipped with an appropriate level of multimedia capabilities." Plus, "the law school is set up for wireless networking, so you can work on your computer outside and catch some rays."

Life

Ole Miss is known as a traditional, southern school with a conservative outlook, and not surprisingly, the law school is similarly perceived. While some say that, "most of the students are from Mississippi, and there is a prevailing conservative, Bible Belt mentality," others maintain that the law school is at least more progressive and less homogeneous than the university which houses it. One student tells us, "The law school is actually quite diverse and often at odds with the general campus political climate," a fact that "tends to generate heated debates and intriguing classroom discussions." Professors at Ole Miss run from "one end of the political spectrum to the other." As one student says, "It's nice to be exposed to so many viewpoints—and particularly surprising in a small southern town."

Barbara Vinson, Director of Admissions
School of Law, Room 310, University, MS 38677
Telephone: 662-915-6910 • Fax: 662-915-1289
E-mail: lawmiss@olemiss.edu • Website: www.law.olemiss.edu

By all accounts, life is good at Ole Miss. On campus, the atmosphere is friendly and social, with students forming a "very close knit community." According to one, "We frequent all of the same bars and parties, and interact far more with each other than with anyone outside the law school community." Another says, "At Ole Miss, we work very hard, but we also know how to play hard. Law school is like a big family." One student notes, "Oxford is a wonderful town for a law student, [since it's] laid-back [and there's] tons to do." Another student comments, "The classic beauty of a small southern town, [with its] columned buildings, the town square and, of course, the Grove," is an additional draw. And don't worry, it's not all southern charm and quaintness, there is also "a great party scene, great bars, and great bands." Do be aware, though, that the social life at Ole Miss can be somewhat one-note. In the words of one straight shooter, "Social life involves drinking and football games in The Grove. When the season is over we just drink."

Getting In

In 2003, the average LSAT score for matriculants was 154, with a 3.5 undergraduate GPA. Although LSAT scores and GPA are the two most important factors in an application, students are also evaluated based on the strength of their undergraduate institution, difficulty of the major field of study, personal experience and background, and letters of recommendation. State residency is also considered, with a preference given to Mississippi residents. Applications are due March 1.

ADMISSIONS

Selectivity Rating	**82**
# applications received	1,942
# applicants accepted	387
# acceptees attending	170
Average LSAT	156
LSAT Range	153–159
Average undergrad GPA	3.5
Application fee	$40
Regular application deadline	3/1
Regular notification	4/15
Rolling notification?	Yes
Early application program?	No
Transfer students accepted?	Yes
Evening division offered?	No
Part-time accepted?	No
LSDAS accepted?	Yes

Applicants Also Look At

Mississippi College, University of Alabama, University of Tennessee.

International Students

TOEFL required of international students?	Yes
Minimum Paper TOEFL	625
Minimum Computer TOEFL	263

FINANCIAL FACTS

Annual tuition (resident)	$7,210
Annual tuition (nonresident)	$13,380
Books and supplies	$1,300
Room & board	$13,970
% of aid that is merit-based	90
Average grant	$5,788
Average loan	$15,334
Average debt	$41,632

EMPLOYMENT INFORMATION

Career Rating	**78**
Job placement rate (%)	98
Average starting salary	$62,882
State for bar exam	MS, TN, GA, FL, TX
Pass rate for first-time bar	91

Employers who frequently hire grads: Top regional employers from across the South and Southeast.

Prominent Alumni: C. Trent Lott, U.S. senator; Thad Cochran, U.S. senator; John Grisham, author; Richard Scruggs, attorney for first tobacco case; Robert C. Khayat, chancellor, the University of Mississippi.

Grads employed by field (%):	
Academic	5
Business/industry	6
Government	6
Judicial clerkships	13
Other	2
Private practice	67
Public interest	1

University of Missouri—Columbia
School of Law

INSTITUTIONAL INFORMATION

Public/private	public
Student/faculty ratio	15:1
% faculty female	40
% faculty minority	8
Total faculty	50

SURVEY SAYS . . .

Diverse opinions accepted in classrooms
Great research resources

STUDENTS

Enrollment of law school	426
% male/female	60/40
% out-of-state	20
% full-time	99
% minority	20
% international	1
# of countries represented	5
Average age of entering class	24

ACADEMICS

Academic Experience rating	**81**
Professors interesting rating	80
Professors accessible rating	76
Hours of study per day	4.57

Academic Specialties

Alternative dispute resolution, criminal law, environmental law, intellectual property law, international law, labor law, property, taxation.

Advanced Degrees Offered

LLM in dispute resolution, 1 year.

Combined Degrees Offered

JD/MBA, 4 years; JD/MPA, 4 years; JD/MA economics, 4 years; JD/MA human development and family studies, 4 years; JD/MA educational leadership & policy analysis, 4 years; JD/MA journalism, 4 years; JD/PhD journalism, 5 years; JD/MLS library and information science, 4 years; JD/MS consumer & family economics, 4 years.

Academic Requirements

Clinical Program Required?	No
Legal Writing Course Requirement?	Yes

Academics

"In terms of academic reputation," the University of Missouri—Columbia School of Law "seems to be on the verge of becoming really good." The faculty, which "is a huge strength," is no doubt a large part of the school's forward progress. Professors are "pretty approachable and seem genuinely interested in helping students." One student offers, "Even those who are hard in class are enjoyable to speak with outside of class." The "wonderful [MU administration is] extremely accommodating [and] helpful" as well. "They bend over backward to help students with any and all problems."

Academic programs are solid. The nationally recognized program in alternative dispute resolution is especially noteworthy. "Because of the law school's location, we have easy access to state government, to a research hospital, and to a top-notch journalism school," boasts an MU student. "I believe the law school does an excellent job of creating opportunities to learn in cooperation with other schools and colleges on campus." An array of dual-degree programs includes the standard JD/MBA option as well as a master's program in conjunction with the department of economics. It is also possible to obtain a JD/MA or a JD/PhD with the celebrated School of Journalism. If you do not like any of the existing dual-degree programs, that's fine; you can design your own. "There is a lot of opportunity to explore your own particular interests." Study abroad programs take MU law students to London, Hamburg, and Cape Town. Certificate programs are available in dispute resolution, Center for the Digital and European Union studies. Prospects for life after law school are good. "The alumni are extremely supportive [and MU has] strong ties to Kansas City, Chicago, and St. Louis."

Mizzou's law school facilities are good but not great. The main gripe is there aren't enough outlets near classroom seats for laptop computers. "Someone will eventually trip over those extension cords," warns one student. When class is not in session, there is "a large quantity of outlets to plug in your laptop [in the] great study haven" that is the law library. You'll find "an abundance of study space" and "wonderful" staff there as well.

Donna Pavlick, Assistant Dean
103 Hulston Hall, Columbia, MO 65211
Telephone: 573-882-6042 • Fax: 573-882-9625
E-mail: umclawadmissions@missouri.edu • Website: www.law.missouri.edu

Life

The MU student population is eclectic. "It ranges from the antisocial studyaholics to party animals." On the competition front, MU students are "intelligent and motivated [but not] ultra-competitive." Students agree, "One great thing about this institution [is that there is] very little competition among students. Everyone helps everyone here." A 1L maintains, "From orientation on, there has been a strong bond among a large group of students from various backgrounds. It really makes you feel at home. It is a great place to be and feel like you belong." Another student analogizes, "The students remind me of golfers. Everyone wants to win, but within the course you are only competing against yourself. The final scores will take care of themselves." Hence, "relations among the students are good [and verging on] very enjoyable."

"The students here have found a healthy mix of studying and social activities that allows them to keep their sanity and humanity," relates one student. Law school at MU is "a great experience both socially and academically." For many students, "most evenings are for studying." However, "it seems like there is always some kind of party available on the weekends and sometimes several happy hours during the week." Often, it can be difficult to hit the books. "Passing things up to study or blowing off class to socialize [is easy] because you can always find someone else doing the same thing." One busy student explains, "We go out three nights a week, play intramural sports or just pick up games, and plan charity dinner parties." Another student simplifies the school saying, "While law school has been challenging academically, I think students at Mizzou strive hard for a balance, and I am confident it will pay off in the long run."

Getting In

Admitted students at the 25th percentile have an LSAT score of 157 and a GPA of 3.2. Admitted students at the 75th percentile have an LSAT score of 161 and a GPA of 3.8. If you take the LSAT more than once, Mizzou will use the average of your scores.

EMPLOYMENT INFORMATION

Career Rating	**77**
Job placement rate (%)	97
Average starting salary	$52,640
State for bar exam	MO, IL, TX, KS, CA
Pass rate for first-time bar	88

Employers who frequently hire grads:
Missouri law firms of all sizes; Missouri, federal, and governmental agencies; business, accounting, and insurance industries; and federal and state judges, both inside and outside the Missouri.

Grads employed by field (%):	
Academic	1
Business/industry	8
Government	26
Judicial clerkships	5
Military	1
Private practice	56
Public interest	1

Legal Methods Course Requirement?	Yes
Legal Research Course Requirement?	Yes
Moot Court Requirement?	Yes
Public Interest Law Requirement?	No

ADMISSIONS

Selectivity Rating	**84**
# applications received	1,058
# applicants accepted	319
# acceptees attending	146
Average LSAT	159
LSAT Range	157–161
Average undergrad GPA	3.5
Application fee	$50
Regular application deadline	3/1
Regular notification	rolling
Rolling notification?	Yes
Early application program?	No
Transfer students accepted?	Yes
Evening division offered?	No
Part-time accepted?	Yes
LSDAS accepted?	Yes

Applicants Also Look At

Saint Louis University, University of Missouri—Kansas City, Washington University.

International Students

TOEFL required of international students?	Yes
Minimum Paper TOEFL	600
Minimum Computer TOEFL	250

FINANCIAL FACTS

Annual tuition (resident)	$13,278
Annual tuition (nonresident)	$25,408
Books and supplies	$1,290
Tuition per credit (resident)	$420
Room & board	$7,390
Financial aid application deadline	3/1
% first-year students receiving some sort of aid	90
% receiving some sort of aid	95
% receiving scholarships	39
Average grant	$4,000
Average loan	$16,500
Average debt	$52,334

UNIVERSITY OF MISSOURI—KANSAS CITY
SCHOOL OF LAW

INSTITUTIONAL INFORMATION

Public/private	public
Student/faculty ratio	18:1
% faculty part-time	51
% faculty female	32
% faculty minority	5
Total faculty	62

SURVEY SAYS . . .

Diverse opinions accepted in classrooms
Great research resources
Great library staff
Students love Kansas City, MO

STUDENTS

Enrollment of law school	211
% male/female	58/42
% out-of-state	33
% full-time	94
% minority	8
Average age of entering class	24

ACADEMICS

Academic Experience rating	**71**
Professors interesting rating	76
Professors accessible rating	80
Hours of study per day	4.86

Academic Specialties

Business, & entrepreneurial law; urban, land use, & environmental law; litigation; taxation.

Advanced Degrees Offered

LLM, 1 to 3 years.

Combined Degrees Offered

JD/MBA, 3 to 4 years; JD/MPA, 3 to 4 years; JD/LLM, 3.5 to 4 years.

Academic Requirements

Clinical Program Required?	No
Legal Writing Course Requirement?	Yes
Legal Methods Course Requirement?	No
Legal Research Course Requirement?	Yes
Moot Court Requirement?	Yes
Public Interest Law Requirement?	No

Academics

The University of Missouri—Kansas City School of Law already offers good value, and with the bar-passage rate climbing each year, the investment just looks better and better. Students enjoy being part of a school "new in its success" and support the administration's aspiration to climb the rankings.

UMKC professors provide the thrust behind the upward momentum. "Some particularly big names have arrived recently, and the law school appears to be leapfrogging up the rankings as a result." The adjunct faculty, made up of practitioners, judges, and Congressional representatives, add their perspectives to the mix. Many instructors draw on a background in "prominent public interest work, making the social-service aspects of the law clearly appreciable." That compassion carries over to their students. A 1L writes, "The entire faculty is aware of stressful times and makes general comments of encouragement along the way." Many students express pleasant surprise at having "such student-oriented professors." If anyone misses class, "they will sit with you one-on-one to explain what we went over." After their first year, students have offices in close proximity to faculty offices, creating an integrated community. But come grade time, the generosity of spirit seems to dry up; professors are serious about "weeding people out after the first semester."

The predominant teaching style features somewhat leftist politics (by Missouri standards) and "old-fashioned" Socratic questioning by way of the Inquisition. Apparently, "someone forgot to tell the faculty here that law school isn't supposed to be like the book *One L* anymore." But professors aren't completely without a sense of humor when lecturing and most will "throw in a joke or two just to make sure the students are still awake." The majority appreciates courses' practical focus but beg for more problem-based teaching methods. Many new students would be at a loss were it not for the structured study groups and tutors in place to ease the transition. A 1L writes, "The mentor program is very positive. We are placed with a 2L or 3L that is studying our area of interest. The 1Ls can pick the upper-level student's brains about classes, professors, exams, and outlines."

About half of the lecture halls have been turned into "the classroom of the future," but the rest "still have a 1970s vibe going on." Climate-control issues force people "to wear coats during class on cold days." The library lacks "in terms of atmosphere, seating, and number of volumes," according to a 2L, but the "extremely gifted researchers" on staff "strive to help all who ask." A summer program at the Peking School of Law in Beijing, China, has provided additional resources for students for the past two years, and plans are in the works to start up in Ireland.

Students prepare for the real world at the Child and Family Services Clinic by helping to establish permanency for children. In the words of a 3L, "Working at the clinic really makes you think about the power a law degree can give you and the responsibility to use that power wisely." Some people will parlay these skills into a public-sector job, but most of the career emphasis lies on big-firm litigation. Everyone with a class ranking in the double digits feels abandoned by their friends at career services, but networking can pick up the slack. Faculty members help out by "organizing meet-and-greets with local attorneys to help you begin networking," to the relief of a 1L. "If you are willing to work in the Kansas City area, opportunities abound for graduates of UMKC Law."

Debbie Brooks, Director of Admissions
UMKC School of Law, 5100 Rockhill Road, Kansas City, MO 64110
Telephone: 816-235-1644 • Fax: 816-235-5276
E-mail: law@umkc.edu • Website: www.law.umkc.edu

Life

Incoming classes are divided into three sections, which either gel into supportive groups or devolve to petty infighting. "Gunners" keep the curve respectable and the laid-back environment from losing its edge. Orientation emphasizes that "the competitive aspects of school should not overshadow professionalism and collegiality." The pervasive "Midwestern values" also help to keep things friendly, and since "most everyone understands that we will all be practicing together," there is good reason to keep the backstabbing to a minimum. Law students tend to "have other things going on in their lives"; one nontraditional student appreciates the school's efforts to "help me find a schedule that is conducive to my lifestyle and family obligations." Students see plenty of opportunities "to combine social life and networking while in law school." For example, the Inn program, run by a small group of students, professors, and UMKC alumni practicing in the Kansas City area, coordinates social events as well as field trips to the courthouse or a law firm, fostering continuity and camaraderie in the bar. Faculty and students look forward to the annual Halloween party, Barrister Ball, and school-wide softball tournament. First-years haunt the on-campus lounge, "a 1L's second home," and happy hour always draws a crowd. People inevitably start butting heads over politics, given the split population, but "for the most part, we are accepting of other views and happy to talk with people of differing beliefs." A 2L explains, "While most people come from similar backgrounds, there is enough of a mix to spice things up."

Getting In

Students who don't quite have the numbers to get into Mizzou's Columbia campus still have a shot at Kansas City. Applicants who can't commit to the full-time program may want to consider the part-time "flex" program, which allows students up to five years to complete the JD degree. Applications are accepted any time after September 1, but procrastinators beware—most seats are filled by the end of February.

EMPLOYMENT INFORMATION

Career Rating	**64**
Job placement rate (%)	85
Average starting salary	$46,000
State for bar exam	MO, KS
Pass rate for first-time bar	87

Employers who frequently hire grads: Blackwell Sanders Peper Martin LLP; Bryan Cave LLP; Husch & Eppenberger, LLC; Jackson County Circuit Court; Lathrop & Gage LC.

Prominent Alumni: Harry S. Truman, president of the United States; Charles E. Whittaker, U.S. Supreme Court justice; Clarence Kelley, FBI director; Lynda Conley, first Native American female lawyer.

Grads employed by field (%):	
Academic	1
Business/industry	9
Government	13
Judicial clerkships	12
Military	1
Other	4
Private practice	57
Public interest	3

ADMISSIONS

Selectivity Rating	**70**
# applications received	1,021
# applicants accepted	466
# acceptees attending	211
Average LSAT	153
LSAT Range	151–156
Average undergrad GPA	3.4
Application fee	$50
Regular application deadline	rolling
Regular notification	rolling
Rolling notification?	Yes
Early application program?	No
Transfer students accepted?	Yes
Evening division offered?	No
Part-time accepted?	Yes
LSDAS accepted?	Yes

Applicants Also Look At

University of Kansas, University of Missouri—Columbia.

International Students

TOEFL required of international students?	Yes
Minimum Paper TOEFL	650
Minimum Computer TOEFL	280

FINANCIAL FACTS

Annual tuition (resident)	$12,426
Annual tuition (nonresident)	$24,540
Books and supplies	$1,520
Fees per credit (resident)	$61
Fees per credit (nonresident)	$61
Tuition per credit (resident)	$414
Tuition per credit (nonresident)	$818
Room & board (on/off-campus)	$17,331/$19,711
Financial aid application deadline	3/1
% of aid that is merit-based	94
% receiving scholarships	30
Average grant	$8,284
Average loan	$21,871

UNIVERSITY OF NEBRASKA—LINCOLN
COLLEGE OF LAW

INSTITUTIONAL INFORMATION

Public/private	public
Student/faculty ratio	15:1
% faculty part-time	46
% faculty female	22
% faculty minority	3
Total faculty	63

SURVEY SAYS . . .

Great research resources
Great library staff

STUDENTS

Enrollment of law school	414
% male/female	55/45
% out-of-state	25
% full-time	100
% minority	10
% international	1
# of countries represented	3
Average age of entering class	24

ACADEMICS

Academic Experience rating	**84**
Professors interesting rating	86
Professors accessible rating	88
Hours of study per day	4.96

Academic Specialties

Commercial law, corporation securities law, environmental law, intellectual property law, international law, labor law, litigation, taxation.

Advanced Degrees Offered

JD, 3 years; MLS, 1 year.

Combined Degrees Offered

JD/PhD psychology, 6 years; JD/MA economics, 4 years; JD/MBA, 4 years; JD/MPA, 4 years; JD/political science, 4 years; JD/community of regional planning, 4 years; JD/PhD Ed administration, 5 years; JD/MA international affairs, 4 years.

Academic Requirements

Clinical Program Required?	No
Legal Writing Course Requirement?	Yes
Legal Methods Course Requirement?	No

Academics

The University of Nebraska College of Law boasts "incredible alumni support" and a price that is "hard to beat," especially for in-state students. "Small classes allow lots of contact with the faculty, [and the] particularly accessible and affable [professors at Nebraska] care about your success." Several faculty members "offer a weekly lunch to get to know" the students. There is an "air of encouragement," and classes are not designed to "weed you out." One candid student promises, "There are a few professors I don't enjoy, but all the professors have excellent knowledge of their respective subjects and are more than willing to help you understand the applicable principles." Another student echoes this sentiment saying, "The teachers have a real loyalty to the school and the state. You know they are here because they want to be."

Some students tell us that the "straightforward and helpful" administration always makes students feel like they are a priority, while others complain, "Communication is horrendous. It's impossible to know what is going on at the school."

"Nebraska provides plenty of opportunities to actually learn the skills you'll need to practice." There are "a lot of extra skills classes and speakers." The location "in an intermediate-size city that is also the capital" of Nebraska is a huge plus. "There are opportunities to work in government, at firms, for nonprofit organizations, and in nontraditional legal areas." Nebraska's Criminal Clinic gives students the opportunity to prosecute a wide range of cases, including drug possession, public indecency, fraud, arson, and extortion. Students in the Civil Clinic represent clients in areas as diverse as bankruptcy, divorce, nonprofit incorporation, adoption, and estate planning.

The "circa-1970" classrooms and student lounge areas at Nebraska "could use an overhaul. They lack power supplies in all seats, [and] the *Brady Bunch* décor" is in need of updating. The school's plan to remodel all classrooms with the exception of the auditorium, to include modern décor, additional technology and power supplies in all seats by fall 2005 should resolve some of these concerns. On the bright side, wireless Internet is ubiquitous—even in those unattractive classrooms—and "the rest of the school is newly renovated and looks great." The "remodeled library has great aesthetics [and is otherwise] astounding." One student observes, "There are great quiet areas to study alone, as well as plenty of study rooms to meet in for study groups. A new outdoor courtyard is also nice."

Life

"Midwestern friendliness" permeates both the staff and the student population. "The students are all very nice and are very willing to help out other students," explains a 1L. Except for a few "close-minded [and] self-important people, no one takes themselves too seriously. We know we are here just to learn how to do a job." There is a good mix of nontraditional students at Nebraska, but cultural and ethnic diversity is definitely not Nebraska's strong suit. "The university has come a long way, but has so much further to go," opines one student.

Denice D. Archer, Admissions Coordinator
PO Box 830902, Lincoln, NE 68583-0902
Telephone: 402-472-2161 • Fax: 402-472-5185
E-mail: lawadm@unl.edu • Website: http://law.unl.edu

The law school is located a mile away from the main city campus, which makes "going out to lunch and other social activities harder." The plus side is that law students "never have to worry about parking." Also, "the cost of living in Nebraska is very affordable."

"Socially, you can be as involved as you want." One student says, "The school and its organizations sponsor a ton of social events and mentoring programs so that the possibilities are there if you are looking for them." "If anything, our law school is too social," writes one student. "The Student Bar Association does not act as a student government, but rather as a Student Beer Association." One student says, "It is Nebraska, so there's not a great club scene." For students in need of something more cosmopolitan, the brighter lights of Omaha are "not far away."

Getting In

More than two out of every five applicants are accepted by the University of Nebraska College of Law, and in terms of law schools admissions, those odds are pretty good for applicants. If you were an honors student in college, even without a knockout LSAT score, you should consider applying. Admitted students at the 25th percentile have an LSAT score of 152 and a GPA of 3.4. Admitted students at the 75th percentile have an LSAT score of 159 and a GPA of 3.8.

EMPLOYMENT INFORMATION

Career Rating	**78**
Job placement rate (%)	94
Average starting salary	$48,696
State for bar exam	NE, NY, NV, TX, MO
Pass rate for first-time bar	93

Employers who frequently hire grads: Small law firms and state government.

Prominent Alumni: Ted Sorensen, special counsel to President John F. Kennedy; Harvey Perlman, chancellor, University of Nebraska—-Lincoln; Ben Nelson, U.S. senator and former governor of Nebraska; Lee Rankin, former solicitor general of the United States; John Hendry, chief justice of the Nebraska Supreme Court.

Grads employed by field (%):	
Academic	2
Business/industry	11
Government	17
Judicial clerkships	4
Military	2
Other	3
Private practice	47
Public interest	2

Legal Research Course Requirement?	Yes
Moot Court Requirement?	No
Public Interest Law Requirement?	No

ADMISSIONS

Selectivity Rating	**78**
# applications received	824
# applicants accepted	342
# acceptees attending	136
Average LSAT	156
LSAT Range	152–159
Average undergrad GPA	3.7
Application fee	$25
Regular application deadline	3/1
Regular notification	rolling
Rolling notification?	Yes
Early application program?	No
Transfer students accepted?	Yes
Evening division offered?	No
Part-time accepted?	No
LSDAS accepted?	Yes

Applicants Also Look At

Creighton University, Drake University, University of Denver, University of Idaho, University of Iowa, University of Kansas, University of Wyoming.

International Students

TOEFL required of international students?	Yes
Minimum Paper TOEFL	600
Minimum Computer TOEFL	250

FINANCIAL FACTS

Annual tuition (resident)	$6,723
Annual tuition (nonresident)	$18,837
Books and supplies	$1,230
Room & board (on/off-campus)	$9,130/$9,622
% first-year students receiving some sort of aid	80
% receiving some sort of aid	80
% of aid that is merit-based	38
% receiving scholarships	50
Average grant	$5,220
Average loan	$12,807
Average debt	$42,614

UNIVERSITY OF NEVADA—LAS VEGAS
WILLIAM S. BOYD SCHOOL OF LAW

INSTITUTIONAL INFORMATION

Public/private	public
Student/faculty ratio	13:1
% faculty part-time	31
% faculty female	40
% faculty minority	15
Total faculty	55

SURVEY SAYS . . .

Great research resources
Abundant externship/internship/ clerkship opportunities
Beautiful campus

STUDENTS

Enrollment of law school	467
% male/female	53/47
% full-time	65
% minority	22
# of countries represented	1
Average age of entering class	28

ACADEMICS

Academic Experience rating	**84**
Professors interesting rating	80
Professors accessible rating	80
Hours of study per day	4.33

Combined Degrees Offered

JD/MBA, 4 years.

Academic Requirements

Clinical Program Required?	No
Legal Writing Course Requirement?	Yes
Legal Methods Course Requirement?	Yes
Legal Research Course Requirement?	Yes
Moot Court Requirement?	No
Public Interest Law Requirement?	Yes

Academics

A young and recently ABA-accredited law school, many students feel "the greatest strength of Boyd is its newness," which lends a sense of optimism, excitement, and challenge to the campus. Because it's not "steeped in tradition, there's an entrepreneurial spirit here. Everyone senses we're building something special." With a quality teaching staff, top-notch facilities, a talented student body, and reasonable tuition costs, students are confident that their school will continue to climb in the ranks. In fact, this sense of excitement extends throughout the city and state. The only law school in Nevada, students report that "the legal community and the community in general are excited to have us here and the whole city is invested in all of us succeeding."

Professors boast impressive educational and professional backgrounds and are known to be both "intelligent and well respected in their fields." More important, they are "stimulating individuals who are skilled teachers." Students are "consistently amazed by the ease with which the faculty so effectively employs the Socratic Method, such that the student body…is able to break down even the most complex legal scenarios and digest them as fully understandable rules and concepts." Outside the classroom, "professors are extremely approachable, even for a shy student."

The administration is generally regarded as "accessible and very pro-student." A 2L affirms, "The administrators I deal with on any sort of regular basis are fantastic. Not only do they know their stuff; they are anxious to help and are just all-around fabulous people." Students particularly applaud the efforts the administration has made to help new students make the transition into law school, citing the "optional 30-minute classes once a week where we are taught exam skills, note taking, and outlining tips."

Built just a few years ago, classrooms at Boyd are "new and clean" and very high-tech. The "top quality facilities" include "wireless Internet and cable Internet hook-ups throughout the building," as well as "a state-of-the-art library." Off campus, students say that "being the only law school in Nevada, in the middle of one of the fastest growing economies in the United States, opportunities abound." For example, UNLV students "have opportunities for something close to 30 judicial externships each year (out of a class of 150)" and additionally "have extraordinary access to the local, regional, and state governments." When it comes to landing a job after graduation, UNLV is extremely well located. In the city of Las Vegas "the local law firms are eager to hire graduates, and the private sector opportunities in gaming, hospitality, real estate, corporate, entertainment and litigation are abundant and highly lucrative."

Frank Durand, Assistant Dean, Admissions and Financial Aid
4505 Maryland Parkway, Box 451003, Las Vegas, NV 89154-1003
Telephone: 702-895-2440 • Fax: 702-895-2414
E-mail: request@law.unlv.edu • Website: www.law.unlv.edu

Life

While located in the heart of Las Vegas, "most of the students commute into campus . . . and that can put a strain on the nearby social scene." In lieu of a hopping campus life, "student organizations are great and have become central to social events at the school." And students have no trouble making friends among their interesting and talented classmates since "the people make the school." One student writes, "I love coming to school because I've made really great friends and don't mind seeing them everyday."

Commuter student or not, "being in the center of Las Vegas, there is always something to do and somewhere new to go." You may be surprised to learn, however, that law school in Sin City is actually quite serious. At Boyd, "students are very competitive and you can feel that in the air." Some students feel the competitiveness is a product of the high caliber of the student body. A 1L explains that many "of the students in the entering class are in their 40s, and several of them are doctors and dentists, so the bar is set quite high." In addition to their diligence, UNLV students are a fairly homogenous and quite conservative group. One student points out that some of "the faculty is comprised of very liberal individuals from a diverse background, whereas a majority of the students are very conservative and tend to have similar life experiences."

Getting In

When selecting applicants, the admissions committee looks for students with demonstrated academic capability, including depth and breadth of undergraduate course work, grades, concurrent work experience, and extracurricular activities. The school also considers non-academic factors, such as community service and work experience. Older students should feel particularly welcomed at Boyd.

EMPLOYMENT INFORMATION

Career Rating	**70**
Job placement rate (%)	87
Average starting salary	$62,000
State for bar exam	NV, AZ, UT, CA
Pass rate for first-time bar	63

Employers who frequently hire grads:
Local private firms and governmental agencies.

Grads employed by field (%):	
Academic	2
Business/industry	11
Government	6
Judicial clerkships	16
Military	1
Other	1
Private practice	62
Public interest	1

ADMISSIONS

Selectivity Rating	**86**
# applications received	1,889
# applicants accepted	215
# acceptees attending	105
Average LSAT	157
LSAT Range	154–160
Average undergrad GPA	3.4
Application fee	$40
Regular application deadline	3/15
Regular notification	4/30
Rolling notification?	Yes
Early application program?	No
Transfer students accepted?	Yes
Evening division offered?	Yes
Part-time accepted?	Yes
LSDAS accepted?	Yes

Applicants Also Look At

Arizona State University, California Western, Southwestern University School of Law, Thomas Jefferson School of Law, University of the Pacific, University of San Diego, University of Utah.

International Students

TOEFL required of international students?	No
TOEFL recommended of international students?	No

FINANCIAL FACTS

Annual tuition (resident)	$8,900
Annual tuition (nonresident)	$17,800
Books and supplies	$850
Tuition per credit (resident)	$317
Tuition per credit (nonresident)	$635
Room & board (on/off-campus)	$9,140/$8,170
Financial aid application deadline	2/1
% of aid that is merit-based	90
% receiving scholarships	36
Average grant	$4,800
Average loan	$17,300

UNIVERSITY OF NEW MEXICO
SCHOOL OF LAW

INSTITUTIONAL INFORMATION

Public/private	public
Student/faculty ratio	10:1
% faculty female	50
% faculty minority	35
Total faculty	34

SURVEY SAYS . . .

Great library staff

Abundant externship/internship/clerkship opportunities

STUDENTS

Enrollment of law school	340
% male/female	45/55
% full-time	100
% minority	38
% international	1
# of countries represented	3
Average age of entering class	29

ACADEMICS

Academic Experience rating	**87**
Professors interesting rating	90
Professors accessible rating	94
Hours of study per day	4.15

Academic Specialties

Environmental law, international law, Indian law.

Advanced Degrees Offered

JD, 3 years.

Combined Degrees Offered

JD/MA, JD/MS, JD/MAPA master of public administration, JD/MALAS master of arts in Latin American studies. All 4 years.

Academic Requirements

Clinical Program Required?	Yes
Legal Writing Course Requirement?	Yes
Legal Methods Course Requirement?	Yes
Legal Research Course Requirement?	Yes
Moot Court Requirement?	No
Public Interest Law Requirement?	No

Academics

The University of New Mexico School of Law is a place where "students can get a wonderful education, [learning from] excellent professors [in] small classes [among a] diverse student body." Believe it or not, "all of this comes at a very reasonable price, [in] beautiful surroundings." As one student puts it, "UNM Law is the whole enchilada." The law school prides itself on producing graduates who have a "tremendous amount" of practical experience. The clinical program, "mandatory to all law students, reflects the school's commitment to hands-on training." As one student testifies, "The school's emphasis on practical lawyering skills has given me great confidence. I've had appearances in real courtrooms with real cases for which I bore serious responsibility." Since UNM is the only law school in the state, it has some pretty strong connections in the local law community. "We've already met two [U]NM Supreme Court justices, who spent hours with us after class talking about their careers," boasts a student.

The faculty at New Mexico School of Law is highly diverse. Half of the professors are women, and about 35 percent are minorities. There is a low 10 to 1 student to teacher ratio at New Mexico, which helps foster the "close relationships" students say they have with the faculty. "My professors know my history and my goals; they know what I want to do after school, and they provide great support and assistance to help me get there," exclaims one content student. Since professors are "heavily networked into the legal community, the opportunities for collaboration with active attorneys are many." As one student tells us, "Our professors are close friends with the best lawyers in the state and are happy to introduce them all to the students."

Students appreciate the way the "administration always has [its] door open and elicits input from the student body." They host "academic workshops after first year to try and help you succeed [and] a cool mentoring program for students who want to learn from local attorneys and judges." Even Career Services gets good marks—it's headed by a "great director who sends out good job/internship/externship listings all the time." Furthermore, the law school "bends over backward to accommodate" students with special needs, "from wheelchairs and seeing-eye dogs to mothers bringing kids to class on frequent occasion[s] (there is a daycare center on campus)."

Facilities are on the up at UNM, as the law school has "recently doubled with a new addition." The school boasts "modern classrooms with Internet access, and plenty of quiet places to enjoy the New Mexico sunshine and study (lots and lots of windows—windows for ceilings in some places, too)." Also, "there is wireless networking and electrical outlets throughout the building." However, the "availability of parking spaces" is one area that students say could stand to be improved.

Susan Mitchell, Director of Admissions
MSC11 6070, 1 University of New Mexico, Albuquerque, NM 87131-0001
Telephone: 505-277-0958 • Fax: 505-277-9958
Website: http://lawschool.unm.edu

Life

They call New Mexico "the Land of Enchantment" for a reason, explains one student. "The law library has great views of the Rocky Mountains. The classrooms face a lovely golf course." Since the law school is part of the larger university, there are "numerous opportunities to utilize the resources of other departments." There's a student group "for every bent," for example, "'Gay-Lesbian-Bisexual-Transsexual, ACLU, Federalist Society, and NLG.'" Social activities vary widely as well. "The social make-up of the student body is multifaceted, and there are just as likely to be trips to the zoo for students and their children as there are happy-hour gatherings."

Students say that the law school's "small student body makes the environment warm, friendly, and supportive." The diversity in "age, ethnicity, gender, and educational background" is a real source of pride with students. There is a "strong minority presence" making for meaningful "discussion and interaction between all students of all backgrounds." Students are optimistic that the "better understanding and appreciation for people" that they gain through this exposure to such a diverse group will be something they can take "into the 'real world,' [to be incorporated] into their professional and personal lives." The atmosphere at the law school is competitive, but students are still "friendly, [inclined to] help each other out, [and] study together." The political wind blows left at New Mexico School of Law, and while that fits with most of the students, some feel that a conservative voice is shouted down. Even one liberal student imagines that the leftist student body must "sometimes be overwhelming for the more conservative students. Tolerance should be more encouraged in the political and social realm."

Getting In

At New Mexico, admitted students at the 25th percentile have an LSAT score of 151 and a GPA of 3.0. Admitted students at the 75th percentile have an LSAT score of 160 and a GPA of 3.7. New Mexico offers many combined degrees. It is a full-time only institution.

ADMISSIONS

Selectivity Rating	**80**
# applications received	1,044
# applicants accepted	243
# acceptees attending	120
Average LSAT	155
LSAT Range	150–159
Average undergrad GPA	3.3
Application fee	$40
Regular application deadline	2/15
Regular notification	rolling
Rolling notification?	Yes
Early application program?	No
Transfer students accepted?	Yes
Evening division offered?	No
Part-time accepted?	No
LSDAS accepted?	Yes
International Students	
TOEFL required of international students?	Yes

FINANCIAL FACTS

Annual tuition (resident)	$7,568
Annual tuition (nonresident)	$19,900
Books and supplies	$1,236
Room & board (off-campus)	$7,056
Financial aid application deadline	3/1

EMPLOYMENT INFORMATION

Career Rating	**77**
Job placement rate (%)	90
Average starting salary	$48,739
State for bar exam	NM
Pass rate for first-time bar	86

Employers who frequently hire grads:
Private firms, federal and state judges, government and public intrest organizations.

Grads employed by field (%):	
Business/industry	6
Government	19
Judicial clerkships	12
Military	5
Private practice	37
Public interest	21

UNIVERSITY OF NORTH CAROLINA—CHAPEL HILL
SCHOOL OF LAW

INSTITUTIONAL INFORMATION

Public/private	public
Student/faculty ratio	15:1
% faculty part-time	60
% faculty female	40
% faculty minority	11
Total faculty	102

SURVEY SAYS . . .

Great research resources
Great library staff
Students love Chapel Hill, NC

STUDENTS

Enrollment of law school	708
% male/female	47/53
% out-of-state	26
% full-time	100
% minority	26
% international	1
# of countries represented	4
Average age of entering class	25

ACADEMICS

Academic Experience rating	**86**
Professors interesting rating	80
Professors accessible rating	70
Hours of study per day	4.7

Academic Specialties

Civil procedure, commercial law, constitutional law, corporation securities law, criminal law, environmental law, government services, human rights law, intellectual property law, international law, labor law, legal history, legal philosophy, property, taxation.

Combined Degrees Offered

JD/MBA, 4 years; JD/MPA, 4 years; JD/MPPS, 4 years; JD/MPH, 4 years; JD/MRP, 4 years; JD/MSW, 4 years; JDMASA, 4 years; JD/MSLS, 4 years; JD/MSIS, 4 years.

Academic Requirements

Clinical Program Required?	No
Legal Writing Course Requirement?	Yes
Legal Methods Course Requirement?	No

Academics

The School of Law at The University of North Carolina—Chapel Hill is "one of the best public law schools in the country [and arguably] the best bang-for-your-buck law school in the nation" (particularly if you are a resident of the Tar Heel State). Nearly all of the engaging, "intellectually impressive and accessible [professors] seem to really enjoy teaching students." One thunderstruck student claims, "I never realized what good teaching was until I came to UNC Law. If I have a question about class, even if we are two days before an exam, I feel comfortable asking anyone and know that I will get an honest answer." Still, some students feel that "there is a strong liberal bias at the school" and that professors sometimes "bring their political views with them into the classroom." To correct this, they are calling for the law school to "improve on fostering a more diverse political atmosphere." UNC Law's "excellent [administration creates] a positive and supportive environment for the study of law." A satisfied student gloats, "Everyone at the school, from the secretary to the dean, is extremely accessible and willing to take as much time as needed to help individual students. As cheesy as it sounds, there is a family atmosphere here."

Most UNC survey respondents are pretty pleased about their employment prospects. One student credits the Career Services office as being "the greatest strength of UNC. Even when they are too busy for a brief meeting about resumes or cover letters, you can just leave your stuff under the door, and someone will get it back to you by the next day with recommendations about what you should fix." Some note a weakness in the "same place all law schools could improve—better access to different regions of the US when looking for job placement." Jobs in North Carolina and neighboring states are fairly abundant, though, in large part because the law school maintains "strong connections" with in-state employers. A disproportionate percentage of area bigwigs are alumni. Four of the last six state governors and 40 percent of the state judiciary, for example, are UNC Law graduates.

Student organizations and learning opportunities are aplenty. According to one student, "There are lots of organizations to get involved in, and the pro bono program is one of the best." About one-third of all students do some kind of pro bono work—many during the summer or over winter or spring breaks. Students who have performed over 75 hours of pro bono service receive certificates of acknowledgement from the state bar association, and those who perform over 100 hours of pro bono service get special shout-outs at graduation. Other notables include UNC's clinical programs, in which students handle more than 350 civil and criminal cases every year and "really get a lot of hands-on experience" in the process. Joint-degree programs include the standard JD/MBA as well as masters of public policy science and a handful of others. UNC also offers a summer program down under in Sydney, Australia, that concentrates on Pacific Rim issues and semester-long programs in Europe and Mexico.

The general consensus is that facilities at UNC are middling, but in terms of the availability of information, "the resources are outstanding." Also, "the school is improving the technology of each classroom every year." It's a pretty slow process, though. As of now, "half the facilities are brand-new. Once they get around to renovating the other half, they'll be golden."

Michael J. States, Assistant Dean for Admissions
CB# 3380, Van Hecke-Wettach Hall, UNC School of Law Admissions,
Chapel Hill, NC 27599-3380
Telephone: 919-962-5109 • Fax: 919-843-7939
E-mail: law_admission@unc.edu • Website: www.law.unc.edu

Life

"Carolina offers a healthy balance between academic and student life." UNC is home to "a surprisingly easy-going group of students." One student exclaims, "I am constantly amazed by how interesting my classmates are." The academic atmosphere is "very friendly [and] very cooperative, which helps tone down the competitive edge and reduce stress levels." Students say they "are not excessively competitive." Instead, they "help each other learn."

Students insist that "there is no better college town in the United States than Chapel Hill," a southern hamlet of about 44,000 souls that offers a good supply of part-time jobs, affordable housing, and a mild climate. These fine qualities have not gone unnoticed: *Money* magazine named the Raleigh-Durham-Chapel Hill area the "Best Place to Live in the South" in 2000, and *Sports Illustrated* named Chapel Hill "the Best College Town in America" a few years earlier. "The combination of the faculty, the resources, and the town makes for a great three years." As one student puts it, "While you don't go to law school for the social life, it makes a big difference to have something to do when you actually do find free time."

"Social life is good [at Chapel Hill because] on the whole, students are very social outside of class. There are school-sponsored social events in town, and there are always parties being thrown by law students to celebrate a wide array of milestones" (for instance, there is a "we just took our second practice exam" party). However, students complain that there is little to do "for someone who does not drink."

Getting In

It is not as difficult to get admitted at UNC as you might think. Admitted students at the 25th percentile have an LSAT score of 157 and a GPA of 3.4. Admitted students at the 75th percentile have an LSAT score of 165 and a GPA of 3.8. Around 75 percent of the law students at Chapel Hill are residents of North Carolina. This statistic is not a freak of nature as it is far tougher to get admitted from out-of-state than most places.

EMPLOYMENT INFORMATION

Career Rating	**86**
% employed within 9 months	97
Average starting salary	$75,000
State for bar exam	NC, NY, FL, GA, VA
Pass rate for first-time bar	93

Prominent Alumni: John Edwards, senator; Terry Sanford, senator; James Hunt, governor.

Grads employed by field (%):	
Academic	1.6
Business/industry	4 8
Government	9
Judicial clerkships	8.5
Private practice	74
Public interest	5

Legal Research Course Requirement?	Yes
Moot Court Requirement?	No
Public Interest Law Requirement?	No

ADMISSIONS

Selectivity Rating	**91**
# applications received	3,888
# applicants accepted	570
# acceptees attending	237
Average LSAT	162
LSAT Range	157–164
Average undergrad GPA	3.6
Application fee	$70
Regular application deadline	2/1
Regular notification	rolling
Rolling notification?	Yes
Early application program?	No
Transfer students accepted?	Yes
Evening division offered?	No
Part-time accepted?	No
LSDAS accepted?	Yes

Applicants Also Look At

College of William & Mary, Duke University, Emory University, Georgetown University, University of Virginia, Vanderbilt University, Wake Forest University.

International Students

TOEFL required of international students?	Yes
Minimum Paper TOEFL	600
Minimum Computer TOEFL	250

FINANCIAL FACTS

Annual tuition (resident)	$11,118
Annual tuition (nonresident)	$23,036
Books and supplies	$900
Room & board	$11,292
% first-year students receiving some sort of aid	85
% receiving some sort of aid	83
% of aid that is merit-based	6
% receiving scholarships	66
Average grant	$3,313
Average loan	$18,748
Average total aid package	$22,803

University of North Dakota
School of Law

INSTITUTIONAL INFORMATION

Public/private	public
Student/faculty ratio	7:1
% faculty part-time	59
% faculty female	48
% faculty minority	13
Total faculty	27

SURVEY SAYS . . .

Diverse opinions accepted in classrooms
Great library staff
Abundant externship/internship/clerkship opportunities
Good social life

STUDENTS

Enrollment of law school	200
% male/female	51/49
% full-time	100
% minority	6
% international	3
# of countries represented	1

ACADEMICS

Academic Experience rating	**62**
Professors interesting rating	75
Professors accessible rating	82
Hours of study per day	4.56

Advanced Degrees Offered

JD, 3 years.

Combined Degrees Offered

JD/MPA, 4 years.

Academic Requirements

Clinical Program Required?	No
Legal Writing Course Requirement?	Yes
Legal Methods Course Requirement?	Yes
Legal Research Course Requirement?	Yes
Moot Court Requirement?	No
Public Interest Law Requirement?	No

Academics

If you are looking for a legal education at bargain basement prices, look no further than the University of North Dakota School of Law, where a "valuable and enriching education" can be had for an "extremely low price." Despite its affordability, quality teaching is a cornerstone of the academic experience at UND, and at least one student is "more entertained while sitting in my first-year classes than I am watching prime-time TV." On top of their ability to keep their students' attention, "the faculty really wants students to succeed" and strive to make the material accessible. In doing so, "they use the Socratic Method, but not as a scare tactic." Professors are nothing if not personable; a 2L recalls that "on my first day, I wandered into the faculty lounge and was greeted by name by a professor who had taught my mother at the same law school 15 years earlier! He remembered when I was 5 years old and Mom had brought me to class when the babysitter was sick."

In addition to professors, the "administration clearly demonstrates an intention to help each student succeed in law school and beyond." Yet students feel that despite the intimate atmosphere, they give up little in terms of diversity and quality of courses and clinical experiences. Even so, students point out some weaknesses in the school's curriculum and course offerings. For example, some would like better programs in criminal and international law, as well as more emphasis on legal writing and research skills. A 3L adds, "This law school is in the middle of one of the greatest agricultural areas of the U.S. However, it is not a center for agricultural law."

In addition to foundational course work, "several legal research courses are offered as part of the curriculum, as well as voluntary training sessions that focus on developing your individual research skills." On top of that, "practical experience is encouraged through things like moot court, trial advocacy competitions, and trial advocacy classes." Students also tell us that "the North Dakota Law Review is also a great opportunity to test and develop your legal research and writing skills" and that the school offers "a summer program abroad in Norway." The school is also proactive in seeking externships and clerkship opportunities within the state, and "Career Services, including internship placements, summer and full-time employment opportunities, is very helpful." In addition, "the North Dakota Supreme Court selects graduating UND students as clerks each year."

In terms of enrollment, UND Law is tiny compared to other law schools, but students feel it is just the right size, "small enough to cater to individual students' interests and needs and large enough to have a good reputation nationally and internationally."

On campus, "facilities, particularly classrooms and the library, need more space and modernization," but students are satisfied with the level of bandwidth available, pointing out that "there is wireless Internet throughout the building, and even outside" and that professors make good use of technology in the classroom. Students report that the research facilities are excellent and "research representatives from LexisNexis or Westlaw are available at all times to help out."

Linda D. Kohoutek, Admissions & Records Associate
Centennial Drive, PO Box 9003, Grand Forks, ND 58202
Telephone: 701-777-2260 • Fax: 701-777-2217
E-mail: myszkowski@law.und.edu • Website: www.law.und.nodak.edu

Life

On this low-key campus, "classmates regularly coordinate group outings to local spots and really seem to get along with everyone." A number of clubs and student groups draw active members, and many make mention of the school's annual social events, like the "fabulous Halloween party" and the annual "Malpractice Bowl, in which the law school students play a football game against the medical students." Hometown Grand Forks gets the thumbs-up, and students tell us that "there are plenty of places to go for students who need to unwind."

In terms of demographics, "more diversity among the student body and faculty would be beneficial." While a few students claim the politics of the school leans to the left, most feel that UND "is a very conservative law school in a very conservative university in a very conservative town." Whatever their politics, "debates and discussions are always brewing between students." "Whether we are in class, studying, or out at the bar, there is always something to disagree on and challenge each other." However, students insist that they are respectful of all viewpoints and opinions, and, "aside from election time, there have been almost no squabbles."

Getting In

While there is no specific pre-law course work required for admission, demonstrated oral and written communication skills are paramount to an admissions decision at University of North Dakota. The applicant's undergraduate record, LSAT scores, and letters of recommendation are the most heavily weighted factors in an admissions decision; however, the school will consider all factors that may suggest a student is capable of completing a rigorous legal curriculum.

ADMISSIONS

Selectivity Rating	**68**
# applications received	382
# applicants accepted	153
# acceptees attending	69
Average LSAT	151
LSAT Range	147–155
Average undergrad GPA	3.5
Application fee	$35
Regular application deadline	4/1
Regular notification	rolling
Rolling notification?	Yes
Early application program?	No
Transfer students accepted?	Yes
Evening division offered?	No
Part-time accepted?	No
LSDAS accepted?	Yes
International Students	
TOEFL required of international students?	No
TOEFL recommended of international students?	No

FINANCIAL FACTS

Annual tuition (resident)	$7,032
Annual tuition (nonresident)	$14,900
Books and supplies	$900
Room & board	$8,100
Financial aid application deadline	4/15
% first-year students receiving some sort of aid	91
% receiving some sort of aid	87
% of aid that is merit-based	1
% receiving scholarships	39
Average grant	$500
Average loan	$16,500
Average total aid package	$16,700
Average debt	$48,800

EMPLOYMENT INFORMATION

Career Rating	**64**
% employed within 9 months	92
Average starting salary	$40,900
State for bar exam	ND, MN, TN, CA, IL
Pass rate for first-time bar	90

Employers who frequently hire grads:
Judicial systems and private firms.

Grads employed by field (%):	
Business/industry	7
Government	14
Judicial clerkships	15
Military	3
Other	1
Private practice	52
Public interest	8

University of Notre Dame
Law School

INSTITUTIONAL INFORMATION

Public/private	private
Student/faculty ratio	16:1
Affiliation	Roman Catholic
% faculty part-time	42
% faculty female	32
% faculty minority	8
Total faculty	78

SURVEY SAYS . . .

Diverse opinions accepted in classrooms
Great library staff

STUDENTS

Enrollment of law school	553
% male/female	56/44
% out-of-state	93
% full-time	100
% minority	21
% international	1
# of countries represented	25
Average age of entering class	24

ACADEMICS

Academic Experience rating	**91**
Professors interesting rating	96
Professors accessible rating	87
Hours of study per day	4.92

Academic Specialties

Human rights law, international law.

Advanced Degrees Offered

LLM in international human rights, 1 year; J/SD in international human rights, 3 to 5 years, including 1 year of residency; LLM in international comparative law (London campus only), 1 academic year.

Combined Degrees Offered

JD/MBA, 4 years; JD/ME, 4 years; JD/MA in English, 3 to 4 years.

Academic Requirements

Clinical Program Required?	No
Legal Writing Course Requirement?	Yes
Legal Methods Course Requirement?	Yes
Legal Research Course Requirement?	Yes

Academics

The University of Notre Dame Law School's motto is "Educating a different kind of lawyer," and it's "a commitment Notre Dame takes very seriously." Students tell us that the school fosters a social consciousness by making "values, morality, and social responsibility a part of class discussions, [and by approaching law as] a professional tool students are taught to understand in order to play strong, ethical roles" after graduation. Also to this end, Notre Dame has "established a loan forgiveness plan [and] has a lot of support for students interested in public interest or government jobs." While some feel stifled by the Catholic flavor and conservatism of Notre Dame, others embrace its ideals.

Students say most of their professors "possess a wonderful ability to both educate and entertain" that makes it a pleasure to go to class. Students appreciate that the faculty is "always available and accessible both before and after class" to help with problems. "There is a large amount of interaction between students and the faculty. I have had more than a few professors over for dinner or met up with them for drinks or a meal and discussion," one student tells us. This kind of interaction may be the result of "the 'open-door' policy at Notre Dame Law School, [which] creates an environment that is exceptionally conducive to the fostering of strong relationships between professors and individual students." Some students do harp that the school hires too many adjunct professors.

Notre Dame boasts a number of interesting academic offerings, like a really cool year-long London program. It's an "opportunity to learn from some of Europe's greatest scholars from Oxford, Cambridge, and University College London in one of the world's great centers of politics, culture, and commerce." Another unique opportunity is that students are allowed to do "directed readings, where you, in essence, create your own class and work under the direction of a professor." Outside of class, the law school sponsors speakers almost every week. "Having the opportunity to hear government officials, judges, lawyers, etc., speak about political and legal issues really enriches our academic studies and provokes questions and ideas," a student gleams.

Feelings on the administration are varied. While some say the dean "is very disconnected from the student body [and claim that] change is hard to come by," others have no complaints. One student extols, "Notre Dame's administration could not be better. From the dean on down, they are some of the friendliest, most helpful people I could hope to encounter. The registrar makes an extra effort to get grades out on time. The admissions office goes above and beyond to make prospective students feel welcome."

While the campus with the Golden Dome is, on the whole, "absolutely gorgeous," the law school building "needs to be renovated and expanded." Currently, "classrooms are cramped and a lack of available rooms limits the school's ability to offer classes." Another student adds, "Classroom temperature is a frequent problem." Yet maybe these aren't bad things? One student likened the law school to an "elderly relative's house—hot, crowded, and antiquated, yet strangely comforting and cozy." The word is that "plans for an enormous addition to the law school are in the works," so perhaps things will be looking up in the near future.

CHARLES W. ROBOSKI, DIRECTOR OF ADMISSIONS AND FINANCIAL AID
NOTRE DAME LAW SCHOOL PO BOX 959, NOTRE DAME, IN 46556-0959
TELEPHONE: 574-631-6626 • FAX: 574-631-5474
E-MAIL: LAWADMIT@ND.EDU • WEBSITE: WWW.LAW.ND.EDU

Life

Located in the middle of northern Indiana, South Bend is not exactly the most happening spot in the world. But, the "locals are kind, the area is safe, there are decent bars and restaurants, [and, at least, there is] not a lot to distract you from studying." Plus, "the small-town atmosphere breeds a cohesive and friendly student body." As one student says, "The sense of community is one of the reasons that I chose Notre Dame." Maybe that's why Notre Dame's alumni network is one of the "largest and strongest in the country." Another student says, "Alumni love this place and are always glad to meet a Domer."

While Notre Dame may "attract students from all over, the student body is very homogenous: white, Catholic, and conservative on social issues." Many students call out for "more diversity" and not just ethnic diversity, either. "This place needs more married students with kids, students with handicaps, and older people with life experience," says one student. Overall, students are happy with their "extremely bright, funny" classmates. "There are of course the prototypical law school nerds with whom any conversation is unbearable," explains one student, "but there are also many fun people who lead a balanced life of studying, partying, and non-law related activities."

Competitiveness rears its ugly head around exam time, "but for the most part people are very helpful—willing to exchange notes, outlines, help answer questions," and so on. "The dog-eat-dog mentality that prevails at other law schools is nowhere to be found at Notre Dame," students assure us.

Getting In

Admitted students to Notre Dame at the 25th percentile have an LSAT score of 161 and a GPA of 3.4. Admitted students at the 75th percentile have an LSAT score of 166 and a GPA of 3.8.

EMPLOYMENT INFORMATION

Career Rating	**96**
% employed within 9 months	98
Average starting salary	$98,826
State for bar exam	IL
Pass rate for first-time bar	97

Employers who frequently hire grads:
Major law firms in locations throughout the country and abroad, judges at all levels, government agencies, corporations, and public interest organizations.

Grads employed by field (%):

Academic	1
Business/industry	4
Government	6
Judicial clerkships	15
Military	3
Private practice	69
Public interest	2

Moot Court Requirement?	Yes
Public Interest Law Requirement?	No

ADMISSIONS

Selectivity Rating	**92**
# applications received	3,773
# applicants accepted	516
# acceptees attending	178
Average LSAT	164
LSAT Range	162–167
Average undergrad GPA	3.5
Application fee	$55
Regular application deadline	3/1
Regular notification	rolling
Rolling notification?	Yes
Early application program?	Yes
Early application deadline	11/1
Early application notification	12/15
Transfer students accepted?	Yes
Evening division offered?	No
Part-time accepted?	No
LSDAS accepted?	Yes

Applicants Also Look At

Boston College, Boston University, The George Washington University, Georgetown University, Northwestern University, University of Southern California, Vanderbilt University.

International Students

TOEFL required of international students?	Yes

FINANCIAL FACTS

Annual tuition	$29,740
Books and supplies	$5,855
Room & board	$5,945
Financial aid application deadline	1/15
% of aid that is merit-based	95
% receiving scholarships	63
Average grant	$12,385
Average loan	$27,229
Average debt	$75,417

UNIVERSITY OF OREGON
SCHOOL OF LAW

INSTITUTIONAL INFORMATION

Public/private	public
Student/faculty ratio	9:1
% faculty part-time	42
% faculty female	35
% faculty minority	15
Total faculty	56

SURVEY SAYS . . .

Great research resources
Beautiful campus

STUDENTS

Enrollment of law school	514
% male/female	57/43
% out-of-state	55
% full-time	100
% minority	15
% international	1
Average age of entering class	25

ACADEMICS

Academic Experience rating	**82**
Professors interesting rating	78
Professors accessible rating	88
Hours of study per day	5.09

Academic Specialties

Commercial law, constitutional law, corporation securities law, criminal law, environmental law, government services, human rights law, international law, labor law, legal history, property, taxation.

Academic Requirements

Clinical Program Required?	No
Legal Writing Course Requirement?	Yes
Legal Methods Course Requirement?	Yes
Legal Research Course Requirement?	Yes
Moot Court Requirement?	No
Public Interest Law Requirement?	No

Academics

"Resources are endless" at the University of Oregon School of Law, a "relatively small, first-rate" public law school in a great college town. The "very teaching-oriented [professors bring] impressive academic credentials, as well as significant real-world experience" to the classroom. They also bring "PowerPoint presentations, web-based content, hypotheticals, and team projects." Critics call the faculty "politically nondiverse [and note that] some [professors] are dry academics." Outside the classroom, "all of the faculty and staff are very interested in getting to know students [and are] very accessible." Also, "a bunch of the faculty members are in a band, and they are actually very good. They play at various student events." When they aren't playing gigs, "the professors beg students to go to lunch with them [and] go out of their way to form relationships." Many students praise the "supportive, flexible," and generally likeable administration. "For example," illustrates one student, "our dean wrote the book on federal rules of evidence, but is at all of the football games talking to students at the tailgating party." Critics, however, cite "an insufferable mess of red tape [and a price tag that is] too expensive for a state school."

The "amazing, comfortable, beautiful, and state-of-the-art" facility that houses the law school is "brand-new [and] as good as they come." Students tell us it "even comes complete with enviro-friendly garbage cans." The "very comprehensive [research library is] open early and late each day. Laptops are required, and the law school is wired for high-speed and wireless access." One student observes that you "can't walk more than about five feet in the building without walking by an Ethernet jack."

"U of O Law has outstanding hands-on programs for second- and third-years." There is a strong "legacy of pro bono work" too. You shouldn't be too surprised to learn that this law school boasts one of the top environmental law programs in the country. Students in the Environmental Law Clinic develop cutting-edge, previously untested legal theories. The Criminal Defense Clinic and Criminal Prosecution Clinic are notable as well. A host of certificate programs include law and entrepreneurship, ocean and coastal law, and intellectual property. Several students gripe that the school could use "a more extensive business program [and more] variety in course offerings." One student explains, "There is not much focus on business law. This school has students with a mind for other areas, like public interest."

Career-wise, you are in luck if you want to work in the Beaver State. But "be prepared to work hard if you want to find a job outside of Oregon." Note also that "Portland has become a tougher legal employment market in recent years because it is nationally "a desirable place to live." Consequently, "the big Portland firms can just as easily hire students from elsewhere."

Admissions Office, Assistant Dean of Admissions
1221 University of Oregon, Eugene, OR 97403-1221
Telephone: 541-346-3846 • Fax: 541-346-3984
E-mail: admissions@law.uoregon.edu • Website: www.law.uoregon.edu

Life

"The students, faculty, and staff create a community that is dedicated to the mutual endeavor of making the three-year experience of law school as beneficial and enjoyable as it can be," writes one student. "Students are very friendly. Competition is not fierce. My computer crashed, and I lost several days worth of notes, and no fewer than five people offered me their notes without my asking." Students also report that "from day one," the school stresses the fact that eventually the students will have to work with each other, "and so we don't want to mislead each other or inhibit anyone in any way."

The "gorgeous campus setting [and] views of Pacific Northwest forests" certainly don't add stress to anyone's life. Winter months are rainy, but temperatures are moderate all year round. Running, jogging, hiking—outdoor activities in general—are a big deal. "Students form informal groups for basketball, running, kayaking, etc. Every afternoon, there are e-mails letting you know" about the next athletic event. Whether they want to or not, students are also able to stay in shape by walking back and forth from their cars to class. "Parking is nonexistent. You can buy a parking pass, also known as a 'hunting license,' as in 'hunting for a place to park.'"

Getting In

Admission is selective. Admitted students have an average LSAT score of 159 and an undergraduate GPA of 3.4. If you take the LSAT more than once, U of O will take your highest score. Obviously, many Oregon residents apply. But don't let out-of-state residency stop you. In recent years nonresident students have composed 60 percent of the law school population. Also, it's full-time or nothing at U of O. The school does not accommodate part-time or evening students.

ADMISSIONS

Selectivity Rating	**81**
# applications received	1,896
# applicants accepted	648
# acceptees attending	185
Average LSAT	159
LSAT Range	156–161
Average undergrad GPA	3.4
Application fee	$50
Regular application deadline	3/1
Regular notification	4/1
Rolling notification?	Yes
Early application program?	No
Transfer students accepted?	Yes
Evening division offered?	No
Part-time accepted?	No
LSDAS accepted?	Yes
International Students	
TOEFL required of international students?	Yes
Minimum Paper TOEFL	650

FINANCIAL FACTS

Annual tuition (resident)	$15,175
Annual tuition (nonresident)	$19,075
Books and supplies	$800
Room & board (off-campus)	$7,740
Financial aid application deadline	2/1
% first-year students receiving some sort of aid	93
% receiving some sort of aid	89
% receiving scholarships	54
Average grant	$3,187
Average loan	$21,000
Average total aid package	$21,285
Average debt	$57,590

EMPLOYMENT INFORMATION

Career Rating	**76**
% employed within 9 months	90
Average starting salary	$52,256
State for bar exam	OR
Pass rate for first-time bar	89

Employers who frequently hire grads:
Law firms from Portland (OR), Eugene (OR), Seattle, and San Francisco areas; O'Melveny & Myers firm from Los Angeles; federal courts; Oregon Appellate Courts, Lane County, and Portland area county circuit courts; Oregon Department of Justice, Washington attorney general's offices, and Western public defender's offices.

Grads employed by field (%):	
Academic	8
Business/industry	12
Government	10
Judicial clerkships	20
Military	2
Private practice	44
Public interest	4

UNIVERSITY OF THE PACIFIC
McGEORGE SCHOOL OF LAW

INSTITUTIONAL INFORMATION

Public/private	private
Student/faculty ratio	17:1
% faculty part-time	37
% faculty female	39
% faculty minority	12
Total faculty	75

SURVEY SAYS . . .

Diverse opinions accepted in classrooms
Great library staff
Beautiful campus

STUDENTS

Enrollment of law school	1,104
% male/female	52/48
% full-time	65
% minority	20
# of countries represented	13
Average age of entering class	24

ACADEMICS

Academic Experience rating	**76**
Professors interesting rating	73
Professors accessible rating	75
Hours of study per day	4.24

Academic Specialties

Advocacy and dispute resolution, criminal law, environmental law, government law, intellectual property law, international law, taxation.

Advanced Degrees Offered

JD, 3 years; JD, 4 years; JSD international water law; LLM transnational business practice, 1 year; LLM international law, 1 year; LLM government and public policy, 1 year.

Combined Degrees Offered

JD/MBA, JD/MPPA, JD/MA, or MS upon approval. All concurrent degrees are planned for 4 years.

Academic Requirements

Clinical Program Required?	No
Legal Writing Course Requirement?	Yes
Legal Methods Course Requirement?	No

Academics

Located in the capital of the Golden State, the University of the Pacific McGeorge School of Law offers a modern, pragmatic, and rigorous legal education to over 1,000 future lawyers. Practical experience is fundamental to instruction at McGeorge. One 2L writes, "Every single one of my professors has actually practiced law at some point in his or her career, and so I know that the advice and insight is actually meaningful and not just theoretical." On top of that, every student is required to successfully complete a rigorous program in legal writing and research. Also, "the appellate and international advocacy programs are very good. Both courses are challenging for second-year students but prepare students well for the everyday practice of law with their emphasis on brief writing and oral argument." Real-world experiences are also emphasized outside the classroom. Crediting the school's favorable location, law students report that "the availability and ease with which students are able to obtain externships is fantastic!" In addition, almost every student singles out for praise the school's "excellent study abroad programs," and "excellent moot court and mock trial competition teams."

With a sizable student body, McGeorge is able to offer "one of the broadest curricula in the nation," boasting "over 140 courses and 6 specializations." Even so, McGeorge students must complete a high number of required classes to receive the JD, the majority of which, we are told, are both rigorous and challenging. A 3L insists, "McGeorge is one of the harder, more disciplined law programs." In fact, students inform us that in the first year you can expect "an average of six to eight hours a day of reading." But there's a light at the end of the tunnel. "McGeorge is notorious for 'weeding' people out after the first year, but if you make it through that first year, it's pretty smooth sailing," assures a 3L. On that note, students claim that despite the challenges, classes are extremely stimulating and well worth the effort you put in. A 2L writes, "This has been the most difficult, yet rewarding academic experience of my life." On top of that, the faculty is readily available to help students who are struggling with the material.

Aesthetically speaking, students say, "much of the school's facilities are dated and need renovating," especially the 1970s-era library. However, "the administration is working to improve the quality of education and the image of the school," and many tell us that the "school has been steadily beautified and upgraded." In general, students are pleased to report that the administration "is aggressively reshaping itself academically and physically to be a more recognized (and higher-rated) law school." At the same time, a number of students express concerns that "the administration at McGeorge has become overly focused on improving the school's reputation and has lost sight of its most important commodity: its students." Students do feel that the dean listens and responds to their concerns, however. "With the arrival of Dean Parker, whose first year was my first year," writes one 3L, "every needed improvement was put on a 'to do' list, and she is getting things done. She has been relentless, no detail too small, and the school continues to improve in all aspects."

Students assure us that, "within the Northern California legal community, McGeorge is known for producing top-rate practicing attorneys," and students are able to find excellent jobs, especially in-state. A 3L explains, "Many of the local employers know that even though other schools may have a better GPA, a McGeorge graduate has the good foundation and is ready to hit the ground running, rather than needing extensive training." While the school's connections run deepest within hometown Sacramento, McGeorge alumni currently practice in every state in the nation.

ADAM W. BARRETT, ASSISTANT DEAN & DIRECTOR OF ADMISSIONS
3200 FIFTH AVENUE, SACRAMENTO, CA 95817
TELEPHONE: 916-739-7105 • FAX: 916-739-7134
E-MAIL: ADMISSIONSMCGEORGE@PACIFIC.EDU • WEBSITE: WWW.MCGEORGE.EDU

Life

With such demanding course work, it is no surprise that some McGeorge students can be rather competitive in the classroom. Students insist, however, that friendliness overrides any of the negative implications of their academic rivalries. "McGeorge students are competitive, but there manages to be a collegial attitude despite the competitiveness." A 3L likewise reasons, "Obviously you can't take the competitive nature out of law school entirely, but there is a general feeling of goodwill and friendship toward your fellow students." For example, "the Bar Review every Thursday night is a well-attended drink fest" held at a different Sacramento location each week. If you are looking for a very close-knit campus community, however, McGeorge will disappoint you. While "people form close relationships with those in their class, the school is too large to feel a real sense of community."

Most students describe their classmates as being slightly more politically conservative, but there's also a healthy balance of liberals to even things out; the school is large enough to promote some difference of opinion and background on campus. A 1L shares, "There are a wide range of student clubs, from the Federalist Society to the Lambda GLBT side." In addition, the school's evening program encourages students of different ages and backgrounds to join the community. When it comes to lifestyle, students approve of affordable Sacramento, telling us that the city "is becoming a great place to live with all new restaurants, lots of culture, and a fun nightlife." However, the school itself is located in a dodgy part of town, described by many as "crime riddled" and "sort of scary." A small number of students feel safety is an issue, so the school attempts to keep the campus safe, and "the campus police are visible, especially after dark when students are going home."

Getting In

At McGeorge, the most important factors in an admissions decision are a student's previous academic record, LSAT scores, graduate school or postcollege career experience, and community service or extracurricular activities. McGeorge also looks for students who might add a diversity of background or perspective to the campus community.

EMPLOYMENT INFORMATION

Career Rating	**73**
Job placement rate (%)	98
Average starting salary	$64,412
State for bar exam	CA, NV, HI, OR, DC
Pass rate for first-time bar	68

Prominent Alumni: Scott Boras, sports agent/baseball; Bill Lockyer, attorney general/California government; Steve Martini, novelist; Johnnie Rawlinson, U.S. Court of Appeals, ninth circuit.

Grads employed by field (%):	
Academic	2
Business/industry	15
Government	22
Judicial clerkships	3
Private practice	54
Public interest	3

Legal Research Course Requirement?	Yes
Moot Court Requirement?	Yes
Public Interest Law Requirement?	No

ADMISSIONS

Selectivity Rating	**81**
# applications received	3,489
# applicants accepted	1,043
# acceptees attending	361
Average LSAT	158
LSAT Range	156–160
Average undergrad GPA	3.2
Application fee	$50
Regular application deadline	5/1
Regular notification	rolling
Rolling notification?	Yes
Early application program?	No
Transfer students accepted?	Yes
Evening division offered?	Yes
Part-time accepted?	Yes
LSDAS accepted?	Yes

Applicants Also Look At

Loyola Marymount University, Santa Clara University, University of California—-Davis, University of California—-Hastings, University of San Francisco.

International Students

TOEFL required of international students?	Yes
Minimum Paper TOEFL	600

FINANCIAL FACTS

Annual tuition	$29,275
Books and supplies	$800
Tuition per credit	$998
Room & board	$11,520
% first-year students receiving some sort of aid	95
% receiving some sort of aid	93
% of aid that is merit-based	94
Average grant	$8,164
Average loan	$27,290
Average total aid package	$34,032
Average debt	$89,982

University of Pennsylvania
Law School

INSTITUTIONAL INFORMATION

Public/private	private
Student/faculty ratio	13:1
% faculty part-time	53
% faculty female	29
% faculty minority	12
Total faculty	144

SURVEY SAYS . . .

Diverse opinions accepted in classrooms
Great research resources
Great library staff
Abundant externship/internship/clerkship opportunities

STUDENTS

Enrollment of law school	827
% male/female	53/47
% full-time	100
% minority	31
% international	3
# of countries represented	14
Average age of entering class	24

ACADEMICS

Academic Experience rating	**95**
Professors interesting rating	86
Professors accessible rating	87
Hours of study per day	4.24

Academic Specialties

Civil procedure, commercial law, constitutional law, corporation securities law, criminal law, environmental law, government services, human rights law, intellectual property law, international law, labor law, legal history, legal philosophy, property, taxation.

Advanced Degrees Offered

JD, LLM, S/JD, LLCM.

Combined Degrees Offered

JD/MBA, JD/MA or PhD in economics, JD/PhD in public policy and management, JD/MA or PhD in philosophy, JD/PhD American legal history, JD/MA in Islamic studies, JD/MCP, JD/MSW, JD/MBioethics, JD/MA public policy communications, JD/MD.

Academics

The "venerable, world-class" University of Pennsylvania Law School "opens up a lot of doors for its students professionally [and is] very accommodating of cross-disciplinary studies." The JD/MBA with the Wharton School of Business is an obvious draw. A profusion of joint-degree programs also includes combining a JD with an MA in Islamic studies, a PhD in philosophy, or a Master's of bioethics in conjunction with the Center for Bioethics, among others. If you seek a more traditional career path, don't worry. A wealth of journals, moot court opportunities, and clinical courses ensures the production of "real practicing lawyers, [and Penn] tends to attract an enormous number of recruiters." As you might expect, virtually every graduate gets a "well-paying" gig, often at a large firm in the Northeast. Penn's public service requirement is also a hit. "The requirement (70 hours before graduation) doesn't overburden even the heaviest course load, and Penn "offers a wide range of options for every student's taste."

There are a few professors who "really shouldn't be teaching fellow human beings anything" but, overall, "classes tend to be engaging." One student notes, "Expectations are usually reasonable, and you know in advance when they'll be highly demanding." Most professors are interesting, and some are even "hysterically funny." Almost all are very accessible. "I have never come across a situation where a professor seemed even the least bit inaccessible," swears one student. It is also "common to see professors having lunch with students." The "warm and fuzzy" administration runs the law school very well, but at times comes off to some students as "completely unresponsive to student concerns." The biggest gripe among students at Penn is probably the "poorly organized legal writing program, [which is] currently taught by 3Ls." One student says, "Students tend not to care [about legal writing,] and teachers don't have very high expectations." Another student continues, "Replacing a few fluffy courses with more practical ones would be appreciated" by many students.

The "bright, quiet, state-of-the-art [library has] every reference you might ever need [and is] an extremely comfortable place to spend long hours." Other facilities "range from magnificent to abysmal," though. Students say, "A few classrooms [are terrible thanks to] acoustic nightmares [and] hard plastic seats that might have been scavenged from an elementary school tag sale." Climate control in classrooms is also an issue. Many "beautiful, modern classrooms" have been added in recent years, though, with "more renovations on the way. All classrooms now have wireless Internet access," too.

Life

"Some of the coolest, smartest people go to Penn." These students are "genuine, focused, [and] motivated." They're also "self-important [and possessed of] so much collective hubris that it's amazing the gods of Olympus haven't smote the school for its excessive pride." Overall, though, "Penn has a remarkably low quotient of people you absolutely want to avoid knowing." But, "does everyone who goes to this school have to be from New York City?" asks one student. No, but "there's a subtextual competition between certain groups to be New-Yorker-than-thou here." Also, most students and professors "range between liberal and extremely liberal on the political spectrum." Some students say that, as a result, "non-PC views are not tolerated, [and] you'll be treated dismissively [if you don't] already adhere to a liberal worldview." Others disagree. "As a conservative student I have felt very comfortable expressing myself in all situations," writes one such student.

Derek E. Meeker, Associate Dean, Admissions & Financial Aid
3400 Chestnut Street, Philadelphia, PA 19104-6204
Telephone: 215-898-7400 • Fax: 215-573-2025
E-mail: admissions@law.upenn.edu • Website: www.law.upenn.edu

A handful of "hyper-competitive gunners" notwithstanding, students nearly unanimously tell us, "Penn's greatest strength is its non-competitive, collegial nature. The collegiality is almost scary," really. One student asks, "Is this Philadelphia or Santa Cruz?" Students aren't ranked against each other, meaning that they "have no incentive not to help each other." Consequently, "outlines circulate like mad." One student recalls, "I had six different property outlines."

Socially, "you can find any social scene you are looking for here." There are "frequent speakers and good events. A ton of kick-ass parties, which always have tons of free beer," are an appropriate counter to the highbrow out-of-class offerings, say students. "Active student groups" proliferate as well, and "there are lots of open invitations to join a pick-up game of basketball or do some picnic somewhere." Students say, "Every Wednesday and Thursday law students congregate at Center City bars" to socialize and blow off steam. Regarding the school's location, students say "the low cost of living is really nice," though, and "Philly is a great city for students."

Getting In

Admission to Penn Law is superselective. Admitted students at the 25th percentile have a GPA of 3.5 and an LSAT score of 166. Admitted students at the 75th percentile have a GPA of 3.8 and an LSAT score of 171. Even if you're that good, you're going to need a little sprinkling of luck to get in.

EMPLOYMENT INFORMATION

Career Rating	**97**
Job placement rate (%)	100
Average starting salary	$125,000
State for bar exam	NY
Pass rate for first-time bar	92

Employers who frequently hire grads:
Variety of major corporate law firms nationwide, prestigious national fellowship organizations and public interest organizations, federal and state judges.

Grads employed by field (%):	
Business/industry	2
Government	4
Judicial clerkships	22
Private practice	69
Public interest	3

Academic Requirements

Clinical Program Required?	No
Legal Writing Course Requirement?	Yes
Legal Methods Course Requirement?	Yes
Legal Research Course Requirement?	Yes
Moot Court Requirement?	No
Public Interest Law Requirement?	Yes

ADMISSIONS

Selectivity Rating	**97**
# applications received	5,189
# applicants accepted	825
# acceptees attending	257
Average LSAT	169
LSAT Range	166–171
Average undergrad GPA	3.7
Application fee	$70
Regular application deadline	2/15
Regular notification	rolling
Rolling notification?	Yes
Early application program?	Yes
Early application deadline	11/1
Early application notification	12/31
Transfer students accepted?	Yes
Evening division offered?	No
Part-time accepted?	No
LSDAS accepted?	Yes

Applicants Also Look At

Columbia University, Georgetown University, Harvard University, New York University.

International Students

TOEFL required of international students?	No
TOEFL recommended of international students?	No

FINANCIAL FACTS

Annual tuition	$34,920
Books and supplies	$975
Room & board	$10,884
Financial aid application deadline	3/1
% first-year students receiving some sort of aid	73
% receiving some sort of aid	78
% of aid that is merit-based	16
% receiving scholarships	37
Average grant	$12,600
Average loan	$31,500
Average total aid package	$34,800
Average debt	$88,500

UNIVERSITY OF PITTSBURGH
SCHOOL OF LAW

INSTITUTIONAL INFORMATION

Public/private	public
Student/faculty ratio	15:1
% faculty part-time	54
% faculty female	25
% faculty minority	15
Total faculty	118

SURVEY SAYS . . .

Diverse opinions accepted in classrooms
Great research resources
Great library staff

STUDENTS

Enrollment of law school	720
% male/female	55/45
% out-of-state	30
% full-time	100
% minority	13
% international	2
# of countries represented	4
Average age of entering class	24

ACADEMICS

Academic Experience rating	**74**
Professors interesting rating	70
Professors accessible rating	70
Hours of study per day	4.06

Academic Specialties

Civil procedure, corporation securities law, environmental law, health law, intellectual property law, international law, taxation.

Advanced Degrees Offered

Master of laws LLM for foreign-trained attorneys, a program that allows foreign-trained lawyers to study common law in a U.S. context.

Combined Degrees Offered

JD/MPA, law and urban and public administration, JD/MPIA, law and international affairs, JD/MBA, law and business administration, JD/MPH, law and public health, JD/MA, law and medical ethics, JD/MS, law and public management (in conjunction with Carnegie Mellon U.), JD/MBA (in conjunction with Tepper School—Carnegie Mellon U.).

Academics

If you are interested in international law, you really should take a close look at the University of Pittsburgh School of Law. Numerous international study opportunities and international internships include the ultra-cool Law at Sea program, which allows students to earn seven law school credits while en route to such exotic ports of call as Spain, Greece, Norway, Poland, Belgium, and Croatia. You can also combine law with language study by taking courses in Chinese, German, and Japanese (among others) while getting your JD. While some students gripe that "too much emphasis is placed on policy discussions and not enough time is spent on practical lawyering skills," others tell us that Pitt's broad array of practical courses is just poorly publicized. "Pitt offers a variety of classes that provide practical experience," explains a 3L. "I found these classes to be most helpful. I just wish I knew about them sooner." Excellent law clinics, including tax and civil practice, provide abundant "opportunities for specialization and hands-on experience." Certificate programs are available in intellectual property, health law, environmental law, and, of course, international law.

The "remarkable [and] committed" faculty is mostly an "energetic and enthusiastic" bunch. Many professors "truly care about students and seem like they have a stake in their success." They are "nationally recognized theorists and practitioners [who remain] accessible and accommodating." One student gushes, "I have never met professors who are so dedicated to teaching and conveying a bit of their vast knowledge. They're genuine people and quite entertaining in class." There are "a few glaring exceptions," though. "Some of the professors here are outstanding," explains one student. "Some of the professors are adequate, but not outstanding." Still others are content to merely "lecture and leave."

Reviews of the administration are mixed. Critics argue that the "very unreliable [administration is] unduly rigid in some seemingly inane ways." Supporters call the administration "fabulous" and say that "the typical university bureaucratic red tape doesn't occur." One student complains, "It's like some sort of cruel joke the way they schedule classes." Students criticize Career Services as well. "The staff is inexperienced and ineffective at reaching out to all students," although the addition of new staff members that hold JD degrees will hopefully address these complaints. On the plus side, "Pittsburgh is a great city with a lot of opportunity if you are willing to look beyond the big firms." Clerkships and externships are plentiful, and summer employment is easy to find.

Pitt Law's facilities are "appropriately modern." Students say, "There is a surreal aura that surrounds the building"—in a good way, at least once you get past the "1970s-style, communist-compound" facade and the lack of natural sunlight. Inside, Pitt's facilities are "state-of-the-art, comfortable, [and] conducive to learning." Classrooms "have been recently renovated [and most come complete with] computers, PowerPoint, and video equipment." One student claims, "Getting the wireless and wired Internet connections working in all seats of all classrooms" would be an improvement, though. "The library is terrific. The accessibility of resources can't be beat," praises one student. "I can find everything I need there and help is always available."

Fredi G. Miller, Assistant Dean for Admissions and Financial Aid
3900 Forbes Avenue, Pittsburgh, PA 15260
Telephone: 412-648-1413 • Fax: 412-648-2647
E-mail: admissions@law.pitt.edu • Website: www.law.pitt.edu

Life

"School morale and pride [are high, and] there is a strong bond [among the] wonderful, cordial, [and] cooperative" Pitt students. "Most people are happy to share notes or explain a concept that someone is confused about. Students are encouraged to help each other learn rather than compete against each other, which makes for a warmer and less cutthroat atmosphere." It is also noted that "students are willing to give outlines to each other and even help one another in searching for jobs."

"The social atmosphere [at Pitt Law] is one of its strengths. There is not a lot of school community," though. In many respects, the students do their own thing. It is not unusual for students to form small and more or less autonomous cliques. Friendships within the cliques are tight, though. "I have become amazing friends with the students in my section," explains one student. "I've made friends I'll have for life," relates another.

Off campus, the culturally vibrant city of Pittsburgh has a lot to offer. The School of Law is located in the center of a neat, "very friendly" area. Excellent restaurants and bars are easily accessible. The cost of living is low. Pittsburgh is perennially rated among the Top 10 cities in the United States in which to live and work. It is also one of the safest cities in North America. But be warned, "parking is a nightmare."

Getting In

Incoming students at the 25th percentile have an LSAT score of 158 and a GPA of 3.1. Incoming students at the 75th percentile have an LSAT score of 162 and a GPA of 3.6. If you've taken the LSAT more than once, it's not a problem; Pitt Law considers your highest score when making its admission decision.

EMPLOYMENT INFORMATION

Career Rating	**76**
% employed within 9 months	98
Average starting salary	$66,000
State for bar exam	PA, VA, MD, NY, CA
Pass rate for first-time bar	82.5

Employers who frequently hire grads: Buchanan Ingersoll; Kirkpatrick & Lockhart; Morgan, Lewis, & Bockius; Jones Day; Pepper Hamilton; Eckert Seamans; Vorys Sater; Seymour & Pease.

Prominent Alumni: Richard Thornburg, former U.S. attorney general; Orrin Hatch, senator, Utah; Joseph Weis, senior judge for the third circut; Ruggerio Aldisert, senior judge for the ninth circuit.

Grads employed by field (%):	
Academic	2
Business/industry	15
Government	7
Judicial clerkships	9
Military	2
Private practice	63
Public interest	2

Academic Requirements

Clinical Program Required?	No
Legal Writing Course Requirement?	Yes
Legal Methods Course Requirement?	No
Legal Research Course Requirement?	Yes
Moot Court Requirement?	No
Public Interest Law Requirement?	No

ADMISSIONS

Selectivity Rating	**82**
# applications received	2,209
# applicants accepted	697
# acceptees attending	248
Average LSAT	160
LSAT Range	158–162
Average undergrad GPA	3.3
Application fee	$55
Regular application deadline	3/1
Regular notification	rolling
Rolling notification?	Yes
Early application program?	No
Transfer students accepted?	Yes
Evening division offered?	No
Part-time accepted?	No
LSDAS accepted?	Yes

Applicants Also Look At

American U., Case Western Reserve U., The George Washington U., Penn State U. MBA, Temple U., U. of Maryland, Villanova U.

International Students

TOEFL required of international students?	Yes
Minimum Paper TOEFL	600
Minimum Computer TOEFL	250

FINANCIAL FACTS

Annual tuition (resident)	$18,494
Annual tuition (nonresident)	$27,390
Books and supplies	$1,210
Room & board	$12,490
Financial aid application deadline	3/1
% first-year students receiving some sort of aid	85
% receiving some sort of aid	85
% of aid that is merit-based	25
% receiving scholarships	46
Average grant	$10,000
Average loan	$22,680
Average debt	$68,777

University of Richmond
School of Law

INSTITUTIONAL INFORMATION

Public/private	private
Student/faculty ratio	15:1
% faculty part-time	54
% faculty female	32
% faculty minority	4
Total faculty	105

SURVEY SAYS . . .

Great research resources
Beautiful campus

STUDENTS

Enrollment of law school	480
% male/female	53/47
% out-of-state	55
% full-time	100
% minority	11
% international	3
# of countries represented	27
Average age of entering class	24

ACADEMICS

Academic Experience rating	**84**
Professors interesting rating	77
Professors accessible rating	81
Hours of study per day	4.75

Academic Specialties

Civil procedure, commercial law, constitutional law, corporation securities law, criminal law, environmental law, intellectual property law, international law, labor law, legal history, property, taxation.

Advanced Degrees Offered

JD, 3 years.

Combined Degrees Offered

JD/MBA, 4 years; JD/MURP, master's in urban planning, 4 years; JD/MHA, master's in health administration, 4 years; JD/MSW, social work, 4 years; JD/MPA, master's in public administration, 4 years.

Academic Requirements

Clinical Program Required?	No
Legal Writing Course Requirement?	Yes
Legal Methods Course Requirement?	Yes

Academics

Students at the University of Richmond School of Law contend that it is "deserving of a stronger national reputation." The "first-year program is solidly grounded in the fundamentals and includes a strong emphasis on legal thinking and writing" in the form of the four-semester lawyering skills curriculum. "There is a strong emphasis on practical skills" as well. "The practical experiences afforded [to] students are extremely varied and relevant, [for the city of Richmond,] students have access to clinical experiences with the U.S. Fourth Circuit Court of Appeals, U.S. District Court, and the Supreme Court and Court of Appeals of Virginia." Many municipal courts are located near the school as well, "as is the whole of state government—the legislature, the attorney general, and executive agencies."

Professors show a "willingness to stop everything and spend time helping students with class work, job hunting, or life in general." They are "very adept at explaining difficult material," too. Also, in the "very small [classes,] professors actively memorize names, faces, and interests." So "don't think that you can be a wallflower here." Students say, "Professors are definitely fans of the Socratic Method, [and] you will feel their wrath if you haven't done the reading. The administration is extremely competent and accessible, [often going] out of its way to provide students with a fostering environment, guidance, and a strong alumni network." There are complaints, like "tuition is too high," course selection "is slim," and there is "an over-reliance on adjunct faculty to provide the upper-level curriculum." These part-time professors "can be hit-or-miss." Still, "it's hard to argue with the fact that two of the 2L law skills instructors are State Supreme Court Justices."

Some students say that "Career Services is especially great. They run all kinds of programs and are always willing to drop what they're doing to go over another cover letter with you or to help you with whatever crisis you might be having." The law school is "well connected" in Virginia. This is "the school to attend if you plan to practice in the Richmond area." Other students say that's exactly the problem. "The CSO at Richmond is really only prepared to assist students in finding a job in Virginia and the Richmond metro area, [not] in the other 49 states. If you want to go anywhere else, you are on your own."

The facilities are excellent. "A large lake in the middle of campus, gothic-style [architecture, and] lots of huge trees provide a serene setting for students to engage in the study of law." On the inside, "UR must be one the most wired law schools in the United States." Amenities include "wireless Internet, video camera and playback, surround sound, and a moot courtroom that makes the Supreme Court jealous." Students are "required to buy laptops, [and] every classroom and study carrel" is Internet-enabled. "The bathrooms badly need renovation," though, and the library "could be more attractive," but it is definitely practical.

Life

"Most of the students are really friendly [and] relaxed" at Richmond. "There's very little cutthroat competition [because] the harsh, competitive nature of law school, although present, is muted by the ever-present push to create a warm atmosphere." One student admits, "There is a healthy dose of competitiveness, but it's just that: healthy."

Michelle Rahman, Associate Dean for Admissions
Law School Admissions Office, University of Richmond, VA 23173
Telephone: 804-289-8189 • Fax: 804-287-6516
E-mail: lawadmissions@richmond.edu • Website: http://law.richmond.edu

Students call the "lack of diversity [within the law school] a big problem." The University of Richmond isn't nicknamed "University of Rich Kids" for nothing. Students "tend to be very Republican" and conservative, but there is also a strong, close-knit liberal community." Mostly, politics is a sideshow at best. "There is no political activism at our law school." There are "numerous school-sponsored events," though. "Hardly a week goes by when there is not at least one opportunity for free food. The school finances on-site parties for students [with kegs and food] about five times each semester, and the Student Bar Association throws a Halloween party every year." School-wide socials are called Down Unders, and they are reportedly legendary. There are "not many social opportunities for older students, married students, or those who may live a distance from the school."

The surrounding city of Richmond is the capital city of Virginia. It's "a great city to live and study in—not too small to be boring, not too big to be a distraction." Students say Richmond is "really beautiful [and replete] with lots of great old houses. Also, it's only 90 minutes to Washington, DC or Virginia Beach." At some point, pretty much "every student falls in love with the city and wants to stay here after graduation."

Getting In

Admitted students at the 25th percentile have an LSAT score of 159 and a GPA of 3.16. Admitted students at the 75th percentile have an LSAT score of 163 and a GPA of 3.61. Those are competitive, but not absolutely forbidding numbers. A little less than one in four applicants are accepted.

EMPLOYMENT INFORMATION

Career Rating	**79**
% employed within 9 months	93
Average starting salary	$58,551
State for bar exam	NC, NY, FL, VA, DC
Pass rate for first-time bar	95

Employers who frequently hire grads: Baker Botts, Christian & Barton, Hirschler Fleischer, Hogan & Hartson, Hunton & Williams, Jackson & Kelly, Kaufman & Canoles, Kennedy Covington, Leclair Ryan.

Prominent Alumni: Lawrence L. Koontz, justice, Virginia Supreme Court; Harvey E. Schlesinger, U.S. District Court judge, middle district of Florida.

Grads employed by field (%):	
Business/industry	15
Government	5
Judicial clerkships	21
Military	3
Private practice	52
Public interest	2

Legal Research Course Requirement?	Yes
Moot Court Requirement?	Yes
Public Interest Law Requirement?	No

ADMISSIONS

Selectivity Rating	**86**
# applications received	2,400
# applicants accepted	553
# acceptees attending	158
Average LSAT	161
LSAT Range	159–163
Average undergrad GPA	3.4
Application fee	$35
Regular application deadline	1/15
Regular notification	4/15
Rolling notification?	Yes
Early application program?	No
Transfer students accepted?	Yes
Evening division offered?	No
Part-time accepted?	No
LSDAS accepted?	Yes

Applicants Also Look At

American University, College of William & Mary, George Mason University, The George Washington University, University of Virginia, Wake Forest University, Washington and Lee University.

International Students

TOEFL required of international students?	Yes
TOEFL recommended of international students?	Yes
Minimum Paper TOEFL	650

FINANCIAL FACTS

Annual tuition	$25,510
Books and supplies	$1,200
Tuition per credit	$1,270
Room & board (on/off-campus)	$5,664/$8,100
Financial aid application deadline	2/25
% first-year students receiving some sort of aid	87
% receiving some sort of aid	94
% of aid that is merit-based	22
% receiving scholarships	78
Average grant	$7,410
Average loan	$27,390
Average total aid package	$30,555
Average debt	$74,025

University of St. Thomas*

School of Law

INSTITUTIONAL INFORMATION	
Public/private	private
Student/faculty ratio	14:1
Affiliation	Roman Catholic

SURVEY SAYS . . .

Great library staff
Beautiful campus
Students love Minneapolis, MN

STUDENTS	
Enrollment of law school	362
% male/female	49/51
% full-time	100
% minority	15

ACADEMICS	
Academic Experience rating	**83**
Professors interesting rating	93
Professors accessible rating	90
Hours of study per day	4.98

Combined Degrees Offered

JD/MBA; Catholic studies, JD/MA; public policy, JD/MA; professional psychology, JD/MA; social work, JD/MSW.

Academic Requirements	
Clinical Program Required?	No
Legal Writing Course Requirement?	No
Legal Methods Course Requirement?	No
Legal Research Course Requirement?	No
Moot Court Requirement?	No
Public Interest Law Requirement?	No

Academics

If you are passionate, opinionated, and love a great debate, you will fit right in at the University of St. Thomas School of Law. On this spirited (and spiritual) campus, "the administration and faculty encourage rigorous debate in the community," and "ideas are challenged from the left and the right." But don't worry about entering a war zone. While "students are not shy about expressing differing opinions," the whole community maintains an attitude that is respectful and collegial. All viewpoints, no matter how radical, are accepted at UST, a place where "even the most conservative students have established life-long friendships with the most liberal students." A student jokes, "I wish Congress could learn to cooperate the way the students have here at UST. The freedom to express one's religious, social, and political views here is liberating!"

A Catholic institution, UST "strongly encourages students to evaluate their behavior as a lawyer with their values, morals, and beliefs" and "promotes integration of spiritual values into professional practice." The school also places an "emphasis on social justice." While students praise the open-minded attitude that pervades the campus, prospective students should be aware of the Catholic influence on the community. "Make no mistake that it is a Catholic law school," advises one first-year student. "We pray before class begins and every event is related to Catholic issues." Even so, UST students say that the stress on moral thinking is valuable, even for non-Catholics. A 1L explains, "I am not Catholic, and I appreciate the emphasis on thinking about how my values will impact my career as an attorney."

University of St. Thomas School of Law is about as young as they come, having graduated its first JD class in May 2004. One decided benefit to attending such a new institution is getting to study in clean, modern, freshly built facilities. Students rave about UST's "absolutely beautiful" building in downtown Minneapolis, which boasts "an amazing library, state-of-the-art technology, and ample space for students to gather." There's also a palpable excitement within the campus environment, as the students and faculty work to build a name for the school. "It is very easy to access the faculty and administration with concerns regarding the direction in which the law school is going," reports one student. There are drawbacks, too, to the newness of the school, like the fact that "many of the bureaucratic processes have not solidified yet." This lack of formalized procedures "can produce unnecessary obstacles" or lead to an absence of communication between students and the administrative brass.

Despite how young the school is, St. Thomas has already assembled an outstanding team of accomplished, accessible, and talented faculty. "The faculty members with whom I have had contact are not only brilliant scholars and exceptional teachers, but they also care deeply about the students they teach," writes one student. "UST Law has extremely bright and energetic faculty who are accessible and really care about the students," adds another. Some would like to see the administration work harder to recruit minority faculty, however, but "there is a broad range of diversity among the faculty" in terms of politics, opinion, and teaching style.

*Provisionally approved by the ABA

Cari Haaland, Director of Admissions
1000 LaSalle Avenue, Minneapolis, MN 55403
Telephone: 651-962-4895 • Fax: 651-962-4876
E-mail: lawschool@stthomas.edu • Website: www.stthomas.edu/law

Graduates are in good shape if they want to practice in the Twin Cities. University of St Thomas is located "close to a great number of businesses and law firms—many of whom have become involved in the school." The school makes the most of its location through an "excellent mentoring program" in which "each student is assigned a personal mentor for each of their three years." The school also offers a variety of other extracurricular programs to help students succeed, such as "a free academic success program to prepare students for the rigors of law school" and "frequent symposiums about various topics of interest," which are described as "a favorite with students." With a focus on social justice, the school also promotes other community-based projects, including the fall and spring "day of service" program.

Life

Students at St. Thomas love a debate, but they also know when to lay down their arguments and have some fun together. "Regardless of what is said in class, be it a conversation about abortion, gay rights, or living wages, we can always find time to walk across the street and have a beer," writes one student. Indeed, competition is kept at bay, and students say they "help each other learn" and that "most students participate in a study group or two." When they aren't hitting the books, students take advantage of downtown Minneapolis, where "there are many places to go grab lunch or a beer after a tough week of class." On campus, there is a "strong social life" and students enjoy events reminiscent of college, such as "a Halloween party, a talent show, a spring fling, Bar Review parties every Thursday night, [and] the annual chili cook-off."

Getting In

University of St. Thomas evaluates students on the following six criteria: LSAT score, undergraduate grades, writing skills, leadership potential, motivation, and demonstrated ability to contribute to UST's mission of promoting ethics in the law. In fall 2004, the median LSAT score for entering students was 156.

ADMISSIONS

Selectivity Rating	**74**
# applications received	746
# applicants accepted	369
# acceptees attending	147
Average LSAT	156
LSAT Range	152–160
Average undergrad GPA	3.4
Application fee	$50
Regular application deadline	7/1
Regular notification	rolling
Rolling notification?	Yes
Early application program?	No
Transfer students accepted?	Yes
Evening division offered?	No
Part-time accepted?	No
LSDAS accepted?	Yes

International Students

TOEFL required of international students?	Yes

FINANCIAL FACTS

Annual tuition	$24,630
Books and supplies	$1,300
Average grant	$22,048
Average loan	$12,000

University of San Diego
School of Law

INSTITUTIONAL INFORMATION

Public/private	private
Student/faculty ratio	15:1
Affiliation	Roman Catholic
% faculty part-time	37
% faculty female	30
% faculty minority	12
Total faculty	92

SURVEY SAYS . . .

Beautiful campus
Students love San Diego, CA

STUDENTS

Enrollment of law school	1,040
% male/female	55/45
% out-of-state	30
% full-time	74
% minority	28
Average age of entering class	24

ACADEMICS

Academic Experience rating	**80**
Professors interesting rating	83
Professors accessible rating	70
Hours of study per day	4.14

Academic Specialties

Administrative law, children's advocacy, civil procedure, commercial law, constitutional law, criminal law, human rights law, intellectual property law, international law, public interest law, taxation.

Advanced Degrees Offered

JD, 3 years day, 4 years evening; master of law, general, taxation, business and corporate, international, comparative law for foreign attorneys, approximately 1 year.

Combined Degrees Offered

JD/MBA; JD/MA, master of arts in international relations; JD/IMBA, international master in business administration.

Academic Requirements

Clinical Program Required?	No
Legal Writing Course Requirement?	Yes

Academics

The University of San Diego School of Law offers a "rigorous academic program [in a] laid-back" sunny Southern California setting. Students at this mid-sized private school rave about their professors' ability to instill "an excitement about the law profession, [leaving students] eager to learn more." This "outstanding [faculty] inspires admiration and confidence" in its pupils. Students are impressed at how professors manage to snag "high profile legal scholars, including Supreme Court justices, to judge competitions and give lectures." It also "appears that the school is constantly recruiting more renowned professors every semester." USD's laid-back atmosphere means professors are relaxed, and "Socratic embarrassments are less painful." One student relays that if professors "call on you, and you indicate that you're not prepared, they'll say 'sorry!'" Professors know students on a personal level, and they are easily "accessible out of the classroom." One student attests, "The professors are wonderful, but you'd better go to class because they know who is there and who isn't."

Students at USD feel the administration could use a little work. The registration process "is unwieldy and disorganized, [and getting classes] is very hard even as a third-year." Plus, adding or dropping a class can be a total hassle. However, students say that the administration is "efficient, [or, at least,] good about letting us know about the really important things." There is some harping about USD's "bizarre 93-point grading system, [that is] like no other in the world." People find it "confusing" and fear that potential employers may not understand it either. One positive note on the career front is USD's "strong network of lawyers in San Diego, [alums who are] very loyal and happy to mentor new USD graduates." A law degree from USD "provides a great 'in' at local firms, many of which are composed completely of USD alumni."

The facilities at USD are beautiful on the outside, but a bit low-tech on the inside. Fortunately, the technology concerns of the students have been addressed as wireless internet is now available in most classrooms and the library. Students also complain of "broken chairs and power outlets." But the "beautiful" law library, the "largest in the county," is a certainly a perk. At USD, the research facilities are "extensive, helpful librarians [along with] a funny and smiling student employee" are always around to help. If only there were "more comfortable chairs [and] more Internet connections," students might be satisfied.

Life

Students love that San Diego is "a big, multicultural city that still manages to retain a small-town feeling." The "location, weather, and urban planning [make] a city with lots to offer without the downsides of larger cities like air pollution and outrageous traffic congestion." The USD campus itself is "beautiful"—there are "manicured lawns and palm trees and fountains all on a bluff overlooking Mission Bay." One student gloats, "We often study by the beach and think about how lucky we are."

Carl Eging, Assistant Dean of Admissions and Financial Aid
5998 Alcala Park, San Diego, CA 92110
Telephone: 619-260-4528 • Fax: 619-260-2218
E-mail: jdinfo@SanDiego.edu • Website: www.law.sandiego.edu

Maybe it's the "sunny weather that allows for the happy dispositions [at USD, but] everyone's pretty cheery." While there's some element of competition, for the most part, students are laid-back and helpful. "With the exception of a few cutthroats, most students seem a little apologetic about the inevitable competition that hits in November and April." Students say, "There are definitely people who don't mind sharing outlines and notes." Plus, there is a "mentoring program with 1Ls and upper classmen, which provides a great support network" for students adjusting to the pressures of the first year. Socially, "there is a lot to do to meet people and get involved." The Bar Review "held almost every weekend at a different local bar or club, [is a] fun way to get to know San Diego and some of your classmates," notes one student. "The SBA Halloween Party and Spring Party are also a great time," though not everyone enjoys these activities. One student actually grumbles, "The social life at my law school is too good—law school is not supposed to be fun." Politically, students lean toward the right. It's a Catholic school, although students say, "You would never know it. Those who want to participate in religious services can find them, but they are not thrust upon anyone." That doesn't mean students don't wish for "more multicultural or multireligious events [and] more diversity" in general.

Getting In

At San Diego, admitted students at the 25th percentile have an LSAT score of 160 and a GPA of 3.2. Admitted students at the 75th percentile have an LSAT score of 164 and a GPA of 3.6. San Diego offers several joint degrees and also accepts part-time and evening students.

EMPLOYMENT INFORMATION

Career Rating	**81**
% employed within 9 months	90
Average starting salary	$75,400
State for bar exam	CA, NV, AZ
Pass rate for first-time bar	79

Employers who frequently hire grads: Gibson Dunn & Crutcher, Cooley Godward, Gray Cary, Pillsbury Winthrop, Department of Justice, Luce Forward, Heller Ehrman, Snell & Wilmer.

Prominent Alumni: Rochelle Berkley, congresswoman from Nevada; Michael Thorsness, Thorsness, Bartolotta and McGuire; Michael Ferrara, Ferrara, Rosetti, & DeVoto.

Grads employed by field (%):	
Academic	1
Business/industry	13
Government	10
Judicial clerkships	3
Military	1
Other	2
Private practice	65
Public interest	5

Legal Methods Course Requirement?	No
Legal Research Course Requirement?	Yes
Moot Court Requirement?	Yes
Public Interest Law Requirement?	No

ADMISSIONS

Selectivity Rating	**87**
# applications received	6,020
# applicants accepted	1,374
# acceptees attending	352
Average LSAT	163
LSAT Range	160–164
Average undergrad GPA	3.4
Application fee	$50
Regular application deadline	rolling
Regular notification	rolling
Rolling notification?	Yes
Early application program?	No
Transfer students accepted?	Yes
Evening division offered?	Yes
Part-time accepted?	Yes
LSDAS accepted?	Yes

Applicants Also Look At

Loyola Marymount University, Santa Clara University, University of California—-Davis, University of California—-Hastings, University of California—-Los Angeles, University of San Francisco, University of Southern California.

International Students

TOEFL required of international students?	Yes
Minimum Paper TOEFL	600
Minimum Computer TOEFL	250

FINANCIAL FACTS

Annual tuition	$30,670
Books and supplies	$867
Fees per credit	$1,035
Tuition per credit	$1,035
Room & board	$15,987
Financial aid application deadline	3/1
% first-year students receiving some sort of aid	85
% receiving some sort of aid	83
% receiving scholarships	37
Average grant	$14,000
Average loan	$26,000
Average total aid package	$43,500
Average debt	$71,400

UNIVERSITY OF SAN FRANCISCO
SCHOOL OF LAW

INSTITUTIONAL INFORMATION

Public/private	private
Student/faculty ratio	17:1
Affiliation	Roman Catholic
% faculty part-time	64
% faculty female	30
% faculty minority	20
Total faculty	89

SURVEY SAYS . . .

Great research resources
Great library staff
Beautiful campus
Students love San Francisco, CA

STUDENTS

Enrollment of law school	716
% male/female	49/51
% out-of-state	20
% full-time	82
% minority	31
% international	1
Average age of entering class	26

ACADEMICS

Academic Experience rating	**85**
Professors interesting rating	80
Professors accessible rating	86
Hours of study per day	4.8

Academic Specialties

Intellectual property law, international law, public interest.

Advanced Degrees Offered

Master of laws LLM in international transactions and comparative law, 1 year; master of laws LLM in intellectual property, 1 year.

Combined Degrees Offered

JD/MBA, 4 years.

Academic Requirements

Clinical Program Required?	No
Legal Writing Course Requirement?	Yes
Legal Methods Course Requirement?	No
Legal Research Course Requirement?	Yes
Moot Court Requirement?	Yes

Academics

A pretty, private school with a relaxed California attitude, University of San Francisco is a remarkably accommodating and comfortable place to study law. While course work is rigorous, students appreciate the small class sizes, as well as the personal relationships they develop with the teaching and administrative staff. So while you may expect all the typical challenges of law school at USF, you never have to worry about being singled out or sabotaged. A 1L shares, "All my professors are amazing in their respective ways and foster a comfortable learning atmosphere, which was quite a departure from the horror stories I heard about the first year." Another adds, "Professors are all experienced both in the classroom and in practice. This faculty is more impressive than I had expected, but there's no pretension."

Outside of the lecture hall, students feel at ease with their accomplished teachers, turning to them as mentors and friends. Students maintain that "more than anything, the faculty and staff want to see you succeed" and that professors "make themselves available at all times and always take extra time in answering your questions." Such close interactions aren't restricted to the classroom or office hours, either: "I have shared numerous meals, drinks, and laughs with professors who treat me like a colleague," recalls one seasoned 3L.

With this kind of precedent set by the faculty, the whole campus follows suit, creating a learning atmosphere that is decidedly intimate and cooperative. At USF, "students are supportive and down to earth...the librarians offer great advice, and the facilities are pleasant and comfortable to be in." On that note, "all the facilities are brand, spanking-new," and "the views from the library and the lounge are spectacular."

Many students feel that the best part of a USF education is the school's "high emphasis on integrity and public interest law," a "commitment to training socially responsible attorneys." In support of its progressive vision, "USF has numerous clinical opportunities through which students are able to gain practical legal experience under faculty and practitioner supervision." Students are active in many political and community issues, such as "closing down the School of the Americas, water resource allocation in the Western US, and custodial care within the Family Courts." In addition, "every summer students travel to the Hague to take part in the Human Rights Commission of the UN and others travel to the Deep South to take part in defending Death Row inmates." While the school's mission and philosophy may encourage students to seek public interest positions after graduation, many point out that it's difficult to make ends meet in a public service career after graduating from a private law school in pricey San Francisco. Many feel that "considering the crushing debt burden that a USF graduate emerges with, [the school] needs to place more resources toward loan repayment and forgiveness programs in order to ensure that competent young attorneys can feel comfortable going into public interest positions."

Financial worries aside, students have nothing but praise for the USF administration. "Things get done quickly and efficiently" here. "You don't have to wait in long lines or deal with mean and bitter staff like at so many public institutions." In addition, students applaud the administration for taking "consistent and deliberate steps in increasing the caliber of both the faculty and the facilities." Over the past decade, "the quality of the incoming students [has been] increasing and the profile of the faculty rising." On top of that, students appreciate the "many resources available for extra help," such as "a useful

ALAN GUERRERO, DIRECTOR OF ADMISSIONS
2130 FULTON STREET, SAN FRANCISCO, CA 94117
TELEPHONE: 415-422-6586 • FAX: 415-422-6433
E-MAIL: LAWADMISSIONS@USFCA.EDU • WEBSITE: WWW.LAW.USFCA.EDU

(free) tutoring program, which gives us the opportunity to learn from former students who have excelled."

Life

Perched on a hilltop in one of the world's most famous cities, "USF's location in San Francisco gives it a unique vibe as well as exposure to all that the city offers." USF students take advantage of their ideal surroundings through the "weekly bar nights" and report that there are "always a multitude of things to do a heartbeat away: museums, opera, hiking, nightclubs. You name it, San Francisco's got it!" On campus, "the general academic atmosphere is welcoming, not fierce and competitive." A 2L elaborates, "Students are driven, but not out to get each other, and I really appreciate that about the school." In addition, the school boasts a number of campus clubs and activities. A 3L writes that "our politically active student body has started over 15 new student organizations in the last two years, and student-sponsored activities are actively supported by the administration."

USF values a diverse and progressive educational experience, and this attitude is reflected in the student body. "Every class is diverse, not just in terms of race or gender but also in terms of experience and knowledge. I am always learning something new from a fellow classmate," writes one 2L. Students from USF, however, also have some things in common. For example, "the average student has taken time off after college," and the student population tends to be very liberal in their politics, which is not surprising given the school's location and commitment to public service. A 3L warns, "I would not recommend USFSL if you are a militant Rush Limbaugh/Ann Coulter Republican. You will find yourself in a very small minority."

Getting In

University of San Francisco carefully evaluates each applicant's pre-law transcripts and curriculum, admitting students whose undergraduate coursework demonstrates success in a broad set of liberal arts courses, as well as an emphasis on oral and written skills. Last year, the school received over 4,500 applications for just 250 first-year spots. The biggest five feeder undergraduate schools are all members of the University of California system.

EMPLOYMENT INFORMATION

Career Rating	**79**
% employed within 9 months	90
Average starting salary	$78,700
State for bar exam	CA
Pass rate for first-time bar	65

Employers who frequently hire grads: Bingham & McCutcheon; Morgan, Lewis & Brockius; Reed Smith; Wilson, Sonsini, Goodrich & Rosati.

Prominent Alumni: Justice Ming Chin, California Supreme Court; Kevin Ryan, U.S. attorney; Judge Saundra B. Armstrong, U.S. District Court Northern California.

Grads employed by field (%):

Academic	1
Business/industry	11
Government	13
Judicial clerkships	3
Other	12
Private practice	58
Public interest	2

Public Interest Law Requirement?	No

ADMISSIONS

Selectivity Rating	**84**
# applications received	4,581
# applicants accepted	1,122
# acceptees attending	257
Average LSAT	160
LSAT Range	157–162
Average undergrad GPA	3.3
Application fee	$60
Regular application deadline	2/1
Regular notification	rolling
Rolling notification?	Yes
Early application program?	No
Transfer students accepted?	Yes
Evening division offered?	Yes
Part-time accepted?	Yes
LSDAS accepted?	Yes

Applicants Also Look At

Golden Gate University, Loyola Marymount University, Santa Clara University, University of California—Davis, University of California—Hastings, University of the Pacific, University of San Diego.

International Students

TOEFL required of international students?	Yes
Minimum Paper TOEFL	600
Minimum Computer TOEFL	250

FINANCIAL FACTS

Annual tuition	$28,977
Books and supplies	$900
Fees per credit	$2
Tuition per credit	$1,037
Room & board (on/off-campus)	$9,780/$12,000
Financial aid application deadline	2/15
% first-year students receiving some sort of aid	92
% receiving some sort of aid	90
% of aid that is merit-based	16
% receiving scholarships	30
Average grant	$10,950
Average loan	$28,500
Average total aid package	$24,000
Average debt	$79,143

University of South Carolina

School of Law

INSTITUTIONAL INFORMATION

Public/private	public
Student/faculty ratio	17:1
% faculty female	22
% faculty minority	4
Total faculty	45

SURVEY SAYS . . .

Diverse opinions accepted in classrooms

Great library staff

STUDENTS

Enrollment of law school	759
% male/female	56/44
% out-of-state	20
% full-time	100
% minority	10
# of countries represented	3
Average age of entering class	24

ACADEMICS

Academic Experience rating	**73**
Professors interesting rating	79
Professors accessible rating	66
Hours of study per day	4.39

Academic Specialties

Corporation securities law, environmental law, international law, property, taxation.

Advanced Degrees Offered

JD, 3 years.

Combined Degrees Offered

JD/master's in international business, 4 years; JD/MBA, 4 years; JD/master of public administration, 4 years; JD/master's in criminal justice, 4 years; JD/master's in economics, 4 years; JD/master's in accounting, 4 years; JD/master's in social work, 4 years; JD/master's in environmental sciences, 4 years; JD, earth, environmental resource management; JD/masters in human resources; JD/masters in health administration.

Academic Requirements

Clinical Program Required?	No
Legal Writing Course Requirement?	Yes

Academics

Students primarily come to University of South Carolina School of Law to gain "a solid practical education" in the law. Interestingly, the University of South Carolina is currently the only ABA accredited law school in the state and thusly "enjoys a premium on some very bright SC students." Furthermore, since it is the lone accredited law school statewide, students tend to monopolize judicial clerkships in the Palmetto State. While "there is not a huge selection of classes," many students say that the greatest strengths of the school are "the various programs of emphasis available," including environmental and business law.

At South Carolina, there is a consensus that while some professors are "very good, involved with the students [and] come to class prepared and ready to inspire," the teachers are really "a mixed bag." One student explains, "Professors are hit-or-miss: some are fantastically intelligent and stimulating, others are grumpy and drab." But as one wag points out, "It is widely accepted that they are the best in the state." When they finish with the wisecracks about their professors, some students raise concerns about losing their instructors to other law schools.

Students appreciate that the administration is doing "the best they can trying to run a law school on a shoestring." Students say, "The administration is helpful and attentive to student needs. The Student Affairs Office is especially good, and the Career Services office tries the best it can." There is an excitement running through the student body about the new dean who is "fresh with vision and passion." One student thinks the new dean is "going to inject the school with a new identity and take it to another level."

With its location in Columbia, the capital of South Carolina, the school allows students access to the South Carolina State Supreme Court and Court of Appeals, and the Federal District Court. One student explains, "The best part about USC is the network both within the school and with the state bar. If you want to practice law in South Carolina, you should attend USC or prepare to explain why you didn't at most job interviews. It's also much easier to get a state or federal clerkship in SC coming from USC than from out-of-state." Furthermore, the alumni base is also very strong, as "over 85 percent [of the lawyers] in the state graduated from this law school and practical experience with them abounds."

Students are quick to point out that the physical plant is in need of a serious facelift: "The law school is decorated in communist Russia circa 1980." Though one student points out the invisible benefit to such Spartan surroundings, "You don't have many distractions to look at!" The law school has attempted a few cosmetic changes, and some ask what you can really complain about when you "have wireless Internet [and] plenty of plugs for laptops." There are whispers of constructing a new building, but many students have their doubts.

803-777-6605, Director of Admissions
701 South Main Street, Columbia, SC 29208
Telephone: 803-777-6605 • Fax: 803-777-7751
E-mail: usclaw@law.law.sc.edu • Website: www.law.sc.edu

Life

The atmosphere at the school is "pleasantly friendly." As in most law schools, "there is an undercurrent of competition," but students tell us that it's "more a sense of competition against the system—the grading curve—than competition against individuals." A "sense of community" pervades the student body, so that "everyone helps everybody else." A student explains further, "There are only one or two [classmates] that I would not feel comfortable hanging out and drinking a beer with after class." Most seem to realize that while "grades and jobs are important, [so is] learning and realizing that [they] will all be practicing together for the next 30 or 40 years." Furthermore, there is "a good selection of active student organizations [and] quite a few social events sponsored by the school as well." It is important to note that the students assure us that the school is "not overly social, [but rather that] there is a good mix" of things to do.

Politically, there are "a lot of liberals and a lot of conservatives [on campus, and] both groups are active and actually get along well."

Getting In

Admitted students at the 25th percentile have an LSAT score of 156 and a GPA of 3.1. Admitted students at the 75th percentile have an LSAT score of 160 and a GPA of 3.6. The law school admits full-time students only, but the school offers several interesting joint degree opportunities.

Legal Methods Course Requirement?	No
Legal Research Course Requirement?	Yes
Moot Court Requirement?	No
Public Interest Law Requirement?	No

ADMISSIONS

Selectivity Rating	**83**
# applications received	1,612
# applicants accepted	480
# acceptees attending	240
Average LSAT	158
LSAT Range	156–160
Average undergrad GPA	3.5
Application fee	$60
Regular application deadline	3/1
Regular notification	rolling
Rolling notification?	Yes
Early application program?	No
Transfer students accepted?	Yes
Evening division offered?	No
Part-time accepted?	No
LSDAS accepted?	Yes

International Students

TOEFL required of international students?	Yes

FINANCIAL FACTS

Annual tuition (resident)	$14,118
Annual tuition (nonresident)	$28,534
Books and supplies	$800
Room & board	$15,358
Financial aid application deadline	4/15
% receiving some sort of aid	79
% of aid that is merit-based	20
Average grant	$1,200
Average loan	$20,655
Average total aid package	$21,876
Average debt	$46,025

EMPLOYMENT INFORMATION

Career Rating	**75**
% employed within 9 months	97
Average starting salary	$51,220
State for bar exam	SC, NC, GA, TX, CA, FL, CO, DC, NY, NH, VA
Pass rate for first-time bar	85

Employers who frequently hire grads: Nelson Mullins Riley & Scarborough; Kennedy, Covington, Lobdell, & Hickman; Alston and Bird.

Prominent Alumni: Richard W. Riley, former U.S. Secretary of Education; Lindsay Graham, U.S. Senate; Karren J. Williams, Court of Appeals, Fourth Circuit; Joe Wilson, U.S. Congress.

Grads employed by field (%):	
Business/industry	6
Government	9
Judicial clerkships	27
Private practice	54
Public interest	3

THE UNIVERSITY OF SOUTH DAKOTA
SCHOOL OF LAW

INSTITUTIONAL INFORMATION

Public/private	public
Student/faculty ratio	17:1
% faculty part-time	1
% faculty female	19
Total faculty	16

SURVEY SAYS . . .

Diverse opinions accepted in classrooms
Great research resources
Great library staff

STUDENTS

Enrollment of law school	252
% male/female	56/44
% out-of-state	35
% full-time	99
% minority	7
% international	1
# of countries represented	2
Average age of entering class	25

ACADEMICS

Academic Experience rating	**67**
Professors interesting rating	71
Professors accessible rating	85
Hours of study per day	4.45

Academic Specialties

Environmental law, Indian law.

Combined Degrees Offered

JD/MBA, JD/MPA professional accountancy, JD/M education administration, JD/M English, JD/M history, JD/M political science, JD/M public administration, JD/M psychology, JD/M administrative studies.

Academic Requirements

Clinical Program Required?	No
Legal Writing Course Requirement?	Yes
Legal Methods Course Requirement?	Yes
Legal Research Course Requirement?	Yes
Moot Court Requirement?	No
Public Interest Law Requirement?	No

Academics

If you plan to practice law in the Mount Rushmore state, the University of South Dakota is the best place to lay the foundation for your career. If you want to study the law in South Dakota at an ABA-accredited law school, USD is the only place to do it. As such, attending USD has many advantages. Simply put, "USD students have unparalleled access to members of the South Dakota bar." And the school's ongoing "relationship with practicing attorneys and judges in the state provides an opportunity for quality hands-on education and guidance." The result of all this South Dakotan legal interconnectivity? "It is commonplace to find members of the SD Supreme Court, the attorney general, the governor of SD, local politicians, leaders of the various Indian Nations, SD state bar leaders, and numerous accomplished USD Law alumni walking the halls here." As if that weren't enough, USD offers a unique opportunity: "For one entire week each spring semester, the SD Supreme Court holds session at the USD Law School, taking great care to pick interesting and difficult cases to hear before the student body."

In addition to enhancing their educational experience, the school's legal connections create many opportunities for practice after graduation. A student explains, "South Dakota is a small bar, and the majority of lawyers in SD went to USD, and they look within the state to recruit first." Some feel, however, that the school is too singularly focused on South Dakota and that "students aren't encouraged to look for positions outside of the fall interview days or out of state." Some also feel their career opportunities could be enhanced with the addition of more practical, hands-on opportunities, such as moot court activities and internships.

Reflecting the small population of its home state, USD boasts a tiny student body and a good student-teacher ratio. Students say the small enrollment benefits them because they "get to know teachers and administrators on a much more personal basis." The result is a supportive academic atmosphere in which students look upon faculty and staff as mentors, not just instructors. Here you can expect to be a part of "a small and extremely close-knit community" where "the faculty and administration have a genuine concern for their students." "Professors take the time to work with us in the academic setting," writes one student, "but are interested in getting to know us personally outside of the classroom as well." Indeed, USD students agree that their professors and classmates have relationships that extend beyond the law. For example, one proud student boasts, "I've played golf with the dean, I've shared single malt scotches with a few professors, and I've spent countless hours discussing my personal life with members of the administration."

The school's affordable price tag is the icing on the cake. Without exception, students describe USD as a great bargain. Some go so far as to say it is "surely one of America's best kept secrets" and "a flat-out steal of a legal education." "You cannot beat the price, and the legal instruction is on par, and may even exceed, some of the top schools." With so much to offer for so little cash, it's also not surprising that USD boasts "an extremely low attrition rate."

JEAN HENRIQUES, ADMISSION OFFICER/REGISTRAR
414 EAST CLARK STREET, VERMILLION, SD 57069-2390
TELEPHONE: 605-677-5443 • FAX: 605-677-5417
E-MAIL: LAWREQ@USD.EDU • WEBSITE: WWW.USD.EDU/LAW

Life

Students describe their classmates as friendly and studious and tell us that the school maintains "a good blend of traditional and nontraditional students." But while "the correct harmony between the 'real' world and the 'academic' world are represented in every class," South Dakota isn't a very ethnically or culturally diverse state. As one student succinctly puts it, "Though USD tries, our student body diversity is sorely lacking." Located in a small town, USD is a tight-knit community where students socialize, study together, and build lasting friendships. In fact, "law students have been going to the same bar for what seems to be forever, so there is rarely a question of where to find your friends." While most students love the friendly and intimate atmosphere, some would prefer a more cosmopolitan environment. One disgruntled student goes so far as to describe the law school as offering an "overpriced high-school atmosphere, under the best of circumstances."

Getting In

The University of South Dakota School of Law seeks students who demonstrate intelligence, a strong desire to practice law (especially in the state of South Dakota), and commitment to helping others through legal advocacy. You are a competitive applicant here with a solid B undergraduate GPA and an LSAT score above 153.

EMPLOYMENT INFORMATION

Career Rating	**61**
% employed within 9 months	92
Average starting salary	$38,251
State for bar exam	SD, WI, IA, ND, SC
Pass rate for first-time bar	71

Employers who frequently hire grads: Eighth circuit court of appeals; U.S. district court; South Dakota Supreme Court; South Dakota Circuit Court; Minnehaha public defender, firms.

Prominent Alumni: Tim Johnson, U.S. senator; David Gilbertson, chief justice, South Dakota Supreme Court; Roger Wollman, U.S. Court of Appeals for the Eighth Circuit.

Grads employed by field (%):	
Business/industry	2
Government	23
Judicial clerkships	34
Other	2
Private practice	39

ADMISSIONS

Selectivity Rating	**73**
# applications received	469
# applicants accepted	169
# acceptees attending	73
Average LSAT	153
LSAT Range	150–156
Average undergrad GPA	3.3
Application fee	$35
Regular application deadline	rolling
Regular notification	rolling
Rolling notification?	Yes
Early application program?	No
Transfer students accepted?	Yes
Evening division offered?	No
Part-time accepted?	Yes
LSDAS accepted?	Yes

Applicants Also Look At

Creighton University, Drake University, Oklahoma City University, University of Nebraska—Lincoln, University of North Dakota, University of Wyoming, Washburn University.

International Students

TOEFL required of international students?	Yes
Minimum Paper TOEFL	600
Minimum Computer TOEFL	250

FINANCIAL FACTS

Annual tuition (resident)	$4,074
Annual tuition (nonresident)	$11,807
Books and supplies	$1,000
Fees per credit (resident)	$114
Fees per credit (nonresident)	$114
Tuition per credit (resident)	$136
Tuition per credit (nonresident)	$394
Room & board (on/off-campus)	$3,700/$5,937
% first-year students receiving some sort of aid	94
% receiving some sort of aid	91
% of aid that is merit-based	90
% receiving scholarships	25
Average grant	$1,000
Average loan	$18,434
Average total aid package	$18,851
Average debt	$53,500

University of Southern California
Law School

INSTITUTIONAL INFORMATION

Public/private	private
Student/faculty ratio	13:1
% faculty part-time	50
% faculty female	38
% faculty minority	16
Total faculty	106

SURVEY SAYS . . .

Diverse opinions accepted in classrooms
Great research resources
Great library staff
Abundant externship/internship/clerkship opportunities

STUDENTS

Enrollment of law school	630
% male/female	52/48
% out-of-state	47
% full-time	100
% minority	41

ACADEMICS

Academic Experience rating	**88**
Professors interesting rating	87
Professors accessible rating	86
Hours of study per day	3.74

Academic Specialties

Civil procedure, commercial law, constitutional law, corporation securities law, criminal law, environmental law, government services, human rights law, intellectual property law, international law, labor law, legal history, legal philosophy, property, taxation.

Advanced Degrees Offered

JD, 3 yrs.; LLM, 1 yr.; MCL, 1 yr.

Combined Degrees Offered

JD/MBA, JD/MPA, JD/PhD in economics, JD/MA in economics, JD/MA in international relations, JD/MA in communications management, JD/MA in philosophy, JD/MA in religion, JD/MSW, JD/master of real estate development, JD/master's of business taxation, JD/MS in gerontology, JD/MPP, JD/PHD California Institute of Tech., JD/MA in political science, JD/PHD in political science.

Academics

"Get ready to pay big bucks" if you want to go to the small University of Southern California Law School, home of "sun, sand, surf, cerveza, and civ pro. You get what you pay for, [though, and] the financial aid is great." Some of USC's strengths include, "small class sizes, [a] strong alumni network, [and a] cooperative learning environment." Students say, "The administration is incredibly friendly, helpful, and supportive." An "interdisciplinary approach" to legal studies is also a huge hit. Most faculty members "seem to have advanced degrees in law and another field." In addition, "there seems to be a special emphasis on teaching ability" among the USC faculty. These "incredibly accomplished and highly intelligent [professors are] also very welcoming" outside the classroom. So when the admissions staff "tells you that the professors are easy to access and talk to, they are telling the truth." Even academic "superstars are concerned with the students needs [and] respond to e-mails usually within a few hours." One student says, "Sure, they're on TV or in the paper, but they consider themselves professors first, and it shows in the classroom."

Job prospects are "great," according to students. "Career Services is very focused on guiding [students] into $130K-plus firm jobs" (though "there are lots of other opportunities" as well). "USC is the place to find higher salaries and the best job opportunities in the West Coast, especially Los Angeles." USC's legendary alumni network does wonders in this regard. If you don't want to work in Southern California, that's cool, too. "The 'Trojan family' runs strong throughout the country."

Students have a few gripes. There is a lack of "merit-based scholarships" for 2Ls and 3Ls. "Writing skills are not stressed enough," either. "They grade student legal writing classes on a curve, [which] seems ridiculous." Also, you won't be inundated with black-letter law at USC, which pleases some students and irks others. "I would like to pass the bar," asserts one student, "so a reduction in legal theory would be much appreciated." Furthermore, "there is not a huge range of classes or clinics." However, there are "superb" opportunities for clinical experience that are available at USC including the intellectual property clinic and "unique" post-conviction clinic, "which allows you to represent inmates in parole hearings as well as in court."

Students don't mince words with regard to the "generally drab, outdated, [and] depressing" law school exterior, calling it "an eyesore on the otherwise stunningly beautiful campus." According to one student, this "concrete cell-block [may or may not be] the ugliest building ever." On the bright side, "the classrooms are functional, [and] there is a lot of technology" all over campus. The library was recently renovated and a $1.5 million cafe was added this year.

Life

The "very politically liberal" students at USC are "laid-back [and] easy-going, with just a hint of pretentiousness." You'll find "a disturbing number of trust babies [and many] insanely privileged kids straight out of undergrad" as well. "The school has a reputation for being a 'friendly' place where people are not competetive," says one student. "This is completely true." Indeed most students find the "combination of camaraderie and competitiveness [to be] ideal. You're able to make friends and have an intense academic environment at the same time."

William Hoye, Associate Dean
USC Law School, Los Angeles, CA 90089-0074
Telephone: 213-740-2523 • Fax: 213-740-4570
E-mail: admissions@law.usc.edu • Website: www.law.usc.edu/

USC is "an extremely fun place to go to law school." It's nourishing, too. There is "lots of free food for club meetings and seminars." One student admits, "Throughout my first year, I spent next to nothing on food. My school fed me!" Students report, "During first year, students do not frequently attend social events together, [but] during second and third years, [social participation] increases dramatically as does the overall social life of the school." A popular social event is the Bar Review, which is held "every week at different LA hot spots [and] is a social paradise." One student says, "They are constantly organizing activities [as well, including] speakers, roundtables, and volleyball tournaments."

One potential downside to attending USC is that students usually choose to commute from numerous regions throughout LA due to the school's ultra-urban, downright rundown [location] amid impoverished neighborhoods." One student writes, "Few law students have less than a 30-minute commute." Students hasten to add that despite being somewhat dilapidated, the school's surroundings are generally "safe and secure." Also, "there are lots of cool places to live scattered throughout the Los Angeles area, [and] traffic is not so bad that a short commute will kill you."

Getting In

Admission to USC Law School is competitive. The school receives 7,000 applications for a little over 200 slots. The average LSAT score of students admitted to USC is 166 and the average GPA is 3.7.

EMPLOYMENT INFORMATION

Career Rating	**90**
% employed within 9 months	94.6
Average starting salary	$110,000
State for bar exam	CA, NY, DC, WA, TX
Pass rate for first-time bar	90

Employers who frequently hire grads: Private firms, corporations, federal judges, government, public interest nonprofits.

Prominent Alumni: Justice Joyce Kennard, California Supreme Court; Larry Flax, California Pizza Kitchen founder; Judge Dorothy Nelson, Court of Appeals, ninth circuit; Walter Zifkin, CEO of William Morris Agency; Carlos Moorehead, U.S. congressman.

Grads employed by field (%):	
Academic	2
Business/industry	18
Government	4
Judicial clerkships	1
Military	1
Private practice	70
Public interest	4

Academic Requirements

Clinical Program Required?	No
Legal Writing Course Requirement?	Yes
Legal Methods Course Requirement?	No
Legal Research Course Requirement?	Yes
Moot Court Requirement?	Yes
Public Interest Law Requirement?	No

ADMISSIONS

Selectivity Rating	**90**
# applications received	7,677
# applicants accepted	1,376
# acceptees attending	203
Average LSAT	166
LSAT Range	163–167
Average undergrad GPA	3.7
Application fee	$70
Regular application deadline	2/1
Regular notification	rolling
Rolling notification?	Yes
Early application program?	No
Transfer students accepted?	Yes
Evening division offered?	No
Part-time accepted?	No
LSDAS accepted?	Yes

Applicants Also Look At

Georgetown University, New York University, Stanford University, University of California—Berkeley, University of California—Los Angeles.

International Students

TOEFL required of international students?	No
TOEFL recommended of international students?	Yes

FINANCIAL FACTS

Annual tuition	$34,882
Books and supplies	$1,284
Room & board	$10,222
Financial aid application deadline	2/15
Average grant	$11,476
Average loan	$31,488
Average debt	$87,218

UNIVERSITY OF TENNESSEE
COLLEGE OF LAW

INSTITUTIONAL INFORMATION

Public/private	public
Student/faculty ratio	11:1
% faculty part-time	41
% faculty female	37
% faculty minority	7
Total faculty	70

SURVEY SAYS . . .

Great research resources
Beautiful campus

STUDENTS

Enrollment of law school	452
% male/female	50/50
% out-of-state	20
% full-time	100
% minority	13
Average age of entering class	24

ACADEMICS

Academic Experience rating	**90**
Professors interesting rating	90
Professors accessible rating	93
Hours of study per day	4.32

Academic Specialties

Advocacy, business transactions, dispute resolutions.

Advanced Degrees Offered

JD, 3 years, 6 semesters.

Combined Degrees Offered

JD/MBA, 4 years; JD/MPA, 4 years.

Academic Requirements

Clinical Program Required?	No
Legal Writing Course Requirement?	No
Legal Methods Course Requirement?	Yes
Legal Research Course Requirement?	No
Moot Court Requirement?	No
Public Interest Law Requirement?	No

Academics

When its students praise the University of Tennessee College of Law, they usually save their most enthusiastic cheers for its ability to "get students practical experience outside the classroom." The law school building houses a legal clinic, which "is a testament to its commitment to students learning practical knowledge balanced against academic instruction." Students love the fact that they can make the decisions as to how to grow in their education. "If you are business-minded, there is the business clinic. Advocacy your cup of tea? Then there is the advocacy clinic." Furthermore, "there are criminal internships, a new domestic violence program, and the list goes on." In the classroom, "the Socratic Method is limited typically to the first year of required courses, and then the professors begin getting your mind ready for the competitive world of law." One complaint seems to be that the college does not offer a broad enough range of classes to choose from each semester.

Students are glad that their college hires professors that are not only "distinguished in the field of law, [but are also] enthusiastic and personable." Students are amazed at the lengths some professors go to be available to them. For example, one student tells us, "When my evidence professor has to be out of town for a couple of days (even if it is on the weekend), he will give us the number to the hotel where he is staying and his mobile number, so we are never out of touch." Students feel the professors "treat them like colleagues rather than just law students." Even when they are not expecting it, professors are there for their students. One impressed student says, "I was sitting in the library complaining about and struggling with the tort concept of proximate cause, when a professor heard me and offered to explain the concept to me. I am not even in his class, nor did he know me. That is why I am proud to attend my law school: I am part of a family."

The administration at the college gets high marks from demanding students. The dean is "amazing, very warm and friendly, [and that] really sets the tone of the law school community." The people in the financial aid office "work extremely hard and really remove a great deal of stress from the students." Even the IT department get its props, since it "can fix practically anything that goes wrong with a laptop." From day one, students feel like they know what's going on at school and that they belong there. One student brings it together, "It really is a school where the students are the focus."

The college has "wireless Internet access throughout the school building," a huge plus for researching. The library facilities are "expansive and extremely comfortable, [and] all classrooms are set up to allow use of a laptop." One student gushes, "If you have to stay in one building for eight hours a day, this is a beautiful place to do it!"

DR. KAREN R. BRITTON, DIRECTOR OF ADMISSIONS, FINANCIAL AID AND CAREER SERVICES
1505 WEST CUMBERLAND AVENUE, KNOXVILLE, TN 37996-1810
TELEPHONE: 865-974-4131 • FAX: 865-974-1572
E-MAIL: LAWADMIT@LIBRA.LAW.UTK.EDU • WEBSITE: WWW.LAW.UTK.EDU

Life

Students describe the college as "the kind of place where you say hi to everyone you pass, whether you know them or not." Students sense "that everyone wants you to excel [in this] amazingly supportive environment." One student notes, "It's a very close-knit community." Socially, students feel at home among their fellow classmates. "I have made more friends in the few months that I have been in law school than I did in four years of undergrad," one student proudly states. One reason there is such a sense of belonging may be because UT has "numerous student organizations, ranging from the Black Law Student Association, to LAMBDA, to the Federalist Society." The camaraderie could also stem from the SBA hosting a "rump court" every Thursday night at a local watering hole, in addition to throwing Chilla (the Halloween party), organizing a riverboat cruise, and numerous other functions. Another possibility is the school itself, which "hosts a welcoming cocktail party, an awards dinner, and a professor-student Martin Luther King Day luncheon."

When you live in Knoxville, you are only "two hours from the Great Smoky Mountain National Park, [which provides] a beautiful place to get away for a weekend and spend time in your books," and only two and a half hours from Nashville.

Getting In

Students admitted to Tennessee at the 25th percentile have an LSAT score of 155 and a GPA of 3.3. Admitted students at the 75th percentile have an LSAT score of 160 and a GPA of 3.7. The school enrolls fewer than 500 students and is a full-time only institution.

EMPLOYMENT INFORMATION

Career Rating	**78**
Job placement rate (%)	97
Average starting salary	$59,090
State for bar exam	TN
Pass rate for first-time bar	89

Employers who frequently hire grads: Law firms, judges, government agencies, corporations, public interest organizations, and academic institutions.

Prominent Alumni: Howard H. Baker Jr., government/public service; Joel A. Katz, entertainment lawyer; Jim Hall, former chair, NTSB; Art Stolnitz, former vice president, Warner Bros.; Penny White, former Tennessee Supreme Court justice.

Grads employed by field (%):	
Academic	1
Business/industry	7
Government	3
Judicial clerkships	10
Military	2
Private practice	75
Public interest	2

ADMISSIONS

Selectivity Rating	**86**
# applications received	1,556
# applicants accepted	316
# acceptees attending	156
Average LSAT	158
LSAT Range	155–161
Average undergrad GPA	3.6
Application fee	$15
Regular application deadline	3/1
Regular notification	3/15
Rolling notification?	Yes
Early application program?	No
Transfer students accepted?	Yes
Evening division offered?	No
Part-time accepted?	No
LSDAS accepted?	Yes

Applicants Also Look At

Mercer University, Samford University, University of Georgia, University of Kentucky, University of Memphis, University of North Carolina at Chapel Hill, Vanderbilt University.

International Students

TOEFL required of international students?	Yes
Minimum Paper TOEFL	213

FINANCIAL FACTS

Annual tuition (resident)	$7,734
Annual tuition (nonresident)	$20,472
Books and supplies	$1,360
Fees per credit (resident)	$58
Fees per credit (nonresident)	$86
Tuition per credit (resident)	$430
Tuition per credit (nonresident)	$1,138
Room & board	$7,400
Financial aid application deadline	3/1
% first-year students receiving some sort of aid	91
% receiving some sort of aid	89
% receiving scholarships	36
Average grant	$7,240
Average loan	$17,328
Average total aid package	$18,840
Average debt	$46,511

University of Texas at Austin
School of Law

INSTITUTIONAL INFORMATION

Public/private	public
Student/faculty ratio	17:1
% faculty part-time	39
% faculty female	30
% faculty minority	11
Total faculty	114

SURVEY SAYS . . .

Diverse opinions accepted in classrooms
Great research resources
Great library staff
Students love Austin, TX

STUDENTS

Enrollment of law school	1,503
% male/female	55/45
% out-of-state	16
% full-time	100
% minority	28
% international	1
# of countries represented	18
Average age of entering class	25

ACADEMICS

Academic Experience rating	**90**
Professors interesting rating	84
Professors accessible rating	68
Hours of study per day	3.54

Academic Specialties

Commercial law, constitutional law, criminal law, environmental law, international law, labor law, property.

Advanced Degrees Offered

LLM, 1 year.

Combined Degrees Offered

JD/MBA; JD/MPA in public affairs; JD/MA in Latin American studies; JD/MS in community and regional planning; JD/MA in Russian, East European, & European studies; JD/MA in Middle Eastern studies; informal combined programs leading to the JD & PhD in government, history, or philosophy.

Academic Requirements

Clinical Program Required?	No

Academics

Students at the University of Texas at Austin School of Law receive "the most bang for the buck in Texas" and arguably the best bargain in American legal education. UT boasts a "very ideologically diverse [faculty,] a relatively relaxed atmosphere, [and] unmatched" alumni support. Tuition is "relatively low," and graduates rack up very little debt. The professors are "dedicated, fascinating, [and] hip." Students feel, "There is a serious commitment to teaching [and] a refusal to hire poor teachers." One student writes, "What I particularly appreciate is how they encourage us to try new areas of law. They show such enthusiasm and knowledge in the courses they teach that even the most boring or difficult course can be interesting and not so difficult after all." Another student brags, "In my first semester, I had the leading expert in admiralty law teach torts by singing songs on guitar, a contracts professor who could have been the stunt-double-professor in *The Paper Chase*, and a criminal law professor who clerked for Thurgood Marshall." Also, "The depth of constitutional law instruction is amazing."

Texas has "some great clinics," including a mental health clinic, a capital punishment clinic, and an actual innocence clinic, in which students screen and investigate claims of innocence from prison inmates. "The administration needs to place more emphasis on legal writing skills," though. "The law school clearly values the academic reputation of its graduates more than their ability to practice law," complains one student. "Major tuition hikes" are an additional source of irritation. Public interest law could use more support, too. Students note smaller classes "would be nice." On the plus side, though, "going to such a large law school [guarantees a] wide range of courses."

When the time comes to get a real job, "the academic reputation enjoyed by Texas is unsurpassed in this part of the country." The school is "right in the middle of one of the nation's biggest legal markets [and maintains a] strong presence in the business and law community, [which translates into] ample employment opportunities." If you want to get out of the Lone Star State, no problem: more than 60 percent of the employers who interview on campus are from other states. Also, since 1995, eight UT grads have clerked for the United States Supreme Court. Of course, you can't please everybody. "Career Services focuses too much on students that want to go into a big-firm environment." One student advises, "If you are looking for something different, you are pretty much on your own."

"The facilities are generally nice" at UT. "The law school occupies an oddly cobbled together set of interconnected buildings representing a number of architectural styles." Unfortunately, "the interior (the part that really matters) is bland and uninspiring." Students say, "The cleaning staff is terrible, and more classrooms with plugs at every seat [and] better acoustics" would help. The "pretty [and] wonderfully comprehensive [law library is] one of the largest in the country, [though,] thanks to the generous donations of alumni." Students are pleased that "the school is complete with wireless Internet throughout."

Life

Is UT competitive? It depends on whom you ask. According to one school of thought, "a lot of kids are really tough, [and] competition among 1Ls can be fierce." Others tell us that "UT is a place where people cooperate. Cutthroat competitiveness is a rarity." Still other students say, "It is easy to find a group of slackers who will bond together in laziness."

Monica Ingram, Assistant Dean for Admissions
727 East Dean Keeton Street, Austin, TX 78705-3299
Telephone: 512-232-1200 • Fax: 512-471-2765
E-mail: admissions@mail.law.utexas.edu • Website: www.utexas.edu/law

"Many political, social viewpoints are represented here," but lots of those viewpoints come from Texas. "The high Texas-resident quota for enrollment stifles diversity of students. Therefore, most students are born and raised in Texas, have not traveled abroad, and want to go into corporate law to make a lot of money in order to buy fancy cars and big houses." So, while the law school population is pretty impressively diverse in terms of ethnicity, "the school could improve by having more students with life and work experience, and by accomplishing diversity in other ways than taking lots of kids from El Paso."

Because the school's law student population "is so large, there's not a real feeling of camaraderie." Nevertheless, "UT Law School is very social" and active, if you want it to be (and if you can find a place to park). "There really is something for everyone," promises one student. "There are a wide variety of student organizations, from political or ethnic groups, to journals or practice-oriented organizations, to a hugely successful variety show written, produced, and performed by law students." Students can take advantage of "tons of opportunities to do extracurricular things off-campus" as well. The "absolutely fantastic [and] truly fascinating [metropolis of Austin, Texas is] the nation's best kept secret for fun, music, nature, food, drinks, politics, people, and culture." One student relays that it's "also a nice place to live, work, and go to school, [in spite of] the high cost of living."

Getting In

Admitted students at the 25th percentile have an LSAT score of 161 and a GPA of 3.4. Admitted students at the 75th percentile have an LSAT score of 167 and a GPA of 3.8. If you take the LSAT more than once, the school will average your scores. Note also that nonresident enrollment can only constitute 20 percent of the student body. Hence, it's almost certainly harder to get admitted if you are not a resident of Texas.

EMPLOYMENT INFORMATION

Career Rating	**92**
% employed within 9 months	99
Average starting salary	$91,950
State for bar exam	TX
Pass rate for first-time bar	92

Employers who frequently hire grads:
Baker Botts, LLP; Fulbright & Jaworski, LLP; Vinson & Elkins, LLP; Haynes & Boone, LLP; Bracewell & Patterson, LLP.

Prominent Alumni: Joseph D. Jamail Jr., owner, Jamail & Kolius Law Firm; Kay Bailey Hutchison, United States senator; Frederico Pena, former secretary of transportation; Rodney G. Ellis, Texas State senator.

Grads employed by field (%):	
Academic	1
Business/industry	7
Government	10
Judicial clerkships	13
Military	2
Private practice	61
Public interest	6

Legal Writing Course Requirement?	Yes
Legal Methods Course Requirement?	No
Legal Research Course Requirement?	Yes
Moot Court Requirement?	Yes
Public Interest Law Requirement?	No

ADMISSIONS

Selectivity Rating	**95**
# applications received	6,095
# applicants accepted	956
# acceptees attending	425
Average LSAT	165
LSAT Range	161–167
Average undergrad GPA	3.6
Application fee	$70
Regular application deadline	2/1
Regular notification	4/1
Rolling notification?	No
Early application program?	Yes
Early application deadline	11/1
Early application notification	1/31
Transfer students accepted?	Yes
Evening division offered?	No
Part-time accepted?	No
LSDAS accepted?	Yes

Applicants Also Look At

The George Washington University, Southern Methodist University, University of California—Los Angeles, University of Houston, Vanderbilt University.

International Students

TOEFL required of international students?	Yes
Minimum Computer TOEFL	213

FINANCIAL FACTS

Annual tuition (resident)	$11,480
Annual tuition (nonresident)	$22,620
Books and supplies	$948
Room & board (on/off-campus)	$7,088/$7,742
Financial aid application deadline	3/31
% receiving some sort of aid	93
% of aid that is merit-based	25
% receiving scholarships	93
Average grant	$5,000
Average loan	$18,500
Average total aid package	$27,650
Average debt	$65,000

University of Toledo
College of Law

INSTITUTIONAL INFORMATION

Public/private	public
Student/faculty ratio	13:1
% faculty part-time	35
% faculty female	37
% faculty minority	4
Total faculty	49

SURVEY SAYS . . .

Diverse opinions accepted in classrooms
Abundant externship/internship/clerkship opportunities

STUDENTS

Enrollment of law school	517
% male/female	58/42
% out-of-state	34
% full-time	67
% minority	7
% international	1
# of countries represented	2
Average age of entering class	27

ACADEMICS

Academic Experience rating	**83**
Professors interesting rating	88
Professors accessible rating	90
Hours of study per day	4.3

Academic Specialties

Civil procedure, commercial law, constitutional law, corporation securities law, criminal law, environmental law, government services, human rights law, intellectual property law, international law, labor law, legal history, legal philosophy, property, taxation.

Advanced Degrees Offered

JD, 3 or 4 years.

Combined Degrees Offered

JD/MBA, 3 to 3.5 years; JD/MSE, 3 to 3.5; JD/master's in public administration, 3 to 3.5; JD/master's in criminal justice, 3 to 3.5 years.

Academic Requirements

Clinical Program Required? No

Academics

With faculty who are "both intellectually stimulating and approachable" and "infinite resources," students at the University of Toledo can't stop singing the praises of their friendly, Midwestern school. Take it from an enthusiastic 1L, who exclaims, "the only way to comprehensively encapsulate my educational experience at UT is: Awesome, baby!" In particular, students tells us that the school's most laudable characteristic is the kindness and accessibility of their teachers, who "bend over backward to help students succeed, in academics, job searches, and life in general." Need an illustration? Take this one from a 2L: "Our property professor, who was about to nail us with our final exam, sought us out in the law library to see if we had questions rather than waiting for us to show up at his office hours." No wonder that most students agree that "it's the human component that makes this school shine."

In addition to their friendliness, students praise the quality and diversity of the teaching staff as "a superb mixture of old-fashioned ethical and young, modern, enthusiastic teachers." A 2L writes, "I feel like I can learn every aspect of any type of law just by picking the brains of the professors." Students at Toledo also appreciate the college's strong focus on the practical applications of their education. "The professors have a lot of experience in legal practice," explains one student. "It is always helpful to hear someone talk about actual cases and issues they have dealt with." Another adds, "One of our greatest strengths is the faculty and their real-world experiences. They use these experiences to demonstrate how the law is practiced in the real world."

The practical wisdom imparted by professors is augmented by the college's extensive and active extracurricular programs. At Toledo "there are an enormous number of avenues for students to get a chance to shine: moot court (appellate and trial advocacy), law review, clinics, externships, clerkships, independent research, student bar association, and many more student organizations. A student only has to put forth an effort to get a world of experience."

Students admit that the college "could update the decor, especially in the library," but they are impressed with the level of technology available in the classrooms, which "are designed for the online experience—with SmartBoards and wireless Internet access." Some point out, however, that the human component may not be as modern as the hardware. Students confide that "the SmartBoards occasionally outfox the professors" and that "the wireless networking throughout the building seems to encourage more web surfing than listening."

While most students are enrolled in the traditional, full-time day program, the college also operates an evening program geared toward students with careers or families. According to participants in the evening program, the administration does a good job of catering to the diverse needs of the student body, including student parents. A participant in the evening program explains, "It would be nice to see more events tailored to nontraditional evening students. Other than that I think they do an admirable job." The college also offers several joint degree programs (JD-MPH, JD-ME [engineering], JD-MBA, and JD-MCJ), as well as several certificates of concentration in environmental law, intellectual property law, international law, and labor and employment law.

Carol E. Frendt, Assistant Dean for Admissions
2801 West Bancroft, Toledo, OH 43606
Telephone: 419-530-4131 • Fax: 419-530-4345
E-mail: law.admissions@utoledo.edu • Website: www.utlaw.edu

Life

Students at Toledo say their pretty, suburban campus is a laid-back and friendly place to study law. As part of the University of Toledo, law students can make use of the whole UT campus, which means they have "access to the undergraduate fitness facilities" or "can take part in undergraduate club sports like flag football, softball, and water polo, and attend some sporting events as well." The 500 students enrolled in the law school hail from "a wide range of backgrounds and places" and enjoy a generally non-competitive and collegial atmosphere. Students also enjoy socializing together and many attend the weekly Bar Reviews sponsored by the SBA. Students also like the school's location in the small, Midwestern city of Toledo. In Toledo, "the cost of living is low." However, "if you want a major city, Chicago, Detroit, Cleveland, Cincinnati, and Columbus . . . are only one to four hours away." And if you want an international experience, the Canadian border is about that far away, too.

Getting In

To be accepted by the University of Toledo College of Law for the full-time day program, you should aim for an LSAT score in the high 150s and a B+ undergraduate GPA. The college enrolls around 90 full-time students in each entering class, for which the college receives approximately 1,000 applications annually. Part-time programs are slightly less competitive in their admissions requirements.

EMPLOYMENT INFORMATION

Career Rating	77
% employed within 9 months	97
Average starting salary	$57,143
State for bar exam	OH, MI
Pass rate for first-time bar	83

Employers who frequently hire grads: Shumaker, Loop & Kendrick; Eastman & Smith; Kilpatrick Stockton; Jones Day; McDermott, Will & Emery; Thompson Hine.

Prominent Alumni: Honorable Judith Lanzinger, justice, Ohio Supreme Court; Honorable Deborah Agosti, retired, chief justice, State of Nevada; Joseph Farnan, U.S. District Court, Wilmington, DE; C. Raymond Mullins, U.S. Bankruptcy Court, Atlanta, GA.

Grads employed by field (%):	
Academic	6
Business/industry	14
Government	15
Judicial clerkships	11
Other	4
Private practice	43
Public interest	7

Legal Writing Course Requirement?	Yes
Legal Methods Course Requirement?	No
Legal Research Course Requirement?	Yes
Moot Court Requirement?	No
Public Interest Law Requirement?	No

ADMISSIONS

Selectivity Rating	**82**
# applications received	1,099
# applicants accepted	251
# acceptees attending	86
Average LSAT	157
LSAT Range	153–159
Average undergrad GPA	3.6
Application fee	$40
Regular application deadline	rolling
Regular notification	rolling
Rolling notification?	Yes
Early application program?	No
Transfer students accepted?	Yes
Evening division offered?	Yes
Part-time accepted?	Yes
LSDAS accepted?	Yes

International Students

TOEFL required of international students?	No
TOEFL recommended of international students?	No

FINANCIAL FACTS

Annual tuition (resident)	$11,511
Annual tuition (nonresident)	$21,755
Books and supplies	$1,750
Fees per credit (resident)	$55
Fees per credit (nonresident)	$55
Tuition per credit (resident)	$480
Tuition per credit (nonresident)	$906
Room & board (off-campus)	$7,385
Financial aid application deadline	8/1
% first-year students receiving some sort of aid	98
% receiving some sort of aid	97
% of aid that is merit-based	17
% receiving scholarships	46
Average grant	$10,654
Average loan	$18,774
Average total aid package	$21,708
Average debt	$49,779

UNIVERSITY OF TULSA
COLLEGE OF LAW

INSTITUTIONAL INFORMATION

Public/private	private
Student/faculty ratio	14:1
Affiliation	Presbyterian
% faculty part-time	32
% faculty female	35
% faculty minority	10
Total faculty	72

SURVEY SAYS . . .

Great research resources
Great library staff

STUDENTS

Enrollment of law school	614
% male/female	57/43
% out-of-state	60
% full-time	84
% minority	21
% international	1
# of countries represented	7
Average age of entering class	28

ACADEMICS

Academic Experience rating	**77**
Professors interesting rating	81
Professors accessible rating	91
Hours of study per day	4.25

Academic Specialties

Alternative dispute resolution, environmental law, government services, health law, international law, Native American law, practical skills.

Advanced Degrees Offered

LLM degrees offered in American law for foreign lawyers, and in American Indian and indigenous law (academic or research track). LLM students take a minimum of 24 units over a 1- to 2-year period.

Combined Degrees Offered

History, industrial/organizational psychology, geosciences, biological sciences, anthropology, accounting, taxation, business administration, clinical psychology, computer science, English. Each joint degree program takes approximately 4 years to complete.

Academics

While the academic program at this mid-sized Southwestern law school is undeniably tough, Tulsa law students say they are soothed by their college's friendly environment. With a low student-faculty ratio, students are on a first-name basis with their accomplished instructors. On top of that, "class sizes, for the most part, are small, which encourages class participation." By almost all accounts, professors are "interested, accessible, and knowledgeable in their fields," and outside the lecture hall "the faculty open-door policy is real rather than pro forma." What's more, they consider and support each student as individuals. As one 1L attests, "As a mother of two young children, the staff and faculty here have bent over backward to help me create a schedule that will work for me and my family." "I love the personal feeling at TU Law," echoes a 2L.

Students laud the "outstanding Native American Law program and LL.M. for international students," as well as the new certificate program in entrepreneurial law. Beyond course work, many mention the quality of the school's three legal clinics in health law, older American law, and Creek Nation Indian law, saying that these programs "do amazing work" within the greater community. Indeed, TU students praise the fact that "the student body cares about making a difference." While students get an excellent blend of practical and theoretical education through course work and clinics, many feel the school could improve by "requiring students to take more bar-oriented courses." A 2L explains, "The school should require more courses that prepare students for the bar. We have a lot of flexibility in scheduling, which is wonderful, but when I graduate, I want to make sure I have adequately covered the bar material."

Like the faculty, "the administration is always there to help you." A new dean was just named to lead the college. With regards to that, many feel that "it is important that the new dean continue with the progress that has been made" in the recent past. However, given the "the willingness of the student body to be involved, stay involved, and develop and improve the school," students are optimistic that the college will continue its climb in quality and prestige. Students also tell us that "the research facilities and the library are outstanding," and "the library staff is helpful and knowledgeable and the library has been ranked very well."

As graduation approaches, "Career Services goes out of their way to help you find a job that is right for you." The staff "suggests all types of opportunities that you may not have ever thought of and give you the means to find that perfect job." On top of that, 35 percent of TU students receive scholarship awards and tell us that "the scholarship program is wonderful," ensuring a less stressful postgraduation job search. A 2L writes, "I received a scholarship, and I expect to have NO academic debt when I graduate with a joint JD/Master of Taxation."

George Justice, Assistant Dean of Admissions and Financial Aid
3120 East Fourth Place, Tulsa, OK 74104-3189
Telephone: 918-631-2709 • Fax: 918-631-3630
E-mail: george-justice@utulsa.edu • Website: www.law.utulsa.edu

Life

University of Tulsa attracts students from across the nation and a majority of current students hail from outside Oklahoma. However, "while we have students from a variety of states, the student body is not very diverse in ethnicity." For the size of the student population, however, "the number of student organizations is very broad, and this allows students many leadership opportunities." Off campus, many claim that surrounding Tulsa is a great place to get a JD, and students appreciate the fact that "the cost of living is reasonable enough to live well as a poor student on loans." In addition, "Tulsa is a beautiful town" with all the friendliness of a small community. A 2L writes, "Tulsa is small, but it is nice to see the people you know from school when you go out at night."

On the whole, TU is a friendly and cooperative environment. A 2L warns, however, that "while the students are friendly, there is definitely a competitive edge." Nonetheless, students enjoy being in the trenches with each other, saying their classmates are "unrivaled in their intellect, integrity, and amiability." A 3L writes, "We stress together, eat together, study together, and talk about our wives/husbands together." Adds another, "I have made some of my best friends at the University of Tulsa."

Getting In

Tulsa Law, like all law schools, admits students whose test scores and academic background suggest they will be successful in the study of law. It is also a little more welcoming of older students than many of its peers. Tulsa Law admits students from across the nation, and over half of the student body hails from outside Oklahoma.

EMPLOYMENT INFORMATION

Career Rating	71
% employed within 9 months	87
Average starting salary	$50,238
State for bar exam	OK, TX, MO, FL, GA
Pass rate for first-time bar	82

Employers who frequently hire grads:
Tulsa law firms.

Prominent Alumni: Chadwick Smith, chief of the Cherokee Nation; Drew Edmondson, Oklahoma attorney general; David Barclay Waller, deputy director general, International Atomic Energy Agency.

Grads employed by field (%):	
Academic	5
Business/industry	13
Government	16
Judicial clerkships	4
Military	1
Private practice	58
Public Interest	3

Academic Requirements

Clinical Program Required?	No
Legal Writing Course Requirement?	Yes
Legal Methods Course Requirement?	Yes
Legal Research Course Requirement?	Yes
Moot Court Requirement?	No
Public Interest Law Requirement?	No

ADMISSIONS

Selectivity Rating	**70**
# applications received	1,437
# applicants accepted	535
# acceptees attending	233
Average LSAT	151
LSAT Range	148–162
Average undergrad GPA	3.2
Application fee	$0
Regular application deadline	rolling
Regular notification	rolling
Rolling notification?	Yes
Early application program?	No
Transfer students accepted?	Yes
Evening division offered?	No
Part-time accepted?	Yes
LSDAS accepted?	Yes

Applicants Also Look At

Baylor University, Oklahoma City University, Saint Louis University, Southern Methodist University, Texas Wesleyan University, University of Arkansas—Fayetteville, University of Oklahoma.

International Students

TOEFL required of international students?	Yes

FINANCIAL FACTS

Annual tuition	$23,392
Books and supplies	$1,500
Tuition per credit	$950
Room & board (on/off-campus)	$6,358/$9,820
Financial aid application deadline	4/1
% first-year students receiving some sort of aid	85
% receiving some sort of aid	89
% of aid that is merit-based	25
% receiving scholarships	35
Average grant	$8,500
Average loan	$20,506
Average total aid package	$30,249
Average debt	$76,503

UNIVERSITY OF UTAH
S. J. QUINNEY COLLEGE OF LAW

INSTITUTIONAL INFORMATION

Public/private	public
Student/faculty ratio	13:1
% faculty part-time	51
% faculty female	38
% faculty minority	19
Total faculty	65

SURVEY SAYS . . .

Diverse opinions accepted in classrooms
Great research resources
Great library staff
Students love Salt Lake City, UT

STUDENTS

Enrollment of law school	408
% male/female	60/40
% out-of-state	23
% full-time	100
% minority	11
% international	1
# of countries represented	9
Average age of entering class	28

ACADEMICS

Academic Experience rating	**89**
Professors interesting rating	85
Professors accessible rating	82
Hours of study per day	4.62

Academic Specialties

Commercial law, constitutional law, criminal law, environmental law, government services, international law.

Advanced Degrees Offered

LLM, environmental law, 1 year.

Combined Degrees Offered

JD/MPA, 4 years; JD/MBA, 4 years.

Academic Requirements

Clinical Program Required?	No
Legal Writing Course Requirement?	Yes
Legal Methods Course Requirement?	Yes
Legal Research Course Requirement?	Yes
Moot Court Requirement?	No
Public Interest Law Requirement?	No

Academics

The University of Utah S. J. Quinney College of Law's "small classes amazing faculty," and cheap in-state tuition make it quite a "bang for your buck." Professors are "great mentors [who are] very responsive to questions through e-mail or visits to their offices." In class, most professors "present the material in an interesting way." One student reports, "My contracts professor does such an amazing job of bringing the material to life that I was in a euphoric buzz after learning the contractual staples of offer and acceptance. Let me assure you, these topics are not inherently invigorating." The U's faculty leans "liberal [but is] as intellectually diverse as faculties come." Students say, "The mountains of Utah subsidize faculty salaries, [bringing an] impressive arsenal of legal scholars." A few professors even moonlight as bigwig judges.

"The academic work is rigorous, [and] the small class sizes allow everyone, [1Ls included,] to participate in discussions that can get quite animated." The Socratic method is popular but not overused. "I've found that the faculty at this law school provides an effective balance between the Socratic Method, lecture, and discussion," observes one student. The first-year legal writing program "is extremely well-taught [and] good writing is continuously stressed. Clinical programs are strong." Students do complain, though, that the College of Law does not "offer enough diversity in class times and credits so that students can build efficient schedules," so getting the classes you want can be difficult.

The "ambitious Career Services office" gets mixed reviews. There are abundant opportunities available for clerkships, and "the Salt Lake City legal community is very committed to the law school." However, "Utah is a highly competitive legal job market, [and] access to jobs outside of Utah is terrible." During on-campus interviews, "it's generally just Utah employers, with a few out-of-state employers sprinkled in the mix."

The "not-quite-up-to-par [physical facilities] are a little dated, but they do the job." We hear that "student carrels are the size of a matchbox [and that] classroom tables are uncomfortable." Plus, the U desperately "needs more restroom space," especially in the "horrible" women's rooms. But on the bright side, "technology is impressive [and] the library and computer labs are great," too. Students say, "A fund-raising campaign will soon begin to raise money for a new structure." In the mean time, "some of the class rooms aren't state-of-the-art, and classroom space is limited, but what can you expect from a public law school that hires tremendous faculty and still charges students a reasonable amount for tuition?"

Life

Students at the U cannot agree on just how competitive their "very small" school is. On the one hand, we hear that there's "a definite undercurrent of ladder climbing, [and that certain students] are always talking about how they need to be better than the next guy." On the other hand, "people share notes and outlines a lot." One student explains, "There are always going to be annoying people in class, but one of the best things about this school is how friendly people are and how much they want to help you succeed."

KARIN JACOBSON, COORDINATOR FOR ADMISSIONS
332 SOUTH 1400 EAST, ROOM 101, SALT LAKE CITY, UT 84112-0730
TELEPHONE: 801-581-7479 • FAX: 801-581-6897
E-MAIL: ADMISSIONS@LAW.UTAH.EDU • WEBSITE: WWW.LAW.UTAH.EDU

The average student "is older than the average at other schools," and one student estimates that "about 50 percent" of the students are married and that "of those, at least 50 percent have kids." Ethnic diversity is "very poor," but as one person shrugs, "We are in Utah, after all." Politically, "there are very conservative students who are members of the Church of Jesus Christ of Latter-day Saints, flaming liberals, [and a few] middle-of-the-roaders." Overall, there is a "very cooperative environment, [and students find it] very refreshing to see a die-hard liberal having an earnest and respectful hallway discussion with a hard-core conservative." However, "the university makes efforts to bridge the social divide between Mormon and non-Mormon" students. And not everyone experiences the cooperative environment. "Half the student body won't talk to you," claims one student, "either because you're Mormon or because you're not."

"The quality of life is very high [at the U, where] there are groups for everyone—single, married, minority, gun-rights," you name it. While "the drinking laws here are not the greatest, there are always Bar Reviews, SBA functions, and tailgates" for anyone interested. "Clean, gorgeous [Salt Lake City is a] conservative town [with] a good Western feel to it." One student says, "SLC has lots of culture, good public transportation, tons of sushi restaurants, extremely low housing costs, and truly friendly people." Also, being located just "20 minutes from the mountains [means] the location is fabulous for anyone interested in outdoor sports." Skiing, snowboarding, and mountain biking are "fantastic."

Getting In

The average LSAT score for admitted students is a very, very solid 160. Admitted students at the 25th percentile have an LSAT score of 158 and a GPA of 3.4. Admitted students at the 75th percentile have an LSAT score of 163 and a GPA of 3.8. If you take the LSAT more than once, the U will average your scores, but if you can show an improvement of six points or more, they will take the higher score. You can become a Utah resident after approximately three semesters.

EMPLOYMENT INFORMATION

Career Rating	77
Job placement rate (%)	93
Average starting salary	$64,075
State for bar exam	UT, CA, NV, AZ, ID
Pass rate for first-time bar	88

Prominent Alumni: Roberta Riley, staff attorney for Planned Parenthood of Washington; Honorable Stephen Anderson, Court of Appeals, tenth circuit; Honorable Richard Howe, former chief justice Utah Supreme Court; Tom Green, senior vice president for law & administraton, Dell Computer; Honorable Nancy Rice, Colorado Supreme Court.

Grads employed by field (%):	
Academic	1
Business/industry	13
Government	23
Judicial clerkships	9
Private practice	52
Public interest	2

ADMISSIONS

Selectivity Rating	**86**
# applications received	1,264
# applicants accepted	321
# acceptees attending	132
Average LSAT	160
LSAT Range	156–162
Average undergrad GPA	3.6
Application fee	$50
Regular application deadline	2/1
Regular notification	rolling
Rolling notification?	Yes
Early application program?	No
Transfer students accepted?	Yes
Evening division offered?	No
Part-time accepted?	No
LSDAS accepted?	Yes

Applicants Also Look At

Arizona State University, Brigham Young University, University of Arizona, University of Colorado, University of Denver, University of Oregon, University of Washington.

International Students

TOEFL required of international students?	Yes
Minimum Paper TOEFL	600
Minimum Computer TOEFL	250

FINANCIAL FACTS

Annual tuition (resident)	$9,559
Annual tuition (nonresident)	$21,075
Books and supplies	$1,930
Room & board	$8,190
Financial aid application deadline	3/15
% first-year students receiving some sort of aid	87
% receiving some sort of aid	82
% of aid that is merit-based	13
% receiving scholarships	42
Average grant	$2,852
Average loan	$14,946
Average total aid package	$17,484
Average debt	$44,840

UNIVERSITY OF VIRGINIA
SCHOOL OF LAW

INSTITUTIONAL INFORMATION

Public/private	public
Student/faculty ratio	14:1
% faculty part-time	54
% faculty female	15
% faculty minority	7
Total faculty	170

SURVEY SAYS . . .

Great research resources
Beautiful campus

STUDENTS

Enrollment of law school	1,100
% male/female	58/42
% out-of-state	54
% full-time	100
% minority	17
Average age of entering class	24

ACADEMICS

Academic Experience rating	**98**
Professors interesting rating	94
Professors accessible rating	84
Hours of study per day	3.99

Academic Specialties

Commercial law, constitutional law, corporation securities law, criminal law, environmental law, human rights law, intellectual property law, international law, labor law, legal history, legal philosophy, taxation.

Advanced Degrees Offered

SJD, doctor of juridical science; LLM, master of laws, 1 year, full-time; JD, 3 years, full-time.

Combined Degrees Offered

JD/PhD, government; JD/MA, bioethics, history, government, economics, English, international relations, philosophy, sociology; JD/MBA, administration, 4 years, full-time; JD/MPA; JD/MALD; JD/MPH; JD/MP; JD/MS, accounting.

Academic Requirements

Clinical Program Required?	No
Legal Writing Course Requirement?	Yes

Academics

At the University of Virginia School of Law, "the faculty is an amazing compilation of experts who are focused on the life of the law school and give generously to students." One student writes, "Professors are available to meet with students outside of class to answer questions and even discuss issues and implications well beyond the scope of class." But it is more than accessibility that students admire about their instructors. "I've never met such devoted teachers, interesting individuals, and talented academic minds! The quality of the teaching is far above what I could have ever expected," gushes another student. Yet while their intellectual capacities may reach to the heavens, when it comes to interacting with their students on a social level, Virginia professors are definitely down to earth. "As a student at UVA Law, you will go out to lunch with professors, join them for poker games, and compete against them in softball games," one student assures us. Hence, the widely held belief among Virginia law students that professors bring a "healthy mix of theoretical genius and practical experience to the classrooms, [and that] some even have a sense of humor."

The school's "administration is cooperative and highly accessible [and is also] quick to note the hardworking and high-caliber faculty and students, [but is] never satisfied being 'one of the best'" law schools in the country. Therefore, they are constantly striving to improve the place. Students reserve particular praise for the dean, who is one of "the most brilliant people [many students] have ever met, [has a] magnetic personality, [and is] universally respected by faculty and students." Administrative complaints center on the cost (it's really high, even for residents of Virginia) and the fact that grades "really need to get posted faster. The slow turnaround is especially disadvantageous to 1Ls looking for jobs in the spring." And while "Career Services could stand to broaden its horizons" in terms of the types of firms they bring to campus to interview students, it almost doesn't matter if you limit the conversation to sheer employability of Virginia graduates. "Employers (including judges) know that UVA produces well-trained attorneys" in almost all areas of the law.

As far as programs go, one student tells us, "The law school has recently initiated several interdisciplinary programs utilizing the strengths of the medical and business schools. I think these are great ideas and hope to see them further" developed. There are a few programs, however, that students feel the need to gripe about. "The Legal Research & Writing program is either under-funded or under-appreciated in its value to the students. First-years are graded on a pass/fail basis, with no incentive to work hard, and the [teacher to student] ratio of 1 to 30 in writing classes is terrible for promoting any improvement in legal writing and/or research," writes ones student. "The school needs more resources devoted to public service opportunities," adds another.

The classrooms and facilities at Virginia "are state of the art." There is "a fairly new, nicely designed building, convenient lockers, computer labs and social spaces, and an extensive library with knowledgeable staff." Sometimes law students feel it's "too good because we always have undergraduates and even other graduate students using our library."

Life

The School of Law is nestled in Charlottesville, "the most beautiful place on the eastern seaboard," according to some students. One student tells us that the funny thing about Charlottesville is that "the Northerners think it is Southern. The Southerners think

Susan Palmer, Associate Dean for Admissions
580 Massie Road, Charlottesville, VA 22903-1789
Telephone: 434-924-7351 • Fax: 434-982-2128
E-mail: lawadmit@virginia.edu • Website: www.law.virginia.edu

it is Northern. People from the city think it is the country. And people from the country think it is the city." This "dichotomy makes for a wonderfully inviting place where students can all find things both familiar and new." Furthermore, since the school is in a small town, "there are few alternatives to hanging out with the law school crowd." Therefore, "everyone knows each other, [which engenders a] lack of competition—everyone is always willing to help each other out, sharing outlines and notes rather than tearing out the pages of books or hiding research sources." The school is in the shadows of the "natural beauty of the Blue Ridge Mountains," which brings some serenity to a stressful time and offers for an even more peaceful escape from civilization.

Because "students are divided into 30 person sections, [they] quickly become a family away from home." This family feeling branches out toward many aspects of the school. "Students support each other in the classroom, in the job search, in personal matters, and yes, on the softball field," at Virginia. One student says, "I am [comforted to know that] I will have a legion of classmates from UVA Law who have helped me achieve my goals and who will be cheering for me (as I will be for them) for decades to come." Another student writes, "Within an hour after the first time I missed class, I found five different sets of class notes in my e-mail inbox—all unsolicited." While some think that the school's activities "focus too much on beer and softball, there is plenty to do in terms of political, academic, religious, and cultural activities here." Students are very pleased with the "good social outlets for every type of student. There are a number of relaxed and low key gatherings, high-energy parties, trendy (and not trendy) bars, great outdoor opportunities (Blue Ridge mountains, etc.), and cultural opportunities."

Getting In

Good luck. The University of Virginia School of Law is unquestionably one of the best public law schools in the land. It is no surprise, then, that it's also one of the hardest to get into. Virginia's admitted students at the 25th percentile have an LSAT score of 166 and a GPA of 3.5. Admitted students at the 75th percentile have an LSAT score of 171 and a GPA of 3.8. Virginia is a public institution and enrolls about 1,100 students. The Law school does not offer a part-time or evening program.

EMPLOYMENT INFORMATION

Career Rating	**95**
% employed within 9 months	99
Average starting salary	$100,000
State for bar exam	NY, VA, CA, TX, NJ
Pass rate for first-time bar	94

Employers who frequently hire grads:
Graduates are in all top 100 firms in the country.

Grads employed by field (%):	
Government	3
Judicial clerkships	16
Military	1
Private practice	77
Public interest	3

Legal Methods Course Requirement?	No
Legal Research Course Requirement?	No
Moot Court Requirement?	No
Public Interest Law Requirement?	No

ADMISSIONS

Selectivity Rating	**95**
# applications received	5,475
# applicants accepted	1,024
# acceptees attending	360
Average LSAT	169
LSAT Range	166–171
Average undergrad GPA	3.6
Application fee	$70
Regular application deadline	1/16
Regular notification	4/15
Rolling notification?	Yes
Early application program?	Yes
Early application deadline	10/15
Early application notification	12/16
Transfer students accepted?	Yes
Evening division offered?	No
Part-time accepted?	No
LSDAS accepted?	Yes

Applicants Also Look At

Columbia University, Duke University, The George Washington University, Georgetown University, Harvard University, New York University, University of Pennsylvania.

International Students

TOEFL required of international students?	Yes

FINANCIAL FACTS

Annual tuition (resident)	$24,591
Annual tuition (nonresident)	$29,532
Books and supplies	$1,374
Room & board	$13,726
Financial aid application deadline	2/15
% first-year students receiving some sort of aid	95
% receiving some sort of aid	86
% of aid that is merit-based	27
% receiving scholarships	51
Average grant	$10,900
Average loan	$26,350
Average total aid package	$33,239
Average debt	$62,290

University of Washington
School of Law

INSTITUTIONAL INFORMATION

Public/private	public
Student/faculty ratio	11:1
% faculty part-time	25
% faculty female	39
% faculty minority	13
Total faculty	63

SURVEY SAYS . . .

Great research resources
Great library staff
Beautiful campus
Students love Seattle, WA

STUDENTS

Enrollment of law school	552
% male/female	38/62
% out-of-state	30
% full-time	100
% minority	19
% international	1
# of countries represented	7
Average age of entering class	25

ACADEMICS

Academic Experience rating	**85**
Professors interesting rating	73
Professors accessible rating	74
Hours of study per day	4.85

Academic Specialties

Asian law, civil procedure, commercial law, constitutional law, corporation securities law, criminal law, dispute resolution, environmental law, government services, health law, human rights law, intellectual property law, international and comparative law, labor law, legal history, legal philosophy, property, taxation.

Advanced Degrees Offered

LLM, Asian law, law of sustainable international development, taxation, intellectual property, 1-year full-time programs. Taxation/IP are evening degree programs and may be full- or part-time.

Academic Requirements

Clinical Program Required?	No

Academics

According to students, the goal of the University of Washington School of Law is to "do all the weeding in the admissions process so that everyone who makes it in can and should graduate. This means that there is no pressure to compete or flunk out." Academically, the administration and teaching staff "tries to deemphasize the 'cutthroat competition' aspects of law school and allow students to focus on learning." Here you will find "relaxed and open faculty who place a serious emphasis on teaching quality." "The professors are all easy-going and only practice a Socratic-light Method. That is, you either know well in advance when you'll be called on in class or, if you're called on randomly, they won't grill you until you start crying," writes a 1L. While they go easy in the classroom, UW professors are nonetheless top-notch. "The professorial staff that I have encountered has been exceptional. Each one has a unique style of instruction and educational background," writes a 2L.

With a student faculty ratio of 11:1, "each 1L has at least one or two classes of 30 students," so there is plenty of opportunity to work one-on-one with profs. On top of that, "professors are eager to discuss almost anything" and make an effort to be available to students outside of the classroom. A 2L recounts, "The professors are not only brilliant, but they actually care about the students. I've had professors take me out to coffee or lunch just because I needed someone to talk to." Students single out the school's taxation and intellectual property programs for praise and applaud the fact that "professional responsibility and pro bono work is stressed" throughout the curriculum. Despite the progressive focus in the curriculum, students admit that the UW population is fairly homogeneous and that the "school desperately needs more professors of color."

Like the teaching staff, the UW administration is "organized, accessible, highly competent, and, most important, kind." In particular, many students tell us that "Dean Joe Knight is an inspiring and motivating force of nature and all-around great guy." In addition to its positive attitude, the administration at UW works hard to support students in their personal lives, not just academically. Among the most striking examples is that "the school offers unlimited, free psychotherapy with the country's leading lawyer psychologist." "Given that law school drives us crazy," comments one 2L, "he is an invaluable resource." The school is also "incredibly family- and child-friendly." In fact, on every level, UW expects students to have a life outside law school. A satisfied 2L adds, "While UW has provided me with all the necessary tools and connections to pursue a stellar career, I can still take time on the weekends to ski, kayak, and even run marathons. This place has allowed me to maintain and nurture all the facets of my life. It's quite rare." In fact, the environment is so non-competitive and encouraging that a 2L goes so far as to suggest that "if you want a school where you can find out how you rank and how you are doing, don't go here."

The school recently built "new, state-of-the-art facilities" funded by Seattle's most famous resident, Bill Gates. The law library, "with its towering skylights and ample use of windows, is affectionately known on campus as the 'shark tank' [and] swarms with undergrads because it's the best place on campus to study." While the quality and technological capabilities of the facility are indisputable, many lament the fact that "the physical space of the law school is not the most student-user friendly," as "there are few spaces for students to congregate, and none, other than classrooms, where more than 50 to 75 people could meet at once."

KATHY SWINEHART, ADMISSIONS SUPERVISOR
WILLIAM H. GATES HALL, BOX 353020, SEATTLE, WA 98195-3020
TELEPHONE: 206-543-4078 • FAX: 206-543-5671
E-MAIL: LAWADM@U.WASHINGTON.EDU • WEBSITE: WWW.LAW.WASHINGTON.EDU

Life

Think of law school. Now, think of its opposite. "I've been shocked that being around a bunch of lawyers can feel so little like being around a bunch of lawyers," writes one 1L. But the UW student body is more than just friendly faces; it is a group of extremely talented and accomplished individuals. "The single greatest strength of the law school is the range of experience of the student body. We have students that hold science PhDs, we have Olympic-caliber athletes, we have professional writers, and any profession in between,". comments one student. The community comprised of these individuals is active in a wide range of social and philanthropic activities, which means that "it's easy to get involved with student groups and do something relevant."

While UW has a famously "mellow, welcoming environment," students are diligent and studious, which leads to some "healthy competition" in an overall atmosphere of teamwork and support. When they aren't studying, students maintain active personal lives, and many are eager to socialize with their classmates in the evenings or on the weekends. "No one is obsessed with school, and someone throws a party just about every weekend (except during finals)," reports a 2L. You will not, however, encounter the "work hard, play hard" attitude prevalent at many other law schools. "There is also the famous 'Seattle reserve' to contend with: people aren't unfriendly, but they don't necessarily bounce around the halls in ecstasy, either."

Getting In

It's tough getting admitted to the University of Washington, but the school follows your basic law school admissions policy: It puts heavy weight on applicants' undergraduate records and LSAT scores, also considering letters of recommendation, work and volunteer experience, and personal statements. The vast majority of enrollees (about 70 percent) are residents of Washington State; however, residency is not a major factor in an admissions decision.

EMPLOYMENT INFORMATION

Career Rating	**86**
% employed within 9 months	99
Average starting salary	$85,000
State for bar exam	WA
Pass rate for first-time bar	85

Employers who frequently hire grads: Darby & Darby, Davis Wright Tremaine, Littler Mendelson, National Association of State PIRGs, Orrick Herrington, Perkins Coie, Stoel Rivesl. .

Prominent Alumni: Tom Foley, former speaker, U.S. House of Representatives; Gerry Alexander, chief justice, Washington Supreme Court; Betty Fletcher, judge, U.S. Court of Appeals, ninth circuit.

Grads employed by field (%):	
Academic	4
Business/industry	8
Government	17
Judicial clerkships	14
Private practice	51
Public interest	6

Legal Writing Course Requirement?	Yes
Legal Methods Course Requirement?	Yes
Legal Research Course Requirement?	No
Moot Court Requirement?	No
Public Interest Law Requirement?	Yes

ADMISSIONS

Selectivity Rating	**90**
# applications received	2,413
# applicants accepted	502
# acceptees attending	181
Average LSAT	163
LSAT Range	159–166
Average undergrad GPA	3.7
Application fee	$50
Regular application deadline	1/15
Regular notification	4/1
Rolling notification?	No
Early application program?	No
Transfer students accepted?	Yes
Evening division offered?	No
Part-time accepted?	No
LSDAS accepted?	Yes

Applicants Also Look At

The George Washington U., Georgetown U., Seattle U., U. of California—Berkeley, U. of California—Hastings, U. of California—Los Angeles, U. of Southern California.

International Students

TOEFL required of international students?	No
TOEFL recommended of international students?	No

FINANCIAL FACTS

Annual tuition (resident)	$13,634
Annual tuition (nonresident)	$19,934
Books and supplies	$1,500
Room & board	$15,000
Financial aid application deadline	2/28
% first-year students receiving some sort of aid	75
% receiving some sort of aid	76
% of aid that is merit-based	9
% receiving scholarships	41
Average grant	$5,500
Average loan	$18,688
Average total aid package	$24,188
Average debt	$40,234

UNIVERSITY OF WISCONSIN—MADISON
LAW SCHOOL

INSTITUTIONAL INFORMATION

Public/private	public
Student/faculty ratio	12:1
% faculty female	38
% faculty minority	15
Total faculty	66

SURVEY SAYS . . .

Diverse opinions accepted in classrooms
Great research resources
Great library staff
Abundant externship/internship/clerkship opportunities
Students love Madison, WI

STUDENTS

Enrollment of law school	843
% male/female	55/45
% full-time	94
% minority	30
Average age of entering class	26

ACADEMICS

Academic Experience rating	**79**
Professors interesting rating	77
Professors accessible rating	69
Hours of study per day	3.86

Academic Specialties

Biotechnology law, constitutional law, corporation securities law, criminal law, environmental law, government services, human rights law, intellectual property law, international law, Islamic law, labor law, legal history, legal philosophy.

Advanced Degrees Offered

JD, LLM, S/JD.

Combined Degrees Offered

Joint degree with environmental studies, business, sociology, political science, library information studies, Latin American studies, and philosophy.

Academic Requirements

Clinical Program Required?	No
Legal Writing Course Requirement?	Yes

Academics

The University of Wisconsin Law School in Madison is an "incredible bargain for in-state students." Even better, you "do not have to take the Wisconsin Bar" if you graduate from UW (or Marquette), provided that you pass certain courses, get decent grades, and pass the character and fitness examination. Naturally, "this is a huge plus!" Another draw is UW Law School's "'law in action' approach, [which seeks to provide] hands-on exposure to the practice of law." To this end, a "multitude [of] incredibly well-tailored [clinical opportunities and] an excellent judicial internship program" await you. "We have so many clinical programs," brags one student, "that if you leave Wisconsin without practical experience, you must have avoided it." Another student comments that there are "a zillion potential internships"—many in the public service sector—also available. And the law school's location "right in the state's capital city [provides] enormous opportunities" in state government and state and federal courts. The administration is "flexible and helpful." The "ridiculously qualified, accessible, well-informed, and passionate [professors are] the kind of people you'd want to have to your house for a dinner party." In class, "the professors use a modified Socratic Method, in which they encourage us to expand our thinking, and with no humiliation." Though a few professors are "too academic [or just] going through the motions, [most] love their area of law, enjoy teaching, [and skillfully] relate theory to real life." On the negative side, some classes "are far too large [and the] bizarre, indecipherable grading scale [used at Wisconsin Law] should be replaced." One student divulges, "Everyone thinks that it could be a little more challenging. I felt like I was back in grade school." Career Services could stand to be "a little more proactive," but, either way, if you are looking to work in Milwaukee, Chicago, or Minneapolis, a degree from UW Law will kick open many doors.

The UW Law School building "was totally overhauled [a few years ago] with a lot of glass and steel." While some say "it looks great," they mostly agree that "in winter it can seem a little stark." Harsher critics say, "Sometimes, [it] resembles a prison." The atrium "gets dark and spooky after sunset [and] brings reminders of the Death Star's infrastructure." Beyond the atrium, the building is "difficult to navigate." "Most of the classrooms are nice and comfortable, [but] awful acoustics [and] florescent lighting plague [some of the more] uninspired" classrooms. Also, "they should improve the common areas and eating areas, which are outdated and poorly kept." One students claims, "The school needs to spend more money on (of all things) janitorial upkeep," especially with regard to the "restrooms," which are in "need [of] serious facelifts." "The Grand Reading Room is gorgeous, [though,] with high ceilings [and] a huge window looking out over campus." Overall, "the law school is not an unpleasant environment for as much time as we all end up spending there."

Life

The "very accomplished, down-to-earth [students at UW Law are] diverse in ethnicity, economic background, marital status, and age." It's "a good blend of East Coast drive, Midwestern practicality, Southern warmth, and West Coast innovation." However, while "there's a group for everyone, [the] degree of mixing among those groups" is often limited. "Cliques form almost immediately." Students are "ideologically diverse, [too, but overall] way too politically liberal" for some tastes. Not for nothing is Madison "nicknamed Berkeley East." One student explains that while "you have your competitive and uptight students, [the environment is] surprisingly relaxed and jovial." Students acknowledge that "classroom discussions are intelligent and exciting." One student

M. Elizabeth Kransberger, Assistant Dean for Admissions and Financial Aid
975 Bascom Mall, Madison, WI 53706
Telephone: 608-262-5914 • Fax: 608-263-3190
E-mail: admissions@law.wisc.edu • Website: www.law.wisc.edu

writes, "Students seem to study plenty, but aren't pulling their hair out." Another student advises, "Come to Wisconsin if you want to go to school with a lot of normal people with normal lives. Some of my fellow students might have been neurotic, competitive law school freaks were it not for the overall ethos of this school."

According to one student, the social life is "a perfect mix of studying hard and partying hard. We're just like UW—Madison undergrad in that respect." Beyond the drinking scene, "the law school is constantly putting together lectures and activities and there's a student group for everyone." "There is even a weekly social function called Donuts with Faculty." Another student continues, "There is also an annual competition against the medical school called Dean's Cup, which involves all sorts of events from tug-of-war to trivia to flag football to ping-pong and bowling." "Tons of law students show up to each competition [in hopes of] thrashing" the med school.

Once you acclimate to the "frozen tundra, [the] progressive, intellectual town" of Madison is "a really fun place to live for three years." Students say, it's "a crazy little island of overeducated liberal activists. It's definitely hard to get bored." Another important social aspect at UW is that "law students are frequent attendees of Wisconsin football and basketball games and can be found at cheap undergrad beer bars throwing back drink specials or listening to jazz at classy martini bars on the Capitol Square." Madison has "politics, boating, running, biking, museums, kayaking," and virtually everything else under the sun. "There's always something to do, so buckling down takes a lot of self-restraint."

Getting In

Incoming students at the 25th percentile have an LSAT score of 155 and a GPA of 3.5. Incoming students at the 75th percentile have an LSAT score of 163 and a GPA of 3.6. In addition to the traditional criteria for law school admission (GPA, LSAT scores, essays, and the like), UW Law School makes a huge deal out of diversity. Everything else being equal, if you have an advanced degree, an unusual background, or are in any other way a unique or nontraditional student, you have a better shot at getting admitted. Finally, note that residents of Minnesota can attend the University of Wisconsin at a special reduced tuition rate.

EMPLOYMENT INFORMATION

Career Rating	**89**
% employed within 9 months	98
Average starting salary	$71,041
State for bar exam	WI
Pass rate for first-time bar	100

Employers who frequently hire grads: Foley & Lardner, Sidley & Austin, Mayer Brown Rowe & Maw, Jenner & Block, Dewey Ballantine, Quarles & Brady, Godfrey & Kahn.

Prominent Alumni: Tommy Thompson '66: Former Sec. of Health & Human Services, former Governor, State of Wisconsin; Tammy Baldwin '89: U.S. House of Representatives, Madison, WI

Grads employed by field (%):	
Business/industry	9
Government	14
Judicial clerkships	9
Private practice	66
Public interest	2

Legal Methods Course Requirement?	Yes
Legal Research Course Requirement?	Yes
Moot Court Requirement?	No
Public Interest Law Requirement?	No

ADMISSIONS

Selectivity Rating	**85**
# applications received	3,411
# applicants accepted	747
# acceptees attending	274
Average LSAT	159
LSAT Range	155–163
Average undergrad GPA	3.4
Application fee	$45
Regular application deadline	2/1
Regular notification	rolling
Rolling notification?	Yes
Early application program?	No
Transfer students accepted?	Yes
Evening division offered?	No
Part-time accepted?	Yes
LSDAS accepted?	Yes

International Students

TOEFL required of international students?	Yes

FINANCIAL FACTS

Annual tuition (resident)	$11,380
Annual tuition (nonresident)	$28,570
Books and supplies	$2,040
Room & board (on/off-campus)	$6,940/$6,840
Financial aid application deadline	3/1
% first-year students receiving some sort of aid	94
% receiving some sort of aid	90
% of aid that is merit-based	45
% receiving scholarships	22
Average grant	$7,000
Average loan	$12,797
Average total aid package	$18,500
Average debt	$58,724

University of Wyoming
College of Law

INSTITUTIONAL INFORMATION

Public/private	public
Student/faculty ratio	16:1
% faculty part-time	25
% faculty female	54
% faculty minority	8
Total faculty	24

SURVEY SAYS . . .

Diverse opinions accepted in classrooms

STUDENTS

Enrollment of law school	228
% male/female	58/42
% out-of-state	41
% full-time	100
% minority	10
% international	2
# of countries represented	4
Average age of entering class	28

ACADEMICS

Academic Experience rating	**65**
Professors interesting rating	64
Professors accessible rating	94
Hours of study per day	4.36

Academic Specialties

Environmental law, natural resources law.

Advanced Degrees Offered

JD, 3 years.

Combined Degrees Offered

JD/MPA, 3.5 years; JD/MBA, 3.5 to 4 years.

Academic Requirements

Clinical Program Required?	No
Legal Writing Course Requirement?	Yes
Legal Methods Course Requirement?	No
Legal Research Course Requirement?	Yes
Moot Court Requirement?	Yes
Public Interest Law Requirement?	No

Academics

Offering knowledgeable professors, small class sizes, and ample practical learning opportunities throughout the state, the tiny College of Law at the University of Wyoming is the ideal training ground for future lawyers of Wyoming. With only 80 students in each entering class, UW students say they get loads of individual attention from their professors. As one student notes, "The University of Wyoming College of Law has an excellent student to professor ratio. I feel like I have as much opportunity as possible to interact with my professors on a personal and educational level." Another student adds, "This law school encourages even the bottom-ranked [students] to do their best. Every single student has access to all the professors, the deans, and the library with little inconvenience."

Students warn, however, that small classes are more challenging than large lectures, as students are required to keep up with the heavy workload and are personally accountable to their instructors. As one student cautions, "Forget about trying to slip through the cracks at this law school. The small, close environment requires your full participation in the class discussions." Even so, students say their professors are friendly and encouraging and not out to "get" slackers. One student comments, "Professors are engaging and yet maintain a sense of compassion." That is, unless you're a conservative. One such student tell us, "There are way too many traditional liberal law professors here who have a preset agenda [and] who don't tolerate conservative or libertarian thought or discussion."

The college offers a wide range of excellent practical and clinical opportunities, "The externship and clinic programs are plentiful enough to give every student a chance at an externship of their choice." In fact, Wyoming students are easily integrated into the legal landscape of the Equality State during the course of their three years. A first-year tells us, "Wyoming is a very large small town. The law school is part of that, and I feel that attending this law school has introduced me to many lawyers in Wyoming and the practice of law in Wyoming, generally." Another student agrees, "The close-knit legal community of Wyoming is the greatest strength of this law school. The students have immeasurable access to state and federal courts and practicing attorneys in Wyoming. Each student could get to know the justices of the Wyoming Supreme Court personally if they wanted to." In fact, a student says, "3Ls have ample opportunities to engage in litigation and other lawyering skills in the courtroom." Unfortunately, students complain that it can be difficult to get a job outside Wyoming. One student puts it bluntly, "This law school needs to assert its influence more in the Rocky Mountain region."

As a small public school in a sparsely populated state, University of Wyoming did not, until recently, have the resources necessary to update their academic facilities or classrooms, nor to fully integrate modern technology into the academic environment. The classrooms, while having "plenty of space," don't offer much in the way of electrical outlets. While over half the classrooms now have data ports at each seat, one student still points out that "in this age of laptop computers, it is a problem." Complaints about the lack of computer terminals and Internet access on campus also circulate. Most students are forgiving of the lackluster facilities, however, especially when they consider the excellent quality and low cost of their education. As one optimist student cracks, "Wyoming's building comes right out of the 70s, with its yellow tabletops and Pleather-covered chairs. However, it has a certain comfort that you can't find at the newer buildings."

Carol Persson, Coordinator of Admissions
Department 3035, 1000 East University Avenue, Laramie, WY 82071
Telephone: 307-766-6416 • Fax: 307-766-6417
E-mail: lawadmis@uwyo.edu • Website: www.uwyo.edu/law

Life

Students say you can find fresh air, friendly people, and no traffic jams in Laramie. On top of that, students like the fact that, "the cost of living in Wyoming is very reasonable—if not modest." They do warn, however, that "the town offers little social activities beyond bars and movies." Even so, campus life is collegial and social. One student glows, "The distinction between 1Ls, 2Ls, and 3Ls relates primarily to course work—socially the University of Wyoming College of Law functions like a family." In fact, a student tells us, "Students here become lifelong friends and colleagues. Some students warn, however, that things can get a little too close on this small campus. One student writes, "Careful of the rumor mill here. If you sneeze, 10 minutes later everyone will know how loud it was and in whose general direction the phlegm flew." What it lacks in terms of anonymity, however, the student body makes up for in terms of diversity. Students tell us that the school is welcoming to all cultures, ages, and walks of life. In the words of one older student, "Most of the students here are nontraditional students, many with children, making it a very family-friendly environment."

Getting In

University of Wyoming grants admission to students who demonstrate a strong academic record and strong LSAT scores. Last year, admitted students in the 25th to 75th percentile scored within the 151–156 range on the LSAT and had an average undergraduate GPA of 3.3. University of Wyoming will also consider a student's relevant legal experience. The average age of matriculating students is 28.

EMPLOYMENT INFORMATION

Career Rating	**62**
% employed within 9 months	90
Average starting salary	$44,544
State for bar exam	WY
Pass rate for first-time bar	69

Employers who frequently hire grads: Government (attorney general, district and federal courts, public defender, county attorney), general practice firms.

Prominent Alumni: Gerry Spence, trial lawyer, author, television commentator; Mike Sullivan, former U.S. ambassador to Ireland & former governor of Wyoming; Alan K. Simpson, former U.S. senator, Wyoming, political commentator.

Grads employed by field (%):	
Business/industry	5
Government	21
Judicial clerkships	22
Private practice	46
Public interest	6

ADMISSIONS

Selectivity Rating	**75**
# applications received	765
# applicants accepted	191
# acceptees attending	78
Average LSAT	152
LSAT Range	149–156
Average undergrad GPA	3.3
Application fee	$50
Regular application deadline	3/1
Regular notification	4/15
Rolling notification?	Yes
Early application program?	Yes
Early application deadline	2/1
Early application notification	3/15
Transfer students accepted?	Yes
Evening division offered?	No
Part-time accepted?	No
LSDAS accepted?	Yes

Applicants Also Look At

Drake University, The University of Akron, University of California—Davis, University of Colorado, University of Kansas, The University of South Dakota, Whittier College.

International Students

TOEFL required of international students?	Yes
Minimum Paper TOEFL	525
Minimum Computer TOEFL	195

FINANCIAL FACTS

Annual tuition (resident)	$6,519
Annual tuition (nonresident)	$13,779
Books and supplies	$1,000
Room & board	$8,616
Financial aid application deadline	3/1
% first-year students receiving some sort of aid	89
% receiving some sort of aid	86
% of aid that is merit-based	18
% receiving scholarships	79
Average grant	$1,610
Average loan	$16,579
Average total aid package	$18,181
Average debt	$37,340

VALPARAISO UNIVERSITY
SCHOOL OF LAW

INSTITUTIONAL INFORMATION

Public/private	private
Student/faculty ratio	17:1
Affiliation	Lutheran
% faculty part-time	34
% faculty female	38
% faculty minority	1
Total faculty	56

SURVEY SAYS . . .

Diverse opinions accepted in classrooms
Great research resources
Abundant externship/internship/ clerkship opportunities

STUDENTS

Enrollment of law school	559
% male/female	49/51
% out-of-state	65
% full-time	92
% minority	9
% international	1
# of countries represented	6
Average age of entering class	25

ACADEMICS

Academic Experience rating	**73**
Professors interesting rating	78
Professors accessible rating	81
Hours of study per day	4.85

Academic Specialties

Civil procedure, commercial law, constitutional law, corporation securities law, criminal law, environmental law, government services, human rights law, intellectual property law, international law, labor law, legal history, legal philosophy, property.

Advanced Degrees Offered

JD, 3 years full-time, 5 years part-time; LLM, 1 year full-time.

Combined Degrees Offered

JD/MBA, JD/CMHC, JD/PSY, JD/MA international commerce and policy, JD/MA sports administration, JD/MALS create your own program.

Academics

For students seeking a small and community-oriented law school, they should know that a "truly personal manner of teaching" is what distinguishes a Valparaiso education. At Valpo, small class sizes are the rule and classes are generally taught through the Socratic Method and group discussion. Students call their professors "true scholars" as well as great teachers and describe classes as "thorough, difficult, rewarding, and fair." They're also enjoyable; take it from this 1L, who tells us, "There is never a day when you don't laugh. The professors here combine a fun and open learning atmosphere while maintaining professionalism and responsibility for the material."

In addition to their flair for teaching, Valpo professors are some of the friendliest in the business. They "go out of their way to make sure that you are at ease with them and the school" and help to engender in a students a feeling of community. In addition to the campus wide "open-door policy," Valpo professors are generous with their time, willing to support students academically, personally, and socially. For example, they are "ready, willing, and able to step up and act as judges for moot court competitions and to help with practice rounds." They're also not above showing up for student parties, dinners, and various extracurriculars. A great "example of this is Cardozo Cup, our fall softball tournament. The faculty and staff come out in force for this event and form their own team to play the various classes of students."

Valparaiso augments its traditional legal course work with an extensive legal writing and research program. Whereas many law schools limit their legal writing courses to the first year, at Valpo "legal writing skills are not only stressed in the first year, but throughout your time" here, as the program includes "a full year dedicated to legal research and three years dedicated to legal writing." These skills are extremely valuable in the real world: "Several of us who worked at large firms were the only summer associates who did not have significant problems transferring our skills to a practical environment, and the employers noticed," writes one 3L. On top of the legal writing program, "there are a lot of practical, hands-on experiences available," including the school's "great clinical program, which is really respected in the community." In addition, "externship opportunities abound" with a list of possible placements including "local prosecutors, in-house work for hospitals and steel corporations, the United States Attorney's Office, federal judicial externships, state judicial exterships, and nonprofits." A 2L exclaims, "My first summer I had the opportunity to work with the Federal Community Defender's office on a death penalty case. Talk about an education!"

In most cases, Valpo students go on to take jobs in regional firms, and "if you are from the Midwest and want to stay, Valparaiso has great contacts, and the alumni are very faithful." By most accounts, "the Career Center is very motivated to help the students and truly care about the results," though some would like to see more support for career searches on a national level. Many students confide that, until recently, Career Services at Valparaiso struggled to place students in big firm jobs in metropolitan areas; however, students say that the administration "has really listened to our needs and helped improve job placement." A 3L attests, "I found a great job, as did my fiancée and a lot of my friends here. The 2L class below us has amazing job placement all over the Chicago area and Indianapolis, as well as other cities in Indiana and Michigan."

Tony Credit, J.D. Executive Director of Admissions
Wesemann Hall, Valparaiso, IN 46383
Telephone: 888-825-7652 • Fax: 219-465-7808
E-mail: valpolaw@valpo.edu • Website: www.valpo.edu/law/

Life

Life on this small town campus is lively, active, and extremely social. Students keep busy through a wide variety of extracurricular clubs, and "there is always a social event, guest lecturer, charity drive, or similar happening taking place." What's more, it's easy to make friends in this open, community-oriented environment; "I'm friends with everyone in my class and have a very personal relationship with my professors," writes one 3L. An enthusiastic 1L brags, "All the social events, which are nearly weekly, revolve around my two favorite things: free food and free beer." If that weren't enough, there is a long list of annual events for students and faculty, which include "a softball competition, a Halloween costume party, the boat cruise, the spring play that students and faculty put on together as a fund-raiser, a big Spring Ball, Law Week, which consists of tons of competitions, and end-of-the-year dinners and banquets."

While the environment is decidedly collegial, not all Valpo students hail from the same background or viewpoint and, especially when it comes to politics, they are surprisingly diverse. At Valparaiso, you can expect lively classroom debates, as "some students are very strong liberals and some are extremely conservative." On this friendly campus, however, "there is always a place for someone, no matter what their political beliefs," and students welcome the liveliness and interest that diversity brings to the campus. Debates aside, you won't find competitiveness at Valparaiso, where "there is a strong sense of community among students" and everyone looks out for everyone else. According to newbies, "2Ls and 3Ls are always there to answer questions and lend a helping hand."

Getting In

To apply to Valparaiso, you must submit a completed application, a personal statement, two letters of recommendation, an undergraduate transcript, and LSAT scores. While LSAT score and GPA are important factors in an admissions decision, Valparaiso also considers a candidate's background, work experience, contribution to the community, and commitment to the study of law.

EMPLOYMENT INFORMATION

Career Rating	**70**
% employed within 9 months	81.3
Average starting salary	$50,795
State for bar exam	IN, IL, MI, WI, GA
Pass rate for first-time bar	80

Prominent Alumni: Stephan Todd, vice president law & environment U.S. Steel Corporation; Cornell Boggs, vice president and general counsel, Tyco Plastics & Adhesives; Honorable Nancy Vaidik, justice, Indiana Court of Appeals; Koreen Ryan, senior council, South Asia McDonald's Corporation; Honorable Robert Rucker, justice, Supreme Court of Indiana.

Grads employed by field (%):	
Academic	1
Business/industry	16
Government	12
Judicial clerkships	4
Military	1
Private practice	63
Public interest	2

Academic Requirements

Clinical Program Required?	No
Legal Writing Course Requirement?	Yes
Legal Methods Course Requirement?	Yes
Legal Research Course Requirement?	Yes
Moot Court Requirement?	No
Public Interest Law Requirement?	Yes

ADMISSIONS

Selectivity Rating	**75**
# applications received	2,386
# applicants accepted	583
# acceptees attending	164
Average LSAT	153
LSAT Range	150–155
Average undergrad GPA	3.2
Application fee	$50
Regular application deadline	4/1
Regular notification	rolling
Rolling notification?	Yes
Early application program?	No
Transfer students accepted?	Yes
Evening division offered?	No
Part-time accepted?	Yes
LSDAS accepted?	Yes

International Students

TOEFL required of international students?	Yes
Minimum Paper TOEFL	575
Minimum Computer TOEFL	230

FINANCIAL FACTS

Annual tuition	$24,670
Books and supplies	$3,350
Fees per credit	$22
Tuition per credit	$965
Room & board	$6,600
Financial aid application deadline	4/1
% first-year students receiving some sort of aid	95
% receiving some sort of aid	95
% of aid that is merit-based	35
% receiving scholarships	73
Average grant	$15,214
Average loan	$18,500
Average total aid package	$35,492
Average debt	$52,038

VANDERBILT UNIVERSITY
LAW SCHOOL

INSTITUTIONAL INFORMATION

Public/private	private
Student/faculty ratio	16:1
% faculty part-time	39
% faculty female	31
% faculty minority	18
Total faculty	67

SURVEY SAYS . . .

Beautiful campus

STUDENTS

Enrollment of law school	632
% male/female	52/48
% out-of-state	70
% full-time	100
% minority	25
% international	4
# of countries represented	8
Average age of entering class	24

ACADEMICS

Academic Experience rating	**90**
Professors interesting rating	90
Professors accessible rating	84
Hours of study per day	4.21

Academic Specialties

Civil procedure, commercial law, constitutional law, corporation securities law, criminal law, environmental law, government services, human rights law, intellectual property law, international law, labor law, legal history, legal philosophy, property, taxation. Students can also craft their own specializations.

Advanced Degrees Offered

LLM program, 1 year.

Combined Degrees Offered

JD/MBA, 4 years; JD/MA, 5 years; JD/PhD, 7 years; JD/MDiv, 5 years; JD/MTS, 4 years; JD/MD, 6 years; JD/MPP, 4 years; LLM/MA of Latin American studies, 2 years.

Academic Requirements

Clinical Program Required?	No
Legal Writing Course Requirement?	Yes

Academics

Vanderbilt University Law School has long enjoyed a reputation as a national powerhouse. Students tell us that Vandy grads are "highly sought after by firms in Chicago and New York" and every other major legal market from Dallas to Birmingham to Washington, DC. This "freedom to go wherever you want after graduation [is due in large part to the] dedicated [and] accessible women in the Career Development Office, [who students feel] should be sainted." While some complain that "many students with lower GPAs feel shut out," and that Career Services is too "large-firm oriented," most concur that the staff gives you "their full attention (even when you just drop in unannounced) and makes sure that you have the best possible opportunity to get the job you want."

"All levels [of the] helpful, compassionate [administration and staff] beam with personality, creating a comforting and encouraging community-like atmosphere." Vanderbilt's "brilliant yet accessible [faculty] is flatly one of the best in the country." Professors "are amazingly diverse, not only in ethnicities, but in their beliefs, backgrounds, and viewpoints." Most students also find the professors "amusing [and] charismatic." One student says, "I was afraid I'd be bored to tears for three years of law school, but I was pleasantly surprised by the enthusiasm and energy professors bring to the classroom." Students observe, "The small class size allows for close relationships among students and faculty." Outside of class, the "extremely approachable [professors] treat you as a client, not a nuisance."

Vanderbilt's "wooded and well-kept campus [is] beautiful." The "gorgeous building [that houses the law school boasts] huge expanses of windows and nice study nooks, [a law library] built into the center of the school, [and] an open-air cafe." One student says, "It makes for a nice place to spend 40-plus hours a week." The "newly renovated [library] has just about anything you need" with the possible exception of more space. "The study areas are often packed. More tables, desks, and study areas in general would be helpful." You will also find Internet ports in most classrooms and "WiFi throughout the campus."

Among students' gripes is lack of course offerings. There is only "sparse course selection in some areas [and] one area that the law school could stand to improve is its support of public interest law." One student laments that "the bread-and-butter classes that are consistently offered [are aimed primarily at] students going into the normal corporate practice at a big law firm," wishing there was more variety and practical classes. "Registration is needlessly complicated" as well. There is a "nearly unanimous feeling" here that the "unrealistic, poorly taught, and dull" courses in legal writing are a "subjective crapshoot."

Life

Both ethnically and geographically, "the law school has great diversity." Though "privilege and elitism" can be palpable at times and a contingent of "gossipy backstabbers and snotty socialites [certainly exists], an incredibly relaxed atmosphere" generally prevails. Most students are "pretty laid-back, [perhaps} too laid-back." One student notes, "Really, this is a collegial place. The students are competitive, but more so with themselves or other schools than with each other. We're a pretty friendly bunch." Furthermore, "Study groups abound, [and] students are more likely to copy [notes] for each other than to hide them from each other," explains one student. "Vanderbilt is a relatively small school so everyone has to be friendly or we'd kill each other. Southern hospitality definitely applies" on this campus.

Richelle Acker, Acting Director of Admissions
131 Twenty-first Avenue South, Nashville, TN 37203
Telephone: 615-322-6452 • Fax: 615-322-1531
E-mail: admissions@law.vanderbilt.edu • Website: www.law.vanderbilt.edu

The upshot of all this cordiality and community is that "you will actually have fun at Vandy Law. Socially, it's more fun than college. Everyone studies hard and plays hard. It's a very supportive, fun atmosphere." One student says, "The student body seems to balance fun with studying (other than during exams), and this makes Vanderbilt students happier than most." Vanderbilt's Bar Review is a weekly Thursday pilgrimage. "It's a great way to bond with your classmates and occasionally bond with other classes." Another student explains, "You're definitely studying hard during the week, but come Thursday night, students like to party." Some students at Vandy never tire of the vibrant party scene, while others complain that "the law school's social life encourages some immaturity."

The surrounding area is certainly conducive to an active life outside of law school. "There is small downtown area at one end of campus with a number of restaurants, bars, and coffee shops." Also, rollicking downtown Nashville is less than two miles away. "Nashville is not as country music-based as I thought it would be," reports a supremely impressed out-of-towner. "The night life is very exciting, and there are a lot of bars, pool halls, dance clubs, and concerts to frequent."

Getting In

Roughly 3,800 starry-eyed applicants seek admission to Vanderbilt each year. Fewer than 800 are accepted. Suffice to say, it ain't easy to get admitted. The average GPA of admitted students is 3.6. The average LSAT is 165.

Legal Methods Course Requirement?	Yes
Legal Research Course Requirement?	Yes
Moot Court Requirement?	No
Public Interest Law Requirement?	No

ADMISSIONS

Selectivity Rating	**91**
# applications received	3,770
# applicants accepted	763
# acceptees attending	227
Average LSAT	165
LSAT Range	164–166
Average undergrad GPA	3.6
Application fee	$50
Regular application deadline	3/15
Regular notification	4/15
Rolling notification?	Yes
Early application program?	Yes
Early application deadline	11/1
Early application notification	12/15
Transfer students accepted?	Yes
Evening division offered?	No
Part-time accepted?	No
LSDAS accepted?	Yes

Applicants Also Look At

Cornell University, Duke University, Emory University, The George Washington University, Georgetown University, Washington and Lee University, Washington University.

International Students

TOEFL required of international students?	Yes

FINANCIAL FACTS

Annual tuition	$31,900
Books and supplies	$1,426
Room & board (off-campus)	$10,684
Financial aid application deadline	2/15
% first-year students receiving some sort of aid	98
% receiving some sort of aid	87
% of aid that is merit-based	59
% receiving scholarships	55
Average grant	$13,000
Average loan	$18,000
Average total aid package	$50,070
Average debt	$80,300

EMPLOYMENT INFORMATION

Career Rating	**92**
% employed within 9 months	98
Average starting salary	$100,674
State for bar exam	TN, GA, NY, TX, FL
Pass rate for first-time bar	91

Employers who frequently hire grads:
King & Spalding; Alston & Bird; Sherman & Sterling; Kirkland & Ellis; Bass, Berry, & Sims; Waller, Lansden, Dortch, & Davis; Locke, Liddell, & Sapp.

Grads employed by field (%):	
Academic	1
Business/industry	4
Government	5
Judicial clerkships	11
Military	2
Private practice	75
Public interest	2

VERMONT LAW SCHOOL

INSTITUTIONAL INFORMATION

Public/private	private
Student/faculty ratio	17:1
% faculty female	53
% faculty minority	1
Total faculty	49

SURVEY SAYS . . .

Great library staff
Beautiful campus

STUDENTS

Enrollment of law school	545
% male/female	48/52
% out-of-state	90
% full-time	100
% minority	16
% international	2
# of countries represented	5
Average age of entering class	26

ACADEMICS

Academic Experience rating	**68**
Professors interesting rating	70
Professors accessible rating	73
Hours of study per day	4.11

Academic Specialties

Civil procedure, commercial law, constitutional law, corporation securities law, criminal law, environmental law, government services, human rights law, international law, labor law, legal history, legal philosophy, property, taxation.

Advanced Degrees Offered

JD, 3 years; MSEL, master of studies in environmental law, 1 year; LLM, 1 year.

Combined Degrees Offered

JD/master of studies in environmental law, 3 years total, 6 regular semesters and 2 summer semesters.

Academic Requirements

Clinical Program Required?	No
Legal Writing Course Requirement?	Yes
Legal Methods Course Requirement?	Yes

Academics

One of the "nation's best" environmental law programs and a "beautiful [and] isolated" setting are the major draws at Vermont Law School. The motto at this independent private school, located in a small town "in the middle of the Green Mountains," is "Law for the Community and the World." Students are indeed impressed with the "extensive" range of environmental law courses offered and by the school's "strong commitment to environmental ethics and civil rights," too. "VLS is a friendly, nurturing, open-minded school that does not lose focus of the good that law can do for others, not just for lawyers," says one happy student. VLS "holds true to its values"—the trustees even distribute part of the law school endowment "to socially responsible investments." But some students feel that VLS is a little too focused on environmental law and say a "broader range of programs" would be a serious improvement. "It's awful that there are tons of environmental classes but only one section of evidence," says one critic. "Last time I checked, environmental law wasn't a covered subject on the bar, whereas evidence is."

The "caring professors really work hard [to help students] understand the information rather than just bulldozing straight through content." One student says, "I love my teachers, and they really get me excited about the course work, which is particularly important with the amount of work you are required to do." A more circumspect student discloses, "I have had both the best and worst professors of my life here. There are a couple of faculty members that I feel are not qualified to be teaching law." Academics can be "very one-sided" as well, strongly tilting toward leftist activism.

The biggest complaint among VLS students is about "difficult" career prospects. While "VLS is a great law school, and it produces very talented attorneys, [it is] located in a remote area and is still fairly young, [and therefore,] not well known outside of the environmental community." One students mentions that networking outside of New England [or even] outside of Vermont" can be a challenge. "The students here can compete academically and professionally with those from any other law school," attests one student, "yet we often do not have the opportunity due to poor career assistance resources."

Vermont Law's "compact but efficient [campus] lacks a lot of the resources of a university-affiliated law school." Also, the "IT department is less than stellar." However, "classrooms and lecture halls are new [and] wired." Students like the fact that most "have a wireless signal [as well,] so you can surf when the professor goes off on an incoherent tangent." Also, not at all surprisingly, the campus is "environmentally friendly, [what with] biodegradable toilets and all."

Kathy Hartman, Associate Dean for Enrollment Management
Chelsea Street, South Royalton, VT 05068-0096
Telephone: 888-277-5985 • Fax: 802-763-7071
E-mail: admiss@vermontlaw.edu • Website: www.vermontlaw.edu

Life

If a "remote location [in central Vermont] right off of a postcard" is your thing, you will love it at VLS. It is "a small school in a minor railroad village not close to anything, [not even] supermarkets or FM radio signals." One student analogizes,"most people [compare life at VLS] to living in a fish bowl." One student says, "There's a local organic grocer, a seasonal farmers market, a video store, and two local bars," taking inventory of the surroundings. So what about the rest? "Most shopping for groceries and clothing is done in New Hampshire or Burlington. Both are more than a half-hour drive [away]." One student confesses, "I used to feel like a hick whenever I visited New York City. Now, Hanover, New Hampshire, has the same effect on me."

While the pace in Vermont might be "a little slow," students agree that the small-town life "encourages studying." There are also "more clubs and student organizations on campus than you can shake a stick at." On campus, "there seems to be a little too much partying going on at times." Students note, "Recreational opportunities" abound. "Good skiing [is just] 20 to 30 minutes" away. If you're craving the urban life, the "hip, but small city" of Burlington is a good fix. Plus the bright lights and tasty poutine of Montreal are just a little over two hours away.

"For the most part, [Vermont Law students are] decent and cooperative." The small size of the school makes it "impossible to be anonymous." Students say the "close-knit" community of Vermont Law School is "impressive." It's "comfortable while at the same time there is a strong sense of professionalism." While "attending Vermont Law School is not for everyone, [it is] ideal for those who love nature and the outdoors, [those] who enjoy being cradled by the Green Mountains [while being] maple-syrup fed."

Getting In

Admitted students at the 25th percentile have an LSAT score of 149 and a GPA of 2.8. Admitted students at the 75th percentile have an LSAT score of 157 and a GPA of 3.3.

EMPLOYMENT INFORMATION

Career Rating	**63**
Job placement rate (%)	94
Average starting salary	$43,000
State for bar exam	VT, MA, NY, CO, CA
Pass rate for first-time bar	60

Employers who frequently hire grads:
Federal & state judges in the Northeast; law firms throughout New England; Beveridge & Diamond in Washington, DC; federal & state agencies; and public interest organizations.

Prominent Alumni: Glenn Berger, partner, Skadden Arps; Charles DiLeva, lead environmental counsel, World Bank; Linda Smiddy, professor of law, Vermont Law School.

Grads employed by field (%):

Academic	3
Business/industry	18
Government	9
Judicial clerkships	14
Military	2
Private practice	40
Public interest	13

Legal Research Course Requirement?	Yes
Moot Court Requirement?	Yes
Public Interest Law Requirement?	No

ADMISSIONS

Selectivity Rating	**70**
# applications received	1,015
# applicants accepted	532
# acceptees attending	203
Average LSAT	154
LSAT Range	151–157
Average undergrad GPA	3.3
Application fee	$50
Regular application deadline	3/15
Regular notification	4/1
Rolling notification?	Yes
Early application program?	No
Transfer students accepted?	Yes
Evening division offered?	No
Part-time accepted?	No
LSDAS accepted?	Yes

Applicants Also Look At
Albany Law School, Franklin Pierce Law Center, Lewis & Clark College, Pace University, Suffolk University, University of Colorado, University of Denver.

International Students

TOEFL required of international students?	Yes
Minimum Paper TOEFL	600

FINANCIAL FACTS

Annual tuition	$26,522
Books and supplies	$950
Room & board (off-campus)	$9,253
Financial aid application deadline	3/1
% first-year students receiving some sort of aid	90
% receiving some sort of aid	90
% of aid that is merit-based	31
% receiving scholarships	53
Average grant	$6,800
Average loan	$18,500
Average total aid package	$31,500
Average debt	$85,400

VILLANOVA UNIVERSITY
SCHOOL OF LAW

INSTITUTIONAL INFORMATION

Public/private	private
Student/faculty ratio	17:1
Affiliation	Roman Catholic
% faculty part-time	56
% faculty female	60
% faculty minority	11
Total faculty	111

SURVEY SAYS . . .

Diverse opinions accepted in classrooms
Great library staff
Abundant externship/internship/clerkship opportunities
Students love Villanova, PA

STUDENTS

Enrollment of law school	762
% male/female	51/49
% out-of-state	36
% full-time	100
% minority	17
% international	1
# of countries represented	4
Average age of entering class	23

ACADEMICS

Academic Experience rating	**82**
Professors interesting rating	88
Professors accessible rating	80
Hours of study per day	4.71

Academic Specialties

International taxation, clinics. Courses are offered in a broad range of specialties.

Advanced Degrees Offered

JD, 3 years; LLM, tax, 24 credits.

Combined Degrees Offered

JD/MBA, 3 to 4.5 years; JD/PhD, psychology, 7 to 8 years; JD/LLM, taxation, 3.5 to 4 years.

Academic Requirements

Clinical Program Required?	No
Legal Writing Course Requirement?	Yes
Legal Methods Course Requirement?	No

Academics

At Villanova University School of Law, students receive a strong, well-rounded legal education through a blend of lecture, discussion, and serious hands-on experience. Students say the teaching staff is the heart and soul of the program, bringing both a practical background and a personal touch to their classes. One first-year student glows, "Instructors are all extremely intelligent and have a wealth of real-world experience, yet remain in touch with students." In fact, he tells us, "My law school professors are much more helpful and approachable than my undergrad professors were." A case in point, another student recounts, "My civil procedure professor memorized the names of all 60 students in the class by the second day." Likewise, students say there is a spirit more of camaraderie than competition between classmates. One explains, "The student body is bright and academically diligent, but not cutthroat. I have never encountered a student who wasn't willing to share notes or an outline."

Villanova takes a fairly traditional approach to introductory course work, and students say "there is still a heavy reliance on the Socratic Method and many classes use a lecture format (especially in the first year)." In the next two years, students continue studying the basic principals of law, while adding elective courses to their schedule. Experiential learning is emphasized throughout the curriculum, and students dole out praise for the school's strong legal writing and research courses, simulation programs, clinics, and externships. For example, students tell us, "The legal writing sections are small, making feedback more specific to each student," and moot court participants get to "argue at least five times in front of a panel of students and faculty members before ever going to an interschool competition." In addition, students get their feet wet through participation in real legal work through the school's active pro bono services. One student says, "The students and staff have a strong commitment to community service and pro bono work, and at many programs you can find students and faculty with their sleeves rolled up." However, the opportunities for services are slightly restricted by the administration's commitment to Catholic values and students who earn a fellowship are forbidden "to work for pro-choice organizations." Still, another student reassures the nonreligious, "Catholicism is overbearing, but being anti-religion myself, I have never found it to be a problem, as long as you can handle crucifixes in the classrooms."

Religious iconography aside, Villanova students cannot stop griping about the school's old, ramshackle facilities. One student laments, "[The] severe lack of classrooms, computers, parking spots, hallways, lockers, and space in general, greatly handicap students' ability to benefit from Villanova's top-notch professors and academic programs." How bad can it be? A student jokes, "As you descend into the lower levels of the library, you swear you are approaching the gates of hell and not the legislative materials area." The good news is that the school has recently announced plans to build a brand new state-of-the-art law school on a site adjacent to the University's suburban Philadelphia campus.

While they may complain that the surroundings feel like a run-down junior high school, students also say they leave Villanova well-prepared for their professional career in the adult world. Life after law school is good for Villanova alumni, especially in the tri-state area where "law firms and other legal organizations love Villanova grads." Students insist that "opportunities for practical experience are abundant," and the Career Services professionals "work diligently for students interested in public interest/public service/government careers as well as many other students." One student claims that Career Services "helped me achieve job offers for both summers during law school and

David P. Pallozzi, Assistant Dean for Admissions
299 North Spring Mill Road, Villanova, PA 19085
Telephone: 610-519-7010 • Fax: 610-519-6291
E-mail: admissions@law.villanova.edu • Website: law.villanova.edu

helped me obtain offers for full-time employment upon graduation even though my grades were not in the top 25 percent of my class."

Life

When they are not hitting the books, Villanova students unwind at the many bars, clubs, and restaurants in Philadelphia, as well as at campus events. A student assures us, "The school encourages students to maintain a social life and keep a balance between work and play. We have many social events during the year that actually make law school fun." According to another, "It is a young student body, so people tend to go out frequently to local bars, and the Student Bar Association holds several annual events." Still, many students choose to maintain a life outside of school, living off-campus with their friends or spouses. One student advises, "There is a bar that students usually hang out at which can be fun, but sometimes after seeing these people all day and every day, it's good to do something away from the law school crowd." Luckily, that is easy to accomplish at Villanova. "The school is in a great location. It is 25 minutes from Philadelphia, as well as a short drive from NYC, DC, Baltimore, the beaches, and skiing!" Most students say that they get along with their classmates, though some say the student body is oppressively homogenous. One student observes, "I can count on my right hand the number of minority students enrolled at VLS. The interaction between minorities and white students is minimal, despite the facade of 'intercommunity organizations.'"

Getting In

To be considered for admission at Villanova University School of Law, students need to have an LSAT score of at least 150, with the average score for matriculants at about 160. Most students admit having a strong undergraduate GPA, with an average of about 3.4. However, Villanova may consider students with a lower GPA if they offer other important qualities, such as commitment to service, volunteer work, or unique professional experience. The majority of students who enter do so within a year or two of college, and the average age of a Villanova student in their first year is 24. Admissions are made on a rolling basis, beginning in late December.

EMPLOYMENT INFORMATION

Career Rating	**83**
% employed within 9 months	95
Average starting salary	$67,972
State for bar exam	PA, NJ, NY, DE
Pass rate for first-time bar	84

Employers who frequently hire grads: State judges and government; law firms in Philadelphia, New York, New Jersey, DC, and Delaware.

Prominent Alumni: Ed Rendell, governor of Pennsylvania; Sandra Schultz-Newman, justice, Supreme Court of Pennsylvania; Kathryn Lewis, judge, Court of Common Pleas; Pat O'Connor, founder, Cozen-O'Connor.

Grads employed by field (%):	
Business/industry	8.7
Government	7.8
Judicial clerkships	21.2
Private practice	61.5
Public interest	2

Legal Research Course Requirement?	Yes
Moot Court Requirement?	Yes
Public Interest Law Requirement?	No

ADMISSIONS

Selectivity Rating	**84**
# applications received	2,924
# applicants accepted	921
# acceptees attending	248
Average LSAT	161
LSAT Range	157–162
Average undergrad GPA	3.5
Application fee	$75
Regular application deadline	3/1
Regular notification	rolling
Rolling notification?	Yes
Early application program?	No
Transfer students accepted?	Yes
Evening division offered?	No
Part-time accepted?	No
LSDAS accepted?	Yes

Applicants Also Look At

American University, Boston College, Fordham University, New York Law School, Temple University, Tulane University, University of Notre Dame.

International Students

TOEFL required of international students?	No
TOEFL recommended of international students?	Yes
Minimum Paper TOEFL	550
Minimum Computer TOEFL	210

FINANCIAL FACTS

Annual tuition	$26,190
Books and supplies	$3,895
Room & board (off-campus)	$11,700
% first-year students receiving some sort of aid	81
% receiving some sort of aid	81
% of aid that is merit-based	2
% receiving scholarships	16
Average grant	$8,425
Average loan	$34,507
Average total aid package	$10,358
Average debt	$89,193

WAKE FOREST UNIVERSITY
SCHOOL OF LAW

INSTITUTIONAL INFORMATION

Public/private	private
Student/faculty ratio	12:1
% faculty part-time	26
% faculty female	24
% faculty minority	16
Total faculty	45

SURVEY SAYS . . .

Diverse opinions accepted in classrooms
Great research resources
Beautiful campus

STUDENTS

Enrollment of law school	480
% male/female	52/48
% out-of-state	71
% full-time	98
% minority	15
% international	3
# of countries represented	35
Average age of entering class	25

ACADEMICS

Academic Experience rating	**93**
Professors interesting rating	95
Professors accessible rating	92
Hours of study per day	5.05

Academic Specialties

Commercial law, constitutional law, corporation securities law, criminal law, international law, labor law, taxation.

Advanced Degrees Offered

LLM in American law, 1 year. Matriculated candidates are graduates of foreign law schools who plan to return to their native countries to practice.

Combined Degrees Offered

JD/MBA. Students may complete both degrees in 4 years rather than 5.

Academic Requirements

Clinical Program Required?	No
Legal Writing Course Requirement?	Yes

Academics

"Wake is great!" That's the general consensus at tiny Wake Forest University School of Law, where you will find a "friendly [administration,] small class sizes, [and] very accessible" professors. Each entering class of 160 students "is divided into four sections of 40. "The small class sizes allow students to form relationships with the professors [and create] a great atmosphere for discussions."

Students tell us that their "amazing, brilliant, [and] committed [professors are] passionate about the law [and] personally invested in your success." One student says, "Professors love their jobs, [and teaching is] their top priority." Another student gushes, "The professors care so much. In addition to always welcoming students into their office at any time, they play football with us, have dinner parties with us, and even join us occasionally for post-exam celebrations." Back in the "mostly serious" classroom, the Socratic Method is alive and well, but "the experience is more of a free exchange of ideas." Though "the professors do not make the classes easy, [they] always look for opportunities to liven things up." One student adds, "Plus, we have a professor that goes by the name 'Mad Dog.' Can you beat that?"

Wake Forest boasts an excellent JD/MBA program and "much of the course work is geared toward students who want to practice corporate law." Students agree, "There is great breadth in the courses offered, [but registration can be] really frustrating [because it seems like classes are] all offered on the same days at the same times." Students' "access to local attorneys and renowned judges" is abundant. Students prize the Litigation Clinic ("it's the best thing at school") and the Elder Law Clinic. They say that, generally, there are "lots of opportunities to get involved with resume-building activities." Depending on who you talk to, courses in legal writing and research are either "spotty at best" or adept at producing "top-notch legal writers."

Student opinion with regard to Career Services is split. Some say Career Services "does a great job [and] will do everything they can to help you find the perfect fit." Others contend that it is "stuck in the dark ages." Some students do not like the fact that "if you want to work outside North Carolina, the office is of almost no help." Dissatisfied students clamor for "more access to the Northeast." Luckily, "Wake is currently expanding its prospective employer base beyond the Southeast, [a trend which] needs to continue."

If you like "brick, green lawns, and great landscaping," you'll like Wake Forest's "beautiful" campus. However, the design of the law school itself gives rise to myriad complaints. "To get anywhere you have to go up two floors, then back down two floors, just because no one thought to put a door in the right place," says one student. "Fighting a dense crowd to get to your next class can induce claustrophobia." There are "not enough bathrooms." And classrooms are "absolutely frigid," note students. "I sort of miss being able to feel my toes," ruminates one first-year student. On the plus side, computer access is "ample," and, outside of temperature control problems, the classrooms are "oddly comfortable." One student mentions that the library has "plenty of study carrels on floors that have windows, which is a wonderful bonus you don't know you'll love until you've been there for hours straight."

Melanie E. Nutt
PO Box 7206 Reynolda Station, Winston-Salem, NC 27109
Telephone: 336-758-5437 • Fax: 336-758-3930
E-mail: admissioins@law.wfu.edu • Website: www.law.wfu.edu

Life

"The greatest strength of Wake Forest Law is collegial atmosphere." However, there is also "an air of competition at Wake Forest that students do not like to admit." One student says, "All the students are concerned about getting good grades and excelling, but the general consensus is that there needs to be a balance between school and life." So, luckily, "it never becomes an unpleasant cutthroat environment." Wake's small size helps to foster "a sense of community and a fertile learning environment, [which is] perfect for facilitating growth and friendship." Or, as one student profoundly observes, "It's like elementary school, only taller."

Outside the classroom, there's plenty happening on campus—everything "from free flu shots to lectures with Maya Angelou about First Amendment issues." One student claims, "We also have an incredible list of speakers that come for the lunch hour, where lunch is served by the school. That's a really nice bonus on a budget." Off-campus, "Winston-Salem is a wonderful city." Students say, "It is just the right size because it is large enough to have things to see and do [yet] small enough to not have traffic and overcrowding." While it's "not the hotbed of progressive urban culture, there are plenty of festivals, restaurants, national parks, and some concerts." It is also good to note that "the mall is a 15-minute drive [away]." Some students long for "better nightlife." Others tell us that students "know how to throw-down and have fun." One student comments, "If you thought undergrad was the time for drinking, you were so wrong." Another student continues, "The legal fraternity and the SBA [usually put together] one law school program a week outside of class, so we can just relax together and get to know one another."

Getting In

The average admitted student has a GPA of 3.4 and an LSAT score of 162. Over 70 percent of the law student population hails from a state other than North Carolina.

EMPLOYMENT INFORMATION

Career Rating	**77**
% employed within 9 months	95
Average starting salary	$63,831
State for bar exam	NC, VA, NY, GA, FL
Pass rate for first-time bar	92

Employers who frequently hire grads: For a representative list, see Career Services Website at www.law.wfu.edu.

Grads employed by field (%):	
Business/industry	5
Government	15
Judicial clerkships	13
Military	2
Other	2
Private practice	63
Public interest	1

Legal Methods Course Requirement?	No
Legal Research Course Requirement?	Yes
Moot Court Requirement?	No
Public Interest Law Requirement?	No

ADMISSIONS

Selectivity Rating	**88**
# applications received	2,433
# applicants accepted	493
# acceptees attending	157
Average LSAT	162
LSAT Range	160–165
Average undergrad GPA	3.4
Application fee	$60
Regular application deadline	4/1
Regular notification	4/15
Rolling notification?	Yes
Early application program?	No
Transfer students accepted?	Yes
Evening division offered?	No
Part-time accepted?	No
LSDAS accepted?	Yes

Applicants Also Look At

American University, College of William & Mary, Emory University, The George Washington University, Tulane University, University of North Carolina at Chapel Hill, Vanderbilt University.

International Students

TOEFL required of international students?	No
TOEFL recommended of international students?	Yes
Minimum Paper TOEFL	650

FINANCIAL FACTS

Annual tuition	$26,400
Books and supplies	$800
Room & board (off-campus)	$12,000
Financial aid application deadline	5/15
% first-year students receiving some sort of aid	78
% receiving some sort of aid	78
% of aid that is merit-based	74
% receiving scholarships	36
Average grant	$18,825
Average loan	$30,128
Average debt	$73,600

WASHBURN UNIVERSITY
SCHOOL OF LAW

INSTITUTIONAL INFORMATION

Public/private	public
Student/faculty ratio	14:1
% faculty part-time	20
% faculty female	44
% faculty minority	27
Total faculty	31

SURVEY SAYS . . .

Diverse opinions accepted in classrooms
Great research resources
Great library staff

STUDENTS

Enrollment of law school	462
% male/female	56/44
% full-time	100
% minority	12
% international	1
Average age of entering class	26

ACADEMICS

Academic Experience rating	**77**
Professors interesting rating	82
Professors accessible rating	87
Hours of study per day	4.06

Academic Specialties

Advocacy, commercial law, corporation securities law, criminal law, environmental law, family law, rural law, taxation.

Advanced Degrees Offered

JD, 90 credit hours, 3 years.

Academic Requirements

Clinical Program Required?	Yes
Legal Writing Course Requirement?	Yes
Legal Methods Course Requirement?	Yes
Legal Research Course Requirement?	No
Moot Court Requirement?	No
Public Interest Law Requirement?	No

Academics

When doling out praise for their school, Washburn University School of Law students hardly know where to begin. From small class sizes to wireless Internet service and an active legal clinic program, Washburn University provides everything a student would hope to find in a law school program. It won't even break the bank, either, since "the tuition is very reasonable, and the cost of living in Topeka is extremely low." Academically, students say that Washburn's rigorous curriculum leaves them well prepared for a professional career. In particular, the school is known for its strong preparation of trial lawyers. "Washburn's greatest strength is in the training of future litigators. From the original *Brown v. Board of Education* attorneys to those who brought down the 'Keating 5,' Washburn has a knack for producing top-flight court-room attorneys."

Although the school offers first-rate litigation training, it isn't packed with a bunch of cutthroat court sharks. In fact, students at this "kinder, gentler" law school say that the environment is friendly, open, and intimate, and has professors who encourage cooperation instead of competition. Students praise "the incredibly supportive atmosphere created by the administration and faculty." Indeed, Washburn faculty and staff make a concerted effort to promote a sense of community on campus. One professor, for example, "started the second day of class by naming all 75 students by first and last name. He only got one wrong." Students tell us that "the faculty goes to pains to encourage students to stop into their offices, and frequently the visits are less about the business of class than whatever is on the student's mind." In the classroom, "Professors have a genuine interest in teaching and are still excited about what they teach; it is quite evident they love what they are doing."

The facilities at Washburn get decent marks from students. "The library is airy and has more computer terminals than users. The classrooms are spacious and amply equipped with modern technology that is regularly used by even the most ancient faculty members." Few complaints include that "the building is outdated" and that "wireless Internet access is not always working." Parking could also be much better, especially if they could do something about those pesky undergraduates who "take up most of the law school's parking lot."

Students give thumbs up to Career Services, saying that Washburn's strong local reputation assures them good jobs after graduation. "The school has a great regional reputation and seems to be gaining prestige across the country," a student assures. However, many lament the fact that Washburn isn't well known outside of the Midwest and would like to see Career Services "broaden the university's horizons beyond the Midwest-centric focus [and] attract employers from beyond Kansas's neighboring states." On a positive note, because Washburn is located in state capital Topeka, a town with "both district and supreme courts, [there are] a lot of good job opportunities" available before and after graduation.

Karla Beam, Director of Admissions
1700 College, Topeka, KS 66621-1140
Telephone: 785-231-1185 • Fax: 785-232-1120
E-mail: admissions@washburnlaw.edu • Website: http://washburnlaw.edu

Life

On campus, the vibe is friendly and social. Students say that their peers, "while competitive, will still help out a struggling classmate." Outside of class, students bond through the many campus clubs, social events, and school-sponsored speakers. "From volunteering to partying, one group always has something going on." If you go to the right "gatherings, meetings and parties, [you] can usually find free food at least twice a week." One cool thing is that "the Student Bar Association hosts debates on issues and between political candidates. Recently, there was one focusing on homosexuality featuring Washburn lawyers, gay activists, and America's leading hate-monger Fred Phelps." Washburn seems to be a pretty tolerant place, where there exists "a genuine acceptance of people from all backgrounds. The student body is remarkably diverse considering the school is located in the middle of Kansas." Politically, "students are in the middle with a slight lean to the right, although there are a few extremists on each side."

Washburn is located in Topeka, Kansas, a city that has "all the conveniences of a big city," but is still small (therefore its citizens enjoy a lower cost-of-living). Yet, students aren't exactly wild about Topeka and warn that the metropolitan area doesn't offer much to do. One student laments, "If the school could just be picked up and flown about five miles out of Topeka, things would be much nicer." Another student gripes, "The town is ridden with crime and the citizens are shifty-eyed." But to look on the bright side, the fact that "Topeka isn't exactly a hot-bed of social activities" means there's "more time to study, so it's not entirely a bad thing." Hey, and if you really don't like it, "you can always live in Lawrence and commute."

Getting In

Washburn evaluates prospective students on the basis of their LSAT scores and GPAs, as well as a number of other factors derived from their applications, transcripts, personal statements, and letters of recommendation. In the past application season, admitted students to Washburn had an average LSAT score of 153 and an average GPA of 3.23.

EMPLOYMENT INFORMATION

Career Rating	**68**
% employed within 9 months	97
Average starting salary	$45,931
State for bar exam	KS
Pass rate for first-time bar	82

Prominent Alumni: Lillian A. Apodaca, former president Hispanic Bar Association; Robert J. Dole, former U.S. senator; William H. Kurtis, journalist/American justice; Delano E. Lewis, former ambassador to South Africa; Ron Richey, chair of executive committee of Torchmark Corp.

Grads employed by field (%):	
Academic	2
Business/industry	13
Government	16
Judicial clerkships	6
Military	3
Private practice	51
Public interest	9

ADMISSIONS

Selectivity Rating	**74**
# applications received	1,172
# applicants accepted	370
# acceptees attending	157
Average LSAT	153
LSAT Range	151–156
Average undergrad GPA	3.2
Application fee	$40
Regular application deadline	4/1
Regular notification	6/1
Rolling notification?	Yes
Early application program?	No
Transfer students accepted?	Yes
Evening division offered?	No
Part-time accepted?	No
LSDAS accepted?	Yes

International Students

TOEFL required of international students?	No
TOEFL recommended of international students?	Yes

FINANCIAL FACTS

Annual tuition (resident)	$11,842
Annual tuition (nonresident)	$19,499
Books and supplies	$1,457
Tuition per credit (resident)	$382
Tuition per credit (nonresident)	$629
Room & board	$11,527
Financial aid application deadline	4/1
% first-year students receiving some sort of aid	96
% receiving some sort of aid	97
% receiving scholarships	46
Average loan	$17,787
Average total aid package	$18,600
Average debt	$40,866

WASHINGTON AND LEE UNIVERSITY
SCHOOL OF LAW

INSTITUTIONAL INFORMATION

Public/private	private
Student/faculty ratio	11:1
% faculty part-time	41
% faculty female	25
% faculty minority	10
Total faculty	61

SURVEY SAYS . . .

Diverse opinions accepted in classrooms
Great research resources
Great library staff

STUDENTS

Enrollment of law school	399
% male/female	57/43
% out-of-state	85
% full-time	100
% minority	18
% international	1
# of countries represented	12
Average age of entering class	25

ACADEMICS

Academic Experience rating	**96**
Professors interesting rating	98
Professors accessible rating	99
Hours of study per day	3.93

Advanced Degrees Offered

Master of law LLM in United States law.

Academic Requirements

Clinical Program Required?	No
Legal Writing Course Requirement?	Yes
Legal Methods Course Requirement?	No
Legal Research Course Requirement?	No
Moot Court Requirement?	No
Public Interest Law Requirement?	No

Academics

Students at tiny, "top-notch" Washington and Lee University School of Law speak of their academic experience in exceptionally glowing terms. Classes are "small," the administration "really listens to the students," the library staff and computer facilities are "excellent," and the faculty-to-student ratio is "very low." Plus, the school "has a low price [and] gives away a ton of money in scholarships." About the only complaints we hear are that "there are not many advanced classes in particularized fields" and that students would like to see "a wider range of classes" in general.

"Washington and Lee's professors love to teach [and] more important, they are great teachers." These "extremely accessible professors are smart and not snobby," according to one emphatic student. "They know everyone's name [and] want to help you along the way." Though "the professors keep everything at a fast pace, [students] are given the opportunity to keep up with them [thanks to a] genuine [and very popular] open-door policy, [which] provides for lots of interaction" between students and professors. "It's not uncommon to be invited to a professor's home for dinner. You really get to know them and their families. You can even play pick-up basketball with your professors," if the mood strikes you. Eventually, "when the time comes to get recommendations, it's no problem. You have access to people who have gotten to know you personally and professionally."

Washington and Lee's "very practical [legal writing program holds students] to extremely high standards." Students take classes, including the intensive writing course, in "small sections." This means that "the professor (who is always a tenured or tenure track professor—never a student or teaching assistant) really gets to know your writing and has one-on-one feedback sessions with you about your memos and motions." Clinical programs are also exceptional. The unique Virginia Capital Case Clearinghouse allows a few lucky students to assist in death-penalty cases and to publish an online journal devoted to the law of capital punishment. Students in the Black Lung Clinic represent coal miners seeking federal disability payments because they have contracted pneumoconiosis (a debilitating and sometimes fatal respiratory condition caused by the inhalation of coal dust). Black Lung students get to match wits against big-time attorneys for the coal industry. If you want to fight the power, this is your chance.

"The carpet and building design [at W&L are] from the 70s, [but the] awesome, state-of-the-art [classrooms boast] big, comfy adjustable chairs, high-tech visual equipment [and,] of course, wireless Internet." You'll even find "automated shades" in this building. "Metal comes down over the windows and everything" when overhead projectors are used in class. We guess you have to be there, but students assure us that the experience is pretty cool. Another huge plus is that the library is "open 24 hours a day."

Andrea Hilton Howe, Director of Admissions
Sydney Lewis Hall, Lexington, VA 24450
Telephone: 540-458-8503 • Fax: 540-458-8586
E-mail: lawadm@wlu.edu • Website: www.law.wlu.edu

Life

Washington and Lee is a "very small" law school in a very small town "out in the middle of nowhere." On the plus side, the "idyllic, rural, [and] peaceful [location] allows you to focus on law school rather than the additional stresses of life in the city." One student says, "The setting is beautiful, [and] there is nothing more lovely than Lexington for hiking, driving, and going to wineries or waterfalls." However, "it gets cold [in the winter], and the place is so remote that nobody knows it exists."

While "there are cliques and cool kids [at W&L,] there is an undeniable sense of community" among the law students. "The best thing about Washington and Lee Law School is that there is a great collegial atmosphere," relates a happy student. "We find a way to be driven while still supporting each other." Students say, "The family-like atmosphere allows for the building of great friendships and academic collaboration. Everyone is supportive [and] super-nice." There is "virtually no competition, which is good [since] there is nowhere to hide."

"The social atmosphere is a lot like high school." There are "very few places to hang out outside of school, [and] most people don't have friends outside of the law school in Lexington." The result is "a unique social bubble, [which] can be great and terrible at the same time." One student analogizes, "It's like going to boarding school without the dorms." There is also "a lot of alcohol, even at the family-oriented stuff." One student explains, "We engage in lots of social activities together, from sports to parties to lectures." Football, volleyball, softball, and intramural sports in general are also very popular.

Getting In

Washington and Lee is one of the best law schools in the country and admission requirements are fairly lofty. Enrolled students at the 25th percentile have an LSAT score of 163 and a GPA of 3.1. Enrolled students at the 75th percentile have an LSAT score of 167 and a GPA of 3.7. W&L does not offer a part-time or evening program.

EMPLOYMENT INFORMATION

Career Rating	**73**
% employed within 9 months	93
Average starting salary	$67,386

Grads employed by field (%):	
Academic	1
Business/industry	6
Government	4
Judicial clerkships	24
Other	4
Private practice	55
Public interest	3

ADMISSIONS

Selectivity Rating	**90**
# applications received	3,710
# applicants accepted	713
# acceptees attending	128
Average LSAT	166
LSAT Range	162–167
Average undergrad GPA	3.5
Application fee	$50
Regular application deadline	2/1
Regular notification	4/1
Rolling notification?	Yes
Early application program?	No
Transfer students accepted?	Yes
Evening division offered?	No
Part-time accepted?	No
LSDAS accepted?	Yes

Applicants Also Look At

College of William & Mary, University of Virginia, Vanderbilt University.

International Students

TOEFL required of international students?	Yes

FINANCIAL FACTS

Annual tuition	$25,300
Books and supplies	$1,500
Room & board (off-campus)	$13,179
Financial aid application deadline	2/15
% first-year students receiving some sort of aid	95
% receiving some sort of aid	97
% of aid that is merit-based	100
% receiving scholarships	81
Average grant	$12,572
Average loan	$26,707
Average total aid package	$34,613
Average debt	$56,026

Washington University
School of Law

INSTITUTIONAL INFORMATION

Public/private	private
Student/faculty ratio	14:1
% faculty part-time	50
% faculty female	35
% faculty minority	2
Total faculty	116

SURVEY SAYS . . .

Great research resources
Beautiful campus

STUDENTS

Enrollment of law school	756
% male/female	58/42
% full-time	99
% minority	18
% international	5
# of countries represented	10
Average age of entering class	23

ACADEMICS

Academic Experience rating	**89**
Professors interesting rating	88
Professors accessible rating	89
Hours of study per day	4.23

Academic Specialties

Civil procedure, commercial law, constitutional law, corporation securities law, criminal law, environmental law, government services, human rights law, intellectual property law, international law, labor law, legal history, legal philosophy, property, taxation.

Advanced Degrees Offered

JD; JSD; LLM for foreign lawyers; LLM in taxation; LLM in intellectual property and technology law.

Combined Degrees Offered

JD/MBA; JD/MS in economics; JD/MSW in social work; JD/MA in Jewish, Islamic, & Near Eastern studies; JD/MA in East Asian studies; JD/PHD in political science, JD/MA in health administration.

Academic Requirements

Clinical Program Required?	No

Academics

Washington University School of Law "excels at being a small school with a drive to succeed at everything it touches." One student adds, "An apparently bottomless bucket of money" certainly helps. The curriculum "is both broad and deep. Whether you're more of a thinker or a doer, there are plenty of endeavors available to you." The workload "is challenging but not suicide-inducing." There is a variety of curriculum including "plenty of journals, moot court teams, public interest opportunities, [and] unparalleled" clinical programs.

The "flexible and responsive [administration] does an excellent job of interacting with students and listening to concerns." Students note a commitment by the administration at Washington University to making it "a top-notch law school." A few professors are "truly horrible, [but most fall in the] truly excellent" end of the spectrum. They are "leading academics [who] range from strictly Socratic to almost entirely lecture" in their classroom styles and "foster spirited discussions concerning the policy considerations behind the law." One awed student writes, "I am amazed at the quality and dedication of most of the professors." The faculty is "very accessible and approachable" as well. "The open-door policy that every law school claims to have is actually real here," declares one student.

Career-wise, "WashU provides great opportunities for students who wish to stay in Missouri but also maintains contacts with legal employers all over the country." The specialty of the "efficient [Career Services office is providing] excellent opportunities for students to work in major Midwestern cities like Chicago, St. Louis, Kansas City, and Minneapolis." Some students gripe that "Career Services could be more nationally focused," though. "Our alumni are not very spread out throughout the United States, so we sometimes have to explain our pedigree and prestige when we're interviewing out of town," writes one student. Also, "there needs to be a broader range of focus, [including opportunities in] public interest, government, and alternative legal professions."

Students attend classes in a "big, bright, extraordinary, [and pretty much] brand-new [building] named after the largest brewery in the United States." Visually, it "resembles a castle in some respects." One student notes, "Busch's beer may be fairly characterized as mundanely ordinary, but Anheuser-Busch Hall is superb." Students say, "Slate roofs, very elegant aesthetics, [and] gargoyles representing the legal profession welcome students into its modern, yet traditional halls. It's a pleasant place to spend all your time." State-of-the-art technology and wireless Internet are nice perks, too. Another student exclaims, "A [great] library [is home to an] easily accessible, exceptionally knowledgeable," and well-liked staff.

Janet Bolin, Associate Dean of Admissions and Financial Aid
1 Brookings Drive, Campus Box 1120, St. Louis, MO 63130-4899
Telephone: 314-935-4525 • Fax: 314-935-8778
E-mail: admiss@wulaw.wustl.edu • Website: http://law.wustl.edu

Life

Students at Washington University tell us that their law school is "remarkably friendly [and that a] non-competitive atmosphere" pervades. What's more, "The social scene is sweet." Throughout the fall and spring, the courtyard in the center of the building is "a great place" for reading, eating lunch, "or just hanging out with friends." The law school also sponsors "free beer and snacks every Friday, [and] the whole school—including professors—usually attends." One student reports, "With both students and professors often living within minutes of the school, both tend to spend quite a bit of time in the library at off-hours and socializing at happy hours." Additionally, different student groups host numerous events. "The gay and lesbian support groups had professional drag queens come in for a show," recalls one student. Also, "the women's law caucus hosts an auction each spring to raise money for the summer stipend program," writes another. Yet another student says, "Our student government is outstanding and throws an awesome Halloween party [and] Barrister's Ball." Intramural sports are quite popular, too. "Law students love taking on each other, the med school, and the cross-quad rival, the business school."

Off-campus, "the surrounding area is decent." If there is a "problem with the school, [it is its location] in St. Louis, [which] could use some upgrades. "One student explains, "St. Louis lacks 21- to 30-year-old intellectuals outside of its great graduate schools." Luckily, these students are able to "come together at bars and other functions." Another student reports, "There are bar-sponsored parties and socials, and our class picks a bar every week to frequent. So we drink a lot."

Getting In

Washington University is one of the hardest schools in the Midwest to get into, but it is by no means impossible. The mean LSAT score for entering students is 164. The mean GPA is 3.6.

EMPLOYMENT INFORMATION

Career Rating	**60***
Average starting salary	$79,135
State for bar exam	MO, IL, CA, NY

Employers who frequently hire grads:
Bryan Cave, Winston & Strawn, Paul Weiss, Arnold & Porter, public defender, state attorney general.

Grads employed by field (%):	
Academic	2
Business/industry	7
Government	12
Judicial clerkships	7
Private practice	68
Public interest	4

Legal Writing Course Requirement?	Yes
Legal Methods Course Requirement?	No
Legal Research Course Requirement?	Yes
Moot Court Requirement?	No
Public Interest Law Requirement?	No

ADMISSIONS

Selectivity Rating	**89**
# applications received	3,113
# applicants accepted	802
# acceptees attending	235
Average LSAT	165
LSAT Range	162–167
Average undergrad GPA	3.6
Application fee	$70
Regular application deadline	3/1
Regular notification	4/15
Rolling notification?	No
Early application program?	Yes
Early application deadline	12/1
Early application notification	12/15
Transfer students accepted?	Yes
Evening division offered?	No
Part-time accepted?	No
LSDAS accepted?	Yes

Applicants Also Look At

Boston College, Boston U., The George Washington U., Georgetown U., Northwestern U., U. of Southern California, Vanderbilt U.

International Students

TOEFL required of international students?	No
TOEFL recommended of international students?	Yes
Minimum Paper TOEFL	600

FINANCIAL FACTS

Annual tuition	$32,590
Books and supplies	$1,000
Room & board (off-campus)	$7,300
Financial aid application deadline	3/1
% first-year students receiving some sort of aid	90
% receiving some sort of aid	92
% of aid that is merit-based	100
% receiving scholarships	65
Average grant	$10,000
Average loan	$33,000
Average total aid package	$45,000
Average debt	$83,700

WAYNE STATE UNIVERSITY
LAW SCHOOL

INSTITUTIONAL INFORMATION

Public/private	public
Student/faculty ratio	23:1
% faculty part-time	59
% faculty female	39
% faculty minority	12
Total faculty	33

SURVEY SAYS . . .

Diverse opinions accepted in classrooms
Great research resources
Abundant externship/internship/clerkship opportunities

STUDENTS

Enrollment of law school	725
% male/female	52/48
% out-of-state	3
% full-time	71
% minority	15
# of countries represented	91
Average age of entering class	25

ACADEMICS

Academic Experience rating	**69**
Professors interesting rating	77
Professors accessible rating	76
Hours of study per day	3.26

Advanced Degrees Offered

JD, 3 years full-time; LLM, 1 year full-time.

Combined Degrees Offered

JD/MBA, 4 years; JD/MA, history and political science, 4 years; JD/MA, 4 years; JD/MADR, 4 years.

Academic Requirements

Clinical Program Required?	No
Legal Writing Course Requirement?	Yes
Legal Methods Course Requirement?	No
Legal Research Course Requirement?	Yes
Moot Court Requirement?	Yes
Public Interest Law Requirement?	No

Academics

The Law School at Wayne State University is efficient, low cost, rich in diversity, and favorably located for future lawyers looking to practice in southeastern Michigan. The school's excellent teaching staff draws praises all around and students assure us that "the academics are stellar." This is at least partly attributable to the fact that, as one 2L puts it, "the faculty are amazing and all boast the highest credentials. We are all confident that we are receiving a premiere education." In addition, "most professors are good teachers and dedicated to imparting knowledge."

While the classrooms could use a touch-up, the school's research and technological facilities are top-notch. A 1L reports, "The law library is extremely well-equipped, and Wayne State is continually improving the technological resources." Yet all this quality comes with a very low price tag. Wayne State students insist that "with [in-state] costs of only $13,000 or so a year, Wayne State deserves even greater recognition as an 'excellent value' in education."

Many students at Wayne State say that one of the school's greatest assets is "the wonderful support given by the administrative staff." Honestly attentive to the student body, administrators are "approachable and always give you advice that you can use" and, furthermore, are extremely efficient at their jobs. A 2L claims that "getting things done at the law school is effortless." In particular, many students have kind words for the charismatic new dean, claiming that "in one year, he has turned the administration around and revitalized the faculty and students." A 2L raves, "One of our greatest strengths? Dean Wu! The man's awesome. I mean, come on, how many other law schools have a dean that rides a motorcycle?"

While the Wayne curriculum will provide you with ample doses of legal theory, there is a strong focus on practical aspects of law. Many of the professors are practicing attorneys and incorporate their expertise into classroom instruction. A 2L explains, "The professors at Wayne are the perfect balance between scholars and practicing lawyers. They help you develop the analytical/theoretical tools you need for a long legal career while also breaking it down to what you really need to know in the real world." In addition, there is "an incredible internship program at Wayne that gives students such great real-world exposure to the legal profession." A 2L shares, "I had a judicial internship at the Federal District Court this semester and am participating in the Urban Housing and Community Development Clinic next semester!" While students appreciate the quality and content of their courses and extracurriculars, some feel that "though the faculty is wonderful, it is too small," and that the school needs to "offer a wider range of classes each semester and improve class scheduling." Students are hopeful that the variety of course offerings will widen shortly as the school "will be adding at least four new tenure-track professors in 2005."

One of the greatest attributes of Wayne State is its location. A 2L boasts, "It is a fabulous location for a law school in general because it is so close to the courts and major MI law firms, as well as very close to Canada. That location alone opens up many opportunities that other MI law schools just cannot compete with." However, students are adamant that the location really pays off after graduation and that "if you want to be a lawyer or a judge in Michigan, Wayne is a great place to be." In fact, "over half of the judges and 75 percent of the lawyers practicing in southeast Michigan are Wayne graduates." Additionally, "the alumni are very active and willing to help other graduates."

LINDA FOWLER SIMS, ASSISTANT DEAN FOR RECRUITMENT AND ADMISSIONS
471 WEST PALMER, DETROIT, MI 48202
TELEPHONE: 313-577-3937 • FAX: 313-993-8129
E-MAIL: LAW.INQUIRE@WAYNE.EDU • WEBSITE: WWW.LAW.WAYNE.EDU

Life

If you are looking to relive your undergraduate years, you may be disappointed with Wayne State. Students warn that "Detroit is not a college town" and that "most students commute to Wayne State, which obviously leads to a different environment than if students lived on campus." This cosmopolitan city is nonetheless "an interesting place to go to school—we have big industry, great suburbs, and lots of diversity." On top of that, "a strong portion of the student body gets together and socializes a great deal," and students say it is easy to make friends among their interesting and talented classmates. A 1L remarks, "The student body is awesome. My section is extremely friendly and we spend a great deal of time together. I see my classmates more than I do my family." While "everyone works well together," be aware that "there is a great deal of competition" academically.

Interacting with their classmates is an important part of the educational experience at Wayne, and within the student body, "there is diversity between races, religions, socio-economic, and prior educational backgrounds." Students say Wayne is the type of place where "you can learn first-hand about people whom you may never have had the opportunity to learn about before," as the environment is "very open and rarely uncomfortable." The "wealth of experience in the student body . . . is an extremely important attribute because, as prospective students will come to find out, you tend to learn as much from your fellow students as you do from you professors."

Getting In

Wayne State admits students on a rolling basis, accepting applications after October 1 for an August start date. Wayne State admits students with competitive LSAT scores and a strong academic record; however, the school also considers relevant personal qualities and characteristics demonstrated through previous leadership positions, community service, or communication ability.

EMPLOYMENT INFORMATION

Career Rating	**82**
Job placement rate (%)	93
Average starting salary	$70,808
State for bar exam	MI, NY, IL, CA, GA
Pass rate for first-time bar	80

Employers who frequently hire grads:
Leading law firms in Michigan, in-house legal departments of Fortune 500 and other corporations and governmental agencies.

Grads employed by field (%):	
Academic	4
Business/industry	18
Government	12
Judicial clerkships	1
Private practice	62

ADMISSIONS

Selectivity Rating	**71**
# applications received	974
# applicants accepted	457
# acceptees attending	195
Average LSAT	154
LSAT Range	151–157
Average undergrad GPA	3.3
Application fee	$50
Regular application deadline	rolling
Regular notification	rolling
Rolling notification?	Yes
Early application program?	Yes
Early application deadline	11/1
Early application notification	12/15
Transfer students accepted?	Yes
Evening division offered?	Yes
Part-time accepted?	Yes
LSDAS accepted?	Yes

Applicants Also Look At
DePaul University, Michigan State University College of Law, Thomas M. Cooley Law School, University of Detroit Mercy, University of Michigan.

International Students

TOEFL required of international students?	No
TOEFL recommended of international students?	No

FINANCIAL FACTS

Annual tuition (resident)	$11,865
Annual tuition (nonresident)	$24,576
Books and supplies	$900
Fees per credit (resident)	$22
Fees per credit (nonresident)	$22
Tuition per credit (resident)	$396
Tuition per credit (nonresident)	$819
Room & board	$11,250
Financial aid application deadline	3/15
% first-year students receiving some sort of aid	95
% receiving some sort of aid	85
% of aid that is merit-based	5
% receiving scholarships	65
Average grant	$2,000
Average loan	$18,500
Average total aid package	$21,500
Average debt	$45,000

West Virginia University
College of Law

INSTITUTIONAL INFORMATION

Public/private	public
Student/faculty ratio	16:1
% faculty part-time	11
% faculty female	11
Total faculty	37

SURVEY SAYS . . .

Great research resources
Great library staff

STUDENTS

Enrollment of law school	471
% male/female	54/46
% out-of-state	23
% full-time	98
% minority	8
# of countries represented	2
Average age of entering class	26

ACADEMICS

Academic Experience rating	**61**
Professors interesting rating	61
Professors accessible rating	61
Hours of study per day	4.19

Academic Specialties

Civil procedure, commercial law, constitutional law, corporation securities law, criminal law, environmental law, government services, human rights law, international law, labor law, legal history, legal philosophy, property, taxation.

Advanced Degrees Offered

JD, 3 years.

Combined Degrees Offered

JD/MPA, 4 years; JD/MBA, 4 years.

Academic Requirements

Clinical Program Required?	No
Legal Writing Course Requirement?	Yes
Legal Methods Course Requirement?	Yes
Legal Research Course Requirement?	No
Moot Court Requirement?	No
Public Interest Law Requirement?	No

Academics

"The quality of education" at West Virginia University College of Law "is exceptional for the price of tuition." Dirt-cheap for WV residents, tuition is quite "affordable" for out-of-state students, as well. An "intense" legal research and writing program is one of WVU's biggest strengths and certainly "good preparation" for holding your own in the legal world. One student reports the program "has been extremely beneficial to me in my summer work experiences, where I have enjoyed a significant advantage over many of my peers."

A common student complaint at WVU is that course offerings are "not as broad as they should be. There are no courses in entertainment law, sports law, mergers and acquisitions, and other courses that do not directly have a large demand in West Virginia," which might prove problematic for those who plan to practice out of state. If you do plan on staying put in West Virginia, however, you will be glad to hear that the school has a very strong connection to the local bar. One student explains that because WVU is the "state's only law school, the State Bar [Association] frequently involves the law school in its functions and provides many opportunities for the students."

Most of the faculty is "incredibly caring, respectful, and accessible [and] as a whole have a real dedication to social justice and progress." Professors "make your law school career enjoyable," says one student. But while "many of the professors are good, some are bad, and a few are just plain ugly," report students. "About half the faculty I would rate as top-notch and excellent instructors," says one student. It sounds like if you can figure out who's who, you'll be in the clear. The good news is that "recent hiring represents a shift of moving toward a younger, more vibrant, and better quality law professor." Another student notes approvingly, "The new faculty members are eager to become involved in activities at the law school and tend to treat students more as colleagues." One cool thing about grading at WVU is that it is done anonymously. Worth noting is that faculty is said to be "extremely liberal."

Students give the administration mixed reviews. Some say it's "helpful and supportive," while others say it leaves "a lot to be desired." The Career Services Center comes under a bit of fire. Students complain that they tend "to focus primarily on placing students in large defense firms" and wish they would have more leads in different areas or in nontraditional jobs or jobs out of West Virginia. Students would like to see them be a little more proactive, too. "The law school Career Service Center advises picking up a telephone book and dialing. Seriously," gripes one student. Another students reports, after Career Services was "no help, I found my job as a legal intern in state government on my own after several days of pounding the pavement around town and a mass-mailing of resumes."

Janet Armistead, Assistant Dean for Admissions
PO Box 6130, Morgantown, WV 26506-6103
Telephone: 304-293-5304 • Fax: 304-293-6891
E-mail: wvulaw.admissions@mail.wvu.edu • Website: www.wvu.edu/~law

The law school building "was built in the 70s [and] is essentially a concrete box, comprised of a few classrooms with no windows." Yet, "it has everything," say students, who are particularly "impressed with the library resources." Word has it that the College of Law has "everything you would ever need and more to answer any legal question [and that] the library staff is particularly nice and helpful as well." But, alas, you may want to "bring some ear plugs [since] the library has become the main social area of the school." Finally, it's good to know that WVU is the rare school that can actually boast, "great parking!"

Life

Students claim that the College of Law's campus, located in the Appalachian mountains of West Virginia, provides an "excellent social life." Students say, "Morgantown is your typical college town, [and for entertainment,] there are lots of concerts, and WVU sports are very popular." Students do admit that "Morgantown and WVU are known for drinking in excess [and that] the law school is no exception." However, "if being a party animal is not your scene there is still an abundance of things to do around town."

Students say that their classmates at WVU are "friendly and helpful toward one another," and the overall student body is not cutthroat. "The best thing about this law school is the students," says one of them. "I feel as though the other students are here to help one another, and this minimizes competition." One thing students would like to see improve is the diversity of the student body.

Getting In

West Virginia's admitted students at the 25th percentile have an LSAT score of 149 and a GPA of 3.2. Admitted students at the 75th percentile have an LSAT score of 156 and a GPA of 3.7.

EMPLOYMENT INFORMATION

Career Rating	**65**
Job placement rate (%)	95
Average starting salary	$45,614
State for bar exam	WV
Pass rate for first-time bar	80

Employers who frequently hire grads:
Law firms, government, judicial clerks.

Grads employed by field (%):	
Academic	2
Business/industry	3
Government	3
Judicial clerkships	28
Private practice	59
Public interest	4

ADMISSIONS

Selectivity Rating	**73**
# applications received	674
# applicants accepted	305
# acceptees attending	165
Average LSAT	154
LSAT Range	149–156
Average undergrad GPA	3.4
Application fee	$50
Regular application deadline	2/1
Regular notification	rolling
Rolling notification?	Yes
Early application program?	No
Transfer students accepted?	Yes
Evening division offered?	No
Part-time accepted?	Yes
LSDAS accepted?	Yes

Applicants Also Look At
College of William & Mary, University of Pennsylvania, University of Pittsburgh.

International Students

TOEFL required of international students?	Yes
Minimum Paper TOEFL	600
Minimum Computer TOEFL	250

FINANCIAL FACTS

Annual tuition (resident)	$3,904
Annual tuition (nonresident)	$11,508
Books and supplies	$1,200
Room & board	$11,233
Financial aid application deadline	3/1
% first-year students receiving some sort of aid	35
% receiving some sort of aid	90
% of aid that is merit-based	1
% receiving scholarships	24
Average grant	$1,776
Average loan	$13,945
Average total aid package	$18,635
Average debt	$45,146

Western New England College
School of Law

INSTITUTIONAL INFORMATION

Public/private	private
Student/faculty ratio	13:1
% faculty part-time	49
% faculty female	43
% faculty minority	9
Total faculty	69

SURVEY SAYS . . .

Diverse opinions accepted in classrooms
Great research resources
Great library staff

STUDENTS

Enrollment of law school	585
% male/female	54/46
% out-of-state	67
% full-time	73
% minority	18
% international	9
# of countries represented	6
Average age of entering class	26

ACADEMICS

Academic Experience rating	**64**
Professors interesting rating	70
Professors accessible rating	71
Hours of study per day	4.67

Advanced Degrees Offered

Starting in fall 2005 Western New England College School of Law will begin offering classes toward an LLM in estate planning and elder law. The program can be completed over 2 or 3 years.

Combined Degrees Offered

JD/MRP, masters of regional planning, with the University of Masssachusetts, 4 years; JD/MSW with Springfield College, 4 years; JD/MBA, masters of business administration, with Western New England College, 4 years.

Academic Requirements

Clinical Program Required?	No
Legal Writing Course Requirement?	Yes

Academics

Western New England College School of Law is a small, private institution with an accomplished teaching staff, diverse student body, and growing national reputation. Students report that their classes are "engaging" and that professors are "simply phenomenal," capable of bringing not just expertise, but also passion to the study of law. "The professors are very knowledgeable and interesting. Their enthusiasm about and devotion to the law, especially their areas of specialization, is apparent in every classroom discussion," reports one 1L. Indeed, the "open and inviting" classroom atmosphere inspires student participation and "debate is encouraged both in and out of the classroom." At WNEC "teaching occurs through the Socratic Method (99 percent of the time) and by means of answering students' questions (1 percent)." Therefore, students must come prepared to participate in class and be ready to think on their feet. The effort pays off. WNEC students report that they "easily master Black Letter law" and feel well prepared for the bar exam, as well as future practice.

While courses are tough, the academic environment at WNEC is decidedly supportive and student friendly. From their first day on campus, "each student is appointed a faculty advisor," and the school offers an optional Legal Education Achievement Program (LEAP) for first- and second-year students, designed to help them improve their study and organizational skills. On top of that, Western New England College "places a heavy emphasis on accessibility of the faculty," and students feel comfortable asking their professors for extra guidance. For example, one 2L reports, "During a writing assignment, I called a professor on a Saturday at home, and she called me back! That is a professor who cares!" Beyond academic concerns, WNEC teachers "encourage students to access them outside of the classroom in order to establish a more personal relationship" and some "even go to bars with the students after class." As a result, professors become more like mentors or friends, willing to lend an ear in any manner of discussion. Similarly, the administration at WNEC works to develop a personal connection with students. A 2L elaborates, "The administration is great. You can always get in to see them and the dean interacts with the students quite often when he hosts the Dean's Tea."

Outside traditional course work, students at WNEC build their resumes and experience through the school's numerous extracurricular programs, including "many volunteer opportunities for 1Ls," clinics, simulations, and externship placements in the Boston area. In addition, the administration works to maintain a lively academic atmosphere and "many outstanding lecturers have already spoken on campus by mid-semester." However, while the day students are highly satisfied with the extracurricular activities and programs available to them, participants in the evening program feel their needs are often overlooked; one such student writes, "Most programs and opportunities seem to be geared toward day students," adding that evening and working students are "limited in opportunities because activities, office hours, and training are scheduled during the middle of the day or afternoons."

Students insist that they receive "a quality education that is comparable to (although perhaps less theoretical than) the top-tier law schools," but many do worry that the school's reputation is still lagging behind where it should be. A 2L laments, "If I could change one thing about WNEC Law, I would match the school's reputation with the outstanding education it provides." Students say administrators "do not do enough to promote the school" or its alumni. However, things may change as the school "becomes more of a national draw." In addition to more widespread recruiting, the administration

Michael A. Johnson, Assistant Dean & Director of Admissions
1215 Wilbraham Road, Springfield, MA 01119
Telephone: 413-782-1406 • Fax: 413-796-2067
E-mail: admissions@law.wnec.edu • Website: www.law.wnec.edu

is committed to constant improvement in the curriculum, campus, and facilities. Students tell prospective students to look for updates in a number of other areas. For example, "the classrooms are being updated as we speak," and "the school is expanding its wireless Internet network." On top of that, the school is constantly offering new programs and classes, such as a recently instituted bar review course.

Life

While the WNEC student body is small, the school boasts "a wide age range, race range, and socioeconomic range." As a result, it's not surprising that "not everyone agrees socially or politically." Students insist, however, that the diversity of opinion and background "makes WNEC rich and interesting" and that "disagreements only spark discussion, not argument." Out of class, WNEC students are far from competitive. By almost all accounts "the school environment is relaxed," and students are generally described as "cooperative and helpful with each other." While studious WNEC students have a strong work ethic and desire to succeed, they are always willing to lend a hand to a colleague. A 1L explains, "There is a strong sense that everyone wants to do well, but not at the expense of another."

WNEC is home to a fairly active student body, and there are a number of campus-based social activities and academic clubs that attract the younger day students. Full-timers say that "everyone is friendly and social" and that it is easy to make friends on this small campus. Some would like to see the extracurricular offerings expanded to include more intellectual or professional activities, rather than primarily social events. In addition, some students in the part-time program feel they aren't well-integrated into the campus community, as the majority of activities take place in the afternoons. "I can say that as an evening student, I do feel that we miss out on a lot of things," complains one 2L.

Getting In

WNEC accepts students on a rolling basis for fall admission until March 15 of each year. Among law schools, the admissions process is fairly forgiving, with about two of every five applicants accepted. More than a quarter of students are in the part-time program.

EMPLOYMENT INFORMATION

Career Rating	**70**
% employed within 9 months	81
Average starting salary	$55,535
State for bar exam	CT, MA, NY, NJ, PA
Pass rate for first-time bar	73

Employers who frequently hire grads:
Bingham Dana; Day, Berry, & Howard; Shipman & Goodwin; accounting firms; insurance companies; government agencies.

Grads employed by field (%):	
Academic	1.2
Business/industry	22
Government	13.4
Judicial clerkships	12.2
Military	3.7
Private practice	43.9
Public interest	3.7

Legal Methods Course Requirement?	Yes
Legal Research Course Requirement?	Yes
Moot Court Requirement?	No
Public Interest Law Requirement?	No

ADMISSIONS

Selectivity Rating	**69**
# applications received	1,655
# applicants accepted	674
# acceptees attending	194
Average LSAT	152
LSAT Range	150–156
Average undergrad GPA	3.1
Application fee	$50
Regular application deadline	rolling
Regular notification	rolling
Rolling notification?	Yes
Early application program?	No
Transfer students accepted?	Yes
Evening division offered?	Yes
Part-time accepted?	Yes
LSDAS accepted?	Yes

Applicants Also Look At

Albany Law School, New England School of Law, Quinnipiac University, Roger Williams University, Suffolk University, University of Connecticut.

International Students

TOEFL required of international students?	Yes

FINANCIAL FACTS

Annual tuition	$27,814
Books and supplies	$1,155
Room & board (on/off-campus)	$7,000/$10,025
% first-year students receiving some sort of aid	95
% receiving some sort of aid	98
% receiving scholarships	45
Average grant	$14,069
Average loan	$20,973
Average total aid package	$23,174
Average debt	$75,204

WIDENER UNIVERSITY
SCHOOL OF LAW, DELAWARE CAMPUS

INSTITUTIONAL INFORMATION

Public/private	private
Student/faculty ratio	20:1
% faculty part-time	43
% faculty female	41
% faculty minority	4
Total faculty	108

SURVEY SAYS . . .

Diverse opinions accepted in classrooms
Great research resources
Great library staff

STUDENTS

Enrollment of law school	1,154
% male/female	55/45
% full-time	59
% minority	11
% international	2
# of countries represented	2
Average age of entering class	23

ACADEMICS

Academic Experience rating	**65**
Professors interesting rating	70
Professors accessible rating	72
Hours of study per day	4.53

Academic Specialties

Civil procedure, commercial law, constitutional law, corporation securities law, criminal law, environmental law, international law, health law, trial advocacy.

Combined Degrees Offered

JD/PsyD, 6 years; JD/MBA, 4 years; JD/MMP.

Academic Requirements

Clinical Program Required?	No
Legal Writing Course Requirement?	Yes
Legal Methods Course Requirement?	Yes
Legal Research Course Requirement?	Yes
Moot Court Requirement?	No
Public Interest Law Requirement?	No

Academics

Widener University has "the advantage of being 100 percent focused on the training of legal professionals, since its Delaware campus is small and removed from the undergraduate schools," students say. Another attribute of Widener that students appreciate is the ability to attend part-time or in the day or evening, which provides opportunities "for those individuals who would like to get an advanced degree, but are not able to because of obligations to family and work." Students rave about how their health law and corporate law programs are well-known, which is easy to understand since so many companies incorporate in the state of Delaware (there is no corporate tax in Delaware). Students also appreciate that "Widener Law emphasizes the legal writing aspect, as well as really emphasizing the need to analyze and apply the law, not just memorize definitions." The "out of the classroom opportunities, such as study abroad, student organizations, [and] clinics" also draw positive reviews. If there is a widespread complaint, it is that "the mandatory [grading] curve is too strict."

Students generally agree that "most of the professors, save one or two, have been outstanding and have had a combination of practical experience and teaching experience." Additionally, students are impressed with the faculty's accessibility. "The professors have a great open-door policy and are always available and willing to meet with students." They are "supportive and encouraging" of students' goals.

Most of the people at Widener think the administration "is very people-oriented [and] makes an honest attempt to be available at any time that they can be for questions." Students do have a few criticisms, though. For example, some students feel that it ought "to alter the curriculum to decrease the amount of required classes, thereby allowing students to take more electives and practical courses." Furthermore, students wish the Career Services office would do a little more for the students by attracting more employers to campus.

Most students agree that the facilities at Widener are average. "The buildings are not great, but I am not here for the architecture. The other resources are adequate. The library is sufficient," writes one down-to-earth student. Some think "the computers could be a lot faster," while others appreciate that "the classrooms are finally high-tech, in the sense that we have SMART Boards that allow the teacher to present Internet applications to the classroom."

BARBARA AYARS, ASSISTANT DEAN FOR ADMISSIONS
PO BOX 7474, 4601 CONCORD PIKE, WILMINGTON, DE 19803-0474
TELEPHONE: 302-477-2162 • FAX: 302-477-2224
E-MAIL: LAW.ADMISSIONS@LAW.WIDENER.EDU • WEBSITE: WWW.LAW.WIDENER.EDU

Life

Most students like how "the campus itself is small, enclosed, and a safe atmosphere." Plus, "five minutes off of the Concord Pike are two beautiful parks that are great for running with a friend after classes in the fall and spring." The school is in close proximity to Wilmington, only "a 7-minute drive on 95," which is where some of the major law firms in the area are located. Philadelphia is only 20 minutes away. Additionally, "the capital and Supreme Court are only minutes away." But because a lot of people drive to school, many are desperate for more parking spaces on campus.

"Student groups organize so many activities that anyone could find something to be involved with, and the students are so diverse in beliefs, interests, etc., that everyone will find someone to get along with," a student assures us. Students admit that they are "quite competitive." However, they maintain that "there's a sense of a 'mutual respect' among the students." Many students say that there is "not much of a social life," save the one you'll find at the single campus bar. As one student explains, "The social life here is divided among the people who live on campus and those who don't. People living on campus tend to hang out together, while people living off-campus tend to hang out with their non-law school friends."

Getting In

The admissions stats at Widener are pretty forgiving (as far as law schools go). More than two out of every five applicants are accepted. Admitted students in the 25th percentile have an LSAT score of 151 and a GPA of 2.8. Admitted students at the 75th percentile have an LSAT score of 155 and a GPA of 3.4. The average LSAT score is 153. Widener is a good alternative for students who can't gain admission to the more competitive law schools in or near the cities of New York, Philadelphia, and Washington, DC.

EMPLOYMENT INFORMATION

Career Rating	**71**
% employed within 9 months	90
Average starting salary	$54,000
State for bar exam	PA, NJ
Pass rate for first-time bar	73

Employers who frequently hire grads:
Law firms, judges, corporations, government employers.

Prominent Alumni: Alan Levin, president and CEO, Happy Harry's Inc.; Cynthia Rhoades Ryan, chief counsel, Drug Enforcement Administration; John Flynn, counselor to U.S. Secretary of Labor; Lee A. Solomon, deputy U.S. attorney.

Grads employed by field (%):	
Business/industry	6
Government	7
Judicial clerkships	28
Military	1
Other	1
Private practice	55
Public interest	2

ADMISSIONS

Selectivity Rating	**69**
# applications received	1,939
# applicants accepted	764
# acceptees attending	254
Average LSAT	153
LSAT Range	151–155
Average undergrad GPA	3.1
Application fee	$60
Regular application deadline	5/15
Regular notification	rolling
Rolling notification?	Yes
Early application program?	No
Transfer students accepted?	Yes
Evening division offered?	Yes
Part-time accepted?	Yes
LSDAS accepted?	Yes

Applicants Also Look At
Hofstra University; Penn State University; Rutgers, The State University of New Jersey—Camden; Temple University; University of Baltimore; Villanova University.

International Students

TOEFL required of international students?	No
TOEFL recommended of international students?	Yes
Minimum Paper TOEFL	550
Minimum Computer TOEFL	220

FINANCIAL FACTS

Annual tuition	$26,800
Books and supplies	$1,000
Tuition per credit	$810
Room & board	$8,300
Financial aid application deadline	4/15
% first-year students receiving some sort of aid	85
% receiving some sort of aid	85
% of aid that is merit-based	11
% receiving scholarships	19
Average grant	$5,291
Average loan	$22,950
Average total aid package	$26,447
Average debt	$68,850

WIDENER UNIVERSITY
SCHOOL OF LAW, HARRISBURG CAMPUS

INSTITUTIONAL INFORMATION

Public/private	private
Student/faculty ratio	21:1
% faculty part-time	41
% faculty female	39
% faculty minority	5
Total faculty	41

SURVEY SAYS . . .

Diverse opinions accepted in classrooms
Great library staff

STUDENTS

Enrollment of law school	513
% male/female	53/47
% full-time	47
% minority	5
% international	1
# of countries represented	2
Average age of entering class	23

ACADEMICS

Academic Experience rating	**72**
Professors interesting rating	74
Professors accessible rating	74
Hours of study per day	4.47

Academic Specialties

Constitutional law, corporation securities law, environmental law, government services, international law, health law.

Combined Degrees Offered

JD/master of science in library sciences in conjunction with Clarion University, 4 years.

Academic Requirements

Clinical Program Required?	No
Legal Writing Course Requirement?	Yes
Legal Methods Course Requirement?	Yes
Legal Research Course Requirement?	Yes
Moot Court Requirement?	No
Public Interest Law Requirement?	No

Academics

Students at Widener School of Law's Harrisburg campus say that their school's greatest asset is its small size, which creates an intimate, supportive, and friendly learning environment. Less than half the size of the Delaware campus, Harrisburg has only about 400 students total. As a result, students say they have ample opportunity to participate in class discussions and to get to know their teachers outside of class. A student attests, "Our school has small classes [that] enable the professors to build individual relationships with each student. They are readily accessible and encourage students to contact them if they have any questions." Also "one-on-one" attention is not the only thing students appreciate about their "high-caliber professors." They praise the faculty's "diverse educational backgrounds, loads of legal experience, [and] mind-boggling" knowledge of the law. It's good to point out class can be pretty fun when your professors are "witty and sometimes wacky."

The administration is popular with some students, less so with others. Some students say that Widener's "powerful" administration "is a joy. They are very open in their communication," and they "really care about the students," doing their best to "make your law school experience—and life after law school—as painless and enjoyable as possible." However, others say that the administration "does not communicate with students," and claim that the administrators pay too much attention to Widener's Delaware campus and not enough to them. Widener's C grading curve is also a source of frustration. Students worry that their curved "grade point averages might not stack up" to their competitors, "causing us to lose out on job opportunities." Students insist that "the curve method of grading must go."

Campus facilities are attractive and modern, although some students say, "There could be more computer access ability in the classrooms (i.e., plugs in all of the desks)." A few students complain of "rather cramped" classrooms and would like to see an update. The library is ample and "staffed by skilled research librarians." Plus, Widener—Harrisburg students benefit greatly from their "sisterhood with the Delaware campus." One students explains, "We can draw on their resources like their expansive library and their cutting-edge electives with seamless ease." Widener students can also tap into the resources of the surrounding city—Widener's location in the state capital, just "minutes away [from the] capitol, commonwealth, and Supreme Court" makes for some great opportunities for "students interested in or working in capital government jobs."

Life

The campus vibe is familial and friendly at Widener University. A student notes, "Because we are a small school, the individual classes are like a Melrose Place of sorts. Everyone knows everyone. It is a small family." Although "sometimes the social environment can be like high school because of how cliquey people get," for the most part, "everyone treats each other great." Students say they "find that the students at Widener are very cooperative and willing to work with each other. Students share notes, study aides, [and] advice."

BARBARA AYARS, ASSISTANT DEAN OF ADMISSIONS
3800 VARTAN WAY, PO BOX 69381, HARRISBURG, PA 17106-9381
TELEPHONE: 717-541-3903 • FAX: 717-541-3999
E-MAIL: LAW.ADMISSIONS@LAW.WIDENER.EDU • WEBSITE: WWW.LAW.WIDENER.EDU

Widener students "come from all walks of life, and as a result, class discussions encompass business, human resources, government, and philosophical perspectives." While students appreciate their classmates' "diversity of student experiences and age range," some say that "there is a strong barrier" and a lack of understanding between the older and younger students. A few call Widener a "commuter school," saying that "people come to class and then disappear," and that "it is very rare that all of the students gather together." But others tell us that "Widener can be a lot of fun if you make an effort to get involved." The "SBA (Student Bar Association) is very active [and hosts] great events with music and spirits all throughout the year for different occasions." One student reports, "We have an annual Barrister's Ball, as well as Halloween parties and the like. We also take part in many community service initiatives through SBA and other clubs. Last week BLSA (Black Law Student Association) sponsored a 'Law Day' for kids to come and see what law school is really like." Off-campus, Harrisburg offers both plentiful professional opportunities and entertainment options. A student tells us, "Harrisburg is a fun, energetic, and thriving area. I hope to find permanent employment and residence in the area."

Getting In

Widener considers LSAT scores and undergraduate GPA to be the two most important factors in an admissions decision. In 2004, admits had an average LSAT score of 151 and an average GPA of 3.2. Widener will average multiple LSAT scores. Students may apply to both the Delaware and Harrisburg campuses with one application.

EMPLOYMENT INFORMATION

Career Rating	**71**
% employed within 9 months	89
Average starting salary	$50,000
State for bar exam	PA, NJ
Pass rate for first-time bar	75

Employers who frequently hire grads:
Law firms, judges, corporations, government employers.

Prominent Alumni: Honorable Mark Cohen, member, Pennsylvania House of Representatives; Honorable Peter J. Daley, member, Pennsylvania Hosue of Representatives; P. Kevin Brobson, partner, Buchanan Ingersoll P.C.

Grads employed by field (%):

Business/industry	2
Government	18
Judicial clerkships	26
Military	2
Private practice	48
Public interest	4

ADMISSIONS

Selectivity Rating	**70**
# applications received	772
# applicants accepted	309
# acceptees attending	132
Average LSAT	151
LSAT Range	149–152
Average undergrad GPA	3.2
Application fee	$60
Regular application deadline	5/15
Regular notification	rolling
Rolling notification?	Yes
Early application program?	No
Transfer students accepted?	Yes
Evening division offered?	Yes
Part-time accepted?	Yes
LSDAS accepted?	Yes

Applicants Also Look At

Hofstra University; New England School of Law; Penn State University; Rutgers, The State University of New Jersey—Camden; Temple University; University of Baltimore; Villanova University.

International Students

TOEFL required of international students?	No
TOEFL recommended of international students?	Yes
Minimum Paper TOEFL	550
Minimum Computer TOEFL	220

FINANCIAL FACTS

Annual tuition	$26,800
Books and supplies	$1,000
Tuition per credit	$810
Room & board	$8,300
Financial aid application deadline	4/1
% first-year students receiving some sort of aid	85
% receiving some sort of aid	87
% of aid that is merit-based	11
% receiving scholarships	18
Average grant	$5,682
Average loan	$24,705
Average total aid package	$26,849
Average debt	$74,115

WILLAMETTE UNIVERSITY
COLLEGE OF LAW

INSTITUTIONAL INFORMATION

Public/private	private
Student/faculty ratio	18:1
Affiliation	Methodist
% faculty part-time	27
% faculty female	25
% faculty minority	10
Total faculty	40

SURVEY SAYS . . .

Diverse opinions accepted in classrooms
Great research resources
Great library staff
Beautiful campus

STUDENTS

Enrollment of law school	466
% male/female	60/40
% out-of-state	64
% full-time	99
% minority	11
% international	1
Average age of entering class	26

ACADEMICS

Academic Experience rating	**69**
Professors interesting rating	68
Professors accessible rating	71
Hours of study per day	4.5

Academic Specialties

Business law, dispute resolution, government services, international law, and comparative law.

Advanced Degrees Offered

LLM in transnational Law, 1 year.

Combined Degrees Offered

Joint degree with Willamette University Atkinson Graduate School of Management, 4-year JD/MBA.

Academic Requirements

Clinical Program Required?	No
Legal Writing Course Requirement?	Yes
Legal Methods Course Requirement?	No
Legal Research Course Requirement?	Yes

Academics

At this small Oregon law school, students are bright and motivated, course work is demanding, and the tough grading curve keeps everyone scrambling for a place at the top. A 3L warns, "One does not associate the word 'humane' with law school. Truthfully, most of the law school curriculum is not humane." Even so, the college maintains a balance between the rigorous academic program and the compassion and community typical to a small school environment. At Willamette, the administration, faculty, and staff couple tough policies with a genuine desire to help students succeed academically and in their subsequent careers. In even the hardest classes, "the professors are down-to-earth people who are very willing to help students." A 1L explains, "The professors do not pull any punches and make sure that we understand that law school is tough. However, they also want us to succeed and therefore work very hard to help us" achieve that end.

With just over 450 students, Willamette's small size is among its most favorable attributes, ensuring face time with the faculty and a highly individualized learning experience. "The small size and accessibility of the faculty is a big plus for me. I attended a small private school and enjoy feeling like more than a number," attests a 3L. Adds another, "The small student body gives us the chance to take smaller classes and really get to interact instead of just shouting out answers all the time." Similarly, the administration remains closely connected to the needs of the student body. In particular, "the dean works very hard to stay involved with the students, including hosting get-togethers at his home." While the school's size is an overwhelming plus to the Willamette experience, there are also the typical sacrifices associated with going to a smaller institution, like limited course offerings and a rather homogeneous faculty. A 3L admits, "We have enough bar classes, but we could use more electives. After second year, I had a hard time finding classes I was interested in that I hadn't already taken."

With a prime location across the street from the Supreme Court of Oregon, Willamette boasts "fabulous opportunities for local externships," a task made easier by the college's "wonderful externship coordinator." However, some feel the school could place more value on practical educational experiences. For example, a 3L does "not feel that we emphasize getting students into externships as much as we could. I think such an opportunity should be more strongly encouraged."

Students praise the school's high-tech classroom and student facilities, including extensive and reliable wireless Internet and a world-class library: "The classroom and research facilities are excellent and the hours cannot be beat. Students are allowed access 24 hours a day," writes one 3L. In addition, the "Willamette University campus is in one of the nicest parts of Salem." Founded more than 120 years ago, Willamette is a fixture in the surrounding community, and the school enjoys a "good local reputation." Students do warn that "Oregon seems to have a weak market for lawyers, so pay is low and competition fierce from other folks who would like to live out west." However, they point out that, with the help of the friendly Career Services department and the college's active alumni network, job prospects are good for Willamette grads.

Carolyn Dennis, Director of Admission
245 Winter Street, SE, Salem, OR 97301-3922
Telephone: 503-370-6282 • Fax: 503-370-6087
E-mail: law-admission@willamette.edu • Website: www.willamette.edu/wucl

Life

While this tiny campus is home to the full spectrum of political views, you won't get much by way of ethnic diversity at Willamette. A 3L admits, "Out of the three law schools in Oregon, Willamette is by far the most conservative and ethnically non-diverse." Even so, there is still a spirit of debate and intellectual diversity within the campus community. In the words of a 3L, "We are pretty much a bunch of white kids, but our politics are diverse, which can make for some fun 'law chat' debates." No matter how heated things get, "students respect each other and appreciate that we are all from different backgrounds and have different future goals."

Students say there is perceptible competition between students in the classroom: "Welcome to law school! It's every woman (or man) for herself!" writes one 3L. Most feel that competitiveness is a result of the college's tough grading policies, combined with the high quality of the student body. At Willamette "the level of academic commitment by the students is extraordinary; people . . . are here because they love the law."

Under any circumstance, Willamette students leave competition in the classroom, saying that, in general, "people are friendly and caring, and there is a general sense of community among the students." A 3L elaborates, "There is some unavoidable competition because of the grade curve, but students don't generally let it interfere with their interpersonal relationships." In fact, "most students are very friendly and most people (at least within each class) know each other to some extent." Don't expect much in terms of social life, however. Campus life is primarily academic as, "a lot of students commute and are just around for school," although the school fees provide some extracurricular activities.

Getting In

Like every other law school, Willamette seeks students whose previous academic record and test scores suggests they will be successful in the law school curriculum. While these factors are the most important in an admissions decision, Willamette also evaluates an applicant's supporting documentation, including letters of recommendation, resume, and personal statement.

EMPLOYMENT INFORMATION

Career Rating	**72**
% employed within 9 months	91
State for bar exam	OR, WA, NV, UT, CA
Pass rate for first-time bar	84.9

Employers who frequently hire grads:
Stoel Rives, Schwabe Williamson Wyatt, Washigton State attorney general, Lane County circuit court, Bulirant Houser Bailey, Miller Nash, Oregon Dept. of Justice, Oregon legislature.

Prominent Alumni: Lisa Murkowski, U.S. Senator from Alaska; Wallace P. Carson, Chief Justice Oregon Supreme Court; Lindsay D. Stewart, Vice President – Law and Corporate Affairs, Nike, Inc.

Grads employed by field (%):	
Academic	1
Business/industry	14
Government	16
Judicial clerkships	7
Military	3
Private practice	57
Public interest	2

Moot Court Requirement?	Yes
Public Interest Law Requirement?	No

ADMISSIONS

Selectivity Rating	**76**
# applications received	1,264
# applicants accepted	504
# acceptees attending	181
Average LSAT	156
LSAT Range	153–158
Average undergrad GPA	3.4
Application fee	$50
Regular application deadline	4/1
Regular notification	rolling
Rolling notification?	Yes
Early application program?	No
Transfer students accepted?	Yes
Evening division offered?	No
Part-time accepted?	No
LSDAS accepted?	Yes

International Students

TOEFL required of international students?	Yes
Minimum Paper TOEFL	600
Minimum Computer TOEFL	250

FINANCIAL FACTS

Annual tuition	$23,400
Books and supplies	$1,300
Room & board	$10,800
Financial aid application deadline	3/1
% first-year students receiving some sort of aid	95
% receiving some sort of aid	93
% of aid that is merit-based	13
% receiving scholarships	43
Average grant	$10,101
Average loan	$29,672
Average total aid package	$32,856
Average debt	$57,414

William Mitchell College of Law

INSTITUTIONAL INFORMATION

Public/private	private
Student/faculty ratio	23:1
% faculty part-time	85
% faculty female	41
% faculty minority	18
Total faculty	234

SURVEY SAYS . . .

Great research resources
Great library staff
Students love St. Paul, MN

STUDENTS

Enrollment of law school	1,078
% male/female	49/51
% out-of-state	29
% full-time	59
% minority	10
% international	1
# of countries represented	6
Average age of entering class	27

ACADEMICS

Academic Experience rating	**72**
Professors interesting rating	70
Professors accessible rating	73
Hours of study per day	4.33

Academic Specialties

Commercial law, criminal law, government services, intellectual property law, international law, labor law, property, taxation.

Advanced Degrees Offered

JD, 3 years full-time, 4 years part-time.

Combined Degrees Offered

Dual degree in conjunction with Minnesota State University—Mankato: JD/MA in public administration and JD/MS in women's studies or community health, 4 years if classes are taken concurrently. Must be completed within 6 years.

Academic Requirements

Clinical Program Required?	No
Legal Writing Course Requirement?	Yes

Academics

William Mitchell College of Law is unique among law schools for its strong evening program. Here, the curriculum for both day and evening programs stresses a practical approach to the law. While first-year students get a dose of "hardcore Socratic teachers," in the second and third years "the professors at Mitchell stress the 'real-world' concept of teaching and actual, practical use of law in the real world." "Many of the specialized upper-division courses are taught by practicing attorneys from large and small firms, industry, and government, all of whom have a commitment to teaching. This provides an unparalleled blend of theory and practical knowledge, along with a little bit of networking!" exclaims one 3L. The school further promotes practical applications of law by augmenting traditional classroom instruction with intensive legal writing and research courses and a dynamic clinical program.

William Mitchell professors are demanding yet "exceptional in their commitment to the students." In fact, every member of the campus community treats individuals with respect and personal attention: "The administration and faculty are easily accessible, the librarians are always there and eager to help with any task, even the security guards always greet people with they enter the building," notes a 3L. Many point out the superb quality of the research facilities and staff. A 2L recounts, "The research librarians are super-helpful. You can e-mail them anytime and typically hear back from them within the hour. They are even happy to help when you call them in a panic from your law clerk job."

William Mitchell was founded as a part-time law school and has since developed a more traditional, full-time program. Still, "40 percent of the students are part-time," and the program preserves much of its original structure and attitude, always keeping the diverse needs of nontraditional or working students in mind. In fact, "you can even switch back and forth between being full-time and part-time." A 2L notes that "the professors understand the rigors of full-time employment while attending law school; they won't coddle you, but they will work with you." While designed to support part-time students, the school's flexible scheduling system benefits those in the full-time programs as well. A 2L explains, "Classes are offered all throughout the day, including evenings, so it is easy to accommodate any type of work or volunteer schedule." However, many students complain that the school's attempt to offer classes at irregular hours results in conflicts for traditional students, as too many mandatory courses overlap during the evening hours: "Class offerings and times could be spread out a bit more. Too often classes I want to take are offered at the same time, so I can only take one," writes one 3L.

"William Mitchell is growing and changing quickly at the moment," and students say it's a propitious time to be a part of the college community. In particular, a new set of administrators has joined the staff, taking positive steps to promote the college and develop its regional and national reputation: "The administration of the college has changed. It is too early to know, but all evidence appears to suggest a forward-thinking, progressive administration interested in enhancing the national public image of the college," writes one student. In addition, the college is physically expanding, and "a new building, student center, and lounge were opened this fall, all of which redefine 'state-of-the-art.'" In fact, the William Mitchell campus draws praises all around for its "beautiful student area for studying and socializing, lots of lockers, beautiful grounds, state-of-the-art classrooms, and many small courtrooms for trial exercises."

Kendra Dane, Assistant Dean and Director of Admissions
875 Summit Avenue, St. Paul, MN 55105
Telephone: 651-290-6476 • Fax: 651-290-6414
E-mail: admissions@wmitchell.edu • Website: www.wmitchell.edu

Life

Given the strength of its evening program, it's not surprising that William Mitchell College of Law attracts many older, nontraditional students who have experience in other career fields. Many say the diversity of the student body is the school's greatest strength, as it "allows people to see how the law would affect different people in different ways." For example, "In my 90-student section we have a doctor, a dentist, two PhDs, a dozen engineers, and almost that many MBAs," writes a 3L. No matter who you are or what your background is, you will feel comfortable at William Mitchell. Whether among kindred spirits or polar opposites, the college promotes tolerance and respect. For example, a 2L tells us, "The law school is extremely supportive of diversity! I specifically chose this law school because of its good standing with the gay community. The school is very GLBT-friendly and supportive."

A friendly college within a friendly city, competition is kept at a minimum at William Mitchell, and "the college provides a collegial atmosphere; most students prefer to work together to learn concepts, rather than compete with each other." For example, "if someone forgets a book for class, another is likely to either forward notes or offer to allow the student to copy his/her book." In particular, many of the evening students claim that they function as a surrogate family, helping each other through the challenges of full-time employment and the legal education. While "students are very, very friendly," you won't find a very social atmosphere on the William Mitchell campus. With many older classmates, "students work hard, but have well-rounded lives outside of school." Even so, there are a few opportunities to get down with your classmates: "The social event held every semester is widely attended and looked forward to by the entire student population."

Getting In

The admissions committee at William Mitchell College of Law evaluates students based on both academic and non-academic factors. Therefore, a student's resume of extracurricular and professional experience is heavily weighted, in addition to grades and LSAT scores.

EMPLOYMENT INFORMATION

Career Rating	**78**
Job placement rate (%)	95
Average starting salary	$56,848
State for bar exam	MN, WI
Pass rate for first-time bar	90

Employers who frequently hire grads: Briggs & Morgan; Faegre & Benson; Gray, Plant, Mooty; Robins, Kaplan, Miller, & Ciresi; and Leonard Street & Deinhard.

Prominent Alumni: Warren E. Burger, chief justice of U.S. Supreme Court; Rosalie Wahl, justice Minnesota Supreme Court (retired); Douglas Amdahl, chief justice Minnesota Supreme Court (retired).

Grads employed by field (%):	
Academic	2
Business/industry	18
Government	11
Judicial clerkships	13
Private practice	54
Public interest	2

Legal Methods Course Requirement?	Yes
Legal Research Course Requirement?	Yes
Moot Court Requirement?	No
Public Interest Law Requirement?	No

ADMISSIONS

Selectivity Rating	**71**
# applications received	1,570
# applicants accepted	823
# acceptees attending	320
Average LSAT	155
LSAT Range	153–158
Average undergrad GPA	3.4
Application fee	$45
Regular application deadline	6/1
Regular notification	rolling
Rolling notification?	Yes
Early application program?	No
Transfer students accepted?	Yes
Evening division offered?	Yes
Part-time accepted?	Yes
LSDAS accepted?	Yes

Applicants Also Look At

Hamline University, St. Thomas University, University of Minnesota.

International Students

TOEFL required of international students?	Yes
Minimum Paper TOEFL	600
Minimum Computer TOEFL	250

FINANCIAL FACTS

Annual tuition	$24,500
Books and supplies	$1,900
Tuition per credit	$806
Room & board (off-campus)	$14,300
Financial aid application deadline	3/15
% first-year students receiving some sort of aid	89
% receiving some sort of aid	90
% of aid that is merit-based	74
% receiving scholarships	44
Average grant	$10,788
Average loan	$18,450
Average total aid package	$29,662
Average debt	$67,882

YESHIVA UNIVERSITY
BENJAMIN N. CARDOZO SCHOOL OF LAW

INSTITUTIONAL INFORMATION

Public/private	private
Student/faculty ratio	17:1
Affiliation	Jewish
% faculty part-time	66
% faculty female	24
% faculty minority	4
Total faculty	123

SURVEY SAYS . . .

Abundant externship/internship/clerkship opportunities
Students love New York, NY

STUDENTS

Enrollment of law school	1,037
% male/female	53/47
% out-of-state	60
% full-time	93
% minority	20
% international	2
# of countries represented	13
Average age of entering class	25

ACADEMICS

Academic Experience rating	**86**
Professors interesting rating	83
Professors accessible rating	81
Hours of study per day	4.43

Academic Specialties

Civil procedure, commercial law, constitutional law, corporation securities law, criminal law, dispute resolution, family law, intellectual property law, international law, legal philosophy, property, public law & regulation, taxation.

Advanced Degrees Offered

JD; LLM in intellectual property law, comparative legal thought, and general studies, 1 year full-time, up to 3 years part-time.

Combined Degrees Offered

JD/LLM in intellectual property law, 7 semesters; JD/MSW, 4 years.

Academic Requirements

Clinical Program Required?	No
Legal Writing Course Requirement?	Yes

Academics

Academic life at "underrated, under-known" Benjamin N. Cardozo School of Law in New York City is pretty exciting. There are "weekly debates featuring legal experts from around the country on topics that run the gamut from post–9/11 national security policy to the impact of labor unions on Major League Baseball." Plus there are lunches or roundtables "every single day with public officials like the New York City Police Commissioner." There is "a strong balance of theory and practice," and Cardozo provides "tons of opportunities for practical experience." The clinics are arguably the "best in the country. One clinical experience, for example, in the tax area may equal three tax courses in terms of the degree of experience and learning opportunities that it provides." Likewise, a participant in Cardozo's Innocence Project tells us, "Spending eight straight hours in the library doesn't seem so bad after you meet a guy who spent 18 years in jail for a crime he didn't commit." Cardozo also boasts a strong intellectual property program, a unique Public Service Scholars program, several "great journals" and study abroad programs, and a bar-passage rate of 88 percent (the state average is 78 percent).

Many students rate the professors at Cardozo as "top-notch. The faculty is composed of nationally recognized scholars who care deeply about their specialized fields of law and their students' progress within it." They are "really enthusiastic about teaching and helping students learn, very interested in helping you to be successful, [and otherwise] the school's greatest asset." Other students say that the professors "vary greatly. Some are amazing, while others are babbling and incoherent." One student remarks, "Cardozo's faculty is a mix of brilliant young stars who have clerked in high places and old-school Socratic Method actors straight out of *The Paper Chase*. My experiences vary so widely from those of 1Ls in other sections that it's as though we go to different schools." Classes are "relatively small, which allows for more flexible and unconventional methods of teaching, and for great interaction with faculty members." Students write, "Most classes are high-energy, interactive experiences, and students tend to stay on top of their reading and participate to the fullest, voluntarily or not."

Cardozo's administration is "friendly [and] accessible, [but] the red tape at Yeshiva could stretch up and down the "floors of our building and around the block," comments one student. Also, registration could be better, and "the administration could do more to improve student quality-of-life." Most students are satisfied with their career prospects. "Although the school's reputation is growing by leaps and bounds," notes one wistful student, "I wish that the school had a better reputation among the hiring firms." Still, internships and clerkships are abundant for students and virtually everyone finds work within a few months after graduation. And the average starting salary for newly minted Cardozo grads isn't so bad at nearly $90,000 per year.

The "terrible" facilities have been "under a slow renovation for the last few years." The new moot court room is "impressive. Two recently completed floors are sparklingly new, and thus the height of the prospective student tour. As the other floors receive the same treatment, the physical plant will improve." Meanwhile, "there is never enough space [and] pillars in the middle of [some classrooms] make it impossible to hear people on the other end of the rooms." Also, technology is not cutting-edge. Cardozo's library has "great reading rooms," but many students complain because it is "closed every Friday night and Saturday." (Cardozo is a Jewish-affiliated law school.)

Robert L. Schwartz, Associate Dean for Admissions
55 Fifth Avenue, New York, NY 10003
Telephone: 212-790-0274 • Fax: 212-790-0482
E-mail: lawinfo@yu.edu • Website: www.cardozo.yu.edu

Life

Besides the fact that the library is closed on Saturdays, "Cardozo does not feel like a religious law school. There are students of every religion, ethnicity, and background." They tell us that they are "exceptionally hardworking and dedicated." One student explains, "We feel that the school is consistently underrated. This gives us a strong bond and sense of community as the underdog."

Students are divided when it comes to the level of competition at Cardozo. Some perceive a "very competitive" atmosphere. Others do not. "The students are more competitive with themselves than with other students," writes a student in the latter camp. "There is generally a very supportive and friendly environment among students."

Cardozo's location in the heart of the Big Apple has both plusses and minuses. Certainly, getting a legal education in the epicenter of the world's capital of business and finance has its perks. If urban life is what you are after, you would be hard-pressed to do better. However, as one student warns, "It is mainly a commuter school," so the law school community can be just so-so. Also, housing comes at a hefty premium in New York City. Some students find housing in Greenwich Village, Tribeca, SoHo, and other nearby neighborhoods. Others aren't so lucky. The law school also has a residence hall, (but space is limited and priority is given to out-of-towners), although it has been possible to accomodate all students in recent years.

Getting In

The mean LSAT score at Cardozo is 154. The mean undergraduate GPA is 3.5. Admitted students at the 25th percentile have an LSAT score of 161 and a GPA of 3.1. Admitted students at the 75th percentile have an LSAT score of 166 and a GPA of 3.6. Normally, if you take the LSAT more than once, Cardozo will average your scores. However, exceptions have been made. If you score significantly better on one LSAT, write an explanatory letter to the admissions committee (unless it states that you took a test prep course with The Princeton Review, and lo and behold, your score shot up). Finally, note that you can enter Cardozo in January and May as well as in September.

EMPLOYMENT INFORMATION

Career Rating	**86**
% employed within 9 months	97.4
Average starting salary	$80,937
State for bar exam	NY
Pass rate for first-time bar	80

Employers who frequently hire grads:
International and national law firms of all sizes, corporations, federal and state judges, district attorney's offices, other state and federal government entities, public interest organizations.

Prominent Alumni: Randi Weingarten, president, United Federation of Teachers; Honorable Sandra J. Feuerstein, judge, U.S. District Court, Eastern District of New York.

Grads employed by field (%):	
Academic	2
Business/industry	14
Government	12
Judicial clerkships	8
Private practice	61
Public interest	3

Legal Methods Course Requirement?	Yes
Legal Research Course Requirement?	Yes
Moot Court Requirement?	No
Public Interest Law Requirement?	No

ADMISSIONS

Selectivity Rating	**89**
# applications received	4,815
# applicants accepted	1,060
# acceptees attending	275
Average LSAT	164
LSAT Range	161–166
Average undergrad GPA	3.5
Application fee	$65
Regular application deadline	4/1
Regular notification	rolling
Rolling notification?	Yes
Early application program?	Yes
Early application deadline	11/15
Early application notification	12/15
Transfer students accepted?	Yes
Evening division offered?	No
Part-time accepted?	Yes
LSDAS accepted?	Yes

Applicants Also Look At

Boston University, Brooklyn Law School, Columbia University, Fordham University, The George Washington University, New York University.

International Students

TOEFL required of international students?	No
TOEFL recommended of international students?	No

FINANCIAL FACTS

Annual tuition	$32,650
Books and supplies	$1,100
Tuition per credit	$1,470
Room & board	$19,500
Financial aid application deadline	4/15
% first-year students receiving some sort of aid	86
% receiving some sort of aid	94
% of aid that is merit-based	62
% receiving scholarships	61
Average grant	$11,338
Average loan	$34,315
Average total aid package	$38,592
Average debt	$89,558

LAW SCHOOL DATA LISTINGS

In this section you will find data listings of the ABA-approved schools not appearing in the "Law School Descriptive Profiles" section of the book. Here you will also find listings of the California Bar Accredited, but not ABA-approved law schools, as well as listings of Canadian law schools. Explanations of what each field of data signifies in the listings may be found in the "How to Use This Book" section.

Appalachian School of Law†

Appalachian School of Law

PO Box 2825, Grundy, VA 24614 United States
Admissions Phone: *276-935-4349* • ***Admissions Fax:*** *276-935-8261*
Admissions E-mail: *aslinfo@asl.edu* • ***Web Address:*** *www.asl.edu*

INSTITUTIONAL INFORMATION

Public/private: Private.
Student/faculty ratio: 20:1
Total faculty: 20
% Faculty Female: 45
% Faculty Minority: 20

STUDENTS

Enrollment of law school: 364
% Male/female: 62/38
% Full-time: 98
% Minority: 9

ACADEMICS

Academic specializations: Alternate dispute resolution.
Advanced degrees offered: JD–3 years.
Grading system: Five-letter alpha with pluses and minuses.
Clinical program required? Yes.
Clinical program description: There is no "clinic" requirement. However, all students are required to participate in school-sponsored externships in the summer following their first year.
Legal writing course requirement? Yes.
Legal writing description: Two semesters of 3 credits each. Instruction in legal analysis and writing.
Legal methods course requirement? Yes.
Legal methods description: Component of legal process course.
Legal research course requirement? Yes.
Legal research description: Component of legal process course.
Moot court requirement? Yes.
Moot court description: Components of the required legal process course generally contain elements of brief writing and oral advocacy.
Academic journals: *Appalachian Journal of Law.*

ADMISSIONS INFORMATION

ADMISSIONS SELECTIVITY RATING: 62
Application fee: $50
Regular application deadline: 4/1
Regular notification: Rolling.
Early application program: No.
LSDAS accepted? Yes.
Average GPA: 2.80
Range of GPA: 2.6–3.3
Average LSAT: 148
Range of LSAT: 146–152
Transfer students accepted? Yes.
Evening division offered: No.
Part-time accepted: No.
Number of applications received: 990
Number of applicants accepted: 457
Number of acceptees attending: 145

RESEARCH FACILITIES

% of JD classrooms wired: 90

FINANCIAL FACTS

Annual tuition: $19,900
Room & board (off-campus): $12,295
Books and supplies: $2,500
Average grant: $6,468
Average loan: $21,372
% receiving some sort of aid: 64
Tuition per credit: $700

INTERNATIONAL STUDENTS

TOEFL required for international students? No.

EMPLOYMENT INFORMATION

Average starting salary: $45,000
State for bar exam: VA, TN, KY, NC, WV
Pass rate for first-time bar: 52
Grads employed by field: Business/industry, 11%; judicial clerkships, 19%; private practice, 69%.

† Provisionally approved by the ABA.

Barry University†

Barry University School of Law

6441 East Colonial Drive, Orlando, FL 32807 United States
Admissions Phone: *866-532-2779* • ***Admissions Fax:*** *321-206-5620*
Admissions E-mail: *lawinfo@mail.barry.edu* • ***Web Address:*** *www.barry.edu/law*

INSTITUTIONAL INFORMATION

Public/private: Private.
Affiliation: Roman Catholic.
Student/faculty ratio: 19:1
Total faculty: 26
% Faculty Part-time: 16
% Faculty Female: 31
% Faculty Minority: 15

STUDENTS

Enrollment of law school: 511
% Out of state: 40
% Male/female: 50/50
% Full-time: 56
% International: 1
% Minority: 23
Average age of entering class: 27

ACADEMICS

Academic specializations: Children and families.
Grading system: Barry utilizes a 4.0 scale with + and - excluding A+.
Clinical program required? No.
Clinical program description: Children and families clinic, mediation externship, public defender externship, state attorney externship, judicial externship, civil government externship, civil poverty externship.
Legal writing course requirement? Yes.
Legal writing description: Legal research and writing spans 2 semesters and introduces essential legal research skills and the development of exceptional legal writing skills. Students complete closed and open memos, appellate briefs, and appellate arguments.
Legal methods course requirement? Yes.
Legal methods description: Legal methods introduces first-year students to the conceptual building blocks of law in the American legal system.
Legal research course requirement? Yes.
Legal research description: Legal research is combined with the legal writing program.
Moot court requirement? No.
Public interest law requirement? Yes.
Public interest law description: Currently, students must complete 10 hours of pro bono work prior to graduation.
Academic journals: *Barry University Law Review.*

ADMISSIONS INFORMATION

ADMISSIONS SELECTIVITY RATING: 62
Application fee: $50
Regular application deadline: 4/1
Regular notification: Rolling.
Early application program: No.
LSDAS accepted? Yes.
Average GPA: 2.90
Range of GPA: 2.6–3.4
Average LSAT: 148
Range of LSAT: 145–153
Transfer students accepted? Yes.
Evening division offered: Yes.
Part-time accepted: Yes.
Applicants also look at: Nova Southeastern University, St. Thomas University, Stetson University, University of Miami.
Number of applications received: 1,500
Number of applicants accepted: 739
Number of acceptees attending: 241

RESEARCH FACILITIES

Research resources available: Westlaw, Lexis, Loislaw.
% of JD classrooms wired: 100

FINANCIAL FACTS

Annual tuition: $24,600
Room & board (off-campus): $10,400
Books and supplies: $1,400
Financial aid application deadline: 6/30
% receiving scholarships: 67
Average grant: $6,779
Average loan: $28,400
% of aid that is merit-based: 16
% receiving some sort of aid: 94
% first year students receiving some sort of aid: 90
Average total aid package: $32,598
Average debt: $70,780
Tuition per credit: $875

INTERNATIONAL STUDENTS

TOEFL required for international students? Yes.
Minimum Paper TOEFL: 600
Minimum Computer-based TOEFL: 250

EMPLOYMENT INFORMATION

Rate of placement: 84
Average starting salary: $57,275
State for bar exam: FL
Pass rate for first-time bar: 49
Grads employed by field: Academic, 6%; business/industry, 26%; government, 23%; military, 2%; private practice, 41%; public interest, 2%.

† Provisionally approved by the ABA.

THE CATHOLIC UNIVERSITY OF AMERICA

Columbus School of Law

Cardinal Station, Washington, DC 20064 United States
***Admissions Phone:** 202-319-5151 • **Admissions Fax:** 202-319-6285*
***Admissions E-mail:** admissions@law.edu • **Web Address:** www.law.edu*

INSTITUTIONAL INFORMATION

Public/private: Private.
Affiliation: Roman Catholic.
Student/faculty ratio: 21:1
Total faculty: 93
% Faculty Part-time: 53
% Faculty Female: 34
% Faculty Minority: 13

STUDENTS

Enrollment of law school: 980
% Male/female: 51/49
% Full-time: 69
% International: 1
% Minority: 17
Average age of entering class: 26

ACADEMICS

Academic specializations: Corporation securities law, international law, labor law, communications, law and public policy.
Advanced degrees offered: JD–3 years, full-time, or 4 years, part-time.
Combined degrees offered: JD/MA programs in accounting, canon law, history, philosophy, psychology, politics, library science, economics, and social work, 3–4 years.
Grading system: Letter grade-based system.
Clinical program required? No.
Clinical program description: General practice clinic, families and the law clinic, advocacy for the elderly, criminal prosecution clinic, DC law students in court, legal externships, SEC training program, externships.
Legal writing course requirement? No.
Legal methods course requirement? Yes.

Legal methods description: Two semesters first year focuses on legal research, writing and advocacy.
Legal research course requirement? No.
Moot court requirement? No.
Public interest law requirement? No.
Academic journals: *Catholic University Law Review, Journal of Communications Law and Policy, Journal of Contemporary Health Law and Policy.*

ADMISSIONS INFORMATION

ADMISSIONS SELECTIVITY RATING: 82
Application fee: $60
Regular application deadline: 3/1
Regular notification: Rolling.
Early application program: Yes.
LSDAS accepted? Yes.
Average GPA: 3.35
Range of GPA: 3.1–3.6
Average LSAT: 158
Range of LSAT: 156–160
Transfer students accepted? Yes.
Evening division offered: Yes.
Part-time accepted: Yes.
Number of applications received: 2,745
Number of applicants accepted: 763
Number of acceptees attending: 235

RESEARCH FACILITIES

Research resources available:
% of JD classrooms wired: 100
School-supported research centers: Lexis-Nexis, Westlaw.

FINANCIAL FACTS

Annual tuition: $29,060
Room & board (off-campus): $12,100
Books and supplies: $1,000
Financial aid application deadline: 4/15
% receiving scholarships: 36
Average grant: $10,068
Average loan: $35,583
% of aid that is merit-based: 10
% receiving some sort of aid: 92
% first year students receiving some sort of aid: 96
Average total aid package: $38,181
Average debt: $92,000
Tuition per credit: $1,060

INTERNATIONAL STUDENTS

TOEFL required for international students? Yes.

EMPLOYMENT INFORMATION

Rate of placement: 92
Average starting salary: $60,000
Employers who frequently hire grads: Akin, Gump, Strauss, Hauer, and Feld, L.L.P.; Clifford, Chance, Rogers, and Wells; Coudert Brothers.
State for bar exam: MD, VA, PA, NY, NJ
Grads employed by field: Academic, 2%; business/industry, 19%; government, 23%; judicial clerkships, 15%; private practice, 38%; public interest, 3%.

CAPITAL UNIVERSITY

Capital University Law School

303 East Broad Street, Columbus, OH 43215-3200 United States
***Admissions Phone:** 614-236-6310 • **Admissions Fax:** 614-236-6972*
***Admissions E-mail:** admissions@law.capital.edu*
***Web Address:** www.law.capital.edu*

INSTITUTIONAL INFORMATION

Public/private: Private..
Affiliation: Lutheran.
Student/faculty ratio: 23:1
Total faculty: 29
% Faculty Part-time: 36
% Faculty Female: 21
% Faculty Minority: 14

STUDENTS

Enrollment of law school: 726
% Out of state: 27
% Male/female: 50/50
% Full-time: 56
% Minority: 13
Average age of entering class: 25

ACADEMICS

Academic specializations: Corporation securities law, environmental law, government services, international law, labor law, taxation, dispute resolution, children and family law, environmental.
Advanced degrees offered: LLM in taxation, 1–6 years; LLM in business, 1–6 years; LLM in business & taxation, 1–6 years; MT, 1–6 years.
Combined degrees offered: JD/MBA: 3.5–6 years; JD/MSN: 3.5–6 years; JD/MSA: 3.5–4 years; JD/MTS: 4–6 years.
Grading system: 4.0 scale, A, A-, B+, B, B-, C+, C, C-, D, E.
Clinical program required? No.
Clinical program description: Although clinical programs are not required, the following is a list of those that are offered: General civil litigation clinic, mediation clinic, general criminal litigation clinic, domestic violence clinic, externships.
Legal writing course requirement? Yes.
Legal writing description: A year-long course covering research, writing, and methods.
Legal methods course requirement? Yes.
Legal methods description: See legal writing.
Legal research course requirement? Yes.
Legal research description: See legal writing.
Moot court requirement? No.
Moot court description: Although not required, the law school has an active intercollegiate moot court program as well as a first-year student moot court competition.
Public interest law requirement? No.
Public interest law description: Although not required, students may receive a certificate for participation in the pro bono program.
Academic journals: *Capital University Law Review.*

ADMISSIONS INFORMATION

ADMISSIONS SELECTIVITY RATING: 63
Application fee: $35
Regular application deadline: Rolling.

Regular notification: Rolling.
Early application program: No.
LSDAS accepted? Yes.
Average GPA: 3.10
Range of GPA: 3.0–3.4
Average LSAT: 150
Range of LSAT: 147–154
Transfer students accepted? Yes.
Evening division offered: Yes.
Part-time accepted: Yes.
Applicants also look at: Cleveland State University, Ohio Northern University, The Ohio State University, The University of Akron, University of Cincinnati, University of Dayton, University of Toledo.
Number of applications received: 1,034
Number of applicants accepted: 599
Number of acceptees attending: 276

RESEARCH FACILITIES

Research resources available: Supreme Court Law Library, Columbus Law Library Association, University Computer Lab, University Clinic and Recreation Center.
% of JD classrooms wired: 100
School-supported research centers: Center for Dispute Resolution, Institute for International Legal Education, Institute for Citizen Education, Institute for Adoption Law.

FINANCIAL FACTS

Annual tuition: $23,345
Room & board (off-campus): $9,471
Books and supplies: $887
Financial aid application deadline: 4/1
% receiving scholarships: 40
Average grant: $6,000
Average loan: $20,400
% of aid that is merit-based: 40
% receiving some sort of aid: 93
% first year students receiving some sort of aid: 94
Average total aid package: $28,737
Average debt: $53,485
Tuition per credit: $621

INTERNATIONAL STUDENTS

TOEFL required for international students? No.

EMPLOYMENT INFORMATION

Rate of placement: 95
Average starting salary: $55,069
Employers who frequently hire grads: Law firms, government agencies, business & corporate employers.
State for bar exam: OH
Pass rate for first-time bar: 62
Grads employed by field: Academic, 2%; business/industry, 28%; government, 11%; judicial clerkships, 8%; military, 1%; private practice, 47%; public interest, 3%.

DUQUESNE UNIVERSITY

School of Law

900 Locust Street, Pittsburgh, PA 15282 United States
Admissions Phone: *412-396-6296* • ***Admissions Fax:*** *412-396-1073*
Admissions E-mail: *campion@duq.edu* • ***Web Address:*** *www.law.duq.edu*

INSTITUTIONAL INFORMATION

Public/private: Private.
Student/faculty ratio: 23:1
Total faculty: 26
% Faculty Female: 21
% Faculty Minority: 16

STUDENTS

Enrollment of law school: 630
% Out of state: 38
% Male/female: 50/50
% Full-time: 65
% Minority: 7
Average age of entering class: 23

ACADEMICS

Combined degrees offered: JD/MBA–4 years; JD/MDiv–5 years; JD/M environmental science and management–4 years; JD/MS taxation–4 years.
Grading system: Numerical system, 4.0 scale. Minimum 3.0 cumulative GPA required to graduate.
Clinical program required? No.
Clinical program description: Development law clinic, criminal justice clinic, family & poverty law clinic.
Legal writing course requirement? Yes.
Legal methods course requirement? Yes.
Legal research course requirement? Yes.
Moot court requirement? No.
Public interest law requirement? No.

ADMISSIONS INFORMATION

ADMISSIONS SELECTIVITY RATING: 60*
Application fee: $50
Regular application deadline: 4/1
Regular notification: Rolling.
Early application program: No.
LSDAS accepted? Yes.
Average GPA: 3.40
Average LSAT: 154
Transfer students accepted? Yes.
Evening division offered: Yes.
Part-time accepted: Yes.

FINANCIAL FACTS

Annual tuition: $19,394
Room & board (off-campus): $8,000
Books and supplies: $1,000
Average grant: $4,500
Average loan: $12,000
% of aid that is merit-based: 50
% receiving some sort of aid: 35
% first year students receiving some sort of aid: 40
Average total aid package: $11,000
Average debt: $35,000

INTERNATIONAL STUDENTS

TOEFL required for international students? Yes.
Minimum Paper TOEFL: 600

EMPLOYMENT INFORMATION

Rate of placement: 97
Average starting salary: $59,693
Employers who frequently hire grads: Reed Smith, Kirkpatrick & Lockhart, Buchanon Ingersoll, Eckert, Seamans.
State for bar exam: PA
Pass rate for first-time bar: 71
Grads employed by field: Academic, 1%; business/industry, 25%; government, 4%; judicial clerkships, 6%; private practice, 61%; public interest, 3%.

FLORIDA A&M UNIVERSITY†

Florida A&M University College of Law

PO Box 3113, Orlando, FL 32802 United States
Admissions Phone: *407-254-3268* • ***Admissions Fax:*** *407-254-3213*
Admissions E-mail: *famulaw.admissions@famu.edu*
Web Address: *www.famu.edu/law*

INSTITUTIONAL INFORMATION

Public/private: Public.
Student/faculty ratio: 13:1
Total faculty: 40

STUDENTS

Enrollment of law school: 293
% Male/female: 40/60
% Full-time: 69
% Minority: 53
Average age of entering class: 33

ACADEMICS

Advanced degrees offered: JD–3 years, full-time student; 4 years, part-time student.
Clinical program required? Yes.
Clinical program description: The law school offers a rigorous traditional curriculum of required and elective courses, complemented by extensive skills training, which includes an intensive 3-year writing program and a strong clinical program. The college of law curriculum is designed to provide students with both the intellectual and practical skills necessary to meet the demands of the modern practice of law by combining theoretical coursework with clinical and practical experiences.
Legal writing course requirement? No.
Legal methods course requirement? Yes.
Legal methods description: The law school will offer a rigorous traditional curriculum of required and elective courses that will be complemented by extensive skills training which includes an intensive 3-year writing program and a strong clinical program. The college of law curriculum is designed to provide students with both the intellectual and practical skills necessary to meet the demands of the modern practice of law by combining theoretical coursework with clinical and practical experiences.
Legal research course requirement? No.
Moot court requirement? No.
Public interest law requirement? Yes.
Public interest law description: Public interest will be an important facet of our educational program. The Florida A&M University College of Law plans to serve the Orlando community by educating lawyers and future leaders to understand the value of helping those in need.

ADMISSIONS INFORMATION

ADMISSIONS SELECTIVITY RATING: 67
Application fee: $20
Regular application deadline: 5/1
Regular notification: Rolling.
Early application program: No.
LSDAS accepted? Yes.
Average GPA: 3.10
Range of GPA: 2.6–3.4
Average LSAT: 148
Range of LSAT: 143–150
Transfer students accepted? No.
Evening division offered: Yes.
Part-time accepted: Yes.
Number of applications received: 540
Number of applicants accepted: 194
Number of acceptees attending: 120

FINANCIAL FACTS

Annual tuition (resident): $7,140
Annual tuition (nonresident): $26,580
Books and supplies: $13,591
Financial aid application deadline: 4/1
% receiving scholarships: 16
Average grant: $1,800
Average loan: $18,500
% receiving some sort of aid: 92
% first year students receiving some sort of aid: 88
Tuition per credit (resident): $239
Tuition per credit (nonresident): $88,600

INTERNATIONAL STUDENTS

TOEFL required for international students? No.

† Provisionally approved by the ABA.

FLORIDA COASTAL SCHOOL OF LAW

Florida Coastal School of Law

7555 Beach Boulevard, Jacksonville, FL 32216 United States
Admissions Phone: *904-680-7710* • ***Admissions Fax:*** *904-680-7777*
Admissions E-mail: *admissions@fcsl.edu* • ***Web Address:*** *www.fcsl.edu*

INSTITUTIONAL INFORMATION

Public/private: Private.
Student/faculty ratio: 20:1

Total faculty: 58
% Faculty Part-time: 46
% Faculty Female: 40
% Faculty Minority: 25

STUDENTS

Enrollment of law school: 685
% Out of state: 60
% Male/female: 54/46
% Full-time: 60
% International: 2
% Minority: 18
Average age of entering class: 26

ACADEMICS

Academic specializations: Civil procedure, commercial law, constitutional law, corporation securities law, criminal law, environmental law, government services, human rights law, intellectual property law, international law, labor law, legal history, legal philosophy, property, taxation.
Advanced degrees offered: JD–2 1/2 to 3 years full-time, 3 1/2 to 4 years part-time.
Grading system: 4.0 scale.
Clinical program required? Yes.
Clinical program description: All students are required to take a skills course or participate in one of the following clinics: Criminal law, civil practice, domestic violence, municipal law, and a international law.
Legal writing course requirement? Yes.
Legal writing description: All students take legal writing in their first full year and they are also required to take an advanced legal writing course in their second or third year. Lawyering Process I focuses on basic research and writing and culminates in the submission of an objective memorandum of law. Lawyering Process II focuses on persuasive writing techniques and culminates in submission of an appellate brief. Students also practice basic oral advocacy skills and participate in appellate arguments.
Legal methods course requirement? Yes.
Legal methods description: First-year students are required to develop legal problem-solving, research, and writing skills and focus upon development and enhancement of lawyering skills in rule-related and professional responsibility contexts.
Legal research course requirement? Yes.
Legal research description: All students take legal research in their first full year and they can elect to take an advanced legal research course in their second or third year.
Moot court requirement? Yes.
Moot court description: The moot court program is voluntary. Students compete in an intramural competition after completion of Lawyering Process II. Students that are selected for moot court may receive academic credit and may compete in national competitions.
Public interest law requirement? No.
Academic journals: *Florida Coastal Law Journal.*

ADMISSIONS INFORMATION

ADMISSIONS SELECTIVITY RATING: 67
Application fee: $50
Regular application deadline: Rolling.
Regular notification: Rolling.
Early application program: No.
LSDAS accepted? Yes.
Average GPA: 3.00
Range of GPA: 2.7-3.3
Average LSAT: 151
Range of LSAT: 149-154
Transfer students accepted? Yes.
Evening division offered: Yes.
Part-time accepted: Yes.
Applicants also look at: Florida State University, Mercer University, Nova Southeastern University, St. Thomas University, Stetson University, University of Florida, University of Miami.
Number of applications received: 4,505
Number of applicants accepted: 1,624
Number of acceptees attending: 305

RESEARCH FACILITIES

Research resources available: University of North Florida and Jacksonville University.
% of JD classrooms wired: 100
School-supported research centers: CALI (Computer Assisted Learning Center), Lexis, Westlaw, LOISLAW, CCH.

FINANCIAL FACTS

Annual tuition: $22,400
Room & board (on/off-campus): $8,046/$12,663
Books and supplies: $1,000
% receiving scholarships: 25
Average grant: $6,200
Average loan: $18,500
% of aid that is merit-based: 11
% receiving some sort of aid: 71
% first year students receiving some sort of aid: 85
Average total aid package: $23,000
Average debt: $50,000

INTERNATIONAL STUDENTS

TOEFL required for international students? No.

EMPLOYMENT INFORMATION

Rate of placement: 94
Average starting salary: $48,000
State for bar exam: FL, GA, TX, TN, SC
Pass rate for first-time bar: 80
Grads employed by field: Academic, 1%; business/industry, 36%; government, 11%; judicial clerkships, 2%; military, 1%; private practice, 47%; public interest, 1%.

FRANKLIN PIERCE LAW CENTER

Franklin Pierce Law Center

Two White Street, Concord, NH 3301 United States
***Admissions Phone:** 603-228-9217* • ***Admissions Fax:** 603-224-4661*
***Admissions E-mail:** admissions@piercelaw.edu*
***Web Address:** www.piercelaw.edu*

INSTITUTIONAL INFORMATION

Public/private: Private.
Student/faculty ratio: 13:1
Total faculty: 81
% Faculty Part-time: 58
% Faculty Female: 24

% Faculty Minority: 1

STUDENTS

Enrollment of law school: 393
% Out of state: 75
% Male/female: 61/39
% Full-time: 100
% International: 6
% Minority: 12
Average age of entering class: 26

ACADEMICS

Academic specializations: Commercial law, human rights law, intellectual property law, health law.
Advanced degrees offered: LLM–1 year; master of intellectual property, commerce & technology (MIPCT)–1 year.
Combined degrees offered: JD/MIPCT–3 years.
Grading system: Anonymous grading using A-plus through F. Students may take electives pass/fail. In all classes with more than 15 students, the mean grade in the class will be no higher than B.
Clinical program required? No.
Clinical program description: Consumer & commercial law clinic, family & housing law clinic, mediation clinic, criminal practice clinic, appellate defender program.
Legal writing course requirement? No.
Legal methods course requirement? Yes.
Legal methods description: Not available.
Legal research course requirement? No.
Moot court requirement? No.
Public interest law requirement? No.
Academic journals: *Pierce Law Review, IDEA: the Journal of Law and Technology, The Germeshausen Newsletter, The Annual Survey of New Hampshire Law.*

ADMISSIONS INFORMATION

ADMISSIONS SELECTIVITY RATING: 69
Application fee: $35
Regular application deadline: 4/1
Regular notification: Rolling.
Early application program: No.
LSDAS accepted? Yes.
Average GPA: 3.20
Range of GPA: 2.9–3.4
Average LSAT: 152
Range of LSAT: 149-156
Transfer students accepted? Yes.
Evening division offered: No.
Part-time accepted: No.
Applicants also look at: Albany Law School, Suffolk University, George Washington University, Vermont Law School, Western New England College.
Number of applications received: 1,583
Number of applicants accepted: 622
Number of acceptees attending: 157

RESEARCH FACILITIES

% of JD classrooms wired: 100
School-supported research centers: High-tech courtroom.

FINANCIAL FACTS

Annual tuition: $25,249
Room & board (off-campus): $9,295
Books and supplies: $3,516
% receiving scholarships: 15
Average grant: $7,400
Average loan: $27,278
% of aid that is merit-based: 57
% receiving some sort of aid: 75
% first year students receiving some sort of aid: 75
Average total aid package: $19,350
Average debt: $77,340

INTERNATIONAL STUDENTS

TOEFL required for international students? Yes.
Minimum Paper TOEFL: 600
Minimum Computer-based TOEFL: 250

EMPLOYMENT INFORMATION

Rate of placement: 97
Average starting salary: $78,442
State for bar exam: NH, MA, NY, DC, CA
Pass rate for first-time bar: 75
Grads employed by field: Academic, 4%; business/industry, 18%; government, 5%; judicial clerkships, 3%; other, 7%; private practice, 56%; public interest, 7%.

HOFSTRA UNIVERSITY

Hofstra University School of Law

121 Hofstra University, Hempstead, NY 11549 United States
***Admissions Phone:** 516-463-5916 • **Admissions Fax:** 516-463-6264*
***Admissions E-mail:** lawadmissions@Hofstra.edu*
***Web Address:** www.hofstra.edu/law*

INSTITUTIONAL INFORMATION

Public/private: Private.
Student/faculty ratio: 18:1
Total faculty: 86
% Faculty Part-time: 52
% Faculty Female: 22
% Faculty Minority: 5

STUDENTS

Enrollment of law school: 1,018
% Male/female: 52/48
% Full-time: 83
% Minority: 18
Average age of entering class: 24

ACADEMICS

Academic specializations: Civil procedure, commercial law, constitutional law, corporation securities law, criminal law, environmental law, government services, intellectual property law, international law, labor law, property, taxation, family law, trial advocacy, international law, health law.
Advanced degrees offered: JD–3 years full-time, 4 years part-time day and evening; LLM–1 year full-time, 2 years part-time.
Combined degrees offered: JD/MBA–4 years; JD/MS in taxation–4 years.
Grading system: Students are marked on the following grade scale: A (4.0), A- (3.67), B+ (3.3), through D (1.00) and F (0.00).
Clinical program required? No.
Clinical program description: Child advocacy clinic, criminal justice clinic, housing rights clinic, mediation clinic and political asylum clinic.
Legal writing course requirement? Yes.

Legal writing description: Legal writing (2 credits) is taken in second semester of first year.
Legal methods course requirement? Yes.
Legal methods description: A 2-week introduction prior to orientation, and variety of sessions during the first semester of first year.
Legal research course requirement? Yes.
Legal research description: Legal research, while not a separate course, begins in the first semester of first year and continues in the legal writing course.
Moot court requirement? Yes.
Moot court description: Appellate advocacy (2 credits) a required course taken in the first semester, second year includes a required appellate argument.
Public interest law requirement? No.
Academic journals: *Law Review, Labor & Employment Law Journal, Family Court Review, Journal of International Business and Law.*

ADMISSIONS INFORMATION

ADMISSIONS SELECTIVITY RATING: 82
Application fee: $60
Regular application deadline: 4/15
Regular notification: Rolling.
Early application program: Yes.
LSDAS accepted? Yes.
Average GPA: 3.40
Range of GPA: 3.0–3.6
Average LSAT: 158
Range of LSAT: 155–159
Transfer students accepted? Yes.
Evening division offered: Yes.
Part-time accepted: Yes.
Applicants also look at: Brooklyn Law School, Fordham University, New York Law School, New York University, Pace University, St. John's University, Yeshiva University.
Number of applications received: 5,539
Number of applicants accepted: 1,458
Number of acceptees attending: 381

RESEARCH FACILITIES

Research resources available: JD students have access to discount Internet service accounts with local service providers.
% of JD classrooms wired: 100
School-supported research centers: Completely wireless Internet and network access both inside and outside of the building.

FINANCIAL FACTS

Annual tuition: $30,824
Room & board (on/off-campus): $9,616/$12,960
Books and supplies: $900
Financial aid application deadline: 4/15
Average grant: $8,553
Average loan: $3,161
% of aid that is merit-based: 50
Tuition per credit: $1,100

INTERNATIONAL STUDENTS

TOEFL required for international students? Yes.
Minimum Paper TOEFL: 580
Minimum Computer-based TOEFL: 237

EMPLOYMENT INFORMATION

Rate of placement: 94
Average starting salary: $68,799
Employers who frequently hire grads: The most prestigious law firms in New York City and Long Island regularly recruit at the law school. Government agencies and public interest organizations are well represented.
State for bar exam: NY, NJ, CT, FL, CA
Grads employed by field: Academic, 1%; business/industry, 12%; government, 13%; judicial clerkships, 6%; private practice, 66%; public interest, 2%.

MARQUETTE UNIVERSITY

Marquette University Law School

Sensenbrenner Hall, PO Box 1881, Milwaukee, WI 53201-1881 United States
Admissions Phone: *414-288-6767* • ***Admissions Fax:*** *414-288-0676*
Admissions E-mail: *law.admission@marquette.edu*
Web Address: *law.marquette.edu*

INSTITUTIONAL INFORMATION

Public/private: Private.
Affiliation: Roman Catholic.
Student/faculty ratio: 15:1
Total faculty: 35
% Faculty Female: 30
% Faculty Minority: 3

STUDENTS

Enrollment of law school: 587
% Out of state: 38
% Male/female: 55/45
% Full-time: 81
% Minority: 11
Average age of entering class: 25

ACADEMICS

Academic specializations: Civil procedure, commercial law, constitutional law, corporation securities law, criminal law, environmental law, government services, intellectual property law, international law, labor law, legal history, property, taxation.
Combined degrees offered: JD/MBA; JD/MA political science; JD/MA political science international relations; JD/MA bioethics. All 4-year programs.
Grading system: A, B, C, D, F.
Clinical program required? No.
Legal writing course requirement? Yes.
Legal writing description: In addition to stressing communication skills in all core classes, Marquette requires you to take specific introductory courses in legal writing, research, and communication.
Legal methods course requirement? Yes.
Legal methods description: Students all need to meet advanced research and advanced oral communication requirements with specially designated courses.
Legal research course requirement? Yes.
Legal research description: Advanced research required.
Moot court requirement? No.
Public interest law requirement? No.
Academic journals: *Marquette Law Review, Intellectual Property Law Review, Sports Law Review, Elder's Advisor.*

ADMISSIONS INFORMATION

ADMISSIONS SELECTIVITY RATING: 71
Application fee: $50

Regular application deadline: 4/1
Regular notification: Rolling.
Early application program: No.
LSDAS accepted? Yes.
Average GPA: 3.30
Range of GPA: 2.9–3.5
Average LSAT: 155
Range of LSAT: 152–157
Transfer students accepted? Yes.
Evening division offered: Yes.
Part-time accepted: Yes.
Applicants also look at: DePaul University, Hamline University, Loyola University Chicago, University of Wisconsin.
Number of applications received: 984
Number of applicants accepted: 490
Number of acceptees attending: 151

RESEARCH FACILITIES

Research resources available: Westlaw, Lexis/Nexis.
% of JD classrooms wired: 10

FINANCIAL FACTS

Annual tuition: $26,176
Room & board (on/off-campus): $10,060/$10,060
Books and supplies: $1,070
Financial aid application deadline: 3/1
Average grant: $10,000
Average loan: $30,000
% of aid that is merit-based: 25
% receiving some sort of aid: 90
% first year students receiving some sort of aid: 85
Average total aid package: $21,550
Average debt: $62,000
Tuition per credit: $895

INTERNATIONAL STUDENTS

TOEFL required for international students? Yes.
Minimum Paper TOEFL: 600
Minimum Computer-based TOEFL: 250

EMPLOYMENT INFORMATION

Rate of placement: 95
Average starting salary: $58,500
Employers who frequently hire grads: Michael Best & Friedrich; Quarles & Brady; Godfrey & Kahn; Von Briesen, Purtell, & Roport; Foley & Lardner; Davis & Kualthay, S.C.; Whyte Hirschboeck Dudek.
State for bar exam: WI
Pass rate for first-time bar: 100
Grads employed by field: Business/industry, 18%; government, 7%; judicial clerkships, 7%; military, 1%; private practice, 63%; public interest, 1%.

NEW YORK LAW SCHOOL

New York Law School

57 Worth Street, New York, NY 10013 United States
***Admissions Phone:** 212-431-2888* • ***Admissions Fax:** 212-966-1522*
***Admissions E-mail:** admissions@nyls.edu* • ***Web Address:** www.nyls.edu*

INSTITUTIONAL INFORMATION

Public/private: Private.
Student/faculty ratio: 17:1

STUDENTS

Enrollment of law school: 1,564
% Male/female: 49/51
% Full-time: 82
% Minority: 18
Average age of entering class: 27

ACADEMICS

Academic specializations: Commercial law, constitutional law, corporation securities law, criminal law, government services, human rights law, intellectual property law, international law, labor law, legal philosophy, taxation.
Advanced degrees offered: JD–3 years full-time, 4 years part-time; LLM in taxation, 1 to 2 years.
Combined degrees offered: JD/MBA with Baruch College–4 years of full-time course load.
Grading system: A–F. Some courses designated pass/fail.
Clinical program required? No.
Clinical program description: Discrimination law enforcement, criminal law, mediation, poverty law, elder law, securities arbitration, employment law.
Legal writing course requirement? Yes.
Legal writing description: Legal writing and research in first year.
Legal methods course requirement? Yes.
Legal methods description: Applied analysis course in first semester.
Legal research course requirement? Yes.
Legal research description: Legal writing and research in first year.
Moot court requirement? No.
Public interest law requirement? No.
Academic journals: *Law Review.*

ADMISSIONS INFORMATION

ADMISSIONS SELECTIVITY RATING: 76
Application fee: $60
Regular application deadline: 4/1
Regular notification: Rolling.
Early application program: No.
LSDAS accepted? Yes.
Average GPA: 3.20
Range of GPA: 3.0–3.4
Average LSAT: 155
Range of LSAT: 153–157
Transfer students accepted? Yes.
Evening division offered: Yes.
Part-time accepted: Yes.
Applicants also look at: Albany Law School, Brooklyn Law School, Hofstra University, Pace University, Roger Williams University, Seton Hall University, Yeshiva University.
Number of applications received: 5,084
Number of applicants accepted: 1,542
Number of acceptees attending: 428

RESEARCH FACILITIES

School-supported research centers: Center for International Law, Center for New York City Law, Center for Professional Values and Practice, Justice Action Center, Institute for Information Law and Policy.

FINANCIAL FACTS

Annual tuition: $36,480
Room & board (on/off-campus): $13,995/$13,995
Books and supplies: $800
Financial aid application deadline: 4/1
Average grant: $7,500
Average loan: $26,000
Tuition per credit: $28,050

INTERNATIONAL STUDENTS

TOEFL required for international students? Yes.
Minimum Paper TOEFL: 600
Minimum Computer-based TOEFL: 250

EMPLOYMENT INFORMATION

Rate of placement: 92
Average starting salary: $75,000
State for bar exam: NY
Pass rate for first-time bar: 72
Grads employed by field: Academic, 1%; business/industry, 14%; government, 11%; judicial clerkships, 7%; other, 11%; private practice, 52%; public interest, 4%.

North Carolina Central University

School of Law

1512 South Alston Avenue, Durham, NC 27707 United States
Admissions Phone: *919-530-7173* • ***Admissions Fax:*** *919-530-6339*
Admissions E-mail: *kalston@nccu.edu* • ***Web Address:*** *www.nccu.edu/law*

INSTITUTIONAL INFORMATION

Public/private: Public.
Student/faculty ratio: 17:1

STUDENTS

Enrollment of law school: 437
% Male/female: 54/46
% Full-time: 77
% Minority: 56
Average age of entering class: 29

ACADEMICS

Advanced degrees offered: JD day program–3 years; JD evening program–4 years.
Combined degrees offered: JD/MBA–4 years; JD/MLS–4 years.
Grading system: A–F.
Clinical program required? No.
Clinical program description: The clinical program offers an exceptional opportunity for law students to obtain practical skills training by representing real clients with real legal issues. The clinic operates year-round, out of a state-of-the-art model law office. Generally, all rising third-year students in good standing are eligible to participate in the clinical program. Clinical students practice law under the supervision of a licensed attorney after completing a required classroom component. The following is a list of clinical experiences offered by the school of law: Civil litigation clinic, criminal litigation clinic, family law clinic, alternative dispute resolution clinic, pro bono legal clinic, small business clinic, and juvenile justice clinic.
Legal writing course requirement? Yes.
Legal writing description: The school of law emphasizes the development of effective writing and analytial skills. This commitment is reflected in an intensive writing program that begins in the first semester and continues through the student's tenure in law school. In the required upper-level writing courses, students will engage in complex critical analyses that result in comprehensive written documents. These courses are appellate advocacy I, legal letters, pleadings and practice, and senior writing (evening program only). For more information, please refer to the law school's bulletin or Web page.
Legal methods course requirement? Yes.
Legal methods description: First-year students must successfully complete legal reasoning and analysis I and II. Legal reasoning and analysis I introduces students to the basics of legal reasoning, analysis, and writing, such as preparing case briefs, identifying issues and key facts, making analogies and distinctions, synthesizing cases, and constructing statutes. The course concludes with a closed-research, objective memorandum of law. Legal reasoning and analysis II covers legal research, analysis, writing, and citation form. Students prepare a research outline and an open-research, objective memorandum of law using the same case problem that was introduced in legal reasoning and analysis I.
Legal research course requirement? Yes.
Legal research description: Legal bibliography is a required first-year, first-semester course. The course includes an overview of legal concepts, such as the structure of the court system, and how law is made. It identifies and describes the sources of law and their search tools in print and electronic format. Students are instructed in the research strategies necessary to find and update the law. Students are introduced to computer-assisted legal research.
Moot court requirement? No.
Moot court description: Students who have excelled in appellate advocacy I are chosen, through in-house moot court competitions, to participate in various regional and national moot court competitions. Participating students must prepare an appellate brief and present an oral argument in a certified competition in order to obtain senior board status and to earn a grade.
Public interest law requirement? No.
Academic journals: *Law Journal.*

ADMISSIONS INFORMATION

ADMISSIONS SELECTIVITY RATING: 75
Application fee: $40
Regular application deadline: 4/15
Regular notification: 4/15
Early application program: No.
LSDAS accepted? Yes.
Average GPA: 3.30
Range of GPA: 2.9–3.6
Average LSAT: 149
Range of LSAT: 143–157
Transfer students accepted? Yes.
Evening division offered: Yes.
Part-time accepted: Yes.
Number of applications received: 2,253
Number of applicants accepted: 304
Number of acceptees attending: 170

RESEARCH FACILITIES

% of JD classrooms wired: 100

School-supported research centers: The law school operates in an IBM PC-compatible environment running Windows 98 and 2000. Two computer labs for word processing, legal research, Internet access and E-mail are maintained in the law library.

FINANCIAL FACTS

Annual tuition (resident): $2,956
Annual tuition (nonresident): $12,060
Room & board (on/off-campus): $6,500/$10,205
Books and supplies: $1,250
Financial aid application deadline: 4/15
% receiving scholarships: 38
Average grant: $2,200
Average loan: $16,500
% of aid that is merit-based: 65
% receiving some sort of aid: 97
% first year students receiving some sort of aid: 96

INTERNATIONAL STUDENTS

TOEFL required for international students? Yes.

EMPLOYMENT INFORMATION

State for bar exam: NC, VA, SC, GA, DC
Grads employed by field: Business/industry, 19%; government, 12%; judicial clerkships, 6%; private practice, 59%; public interest, 4%.

THE PENNSYLVANIA STATE UNIVERSITY

The Dickinson School of Law

150 South College Street, Carlisle, PA 17013 United States
***Admissions Phone:** 717-240-5207* • ***Admissions Fax:** 717-241-3503*
***Admissions E-mail:** dsladmit@psu.edu* • ***Web Address:** www.dsl.psu.edu*

INSTITUTIONAL INFORMATION

Public/private: Public.
Student/faculty ratio: 17:1
Total faculty: 89
% Faculty Part-time: 49
% Faculty Female: 34
% Faculty Minority: 1

STUDENTS

Enrollment of law school: 622
% Out of state: 49
% Male/female: 54/46
% Full-time: 100
% International: 1
% Minority: 18
Average age of entering class: 24

ACADEMICS

Academic specializations: Civil procedure, commercial law, constitutional law, corporation securities law, criminal law, environmental law, government services, human rights law, intellectual property law, international law, labor law, legal history, property, taxation, dispute resolution.
Advanced degrees offered: JD–3 years; LLM in comparative law–1 year.
Combined degrees offered: JD/MBA with Penn State's Smeal College of Business Administration; JD/MBA with Penn State Harrisburg; JD/MPA with Penn State Harrisburg School of Public Affairs; JD/3 environmental pollution control degrees with Penn State Harrisburg; JD/MSIS (information systems) with Penn State Harrisburg; JD/5 counseling degree programs with Shippensburg University.
Grading system: Course grades reported & recorded on numerical basis: 90 and above=distinguished, 85–89=excellent, 80–84=good, 75–79=satisfactory, 70–74=passing, 65–69=conditional failure, below 65=failure.
Clinical program required? No.
Clinical program description: Family law; disability law; elder law; art, sports, and entertainment law; and externships in judges' chambers, district attorneys' and public defenders' offices, government agencies, legal services offices.
Legal writing course requirement? Yes.
Legal writing description: Lawyering skills–first year, 2 semesters. Involves teaching skills such as research, analysis of cases and statutes, writing of legal memoranda and briefs, and oral argument.
Legal methods course requirement? No.
Legal research course requirement? Yes.
Legal research description: Lawyering skills–first year, 2 semesters. Involves teaching skills such as research, analysis of cases and statutes, writing of legal memoranda and briefs, and oral argument.
Moot court requirement? Yes.
Moot court description: Fall semester–second year; classroom meetings on appellate practice issues, briefwriting and oral argument; submission of brief and presentation of oral argument, both for a grade.
Public interest law requirement? No.
Academic journals: *Penn State Law Review, Penn State Environmental Law Review, Penn State International Law Review, Journal of American Arbitration, World Arbitration and Mediation Report.*

ADMISSIONS INFORMATION

ADMISSIONS SELECTIVITY RATING: 77
Application fee: $60
Regular application deadline: 3/1
Regular notification: Rolling.
Early application program: No.
LSDAS accepted? Yes.
Average GPA: 3.30
Range of GPA: 3.1–3.5
Average LSAT: 155
Range of LSAT: 154–157
Transfer students accepted? Yes.
Evening division offered: No.
Part-time accepted: No.
Applicants also look at: American University, Syracuse University, Temple University, University of Pittsburgh, Villanova University, Widener University.
Number of applications received: 2,561
Number of applicants accepted: 699
Number of acceptees attending: 176

RESEARCH FACILITIES

Research resources available: All Penn State libraries and libraries of Big 10. LEXIS, Westlaw, Loislaw, and member libraries of association of college libraries of central Pennsylvania consortium.
% of JD classrooms wired: 100
School-supported research centers: Agricultural Law Research and Education Center, Miller Center for Public InterestAdvocacy, Center for Dispute Resolution, Center for International and Comparative Law.

FINANCIAL FACTS

Annual tuition (resident): $25,250

Annual tuition (nonresident): $25,250
Room & board (on/off-campus): $6,600/$8,280
Books and supplies: $1,100
Financial aid application deadline: 3/1
% receiving scholarships: 50
Average grant: $11,631
Average loan: $25,550
% of aid that is merit-based: 90
Average debt: $75,522

INTERNATIONAL STUDENTS

TOEFL required for international students? No

EMPLOYMENT INFORMATION

Rate of placement: 94
Average starting salary: $50,692
Employers who frequently hire grads: Dickinson graduates are hired by a variety of employers each year including national law firms, small firms, federal and state judges, government agencies, public interest organizations, and other entities.
Prominent alumni: Hon. Thomas Ridge, secretary of homeland security; Hon. Richard Santorum, U.S. senator; Hon. D. Brooks Smith, Third Circuit Court of Appeals; Lisa A. Hook, vice president, AOL/Time-Warner; Hon. J. Michael Eakin, PA Supreme Court.
State for bar exam: PA
Pass rate for first-time bar: 87
Grads employed by field: Business/industry, 7%; government, 12%; judicial clerkships, 27%; military, 3%; other, 1%; private practice, 45%; public interest, 5%.

SAINT LOUIS UNIVERSITY

Saint Louis University School of Law

3700 Lindell Boulevard, St. Louis, MO 63108 United States
***Admissions Phone:** 314-977-2800 • **Admissions Fax:** 314-977-1464*
***Admissions E-mail:** admissions@law.slu.edu • **Web Address:** law.slu.edu*

INSTITUTIONAL INFORMATION

Public/private: Private.
Affiliation: Roman Catholic.
Student/faculty ratio: 17:1
Total faculty: 48
% Faculty Female: 35
% Faculty Minority: 4

STUDENTS

Enrollment of law school: 825
% Out of state: 46
% Male/female: 47/53
% Full-time: 72
% Minority: 11
Average age of entering class: 25

ACADEMICS

Academic specializations: Civil procedure, commercial law, constitutional law, corporation securities law, criminal law, environmental law, government services, human rights law, intellectual property law, international law, labor law, legal history, legal philosophy, property, taxation.
Advanced degrees offered: LLM health law–1 year full-time, 2 years part-time; LLM for foreign lawyers–1 year full-time.
Combined degrees offered: JD/MBA–3 1/2 to 4 years; JD/MHA–4 years; JD/MAPA, JD/MAUA–3 1/2 to 4 years; JD/MPH–4 years.
Grading system: Letter and numerical system, 4.0 scale.
Clinical program required? No.
Clinical program description: In-house clinic, externship program, judicial process clinic, criminal public defender clinic, corporate counsel externship clinic, immigration law project, health law clinic, litigation clinic, housing and finance clinic.
Legal writing course requirement? Yes.
Legal methods course requirement? No.
Legal research course requirement? Yes.
Moot court requirement? No.
Public interest law requirement? No.
Academic journals: *Saint Louis University Law Journal*, *Public Law Review*, and *The Journal of Health Law.*

ADMISSIONS INFORMATION

ADMISSIONS SELECTIVITY RATING: 77
Application fee: $55
Regular application deadline: 3/1
Regular notification: Rolling.
Early application program: No.
LSDAS accepted? Yes.
Average GPA: 3.40
Range of GPA: 3.2–3.7
Average LSAT: 156
Range of LSAT: 153–160
Transfer students accepted? Yes.
Evening division offered: Yes.
Part-time accepted: Yes.
Number of applications received: 1,694
Number of applicants accepted: 644
Number of acceptees attending: 223

RESEARCH FACILITIES

% of JD classrooms wired: 100
School-supported research centers: The law school will be a wireless network facility this upcoming fall.

FINANCIAL FACTS

Annual tuition: $27,250
Room & board (off-campus): $11,988
Books and supplies: $1,040
Financial aid application deadline: 6/3
% receiving scholarships: 43
Average grant: $11,000
Average loan: $24,236
% of aid that is merit-based: 30
% receiving some sort of aid: 92
% first year students receiving some sort of aid: 92
Average total aid package: $26,000
Average debt: $69,796

INTERNATIONAL STUDENTS

TOEFL required for international students? No.
Minimum Computer-based TOEFL: 232

EMPLOYMENT INFORMATION

Rate of placement: 93
Average starting salary: $55,291
Employers who frequently hire grads: Bryan Cave, LLP; Husch & Eppenberger; Lewis, Rice, & Fingersh; Armstrong Teasdale, LLP; Sonnenschein, Nath & Rosenthal; Greensfelder, Hemker & Gale; Blackwell,

Sanders, Peper, Martin; Missouri State Public Defender; Evans & Dixon; Brown & James.
State for bar exam: MO, IL
Pass rate for first-time bar: 80
Grads employed by field: Academic, 3%; business/industry, 16%; government, 9%; judicial clerkships, 4%; private practice, 64%; public interest, 4%.

Southern University

Law Center

A.A. Lenoir Hall, PO Box 9294, Baton Rouge, LA 70813 United States
Admissions Phone: *225-771-5340* • ***Admissions Fax:*** *225-771-7424*
Admissions E-mail: *ESimmons@sus.edu* • ***Web Address:*** *www.sus.edu/sulc*

INSTITUTIONAL INFORMATION

Public/private: Public.
Student/faculty ratio: 14:1
Total faculty: 44
% Faculty Female: 30
% Faculty Minority: 64

STUDENTS

Enrollment of law school: 311
% Out of state: 8
% Male/female: 50/50
% Full-time: 100
% Minority: 66
Average age of entering class: 27

ACADEMICS

Grading system: 4.00 grade point scale; A=90–100; B+=85–89; B=84–80; C+=79–75; C=74–70; D+=65–69; D=64–60; F=59–0.
Clinical program required? No.
Clinical program description: 4 clinics—criminal, juvenile, elder law, administrative/civil; clinical education program is restricted to third-year law students in good standing.
Legal methods course requirement? Yes.
Legal methods description: First year-legal writing 2 hours per semester; 2nd year-adv. leg. writing 1 hours per semester.

ADMISSIONS INFORMATION

ADMISSIONS SELECTIVITY RATING: 60*
Application fee: $25
Regular application deadline: 3/1
Regular notification: Rolling.
Early application program: No.
LSDAS accepted? No.
Average GPA: 2.70
Range of GPA: 2.5–3
Average LSAT: 145
Range of LSAT: 142–148
Transfer students accepted? No.
Evening division offered: No.
Part-time accepted: No.
Number of applications received: 250

RESEARCH FACILITIES

Research resources available: Through a cooperative aggreement with Paul M. Herbert Law Center at Louisiana State University, students at both institutions have unlimited and free access to each institution's facilities and materials.
School-supported research centers: Louisiana Online University Information System (LOUIS) provides access to library holdings to a majority of the academic libraries in Louisiana and the nation via the Web.

FINANCIAL FACTS

Annual tuition (resident): $3,128
Annual tuition (nonresident): $7,728
% first year students receiving some sort of aid: 86

INTERNATIONAL STUDENTS

TOEFL required for international students? No.

EMPLOYMENT INFORMATION

State for bar exam: LA
Pass rate for first-time bar: 31

Stetson University

Stetson University College of Law

1401 61st Street, South Gulfport, FL 33707 United States
Admissions Phone: *727-562-7802* • ***Admissions Fax:*** *727-343-0136*
Admissions E-mail: *lawadmit@law.stetson.edu*
Web Address: *www.law.stetson.edu*

INSTITUTIONAL INFORMATION

Public/private: Private.
Student/faculty ratio: 18:1
Total faculty: 82
% Faculty Part-time: 42

STUDENTS

Enrollment of law school: 920
% Male/female: 47/53
% Full-time: 80
% Minority: 25

ACADEMICS

Academic specializations: International law, advocacy, health law, elder law.
Advanced degrees offered: JD: full-time–3 years, part-time–4 years; JD/MBA–3 years, full-time; LLM–1 year, full-time.
Combined degrees offered: JD/MBA: 3 years for full-time students and 4 years for part-time students.
Grading system: 4.00 point scale.
Clinical program required? No.
Clinical program description: Although not required, the following are the programs that we offer: Alternative dispute resloution clinic, civil government clinic civil poverty clinic, elder consumer protection clinic, employment discrimincation clinis, labor law clinic, local government clinic, public defender clinic and prosecution clinic.
Legal writing course requirement? Yes.
Legal writing description: Two-semester, graded course that focuses on legal research, objective and persuasive writing, and oral advocacy.

Legal methods course requirement? No.
Legal research course requirement? Yes.
Legal research description: Legal research is taught as part of the research and writing course. We focus on print and computer-assisted research. Students have the opportunity to participate in small-group lab sessions.
Moot court requirement? Yes.
Moot court description: First-year students are taught oral advocacy in the second semester of research and writing II. They give 4 oral presentations. Top oralists compete in a first-year appellate advocacy competition for cash prizes and positions on the moot court board.
Public interest law requirement? Yes.
Public interest law description: Students must complete 20 hours of pro bono work before graduation.
Academic journals: *Stetson Law Review, Journal of International Aging Law and Policy.*

ADMISSIONS INFORMATION

ADMISSIONS SELECTIVITY RATING: 78
Application fee: $55
Regular application deadline: Rolling.
Regular notification: Rolling.
Early application program: No.
LSDAS accepted? Yes.
Average GPA: 3.46
Range of GPA: 3.2–3.7
Average LSAT: 153
Range of LSAT: 151–157
Transfer students accepted? Yes.
Evening division offered: Yes.
Part-time accepted: Yes.
Applicants also look at: Barry University, Florida State University, Nova Southeastern University, University of Florida, University of Miami.
Number of applications received: 3,058
Number of applicants accepted: 725
Number of acceptees attending: 299

RESEARCH FACILITIES

Research resources available: Satellite law campus opened near downtown Tampa in January 2004. This facility has computer labs and a library for all students and alumni to use. The facility offers some of the part-time evening courses and includes courtrooms set up with advanced technologies, as well as fully wired classrooms. Additionally, the entire campus will have wireless network access.
% of JD classrooms wired: 100

FINANCIAL FACTS

Annual tuition: $24,760
Room & board (on/off-campus): $8,147/$11,361
Books and supplies: $1,200
% receiving scholarships: 27
Average grant: $9,079
Average loan: $30,000
% of aid that is merit-based: 51
% receiving some sort of aid: 89
% first year students receiving some sort of aid: 72
Average total aid package: $38,000
Average debt: $98,000

INTERNATIONAL STUDENTS

TOEFL required for international students? Yes.
Minimum Paper TOEFL: 600
Minimum Computer-based TOEFL: 250

EMPLOYMENT INFORMATION

Rate of placement: 94
Average starting salary: $54,000
Employers who frequently hire grads: Small, medium, and large firms in the greater Tampa Bay area, state attorney's offices, public defenders office.
Prominent alumni: Justice Carol Hunstein, Supreme Court of Georgia; Hon. Elizabeth Kovachevich, USDC Middle District Florida; Rich McKay, president and GM, Atlanta Falcons; Bruce Jacob, dean emeritus and professor of law, argued Gideon v. Wainwright, 372 U.S. 335 (1963); Rhea F. Law, president and CEO, Fowler White.
State for bar exam: FL, GA, DC, VA, MD
Grads employed by field: Academic, 5%; business/industry, 6%; government, 22%; judicial clerkships, 7%; military, 2%; private practice, 56%; public interest, 2%.

TEXAS SOUTHERN UNIVERSITY

Thurgood Marshall School of Law

3100 Cleburne Avenue, Houston, TX 77004 United States
***Admissions Phone:** 713-313-7114*
***Admissions E-mail:** lawadmit@tsulaw.edu* • ***Web Address:** www.tsulaw.edu*

INSTITUTIONAL INFORMATION

Public/private: Public.
Student/faculty ratio: 17:1
Total faculty: 35
% Faculty Female: 20
% Faculty Minority: 83

STUDENTS

Enrollment of law school: 541
% Male/female: 57/43
% Full-time: 100
% Minority: 77

ACADEMICS

Academic specializations: Commercial law, corporation securities law.
Clinical program required? No.
Legal methods course requirement? No.

ADMISSIONS INFORMATION

ADMISSIONS SELECTIVITY RATING: 61
Application fee: $50
Regular application deadline: 4/1
Regular notification: Rolling.
Early application program: No.
LSDAS accepted? No.
Average GPA: 2.80
Range of GPA: 2.5–3.2
Average LSAT: 141
Range of LSAT: 138–144
Transfer students accepted? Yes.
Evening division offered: No.

Part-time accepted: No.
Number of applications received: 1,460
Number of applicants accepted: 540
Number of acceptees attending: 265

FINANCIAL FACTS

Annual tuition (resident): $4,466
Annual tuition (nonresident): $7,562
Room & board (off-campus): $6,000
Books and supplies: $700

INTERNATIONAL STUDENTS

TOEFL required for international students? No.

EMPLOYMENT INFORMATION

State for bar exam: TX
Pass rate for first-time bar: 68
Grads employed by field: Government, 2%; judicial clerkships, 4%; private practice, 87%; public interest, 5%.

THOMAS M. COOLEY LAW SCHOOL

Thomas M. Cooley Law School

PO Box 13038, 300 South Capitol Avenue, Lansing, MI 48901 United States
Admissions Phone: *517-371-5140* • ***Admissions Fax:*** *517-334-5718*
Admissions E-mail: *admissions@cooley.edu* • ***Web Address:*** *www.cooley.edu*

INSTITUTIONAL INFORMATION

Public/private: Private.
Student/faculty ratio: 22:1
Total faculty: 267
% Faculty Part-time: 70
% Faculty Female: 35
% Faculty Minority: 12

STUDENTS

Enrollment of law school: 2,884
% Out of state: 82
% Male/female: 59/41
% Full-time: 17
% International: 2
% Minority: 20
Average age of entering class: 26

ACADEMICS

Academic specializations: Constitutional law, environmental law, government services, intellectual property law, international law, taxation, business transactions, general practice, litigation, administrative law.
Advanced degrees offered: JD–2 to 5 years; LLM-taxation–1 year full-time; LLM-intellectual property–1 year full-time.
Combined degrees offered: JD/MPA–3 to 6 years with Western Michigan University.
Grading system: In most courses, grades are based on written final exams, administered & graded under a system that assures student anonymity. Proffesors adhere to established grade definitions. The Thomas M. Cooley Law School does not practice grade inflation.
Clinical program required? Yes.
Clinical program description: Cooley Law School offers 4 clinical options:
1) An extensive third-year externship program that places senior students in real work situations throughout the United States with daily or weekly contact with faculty. Placements in prosecutors' offices, with judges, in law firms, with corporate counsel, and legal services programs.
2) Sixty plus, an award-winning in-house clinical program, providing representation to senior citizens in mid-Michigan.
3) Estate planning clinic, an evening or weekend clinic with students providing estate-planning services to seniors.
4) Innocence project, where students use forensic science to aid innocent persons wrongfully convicted of crimes.
Legal writing course requirement? Yes.
Legal writing description: Research and writing (first year) and advanced research and writing (third year) are required of all students. Together, they provide a sequence of courses that train students in clear and effective legal writing using plain English. Students are also trained in book and computer research methods.
Legal methods course requirement? Yes.
Legal methods description: Introduction to law I is required of all students, exposing them to law school briefing, examinations, and jurisprudence.
Legal research course requirement? Yes.
Legal research description: In 2 sequenced courses, students learn both traditional book research and efficient and effective computer research. Research and Writing provides first-year training; advanced research and writing is a third-year course. Additional instuction is available in advanced computer research elective.
Moot court requirement? No.
Moot court description: We offer a first-year moot court competition to all interested students, a second-year class, and several invitation-only competition teams that successfully compete in national programs. Cooley teams have earned best advocate, best brief, and overall winner.
Public interest law requirement? No.
Academic journals: *The Thomas M. Cooley Law Review, The Thomas M. Cooley Journal of Practical and Clinical Law.*

ADMISSIONS INFORMATION

ADMISSIONS SELECTIVITY RATING: 61
Regular application deadline: Rolling.
Regular notification: Rolling.
Early application program: No.
LSDAS accepted? Yes.
Average GPA: 3.01
Range of GPA: 2.7–3.4
Average LSAT: 148
Range of LSAT: 144–151
Transfer students accepted? Yes.
Evening division offered: Yes.
Part-time accepted: Yes.
Applicants also look at: Florida Coastal School of Law, Michigan State University—College of Law, Ohio Northern University, Thomas Jefferson School of Law, University of Detroit Mercy, Wayne State University, Widener University.
Number of applications received: 4,387
Number of applicants accepted: 2,616
Number of acceptees attending: 890

RESEARCH FACILITIES

% of JD classrooms wired: 25
School-supported research centers: Four computer labs that are available in our library to all students. In addition, faculty course pages, a school events calendar, clinical information, our law school catalog, and other information is available to all students through our Website, and provides access at home to many electronic resources. Westlaw and Lexis accounts are provided. In addition, our Academic Resource Center includes another computer lab that pro-

vides access to a variety of CALI instruction materials. Our clinical programs are networked to assist interns and their clients.

FINANCIAL FACTS

Annual tuition: $23,700
Room & board (off-campus): $6,860
Books and supplies: $800
Financial aid application deadline: 12/5
% receiving scholarships: 42
Average grant: $3,447
Average loan: $18,500
% of aid that is merit-based: 35
% receiving some sort of aid: 92
% first year students receiving some sort of aid: 90
Average total aid package: $18,500
Average debt: $82,330
Tuition per credit: $790

INTERNATIONAL STUDENTS

TOEFL required for international students? No.

EMPLOYMENT INFORMATION

Rate of placement: 77
Average starting salary: $47,525
Employers who frequently hire grads: Michigan Court of Appeals prosecutors, legal services programs, Michigan law firms.
Prominent alumni: John Engler, former governor; Bart R. Stupak, U.S. representative; Paul Hillegonds, president, Detroit Renaissance; Jane Markey, Michigan Court of Appeals; Chris Chocola, U.S. representative.
State for bar exam: MI, NY, NJ, FL, IN
Pass rate for first-time bar: 63
Grads employed by field: Academic, 4%; business/industry, 15%; government, 11%; judicial clerkships, 11%; military, 8%; other, 2%; private practice, 47%; public interest, 2%.

TOURO COLLEGE

Jacob D. Fuchsberg Law Center

300 Nassau Road, Huntington, NY 11743 United States
***Admissions Phone:** 631-421-2244 • **Admissions Fax:** 631-421-9708*
***Admissions E-mail:** admissions@tourolaw.edu*
***Web Address:** www.tourolaw.edu*

INSTITUTIONAL INFORMATION

Public/private: Private.
Student/faculty ratio: 17:1
Total faculty: 57
% Faculty Part-time: 21
% Faculty Female: 35
% Faculty Minority: 7

STUDENTS

Enrollment of law school: 719
% Out of state: 18
% Male/female: 55/45
% Full-time: 60
% Minority: 24
Average age of entering class: 28

ACADEMICS

Academic specializations: Commercial law, criminal law, human rights law, intellectual property law, international law, health care law.
Advanced degrees offered: JD–3 years full-time, 4 years part-time; LLM for foreign-trained attorneys–1 year full-time, 3 semesters part-time; LLM general studies–1 year full-time, 3 semesters part-time.
Combined degrees offered: Joint-degree programs: JD/MBA; JD/MPA; JD/MSW (add 1 year of study for joint-degree programs).
Grading system: Clinics and courses: Graded; pro bono work: Pass/fail.
Clinical program required? No.
Clinical program description: Civil rights litigation clinic, elder law clinic, international human rights litigation clinic, family law clinic, judicial clerkship clinic, not-for-profit corporation law, civil practice clinic, criminal law clinic.
Legal writing course requirement? Yes.
Legal writing description: Part of legal methods.
Legal methods course requirement? Yes.
Legal methods description: Two semesters, 2 credits each semester.
Legal research course requirement? Yes.
Legal research description: Part of legal methods.
Moot court requirement? Yes.
Moot court description: Membership is by grade and by competition (combination of brief and oral argument). Members must serve for 4 consecutive semesters.
Public interest law requirement? Yes.
Public interest law description: Satisfied by successful completion of one of the following: a clinic, a course plus 20 hours pro bono work, or 40 hours of pro bono work.
Academic journals: *Touro Law Review.*

ADMISSIONS INFORMATION

ADMISSIONS SELECTIVITY RATING: 68
Application fee: $50
Regular application deadline: Rolling.
Regular notification: Rolling.
Early application program: No.
LSDAS accepted? Yes.
Average GPA: 3.00
Range of GPA: 2.6–3.3
Average LSAT: 150
Range of LSAT: 147–152
Transfer students accepted? Yes.
Evening division offered: Yes.
Part-time accepted: Yes.
Number of applications received: 2,075
Number of applicants accepted: 711
Number of acceptees attending: 286

RESEARCH FACILITIES

% of JD classrooms wired: 100

FINANCIAL FACTS

Annual tuition: $25,210
Room & board (on/off-campus): $15,000/$15,000
Books and supplies: $500
Financial aid application deadline: 5/1
% receiving scholarships: 52
Average grant: $7,500
Average loan: $38,500
% of aid that is merit-based: 53
% receiving some sort of aid: 85
% first year students receiving some sort of aid: 85
Average total aid package: $30,000

Average debt: $65,000
Tuition per credit: $900

INTERNATIONAL STUDENTS

TOEFL required for international students? No.
Minimum Paper TOEFL: 600
Minimum Computer-based TOEFL: 250

EMPLOYMENT INFORMATION

Rate of placement: 94
Average starting salary: $45,000
Employers who frequently hire grads: District attorney's offices, public interest employers, small and medium law firms.
State for bar exam: NY
Pass rate for first-time bar: 63
Grads employed by field: Academic, 3%; business/industry, 23%; government, 21%; judicial clerkships, 2%; private practice, 46%; public interest, 5%.

UNIVERSITY OF BALTIMORE

School of Law

1420 North Charles Street, Baltimore, MD 21201 United States
***Admissions Phone:** 410-837-4459 • **Admissions Fax:** 410-837-4450*
***Admissions E-mail:** lwadmiss@ubmail.ubalt.edu*
***Web Address:** law.ubalt.edu*

INSTITUTIONAL INFORMATION

Public/private: Public.
Student/faculty ratio: 18:1
Total faculty: 104
% Faculty Part-time: 58
% Faculty Female: 32
% Faculty Minority: 11

STUDENTS

Enrollment of law school: 972
% Out of state: 15
% Male/female: 49/51
% Full-time: 69
% International: 1
% Minority: 19
Average age of entering class: 27

ACADEMICS

Academic specializations: Commercial law, corporation securities law, criminal law, environmental law, government services, intellectual property law, international law, labor law, legal history, legal philosophy, property, taxation.
Advanced degrees offered: LLM in taxation, LLM in law of the United States.
Combined degrees offered: JD/MBA; JD/MS in criminal justice; JD/MPA; JD/PhD in policy science in conjuction with the University of Maryland at Baltimore; JD/LLM in taxation; JD/MS in negotiation and conflict management. Most combined degrees add 1 year of study.
Grading system: a 4.0 quality scale from A–F.
Clinical program required? No.
Clinical program description: Family law clinic, criminal practice clinic, community development clinic, appellate advocacy clinic, civil clinic, disability law clinic.
Legal writing course requirement? Yes.
Legal writing description: Students are required to take 3 semesters of legal writing, as well as compete an upper-level writing requirement.
Legal methods course requirement? Yes.
Legal methods description: Part of 3-semester program encompassing legal writing and research.
Legal research course requirement? Yes.
Legal research description: Part of 3-semester writing program.
Moot court requirement? No.
Public interest law requirement? No.
Academic journals: *Law Review, Law Forum, Environmental Law Journal, Intellectual Property Law Journal.*

ADMISSIONS INFORMATION

ADMISSIONS SELECTIVITY RATING: 72
Application fee: $60
Regular application deadline: 4/15
Regular notification: Rolling.
Early application program: No.
LSDAS accepted? Yes.
Average GPA: 3.10
Range of GPA: 2.8–3.5
Average LSAT: 153
Range of LSAT: 149–156
Transfer students accepted? Yes.
Evening division offered: Yes.
Part-time accepted: Yes.
Applicants also look at: American University, The Catholic University of America, University of Maryland, Widener University.
Number of applications received: 2,654
Number of applicants accepted: 849
Number of acceptees attending: 333

RESEARCH FACILITIES

Research resources available:
% of JD classrooms wired: 50

FINANCIAL FACTS

Annual tuition (resident): $15,987
Annual tuition (nonresident): $31,956
Room & board (off-campus): $10,000
Books and supplies: $850
Financial aid application deadline: 4/1
% receiving scholarships: 10
Average grant: $4,000
Average loan: $12,500
% receiving some sort of aid: 68
Average debt: $38,300
Tuition per credit (resident): $745
Tuition per credit (nonresident): $1,158

INTERNATIONAL STUDENTS

TOEFL required for international students? No.

EMPLOYMENT INFORMATION

Rate of placement: 92
Average starting salary: $39,391
Employers who frequently hire grads: Law firms, judges, government agencies, corporations.
Prominent alumni: Peter Angelos, owner of Baltimore Orioles; Joseph Curran, attorney general of Maryland; William D. Shaffer, former govenor, current comptroller of Maryland.
State for bar exam: MD
Pass rate for first-time bar: 72

Grads employed by field: Academic, 1%; business/industry, 6%; government, 13%; judicial clerkships, 31%; private practice, 47%; public interest, 2%.

UNIVERSITY OF DAYTON

University of Dayton School of Law

University of Dayton School of Law, 300 College Park, 112 Keller Hall, Dayton, OH 45469-2760 United States

***Admissions Phone:** 937-229-3555 • **Admissions Fax:** 937-229-4194*

***Admissions E-mail:** lawinfo@notes.udayton.edu*

***Web Address:** www.law.udayton.edu*

INSTITUTIONAL INFORMATION

Public/private: Private.
Affiliation: Roman Catholic.
Student/faculty ratio: 17:1
Total faculty: 41
% Faculty Part-time: 41
% Faculty Female: 39
% Faculty Minority: 12

STUDENTS

Enrollment of law school: 481
% Out of state: 60
% Male/female: 57/43
% Full-time: 100
% Minority: 13
Average age of entering class: 25

ACADEMICS

Academic specializations: Civil procedure, commercial law, constitutional law, corporation securities law, criminal law, intellectual property law, taxation, computer/cyberspace law.
Advanced degrees offered: JD–3 years.
Combined degrees offered: JD/MBA–4 years; JD/MSEd–4 years.
Grading system: Numerical system, 4.0 scale.
Clinical program required? No.
Clinical program description: Students are responsible for assisting low-income clients in real legal disputes. The combination of fieldwork and class sessions helps the students assume the role of lawyer and analyze decisions made in that role.
Legal writing course requirement? Yes.
Legal writing description: There are 3 required semesters of legal research, writing and analysis under the title legal profession I, II, and III (total of 8 letter-graded credits). The courses are client-simulation driven and introduce students to research in several media, objective writing, and persuasive writing and oral argument at the trial and appellate level.
Legal methods course requirement? Yes.
Legal methods description: There are 3 required semesters of legal research, writing, and analysis under the title legal profession I, II, and III (total of 8 letter-graded credits).
Legal research course requirement? Yes.
Legal research description: There are 3 required semesters of legal research, writing, and analysis under the title legal profession I, II, and III (total of 8 letter-graded credits).
Moot court requirement? No.
Moot court description: Second- and third-year students represent the school of law in interschool and national competitions. The course is designed to provide students with an opportunity to develop both written and oral appellate advocacy skills.
Public interest law requirement? No.
Academic journals: *University of Dayton Law Review.*

ADMISSIONS INFORMATION

ADMISSIONS SELECTIVITY RATING: 66
Application fee: $20
Regular application deadline: 5/1
Regular notification: Rolling.
Early application program: No.
LSDAS accepted? Yes.
Average GPA: 3.14
Range of GPA: 2.7–3.3
Average LSAT: 152
Range of LSAT: 150–154
Transfer students accepted? Yes.
Evening division offered: No.
Part-time accepted: No.
Applicants also look at: Capital University, Cleveland State University, Ohio Northern University, Ohio State University, University of Akron, University of Cincinnati, University of Toledo.
Number of applications received: 1,685
Number of applicants accepted: 775
Number of acceptees attending: 183

RESEARCH FACILITIES

Research resources available: Lexis-Nexis, Westlaw, Index master, TA Campus.
% of JD classrooms wired: 100
School-supported research centers: Separate law school servers/network.

FINANCIAL FACTS

Annual tuition: $24,030
Room & board (on/off-campus): $8,900/$8,900
Books and supplies: $900
Financial aid application deadline: 5/1
% receiving scholarships: 49
Average grant: $10,000
Average loan: $23,876
% receiving some sort of aid: 90
% first year students receiving some sort of aid: 90
Average total aid package: $33,699
Average debt: $71,538

INTERNATIONAL STUDENTS

TOEFL required for international students? No.
Minimum Paper TOEFL: 600
Minimum Computer-based TOEFL: 250

EMPLOYMENT INFORMATION

Rate of placement: 85
Average starting salary: $50,100
Prominent alumni: Barbara Gorman, judge, Common Pleas Court; Ron Brown, CEO, Milacron Inc.; Nancy Michaud, vice president & general counsel, Huffy Inc.; Steve Powell, judge, Appellate Court, 12th District; Michael Coleman, mayor, Columbus, Ohio.
State for bar exam: OH, FL, GA, KY, IN
Pass rate for first-time bar: 86
Grads employed by field: Academic, 1%; business/industry, 15%; government, 4%; judicial clerkships, 7%; military, 8%; private practice, 64%; public interest, 1%.

UNIVERSITY OF DETROIT MERCY

School of Law

651 East Jefferson Avenue, Detroit, MI 48226 United States
Admissions Phone: *313-596-0264* • ***Admissions Fax:*** *313-596-0280*
Admissions E-mail: *udmlawao@udmercy.edu*
Web Address: *www.law.udmercy.edu*

INSTITUTIONAL INFORMATION

Public/private: Private.
Affiliation: Roman Catholic.
Student/faculty ratio: 19:1

STUDENTS

Enrollment of law school: 408
% Male/female: 53/47
% Full-time: 64
% International: 11
% Minority: 8
Average age of entering class: 28

ACADEMICS

Academic specializations: Comprehensive legal education with courses in all areas.
Advanced degrees offered: JD–3 years, full-time; JD/MBA–4 years, full-time; JD/LLB–3 years, full-time.
Combined degrees offered: JD/MBA–4 years full-time; JD/LLB–3 years full-time.
Grading system: 4.0 numerical grading system.
Clinical program required? No.
Clinical program description: Urban law clinic, immigration law clinic, externship program.
Legal writing course requirement? Yes.
Legal writing description: First-year, 6-credit, 2-semester course in conjunction with legal theory, analysis, and research.
Legal methods course requirement? Yes.
Legal methods description: Included in first-year, 2-semester, 6-credit applied legal theory and analysis course.
Legal research course requirement? Yes.
Legal research description: First-year, 6-credit, 2-semester applied legal theory and analysis course.
Moot court requirement? Yes.
Moot court description: First-year mandatory moot court program arguing in appellate court.
Public interest law requirement? No.
Academic journals: *University of Detroit Mercy School of Law, Law Review.*

ADMISSIONS INFORMATION

ADMISSIONS SELECTIVITY RATING: 65
Application fee: $50
Regular application deadline: 4/15
Regular notification: Rolling.
Early application program: No.
LSDAS accepted? Yes.
Average GPA: 3.20
Range of GPA: 3.0–3.4
Average LSAT: 150
Range of LSAT: 146–153
Transfer students accepted? Yes.
Evening division offered: Yes.
Part-time accepted: Yes.
Applicants also look at: Michigan State University—College of Law, Wayne State University.
Number of applications received: 543
Number of applicants accepted: 255
Number of acceptees attending: 91

FINANCIAL FACTS

Annual tuition:
Room & board (off-campus): $14,327
Books and supplies: $1,020
Financial aid application deadline: 4/1
% receiving scholarships: 15
Average grant: $10,000
Average loan: $19,300
Average debt: $69,678
Tuition per credit: $798

INTERNATIONAL STUDENTS

TOEFL required for international students? Yes.

EMPLOYMENT INFORMATION

Rate of placement: 93
Average starting salary: $55,500
Employers who frequently hire grads: County prosecutors; Dickinson Wright PLLC; Dykema Gossett PLLC; Michigan Court of Appeals; Butzel Long; Bodman Longley; Howard & Howard; Michigan Supreme Court.
State for bar exam: MI
Pass rate for first-time bar: 81
Grads employed by field: Business/industry, 15%; government, 8%; judicial clerkships, 8%; other, 1%; private practice, 68%.

UNIVERSITY OF LOUISVILLE

Louis D. Brandeis School of Law

University of Louisville, Louisville, KY 40292 United States
Admissions Phone: *502-852-6364* • ***Admissions Fax:*** *502-852-0862*
Admissions E-mail: *lawadmissions@louisville.edu*
Web Address: *www.louisville.edu/brandeislaw/*

INSTITUTIONAL INFORMATION

Public/private: Public.
Student/faculty ratio: 14:1
Total faculty: 39
% Faculty Part-time: 37
% Faculty Female: 33
% Faculty Minority: 10

STUDENTS

Enrollment of law school: 385
% Out of state: 21
% Male/female: 45/55
% Full-time: 75
% International: 1

% Minority: 6
Average age of entering class: 26

ACADEMICS

Advanced degrees offered: JD–3 years full-time, 4 years part-time.
Combined degrees offered: JD/MBA; JD/MSW; JD/MDiv; JD/MA in humanities; JD/MA in political science. All 4 to 5 years.
Grading system: Numerical system on a 4.0 scale.
Clinical program required? Yes.
Clinical program description: Public service program and 6 externship programs.
Legal writing course requirement? Yes.
Legal writing description: 3 credits–basic legal skill writing (first year).
Legal methods course requirement? Yes.
Legal methods description: 3 credits–basic legal skill writing (first year).
Legal research course requirement? Yes.
Legal research description: 1 credit–research & writing (first semester).
Moot court requirement? Yes.
Moot court description: Basic legal skills course requirement, second semester oral arguments.
Public interest law requirement? Yes.
Public interest law description: 30-hour public service requirement.
Academic journals: *Brandeis Law Journal, Journal of Law and Education.*

ADMISSIONS INFORMATION

ADMISSIONS SELECTIVITY RATING: 82
Application fee: $45
Regular application deadline: 5/15
Regular notification: Rolling.
Early application program: No.
LSDAS accepted? Yes.
Average GPA: 3.36
Range of GPA: 3.1–3.8
Average LSAT: 157
Range of LSAT: 153–159
Transfer students accepted? Yes.
Evening division offered: Yes.
Part-time accepted: Yes.
Applicants also look at: Northern Kentucky University, University of Cincinnati, University of Dayton, University of Kentucky, University of Memphis, University of Tennessee, Vanderbilt University.
Number of applications received: 1,198
Number of applicants accepted: 296
Number of acceptees attending: 134

RESEARCH FACILITIES

Research resources available: Westlaw, Lexis, Nexis, CALI, Kentucky Commonwealth Virtual University.
% of JD classrooms wired: 100

FINANCIAL FACTS

Annual tuition (resident): $9,200
Annual tuition (nonresident): $20,760
Room & board (on/off-campus): $13,410/$13,410
Books and supplies: $976
Financial aid application deadline: 4/15
% receiving scholarships: 39
Average grant: $4,000
Average loan: $18,500
% of aid that is merit-based: 100
% receiving some sort of aid: 85
% first year students receiving some sort of aid: 85
Average total aid package: $22,500
Tuition per credit (resident): $384
Tuition per credit (nonresident): $865

INTERNATIONAL STUDENTS

TOEFL required for international students? No.

EMPLOYMENT INFORMATION

Rate of placement: 97
Average starting salary: $50,000
Employers who frequently hire grads: Frost, Brown, & Todd; Dinsmore & Shohl; Greenebaum, Doll, & McDonald; Wyatt, Tarrant, & Combs; Stites & Harbison.
Prominent alumni: Chris Dodd, U.S. senator; Ron Mazzoli, former U.S. congressman; Joseph Lambert, chief justice of Kentucky; Stanley Chauvin, former ABA president; Ernie Allen, director, National Center for Missing & Exploited.
State for bar exam: KY, IN, TN, OH
Pass rate for first-time bar: 77
Grads employed by field: Academic, 1%; business/industry, 13%; government, 8%; judicial clerkships, 8%; private practice, 64%; public interest, 6%.

UNIVERSITY OF MONTANA

School of Law

Admissions Office, Missoula, MT 59812 United States
***Admissions Phone:** 406-243-2698 • **Admissions Fax:** 406-243-2576*
***Admissions E-mail:** heidi.fanslow@umontana.edu*
***Web Address:** www.umt.edu/law*

INSTITUTIONAL INFORMATION

Public/private: Public.
Student/faculty ratio: 19:1
Total faculty: 22
% Faculty Part-time: 18
% Faculty Female: 32
% Faculty Minority: 5

STUDENTS

Enrollment of law school: 241
% Out of state: 29
% Male/female: 56/44
% Full-time: 100
% Minority: 3
Average age of entering class: 28

ACADEMICS

Academic specializations: Environmental law, taxation, Indian law and trial advocacy.
Advanced degrees offered: JD–3 years.
Combined degrees offered: JD/MPA–3 years; JD/MBA–3 years; JD/MS-EVST–4 years.
Grading system: Students are not graded on mandatory curve.
Clinical program required? Yes.
Clinical program description: Criminal defense, Indian, prosecution, legal aid, disability, judicial, environmental, mediation, land use & planning, child support.
Legal writing course requirement? Yes.
Legal writing description: Legal writing and an advanced writing project are required.
Legal methods course requirement? Yes.

Legal methods description: The University of Montana School of Law devotes special attention to legal writing throughout its curriculum. UM's legal writing program has its foundation in the first year, but extends through all 3 years. Research and writing experiences at UM are integrated into many courses. The first year begins with the basics of legal research, analysis, and writing. Students complete several legal memoranda, draft contract provisions, legal pleadings, and 2 briefs to a court, and argue their motions for summary judgment. All second-year students enroll in business transactions, and negotiate and draft business agreements. All students must fulfill our advanced writing requirement by completing a major written piece (and presenting and defending it orally) during their second or third year. To further underscore the inportance of legal writing, roughly half of our elective courses involve writing papers or legal memoranda.
Legal research course requirement? Yes.
Legal research description: One-semester course.
Moot court requirement? No.
Public interest law requirement? Yes.
Public interest law description: Participation in clinical program.
Academic journals: *Montana Law Review, Public Land and Natural Resource Law Review.*

ADMISSIONS INFORMATION

ADMISSIONS SELECTIVITY RATING: 78
Application fee: $60
Regular application deadline: 3/1
Regular notification: Rolling.
Early application program: No.
LSDAS accepted? Yes.
Average GPA: 3.40
Range of GPA: 3.2–3.6
Average LSAT: 155
Range of LSAT: 152–157
Transfer students accepted? Yes.
Evening division offered: No.
Part-time accepted: No.
Applicants also look at: Gonzaga University, Lewis & Clark College, University of Denver, University of Idaho, University of Oregon, University of Wyoming.
Number of applications received: 550
Number of applicants accepted: 178
Number of acceptees attending: 79

RESEARCH FACILITIES

% of JD classrooms wired: 100
School-supported research centers: Westlaw, Lexus, Montlaw.

FINANCIAL FACTS

Annual tuition (resident): $8,710
Annual tuition (nonresident): $17,475
Room & board (on/off-campus): $9,300/$9,300
Books and supplies: $1,010
Financial aid application deadline: 3/1
% receiving scholarships: 40
Average grant: $1,457
Average loan: $14,350
% of aid that is merit-based: 3
% receiving some sort of aid: 88
% first year students receiving some sort of aid: 85
Average total aid package: $14,619
Average debt: $48,504

INTERNATIONAL STUDENTS

TOEFL required for international students? Yes.
Minimum Paper TOEFL: 600

EMPLOYMENT INFORMATION

Rate of placement: 90
Average starting salary: $41,063
Employers who frequently hire grads: Church, Harris, Johnson, and Williams; Moulton, Bellingham, Longo, and Mather; Crowley, Haughy, Hanson, Toole, and Dietrich; Towe, Ball, Enright, MacKey, and Summerfeld; Smith, Walsh, Clark, and Gregoire; Jardine, Stephenson, Blewett, and Weaver; Montana Superior Court.
State for bar exam: MT, WA
Pass rate for first-time bar: 80
Grads employed by field: Academic, 11%; business/industry, 6%; government, 12%; judicial clerkships, 23%; private practice, 35%; public interest, 1%.

UNIVERSITY OF OKLAHOMA

University of Oklahoma College of Law

Andrew M. Coats Hall, 300 Timberdell Road, Norman, OK 73019 United States
***Admissions Phone:** 405-325-4726 • **Admissions Fax:** 405-325-0502*
***Admissions E-mail:** kmadden@ou.edu • **Web Address:** www.law.ou.edu*

INSTITUTIONAL INFORMATION

Public/private: Public.
Student/faculty ratio: 10:1
Total faculty: 55
% Faculty Part-time: 30
% Faculty Female: 20
% Faculty Minority: 9

STUDENTS

Enrollment of law school: 519
% Out of state: 16
% Male/female: 52/48
% Full-time: 100
% Minority: 19
Average age of entering class: 24

ACADEMICS

Academic specializations: Civil procedure, commercial law, constitutional law, corporation securities law, criminal law, environmental law, intellectual property law, international law, labor law, property, taxation.
Advanced degrees offered: None.
Combined degrees offered: JD/MBA–4 years; JD/MPH–4 years; JD/generic dual degree–4 years.
Grading system: 12-point grading scale: 12=A+, 11=A, 10=A-, 9=B+, 8=B, 7=B-, 6=C+, 5=C, 4=C-, 3=D+, 2=D, 1=D-, 0=F.
Clinical program required? No.
Clinical program description: Judicial clinic, civil clinic, criminal defense clinic.
Legal writing course requirement? Yes.
Legal writing description: Required first-year course, fall and spring semesters, includes research & writing and oral advocacy.
Legal methods course requirement? No.
Legal research course requirement? Yes.
Legal research description: Required first-year course, fall and spring semesters, includes research & writing and oral advocacy.

Moot court requirement? No.
Public interest law requirement? No.
Academic journals: *Oklahoma Law Review, American Indian Law Review, Oklahoma Journal of Law and Technology.*

ADMISSIONS INFORMATION

ADMISSIONS SELECTIVITY RATING: 83
Application fee: $50
Regular application deadline: 3/15
Regular notification: Rolling.
Early application program: No.
LSDAS accepted? Yes.
Average GPA: 3.64
Range of GPA: 3.3–3.8
Average LSAT: 156
Range of LSAT: 153–160
Transfer students accepted? Yes.
Evening division offered: No.
Part-time accepted: No.
Number of applications received: 1,307
Number of applicants accepted: 321
Number of acceptees attending: 172

RESEARCH FACILITIES

Research resources available: Westlaw, Lexis & Nexus, Wilsonweb, CCH, LegalTrac.
% of JD classrooms wired: 60

FINANCIAL FACTS

Annual tuition (resident): $7,848
Annual tuition (nonresident): $17,777
Room & board (on/off-campus): $13,091/$14,360
Books and supplies: $950
Financial aid application deadline: 3/1
% receiving scholarships: 68
Average grant: $2,000
Average loan: $15,911
% of aid that is merit-based: 58
% receiving some sort of aid: 89
% first year students receiving some sort of aid: 89
Average total aid package: $17,911
Average debt: $47,733

INTERNATIONAL STUDENTS

TOEFL required for international students? No.

EMPLOYMENT INFORMATION

Rate of placement: 95
Average starting salary: $54,765
Employers who frequently hire grads: McAfee & Taft; Crowe & Dunlevy; McKinney & Stringer; Conner & Winters; Gable & Gotwals; Hall, Estill, Hardwick, Gable, & Nelson; Phillips, McFall, McCaffrey, McVay, & Murray; U.S. government; State of Oklahoma.
Prominent alumni: Frank Keating, former governor of Oklahoma; David L. Boren, president of O.U. (former U. S. senator); William T. Comfort, president CitiCorp Venture Capital; Robert Henry, judge, 10th Circuit Court of Appeals; Andrew M. Coats, dean, O.U. law, (former mayor of Oklahoma City).
State for bar exam: OK, TX, CO, MO, CA
Pass rate for first-time bar: 91
Grads employed by field: Academic, 4%; business/industry, 6%; government, 19%; judicial clerkships, 1%; military, 4%; private practice, 63%; public interest, 3%.

WESTERN STATE UNIVERSITY†

Western State University College of Law

1111 North State College Boulevard, Fullerton, CA 92831 United States
***Admissions Phone:** 714-459-1101 • **Admissions Fax:** 714-441-1748*
***Admissions E-mail:** adm@wsulaw.edu • **Web Address:** www.wsulaw.edu*

INSTITUTIONAL INFORMATION

Public/private: Private.
Student/faculty ratio: 24:1
Total faculty: 41
% Faculty Part-time: 39
% Faculty Female: 37
% Faculty Minority: 15

STUDENTS

Enrollment of law school: 510
% Out of state: 19
% Male/female: 48/52
% Full-time: 56
% International: 2
% Minority: 40
Average age of entering class: 27

ACADEMICS

Academic specializations: Criminal law.
Advanced degrees offered: JD–4 years part-time, 3 years, full-time.
Grading system: Based on a 4.0 scale.
Clinical program required? No.
Clinical program description: WSU's Legal Clinic assists low income persons with common legal poroblems such as landlord-tenant and family law disputes.
Legal writing course requirement? Yes.
Legal writing description: Incorporated into professional skills I & II and advocacy courses.
Legal methods course requirement? No.
Legal research course requirement? Yes.
Legal research description: Incorporated into professional skills I & II and advocacy courses.
Moot court requirement? Yes.
Moot court description: Incorporated into the advocacy course.
Public interest law requirement? No.
Academic journals: *Law Review.*

ADMISSIONS INFORMATION

ADMISSIONS SELECTIVITY RATING: 63
Application fee: $50
Regular application deadline: Rolling.
Regular notification: Rolling.
Early application program: No.
LSDAS accepted? Yes.
Average GPA: 3.00
Range of GPA: 2.7–3.2
Average LSAT: 147
Range of LSAT: 145–149
Transfer students accepted? Yes.
Evening division offered: Yes.

Part-time accepted: Yes.
Applicants also look at: California Western, Chapman University, Golden Gate University, Loyola Marymount University, Southwestern University School of Law, Thomas Jefferson School of Law, Whittier College.
Number of applications received: 1,523
Number of applicants accepted: 656
Number of acceptees attending: 209

RESEARCH FACILITIES

Research resources available: CSU Fullerton
% of JD classrooms wired: 50
School-supported research centers:

FINANCIAL FACTS

Annual tuition: $24,680
Room & board (off-campus): $11,739
Books and supplies: $810
Financial aid application deadline: 3/2
% receiving scholarships: 54
Average grant: $8,000
Average loan: $20,303
% of aid that is merit-based: 13
% receiving some sort of aid: 92
% first year students receiving some sort of aid: 92
Average total aid package: $29,692
Average debt: $66,000
Tuition per credit: $16,600

INTERNATIONAL STUDENTS

TOEFL required for international students? Yes.
Minimum Paper TOEFL: 600
Minimum Computer-based TOEFL: 250

EMPLOYMENT INFORMATION

Rate of placement: 89
Average starting salary: $63,100
Employers who frequently hire grads: Medium-sized law firms, district attorneys, public defenders, corporations, state governments, federal governments.
Prominent alumni: Ross Johnson, CA state senator; Joseph Mederow, chief counsel, UPS; Nancy Zeltzer, managing partner, Lewis, Brisbois, Bisgard, & Smi; Chuck Middleton, chief asst. D.A., Orange County, CA; Pamela Iles, judge, Orange County Superior Court.
State for bar exam: CA, AZ, TX, OR, FL
Pass rate for first-time bar: 43
Grads employed by field: Academic, 3%; business/industry, 22%; government, 22%; judicial clerkships, 1%; private practice, 48%; public interest, 3%.

† Provisionally approved by the ABA.

WHITTIER COLLEGE

Whittier Law School

3333 Harbor Boulevard, Costa Mesa, CA 92626 United States
Admissions Phone: *714-444-4141* • ***Admissions Fax:*** *714-444-0250*
Admissions E-mail: *info@law.whittier.edu*
Web Address: *www.law.whittier.edu*

INSTITUTIONAL INFORMATION

Public/private: Private.
Student/faculty ratio: 20:1
Total faculty: 91
% Faculty Part-time: 58
% Faculty Female: 48
% Faculty Minority: 11

STUDENTS

Enrollment of law school: 1,006
% Out of state: 30
% Male/female: 47/53
% Full-time: 67
% International: 2
% Minority: 37
Average age of entering class: 27

ACADEMICS

Academic specializations: Criminal law, intellectual property law, international law, children's rights, health law.
Advanced degrees offered: JD–3 years full-time, 4 years part-time; LLM in foreign legal studies–24 credits, 1 year.
Grading system: Letter and numerical system, 55 to 100–point scale. Cumulative grade of 77 required for good standing.
Clinical program required? No.
Clinical program description: Whittier Law School offers a variety of clinical opportunities for students through several on-campus, live client clinics, and off-site externship placements. Up to 15 students per term can enroll in 3 clinics that are part of the law school's center for children's rights. Students can choose from the special education clinic, guardianship and adoption clinic, family law and domestic violence clinic or health law clinic. All of the clinics are designed to prepare law students to represent children in the legal system. Students provide direct advocacy under the supervision of attorney staff. General off-site clinical externships are available to all students after their first year of study. Placements are available in public-interest legal agencies, governmental offices, and judicial chambers throughout southern California. The law school also offers a substantial street law program, allowing law students the opportunity to provide legal education to at-risk children and youth.
Legal writing course requirement? Yes.
Legal writing description: Six units of legal writing required for graduation.
Legal methods course requirement? No.
Legal research course requirement? Yes.
Legal research description: Legal research is part of the 6 units of required legal writing for graduation.
Moot court requirement? Yes.
Moot court description: The moot court component of the first-year required legal skills course is designed to enhance oral advocacy skills. Students pair up to argue against another pair of students before a panel of 3 "judges" who are members of the moot court honors board. They are given both written and oral feedback on their performance. The moot court honors board advances student skills in appellate advocacy. The moot court program provides students an

opportunity to improve their oral advocacy and brief-writing skills. This is accomplished through participation in national and internal appellate competitions and appellate workshops.

Public interest law requirement? No.

Academic journals: *The Whittier Law Review* and *The Whittier Journal of Child and Family Advocacy* are 2 scholarly legal periodicals, edited and published by selected students. The *Law Review* publishes 4 issues per year.

ADMISSIONS INFORMATION

ADMISSIONS SELECTIVITY RATING: 70
Application fee: $50
Regular application deadline: Rolling.
Regular notification: Rolling.
Early application program: No.
LSDAS accepted? Yes.
Average GPA: 3.03
Range of GPA: 2.7–3.3
Average LSAT: 152
Range of LSAT: 150–154
Transfer students accepted? Yes.
Evening division offered: Yes.
Part-time accepted: Yes.
Applicants also look at: California Western, Chapman University, Pepperdine University, Southwestern University School of Law, University of San Diego, University of San Francisco, University of the Pacific.
Number of applications received: 3,070
Number of applicants accepted: 1,010
Number of acceptees attending: 390

RESEARCH FACILITIES

Research resources available: Library, health, gym, and performing arts facilities at Whittier College.
% of JD classrooms wired: 90
School-supported research centers: Dedicated WESTLAW, Lexis and student labs (students need not own their own computer)

FINANCIAL FACTS

Annual tuition: $27,750
Room & board (off-campus): $10,084
Books and supplies: $6,076
Financial aid application deadline: 5/1
% receiving scholarships: 55
Average grant: $6,338
Average loan: $25,696
% of aid that is merit-based: 25
% receiving some sort of aid: 73
% first year students receiving some sort of aid: 82
Average total aid package: $32,033
Average debt: $76,805
Tuition per credit: $925

INTERNATIONAL STUDENTS

TOEFL required for international students? Yes.
Minimum Paper TOEFL: 600
Minimum Computer-based TOEFL: 250

EMPLOYMENT INFORMATION

Rate of placement: 88
Average starting salary: $60,000
Employers who frequently hire grads: Small law firm practices (2-10 attorneys)
Prominent alumni: Florence Marie Cooper, U.S. district judge; Garo Mardirossian, Mardirossian, and Associates, Personal Injury; Judith Ashmann-Gerst, California Court of Appeal; Mablean Ephraim, presiding judge, Divorce Court TV program; Kathleen Strottman, counsel to Senator Mary Landrieu.
State for bar exam: CA
Pass rate for first-time bar: 30
Grads employed by field: Academic, 4%; business/industry, 29%; government, 7%; judicial clerkships, 1%; private practice, 54%; public interest, 5%.

YALE UNIVERSITY

Yale Law School

P.O. Box 208329, New Haven, CT 06520-8329 United States
Admissions Phone: *203-432-4995*
Admissions E-mail: *admissions.law@yale.edu*
Web Address: *www.law.yale.edu*

INSTITUTIONAL INFORMATION

Public/private: Private.
Student/faculty ratio: 7:1
Total faculty: 65
% Faculty Female: 22
% Faculty Minority: 17

STUDENTS

Enrollment of law school: 582
% Male/female: 56/44
% Full-time: 100
% Minority: 30
Average age of entering class: 24

ACADEMICS

Advanced degrees offered: JD–3 years; LLM–1 year; MSL–1 year; JSD–up to 5 years.
Combined degrees offered: JD/PhD history; JD/PhD political science; JD/MS forestry; JD/MS sociology; JD/MS statistics; JD/MBA (w/ Yale School of Management); and others.
Grading system: Honors: Work done in the course is significantly superior. Pass: Successful performance of the work in the course. Low Pass: Work done in the course is below the level of performance.
Clinical program required? No.
Clinical program description: Clinical opportunities are offered through the Jerome N. Frank legal services organization, which links law students with individuals in need of legal help who cannot afford private attorneys. Faculty-supervised students interview clients, write briefs, prepare witnesses, try cases, negotiate settlements, and argue appeals in state and federal courts, including the U.S. Court of Appeals for the Second Circuit and the Connecticut Supreme Court. There are 9 main projects: Advocacy for children and youth, community and economic development, community lawyering, immigration, landlord/tenant, legal assistance, prisons, criminal defense, and complex federal litigation. Students also participate in independent projects at 2 local prosecutors' offices (the New Haven state attorney and the U.S. attorney) and at other public service law offices. Other clinics include the environmental protection clinic and the Allard K. Lowenstein international human rights law clinic. In the second term, students may begin participation in programs managed primarily by students under the supervision of a faculty adviser. These include the capital defense project, the domestic violence temporary restraining order project, the Greenhaven prison project, street law, Thomas Swan barristers' union, Morris Tyler moot court of appeals, and numerous reviews and journals.

Legal writing course requirement? No.
Legal methods course requirement? No.
Legal research course requirement? No.
Moot court requirement? No.
Public interest law requirement? No.
Academic journals: Student-edited publications include the *Yale Law Journal*, *Yale Journal of International Law*, *Yale Journal of Law and Feminism*, *Yale Journal of Law and the Humanities*, *Yale Journal on Regulation*, *Yale Human Rights and Development Law Journal*, and *Yale Law*.

ADMISSIONS INFORMATION

ADMISSIONS SELECTIVITY RATING: 99
Application fee: $70
Regular application deadline: 2/1
Regular notification: Rolling.
Early application program: No.
LSDAS accepted? Yes.
Average GPA: 3.86
Range of GPA: 3.7–3.9
Average LSAT: 171
Range of LSAT: 168–175
Transfer students accepted? Yes.
Evening division offered: No
Part-time accepted: No.
Number of applications received: 3,783
Number of applicants accepted: 248
Number of acceptees attending: 189

RESEARCH FACILITIES

% of JD classrooms wired: 100

FINANCIAL FACTS

Annual tuition: $36,490
Room & board (on-campus): $10,750
Books and supplies: $900
Financial aid application deadline: 3/15
% receiving scholarships: 43
Average grant: $15,465
Average loan: $32,059
% receiving some sort of aid: 79
% first year students receiving some sort of aid: 79
Average debt: $79,354

INTERNATIONAL STUDENTS

TOEFL required for international students? No.
Minimum Paper TOEFL: 600
Minimum Computer-based TOEFL: 250

EMPLOYMENT INFORMATION

Rate of placement: 96
Average starting salary: $85,160
State for bar exam: NY
Pass rate for first-time bar: 96
Grads employed by field: Academic, 2%; business/industry, 3%; government, 4%; judicial clerkships, 43%; private practice, 45%; public interest, 3%.

Cal Northern School of Law

Cal Northern School of Law

1395 Ridgewood Drive, Chico, CA 95973 United States
Admissions Phone: *530-891-6900* • ***Admissions Fax:*** *530-891-3429*
Admissions E-mail: *info@calnorthern.edu*
Web Address: *www.calnorthern.edu*

INSTITUTIONAL INFORMATION

Public/private: Private.
Student/faculty ratio: 4:1
Total faculty: 18
% Faculty Part-time: 100
% Faculty Female: 28

STUDENTS

Enrollment of law school: 75
% Male/female: 100/0
Average age of entering class: 35

ACADEMICS

Advanced degrees offered: JD only–4-year program.
Clinical program required? No.
Legal writing course requirement? Yes.
Legal writing description: Legal writing is required in the first year and advanced legal writing is required in the fourth year.
Legal methods course requirement? Yes.
Legal methods description: Legal writing is required in the first year and advanced legal writing is offered in the fourth year.
Legal research course requirement? Yes.
Legal research description: Legal research is required in the first year.
Moot court requirement? Yes.
Moot court description: Fourth year, trial advocacy–15 weeks.
Public interest law requirement? No.

ADMISSIONS INFORMATION

ADMISSIONS SELECTIVITY RATING: 61
Application fee: $50
Regular application deadline: 6/1
Regular notification: 7/3
Early application program: No.
LSDAS accepted? No.
Average GPA: 3.20
Average LSAT: 145
Transfer students accepted? Yes.
Evening division offered: Yes.
Part-time accepted: Yes.
Number of applications received: 37
Number of applicants accepted: 33
Number of acceptees attending: 28

RESEARCH FACILITIES

Research resources available: California State University, Chico and Butte county law library.
% of JD classrooms wired: 100

FINANCIAL FACTS

Annual tuition: $7,590
Books and supplies: $500
Average grant: $250
Average loan: $8,000
% receiving some sort of aid: 5
Tuition per credit: $330

INTERNATIONAL STUDENTS

TOEFL required for international students? No.

EMPLOYMENT INFORMATION

Prominent alumni: Rick Keene, California assemblyman.
State for bar exam: CA
Pass rate for first-time bar: 54

Empire College

Empire College School of Law

3035 Cleveland Avenue, Santa Rosa, CA 95403 United States
Admissions Phone: *707-546-4000* • ***Admissions Fax:*** *707-546-4058*
Admissions E-mail: *info@empcol.edu* • ***Web Address:*** *www.empcol.edu*

INSTITUTIONAL INFORMATION

Public/private: Private.
Student/faculty ratio: 4:1
Total faculty: 47
% Faculty Part-time: 100
% Faculty Female: 17
% Faculty Minority: 2

STUDENTS

Enrollment of law school: 146
% Male/female: 100/0
Average age of entering class: 36

ACADEMICS

Grading system: 90–100=A; 80–89=B; 70–79=C; 65–69=D; Below 65=F.
Clinical program required? No.
Clinical program description: Third- and fourth-year students may clerk in a variety of settings, including private law offices and public agencies such as the district attorney's or public defender's offices.
Legal writing course requirement? Yes.
Legal writing description: One semester.
Legal methods course requirement? No.
Legal research course requirement? Yes
Legal research description: One semester.
Moot court requirement? Yes.
Moot court description: One semester, requiring a written brief and oral argument.
Public interest law requirement? No.

ADMISSIONS INFORMATION

ADMISSIONS SELECTIVITY RATING: 61
Application fee: $50
Regular application deadline: Rolling.
Regular notification: Rolling.
Early application program: No.
LSDAS accepted? No.
Average GPA: 3.10
Range of GPA: 2.5–3.9
Average LSAT: 39
Range of LSAT: 28–70
Transfer students accepted? Yes.
Evening division offered: Yes.
Part-time accepted: Yes.
Number of applications received: 106
Number of applicants accepted: 105
Number of acceptees attending: 96

RESEARCH FACILITIES

% of JD classrooms wired: 10

FINANCIAL FACTS

Annual tuition: $7,119
Books and supplies: $300
Tuition per credit: $339

INTERNATIONAL STUDENTS

TOEFL required for international students? No.

EMPLOYMENT INFORMATION

Employers who frequently hire grads: Office of the district attorney, public defender's office, private, business.
Prominent alumni: Jeanne Buckley, superior court commissioner (ret.); Raima Ballinger, judge, Sonoma County Superior Court; Francisca Tisher, judge, Napa County Municipal Court; Thomas S. Burr, Juvenile Court referee, Merced County Superior Court; Ron Brown, judge, Mendocino County Superior Court.
State for bar exam: CA

GLENDALE UNIVERSITY

Glendale University College of Law

220 North Glendale Avenue, Glendale, CA 91206 United States
***Admissions Phone:** 818-247-0770 • **Admissions Fax:** 818-247-0872*
***Admissions E-mail:** admissions@glendalelaw.edu*
***Web Address:** www.glendalelaw.edu*

INSTITUTIONAL INFORMATION

Public/private: Private.
Student/faculty ratio: 23:1

STUDENTS

Enrollment of law school: 130
% Male/female: 100/0
% Minority: 35
Average age of entering class: 36

ACADEMICS

Advanced degrees offered: JD–4 years.
Clinical program required? No.
Legal writing course requirement? Yes.
Legal writing description: LWR I a, b, c; LWR II a, b, c; LWR III a, b, c.
Legal methods course requirement? No.
Legal research course requirement? Yes.
Legal research description: LWR I, II, III, a, b, c.
Moot court requirement? Yes.
Moot court description: third-year students write briefs and present their cases in oral arguements before a panel of judges.
Public interest law requirement? No.
Academic journals: *Glendale Law Review.*

ADMISSIONS INFORMATION

ADMISSIONS SELECTIVITY RATING: 63
Application fee: $55
Regular application deadline: Rolling.
Regular notification: Rolling.
Early application program: No.
LSDAS accepted? No.
Average GPA: 3.00
Average LSAT: 145
Transfer students accepted? Yes.
Evening division offered: Yes.
Part-time accepted: Yes.
Number of applications received: 100
Number of applicants accepted: 50
Number of acceptees attending: 40

FINANCIAL FACTS

Annual tuition: $9,057
Books and supplies: $500
Tuition per credit: $285

INTERNATIONAL STUDENTS

TOEFL required for international students? No.

EMPLOYMENT INFORMATION

State for bar exam: CA
Pass rate for first-time bar: 50

HUMPHREYS COLLEGE

Humphreys College School of Law

6650 Inglewood Avenue, Stockton, CA 95207 United States
***Admissions Phone:** 209-478-0800 • **Admissions Fax:** 209-478-8721*
***Admissions E-mail:** selopez@humphreys.edu*
***Web Address:** www.humphreys.edu/law/*

INSTITUTIONAL INFORMATION

Public/private: Private.
Student/faculty ratio: 6:1
Total faculty: 12
% Faculty Part-time: 83
% Faculty Female: 17

STUDENTS

Enrollment of law school: 60
% Male/female: 100/0
Average age of entering class: 33

ACADEMICS

Grading system: 90–100, excellent; 80–90, good; 70–79, satisfactory; 55–69, unsatisfactory; below 55, failure.
Clinical program required? No.
Legal methods course requirement? Yes.
Legal methods description: One quarter in both the first and fourth year.
Academic journals:

ADMISSIONS INFORMATION

ADMISSIONS SELECTIVITY RATING: 62
Application fee: $20
Regular application deadline: 6/1
Regular notification: Rolling.
Early application program: No.
LSDAS accepted? No.
Average GPA: 2.80
Average LSAT: 149
Transfer students accepted? Yes.
Evening division offered: Yes.
Part-time accepted: Yes.
Number of applications received: 52
Number of applicants accepted: 32
Number of acceptees attending: 19

FINANCIAL FACTS

Annual tuition: $7,062
Books and supplies: $650
Average loan: $14,658
% receiving some sort of aid: 66
% first year students receiving some sort of aid: 21
Average total aid package: $14,658
Average debt: $48,000
Tuition per credit: $214

INTERNATIONAL STUDENTS

TOEFL required for international students? Yes
Minimum Paper TOEFL: 450

EMPLOYMENT INFORMATION

Rate of placement: 80
Employers who frequently hire grads: D.A. offices; police departments
State for bar exam: CA
Pass rate for first-time bar: 54
Grads employed by field: Academic, 5%; business/industry, 5%; government, 30%; private practice, 60%.

JOHN F. KENNEDY UNIVERSITY

School of Law

100 Ellinwood Way, Pleasant Hill, CA 94523 United States
Admissions Phone: *925-969-3330* • ***Admissions Fax:*** *925-969-3331*
Admissions E-mail: *law@jfku.edu* • ***Web Address:*** *www.jfku.edu/law*

INSTITUTIONAL INFORMATION

Public/private: Private.
Student/faculty ratio: 30:1

STUDENTS

Enrollment of law school: 194
% Male/female: 100/0
Average age of entering class: 36

ACADEMICS

Clinical program required? No.
Legal methods course requirement? No.

ADMISSIONS INFORMATION

ADMISSIONS SELECTIVITY RATING: 65
Application fee: $50
Regular application deadline: 5/30
Regular notification: Rolling.
Early application program: No.
LSDAS accepted? No.
Average GPA: 3.00
Average LSAT: 1
Transfer students accepted? No.
Evening division offered: Yes.
Part-time accepted: Yes.
Applicants also look at: Syracuse University.
Number of applications received: 40
Number of applicants accepted: 30
Number of acceptees attending: 28

RESEARCH FACILITIES

% of JD classrooms wired: 100
School-supported research centers:

FINANCIAL FACTS

Annual tuition: $9,216
Books and supplies: $500
Average grant: $1
Average loan: $1
Tuition per credit: $576

INTERNATIONAL STUDENTS

TOEFL required for international students? Yes.
Minimum Paper TOEFL: 550
Minimum Computer-based TOEFL: 213

Lincoln Law School of Sacramento

3140 J Street, Sacramento, CA 95816 United States
Admissions Phone: *916-446-1275* • ***Admissions Fax:*** *916-446-5641*
Admissions E-mail: *info@lincolnlaw.edu* • ***Web Address:*** *www.lincolnlaw.edu*

INSTITUTIONAL INFORMATION

Public/private: Private.
Student/faculty ratio: 40:1
Total faculty: 25
% Faculty Part-time: 100
% Faculty Female: 20
% Faculty Minority: 10

STUDENTS

Enrollment of law school: 275
% Male/female: 100/0
Average age of entering class: 35

ACADEMICS

Academic specializations: Civil procedure, constitutional law, corporation securities law, criminal law, environmental law, government services, intellectual property law, labor law, legal history, legal philosophy, property, taxation, family law, applied legal reasoning.
Advanced degrees offered: JD–4 year.
Grading system: 4.0 grading system.
Clinical program required? No.
Legal writing course requirement? Yes.
Legal writing description: Two semesters of legal writing required for first-year students.
Legal methods course requirement? Yes.
Legal methods description: Writing law school exams–2 semesters.
Legal research course requirement? Yes.
Legal research description: One semester required for second-year students.
Moot court requirement? Yes.
Moot court description: Summer semester required for second-year students.
Public interest law requirement? No.

ADMISSIONS INFORMATION

ADMISSIONS SELECTIVITY RATING: 61
Application fee: $30
Regular application deadline: Rolling.
Regular notification: Rolling.
Early application program: No.
LSDAS accepted? Yes.
Average GPA: 2.80
Range of GPA: 2.1–4.0
Average LSAT: 145
Transfer students accepted? Yes.
Evening division offered: Yes.
Part-time accepted: Yes.
Applicants also look at: Golden Gate University, Humphreys College, John F. Kennedy University, University of California, Davis, University of the Pacific.
Number of applications received: 150
Number of applicants accepted: 105
Number of acceptees attending: 95

RESEARCH FACILITIES

% of JD classrooms wired: 50
School-supported research centers: Lexis-Nexis

FINANCIAL FACTS

Annual tuition: $7,000
Room & board (off-campus): $6,000
Books and supplies: $500
Financial aid application deadline: 6/1
% receiving scholarships: 20
Average grant: $500
Average loan: $10,000
% of aid that is merit-based: 2
% receiving some sort of aid: 20
% first year students receiving some sort of aid: 10
Average total aid package: $7,000
Average debt: $10,500
Tuition per credit: $350

INTERNATIONAL STUDENTS

TOEFL required for international students? No.

EMPLOYMENT INFORMATION

Rate of placement: 80
Average starting salary: $40,000
Employers who frequently hire grads: District attorney's office; attorney general's office; public defender's office; local private firms.
Prominent alumni: Jan Scully, Sacramento County district attorney; Brad Fenocchio, Placer County district attorney; Robert Holzapfel, Glenn County district attorney; Hon. Gerald Bakarich, Sacramento County Superior Court judge; Hon. Sue Harlan, Amador County Superior Court judge.
State for bar exam: CA, OR, NV, AZ, CO
Pass rate for first-time bar: 60
Grads employed by field: Business/industry, 10%; government, 30%; judicial clerkships, 5%; private practice, 50%; public interest, 5%.

Lincoln Law School of San Jose

Lincoln Law School of San Jose

One North First Street, San Jose, CA 95113 United States
Admissions Phone: *408-977-7227* • ***Admissions Fax:*** *408-977-7228*
Admissions E-mail: *admissionlincoln@earthlink.net*
Web Address: *www.lincolnlawsj.edu/*

INSTITUTIONAL INFORMATION

Public/private: Private.
Student/faculty ratio: 1:1

STUDENTS

Enrollment of law school: 153

ACADEMICS

Clinical program required? No.
Legal methods course requirement? No.

ADMISSIONS INFORMATION

ADMISSIONS SELECTIVITY RATING: 60*
Application fee: $35
Regular application deadline: Rolling.
Regular notification: Rolling.
Early application program: No.
LSDAS accepted? No.
Transfer students accepted? Yes.
Evening division offered: Yes.
Part-time accepted: Yes.

FINANCIAL FACTS

Tuition: $499 per credit hour

INTERNATIONAL STUDENTS

TOEFL required for international students? No.
Minimum Paper TOEFL: 600
Minimum Computer-based TOEFL: 60

MONTEREY COLLEGE OF LAW

Monterey College of Law

404 West Franklin Street, Monterey, CA 93940 United States
Admissions Phone: *831-373-3301* • ***Admissions Fax:*** *831-373-0143*
Admissions E-mail: *wlariviere@montereylaw.edu*
Web Address: *www.montereylaw.edu*

INSTITUTIONAL INFORMATION

Public/private: Private.
Student/faculty ratio: 25:1
Total faculty: 44
% Faculty Part-time: 100
% Faculty Female: 23
% Faculty Minority: 2

STUDENTS

Enrollment of law school: 100
% Male/female: 100/0
Average age of entering class: 35

ACADEMICS

Academic specializations: Civil procedure, commercial law, constitutional law, corporation securities law, criminal law, environmental law, government services, human rights law, intellectual property law, property, taxation.
Advanced degrees offered: JD degree, 4-year evening program.
Grading system: MCL uses a numerical grading system (0 to 100) to reflect academic performance.
Clinical program required? Yes.
Clinical program description: Under the supervision of a clinical studies professor, students give legal advice to clients in a pro bono legal clinic focusing on small claims issues.
Legal writing course requirement? Yes.
Legal writing description: Students are required to complete a 2-semester legal writing course in their first year and a 2-semester advanced legal writing course during their second year.
Legal methods course requirement? Yes.
Legal methods description: Legal writing classes are required in the first and second years. In the third and fourth years, they are integrated into the curriculum.
Legal research course requirement? Yes.
Legal research description: Legal research is a required course for first year students. Computer-assisted legal research is an elective course available after the student's second year of study.
Moot court requirement? Yes.
Moot court description: The Heisler moot court gives students an opportunity to study and write about constitutional issues. Starting with drafting an appellate brief, the semester culminates in a series of hearings, where local judges hear the students' oral arguments on each side of a current civil liberties issue. The public is invited to witness the final round of arguments made by 4 students in front of an appellate panel of judges.
Public interest law requirement? No.

ADMISSIONS INFORMATION

ADMISSIONS SELECTIVITY RATING: 64
Application fee: $75
Regular application deadline: 5/1
Regular notification: Rolling.
Early application program: No.
LSDAS accepted? No.
Average GPA: 3.10
Range of GPA: 2.4–3.9
Average LSAT: 153
Range of LSAT: 141–169
Transfer students accepted? Yes.
Evening division offered: Yes.
Part-time accepted: Yes.
Applicants also look at: Lincoln Law School of San Jose.
Number of applications received: 63
Number of applicants accepted: 48
Number of acceptees attending: 28

RESEARCH FACILITIES

Research resources available: Monterey Courthouse Law Library, Santa Cruz County Law ibrary, Salinas Law library, Watsonville Law Library.

FINANCIAL FACTS

% receiving scholarships: 25
Average grant: $750
Average loan: $5,000
% of aid that is merit-based: 30
% receiving some sort of aid: 55
% first year students receiving some sort of aid: 26
Tuition per credit: $400

INTERNATIONAL STUDENTS

TOEFL required for international students? No.

EMPLOYMENT INFORMATION

Rate of placement: 87
Employers who frequently hire grads: Governmental offices, public agencies, private law firms, public defender's office, district attorney's office.
State for bar exam: CA
Pass rate for first-time bar: 54
Grads employed by field: Business/industry, 25%; government, 5%; private practice, 65%; public interest, 5%.

New College of California

New College of California School of Law

50 Fell Street, San Francisco, CA 94102 United States
Admissions Phone: *415-241-1374* • ***Admissions Fax:*** *415-241-9525*
Admissions E-mail: *Lawadmissions@newcollege.edu*
Web Address: *www.newcollege.edu*

INSTITUTIONAL INFORMATION

Public/private: Private.
Student/faculty ratio: 15:1

STUDENTS

Enrollment of law school: 200
% Out of state: 10
% Male/female: 35/65
% Full-time: 75
% International: 10
% Minority: 35
Average age of entering class: 35

ACADEMICS

Academic specializations: Constitutional law, environmental law, government services, human rights law, labor law, property.
Advanced degrees offered: JD–3 years, full-time; 4 years, part-time.
Grading system: Letter grading, based upon a bar standard.
Clinical program required? No.
Legal writing course requirement? Yes.
Legal writing description: One year legal research and writing.
Legal methods course requirement? Yes.
Legal methods description: One semester.
Legal research course requirement? Yes.
Legal research description: One year legal research and writing.
Moot court requirement? No.
Public interest law requirement? Yes.
Public interest law description: 600–800 hours of public interest internship.
Academic journals: *Journal of Public Interest Law.*

ADMISSIONS INFORMATION

ADMISSIONS SELECTIVITY RATING: 61
Application fee: $45
Regular application deadline: 5/1
Regular notification: Rolling.
Early application program: Yes.
LSDAS accepted? Yes.
Average GPA: 3.00
Range of GPA: 2–4.0
Average LSAT: 145
Transfer students accepted? Yes.
Evening division offered: No.
Part-time accepted: Yes.
Number of applications received: 150
Number of applicants accepted: 110
Number of acceptees attending: 65

FINANCIAL FACTS

Annual tuition: $14,500
Books and supplies: $400
Financial aid application deadline: 8/5
Average grant: $500
Average loan: $18,500
% first year students receiving some sort of aid: 90
Average total aid package: $22,000

INTERNATIONAL STUDENTS

TOEFL required for international students? No.

EMPLOYMENT INFORMATION

Average starting salary:
State for bar exam: CA
Pass rate for first-time bar: 25
Grads employed by field: Government, 10%; private practice, 10%; public interest, 80%.

San Francisco Law School

San Francisco Law School

20 Haight Street, San Francisco, CA 94102 United States
Admissions Phone: *415-626-5550* • ***Admissions Fax:*** *415-626-5584*
Admissions E-mail: *admin@sfls.edu* • ***Web Address:*** *www.sfls.edu*

INSTITUTIONAL INFORMATION

Public/private: Private.
Student/faculty ratio: 25:1
Total faculty: 32
% Faculty Part-time: 100
% Faculty Female: 13
% Faculty Minority: 1

STUDENTS

Enrollment of law school: 115
% Male/female: 100/0
Average age of entering class: 38

ACADEMICS

Advanced degrees offered: JD–4-year program beginning in August; 4 1/2-year program beginning in January.
Grading system: We use the numerical system up to 100.
Clinical program required? No.
Clinical program description: Private practice/judges.
Legal writing course requirement? Yes.
Legal writing description: Advanced legal writing, one semester.
Legal methods course requirement? No.
Legal research course requirement? Yes.
Legal research description: Covers the use of law books, as well as legal research on the Internet, two semesters.
Moot court requirement? Yes.
Moot court description: Teams in a workshop setting, one semester course.

Public interest law requirement? No.
Academic journals: *San Francisco Law Review.*

ADMISSIONS INFORMATION

ADMISSIONS SELECTIVITY RATING: 61
Application fee: $50
Regular application deadline: 6/5
Regular notification: Rolling.
Early application program: No.
LSDAS accepted? No.
Average GPA: 2.80
Range of GPA: 2–3.8
Average LSAT: 148
Transfer students accepted? Yes.
Evening division offered: Yes.
Part-time accepted: Yes.
Number of applications received: 150
Number of applicants accepted: 87

FINANCIAL FACTS

Annual tuition: $6,700
Room & board (off-campus): $25,000
Books and supplies: $350
% of aid that is merit-based: 40
Tuition per credit: $335

INTERNATIONAL STUDENTS

TOEFL required for international students? No.

EMPLOYMENT INFORMATION

Employers who frequently hire grads: SF public defender; SFDA, private sector
Prominent alumni: Edmund G. Brown (late), governor of California; Milton Marks, Jr. (late), California state senator; Leo T. McCarthy, lt. governor of California; Hon. Lynn O'Malley Taylor, judge of the Superior Court; Hon. Henry Needham, judge of the Superior Court.
State for bar exam: CA
Pass rate for first-time bar: 30
Grads employed by field: Academic, 5%; business/industry, 5%; government, 20%; judicial clerkships, 5%; private practice, 60%; public interest, 5%.

SAN JOAQUIN COLLEGE OF LAW

San Joaquin College of Law

901 Fifth Street, Clovis, CA 93612-1312 United States
***Admissions Phone:** 559-323-2100 • **Admissions Fax:** 559-323-5566*
***Admissions E-mail:** jcanalin@sjcl.org • **Web Address:** www.sjcl.org*

INSTITUTIONAL INFORMATION

Public/private: Private.
Student/faculty ratio: 16:1
Total faculty: 36
% Faculty Part-time: 83
% Faculty Female: 45
% Faculty Minority: 14

STUDENTS

Enrollment of law school: 185
% Male/female: 54/46
% Full-time: 13
% Minority: 26
Average age of entering class: 33

ACADEMICS

Academic specializations: Commercial law, corporation securities law, criminal law, environmental law, international law, labor law, taxation.
Advanced degrees offered: JD–3-5 year program; MS taxation–2 years.
Grading system: 100–85 A, 84–75 B, 74–65 C, 64–55 D, 54–0 F.
Clinical program required? Yes.
Clinical program description: Alternative dispute resolution, small claims.
Legal methods course requirement? Yes.
Legal methods description: Legal analysis/research writing.

ADMISSIONS INFORMATION

ADMISSIONS SELECTIVITY RATING: 61
Application fee: $40
Regular application deadline: 6/30
Regular notification: Rolling.
Early application program: No.
LSDAS accepted? No.
Average GPA: 2.90
Range of GPA: 1.8–3.9
Average LSAT: 148
Range of LSAT: 139-174
Transfer students accepted? Yes.
Evening division offered: Yes.
Part-time accepted: Yes.
Number of applications received: 135
Number of applicants accepted: 108
Number of acceptees attending: 91

FINANCIAL FACTS

Annual tuition: $10,212
Books and supplies: $550
% receiving scholarships: 14
Average grant: $1,600
Average loan: $14,500
% of aid that is merit-based: 12
% receiving some sort of aid: 75
% first year students receiving some sort of aid: 75
Average total aid package: $18,500
Average debt: $62,500

INTERNATIONAL STUDENTS

TOEFL required for international students? No.

EMPLOYMENT INFORMATION

Rate of placement: 70
Employers who frequently hire grads: Local DA and DD; various small firms.
State for bar exam: CA
Pass rate for first-time bar: 56
Grads employed by field: Government, 23%; private practice, 70%; public interest, 5%.

Santa Barbara and Ventura Colleges of Law

Santa Barbara College of Law

20 East Victoria Street, Santa Barbara, CA 93101 United States
Admissions Phone: *805-966-0010* • ***Admissions Fax:*** *805-966-7181*
Admissions E-mail: *admit@venturalaw.edu*
Web Address: *www.santabarbaralaw.edu*

INSTITUTIONAL INFORMATION

Public/private: Private.
Student/faculty ratio: 11:1
Total faculty: 19
% Faculty Part-time: 100
% Faculty Female: 26
% Faculty Minority: 5

STUDENTS

Enrollment of law school: 917
% Male/female: 51/49

ACADEMICS

Grading system: Letter grades A–F.
Clinical program required? Yes.
Clinical program description: All off-site (government or private pro bono).
Legal writing course requirement? Yes.
Legal writing description: Basic legal writing–30 hours and adv. legal writing–30 hours.
Legal methods course requirement? No.
Legal research course requirement? Yes.
Legal research description: 30 hours of instruction.
Moot court requirement? No.
Public interest law requirement? No.

ADMISSIONS INFORMATION

ADMISSIONS SELECTIVITY RATING: 71
Application fee: $40
Regular application deadline: Rolling.
Regular notification: Rolling.
Early application program: No.
LSDAS accepted? No.
Average GPA: 3.20
Range of GPA: 3.0–3.5
Average LSAT: 156
Range of LSAT: 153–158
Transfer students accepted? No.
Evening division offered: Yes.
Part-time accepted: Yes.
Applicants also look at: Syracuse University.
Number of applications received: 2,528
Number of applicants accepted: 1,265
Number of acceptees attending: 291

RESEARCH FACILITIES

% of JD classrooms wired: 40

FINANCIAL FACTS

Annual tuition: $22,000
Room & board (on/off-campus): $9,787/$9,787
Books and supplies: $903
% receiving scholarships: 31
Average grant: $8,071
Average loan: $1
% of aid that is merit-based: 7
% receiving some sort of aid: 85
% first year students receiving some sort of aid: 77
Average debt: $60,379

INTERNATIONAL STUDENTS

TOEFL required for international students? No.

EMPLOYMENT INFORMATION

Rate of placement: 96
Average starting salary: $58,000
State for bar exam: CA
Pass rate for first-time bar: 71
Grads employed by field: Academic, 2%; business/industry, 24%; government, 8%; judicial clerkships, 4%; military, 1%; private practice, 58%; public interest, 3%.

Santa Barbara and Ventura Colleges of Law

Ventura College of Law

4475 Market Street, Ventura, CA 93003 United States
Admissions Phone: *805-658-0511* • ***Admissions Fax:*** *805-658-0529*
Admissions E-mail: *vcl@venturalaw.edu* • ***Web Address:*** *www.venturalaw.edu*

INSTITUTIONAL INFORMATION

Public/private: Private.
Student/faculty ratio: 7:1
Total faculty: 19
% Faculty Part-time: 100
% Faculty Female: 32
% Faculty Minority: 5

STUDENTS

Enrollment of law school: 140
% Male/female: 100/0
Average age of entering class: 36

ACADEMICS

Advanced degrees offered: JD–4 year part-time evening program.
Grading system: Alpha system (A–F) on a 4.0 scale.
Clinical program required? Yes.
Clinical program description: Off-campus internships.
Legal writing course requirement? Yes.
Legal writing description: Two separate 2-unit courses are required.

Legal methods course requirement? Yes.
Legal methods description: One-semester course during the first-year curriculum.
Legal research course requirement? Yes.
Legal research description: One 2-unit course is required.
Moot court requirement? No.
Public interest law requirement? Yes.
Public interest law description: 65-hour (1 unit) internship.

ADMISSIONS INFORMATION

ADMISSIONS SELECTIVITY RATING: 60*
Application fee: $45
Regular application deadline: 7/15
Regular notification: 8/1
LSDAS accepted? No.
Average GPA: 2.98
Average LSAT: 149
Transfer students accepted? Yes.
Evening division offered: Yes.
Part-time accepted: Yes.

RESEARCH FACILITIES

% of JD classrooms wired: 100

FINANCIAL FACTS

Annual tuition: $6,195
Books and supplies: $650
Average grant: $1,000
Average loan: $8,000
Tuition per credit: $295

INTERNATIONAL STUDENTS

TOEFL required for international students? No.

EMPLOYMENT INFORMATION

State for bar exam: CA
Pass rate for first-time bar: 33

STUDENTS

Enrollment of law school: 50
% Male/female: 60/40
% Minority: 15
Average age of entering class: 32

ACADEMICS

Legal methods course requirement? Yes.

ADMISSIONS INFORMATION

ADMISSIONS SELECTIVITY RATING: 60*
Early application program: No.
LSDAS accepted? No.
Transfer students accepted? No.
Evening division offered: No.
Part-time accepted: No.
Number of applications received: 50

RESEARCH FACILITIES

Research resources available: Local courthouse library.

FINANCIAL FACTS

Annual tuition: $6,480
Books and supplies: $500
% of aid that is merit-based: 100
Tuition per credit: $200

INTERNATIONAL STUDENTS

TOEFL required for international students? Yes.

EMPLOYMENT INFORMATION

Average starting salary: $30,000
Employers who frequently hire grads: Local law firms, government & state agencies.
State for bar exam: CA
Pass rate for first-time bar: 50

SOUTHERN CALIFORNIA INSTITUTE OF LAW

College of Law

877 South Victoria Avenue, Ventura, CA 93003 United States
***Admissions Phone:** 805-644-2327 • **Admissions Fax:** 805-644-2367*
***Admissions E-mail:** SCILregistrar@lawdegree.com*
***Web Address:** www.lawdegree.com*

INSTITUTIONAL INFORMATION

Public/private: Private.
Student/faculty ratio: 5:1
% Faculty Part-time: 75
% Faculty Female: 50
% Faculty Minority: 10

TRINITY INTERNATIONAL UNIVERSITY

Trinity Law School

2200 North Grand Avenue, Santa Ana, CA 92705 United States
***Admissions Phone:** 714-796-7100 • **Admissions Fax:** 714-796-7190*
***Admissions E-mail:** deaton@tiu.edu • **Web Address:** www.tls.edu*

INSTITUTIONAL INFORMATION

Public/private: Private.
Affiliation: Protestant.

ADMISSIONS INFORMATION

ADMISSIONS SELECTIVITY RATING: 60*
Early application program: No.
LSDAS accepted? No.
Transfer students accepted? No.
Evening division offered: No.
Part-time accepted: No.

INTERNATIONAL STUDENTS

TOEFL required for international students? No.

UNIVERSITY OF LA VERNE

College of Law

320 East D Street, Ontario, CA 91764 United States

***Admissions Phone:** 909-460-2001* • ***Admissions Fax:** 909-460-2082*

***Admissions E-mail:** lawadm@ulv.edu* • ***Web Address:** law.ulv.edu*

INSTITUTIONAL INFORMATION

Public/private: Private.
Student/faculty ratio: 14:1
Total faculty: 25
% Faculty Part-time: 36
% Faculty Female: 28
% Faculty Minority: 12

STUDENTS

Enrollment of law school: 80
% Out of state: 18
% Male/female: 67/33
% Full-time: 74
% International: 5
% Minority: 35
Average age of entering class: 26

ACADEMICS

Academic specializations: Civil procedure, commercial law, constitutional law, corporation securities law, criminal law, environmental law, government services, human rights law, intellectual property law, international law, labor law, legal philosophy, property, taxation, see catalog.
Advanced degrees offered: JD–3 years, full-time; 4 years, part-time.
Combined degrees offered: JD/MBA–4 years; JD/MPA–4 years.
Grading system: Point system.
Clinical program required? No.
Legal writing course requirement? Yes.
Legal writing description: Legal analysis and writing I and II. It is 2 units the first semester where students learn how to write predictively and 1 unit the second semester where students learn how to write persuasively. All students, except for those on Law Review, must take a second year appellate advocacy course where they further develop skills in brief writing. Students in their final year must take and additional course that has a writing requirement such as moot court honors, independent study, or a seminar.
Legal methods course requirement? Yes.
Legal methods description: Legal methods are covered in the first half of legal analysis and writing I.
Legal research course requirement? Yes.
Legal research description: Research I is a 1-unit first-semester course wherein students learn what legal resources are available and how to find legal authority. Proper citation form is also covered.
Moot court requirement? No.
Public interest law requirement? No.
Academic journals: *Law Review (Journal of Juvenile Law).*

ADMISSIONS INFORMATION

ADMISSIONS SELECTIVITY RATING: 61
Application fee: $55
Regular application deadline: Rolling.
Regular notification: Rolling.
Early application program: No.
LSDAS accepted? Yes.
Average GPA: 3.01
Range of GPA: 2.6–3.4
Average LSAT: 149
Range of LSAT: 147–152
Transfer students accepted? Yes.
Evening division offered: Yes.
Part-time accepted: Yes.
Applicants also look at: Loyola Marymount University, Southwestern University School of Law, University of Maryland, Western State University, Whittier College.
Number of applications received: 467
Number of applicants accepted: 291
Number of acceptees attending: 80

RESEARCH FACILITIES

% of JD classrooms wired: 100

FINANCIAL FACTS

Annual tuition: $22,700
Room & board (off-campus): $8,334
Books and supplies: $4,464
Financial aid application deadline: 3/2
% receiving scholarships: 69
Average grant: $12,900
Average loan: $18,500
% receiving some sort of aid: 90
% first year students receiving some sort of aid: 86
Average total aid package: $28,500
Average debt: $60,000
Tuition per credit: $750

INTERNATIONAL STUDENTS

TOEFL required for international students? Yes.
Minimum Paper TOEFL: 550
Minimum Computer-based TOEFL: 213

EMPLOYMENT INFORMATION

Rate of placement: 100
Employers who frequently hire grads: County governments & private law firms.
Prominent alumni: Hon. Peter H. Norell, presiding judge, Superior Court San Bernardino, CA; Thomas M. Finn, senoir commissioner, Dublin, Ireland; Hon. Dennis Aichroth, judge, Superior Court, Los Angeles; Hon. Roberta McPeters, judge, Superior Court, San Bernardino, CA; Hon. Jean Pfeiffer Leonard, judge, Juvenile Court, Riverside, CA.
State for bar exam: CA
Pass rate for first-time bar: 82

University of West Los Angeles

School of Law

1155 West Arbor Vitae Street, Inglewood, CA 90301-2902 United States
Admissions Phone: *310-342-5254* • ***Admissions Fax:*** *310-342-5295*
Admissions E-mail: *lfreeman@uwla.edu* • ***Web Address:*** *www.uwla.edu*

INSTITUTIONAL INFORMATION

Public/private: Private.
Student/faculty ratio: 30:1
Total faculty: 36
% Faculty Part-time: 81
% Faculty Female: 19
% Faculty Minority: 17

STUDENTS

Enrollment of law school: 262
% Male/female: 45/55
% Full-time: 13
% Minority: 24

ACADEMICS

Advanced degrees offered: JD–3 year, full-time; 4 year, part-time.
Grading system: Letter grade, 4-point scale.
Clinical program required? No.
Clinical program description: Credit for judicial and public agencies externships (legal aid).
Legal writing course requirement? Yes.
Legal writing description: Three courses are required, a basic research and writing course after the first year and then an advanced writing class in the second year followed by moot court.
Legal methods course requirement? Yes.
Legal methods description: First semester required course for all students.
Legal research course requirement? Yes.
Legal research description: Basic course required after completion of the first year. Students learn how to use the print and online research tools.
Moot court requirement? No.
Public interest law requirement? No.
Academic journals: *UWLA Law Review.*

ADMISSIONS INFORMATION

ADMISSIONS SELECTIVITY RATING: 64
Application fee: $55
Regular application deadline: Rolling.
Regular notification: Rolling.
Early application program: No.
LSDAS accepted? No.
Average GPA: 3.10
Range of GPA: 2–3.9
Average LSAT: 148
Transfer students accepted? Yes.
Evening division offered: Yes.
Part-time accepted: Yes.
Number of applications received: 59
Number of applicants accepted: 28
Number of acceptees attending: 17

FINANCIAL FACTS

Annual tuition: $15,795
Books and supplies: $1,000
Financial aid application deadline: 3/1
% receiving scholarships: 5
Average grant: $18,500
Average loan: $18,500
% receiving some sort of aid: 90
% first year students receiving some sort of aid: 80
Average total aid package: $18,500
Average debt: $70,000
Tuition per credit: $585

INTERNATIONAL STUDENTS

TOEFL required for international students? Yes.
Minimum Paper TOEFL: 550
Minimum Computer-based TOEFL: 213

EMPLOYMENT INFORMATION

Rate of placement: 25
Prominent alumni: Paula Zinneman, California real estate commissioner; Gail Margolis, director, mental health services, state of CA; Hon. Ron Skyers, judge, LA Superior Court; Lael Rubin, district attorney's office.
State for bar exam: CA
Pass rate for first-time bar: 30

DALHOUSIE

Dalhousie Law School

Dalhousie Law School, Halifax, NS B3P 1P8 Canada

Admissions Phone: *902-494-2068* • ***Admissions Fax:*** *902-494-1316*

Admissions E-mail: *Rose.Godfrey@dal.ca*

Web Address: *www.dal.ca/law/admission.html*

INSTITUTIONAL INFORMATION

Public/private: public
Student/faculty ratio: 13:1
Total faculty: 35
% Female: 45
% Minority: 6

STUDENTS

Enrollment of law school: 464
% Out of state: 88
% Male/female: 45/55
% Full-time: 98
% Minority: 12
Average age of entering class: 24

ACADEMICS

Academic specializations: Commercial law, corporation securities law, environmental law, international law.
Advanced degrees offered: LLM, JSD.
Combined degrees offered: LLB/MBA; LLB/MLIS; LLB/MPA; LLB/MHSA. All 4 years.
Clinical program required? No.
Clinical program description: Legal aid clinic.
Legal writing course requirement? Yes.
Legal writing description: Required course, first year.
Legal methods course requirement? No.
Legal research course requirement? Yes.
Legal research description: Required course, first year.
Moot court requirement? Yes.
Moot court description: Mandatory moot, second year.
Public interest law requirement? No.
Academic journals: Dalhousie Law Journal, Dalhousie Journal of Legal Studies, Canadian Journal of Law and Technology.

ADMISSIONS INFORMATION

ADMISSIONS SELECTIVITY RATING: 90
Application fee: $65
Regular application deadline: 2/28
Regular notification: 4/1
Early application program: No.
LSDAS accepted? No.
Average GPA: 3.80
Average LSAT: 161
Transfer students accepted? Yes.
Evening division offered: No.
Part-time accepted: Yes.
Applicants also look at: Arizona State University, McGill University, Queen's University, University of British Columbia, University of Toronto, York University.
Number of applications received: 1,285
Number of applicants accepted: 279
Number of acceptees attending: 162

RESEARCH FACILITIES

% of JD classrooms wired: 100
School-supported research centers: Dalhousie legal aid clinic, health law institute, law and technology institute, marine and environmental law institute.

FINANCIAL FACTS

Annual tuition: $9,492
Room & board (on-campus): $3,500
Books and supplies: $1,200
Financial aid application deadline: 10/31
Average grant: $4,212
Average loan: $8,000
% of aid that is merit-based: 43
Average total aid package: $2,500

INTERNATIONAL STUDENTS

TOEFL required for international students? Yes.
Minimum Paper TOEFL: 600

EMPLOYMENT INFORMATION

Rate of placement: 93
Employers who frequently hire grads: Law firms, government, courts.
Grads employed by field: Academic, 1%; business/industry, 5%; government, 5%; judicial clerkships, 5%; private practice, 80%.

MCGILL UNIVERSITY

McGill Faculty of Law

3674 Peel Street, Montreal, QC H3A 1W9 Canada

Admissions Phone: *514-398-3544*

Admissions E-mail: *gradadmissions.law@mcgill.ca*

Web Address: *www.law.mcgill.ca*

INSTITUTIONAL INFORMATION

Public/private: private

ADMISSIONS INFORMATION

ADMISSIONS SELECTIVITY RATING: 60*
Application fee: $60
Regular application deadline: 3/1
Early application program: No.
LSDAS accepted? No.
Transfer students accepted? No.
Evening division offered: No.
Part-time accepted: No.

FINANCIAL FACTS

Annual tuition (In-province/Out of-province/International): $3,036/$5,951/$13,082
Room & board (on-campus): $9,600
Books and supplies: $800

INTERNATIONAL STUDENTS

TOEFL required for international students? Yes.
Minimum Paper TOEFL: 600
Minimum Computer-based TOEFL: 250

QUEEN'S UNIVERSITY

Faculty of Law, Queen's University

Macdonald Hall, Union Street, Queen's University
Kingston, ON K7L 3N6 Canada
***Admissions Phone:** 613-533-2220* • ***Admissions Fax:** 613-533-6611*
***Admissions E-mail:** llb@post.queensu.ca* • ***Web Address:** law.queensu.ca*

INSTITUTIONAL INFORMATION

Public/private: public
Student/faculty ratio: 6:1
Total faculty: 78
% Part-time: 69
% Female: 36

STUDENTS

Enrollment of law school: 480
% Male/female: 48/52
% Full-time: 97
Average age of entering class: 25

ACADEMICS

Academic specializations: Civil procedure, commercial law, constitutional law, corporation securities law, criminal law, environmental law, government services, human rights law, intellectual property law, international law, labor law, legal history, legal philosophy, property, taxation.
Advanced degrees offered: The master of law (LLM) program, administered jointly by the faculty of law and the school of graduate studies and research, is designed to enable students of high academic merit to pursue advanced study independent research and coursework.
Combined degrees offered: MIR/LLB cooperative combined degree program. This co-operative program is a 4-year, full-time combined degree program offered by the school of industrial relations and the faculty of law. Graduate training in industrial relations is combined with a degree in law in order to meet the increasing demand for industrial relations specialists with legal backgrounds. MPA/LLB cooperative combined degree program. The MPA/LLB co-operative program is a 4-year, full-time combined degree program offered by the school of policy studies and the faculty of law to facilitate a closer integration of studies in law and public policy so that students are able to apply their knowledge and understanding to the resolution of theoretical and practical problems in either discipline and at the interstices of these disciplines. The public administration curriculum offers students training in policy analysis and management, while the LLB curriculum offers students the substantive knowledge necessary for successful policy implementation and interpretation. Co-operative placements will be provided at the Federal Department of Justice or the provincial Ministry of the Attorney General, and have been approved by the Law Society of Upper Canada to be the equivalent of articles.
Grading system: The current grading system for the faculty of law is as follows: A exceptional, A-minus excellent, B+ very good, B good, B-minus satisfactory, C+ fair, C adequate, D marginal, F failure, PA pass, H honors, PN pass no honors available in this course.
Clinical program required? No.
Clinical program description: Clinical programs offered: Clinical correctional law, clinical litigation, and clinical family. There is a practice skills degree requirement that can be satisfied by completion of clinical programs and other related courses. See http://www.law.queensu.ca/students/LLB_Programs/index.php
Legal writing course requirement? Yes.
Legal writing description: First-year resource program and small sections: Small section professors in conjunction with library staff have primary responsibility for a program of introduction to legal education and legal skills, with a particular emphasis on legal research and writing. A substantial term paper requirement must be completed during their upper years, students must complete a minimum of 1 substantial paper of term paper standard. In order to qualify as a substantial paper, a paper should be on a topic capable of sustained development, should appropriately develop the topic and should, ordinarily and depending on the topic, bear some of the following characteristics: development of an idea or set of ideas in a way which relates the idea or ideas to the body of thought on the topic; mastery of and clear statement of a complicated body of law making up the topic; development of ideas from a discipline other than law in a way helpful to resolution of the problems making up the topic; development of factual material in such a way helpful to resolution of the problems making up the topic. A paper does not qualify as a substantial paper merely because it is original or good or because it shows a large amount of work. A paper does not fail to qualify as a substantial paper merely because, being a memorandum or a draft of a statute with accompanying comments, it does not take the form of a scholarly essay. Papers must be graded by a faculty member to meet this degree requirement.
Legal methods course requirement? Yes.
Legal methods description: Practice skills requirement: A "Legal Methods" course, or practice skills course, is one that gives students significant opportunity to undertake legal research and to develop skills of drafting, client interaction, oral advocacy, negotiation or mediation, or offer students a clinical legal experience.
Legal research course requirement? No.
Moot court requirement? Yes.
Moot court description: Each student completes a course in appellate advocacy in second year, involving oral advocacy and preparation of factums in small classes of approximately 16 students. Students argue a moot in teams of 4 at the conclusion of the course. Additional opportunities for oral advocacy are provided through competitive moots. See http://www.queensu.ca/calendars/law/MootsandOralAdvocacy_1914.htm.
Public interest law requirement? Yes.
Public interest law description: First-year curriculum includes innovative first year resource program with enrichment in areas such as ethics, perspectives, diversity and skills.
Academic journals: *The Queen's Law Journal.*

ADMISSIONS INFORMATION

ADMISSIONS SELECTIVITY RATING: 98
Application fee: $175
Regular application deadline: 11/1
Regular notification: Rolling.
Early application program: No.
LSDAS accepted? No.
Average GPA: 3.70
Range of GPA: 3.0-4.0
Average LSAT: 160
Range of LSAT: 153-174
Transfer students accepted? Yes.
Evening division offered: No.
Part-time accepted: Yes.
Applicants also look at: Dalhousie, McGill University, University of British Columbia, University of Calgary, University of Ottawa, University of Toronto, York University.

Number of applications received: 2,361
Number of applicants accepted: 164
Number of acceptees attending: 158

RESEARCH FACILITIES

Research resources available: National and international study programs. Queen's provides opportunities for students to enrich their LLB studies by attending other universities for a semester. Students may earn credit toward their degree with one of the faculty's highly regarded exchange partners across Canada and abroad: University of Sydney—Australia; University of Melbourne—Australia; University of New South Wales—Australia; University of Groningen—Netherlands; Universite Jean Moulin—Lyon, France; University de Sherbrooke—Quebec; Canada Exchange Scholars Program Canada; City University, Hong Kong; National University of Singapore. Students can also spend a spring semester enrolled in the international study centre in East Sussex, U.K. Queen's faculty of law and school of business have created this module as another way to integrate international law and business into legal studies. Students will earn degree credits as they live and study at the Herstmonceux castle estate which has been designed as a unique learning environment in which students, scholars, and citizens from around the world can meet to study and work towards common goals.
% of JD classrooms wired: 85
School-supported research centers: Educational technology. The William R. Lederman law library is highly regarded for its leadership role in continually using technology to provide better access to legal information from around the world; access that is crucial for effective teaching, research, and analysis. The electronic law library is a major initiative to provide as much direct electronic access as possible to the desktops of our students and faculty. Queen's Law provides full access to its impressive electronic resources through the faculty's ample computer workstations in the law library and with wireless Internet connections throughout Macdonald Hall.
Clinical programs. Queen's Law clinical courses: Clinical correctional law, clinical litigation practice, and clinical family law. Clinical correctional law is associated with the correctional law project, and is a course unique in Canada. Students provide legal advice and representation to prisoners in the federal penitentiaries in the Kingston area. While taking part in clinical litigation practice, students provide legal advice and representation to disadvantaged members of our community and full-time Queen's students, under the auspices of Queen's legal aid. Students participating in clinical family law find clinical placements with children's and family law related agencies, the Superior Court of Justice-Family Court, or with a local family law practitioner.
Co-operative combined degree programs. The master of industrial relations/bachelor of laws (MIR/LLB) and the master of public administration/bachelor of laws (MPA/LLB). The MIR/LLB program is offered with the school of industrial relations at Queen's University in order to meet the profession's increasing demand for specialists in the industrial relations area. The innovative MPA/LLB co-operative combined degree program is offered in partnership with the school of policy studies at Queen's. Through the MPA/LLB program, students will become specialists in law and public policy. Students will benefit from the strong reputation and connections of both Queen's faculty of law and Queen's school of policy studies with government policymakers.

FINANCIAL FACTS

Annual tuition (resident): $8,961
Annual tuition (nonresident): $18,650
Room & board (on/off-campus): $4,503
Books and supplies: $1,850
Financial aid application deadline: 10/31
Average grant: $2,630
Average loan: $4,752
% receiving some sort of aid: 69
% first year students receiving some sort of aid: 60

INTERNATIONAL STUDENTS

TOEFL required for international students? Yes.
Minimum Paper TOEFL: 600
Minimum Computer-based TOEFL: 250

EMPLOYMENT INFORMATION

Rate of placement: 96
Prominent alumni: Mr. Justice Thomas Cromwell, Nova Scotia Court of Appeal.
Grads employed by field: Academic, 2%; business/industry, 1%; government, 8%; judicial clerkships, 3%; other, 2%; private practice, 79%; public interest, 1%.

UNIVERSITE DE MONTREAL

Faculte de Droit

PO Box 6128, Stn. Centre-Ville, Monteal, Quebec Canada Montreal, QC H3C 3J7 Canada
***Admissions Phone:** 514-343-6125 • **Admissions Fax:** 514-343-2030*
***Admissions E-mail:** monique.bourbonnais@umontreal.ca*
***Web Address:** www.droit.umontreal.ca*

INSTITUTIONAL INFORMATION

Public/private: public
Student/faculty ratio: 16:1
Total faculty: 60
% Female: 28
% Minority: 2

STUDENTS

Enrollment of law school: 945
% Male/female: 32/68
% Full-time: 93
% International: 1

ACADEMICS

Academic specializations: Civil procedure, commercial law, constitutional law, corporation securities law, criminal law, environmental law, government services, human rights law, intellectual property law, international law, labor law, legal history, legal philosophy, property, taxation.
Advanced degrees offered: LLD–3 years; general LLM–1 to 2 years; specialized LLM or graduate studies degree (DESS), 1 year, in notarial law, tax law, business law, information technologies, international and transational law, North American bommon law and e-commerce.
Grading system: GPA from 1 to 4.
Clinical program required? No.
Legal writing course requirement? Yes.
Legal writing description: A mandatory seminar is devoted to the preparation of an essay.
Legal methods course requirement? No.
Legal research description: 3 credits of teaching and assignements during the first year.
Moot court requirement? No.
Public interest law requirement? No.
Academic journals: *Revue juridique Thémis*; *Revue québécoise de droit international.*

ADMISSIONS INFORMATION

ADMISSIONS SELECTIVITY RATING: 87
Application fee: $40
Regular application deadline: 4/1
Regular notification: 5/1
Early application program: No.
LSDAS accepted? No.
Average GPA: 3.00
Transfer students accepted? Yes.
Evening division offered: No.
Part-time accepted: No.
Number of applications received: 2,072
Number of applicants accepted: 428
Number of acceptees attending: 335

FINANCIAL FACTS

Annual tuition (resident): $1,400
Annual tuition (nonresident): $4,200
Books and supplies: $600
Average loan: $3,456

INTERNATIONAL STUDENTS

TOEFL required for international students? No.

EMPLOYMENT INFORMATION

Prominent alumni: Hon. Michel Bastarache, justice of the Supreme Court of Canada; Hon. Marie Deschamps, justice of the Supreme Court of Canada; Louise Arbour, U.N. high commissioner for refugees, ex-JSCC; Philippe Kirsch, president, International Criminal Court; Morris Rosenberg, deputy minister, Health Canada.
State for bar exam: QC, NY
Pass rate for first-time bar: 79

UNIVERSITÉ DE SHERBROOKE

Faculté de droit

2500, Boulevard de l'Université, Sherbrooke, QC J1K 2R1 Canada
Admissions Phone: *800-267-8337* • ***Admissions Fax:*** *819-821-7652*
Admissions E-mail: *information@usherbrooke.ca*
Web Address: *www.usherbrooke.ca*

INSTITUTIONAL INFORMATION

Public/private: private

ADMISSIONS INFORMATION

ADMISSIONS SELECTIVITY RATING: 60*
Early application program: No.
LSDAS accepted? No.
Transfer students accepted? No.
Evening division offered: No.
Part-time accepted: No.

INTERNATIONAL STUDENTS

TOEFL required for international students? No.

UNIVERSITY OF BRITISH COLUMBIA

Faculty of Law

1822 East Mall, Vancouver, BC V6T 1Z1 Canada
Admissions Phone: *604-822-6303* • ***Admissions Fax:*** *604-822-8108*
Admissions E-mail: *admissions@law.ubc.ca* • ***Web Address:*** *www.law.ubc.ca*

INSTITUTIONAL INFORMATION

Public/private: public
Student/faculty ratio: 15:1
Total faculty: 40
% Female: 50
% Minority: 10

STUDENTS

Enrollment of law school: 723
% Out of state: 27
% Male/female: 50/50
% Full-time: 90
% International: 1
% Minority: 10
Average age of entering class: 26

ACADEMICS

Academic specializations: Civil procedure, commercial law, constitutional law, corporation securities law, criminal law, environmental law, government services, human rights law, intellectual property law, international law, labor law, legal history, legal philosophy, property, taxation, alternative dispute resolution.
Advanced degrees offered: The bachelor of laws (LLB) degree is a 3-year program, full-time; the master of laws (LLM) degree is a 12-month program; the doctorate (PhD) judge degree is a 1- to 2-year program.
Combined degrees offered: The combined LLB/MBA program is 4 years in length and is administered jointly by the faculty of commerce and the faculty of law. Students are required to complete 86 credits in law and 45 credits in the MBA program.
The combined LLB/MA(MAPPS) permits students to obtain the degrees of LLB and MA in Asia Pacific policy studies (MAPPS) through combined enrollment in the faculty of law and the institute of Asian research. The program is 3 years in length and requires students to take 86 law credits (excluding IAR 500) and 30 MAPPS credits.
Grading system: Grades are given in percentages.
Clinical program required? No.
Clinical program description: Although students are not required to participate in the clinical program many students do participate for the experience. Participation in the program allows students a well-rounded education, where the theory learned in the classroom is applied in a practical setting.
The law students legal advice program (LSLAP) is a student-run organization that provides legal advice to those who would otherwise not be able to afford such assistance. The program has grown from a small summer experiment to being the second largest provider of free legal services in the province of British Columbia. LSLAP operates student staffed clinics throughout the Lower Mainland area making our law students an invaluable legal resource in the province. Participation in the program affords students a well-rounded education, where theory learned in class is applied in a practical setting. LSLAP memebrs provide a wide variety of services for their clients, all under the strict guidance of the program's supervising lawyer. Student's may provide solicitor's work such as

drafting wills, assisting clients with uncontested divorces and advising the clients on such areas of law as contracts and civil liberties. Students may also perform barrister's work, appearing on behalf of clients in court and before tribunals. The clinicians are competent to defend persons in Provincial Criminal Court. Students may appear before Small Claims Court and before various tribunals concerning worker's compensation, employment insurance, welfare and landlord/tenant issues. LSLAP also operates specialized legal clinics for students that have particular interests: The women's clinic, the persons with AIDS clinic, the street youth clinic, the Chinese clinic, and the First Nations clinic.

Legal writing course requirement? Yes.

Legal writing description: The legal research and writing program is 1 full year during the first year of study. Students will learn proper legal research and writing formatting, learn where to find the legal tools they require to complete memos and serve clients.

Legal methods course requirement? No.

Legal research course requirement? Yes.

Legal research description: The legal research and writing program is 1 full year during the first year of study. Students will learn proper legal research and writing formatting, learn where to find the legal tools they require to complete memos and serve clients.

Moot court requirement? Yes.

Moot court description: All first-year students are required to participate in a moot court program as part of their first-year curriculum. They must write an appeal factum and participate as an advocate in the mock appeal in the mock appeal in front of a bench of legal practitioners acting as judges. Students will wear robes and receive feedback from the judges.

Public interest law requirement? No.

Academic journals: *Law Review, Canadian Journal of Family Law, Insolvency Journal.*

ADMISSIONS INFORMATION

ADMISSIONS SELECTIVITY RATING: 90

Application fee: $80

Regular application deadline: 2/1

Regular notification: Rolling.

Early application program: Yes.

LSDAS accepted? No.

Average GPA: 3.81

Average LSAT: 163

Range of LSAT: 152–175

Transfer students accepted? Yes.

Evening division offered: No.

Part-time accepted: Yes.

Applicants also look at: University of Alberta, University of Calgary, University of Toronto, University of Victoria, York University.

Number of applications received: 1,862

Number of applicants accepted: 472

Number of acceptees attending: 206

RESEARCH FACILITIES

Research resources available: Quicklaw, Westlaw Lexus-Nexus, Canadian Bar Association.

% of JD classrooms wired: 100

School-supported research centers: Center for Asian legal studies; Chinese legal studies; Southeast Asian legal studies; Center for feminist legal studies; First Nations legal studies program, environment, sustainable development & law; International Center for Criminal Law Reform and Criminal Justice Policy, dispute resolution program, legal history, cyberspace law.

FINANCIAL FACTS

Annual tuition (resident): $9,000

Annual tuition (nonresident): $17,000

Room & board: $27,018

Books and supplies: $1,400

Financial aid application deadline: 5/15

% receiving scholarships: 40

Average loan: $7,350

% of aid that is merit-based: 50

% receiving some sort of aid: 70

% first year students receiving some sort of aid: 70

Average total aid package: $7,500

Average debt: $25,000

Tuition per credit (resident): $281

Tuition per credit (nonresident): $281

INTERNATIONAL STUDENTS

TOEFL required for international students? No.

EMPLOYMENT INFORMATION

Rate of placement: 90

Average starting salary: $51,000

Employers who frequently hire grads: British Columbia law firms and government agencies (including Vancouver Island and interior), Ontario law firms and government agencies, Alberta law firms and government agencies, New York law firms, Canadian public interest groups, Canadian courts.

Prominent alumni: Frank Iacobucci, justice Supreme Court of Canada; Lance Finch, chief justice of British Columbia; Kim Campbell, former prime minister of Canada; Don Brenner, chief justice of British Columbia Supreme Court; Ujjal Dosanjh, former premier of British Columbia and attorney general.

State for bar exam: BC, AB, NY, MA, ON

Pass rate for first-time bar: 99

Grads employed by field: Academic, 4%; government, 2%; judicial clerkships, 9%; other, 1%; private practice, 74%; public interest, 1%.

UNIVERSITY OF CALGARY

Faculty of Law

Room 3390, Murray Fraser Hall, 2500 University Drive NW,
Calgary, AB T2N 1N4 Canada
Admissions Phone: *403-220-8154* • ***Admissions Fax:*** *403-210-9662*
Admissions E-mail: *law@ucalgary.ca* • ***Web Address:*** *www.law.ucalgary.ca/*

INSTITUTIONAL INFORMATION

Public/private: public

Student/faculty ratio: 15:1

Total faculty: 17

% Female: 47

STUDENTS

Enrollment of law school: 218

% Male/female: 44/56

% Full-time: 100

Average age of entering class: 26

ACADEMICS

Academic specializations: Environmental law, natural resource, law legal-skills program.

Advanced degrees offered: LLB–3 years; LLM–15 to 18 months.

Combined degrees offered: LLB/MBA–4 years law and masters of business administration; LLB/MEDes law and masters of environmental design.

Grading system: 11-band grading system; 4-point scale.
Clinical program required? Yes.
Clinical program description: Clinical programs are not required. However, the following are offered: Criminal seminar, family seminar, naural resources seminar, business seminar.
Legal methods course requirement? Yes.
Legal methods description: Contact school for this information.

ADMISSIONS INFORMATION

ADMISSIONS SELECTIVITY RATING: 99
Application fee: $60
Regular application deadline: 2/1
Regular notification: Rolling.
Early application program: No.
LSDAS accepted? No.
Average GPA: 3.51
Range of GPA: 2.5–4.0
Average LSAT: 71
Range of LSAT: 26–99
Transfer students accepted? Yes.
Evening division offered: No.
Part-time accepted: Yes.
Applicants also look at: University of Alberta, University of British Columbia, University of Saskatchewan.
Number of applications received: 877
Number of applicants accepted: 75
Number of acceptees attending: 75

RESEARCH FACILITIES

Research resources available: Canadian institute for resources law (CIRL); Alberta civil liberties research center (ACCRC).

FINANCIAL FACTS

Annual tuition (resident): $10,500
Annual tuition (nonresident): $10,500
Room & board (on/off-campus): $7,000/$10,000
Books and supplies: $1,800

INTERNATIONAL STUDENTS

TOEFL required for international students? Yes.
Minimum Paper TOEFL: 600
Minimum Computer-based TOEFL: 250

EMPLOYMENT INFORMATION

Rate of placement: 90
State for bar exam: AB

UNIVERSITY OF NEW BRUNSWICK

Faculty of Law

Law Admissions Office, Faculty of Law, PO Box 44271, Fredericton, NB E3B 6C2 Canada
***Admissions Phone:** 506-453-4693* • ***Admissions Fax:** 506-458-7722*
***Admissions E-mail:** lawadmit@unb.ca* • ***Web Address:** www.law.unb.ca*

INSTITUTIONAL INFORMATION

Public/private: public

STUDENTS

Enrollment of law school: 235
% Male/female: 47/53
% Full-time: 100
% International: 3
Average age of entering class: 25

ADMISSIONS INFORMATION

ADMISSIONS SELECTIVITY RATING: 86
Application fee: $50
Regular application deadline: 3/1
Regular notification: 3/2
Early application program: No.
LSDAS accepted? No.
Average GPA: 3.70
Range of GPA: 3.2–4.0
Average LSAT: 159
Range of LSAT: 151–173
Transfer students accepted? Yes.
Evening division offered: No.
Part-time accepted: No.
Applicants also look at: Dalhousie.
Number of applications received: 911
Number of applicants accepted: 209
Number of acceptees attending: 84

FINANCIAL FACTS

Annual tuition (resident): $6,972
Annual tuition (nonresident): $6,972
Room & board (on-campus): $5,938
Books and supplies: $1,500
Financial aid application deadline: 1/1

INTERNATIONAL STUDENTS

TOEFL required for international students? No.

EMPLOYMENT INFORMATION

Rate of placement: 87

University of Saskatchewan

University of Saskatchewan College of Law

College of Law, University of Saskatchewan, 15 Campus Drive Saskatoon, SK S7N 5A6 Canada

Admissions Phone: *306-966-5045* • ***Admissions Fax:*** *306-966-5900*

Admissions E-mail: *law_admissions@usask.ca*

Web Address: *www.usask.ca/law/*

INSTITUTIONAL INFORMATION

Public/private: public

ADMISSIONS INFORMATION

ADMISSIONS SELECTIVITY RATING: 60*
Early application program: No.
LSDAS accepted? No.
Transfer students accepted? No.
Evening division offered: No.
Part-time accepted: No.

INTERNATIONAL STUDENTS

TOEFL required for international students? No.

University of Toronto

Faculty of Law

78 Queens Park, Toronto, ON M5S 2C5 Canada

Admissions Phone: *416-978-3716* • ***Admissions Fax:*** *416-978-7899*

Admissions E-mail: *law.admissions@utoronto.ca*

Web Address: *www.law.utoronto.ca*

INSTITUTIONAL INFORMATION

Public/private: public
Student/faculty ratio: 10:1
Total faculty: 55
% Female: 33

STUDENTS

Enrollment of law school: 589
% Male/female: 50/50
% Full-time: 99
% Minority: 30
Average age of entering class: 25

ACADEMICS

Advanced degrees offered: Master of laws (LLM)–1 year; doctor of juridical science (SJD)–1 year plus thesis; master of studies in law (MSL)–1 year.
Combined degrees offered: JD/MBA–4 years; JD/MSW–4 years; JD/MA (criminology)–3 years; JD/MA (economics)–3 years; JD/MA in political science, collaborative program in international relations–3 years; JD/MA (Russian and East European studies)–4 years; JD/MIST (masters of information studies); collaborative program in environmental studies–3 years; JD/PhD (economics)-4 years plus dissertation; JD/PhD (philosophy)-4 years plus dissertation; JD/PhD (political science) 4 years plus dissertation.
Grading system: Letter grades A, B+, B, C+, C, D, F. Students who are in the top 10% of the class each year are awarded "A honors standing." Students are not ranked except as disclosed on the prize list.
Clinical program required? No.
Clinical program description: UT does not require students to participate in a clinic program; however, we offer several vibrant and interesting clinical opportunities, and a majority of students take part in at least 1 clinic program: Center for Spanish-speaking people, advocates for injured workers, downtown legal services, international human rights clinic, artists' legal advice services, Barbra Schlifer commemorative clinic.
Legal writing course requirement? Yes.
Legal writing description: Students must complete writing assignments in their first year as part of their first-year program in their "small group" (see below).
Legal methods course requirement? Yes.
Legal methods description: The cornerstone of the first-year curriculum is the "small group," which permits students to study 1 of the first-year subjects with a member of the faculty and 15 classmates. The "small group" introduces students to the techniques of legal research and writing in a personal and direct setting with a member of the teaching faculty.
Legal research course requirement? Yes.
Legal research description: As part of the "small group" in first year, students are introduced the many elements of legal research.
Moot court requirement? Yes.
Moot court description: Every student is required to participate in a moot and its successful completion is an academic requirement. Students complete their moot in second term of second or third year. Students may also fulfill the mooting requirement through participation in a competitive moot.
Public interest law requirement? No.
Public interest law description: Students are not required to complete a public interest requirement, however, many of our students participate in our pro bono students Canada program, which offers students volunteer placements with pro bono organizations, and summer internships doing pro bono work.
Academic journals: *University of Toronto Faculty of Law Review, Journal of Law & Equality, Indigenous Law Journal, Journal of International Law and International Relations.*

ADMISSIONS INFORMATION

ADMISSIONS SELECTIVITY RATING: 98
Application fee: $50
Regular application deadline: 11/1
Regular notification: 1/4
Early application program: No.
LSDAS accepted? No.
Average GPA: 3.80
Range of GPA: 3.7–4.0
Average LSAT: 166
Range of LSAT: 157–180
Transfer students accepted? Yes.
Evening division offered: No.
Part-time accepted: Yes.
Applicants also look at: Columbia University, Harvard University, McGill University, Northern Illinois University, University of California—Berkeley, University of Victoria, York University.
Number of applications received: 1,896
Number of applicants accepted: 273
Number of acceptees attending: 182

RESEARCH FACILITIES

% of JD classrooms wired: 95

FINANCIAL FACTS

Annual tuition (resident): $16,000
Annual tuition (nonresident): $23,195
Room & board (on/off-campus): $10,250/$8,900
Books and supplies: $1,100
Financial aid application deadline: 5/15
% receiving scholarships: 46
Average grant: $7,207
Average loan: $12,104
% of aid that is merit-based: 3
% receiving some sort of aid: 53
% first year students receiving some sort of aid: 48
Average total aid package: $19,311
Average debt: $33,437
Tuition per credit (resident): $8,000
Tuition per credit (nonresident): $11,598

INTERNATIONAL STUDENTS

TOEFL required for international students? No.

EMPLOYMENT INFORMATION

Rate of placement: 95
Average starting salary: $50,000
Employers who frequently hire grads: All major Toronto law firms, all provincial and federal government departments, many large New York and Boston law firms, large and midsize Vancouver, Halifax and Calgary law firms.
Prominent alumni: Justice Frank Iacobucci, interim president, University of Toronto; Justice Rosalie Abella, Supreme Court of Canada; Justice Bonnie Croll, judge, Ontario Superior Court of Justice; The Hon. Paul Martin, prime minister of Canada.
State for bar exam: NY, MA, CA
Grads employed by field: Business/industry, 1%; government, 8%; judicial clerkships, 8%; private practice, 80%; public interest, 1%.

UNIVERSITY OF VICTORIA

University of Victoria, Faculty of Law

PO Box 2400, STN CSC, Victoria, BC V8W 3H7 Canada
***Admissions Phone:** 250-721-8151* • ***Admissions Fax:** 250-721-6390*
***Admissions E-mail:** lawadmss@uvic.ca* • ***Web Address:** www.law.uvic.ca*

INSTITUTIONAL INFORMATION

Public/private: public
Student/faculty ratio: 7:1
Total faculty: 57
% Part-time: 47
% Female: 33
% Minority: 5

STUDENTS

Enrollment of law school: 365
% Out of state: 50
% Male/female: 44/56
% Full-time: 96
% Minority: 20
Average age of entering class: 25

ACADEMICS

Academic specializations: Environmental law, intellectual property law, international law, legal history, property, alternative dispute resolution, aboriginal law.
Advanced degrees offered: LLM and PhD program commencing 2004/2005 academic year.
Combined degrees offered: Bachelor of laws/master's of public administration (LLB/MPA)–4 years; bachelor of laws/master's of business administration (LLB/MBA)–4 years; bachelor of laws/master's of international relations (LLB/MIA)–3.5 years; bachelor of common law/bachelor of civil law (LLB/BCL)–4.5 years; bachelor of laws/master of arts in indigenous government (LLB/MAIG)–4 years.
Grading system: 9-point system: 9=A+, 8=A, 7=A-, 6=B+, 5=B, 4=B-, 3=C+, 2=C, 1=D, 0=F.
Clinical program required? No.
Clinical program description: Although it is not mandatory that students participate in any clinical programs, the following is a list of those we offer or recommend: Law 349—business law clinic: Students apply knowledge gained in earlier courses to assist small business owners in assessing their legal requirements; law 350—clinical law term: Provides students with the opportunity to integrate legal theory, legal skills, and public service in a community law office; law 353—environmental law centre clinic: Students study theory, conduct research projects, and engage in public interest environmental lawyering.
Legal writing course requirement? Yes.
Legal writing description: Law 110—legal research and writing. This 8-month course acquaints first-year students with the variety of materials in the law library and provides a knowledge of basic legal research techniques. Through a variety of written assignments, students become familiar with accepted principles pertaining to proper citation in legal writing and develop a degree of proficiency in legal writing and research.
Legal methods course requirement? Yes.
Legal methods description: Law 104—The Law, Legislation, and Policy is an 8-month course during first year that considers the development and interpretation of legislation.
Legal research course requirement? Yes.
Legal research description: Part of the law 110 as listed above under the legal writing course requirement.
Moot court requirement? Yes.
Moot court description: All students in first year must complete a moot court exercise as part of the legal research and writing course. In upper years, there are optional competitive mooting programs that students can take part in for course credit.
Public interest law requirement? No.
Academic journals: *APPEAL: Review of Current Law and Law Reform.*

ADMISSIONS INFORMATION

ADMISSIONS SELECTIVITY RATING: 97
Application fee: $50
Regular application deadline: 2/1
Regular notification: 5/31
Early application program: No.
LSDAS accepted? No.
Average GPA: 3.90
Range of GPA: 3.5–4.0
Average LSAT: 164
Range of LSAT: 156–177
Transfer students accepted? Yes.
Evening division offered: No.
Part-time accepted: Yes.
Applicants also look at: University of British Columbia, University of Toronto.
Number of applications received: 1,184

Number of applicants accepted: 207
Number of acceptees attending: 105

RESEARCH FACILITIES

% of JD classrooms wired: 90

FINANCIAL FACTS

Annual tuition (resident): $5,649
Annual tuition (nonresident): $16,948
Room & board (on/off-campus): $9,700/$13,000
Books and supplies: $2,000
Financial aid application deadline: 6/20
Average grant: $2,500
Average loan: $10,000
% of aid that is merit-based: 40
Average total aid package: $1,500
Average debt: $23,000
Tuition per credit (resident): $341
Tuition per credit (nonresident): $962

INTERNATIONAL STUDENTS

TOEFL required for international students? Yes.
Minimum Paper TOEFL: 600
Minimum Computer-based TOEFL: 250

EMPLOYMENT INFORMATION

Rate of placement: 84
Employers who frequently hire grads: Local, provincial, and national law firms; federal and provincial government; judicial clerkships; and non-profit organizations.
Grads employed by field: Government, 5%; judicial clerkships, 8%; private practice, 67%; public interest, 3%.

THE UNIVERSITY OF WESTERN ONTARIO

The University of Western Ontario Faculty of Law

Administrative Wing, Faculty of Law London, ON N5X 3T5 Canada
***Admissions Phone:** 519-661-3347 • **Admissions Fax:** 519-661-2063*
***Admissions E-mail:** lawapp@uwo.ca • **Web Address:** www.law.uwo.ca*

INSTITUTIONAL INFORMATION

Public/private: public
Student/faculty ratio: 7:1
Total faculty: 64
% Part-time: 49
% Female: 43

STUDENTS

Enrollment of law school: 165
Average age of entering class: 25

ACADEMICS

Academic specializations: Criminal law, intellectual property law, taxation.
Advanced degrees offered: LLB (3 years); LLM (1 year-research based).
Combined degrees offered: HBA/LLB; BESc/LLB (4 degree programs in engineering); BSc (computer science)/LLB; honors BA (history)/LLB; BA (kin)/LLB; honors BA (MIT)/LLB; honors BA (political science)/LLB; LLB/MBA; PhD philosophy.
Grading system: Students are graded by letter grade: A+ excellent 90–100%, A excellent 85–89%, A- excellent 80–84%, B+ good 77–79%, B good 73–76%, B- good 70–72%, C+ competent 67–69%, C competent 63–66%, C- competent 60–62%, D marginal pass 50–59%.
Clinical program required? No.
Clinical program description: Litigation practice, advanced litigation practice, arbitration law & procedure, case studies in business law, clinic in criminal law practice, criminal law advocacy, family law practice and procedure, community legal services clinic, western business law clinic, the sport solution, the dispute resolution center.
Legal writing course requirement? Yes.
Legal writing description: As part of the first-year course: Legal research writing & advocacy.
Legal methods course requirement? Yes.
Legal methods description: As part of the first-year course: Legal research writing & advocacy.
Legal research course requirement? Yes.
Legal research description: As part of the first-year course: Legal research writing & advocacy. Upper-year elective: Advanced legal research (offered in fall term and in spring term).
Moot court requirement? Yes.
Moot court description: As part of the first-year small-group program, students are required to participate in a moot in the fall term. Upper-year students can participate in a voluntary moot court program, the winners of which are invited to participate in external moot competitions.
Public interest law requirement? No.
Academic journals: *The Canadian Journal of Law & Jurisprudence.*

ADMISSIONS INFORMATION

ADMISSIONS SELECTIVITY RATING: 60*
Application fee: $75
Regular application deadline: 11/1
Early application program: No.
LSDAS accepted? No.
Average GPA: 3.70
Transfer students accepted? Yes.
Evening division offered: No.
Part-time accepted: Yes.
Number of applications received: 2,360

RESEARCH FACILITIES

Research resources available: Information technology services
% of JD classrooms wired: 100

FINANCIAL FACTS

Annual tuition (resident): $9,750
Books and supplies: $1,300
Financial aid application deadline: 4/1

INTERNATIONAL STUDENTS

TOEFL required for international students? Yes.

EMPLOYMENT INFORMATION

Rate of placement: 96
Average starting salary: $50,000
Grads employed by field: Business/industry, 8%; government, 5%; judicial clerkships, 2%; other, 15%; private practice, 70%.

University of Windsor

University of Windsor, Faculty of Law

Faculty of Law, 401 Sunset, Windsor, ON N9B 3P4 Canada
Admissions Phone: *519-253-3000* • ***Admissions Fax:*** *519-973-7064*
Admissions E-mail: *lawadmit@uwindsor.ca*
Web Address: *www.uwindsor.ca/law*

INSTITUTIONAL INFORMATION

Public/private: public
Student/faculty ratio: 22:1

STUDENTS

Enrollment of law school: 516
% Male/female: 40/60
% Full-time: 98
Average age of entering class: 26

ACADEMICS

Academic specializations: Civil procedure, commercial law, constitutional law, corporation securities law, criminal law, environmental law, human rights law, intellectual property law, international law, labor law, legal history, legal philosophy, property, taxation, intellectual property.
Combined degrees offered: MBA/LLB–3 to 4 years; JD/LLB–3 years.
Grading system: 13 point.
Clinical program required? No.
Clinical program description: Legal assistance of Windsor, community legal aid, University of Windsor mediation service, probono students of Canada.
Legal writing course requirement? Yes.
Legal writing description: One academic year (law I) a series of assignments, culminating in the moot court.
Legal methods course requirement? Yes.
Legal methods description: Part of the legal research and writing course, see "legal writing" above.
Legal research course requirement? Yes.
Legal research description: Part of the legal resesarch and writing course, see "legal writing" above.
Moot court requirement? Yes.
Moot court description: Required component of the legal research and writing course in law I.
Public interest law requirement? No.
Academic journals: *Windsor Review of Legal and Social Issues.*

ADMISSIONS INFORMATION

ADMISSIONS SELECTIVITY RATING: 60*
Application fee: $50
Regular application deadline: 1/11
Regular notification: Rolling.
Early application program: No.
LSDAS accepted? No.
Transfer students accepted? Yes.
Evening division offered: No.
Part-time accepted: Yes.
Number of applications received: 1,828
Number of acceptees attending: 147

RESEARCH FACILITIES

% of JD classrooms wired: 50
School-supported research centers: CARC (Canadian-American research centre for law and policy), IPLI (intellectual property law institute), and JD/LLB program with with University of Detroit Mercy Law School.

FINANCIAL FACTS

Annual tuition (resident): $9,268
Annual tuition (nonresident): $14,053
Room & board (on-campus): $4,218
Books and supplies: $1,315
Average grant: $750
Average loan: $9,350
% of aid that is merit-based: 60

INTERNATIONAL STUDENTS

TOEFL required for international students? No.

EMPLOYMENT INFORMATION

Rate of placement: 98
Employers who frequently hire grads: Law firms.
State for bar exam: ON, AB, BC, NS, NF
Pass rate for first-time bar: 99
Grads employed by field: Business/industry, 1%; government, 28%; judicial clerkships, 1%; private practice, 70%.

York University

Osgoode Hall Law School

4700 Keele Street, Toronto, ON M3J 1P3 Canada
Admissions Phone: *416-736-5712* • ***Admissions Fax:*** *416-736-5618*
Admissions E-mail: *admissions@osgoode.yorku.ca*
Web Address: *www.osgoode.yorku.ca*

INSTITUTIONAL INFORMATION

Public/private: public
Student/faculty ratio: 8:1
Total faculty: 134
% Part-time: 40
% Female: 40

STUDENTS

Enrollment of law school: 954
% Male/female: 48/52
% Full-time: 100
% Minority: 30
Average age of entering class: 24

ACADEMICS

Academic specializations: International law, taxation, litigation.
Advanced degrees offered: LLM; D Jur.
Combined degrees offered: JD(NYU)/LLB–4 years; LLB/MBA–4 years; LLB/MES–4 years.
Grading system: A+, A, B+, B, C+, C, D+, D, F, allowed (See handbook at: www.osgoode.yorku.ca).
Clinical program required? No.

Clinical program description: Immigration and refugee, business (small business intensive and mergers & acquisitions intensive), criminal, aboriginal, poverty law (Parkdale and CLASP-2 legal aid clinics), innocence project.
Legal writing course requirement? Yes.
Legal writing description: Mandatory course, year-long assessment. Case comments, memos, and factum.
Legal methods course requirement? No.
Legal research course requirement? Yes.
Legal research description: Combined with legal writing as above.
Moot court requirement? Yes.
Moot court description: All first-year students complete a moot as part of their legal research and writing course. In addition, both first- and upper-year students participate in Osgoode's excellent competitive mooting program.
Public interest law requirement? No.
Academic journals: *Osgoode Hall Law Journal.*

ADMISSIONS INFORMATION

ADMISSIONS SELECTIVITY RATING: 87
Application fee: $75
Regular application deadline: 11/1
Regular notification: Rolling.
Early application program: No.
LSDAS accepted? No.
Average GPA: 3.80
Average LSAT: 82
Transfer students accepted? Yes.
Evening division offered: No.
Part-time accepted: No.
Number of applications received: 2,418
Number of applicants accepted: 569
Number of acceptees attending: 298

RESEARCH FACILITIES

% of JD classrooms wired: 60
School-supported research centers: Center for public law & policy, institute for feminist legal studies, Nathanson center for the study of organized crime and corruption.

FINANCIAL FACTS

Annual tuition (resident): $12,000
Annual tuition (nonresident): $12,000
Room & board (on/off-campus): $10,000
Books and supplies: $1,300
Financial aid application deadline: 9/5
% receiving scholarships: 20
Average grant: $5,000
Average loan: $10,000
% of aid that is merit-based: 25
% receiving some sort of aid: 55
Average total aid package: $5,000

INTERNATIONAL STUDENTS

TOEFL required for international students? Yes.
Minimum Computer-based TOEFL: 250

EMPLOYMENT INFORMATION

Rate of placement: 92
Average starting salary: $45,000
Employers who frequently hire grads: Toronto: Aird & Berlis LLP; Baker & McKenzie; Bennet Jones LLP; Bereskin & Parr; Blake, Cassels, & Graydon LLP; Borden, Ladner, Gervais LLP; Cassels, Brock, & Blackwell LLP; Davies, Ward, Phillips, & Vineberg LLP; Davis & Company; department of justice, Ontario.
State for bar exam: ON
Pass rate for first-time bar: 98
Grads employed by field: Academic, 1%; business/industry, 3%; government, 9%; judicial clerkships, 5%; other, 3%; private practice, 77%; public interest, 2%.

Contact Listings for Additional Canadian Law Schools

Carleton University

Department of Law

C473 Loeb
1125 Colonel By Drive,
Ottawa, On K1S 5B6, Canada
Admissions Phone: *(613) 520-3690* • ***Admissions Fax:*** *(613) 520-4467*
Admissions E-mail: *law@carleton.ca*

Laurentian University

Department of Law and Justice

Dr. Charlotte Neff, Chair
935 Ramsey Lake Road, Arts Building, Room A-308
Sudbury, On P3E 2C6, Canada
Admissions Phone: *(705) 675-1151* • ***Admissions Fax:*** *(705) 675-4823*
Admissions E-mail: *cneff@laurentian.ca*

Université du Québec à Montréal

Faculte de science politique et de droit, Claudette Jodoin, Registrariat
870, boulevard de Maisonneuve Est, Bureau T-3600,
Case postale 6190, succursale Centre-Ville
Montréal, QC H3C 4N6, Canada
Admissions Phone: *(514) 987-3132* • ***Admissions Fax:*** *(514) 987-8932*
Admissions E-mail: *admission@uqam.ca*

Université Laval

Faculté de droit Université Laval

Céline Cyr, Conseillère à la gestion des études
Bureau du registraire, Pavillon Jean-Charles-Bonenfant
Pavillon Charles-De Koninck, QC GIK 7P4, Canada
Admissions Phone: *(418) 656-3080* • ***Admissions Fax:*** *(418) 656-5216*
Admissions E-mail: *info@vrdri.ulaval.ca*

Université de Moncton

Universite' de Moncton Facute' de droit

Lise Briard, Adjointe administrative et agente de recrutement
Faculte' de droit, Universite' de Moncton
Moncton, NB E1A 3E9, Canada
Admissions Phone: *506-858-4564* • ***Admissions Fax:*** *506-858-4534*
Admissions E-mail: *edr@umoncton.ca*

University of Alberta

University of Alberta Faculty of Law

Diane Mirth, Director of Admissions
University of Alberta, Law Centre
Edmonton, AB T6G 2H5, Canada
Admissions Phone: *(780) 492-3115* • ***Admissions Fax:*** *(780) 492-4924*
Admissions E-mail: *dmirth@law.ualberta.ca*

University of Manitoba

University of Manitoba Faculty of Law

Marcy Hayward covering for Jody Dewbury
Junior Admissions Officer for Law School
424 University Centre, Winnipeg, MB R3T 2N2, Canada
Admissions Phone: *204-474-8808* • ***Admissions Fax:*** *204-474-7554*
Admissions E-mail: *admissions@umanitoba.ca*

University of Ottawa

University of Ottawa Faculty of Law

Geneviève Hogan-Rancourt, Admission Officer, Fauteux Hall, room 237
P.O. Box 450, Stn. A, 57 Louis Pasteur St.
Ottawa, ON K1N 6N5, Canada
Admissions Phone: *(613) 562-5800 x3288* • ***Admissions Fax:*** *(613) 562-5124*
Admissions E-mail: *ghogan@uottawa.ca*

University of Victoria Faculty of Law (Akitsiraq)

Akitsiraq Law School

Shelley Wright, Northern Director, Akitsiraq Law School Program
PO Box 2292, Iqaluit, NU X0A 0H0, Canada
Admissions Phone: *(250) 721-8151* • ***Admissions Fax:*** *(250) 721-6390*
Admissions E-mail: *lawadmss@uvic.ca*

School Says

In this section you'll find schools with extended listings describing admissions, curriculum, internships, and much more. This is your chance to get in-depth information on programs that interest you. The Princeton Review charges each school a small fee to be listed, and the editorial responsibility is solely that of the university.

CALIFORNIA WESTERN SCHOOL OF LAW

AT A GLANCE

California Western School of Law offers JD and LLM degrees. Founded in 1924, the school is fully accredited by the American Bar Association and is a member of the Association of American Law Schools. The school focuses on educating creative, versatile graduates with a wide perspective on today's complex legal challenges.

CAMPUS & LOCATION

California Western is located in downtown San Diego, California's second largest city. The campus is close to the metropolitan region's courthouses, leading law firms and government agencies. The school is also a convenient distance to more than 70 miles of beaches, Balboa Park and its world-famous San Diego Zoo, the Gaslamp District with its vibrant nightlife and restaurants, as well as a wide variety of residential neighborhoods.

DEGREES OFFERED

California Western has full-time and part-time day programs for students seeking a JD degree.

The JD program offers areas of concentration that provide a rigorous and thorough academic experience in the following six fields: Child, family & elder law; creative problem solving; criminal justice; intellectual property, telecommunications and technology regulation; international law; and labor & employment law. California Western offers JD/PhD dual degrees in political science and history in conjunction with the University of California, San Diego, and JD/MSW and JD/MBA dual degrees with San Diego State University.

The school also offers two graduate legal degrees. The LLM in trial advocacy specializing in Federal criminal law combines classroom instruction, advocacy skills training, and real-world practice experience in a federal defender office. The master of laws in comparative law (LLM)/master of comparative law (MCL) program is designed to introduce foreign attorneys to a basic working knowledge of the U.S. legal system and the practice of law in the United States.

CENTERS & INSTITUTES

California Western is home to several innovative legal centers and institutes that allow students to become actively involved in today's key legal issues.

The Institute for Criminal Defense Advocacy, founded in 1991, operates the Trial Skills Academy, the California Innocence Project, the California Sentencing Project, the LLM in trial advocacy in Federal criminal law, and the street law program for inner-city high school students.

The California Innocence Project is a law school clinical program that is nationally renowned for successfully freeing wrongfully-convicted inmates. California Western professors and students spend countless hours reinvestigating cases and filing briefs on behalf of inmates who maintain their innocence. By uncovering new evidence—including false eye-witness identifications and unreliable trial testimony in several cases—the California Innocence Project has helped secure the release of inmates who served a combined 56 years in prison for crimes they did not commit.

The Center for Creative Problem Solving develops curriculum, research, and projects to educate students and lawyers in methods for preventing problems where possible, and creatively solving legal problems that do exist. The center focuses both on using the traditional analytical process more creatively and on using nontraditional problem solving processes, drawn from business, psychology, economics, neuroscience, and sociology among others.

The Institute of Health Law Studies, founded at California Western in 2004, focuses on expanding understanding of law and policy in the medical and legal fields. IHLS performs research, participates in advocacy activities, engages in community service, and provides education to advance its mission of "Improving health care today…for all our tomorrows."

FACILITIES

The school's campus includes a state-of-the-art library dedicated in 2000. The library holds more than 297,000 volumes, approximately 3,870 serial subscriptions, microforms currently equivalent to 137,000 volumes, audio and video tapes, computer software, and interactive videos. The library also offers an excellent computer lab.

Classes are held in an elegant, historic building at 350 Cedar Street in downtown San Diego. The building is a San Diego landmark that has been refurbished and updated. It houses the California Western's Gafford Moot Courtroom, offices for the school's numerous student organizations, a modern student lounge and study area, and other facilities.

FINANCIAL AID

California Western facilitates students' ability to finance their education through a comprehensive financial aid program, including loans, and work-study opportunities. Eighty-nine percent of the students at California Western borrow funds to help meet academic expenses. A number of merit-based scholarships are also available and are administered through admissions and academic departments.

FACULTY

California Western has 43 full-time faculty members who are complemented by adjunct professors teaching courses for specific interests. The school places great emphasis on maintaining a collegial environment that promotes easy access to professors. Faculty members are widely published and actively research in the following areas: Advocacy and dispute resolution, constitutional/civil rights law, corporate law, criminal law, family law, international law/comparative law, Internet law, real estate law, sexual discrimination/harassment, and other special areas.

STUDENTS

California Western's student body includes approximately 900 students from diverse cultural, ethnic, and religious backgrounds, work experiences, and age groups. The school has more than 30 student organizations. The Office of Student and Diversity Services offers a wide range of services to students with the goal of promoting a healthy and productive law school community.

ADMISSIONS

While the admissions process is highly competitive, all applications are thoroughly reviewed and considered. Early application is encouraged. The school has rolling admissions and acceptance may be more competitive for applicants whose files are received closer to the application deadline. The application deadline for August enrollment is April 1 for new students and July 15 for transfer students. Application deadline for the January class is November 1 for new students and November 15 for transfer and visiting students.

CAREER SERVICES & PLACEMENT

The Career Services department works aggressively to provide assistance for all students and alumni. The office facilitates access to law firms, public interest organizations, and government agencies for students seeking summer associate, law clerk, and attorney positions. While many graduates choose to stay in Southern California, the office receives job listings from firms and agencies throughout the country. Many of the job listings come from California Western's impressive network of alumni residing in all 50 states and 11 foreign countries.

CHAPMAN UNIVERSITY

School of Law

AT A GLANCE

Chapman Law, housed in the beautifully appointed $30 million Donald P. Kennedy Hall, is far from the world of dusty books and time-worn halls. The Law School marries the ethical heritage of our profession with the cutting-edge technology of the twenty-first century. Our administration and faculty are dedicated to providing each student with the most advanced educational programs, the latest technologies, and the most extensive resources possible. You will discover a rigorous curriculum of required and elective course work taught by an accomplished and experienced faculty. Programs of study include: Juris doctor certificate programs: tax law environmental, land use, and real estate law advocacy and dispute resolution; joint JD/MBA with Chapman's George L. Argyros School of Business; LLM program in taxation; clinical programs in tax law, elder law, constitutional litigation, and appellate practice.

CAMPUS & LOCATION

The Chapman University School of Law is the only law school in Orange County located on a university campus. The campus setting presents many opportunities to develop interdisciplinary courses and degree programs with other schools of the university. The site was once part of the fabled Rancho Santiago de Santa Ana, a huge tract granted by the Mexican government in 1810. A prominent Los Angeles lawyer, Alfred Beck Chapman, and his law partner, Andrew Glassell, acquired a large portion of the ranch in 1868 and laid out the town that today is called Orange. In 1872, Mr. Chapman donated to the town the land on which the new law building is located.

DEGREES OFFERED

Chapman University School of Law offers the traditional Juris doctor, the LLM degree in taxation law, and a dual JD/MBA degree.

PROGRAMS & CURRICULUM

The Law School requires 88 academic credits for graduation. First-year courses are required and cover traditional subjects: contracts, torts, civil procedure, property, criminal law, and legal research and writing. Several upper-level courses are also required in the following areas: constitutional law, corporations, evidence, federal income taxation, and professional responsibility. Students may choose to focus their electives in one of three certificate areas: taxation, environmental/real estate/land use, or advocacy and dispute resolution. Clinic offerings include courses in appellate practice, elder law, constitutional litigation, and tax law.

FACILITIES

Kennedy Hall, home to the law school, was completed in June 1999. Rising four stories, the structure offers an efficient and pleasant learning environment for students. Classrooms and seminar rooms are equipped with state-of-the-art technology for enhanced teaching and learning and are capable of accommodating future changes in electronic, visual, and on-site learning. The library occupies one wing of the building. Two courtrooms, one designed for trials and the other for appellate hearings, provide fully equipped facilities for trial advocacy exercises, mock trial and moot court competitions, and formal hearings by visiting courts. Student lounges and facilities for student organizations and publications ensure that the law school experience at Chapman will be both productive and pleasant.

FACULTY

Chapman Law School has assembled an impressive array of faculty (including three former U.S. Supreme Court clerks) who are excellent teachers, accomplished scholars and outstanding mentors to students. The 2004 student/faculty ratio was 18:1. Students have easy access to the faculty and frequent opportunities to engage them in both formal and informal settings. Students are organized into small first-year sections of 60 to 65 students each.

STUDENTS

Chapman University School of Law is an ideal environment for learning. The total student body of the Law School numbers about 500. We anticipate approximately 185 students for the 2005 entering class. The first-year students will be divided into three tracks of 60–65 students each. They will be further divided into considerably smaller sections of 12 to 15 students for the legal research and writing component. For the past two years, the minority representation of the entering class has been 33 percent. The average age has been in the mid-twenties for the same time period. With respect to geographic representation, 10 to 15 percent of the 2004 entering class was from states other than California.

ADMISSIONS

Chapman University School of Law has a rolling admissions policy and generally accepts applications until the class is full, typically in May or early June of each year. The admissions process is highly competitive with over 2,500 applications for only 185 seats in the entering class. Applicants are required to submit a formal application, a personal statement, a resume, two letters of recommendation, a $60 nonrefundable application fee, and the LSDAS report from the Law School Admission Council (LSAC). The LSDAS report generally includes your LSAT score(s), official transcript(s), and letters of recommendation. Applicants should be advised that the law school averages LSAT scores and does not accept LSAT scores before February 2001 for the 2005 entering class.

SPECIAL PROGRAMS

In addition to its three certificate programs and its clinical and externship programs, Chapman Law School offers a special JD/MBA joint degree opportunity. This program affords students the ability to obtain two separate, accredited professional degrees in a shorter period than would normally be required to obtain the degrees independently. The adequately-prepared student may obtain both degrees in four years rather than the typical five years. Chapman's George L. Argyros School of Business and Economics is AACSB accredited. Chapman Law School also offers a master of laws in taxation (LLM), and students in the JD program who are well prepared in the taxation area are permitted with permission to take courses otherwise open only to LLM students.

CAREER SERVICES & PLACEMENT

Chapman Law students successfully find satisfying employment with the assistance of the professionals in the Career Services Office. The office strives to provide Chapman students with the necessary skills to navigate the legal job market and to market the law school and its students to legal employers. The office provides a host of programs designed to teach students job searching skills, educate students about their career options, and provide students with an opportunity to meet with potential employers.

COLUMBIA UNIVERSITY

AT A GLANCE

Columbia Law School is distinguished, perhaps uniquely among leading U.S. law schools, as an international center of legal education that stimulates its students to consider the full dimensions of the possibility of the law—as an intellectual pursuit, as a career, and as an instrument of human progress. The character of academic and social life at Columbia is fiercely democratic, dynamic, creative, and innovative. The law school is especially committed to educating students of differing perspectives, from diverse backgrounds, and with varied life experiences.

Professional prospects for Columbia law graduates are quite extraordinary. Our graduates proceed to productive careers in every conceivable arena of private practice. But, it should be emphasized that while Columbia-trained attorneys are especially well-regarded for their work in corporate law and finance, an unusually high number also serve as state and federal judges, prosecutors, civil and human rights advocates, legal scholars, public defenders, entrepreneurs, business executives, elected government officials, and national and international leaders. Many Columbia law alumni/ae contribute significantly to the shaping of U.S. culture at large. Currently our graduates serve in leadership roles across the fields of art, music, film, publishing, science, professional athletics, philanthropy, and higher education.

CAMPUS & LOCATION

Columbia law school recently completed a $133 million physical expansion and renewal project, ensuring that our facilities are among the finest of any law school in the country. Our main building, Greene Hall, has undergone significant expansion and improvement, devoted primarily to our students—a spacious new entrance and foyer, library renovations, and the creation of a student commons that includes a student lounge and café. New seminar rooms and state-of-the-art multimedia classrooms have also been designed to provide students with full Internet and other legal research access. Across the street from Greene Hall is William C. Warren Hall, home to the *Columbia Law Review,* Morningside Heights Legal Services (a law school clinic serving our community), and the Center for Public Interest Law.

William and June Warren Hall opened in 1999 and includes amphitheater-style classrooms equipped with modern teaching resources, a center for the law school's international programs, and conference facilities. It is also home for the center for student services, which includes the offices of admissions, financial aid, registration services, and the dean of students office. And Lenfest Hall, a gracious apartment complex for law students, opened in August 2003.

The renovation and expansion of the law school's facilities have greatly enhanced the quality of life and learning at Columbia. Students have a superb learning environment that is conducive to community building and social and intellectual engagement and reflects the changing nature of legal education in the twenty-first century.

FACILITIES

One of the largest and most comprehensive law collections in the world, Columbia's library is especially rich in U.S. law and legal history; international law; comparative law; Roman law; and the legal literature of the major European countries, China, and Japan. Access to the Internet and CD-ROMs provide additional resources with materials from Germany, South Africa, and a wide range of international organizations. In addition, the many libraries of the university, containing more than seven million volumes, are available to law students.

Research centers, special programs research centers, and special programs include: Kernochan Center for Law, Media, and the Arts; Silver Program in Law, Science, and Technology; Center for Law and Philosophy; Center for Law and Economic Studies; Center for the Study of Law and Culture; Rubin Program for Liberty and Equality through Law; Center for Public Interest Law; Public Interest Law Initiative in Transitional Societies; Human Rights Institute; Parker School of Foreign and Comparative Law; Center for Chinese Legal Studies; Center for Japanese Legal Studies; Center for Korean Legal Studies; European Legal Studies Center; the Legislative

Drafting Research Fund; and programs in alternative dispute resolution and in law and history.

Columbia has a special commitment to clinical education, which places the student in the role of a lawyer doing a lawyer's actual work under intensive faculty supervision. Some examples of clinical opportunities are lawyering in the digital age, law and the arts, nonprofit organizations, prisoners and families, child advocacy, mediation, environmental law, and human rights. Unique to Columbia is a summer program that places 60 to 70 students in civil rights and human rights internships in law firms and organizations throughout this country and around the world.

STUDENTS

Columbia continues to place among the handful of the most highly selective JD programs in our nation—as evaluated by the principal criteria used to measure admissions selectivity (application volume, acceptance rates, LSAT scores, and academic performance). Indeed, in recent years, the demand for a Columbia legal education has never been greater, and the academic credentials of our entering classes are stronger than ever. Columbia's JD student body is further distinguished by standing as one of the most culturally diverse among U.S. leading law schools. People who choose to study law at Columbia hail from the small towns, farms, and suburbs of the West, Midwest, and South; the industrial corridors and Ivy halls of the Northeast; the inner cities of every major U.S. metropolis; and the international centers of Europe, Asia, Africa, and Latin America.

Each entering class reflects the broad range of economic, ethnic, and cultural backgrounds found in the United States. And from around the world, we welcome students who will enrich learning at Columbia and thereafter advance the developing legal cultures of their homelands.

With the largest number and percentage of international students in its JD program of any leading law school; with the highest percentage of students of color; with its students hailing from 43 states, 44 foreign countries, and more than 230 different colleges and universities; and with approximately 15 percent of its JD students having earned at least one graduate or professional degree before studying law, Columbia's student body abounds with a diversity of life experiences, cultural backgrounds, and intellectual perspectives.

ADMISSIONS

Columbia University School of Law

435 West 116th Street

New York, NY 10027

Telephone: 212-854-2670

Fax: 212-854-1109

E-mail: admissions@law.columbia.edu

Website: www.law.columbia.edu.

DUKE UNIVERSITY

AT A GLANCE

Duke Law School offers a rigorous legal education in an environment well known for being exceptionally collegial and collaborative. Our faculty is composed of top scholars who engage with students in and out of the classroom, and involve them in their research and pro bono activities. First-rate interdisciplinary centers at Duke in the areas of national security, public law, intellectual property, environmental law, international law, and business law generate an especially rich array of academic conferences, speakers, special events, student-run symposia, and specialized courses.

CAMPUS AND LOCATION

Duke University is a magnificent campus, sitting amid hundreds of forested acres in Durham, North Carolina. A diverse and dynamic city of more than 200,000 residents ranked among the best places to live in the U.S., Durham is close to Raleigh and Chapel Hill, as well as Research Triangle Park, one of the world's largest planned centers for high-tech research and development. The area enjoys a moderate climate, year-round outdoor recreation, accessible and affordable housing, and a stimulating array of cultural, intellectual, and athletic events, both on and off campus.

ACADEMIC PROGRAMS

Nearly 25 percent of Duke JD students enroll in a joint-degree program. By starting in the summer, students in three years can earn both a JD and an LLM degree in international and comparative law, or an MA in English, public policy, cultural anthropology, economics, political science, history, and a number of other disciplines. The law school also offers four-year professional joint-degree programs that combine the JD with an MBA, an MEM (masters in environmental management), or an MPP (masters in public policy), as well as a joint JD/MD program and several JD/PhD programs. Duke also offers a one-year LLM program in American law for students who have earned law degrees in other countries.

FACULTY

The Duke faculty is among the strongest in the nation. It includes leading scholars in constitutional law, international law, business law, tax, and a number of other areas. No school has a stronger faculty or presence in the field of national security law, nor a better cluster of faculty in fields related to science, technology, and innovation, including intellectual property, health, telecommunications, environmental law, and biotechnology.

Interdisciplinary connections across Duke University enrich teaching and research in the Law School, through such programs as the Center for the Study of the Public Domain; the Program in Public Law; the Center on Law, Ethics, and National Security; the Duke Center for Environmental Solutions; the Center for Genome Ethics, Law, & Policy; and the Duke Global Capital Markets Center. Through their conferences and sponsorship of visits from leading thinkers and innovators, these programs and centers contribute enormously to the intellectual life of the law school and to the quality of legal education afforded to students.

STUDENTS

Duke Law students have extraordinarily diverse backgrounds and experiences. Almost all students come to Duke from other locations, and thus tend to seek a strong community in which they can study and grow intellectually and socially for three years. Students are encouraged to take on leadership roles, and are given many opportunities to reinforce the skills characteristic of the best lawyers, such as teamwork, collaboration, and effective communication.

Students at Duke volunteer for an impressive range of pro bono activities, chosen from hundreds of public service projects in the area. They also participate in dozens of student organizations with a broad range of intellectual and social interests, such as the intellectual property and cyberlaw society, the business law society, the sports and entertainment law society, the women law students association, and the Black law students association. Many students take part in cultural and recreational activities such as the drama society, international week, and the popular student-faculty bowling league. Duke has eight student-run law journals.

SPECIAL PROGRAMS

Duke Law School maintains one of the highest quality clinical education programs in the country. Current clinics include the AIDS Legal Assistance Project, Children's Education Law Clinic, Community Enterprise Clinic, Poverty Law Clinic, Low-Income Taxpayer Clinic, and Animal Law Clinic. In addition, through a Wrongful Convictions seminar and Duke Law School's Innocence Project, students pursue plausible claims of actual innocence by convicted felons.

FACILITIES

Duke Law is nearing completion of an ambitious construction project that is transforming the look and functionality of the school's physical facility. All classrooms are new or recently renovated state-of-the-art teaching environments, and a recently completed wing provides full floors for clinics and law journals.

In 2005, Duke Law topped *The National Jurist's* "Technology Honor Roll;" students can access the Internet in the library, classrooms, courtyard, and most other areas through a university-wide wireless network. Cutting-edge educational technologies enhance teaching and coursework through several unique multi-media projects developed by Duke Law faculty.

CAREER SERVICES

Duke graduates have an extraordinary range of employment opportunities in private practice, judicial clerkships, government service, academic teaching, and public interest organizations. Each year, hundreds of employers from across the country come to campus to participate in an extensive on-campus recruiting program for summer and permanent employment. The Office of Career Services also offers extensive programming throughout all three years, to ensure that students are familiar with the broad range of career opportunities available to them. Duke graduates are highly sought after by employers, and take positions in every major legal market nationally and internationally.

ADMISSIONS

In addition to top grades and LSAT scores, candidates admitted to Duke have demonstrated abilities in other areas such as leadership, community involvement, and intellectual engagement that add to the strength of the School in myriad ways.

EXPENSES AND FINANCIAL AID

Basic tuition at Duke Law School in academic year 2005–2006 is $35,868. Living expenses at Duke are considerably lower than at most other top schools, and 73 percent of students receive some scholarship aid. The Mordecai scholars program offers full or substantial tuition to a carefully selected group of scholars with both a strong academic background and success as leaders. A special program assists students with heavy debt to pursue public interest employment upon graduation.

GOLDEN GATE UNIVERSITY
School of Law

AT A GLANCE
Founded in 1901, Golden Gate University School of Law has developed a reputation for providing a strong balance of theory and practical education. Golden Gate University School of Law is an urban law school that draws on the dynamic environment of the legal/business district of San Francisco.

Students who enter in the fall may attend a full-time day program or a part-time evening program. Full-time students may also begin their studies in January through the midyear admission program. The 1,000 students at the school of law include working professionals and recent college graduates from more than 100 undergraduate and graduate institutions. They come from across the United States and from a number of other nations, and represent a wide spectrum of ethnic, economic, and cultural backgrounds.

CAMPUS & LOCATION
Golden Gate University School of Law is located in the heart of downtown San Francisco, gateway to the Pacific Rim and one of the most beautiful cities in the world. Situated in the middle of the legal and financial districts, Golden Gate University is a short walk from law offices, the business center, and courts. The school is accessible by all forms of public transportation—local San Francisco bus and streetcar traffic, Bay Area Rapid Transit (BART), and buses that travel throughout the Bay Area.

DEGREES OFFERED
The School of Law offers the JD degree, as well as two combined degrees: the JD/MBA with Golden Gate University and the JD/PhD in clinical psychology through the Pacific Graduate School of Psychology.

Golden Gate University School of Law is a center for graduate legal education. People who have earned a law degree can enroll in any of our five LLM (masters of law) programs: environmental law, intellectual property law, international legal studies, taxation, and U.S. legal studies. The school of law also offers a doctorate (SJD) in international legal studies.

PROGRAMS & CURRICULUM
Golden Gate has one of the most extensive clinical programs in the country, offering students excellent opportunities to experience hands-on, practical legal training. Students can participate in three on-site clinics: the Women's Employment Rights Clinic, the Environmental Law and Justice Clinic, and the Innocence Project. Ten field-placement clinics also provide practical experience for students.

SPECIAL PROGRAMS
In addition to the standard JD program, Golden Gate University offers the unique honors lawyering program. In this innovative honors program, students combine classroom learning with the practical experience of full-time apprenticeships in law offices.

EXPENSES & FINANCIAL AID
Golden Gate University School of Law has a full range of programs to help students who need financial assistance. The Admissions and Financial Aid Office provides budget and debt management counseling, evaluates students' financial needs, and determines financial aid awards. Tuition for the 2005–2006 year is $970 per unit. For more information on fees and expenses, see our website at www.ggu.edu.

To attract a highly qualified student body, the School of Law awards to entering students a number of full-tuition and partial-tuition scholarships based solely on academic merit. Criteria include past academic achievement and LSAT results.

FACULTY
Students at Golden Gate University School of Law are taught by an accomplished, diverse faculty who practiced law before teaching. They are experts in a wide range of legal areas—from litigation to labor law, corporate law to criminal law, property development to public interest, environmental law to entertainment law, international law to intellectual property law—and much more. The school of law has 45 full-time faculty members and more than 100 adjunct faculty members.

STUDENTS
The approximately 1,000 students at Golden Gate University School of Law reflect a wide variety of ages; work experience; and cultural, ethnic, and religious backgrounds. Our student population includes students fresh out of undergraduate programs, students with advance degrees, and students returning to school after years in the work force. More than 20 student organizations address the many interests of our diverse student population.

ADMISSIONS
Contact: Assistant Dean for Admissions and Financial Aid

536 Mission Street

San Francisco, CA 94105-2968

Admissions telephone: 415-442-6630 or 800-GGU-4YOU

Admissions fax: 415-442-6631

Admissions E-mail: lawadmit@ggu.edu

Website: www.ggu.edu/law

Application Deadlines: April 15 for fall full-time day program, June 2 for fall part-time evening program, November 15 for January midyear admission program (full-time only).

CAREER SERVICES & PLACEMENT
The Law Career Services Office (LCS) provides a wide variety of services, resources, and programs to guide students and graduates through the career planning process. Services for all first-year students include an online job search guide, workshops on resumes and cover letters, and visits to nearby law offices. Services for all JD and LLM students and graduates include print and online job listings, presentations by graduates on their career experiences, career counseling, job search skills workshops, resume and cover letter review, mock interviews with alumni working in various fields of the legal profession, recruitment programs, specialty area and regional job fairs, and more.

The average starting salary of recent graduates was $50,000, and they were employed as shown below. Private practice: 60 percent; business/industry: 12 percent; government: 11 percent; academic: 7 percent; judicial clerkships: 5 percent; public interest: 5 percent.

HAMLINE UNIVERSITY

School of Law

HAMLINE UNIVERSITY SCHOOL OF LAW

AT A GLANCE

Hamline University School of Law, founded in 1972, is accredited by the American Bar Association (ABA) and a member of the Association of American Law Schools (AALS). Hamline is located in the heart of the Twin Cities of Saint Paul and Minneapolis, noted as "one of the top 10 cities in the U.S." by Cityrating.com.

CAMPUS & LOCATION

Hamline Law School is located among 55 acres of wooded campus in the vibrant, urban centers of Minneapolis/St. Paul. The Twin Cities are home to many corporate headquarters, including 3M, Cargill, Medtronic, Target Corporation, and General Mills. Additionally, the Twin Cities are a center for diverse cultural, social, political and educational opportunities.

DEGREES OFFERED

Hamline Law School offers a full-time three year JD degree and a part-time, four year weekend program. An LLM degree for international lawyers is also offered.

Dual degrees are available in public administration, management, nonprofit management, organizational leadership, and library and information science.

PROGRAMS & CURRICULUM

Hamline's nationally ranked alternative dispute resolution (ADR) program provides a full range of ADR-related programming including a summer institute, January term courses, certificate programs, and a biannual symposium. A new Health Law Center will focus on the growth of health law, federal regulation, tort reform, medical device development and regulation, and ethics. The curriculum also supports 10 organized tracks of study or concentrations. These include: business representation, children and the law, civil dispute resolution, commercial law, criminal law, government and regulatory affairs, intellectual property, international law, labor and employment law, and social justice.

FACILITIES

Hamline Law School's architectural design encourages easy access to faculty and administrative offices. Wireless internet access is available throughout the building. The newly renovated moot courtroom is a technological showplace. Hamline's law library provides modern collections of print, electronic and microform resources. The library contains more than 266,000 volumes and numerous electronic databases. In addition, students have access to the libraries of seven other colleges and universities through a consortium arrangement. The library has a computer lab with 30 personal computers, wireless access, and numerous network ports.

EXPENSES & FINANCIAL AID

Hamline University School of Law is a private school. Full-time tuition for the 2005–2006 academic year is $25,245. Hamline offers merit based scholarships, diversity scholarships and endowed scholarships for first-year students.

FACULTY

Hamline Law School has 39 full-time faculty members: 18 women and 21 men. Adjunct faculty complement the faculty by teaching upper division courses in specialty areas. Hamline has recently invested in growing its faculty, with nationally recognized experts in bio-ethics, intellectual property, international trade, corporate law, and critical race theory. These faculty members join a faculty nationally recognized for scholarship and academic leadership in dispute resolution, commercial law, state constitutional law, and many other fields. The Hamline faculty is committed to an "open door" policy to help students learn and enjoy the law.

STUDENTS

Hamline Law School's student body includes approximately 720 students from diverse backgrounds. As a student-centered community, Hamline student organizations play a key role in the vitality of the Law School environment. More than 20 student organizations focus on students' cultural and professional interests.

ADMISSIONS

The admission selection process emphasizes a rigorous but fair examination of each person's application. In addition to the LSAT and undergraduate GPA, other factors are given significant weight including motivation, personal experiences, employment history, graduate education, maturity, letters of recommendation, and the ability to express one's interest in the study of law.

SPECIAL PROGRAMS

Hamline's nine clinics offer students the opportunity to develop litigation, transactional, and alternative dispute resolution skills. The Practicum Program combines 114 hours of field experience with a classroom component focused on enhancing a student's lawyering skills. Moot court and similar competitions involve legal research, brief writing, and oral argument. Hamline is home to three scholarly journals. Hamline law students staff the Hamline Law Review and the Hamline Journal of Public Law and Policy, and provide editorial assistance for The Journal of Law and Religion. Hamline Law School offers unique study abroad opportunities in Norway, Italy, France, Hungary, England, Israel and Puerto Rico.

CAREER SERVICES & PLACEMENT

The Career Services Office (CSO) provides informational programs, mock interviews, one-on-one counseling, networking opportunities, and an online job bank. It also hosts on-campus interviews for interested employers and works extensively with employers to market Hamline law students.

MASSACHUSETTS SCHOOL OF LAW AT ANDOVER

MISSION

The Massachusetts School of Law at Andover (MSL) offers a full Juris Doctorate degree. MSL's mission is to provide high quality, practical, affordable legal education to deserving persons who have been unfairly excluded from law schools. MSL seeks to give these persons access to the societal advancement that is available, in law and other fields, to people with legal degrees. To accomplish its mission, MSL serves persons from working class backgrounds, minorities, mid-life individuals who seek to change careers, and immigrants. MSL also serves middle class people who have increasingly been shut out of legal education. MSL gives individuals from all these groups a rigorous, useful and affordable legal education so that they can improve their lives and better serve their communities.

CAMPUS & LOCATION

The Massachusetts School of Law at Andover is located approximately 25 miles north of Boston.

THE LEADER IN REFORMING LEGAL EDUCATION

The many reforms MSL has pioneered include: admitting people on the basis of their entire life-record and their considered aspirations, instead of on the basis of LSAT scores; providing students with extensive training in the practical professional skills needed by practicing lawyers; enhancing practical education with intellectual theory by ensuring that sociological, economic, political, and other ideas underlying fields of law are specially discussed in every course; keeping law school costs down so that tuition can be kept low.

PROGRAMS & CURRICULUM

MSL offers both a full-time and part-time program. Students may attend day or evening, or may take a combination of day and evening classes. In addition to the general course of study, students may choose to concentrate their studies in a number of different areas including: Business & corporate law, civil litigation, communication, sports & entertainment law, environmental law, family law, criminal law, finance and asset management law, labor law, juvenile law litigation, land use and planning, intellectual property and real estate.

EXPENSES & FINANCIAL AID

MSL's tuition is only about 50 percent of the average tuition of other private law schools. Currently, the cost is $12,300 per year for full time students. Students pay $410 per credit. The school prides itself on only raising the tuition 4 times in its 17-year history. MSL students are eligible to participate in the Federal Stafford Loan Program.

ADMISSIONS

MSL has a rolling admission policy. The school matriculates incoming students both in the fall session, which begins in August, and the spring session, which begins in January. For the fall class, applications are received and reviewed through July and for the January class through December. All applicants are interviewed and give a written entrance exam on the day of the interview.

FACULTY

MSL incorporates practical and ethical training into its entire curriculum by using expert judges and lawyers. The schools entire faculty engages in some practice, as many medical professors do, in order to bring their practical knowledge to the classroom. In addition to the full time faculty, MSL employs 80 adjunct faculty members all teaching in their area of expertise.

CAREER SERVICES

In addition to the wealth of practical training students obtain through the regular curriculum, MSL offers both legal internships and Judicial Clerkship programs. The Career Services office also helps students with resume writing, organizing job searches and providing contacts for full time positions upon graduation.

SPECIAL PROGRAMS

MSL has entered into articulation agreements to offer students the ability to pursue both their Juris Doctorate degree and MBA simultaneously. MSL currently offers two JD/MBA programs with Nichols College and Fitchburg State College. In addition to the advanced degree options, MSL has 3+3 programs that allow eligible undergraduate students to begin law school after 3 years of undergraduate study. These programs allow students to save both time and money.

www.mslaw.edu

978-681-0800

NORTHERN ILLINOIS UNIVERSITY
College of Law

Northern Illinois University NIU LAW

AT A GLANCE
Established in 1978, NIU Law is a young and dynamic law school located in DeKalb, Illinois approximately 60 miles west of Chicago. Ranked as one of the most diverse law schools in the nation, NIU Law is a place where a diverse society is respected, valued, and also reflected in our student body and administration. NIU Law seeks to prepare its graduates not only for the traditional role of lawyers, but also for the tasks we can now only speculate will be assumed by the law-trained. With a commitment to public interest, NIU Law offers an unmatched value-driven education, affording student the freedom of professional choice without the fear of paralyzing debt loads. To learn more, visit us at http://law.niu.edu.

DEGREES OFFERED
NIU Law offers a full-time day program leading to the JD degree. Part-time study opportunities are available on a limited basis. Dual degree opportunities are available with several graduate-level programs including the master of business administration and master of public administration.

PROGRAMS & CURRICULUM
NIU Law offers its students a broad-based legal education through high quality academic programs taught by well-respected faculty. NIU Law provides practical skills training and a cooperative learning environment with personalized attention. During the summer, electives may be offered on the main campus or through NIU Law's summer abroad study program in France.

Through its practical skills courses and clinical and externship programs, NIU Law provides students with a variety of both theoretical and experiential educational opportunities. This "hands on" experience prepares students to meet the challenges encountered by today's advocate and allows them to competitively enter the legal profession immediately after graduation.

FACILITIES
NIU Law is housed in Swen Parson Hall, an impressive Gothic structure. The facilities promote a community atmosphere in which law faculty and students work and study in close proximity. The facilities feature the David C. Shapiro Memorial Law Library, which provides one of the best ratios of library resources to students.

In keeping with our commitment to providing students with the latest in technology-based learning, the Kenneth C. Chessick Legal Skills Training Center opened in 2004. The center features a deposition room, smart classroom, and high tech courtroom patterned after the Federal model. Designed to simulate the environment found in today's high tech courtroom, students experience the look and feel of a high tech setting and are able to hone their advocacy skills.

EXPENSES & FINANCIAL AID
NIU Law offers its students small class sizes and a quality legal education at an affordable cost. For the 2004–2005 academic year, in-state tuition is $8,346 and out-of-state is $16,692. Out-of-state residents can also qualify for in-state tuition in six months. Scholarships and grants are available for students from a variety of sources. After the first year of law school, students may also qualify for research assistantships.

FACULTY
Recently ranked third in the nation by Princeton Review as having the most diverse faculty, NIU Law faculty are dedicated to their students. Through combined scholarship, practice, and education experience, NIU Law faculty provide students with excellent classroom teaching and professional guidance. The faculty consists of 22 full-time instructors. All have a JD degree and 42 percent have advanced law degrees. Of all the faculty members, 5 percent are Asian/Pacific islander, 21 percent are African American, 11 percent are Hispanic, and 63 percent are Caucasian; 40 percent are women.

STUDENTS
Having approximately 300 students, NIU Law's student body come from universities located coast to coast and reflects a broad spectrum of ethnic, cultural, and geographical diversity. Approximately one-third of our student body is made up of minority students and one-half are female. Our low student-faculty ratio, which is approximately 14 to 1, facilitates a supportive environment with a lively exchange of ideas. The law school provides an atmosphere of shared goals and achievement and a genuine sense of community.

ADMISSIONS
NIU Law is a selective school with a small entering class size, ranging from 115 to 125 out of an applicant pool ranging from 1,200 to 1,600. Factors important for admission include the applicant's undergraduate record, LSAT score, reasons for seeking admission, school or community activities and accomplishments, and employment background. Applicants may submit their application either online or by paper form.

NORTHUMBRIA UNIVERSITY

Northumbria University School of Law

AT A GLANCE

The School of Law at Northumbria University is the largest law department in the north of England. It is renowned for providing excellent legal education and offers the most comprehensive portfolio of courses in the country at both undergraduate and postgraduate levels. The school is well known for its distinctive and innovative courses of study. The school maintains close links with the legal profession and has been validated by both the Law Society of England and Wales and the Bar Council for Legal Education to run postgraduate vocational training courses for prospective barristers and solicitors. In addition, the school is authorized by both the Law Society and the Bar Council to run the only exempting four-year LLB degree in the United Kingdom, a course exempting graduates from the need for further professional vocational training.

CAMPUS & LOCATION

Northumbria University City Campus

The City Campus is in the heart of the Newcastle upon Tyne city centre, only a couple of minutes walk from the main shopping areas and leisure facilities.

The largest of Northumbria's campuses, this is home for all courses in the School Law of Applied Sciences, Arts & Social Sciences, Built Environment, Design, Engineering, Law, Psychology & Sport Sciences, and Newcastle Business School. The City Campus contains the main university library, the students' union building, the language laboratory, the university gallery and the refurbished sports centre which, with its fully-equipped fitness suite, now offers some of the finest facilities of its kind among the country's universities.

Newcastle upon Tyne, in the Northeast of England, is a regional capital and is just two hours and forty minutes away from London by the fastest rail service, while Edinburgh (Scotland's capital) is only an hour away.

DEGREES OFFERED

For North American students we offer the LLB degree, a three-year undergraduate law degree. On successful completion of the degree graduates will have a degree fully recognized by the Law Society of England and Wales and the Bar Council as satisfying the 'academic stage' of a UK legal education.

This degree is also recognized by the New York Bar for the purposes of qualifying to practice in New York after successful completion of the New York State Bar Exam. Other U.S. states recognize the degree as partially satisfying their requirements to practice.

FACILITIES

The school of law offers a wealth of facilities to all students. Whether undertaking full-time, part-time or distance learning programs, the school of provides the kind of facilities that will enable any student to gain the most from their time at the university.

The school has three mock courtrooms, which enable the students to gain real-life exposure to what they can expect to experience in a courtroom scenario. In Sutherland Building, the home of the school of law, we offer IT facilities exclusively for use by law students. The law school has a specialist law library containing practitioner materials and areas for you to study. A greater selection of law books is available in the main university library.

EXPENSES & FINANCIAL AID

You will find that for our law degree, the overall cost of studying at Northumbria represents excellent value for money when compared to U.S. law schools.

The annual tuition fee for overseas students on this program is $13,000.

Northumbria University is currently registered with the U.S. Department of Education to receive federally funded students. Our OPE ID (Federal School Code) is 030295 00

In addition to tuition fees, students should allow enough funds to cover living expenses for the duration of studies. We estimate that the minimum amount required by a single student to cover basic living expenses (e.g. accommodation, heating, food) is between £430 and £530 per month. For a 9-month academic year, this amounts to between approximately £4,000 and £5,000.

FACULTY

The law school has approximately 80 lecturing staff, the vast majority of whom are full-time. They teach the whole range of academic and practitioner subjects including criminal law, constitutional law, tort, contract, property, trusts, business law, employment law, human rights law, medical law, and mental health law.

STUDENTS

At Northumbria University, we want our students to get the very best out of the years spent with us. We want them to look back on their period of study as one which was not only successful in academic terms, but rewarding on a personal and social level. To that end we have developed a comprehensive range of services designed to support students of all ages, nationalities and abilities both in and outside the lecture room. With so much in common we believe that for an American student to study law at Northumbria is a huge opportunity and we have taken steps to make it a reality. We offer you a unique opportunity to enroll on our law degree, study alongside English students, obtain an internationally recognized English legal qualification and then return to the U.S. and qualify as an American lawyer. Add to this the travel and cultural benefits attached to studying abroad and we think that we have created a winning combination for you.

ADMISSIONS

We accept applications on a rolling program. In practical terms the very latest we should receive your application is the end of July in the year that you want to commence your studies. This will permit your application to be processed and for you to make arrangements to come to the UK.

CAREER SERVICES & PLACEMENT

Current figures show that 90 percent of graduates from Northumbria enter employment or further study/training on completion of their studies. Supporting this success is the university's Careers Service, whose advisers are dedicated to helping students plan the next stage of their careers whether it be employment or a further period of study or training. Advisers are trained to offer guidance on choice of occupation and employer, and can assist with CVs, job applications and interview technique. Specialist facilities include psychometric assessment and mock interview practice.

PACE UNIVERSITY

Pace Law School

AT A GLANCE

Pace Law School, a division of Pace University, is fully accredited by the American Bar Association and is a member of the Association of American Law Schools. Known for an outstanding environmental program and excellent clinical opportunities, Pace also offers over 70 electives, more than those offered at most comparable law schools. The school offers an excellent student/faculty ratio (17:1), and over 60 percent of elective classes have less than 20 students enrolled.

CAMPUS & LOCATION

Dedicated entirely to Pace's legal program, the White Plains campus houses the Law School's academic facilities, student activities center, and residence hall. The Law School has recently expanded and now includes a new, state-of-the-art classroom building on its sprawling, 12-acre campus.

DEGREES OFFERED

Pace Law School offers the JD, JD/MBA, JD/MPA, a JD/MEM with Yale University, JD/MA with Bard College, JD/MS with Sarah Lawrence College, an LLM and SJD in environmental law, and an LLM in comparative legal studies.

PROGRAMS & CURRICULUM

The programs of the law school are national in perspective. They do not emphasize the law in any state and are based on the concept that rigorous standards and high-quality teaching can coexist with an atmosphere congenial to learning and enjoyment. Students can obtain certificates in environmental law, international law, and health law by completing a sequence of courses with a specified GPA in the applicable area. Pace offers the opportunity to pursue studies on both a full-time, and part-time basis.

FACILITIES

Pace Law School's campus in White Plains features green space, student housing, recreational facilities and on-site parking. The centerpiece of the campus is the classroom building, which joins four other buildings. The five classrooms in this three-story facility feature horseshoe-shaped seating with raised tiers designed to promote interaction between teachers and students.

EXPENSES & FINANCIAL AID

Tuition for the 2004–2005 year was $31,158. Dannat Hall, the residence center, provides housing for 210 single, full-time students, and features single rooms with Internet access, telephones, voicemail, and cable television. A variety of housing is available off campus in White Plains and the surrounding area. The Admissions Office assists students with securing suitable off-campus accommodations through the housing pages on the law school's Web page.

FACULTY

The law school includes 115 total faculty members, of whom 47 are full-time. Faculty scholarship covers fundamental areas of law such as civil litigation, civil procedure, constitutional law, contracts, evidence, family law, federalism and separation of powers, federal jurisdiction, federal law and procedure, property, and torts. Also covered are specialized areas of the law such as the Americans with Disabilities Act, cable franchising and regulations, children's legal representation, environmental and toxic torts, equal pay, hazardous waste, health care fraud, international commercial law, land use, law of the sea, legal and ethical issues in health care, nonprofit organizations, prosecutorial and judicial ethics, racially motivated violence, securities fraud, and white collar crime. Many of the faculty members are authors of widely circulated legal textbooks and books influential in the profession and are drafters of groundbreaking state laws.

STUDENTS

The entering class of 2004 was a diverse group, representing 29 states and 5 different countries. The average age for the full-time class was 25 and the part-time class was 31. There were over 152 undergraduate schools represented and an 17 percent minority population.

ADMISSIONS

At Pace, as at many law schools, the most important admissions criteria are the undergraduate grade point average (GPA) and the Law School Admissions Test. Reliance on these purely academic criteria is appropriate in making many decisions. Other factors, such as interpreting the GPA by carefully evaluating an applicant's transcript to determine the strength of the curriculum, or the quality of the institution at which undergraduate work was done, are also considered. We also consider other qualities and experience an applicant might have, including a proven capacity for leadership, dedication to community service, excellence in a specific field of work, ethnic and cultural background, a high level of motivation, graduate study in another discipline, work experience, and extracurricular activities.

Pace has instituted an admissions interview program, believing that a personal interview may assist the admissions committee in its decision-making process.

SPECIAL PROGRAMS

The Women's Justice Center is a training, resource, and direct legal services center. Each year the center trains thousands of judges, attorneys, and others who work to eradicate injustice to women. Pace Law students participate in all aspects of the program, including direct representation of clients in family court. The Land Use Law Center teaches students to understand how best to develop and conserve the land. It brings students into the process in their first year of law school in such projects as research and publications, outreach and community service, and project management and technology. The Pace investor rights project addresses the problem of investor justice through grant-funded research and community service activities. Students working with the project gain valuable legal training in this specialized area of investment issues and practice. The Pace London Law program, in affiliation with University College Faculty of Laws, University of London, provides both an academic and an internship experience during the spring semester for 30 to 40 students from Pace and other law schools.

ADDITIONAL INFORMATION

78 North Broadway, White Plains, NY 10603; Admissions Phone: 914-422-4210; Admissions E-mail: admissions@law.pace.edu; website: www.law.pace.edu.

CAREER SERVICES & PLACEMENT

Through a variety of outreach activities, the Office of Career Development actively solicits job listings for part-time, summer, and permanent positions after graduation as well as full-time jobs for evening students while they are in school. In addition to regularly contacting legal employers through mailings and surveys regarding immediate hiring needs, visits with law firms and other organizations are scheduled throughout the year to establish, and maintain relationships that result in the receipt of additional job notices. Respondents to the 2003 graduating class survey reported 87 percent employment within the six months following graduation.

ST. THOMAS UNIVERSITY

School of Law

AT AT GLANCE

St. Thomas University School of Law is a highly-regarded student-centered law school where diversity is cherished, where a commitment to human rights and international law flourishes, and where the Catholic heritage of ethical behavior and public service is paramount.

One of the greatest strengths of our law school is the profound sense of community shared by students, faculty, and administration. Rich in diversity and small in size, the St. Thomas community is one of cohesiveness and collegiality where friendships are valued and differences are embraced.

St. Thomas boasts one of the most culturally diverse student bodies in the country, tied for second among all ABA-approved law schools in student diversity by *U.S. News & World Report*. We are also ranked one of the top five law schools for Hispanic students by *Hispanic Outlook in Higher Education* magazine. True to its Catholic heritage, St. Thomas places an institutional emphasis on social justice and ethical behavior.

CAMPUS AND LOCATION

St. Thomas University School of Law's location in Miami, Florida provides an ideal setting for the study of law. Miami is a vibrant, thriving international community. A hub of domestic and international trade, an innovative center for performing and fine arts, and one of the world's most popular vacation spots, Miami is a dynamic place to live and study. As the gateway to Latin America and the Caribbean, Miami enjoys a rapidly expanding multinational legal community and is home to federal and state trial and appellate courts.

DEGREES OFFERED

St. Thomas University School of Law offers the traditional JD degree as well as joint degrees and advanced degrees including LLM and JSD degrees. The joint degree programs offer St. Thomas Law students the opportunity to complete both the Juris Doctor and the master's degree in the three years it typically takes to complete the Juris Doctor degree alone. The graduate school and the law school accept credits from courses taken at the other school, thereby reducing the total number of credits needed for both degrees, saving the student both time and money. Students may opt for the following degrees: JD/MBA in international business; JD/MBA in accounting; JD/MS in sports administration; JD/MS in marriage and family counseling.

St. Thomas University School of Law also offers advanced degrees: the LLM and JSD in intercultural human rights and in international taxation.

PROGRAMS AND CURRICULUM

Fundamental to our curriculum at St. Thomas University School of Law is the emphasis placed on the development of professional skills. The school of law offers a wide array of opportunities to develop practical lawyering skills to ensure your success in the legal profession upon graduation. Through our extensive clinical and externship offerings, and our in-depth legal writing programs, students participate in a variety of substantive experiences in order to hone the skills necessary for the practice of law.

FACILITIES

The law school is designed to provide our students with an outstanding environment for learning the law. The law library is the heart of the law school housing the cases, statutes, law reviews, monographs and rare documents on which students and faculty depend.

Computers and printers are in abundant supply throughout the library and the library's computer lab, giving students unlimited access to online research services such as LEXIS and WESTLAW and to the Internet. The law library offers Internet access to online databases and has been a leader in applying technology to legal education.

During the past year, our classrooms were refurbished, the moot courtroom and judge's chambers were renovated, and a new moot court competition room was created. A closed circuit television system now broadcasts law school information on plasma screen televisions throughout campus.

EXPENSES AND FINANCIAL AID

Tuition and fees for the JD degree for 2004–2005 are $24,700 per year.

St. Thomas University School of Law offers merit-based scholarships to qualified students. St. Thomas also offers financial assistance apart from scholarships to eligible students in the form of loans, part-time employment and grants.

FACULTY

The faculty at St. Thomas is committed to teaching, scholarship, and service. Our exceptional faculty have earned law degrees, and, in many cases, advanced law degrees, from some of the nation's most prestigious institutions, including Harvard, Yale, Columbia, Michigan, Pennsylvania, Georgetown, and New York University. Their record of publication in the leading law reviews is outstanding, and their practical experience is vast.

STUDENTS

St. Thomas University School of Law offers a rich student life. With more than twenty student organizations to choose from, students easily find activities that appeal to their interests. The Student Bar Association serves as the student government, planning activities and events, as well as working with the administration to communicate the student body's interests and concerns. Students also enjoy the wealth of activities, cultural and sporting events, and nightlife offered in Miami.

ADMISSIONS

Admissions decisions are made by the law school admissions committee which evaluates each applicant's potential for excellence in the study of law. The Law School Admission Test (LSAT) score is a factor; however, consideration will also be given to other factors such as the undergraduate record and grade point average, undergraduate institution, course of study, graduate degrees, work experience, honors, extra-curricular activities, community service, personal statement, and the letter of recommendation. All applicants are welcome to visit the law school and sit in on a class, meet current students, and take a tour.

CAREER SERVICES AND PLACEMENT

With a 94 percent, 89 percent, and 87 percent job placement rate over the past three years, St. Thomas provides first-rate career services that match the needs and interests of students with those of the legal community. St. Thomas graduates are partners in major law firms from Florida to California, and the law school is represented in many of the most prestigious firms in the country. Our Career Services Office is dedicated to guiding students through the career planning process from their first day of law school through their alumni years.

SAMFORD UNIVERSITY

Cumberland School of Law

INTRODUCTION

The Cumberland School of Law, established in 1847 as a part of Cumberland University in Lebanon, Tennessee, is one of the oldest law schools in the country. The school was acquired by Samford University in 1961 and is now known as Samford University, Cumberland School of Law. Today, Samford University is the largest privately supported and fully accredited institution of higher learning in Alabama. The beautiful campus is located in a suburban area of Birmingham, Alabama's largest city. Birmingham is the state's industrial, business, and cultural center. The Cumberland School of Law has been a member of the Association of American Law Schools (AALS) since 1952 and has been accredited by the American Bar Association (ABA) since 1949.

LIBRARY AND PHYSICAL FACILITIES

The Lucille Stewart Beeson Law Library, an $8.4 million, freestanding, Georgian structure, opened in March 1995. The library is visually stunning, as well as superbly functional. This 61,000-square-foot, three-and-one-half story building is connected to the law school by a second-story breezeway. The building's design is intended to make all facilities easily accessible to students with disabilities.

Complete training on Westlaw, LexisNexis, and Legal Trac is part of the first-year curriculum through the *Lawyering and Legal Reasoning* course. All study carrels and conference rooms are wired for data transmission. In addition, law students have full access to the university's four campus libraries, as well as six computer labs.

JOINT-DEGREE PROGRAMS

To broaden their thinking or help them prepare for careers in special fields, Cumberland students may opt to pursue six different joint degrees: JD/MAcc, JD/MBA, JD/MPH, JD/MPA, JD/MDiv, and JD/MS in environmental management.

CENTER FOR BIOTECHNOLOGY, LAW & ETHICS

Dedicated to furthering practical training in the legal disciplines critical to biotechnology, Cumberland's unique program builds on a base of intellectual property, health care, environmental, tort, and natural resources law. The center's specific focus on biotechnology includes issues related to the medical, pharmaceutical, and agricultural sectors and offers students research opportunities.

INTERNATIONAL LAW

Cumberland conducts two ABA-approved international summer programs that are offered at the University of Durham, England, and the University of Victoria, British Columbia. The graduate degree of master of comparative law (MCL) is offered to international law school graduates.

ADVOCACY AND SKILLS TRAINING

Cumberland's emphasis on teaching students the art and science of courtroom advocacy begins in the first-year curriculum, where a six-credit, two-semester course titled *Lawyering and Legal Reasoning* provides students hands-on, practical instruction in prelitigation skills, such as client interviewing, counseling, memorandum preparation, and negotiation; pre-trial litigation skills, including summary judgment motions and making compelling oral arguments; and appellate litigation skills. This intensive course prepares students to work effectively in their first summer clerkships where they may be expected to research cases and write briefs in their first week.

Cumberland has an exceptional record of recent trial-advocacy competition victories, winning both the ABA and ATLA national championships (including several national second-and third-place awards); winning 31 regional championships; and winning the coveted American College of Trial Lawyers' Emil Gumpert Award for Excellence in Teaching Trial Advocacy. The law school also offers a certificate in trial advocacy to recognize students' achievements. Cumberland students have the chance to get class credit and a professional leg up working for Birmingham's major law firms, judges' offices, and corporate legal departments. The clinical curriculum offers second- and third-year students judicial and corporate externships as well as externships in the offices of the IRS, the U.S. Attorney's office, and organizations that serve underrepresented or economically disadvantaged groups. In addition, the Alabama third-year practice rule gives third-year students a chance to practice law under the supervision of a licensed attorney.

ADMISSION

Cumberland School of Law does not use a number index system or formula when choosing who will be admitted. Every applicant's file is thoroughly reviewed by the faculty admissions committee. In addition to the LSAT score and undergraduate GPA, other important factors considered are undergraduate school; grade trend and difficulty of major; extracurricular activities and/or employment while in undergraduate school; whether economic, physical, or other challenges have been overcome; graduate work; scholarly achievements; employment experience; personal statement; and letters of recommendation. Applicants, who because of their backgrounds will bring to the school of law different and enlightening perspectives, will be recognized by the committee. The law school seeks a diverse student body that will make a contribution to the law school and to the legal profession.

Admitted applicants are required to pay a nonrefundable $400 seat deposit that is credited toward tuition. The first installment of $150 is due April 1; the second installment of $250 is due June 15.

STUDENT ACTIVITIES

The Student Bar Association (SBA) functions as the first professional organization of a law student's career. Student bar chapters keep students in touch with job opportunities and bar requirements. In addition to many outstanding organizations, students may also be invited to join one of three national legal fraternities and be inducted into two honorary societies, Order of the Barrister and Curia Honoris. Student–run publications include *Cumberland Law Review*, *American Journal of Trial Advocacy*, and *Pro-Confesso.*

SCHOLARSHIPS

All admitted applicants are automatically considered for merit and recruiting scholarship awards. Various other scholarships are available to outstanding students who distinguish themselves academically, or who make outstanding contributions through leadership in the law school's program, or who demonstrate financial need.

CAREER SERVICES

Through the Career Services Office, the law school assists all law students in locating summer clerkships and part-time and permanent employment upon graduation. Students also receive individual counseling and take part in workshops. The office schedules on-campus interview programs during the fall and spring semesters. Cumberland students and graduates are encouraged to attend well-known recruiting conferences in Chicago, Atlanta, Nashville, and Washington, DC. The Career Services Office surveys each graduating class nine months after graduation, and based on data collected from the most recent graduates (Class of 2003), 96 percent had successfully obtained employment or were attending graduate school.

Cumberland School of Law
800 Lakeshore Drive
Birmingham, AL 35229
Telephone: 205-726-2702, 800-888-7213
Fax: 205-726-2057
E-mail: law.admissions@samford.edu
Website: http://cumberland.samford.edu

SETON HALL UNIVERSITY

School of Law

AT A GLANCE

Seton Hall University School of Law offers JD, LLM, and MSJ degrees, is fully accredited by the American Bar Association, and a member of the Association of American Law Schools. The scholarly resources and the caliber of the faculty provide students with an outstanding legal education and professional opportunities. The rigorous academic program prepared first-time test takers in 2004 to pass the New Jersey State Bar with an 82 percent passage rate, and in New York, an 86 percent passage rate.

CAMPUS & LOCATION

Seton Hall Law School is located in downtown Newark, close to New York City's leading law firms and governmental agencies. Seton Hall is one block away from Newark Penn Station, providing students easy access to Manhattan and New Jersey's suburban cities. The school's convenient location along the northeast region of the United States attracts world-renowned speakers, visiting faculty, and top employers.

DEGREES OFFERED

Seton Hall has a full-time division and part-time evening division for students seeking a JD degree. The JD program requires 85 credits of study and can be completed on a full-time basis in three years or part-time in four years.

Seton Hall Law School offers a joint degree program with University of Medicine of New Jersey/Robert Wood Johnson Medical School where students can obtain a JD/MD in six years. There is a four-year JD/MBA program with Seton Hall University's Stillman School of Business and a four year JD/MADIR program with Seton Hall University's School of Diplomacy and International Relations. Seton Hall Law also offers a dual degree agreement with New Jersey Institute of Technology in which a student may earn a BS degree at NJIT and a JD from Seton Hall. This is a 3+3 arrangement allowing students to earn a bachelor's degree and a JD in six years. Seton Hall also offers two graduate legal degrees. There is an MSJ degree in health, science, and technology and an LLM degree in health law.

PROGRAMS & CURRICULUM

The Center for Social Justice's for-credit clinical programs and pro bono program allow students to engage in a legal apprenticeship, representing actual clients in cases with real-life outcomes. Seton Hall students also receive funding to spend summers with a variety of organizations such as the Urban Justice Center, Mental Health Project; Covenant House of New Jersey, Youth Advocacy Center; International Human Rights Institute; Legal Aid Society of New York; and the NAACP Legal Defense and Educational Fund.

FACILITIES

Seton Hall Law School is located at One Newark Center in a striking five-story, glass-encased building. Students have access to state-of-the-art classrooms that are wirelessly networked. In addition, the law school provides two moot court rooms, a 300-person capacity auditorium, student organization and journal suites, a student lounge, sizeable reading areas, meeting rooms, a chapel, and a cafeteria.

The Peter W. Rodino, Jr., Law Library is located on three floors and accommodates 600 students, including 50 terminals for students to connect to Lexis-Nexis and Westlaw's legal databases. The library contains more than 425,000 volumes and volume equivalents covering a vast assortment of law and law related subjects. Health and environmental law are areas of strength and the library is a depository for U.S. government documents and New Jersey State documents.

EXPENSES & FINANCIAL AID

Seton Hall facilitates each student's ability to finance his or her education through its comprehensive financial aid packages. In the 2004–2005 academic year, the school of law awarded approximately $25 million in financial aid. Ninety-two percent of our students receive financial assistance. Tuition is $1,081 per credit. For more information about costs and financial assistance, visit our website at http://law.shu.edu.

FACULTY

Seton Hall Law has 66 full-time faculty members who are complemented by select adjunct faculty who teach upper-class courses of specific interests. The student/faculty ratio provides students with easy access to faculty. Faculty members are widely published and actively involved in research projects in innovative areas of the law. Among the research subjects that have commanded attention are corporate and tax law, religious liberty, international human rights, property and the public interest, food and drug laws, cyberspace law, bioethics, affirmative action, immigration justice, antitrust, science and the law, environmental policy, and employment discrimination.

STUDENTS

Seton Hall's student body includes approximately 1,277 students from diverse cultural, ethnic and religious backgrounds, work experience, and age groups. The school has more than 30 student organizations that focus on students' cultural and professional interests.

ADMISSIONS

Seton Hall carefully considers each applicant's overall application in the admissions process. So while undergraduate GPA and LSAT scores are important, they are not determinative. The 2004 entering class had a median undergraduate GPA of 3.25 and a median LSAT score of 160.

SPECIAL PROGRAMS

Seton Hall offers six clinical programs in impact litigation, civil litigation, family law, housing & homelessness, immigration and human rights, and juvenile justice that provide students with hands-on experience. In addition Seton Hall also offers externship programs with various governmental and private agencies. The law school also allows students to commit 35 hours a semester working at a nonprofit organization through the school's pro bono program. Students are also able to spend a summer abroad through one of the school's study abroad programs in Cairo, Egypt; Italy; and Galway, Ireland.

CAREER SERVICES & PLACEMENT

Surveys, rankings, and other evidence convincingly demonstrate Seton Hall's quality legal education. Within nine months after graduation, 95 percent of Seton Hall's most recent graduates are employed. Seton Hall also offers real-world experiences and opens career paths for our students. The law school is in close proximity to many of the hundreds of large and small firms in Newark, offering students the opportunity to gain legal experiences as interns, clerks, and summer associates. Moreover, these same law firms serve as major sources of employment after graduation.

Christine Q. Bland
Director of Law School Communications
Seton Hall University School of Law
Room 313, One Newark Center
Newark, NJ 07102
Telephone: (973) 642-8724
Fax: (973) 642-8031
Website: http://law.shu.edu

UNIVERSITY OF MINNESOTA LAW SCHOOL

The University of Minnesota Law School aspires to produce ethical, well-trained lawyers who will effectively advance the practice of law and serve the interests of the nation, and the world. At Minnesota, scholarship and practical service go hand-in-hand.

The law school faculty is comprised of nationally and internationally recognized scholars who are also dedicated and talented classroom and clinical teachers. Members of the current faculty have published more than 200 books, 2,000 research articles, and a variety of printed and electronic materials. They are highly sought as lecturers and contributors for conferences and symposia throughout the world. Our large and outstanding faculty allows us to offer extensive curriculum to support our students' pursuits in all areas of the law.

The integration of lawyering skills into the University of Minnesota's law curriculum begins in the very first year. Students can expect to encounter skills training and exercises not only in the legal writing program but also in substantive classes such as civil procedure, contracts, or property. Training opportunities expand in the second and third years in advanced courses designed to enhance professional skills in more specialized

litigation and transactional practice contexts. This curriculum is central to the University of Minnesota's vision of educating the complete lawyer through the integration of skills, ethics, theory, and practice.

The trial practice program provides students with an intensive exposure to the skills and strategy necessary for trying civil and criminal cases. Students learn trial skills, including procedures, tactics, and persuasion. The program is taught in small sections by prominent federal and state trial court judges. In addition to the traditional trial practice courses, the Law School offers several courses beyond the basics of litigation practice

As part of our commitment to training students in analysis and communication, we require predictive and/or persuasive writing in all three years of our JD program. First year students take a year-long course in legal writing. During the second year, students must either work on a scholarly journal or participate in a moot court program. During the third year, students may continue with a journal or moot court, or may enroll in one of many diverse seminar offerings to complete a third-year legal writing requirement.

Law students in the University of Minnesota's clinical program gain experience representing real clients and deepen their understanding of the relationship between abstract doctrine and real life consequences. The law school's clinical and lawyering skills education programs are among the nation's largest and most distinguished. Providing second- and third-year law students with a unique educational opportunity, the law clinics serve as the law school's own teaching law firm, staffed by faculty and students. Between 50 and 60 percent of the students in each graduating class participate in at least one of our numerous clinical courses. Under the student practice rule adopted by the Minnesota Supreme Court, students enrolled in clinical courses may represent clients in transactions or in court and administrative agency proceedings under the supervision of clinic faculty as early as the summer after the first year. the law school has nine full-time clinical professors (along with a number of adjunct professors) who instruct and supervise students in the clinical programs and provide clinical instruction to an average of 300 student attorney positions per year. Each year, the clinics take on approximately 700 new cases, with student attorneys providing more than 18,000 hours of pro bono legal service to the Twin Cities community, primarily to lower-income individuals who otherwise would have difficulty obtaining representation.

Our eight moot court programs are an integral part of our commitment to practical legal training. All students may participate in one of our diverse moot court programs in their second or third years. The University of Minnesota has one of the strongest intercollegiate moot court records in the country. Over the last fifteen years, our students and teams have won three national and nine regional championships, five national and seventeen regional best brief awards, two national and ten regional oral advocacy awards.

One of our National Moot Court Competition teams was second in the nation in 2004, as was our Giles Sutherland Rich Intellectual Property Moot Court competition team.

The University of Minnesota Law School is one of only a few law schools with both student-edited and faculty-edited scholarly journals, each of which has gained national prominence.

The law school library is world-class, ranking eighth in size among American academic law libraries, and containing more than one million volumes. The Law Library houses exceptional Anglo-American, foreign, comparative, and international law collections, as well as a magnificent rare books collection. the law library remains a leader in the integration of electronic resources into a traditional legal research environment. Law students may use the law library 24 hours a day, 7 days a week.

Our renowned research and policy institutes extend our influence to the state, national, and international communities. Five different research and policy institutes contribute to the law school, the university, and the local community by exploring new frontiers

of research, meeting significant societal needs, and extending public outreach. This includes the Human Rights Center, the Institute on Race & Poverty, the Consortium on Law and Values in Health, Environment & the Life Sciences, the Kommerstad Center for Business Law and Entrepreneurship, and the Minnesota Center for Legal Studies.

Through joint and dual degree programs, the law school offers students the opportunity for interdisciplinary study with the ability to individually tailor career plans while fulfilling the requirements for two degrees.

Our Career Services Office provides a wide variety of services to students and alumni alike. Throughout the year, the CSO invites leading public interest attorneys from Minnesota and around the country to discuss careers in their areas of practice and how they achieved their career successes. It maintains a web-based database of job listings for summer, entry level, and graduate opportunities. CSO staff assists students by providing resume and cover letter review, mock interview practice and fellowship application editing.

WHITTIER COLLEGE

Whittier Law School

AT A GLANCE

Whittier Law School (WLS) offers JD and LLM degrees, and is fully accredited by the American Bar Association and a member of the Association of American Law Schools. Part-time, flexible day, and evening programs are offered. The Law School provides many resources and support with distinguished faculty for a superb legal education and career opportunities.

CAMPUS &LOCATION

Whittier Law School is located in Costa Mesa, just 30 miles from downtown Los Angeles and 20 miles away from Whittier College. A self contained campus on 15-acres in the heart of Orange County, where temperate weather, a sophisticated and dynamic business environment, and cultural and recreational opportunities combine to create a highly desirable location in which to live, learn, and work.

DEGREES OFFERED

Juris Doctor: full-time 3 years.

Juris Doctor: part-time and evening 4 years.

Juris Doctor: accelerated mid-year spring admissions 2 1/2 years. LLM.

PROGRAMS &CURRICULUM

The Law School has nationally recognized centers in Children's Rights, Intellectual Property Law, and International & Comparative Law, which have certificate programs, host fellows, offer externships, sponsor symposia and workshops. WLS has five Clinics serving the public in the following areas: Children's Rights, Special Education, Family Violence, Health Care Access, and Legal Policy. Whittier Law School offers concentrations in Business Law and Criminal Law. The Law School additionally offers an LLM program; public interest law program; 5 ABA-approved summer abroad programs in China, France, Israel, the Netherlands, and Spain; a program in Australia during winter break; moot court; honors board trial and appellate practice/dispute resolution; externships; five clinics in children's rights, family violence, health care access, special education, and legal policy.

FACILITIES

Whittier Law School's 15-acre campus in beautiful Orange County offers the best of Southern California. Cultural and recreational opportunities abound and the Law School's central location between Los Angeles and San Diego provides access to the largest concentration of legal employers in the nation. Students have access to state-of-the-art classrooms with Internet connections. In addition, the Law School provides two moot court rooms, student organization and journal rooms, a student lounge, sizeable reading areas, meeting rooms, and a cafeteria.

The Whittier Law School's 45,000 square-foot library contains in excess of 350,000 volumes to aid students with instruction and research, and serves as a California state and federal depository. The collection includes materials in print, on laser disc, and on microform. Printers are available for the microform materials. Students may study in the Segerstrom Reading Room or one of the many carrels or tables located in the book stacks. For student group meetings there are fourteen Conference Rooms and rooms for viewing videotapes. The library maintains an Adaptive Learning Center for sight-impaired students.

EXPENSES &FINANCIAL AID

Day division (annual): $29,190

Evening division (annual): $ 19,460

Flexible day division (annual): $19,460

Application fee (non-refundable): $50

Student bar association fee (per semester): $40

Whittier Law School has a longstanding tradition of providing students with financial assistance to complete their legal education. The Law School adheres to a need-blind admissions policy, admitting the best students regardless of family financial strength. The Law School also awards numerous tuition scholarships annually and they are based on academic merit and financial need.

FACULTY

Whittier Law School's faculty are nationally acclaimed and committed scholar/professors, each of them with distinguished academic backgrounds, recognized expertise, and successful practice. Also, our faculty provides pro bono service for a variety of public interest organizations, furthering our commitment to public service. Whittier Law's faculty is among the greatest strengths of the school, with their excellent notability and accomplishments.

STUDENTS

Whittier Law School has a student body of a little over a 1,000 students from diverse cultural, ethnic and religious backgrounds, work experience, and age groups. The school has many student organizations that focus on students' cultural, political, and professional interests.

ADMISSIONS

Whittier Law School reviews all factors relevant to an applicant's potential ability to meet the demanding academic standards of the Juris Doctor program. The traditional criteria, undergraduate academic performance and Law School Admissions Test (LSAT) scores, are both employed in admission evaluations. However, there are no "magic numbers." The Faculty Admissions Committee also considers an applicant's resumé, personal statement, and letters of recommendation.

CAREER SERVICES & PLACEMENT

Legal career opportunities abound in Southern California's dynamic legal community. The Whittier Law School Career Services Office provides valuable resources to students beginning in their first year of study and into their attorney careers. The Career Services Office is involved with bar associations and other organizations to promote the law school. The office is actively involved in the National Association for Law Placement (NALP), the Law School Career Advisors of Southern California (LSCA), the Los Angeles Area Legal Recruitment Association (LAALRA), the Orange County Area Legal Recruitment Association (OCALRA), and Equal Justice Works. Whittier Law School pays membership dues for all Whittier Law School students to the Orange County Bar Association (OCBA), the largest bar association in the local community. Membership allows students to meet with attorneys in specialty practice areas and to learn effective networking skills early in their careers.

For Additional Information, contact:

Whitter Law School

Admissions Office

3333 Harbor Boulevard

Costa Mesa, CA, 92626

Telephone: 714-444-4141

Fax: 714-444-0250

Website: www.law.whittier.edu

INDEXES

ALPHABETICAL LIST OF SCHOOLS

T

U

V

W

Y

SCHOOLS BY LOCATION

USA

ALABAMA

ARIZONA

ARKANSAS

CALIFORNIA

COLORADO

CONNECTICUT

DELAWARE

NORTH CAROLINA

NORTH DAKOTA

OHIO

OKLAHOMA

OREGON

PENNSYLVANIA

RHODE ISLAND

SOUTH CAROLINA

SOUTH DAKOTA

TENNESSEE

TEXAS

ABOUT THE AUTHOR

Eric Owens, Esq., attended Cornell College for his undergraduate degree and Loyola University Chicago for law school. He is now an American diplomat.

John Owens, Esq., earned his undergraduate degree in accountancy at the University of Illinois, Urbana-Champaign. He then matriculated at Loyola University Chicago School of Law, where he earned his JD. John works in the tax department of a Chicago law firm. He is currently working on a book, which he hopes to finish up this year. In his spare time, John likes to rock.

Julie Doherty graduated from Stanford University in 1998 with a degree in English. She currently lives in San Miguel de Allende, Mexico, where she works in an art gallery and printmaking studio. She is the co-author of several Princeton Review titles, including *The Best 361 Colleges* and *Planning a Life in Medicine*. She is working on her first novel.

In order to address this problem and try to ease the financial burden on student borrowers, Congress passed the *Consolidation Loan Program* under the *Higher Education Act in 1986*. With this program, student loan borrowers are able to consolidate their multiple Federal Student Loans into one new Loan, while at the same time, extending their repayment term and locking in a fixed interest rate. By doing this, borrowers are able to lower their monthly payments enabling them to avoid delinquency and default.

THE FEDERAL CONSOLIDATION LOAN PROGRAM

The Federal Consolidation Loan Program is a unique program offered by the Federal Government that provides student loan borrowers with the following benefits:

- Lower monthly loan payments.
- Lock in a fixed interest rate for the life of the loan.
- Ability to merge all of the existing eligible federal loans into one new loan thereby making only one payment per month.
- Maintain their existing in-school deferment option if attending a graduate school and have no prepayment penalties. In-school deferment allows borrowers to postpone their payments while they are enrolled at least half time. While in deferment, all subsidized Stafford loans included in the consolidation will accrue zero interest.
- Availability of several repayment plans, including standard level payments, graduated payments, and income-based payments, allowing borrower to select the plan that best meets his or her needs.
- Potential interest rate reductions or other benefits, depending on the lender.

The Federal Consolidation Loan Program could be in the best interest of many students depending on the interest rates at the current time. There are no additional service fees for setting up a Consolidation Loan.

The eligibility guidelines for the program are very simple. In order to be eligible for a consolidation loan, a borrower must:

- Have outstanding loans made under the Federal Family Education Loan Program (FFELP), Direct, Perkins or Health Professions Student Loan (HPSL) program.
- Be in repayment period (including deferment and forbearance) or grace period.
- If a borrower is in default on their loans, certain rules/requirements apply in order to include these loans in the consolidation. Not all lenders will consolidate defaulted loans.
- Although Federal rules do not require a minimum balance many lenders may set minimum balance requirements. Typical minimums range from $5,000 to $10,000.

Qualifying Loans Under the Program:

Several types of student loans are eligible for Consolidation, including:

- Federal Family Education Loan Program (FFELP)
    - Federal Subsidized and Unsubsidized Stafford Loans
    - Federal PLUS Loans
    - Federal Consolidation Loans
- Direct Loan Program
    - Direct Subsidized and Unsubsidized Stafford Loans
    - Direct PLUS loans
    - Direct Consolidation Loans
- Perkins Loan Program
    - Federal Perkins Loans
- Health Profession Student Loans (HPSL)
- Other
    - Federal Education Assistance Loans (HEAL)
    - Federal Nursing Student Loans (NSL)

CONSOLIDATION, WHEN IS THE RIGHT TIME?

A borrower can consolidate their student loans upon the completion of an undergraduate or graduate degree. As for those planning to attend postsecondary school, there are a few things to consider.

One of the great benefits of a higher education is the entitlement to in-school deferment on all federal loans. A borrower is legally entitled to this deferment even if they consolidate their student loans after they receive their undergraduate degree! The Department of Education states that students considered at least half-time (typically a minimum of six credit hours per semester) are not only eligible, but are legally guaranteed in-school deferment.

If this is the case, what is the benefit to consolidating only a portion of your student loans? All Stafford loans have variable interest rates prior to using the FFEL Consolidation Program. Once your loans have been consolidated the interest rate is locked in for the life of the loan and cannot go any higher. This is the primary and obvious reason to consolidate all eligible Stafford loans while still accumulating student loan debt.

The loans that will be taken out for postsecondary school may maintain their variable interest rates until the program is complete or the course load drops below half time. If the current interest rates are low in comparison to past years, you should secure whatever eligible debt you have incurred at these rates and consolidate the postsecondary school loans later. In fact, the option to roll all loans together or consolidate the remaining loans in a completely separate consolidation is something to be decided later.

The Six Month Grace Period = Opportunity for Big Savings

Most know that they do not necessarily have to begin paying off their student loans until six months after graduation. This six months is called a Grace Period or a period in which recently graduated students are awarded time to decide where they are going to live, find a job, etc. before they are required to make payments on their student loan debt.

Despite popular belief, the grace period typically may be the best time to consolidate student loans. When in a grace period, student loan interest rates are actually over a half of a percent lower than when the required payments begin six months after graduation.

STUDENT LOAN INTEREST RATES

Not all student loan borrowers have the same interest rate when they take advantage of the Consolidation Loan Program. This is not due to personal credit or the lender selected, but rather to government rules. A borrower's interest rate is determined by several factors.

FFELP Consolidation is a federal program and the actual interest rate is determined by a set of rules defined by the U.S. Department of Education. The fixed interest rates are determined by taking the weighted average of all of the loans being consolidated and rounding to the nearest 1/8th of a point.

Rates for Stafford and PLUS loans first disbursed on or after July 1, 1998, are adjusted on July 1 of each year based on the results of the last auction of the three-month Treasury bills before June 1st.

Many mailings and advertisements from Consolidation lenders offer the lowest possible rate and interest rate reductions. It is standard practice for companies to offer 0.25 percent reduction for making automatic EFT payments from a checking account. Many also offer a 1 percent interest rate reduction once a certain number of on-time payments have been received. The actual interest rate that is determined by the U.S. Department of Education is the maximum that a lender can charge and is the same from company to company.

Repayment Options

The Federal Consolidation Loan Program allows borrowers to get the best payoff terms without imposing penalties for early repayment. All Stafford loans are initially on a ten-year payoff plan, leaving many to opt for a nonpayment status such as deferment or forbearance when experiencing a cash flow problem in the short-term. Many borrowers want lower monthly payments, which will lengthen the payoff term. Switching to a longer-term payoff plan provides an immediate increase in short-term cash flow. Since there is no pre-payment penalty with the program, a borrower can make aggressive payments towards the principal at any time.

Most lenders do not require a borrower to accept the longer term associated with the repayment plans, so if they are opposed to it, other options exist. At the borrower's request, the servicer of his/her consolidation can adjust the payment plan to a ten-year payoff schedule. Borrowers are initially set up on the following terms based upon the balance of their Consolidation Loan:

- **10 years** for less than $7,500
- **12 years** for $7,500 to $10,000
- **15 years** for $10,000 to $20,000 ($20,000 balance monthly payment drop from $192 to $110)
- **20 years** for $20,000 to $40,000 ($35,000 balance monthly payment drop from $335 to $191)
- **25 years** for $40,000 to $60,000 ($50,000 balance monthly payment drop from $480 to $234)
- **30 years** for $60,000 and above ($100,000 balance monthly payment drop from $960 to $415)

A borrower may choose from the most suitable of four repayment plans:

- **Standard Repayment**

The monthly payment amount is fixed over the life of the Loan. The most popular plan is the level repayment method. Many borrowers choose this plan because they like the security and simplicity of a fixed monthly payment. However, more importantly, the level repayment plan usually is the least expensive in terms of total interest charges. The latter plans cost more because they slow down the repayment of the principal.

- **Graduated Repayment**

The Graduated Repayment Plan can vary from lender to lender, however many lenders offer more affordable interest only payments with the initial installments. After a certain number of the interest only payments the borrower will begin to pay down on the principle, resulting in higher payments. Other lenders offer pay increases every two years on the loans. The loan is repaid in the same timeframe as the Standard Repayment, but the total interest costs are slightly higher. The purpose of this payment plan is to provide the borrower more disposable income immediately upon beginning repayment.

- **Extended Repayment**

  This plan allows the borrower to repay his/her Federal Consolidation Loans over a 25-year period under a level or graduated repayment schedule. To be eligible, the oldest Federal Stafford (subsidized and unsubsidized), Federal PLUS and/or Federal Consolidation Loan must have been disbursed on or after October 7, 1998 (borrowers who have pre-1998 loans can qualify for extended repayment if they consolidate all of the pre-1998 loans). In addition, the combined outstanding balance on all eligible Loans must be at least $30,000.01.

- **Income-sensitive repayment**

  Initial monthly payments are based on monthly earnings and are adjusted annually, according to changes in income.

A new federal loan allows a borrower to consolidate again and restart a brand new term. While extending the repayment term may increase the overall amount of interest paid over the life of the loan, those who have higher debt often find the longer payoff schedule to be acceptable.

In addition to the choice of plans, the borrower can switch from one repayment plan to another at least once a year. There's no extra cost or penalty. All it takes is a phone call to his/her servicer or lender.

MAKING THE RIGHT DECISION

Now that all of the benefits of the Federal Consolidation Loan Program have been explained in their entirety, it is up to you, the borrower, to make the final decision. Find the company that offers the best explanation of terms, or find the one with the best incentives. Remember, the official interest rate formula is the same everywhere. The decision simply becomes a matter of personal choice. So what are you waiting for? Consolidate your student loans today and save money today!

The Graduate Loan Center, based in Chicago, Illinois, helps borrowers manage paying for the high cost of education by offering the Federal Consolidation Loan Program and Private Loan Programs. The Graduate Loan Center works with some of the nation's leading financial institutions, which combined have consolidated well over $1 billion in student loans. Call today to speak with one of our specially trained Financial Aid Advisors.